T0207223

Communications in Computer and Information Science 1886

Rationale

The CCIS series is devoted to the publication of proceedings of computer science conferences. Its aim is to efficiently disseminate original research results in informatics in printed and electronic form. While the focus is on publication of peer-reviewed full papers presenting mature work, inclusion of reviewed short papers reporting on work in progress is welcome, too. Besides globally relevant meetings with internationally representative program committees guaranteeing a strict peer-reviewing and paper selection process, conferences run by societies or of high regional or national relevance are also considered for publication.

Topics

The topical scope of CCIS spans the entire spectrum of informatics ranging from foundational topics in the theory of computing to information and communications science and technology and a broad variety of interdisciplinary application fields.

Information for Volume Editors and Authors

Publication in CCIS is free of charge. No royalties are paid, however, we offer registered conference participants temporary free access to the online version of the conference proceedings on SpringerLink (http://link.springer.com) by means of an http referrer from the conference website and/or a number of complimentary printed copies, as specified in the official acceptance email of the event.

CCIS proceedings can be published in time for distribution at conferences or as post-proceedings, and delivered in the form of printed books and/or electronically as USBs and/or e-content licenses for accessing proceedings at SpringerLink. Furthermore, CCIS proceedings are included in the CCIS electronic book series hosted in the SpringerLink digital library at http://link.springer.com/bookseries/7899. Conferences publishing in CCIS are allowed to use Online Conference Service (OCS) for managing the whole proceedings lifecycle (from submission and reviewing to preparing for publication) free of charge.

Publication process

The language of publication is exclusively English. Authors publishing in CCIS have to sign the Springer CCIS copyright transfer form, however, they are free to use their material published in CCIS for substantially changed, more elaborate subsequent publications elsewhere. For the preparation of the camera-ready papers/files, authors have to strictly adhere to the Springer CCIS Authors' Instructions and are strongly encouraged to use the CCIS LaTeX style files or templates.

Abstracting/Indexing

CCIS is abstracted/indexed in DBLP, Google Scholar, EI-Compendex, Mathematical Reviews, SCImago, Scopus. CCIS volumes are also submitted for the inclusion in ISI Proceedings.

How to start

To start the evaluation of your proposal for inclusion in the CCIS series, please send an e-mail to ccis@springer.com.

Sergio Terzi · Kurosh Madani · Oleg Gusikhin · Hervé Panetto
Editors

Innovative Intelligent Industrial Production and Logistics

4th International Conference, IN4PL 2023 Rome, Italy, November 15–17, 2023 Proceedings

Editors
Sergio Terzi
Politecnico di Milano
Milan, Italy

Kurosh Madani
University of Paris - EST Créteil
Créteil, France

Oleg Gusikhin
Ford Motor Company
Dearborn, MI, USA

Hervé Panetto
University of Lorraine
Nancy, France

ISSN 1865-0929 ISSN 1865-0937 (electronic)
Communications in Computer and Information Science
ISBN 978-3-031-49338-6 ISBN 978-3-031-49339-3 (eBook)
https://doi.org/10.1007/978-3-031-49339-3

This Springer imprint is published by the registered company Springer Nature Switzerland AG
The registered company address is: Gewerbestrasse 11, 6330 Cham, Switzerland

Paper in this product is recyclable.

Preface

This volume contains the proceedings of the 4th International Conference on Innovative Intelligent Industrial Production and Logistics (IN4PL 2023), held in Rome, Italy as a hybrid event, from 15 to 17 November, 2023.

IN4PL is sponsored by the Institute for Systems and Technologies of Information, Control and Communication (INSTICC).

This conference focuses on research and development involving innovative methods, software and hardware, whereby intelligent systems are applied to industrial production and logistics. This is currently related to the concept of Industry 4.0 - an expression reflecting the trend towards automation and data exchange in manufacturing technologies and processes which include cyber-physical systems, the industrial internet of things, industrial robotics, cloud computing, cognitive computing and artificial intelligence. These technologies can be applied to industrial manufacturing and management as well as to supply-chain or logistic problems, involving for example transportation management or the optimization of operations.

In addition to paper presentations, IN4PL's program included three keynote talks by internationally distinguished speakers: Michele Dassisti (Politecnico di Bari, Italy), Resilience and Smart Sustainable Manufacturing Within the Human-centric Paradigm, Hani Hagras (University of Essex, UK), Towards True Explainable Artificial Intelligence for Real-World Applications, and Dimitris Mourtzis (University of Patras, Greece), Digital Twins and Generative AI for 3D Printing.

The conference also included the 17th IFAC/IFIP International Workshop on Enterprise Integration, Interoperability and Networking - EI2N 2023, chaired by Hervé Panetto, Qing Li, and Raquel Sanchis. This workshop contributed to the community with oral presentations (full and short papers), which have also been included in the proceedings book, and a brainstorming session discussing the future trends and challenges for human-centric systems interoperability.

IN4PL received 33 paper submissions from 16 countries, of which 33% were accepted as full papers. The high quality of the papers received imposed difficult choices during the review process. To evaluate each submission, a double-blind paper review was performed by the Program Committee, whose members were highly qualified independent researchers in the IN4PL topic areas.

All accepted complete papers are published by Springer CCIS in the conference proceedings, under an ISBN reference. The proceedings will be abstracted/indexed in DBLP, Google Scholar, EI-Compendex, INSPEC, Japanese Science and Technology Agency (JST), Norwegian Register for Scientific Journals and Series, Mathematical Reviews, SCImago, Scopus, and zbMATH. CCIS volumes are also submitted for inclusion in ISI Proceedings.

We express our thanks to all participants. First to all the authors, whose quality work is the essence of this conference; secondly to all members of the Program Committee and auxiliary reviewers, who helped us with their expertise and valuable time. We also deeply thank the invited speakers for their excellent contributions in sharing their knowledge and vision.

Finally, we acknowledge the professional support of the IN4PL 2023 team for all organizational processes, especially given the need for a hybrid event, in order to make it possible for the IN4PL 2023 authors to present their work and share ideas with colleagues in spite of the logistic difficulties.

We hope you all had an inspiring conference. We hope to meet you again next year for the 5th edition of IN4PL, details of which will soon be available at https://in4pl.scitevents.org/.

November 2023

Sergio Terzi
Kurosh Madani
Oleg Gusikhin
Hervé Panetto

Organization

Conference Co-chairs

Kurosh Madani	Paris-East Créteil University, France
Oleg Gusikhin	Ford Motor Company, USA
Hervé Panetto	University of Lorraine, France

Program Chair

Sergio Terzi	Politecnico di Milano, Italy

Program Committee

Anna Adamik	Lodz University of Technology, Poland
El-Houssaine Aghezzaf	Ghent University, Belgium
Cláudio Alves	Universidade do Minho, Portugal
Zeyar Aung	Khalifa University, UAE
Nouha Baccour	National Engineering School of Sfax of the University of Sfax, Tunisia
Endre Boros	Rutgers University, USA
Patrick Brandtner	University of Applied Sciences Steyr, Austria
Hing Kai Chan	University of Nottingham Ningbo China, China
Vincent Chapurlat	IMT Mines Alès, France
Ferdinando Chiacchio	University of Catania, Italy
Law Chong Seng	Southern University College, Malaysia
Mohammed Dahane	University of Lorraine, France
Mauro Dell'Amico	University of Modena and Reggio Emilia, Italy
Xavier Delorme	École nationale supérieure des mines de Saint-Étienne, France
Alejandro Escudero-Santana	University of Seville, Spain
Piotr Gaj	Silesian University of Technology, Poland
Virginie Goepp	Institut National des Sciences Appliquées de Strasbourg, France
Marvin Gonzalez	College of Charleston, USA
Cathal Heavey	University of Limerick, Ireland
Ayad Hendalianpour	University of Tehran, Iran

Benoît Iung	University of Lorraine, France
Stanislaw Iwan	Maritime University of Szczecin, Poland
Zivana Jakovljevic	University of Belgrade, Serbia
Bernard Kamsu-Foguem	National School of Engineers of Tarbes, France
Arkadiusz Kawa	Institute of Logistics and Warehousing, Poland
Manas Khatua	Indian Institute of Technology Guwahati, India
Mladen Krstic	University of Belgrade, Serbia
Seokcheon Lee	Purdue University, USA
Yongjian Li	Nankai University, China
Sergio Martin	UNED - Spanish University for Distance Education, Spain
Peter Marwedel	TU Dortmund, Germany
Jorn Mehnen	University of Strathclyde, UK
Rafał Michalski	Wroclaw University of Science and Technology, Poland
Marko Mladineo	University of Split, Croatia
Arturo Molina	Tecnológico de Monterrey, Mexico
Young Moon	Syracuse University, USA
Christian Neureiter	Salzburg University of Applied Sciences, Austria
Sang Do Noh	Sungkyunkwan University, South Korea
Stefano Rinaldi	University of Brescia, Italy
David Romero	Tecnológico de Monterrey, Mexico
Vikram Sharma	LNM Institute of Information Technology, India
Neeraj Kumar Singh	National School of Electrical Engineering, Electronics, Computers, Hydraulics and Telecommunications, France
Dongping Song	University of Liverpool, UK
Bruno Vallespir	University of Bordeaux, France
François Vernadat	University of Lorraine, France
Wei Wang	Xi'an Jiaotong Liverpool University, China
Yuehwern Yih	Purdue University, USA
Hongnian Yu	Bournemouth University, UK

Invited Speakers

Dimitris Mourtzis	University of Patras, Greece
Michele Dassisti	Politecnico di Bari, Italy
Hani Hagras	University of Essex, UK

Invited Speakers

Resilience and Smart Sustainable Manufacturing Within the Human-Centric Paradigm

Michele Dassisti

Politecnico di Bari, Bari, Italy

Abstract. Resiliency of a manufacturing system may be defined as that intrinsic feature of a system to persist in the same equilibrium condition or to find, in a reasonable time, a new stable one resulting from a perturbation so that the system itself can pursue the scope of its existence. These features seem up-to-now be deeply tied to the smartness from one side and to sustainability paradigm to the other. The smartness paradigm stems from the appropriate availability of information pertaining to the so called "cyber-world" (the virtual domain where information is stored and managed by physical manufacturing settings) to be used for pursuing manufacturing goals. Information (say digital assets) may have different forms (say, e.g., data, procedures, experience, wisdom, etc.) belonging either to the explicit (i.e., clearly stated and manageable in a formal manner) or to the implicit nature of information (this latter pertaining to the intuition and/or the not yet clearly formalized). Starting from explicit information - but much more from implicit information - we human create models to interpret the world surrounding us: our reality is made of information available to us to the limit where this can resemble to the reality or become the reality itself: virtualisation is just one trivial example of use of explicit geometrical data. Sustainability paradigm in manufacturing activities, on the other hand, will bring even more challenging issues, being deeply interlinked with the measure of resources consumption and use by machines - provided the Digital Twins as well as Cyber Physical Systems are mostly based on explicit information (say, e.g. bid data). But even more important, sustainability struggle will be won endeavouring the potentialities of the human-centred paradigm. The nature of interrelationship between real- (made of man and physical manufacturing settings) and cyber-world (made of digital assets) is swiftly changing shape in the search for improving manufacturing sustainability. Open issues are on the ground about the mutual dependency between smartness and sustainability, such as the emerging field of research named "digitability" in the search for endeavouring the cross fertilisation coming from digitalisation of businesses for sustainability. But how digitability will contribute to resilience of manufacturing systems? And more important, how the human-centred paradigm will change the manufacturing technologies to improve the resilience of manufacturing systems? Will the smartness be the cornerstone of sustainable manufacturing or it may have even implicit drawbacks for workers? A brand-new concept of "cybermanability" can be thus here introduced, to speculate about the more promising cross fertilisation coming from the human-centred paradigm with the physical/cyber-world for the scope of the manufacturing sustainability. These and other related issues came only recently to light in the scientific arena, but still there is room for discussions, in particular about the new role of smart sustainable manufacturing under the human-centred paradigm for resiliency, that can be of great interest to manufacturers in their pursuing the 17 SDG's and - in doing so – in the imagining the future direction of our I5.0 society.

Towards True Explainable Artificial Intelligence for Real-World Applications

Hani Hagras

Computer Science, University of Essex, Colchester, UK

Abstract. The recent advances in computing power coupled with the rapid increases in the quantity of available data has led to a resurgence in the theory and applications of Artificial Intelligence (AI). However, the use of complex AI algorithms could result in a lack of transparency to users which is termed as black/opaque box models. Thus, for AI to be trusted and widely used by governments and industries, there is a need for greater transparency through the creation of human friendly explainable AI (XAI) systems. XAI aims to make machines understand the context and environment in which they operate, and over time build underlying explanatory models that allow them to characterize real-world phenomena. The XAI concept provides an explanation of individual decisions, enables understanding of overall strengths and weaknesses, and conveys an understanding of how the system will behave in the future and how to correct the system's mistakes. In this keynote speech, Hani Hagras introduce the concepts of XAI by moving towards "explainable AI" (XAI) to achieve a significantly positive impact on communities and industries all over the world and will present novel techniques enabling to deliver human friendly XAI systems which could be easily understood, analysed and augmented by humans. This will allow to the wider deployment of AI systems which are trusted in various real world applications. Back to Top

Contents

Invited Speaker

Adaptive Control of 3D Printer Based on Digital Twin Concept

Dimitris Mourtzis(✉), Antonis Varsamis, Stelios Zygomalas, and John Angelopoulos

Laboratory for Manufacturing Systems and Automation, Department of Mechanical Engineering and Aeronautics, University of Patras, 26504 Rio Patras, Greece
mourtzis@lms.mech.upatras.gr

Abstract. The current industrial landscape is characterized by the immense effort towards the digitalization of systems, networks and processes. Under the light of Industry 4.0, digital technologies such as Digital Twins (DT), eXtended Reality (XR), and Additive Manufacturing (e.g. Fused Deposition Modeling – FDM) are considered among other key pillars for completing the digital transformation of manufacturing and production systems/networks. Ultimately, the goal is to enhance system dependability, ensure precise process monitoring, and predict future system failures. Consequently, in this research work the design, development, and implementation of a Digital Twin based framework for monitoring and improving Fused Deposition Modeling (FDM). The focal point of the Digital Twin is to assess the quality of 3D printed components, calculate the experimental result and accordingly adjust the process parameters, via the seamless connection of the physical printer to its DT. As a result, a fundamental aspect of this study revolves around outlining the information flow among the previously mentioned components to optimize FDM process parameters, thus reducing the time and resources squandered due to human inaccuracies. The execution of the proposed framework hinges on the integration of appropriate communication protocols and channels between the physical and virtual counterparts in order to achieve seamless and continuous communication.

Keywords: Fused deposition modelling · Additive manufacturing · Digital twin

1 Introduction

Industry 4.0 is the latest industrial revolution, that emerged in the early twenty-first century and has been characterized by the effect it has on digitalization, automation, and data exchange in manufacturing technologies. It is a concept in which not only objects, but also machines, assembly lines, and even whole factories are unified into a network. Its arrival has brought to the surface a lot of interesting technologies which include the Internet of Things (IoT), Industrial Internet of Things (IIoT), Big Data, Cyber-Physical Systems (CPS), Artificial Intelligence (AI), Additive Manufacturing (AM) and Digital Twins (DT) to name a few. More specifically, AM has been one of the most important

S. Terzi et al. (Eds.): IN4PL 2023, CCIS 1886, pp. 3–17, 2023.
https://doi.org/10.1007/978-3-031-49339-3_1

pillars of Industry 4.0, as it changes the way manufacturing is viewed and the way the design of components is done. AM is considered a manufacturing process where the final product is built layer by layer by melting material in liquid, powder, or solid form while conventional manufacturing processes include cutting tools that cut off material to shape the part, generating material waste and chips. The way that AM processes work, gives designers the freedom to create more intricate and complex parts, while also reducing the total waste of material, in contrast with subtractive manufacturing where such complex geometries cannot be manufactured and there is a lot of waste material which is discarded in the form of chips. Digital Twin technology mainly affects digitalized Smart Factories as they as they rely heavily on data to operate. Therefore, in [1], a DT framework for the optimization of the design phase has been developed under the concept of Zero-Defect Manufacturing, where production optimization is the sole purpose. The utilization of both real data from operational machines and simulation data have been used to assist engineers in designing a more robust machine and adjust the parameters of each component. In [2], the authors designed and developed a framework for an FDM 3D Printer, which was used to monitor and optimize the parameters of the process, by also using a Cloud to store the data for each print. They replaced the firmware and the processor that the 3D printer unit had with a Raspberry Pi and the Klipper firmware so that they could control the 3D printer's stepper motors. Every time a part was created with this process; a log file was uploaded to the cloud database. A digital twin concept [3], is mainly characterized by data and model creation, allowing the interaction of the virtual and physical part. A Digital Twin Structure Model is introduced in the sphere of manufacturing, expanding the knowledge behind this technology. In a DT framework, vast amounts of data are collected, posing a challenge in finding efficient ways to store them.. This paper [4], introduces a new method for digital twin-driven product design, addressing manufacturing data-related challenges in the product lifecycle. Additionally, it presents three practical cases demonstrating the application of digital twins in each phase of a product. Smart production management and control for complex product assembly flours with the use of digital twin technology is presented in [5]. By creating the virtual twin of the shop floor, acquiring real time data, and using it for predictive and control purposes, a complete framework is formed.

The rest of the manuscript is structured as follows. In Sect. 2 a review regarding the most relevant publications on this topic is presented. In Sect. 3, the architecture of the proposed methodology is developed and discussed. In Sect. 4, the results and outcomes of the framework are presented and finally in Sect. 5 conclusions are drawn and future work regarding the topic is suggested.

2 State of the Art

Constant changes and improvements in technologies that were brought with the emergence of Industry 4.0 have prompted the implementation of some of those technologies in many industries to improve their characteristics. Among those, is the Manufacturing industry which has been continuously growing and surpassed the expectations in the years before the pandemic. Digital technologies, provide interconnected intelligent components inside the shop floor that process, analyse and evaluate data from sensors within it,thus playing an important role in boosting productivity and enhancing the competitiveness of the company. The DT technology is a major advantage in manufacturing as it offers simulations and optimization of the production line whilst enabling a detailed visualization of the manufacturing processes that occur on the shop floor, from manufacturing single components to whole assemblies. This paper [6], uses a digital twin framework in a smart manufacturing workshop to optimize the system's behaviour. Diverse manufacturing resources may be established as a dynamic autonomous system to co-create customized items by creating a cyber-physical link via decentralised digital twin models. Another paper [7] introduces an approach using Key Performance Indicators (KPIs) and differentials to identify measured values that can negatively affect production performance. The method utilizes a dashboard and historical data stored in a database, aggregated through an OLAP server. This approach allows the quick identification of root measured values that deviate from expected performance without supervision. Moving in the sphere of the 4th Industrial Revolution where mass customization of products is often employed, a Personalized PSS has been created in [8] to enable the participation of customers in the design phase of new products. A cloud platform has been set up, which acts as the cyberspace that allows communication among the engineers. Four services have been integrated into this framework, an AR and VR application, a DT service and the File and Data Handling Service. In another work [9], it is proposed in intelligent manufacturing the utilization of a Digital Twin will allow for the simulation of the production line therefore increasing its efficiency. It can also provide a monitoring module, that tracks the status of the products and the equipment, acting as a predictive feature. As previously mentioned, DT technology can assist in monitoring applications to improve the understanding of the process. This monitoring module was integrated in [10] for context awareness in WAAM (Wire Arc Additive Manufacturing) monitoring applications with the use of a DT. Two quality metrics, defect expansion, and local anomaly density, were introduced to detect defects in-process. The context-aware monitoring system enabled a quantitative evaluation of defect expansion and densities for various defect types. In another work [11], they have demonstrated the use of nonlinear autoregressive models with exogenous variables, powered by dynamic, recurrent neural networks, to replicate complex simulations of the extrusion process in fused filament fabrication. The NARXs can predict the extrusion rate and compression force with an average error rate of 0.12%, while operating at a much faster computational speed than the original simulation. The NARXs can also be connected to sensors on a real FFF machine, allowing for the creation of a digital twin of the extrusion process that can be used for real-time decision making by an AI machine controller. Moreover, an approach and conceptual design for a digital twin-based virtual part inspection in additive manufacturing were presented in [12]. This paper proposes a concept for a virtual part inspection that combines data from product development and manufacturing to predict the properties of the as-built part. The concept is designed with the digital twin architecture in mind and is integrated into the existing additive manufacturing process chain. Additionally, in [13], an architecture to acquire data for an Additive Manufacturing (3D printing) process is presented, using a set of consolidated Internet of Things (IoT) technologies to collect, verify, and store these data in a trustworthy and secure way. In order to ensure that the data collected from machines is reliable, this paper proposes an architecture that utilizes established Internet of Things (IoT) technologies to gather, validate, and securely store the data. In another work [14], the use of machine learning in the creation of a Digital Twin framework is shown. A data-driven and model-based concept of a Digital Twin with the use of ML, will speed up the development times of manufacturing systems, creating a very accurate DT. A Digital twin-driven manufacturing cyber-physical system (MCPS) for parallel controlling of the smart workshop is proposed in [6], which can optimize the dynamic execution mechanism and assist engineers in equipment configuration and operation. To implement this, a large number of sensors, actuators, and other manufacturing infrastructure devices that contain embedded systems that can interact with each other have to be used, forming a large network of data exchange systems. Additionally, in [15], a framework for transforming a power grid into a Smart Grid using Digital Twin technology is presented. The implementation of this method allows electric energy to be associated with value-added services for customers, enabling energy providers to transition to a serviced and platform-based model. A Cloud platform, a Data Acquisition and Monitoring Systems, a Digital Twin and a Communication framework have been set up for the completion of this work. Furthermore, in [16] a time estimation model for hybrid assembly stations has been developed under the framework of Digital Twins. This proposed model, has a 95% accuracy, and the application has been tested, speeding up the design process by 23%. Lastly, an AR application based on Digital Twins for monitoring laser processes has been discussed in [17]. The framework enables real-time analysis and advanced data visualization of monitoring system performance. The primary objective is to create a dynamic AR environment that simulates the functionalities of the main system, reducing configuration time, cost, and inaccuracies.

3 Proposed System Architecture

In this Section, a Digital Twin architecture for the implementation of an FDM 3D printer is presented to enable the visualization and remote monitoring of the 3D printing process. Further to that, with the integration of the proposed method, the simulation of the printing process becomes feasible. By extension, engineers are capable of adjusting the process parameters to reduce errors and improve the quality of the 3D-printed components. As a result, the provision of predictive functionalities is enabled, thus if a faulty part is designed or a mistake is made in the creation of the geometry, the simulation of the process will be carried out to foresee the outcome before sending the G-Code to the printer. In addition to that, this feature can also save valuable time for the engineer, as the entire process will be simulated in the DT environment. In this work, a combination of engineering and game development software is suggested, where one will have the role of the Digital Twin framework, allowing for the alteration of parameters,, and the other will facilitate the visualization of the proposed process parameters. Furthermore, a real-time monitoring module that delivers continuous feedback on the printing process will be incorporated into the suggested Digital Twin architecture, assisting in the early detection of potential flaws or irregularities in the printed parts. A high-level representation of the proposed system architecture is illustrated in Fig. 1.

For the visualization of the behavior and the sequential activities of the process workflow, a simple Unified Modelling Language (UML) activity diagram was created.

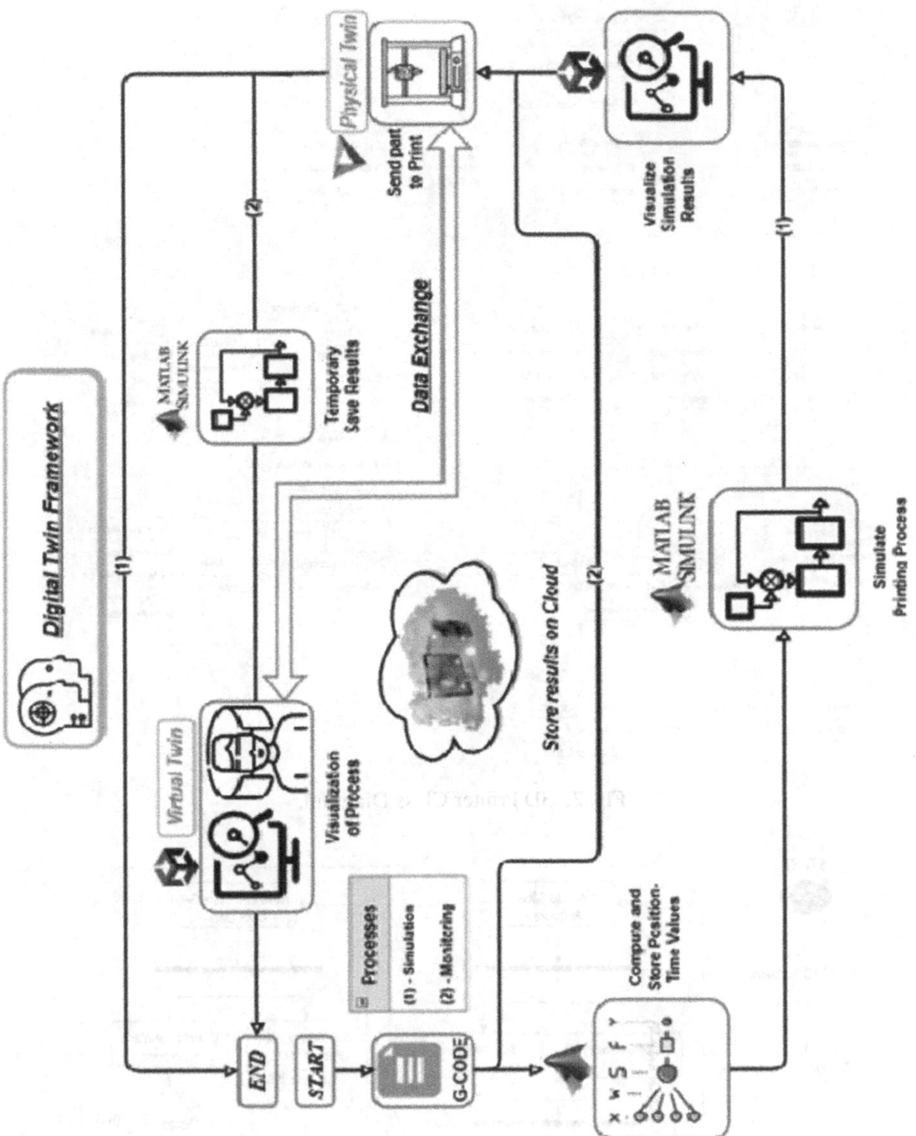

Fig. 1. 3D printer Digital Twin Framework.

The UML is used to model the proposed system, as it is a standardized modelling language that helps to visualize the design of the proposed system. The corresponding UML is presented in Fig. 2.

This will be useful for the user to understand how the process works and how each step is connected to each other. Additionally,, an activity diagram was created to illustrate the flow of the process, as presented in Fig. 3.

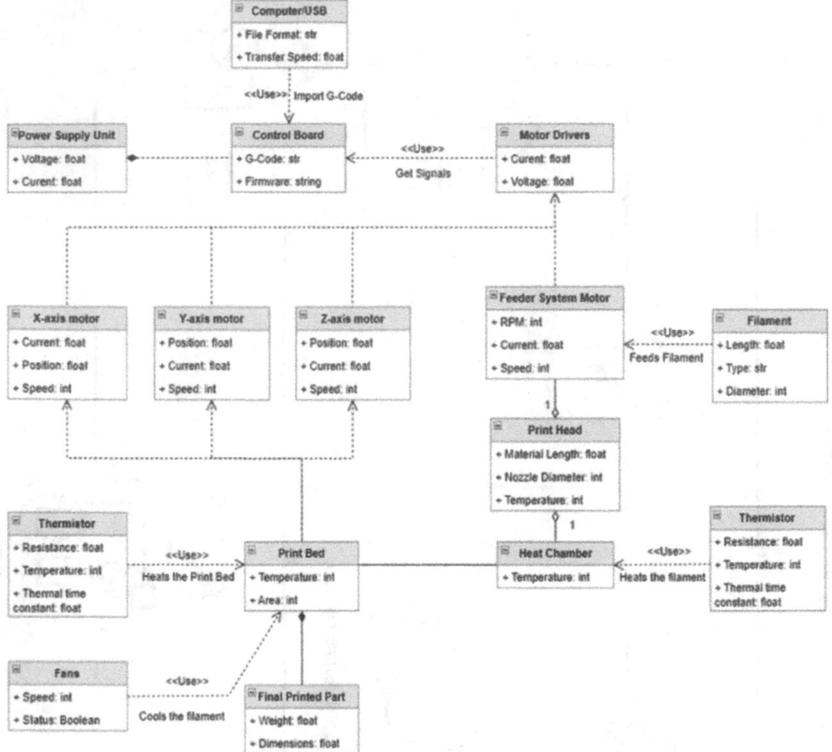

Fig. 2. 3D Printer Class Diagram.

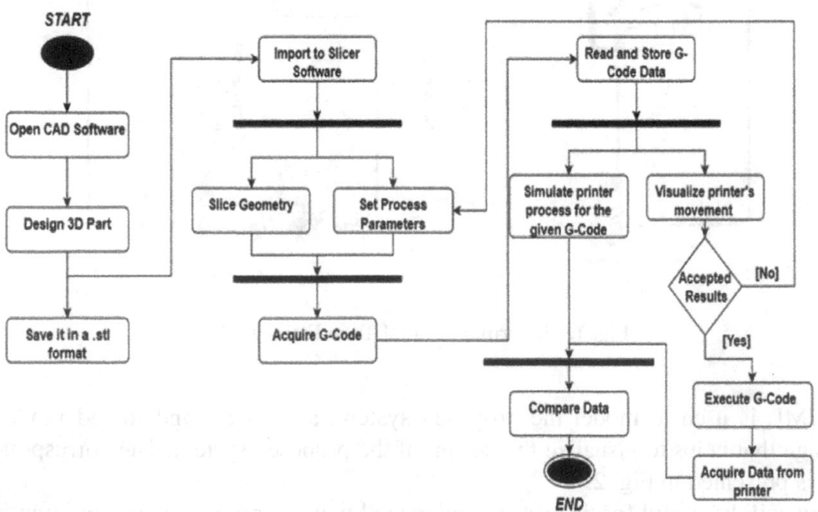

Fig. 3. Process Activity Diagram.

The proposed framework allows the user to collect data from the printer and import it into the model environment, allowing the engineer to monitor the printing process. This can be done in both real-time and simulation time. In simulation time, the monitoring of the process has more of a predictive feature, as it can simulate how the process will continue and if it needs to be stopped before material is wasted. In real-time, the process has a monitoring feature, as it will visualize exactly how the printer responds to the given G-Code commands. This allows for remote monitoring between the computer and the 3D printer without requiring an Internet connection.. A "digital twin" is a continuous cycle of automatic data transfer between the physical and digital worlds without any manual interference in the data transfer. This allows for smooth, flexible, and fast data transfer between the two environments. The received data can provide useful information rather than being simplistic,, which constitutes this process necessary for engineers to gain a deeper understanding of the process parameters. Consequently, engineers are more informed and capable of performing the required adjustments to the physical machine, to achieve the targeted result in terms of printing quality and resource utilization.

4 System Implementation

In this implementation, two software packages were mainly used to create the Digital Twin environment and perform all the necessary computations. The software was used only after the part was designed in CAD (Computer Aided Design) software and sliced with the appropriate slicer software to receive the G-Code file. The Digital Twin model is based on a Sindoh 3DWOX 1 FDM 3D printer. Having that done, the next step was to use MATLAB to analyze the data and create the model. Firstly, the G-Code from the slicer was imported into MATLAB, where it was saved in a matrix format so that every axial movement of the 3D printer could be easily operated. The acquired parameters from G-Code to the MATLAB file are X, Y, and Z (mm) axial movements and F (mm/s) which is the feed rate. The feed rate parameter (F) was used solely to estimate the printing time for each printing process. The time estimation model is critical as it affects the printing sequence of the process. This is because every matrix row that has the X, Y, and Z positions corresponds to a single time value, meaning that if the time value is not correct, the printer may not reach the desired position, leading to a false estimation. The proposed model was created in Simulink, a MathWorks software, that provides a block diagram environment for designing and simulating systems. Simulink can communicate with MATLAB by sharing data from one software to another. The simulated stepper motor of the 3D printer is the model 17PM-KA142B with all three degrees of freedom. In Fig. 3, the block diagram model, created in the Simulink environment, which simulates the unipolar behavior of the 3D printer's stepper motor, is presented. Simulink offers predefined parameterization for certain stepper motors. In our case, a predefined stepper motor was used, similar to the one wanted, adjusting the parameters to the correct ones that match the desired model. The proposed framework has two main applications. Firstly, the platform can be used to simulate the printing process of the part before it begins. Secondly, the application is used for real-time monitoring of the process. For the first application, communication between the server (Simulink) and the client (Unity3D) was established with the use of the UDP communication protocol due to its low latency of data transfer. The second application utilizes a Data Acquisition (DAQ) system to retrieve the axial position data from the 3D printer and send it via a microcontroller, so the process can be monitored.

Fig. 4. i) Digital model of 3D printer in Unity 3D development environment; ii) Augmented Reality visualization of the 3D printer (photo taken from Android smart device).

The simulation of the printing process was handled with Unity by generating a parent material (Sphere) for every framerate (0.02 s), which represents a fixed time step within the software. Due to the fact that the generation of the material requires a vast amount of processing power, the generated spheres were not so frequent, meaning that the simulated deposited material did not form a uniform line. However, this simulation provides us with all the necessary information for monitoring the printing process and spotting flaws in the G-Code of the printed part. For the monitoring application, as previously mentioned, a microcontroller and a Wi-Fi module are used to acquire the axial positions of the 3D printer and send the data to the computer over a network communication protocol such as UDP (Fig. 5).

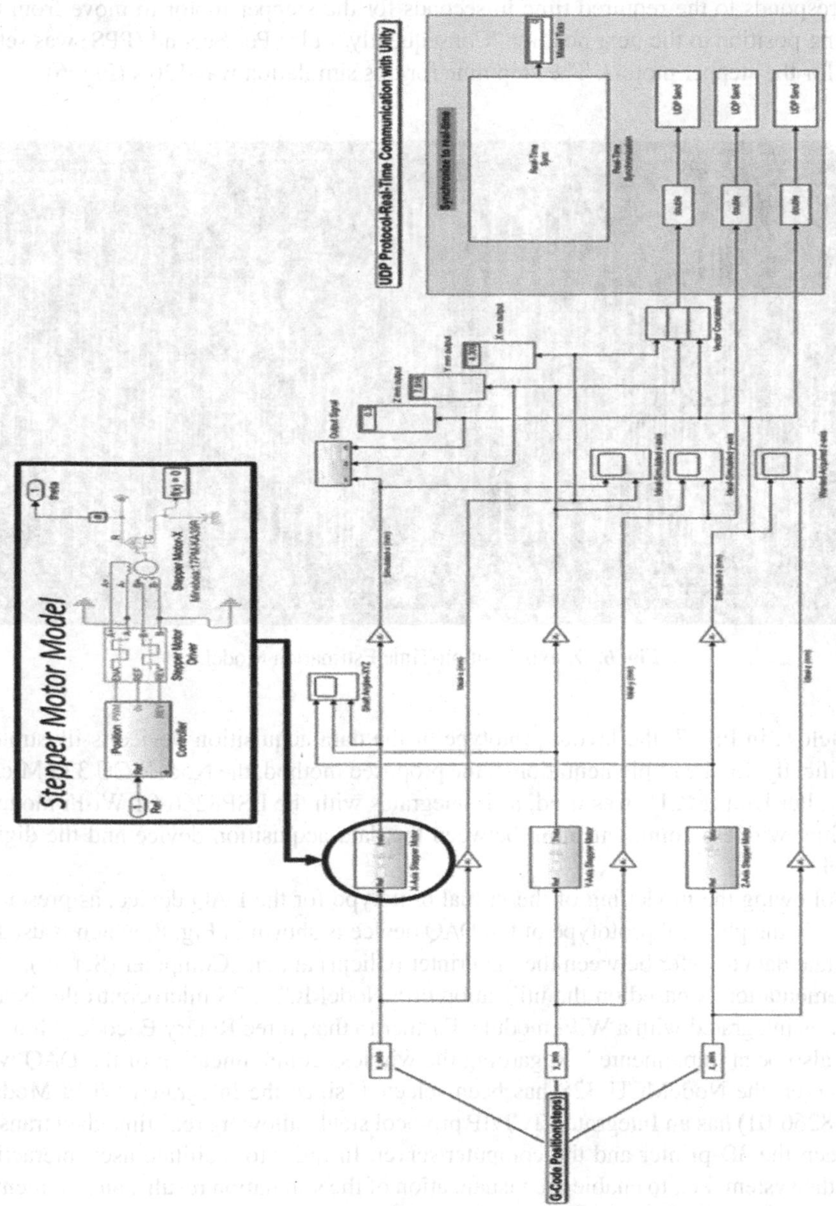

Fig. 5. Block Diagram of 3D Printer Stepper Motors.

The time estimation for each stepper motor is calculated using Eq. 1.

$$t_{Time\ Interval} = \frac{|x_{n+1}| - |x_n|}{200}, \forall n \geq 0 \quad (1)$$

The input for the Simulink stepper motor block diagram, is x (steps)-t (time) matrix, where x is how many steps the stepper motor has completed, to get into position and t corresponds to the required time in seconds for the stepper motor to move from the starting position to the next position. Consequently, Pulse Per Second (PPS) was set to 100, for the stepper motors. The stop time for this simulation was 120 s (Fig. 6).

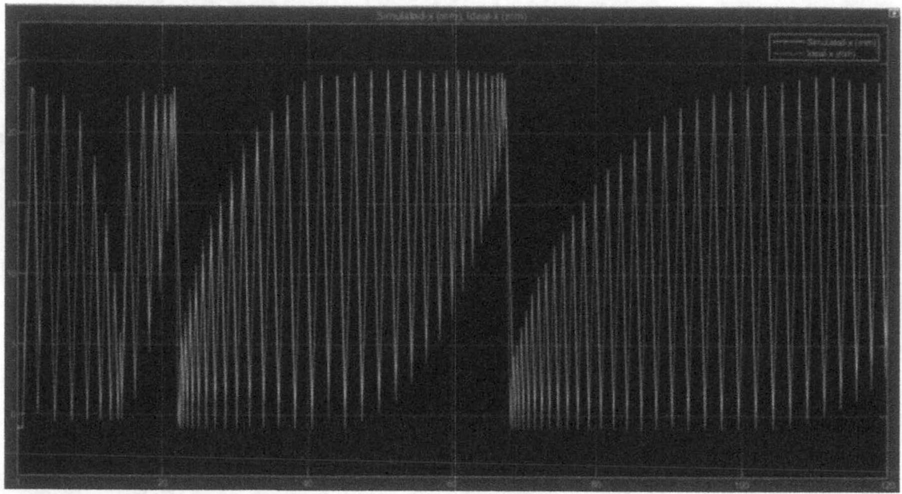

Fig. 6. X axis Position-Time Estimation Model.

Below, in Fig. 7, the layout/prototype of the data acquisition device is illustrated. Specifically, for the implementation of the proposed method, the NodeMCU 32S Micro-Controller Unit (MCU) was used, as it integrates with the ESP8266-01 Wi-Fi module, enabling wireless communication between the data acquisition device and the digital model.

Following the modelling of the virtual prototype for the DAQ device, as presented in Fig. 7, the physical prototype of the DAQ device is shown in Fig. 8, which is used to facilitate data transfer between the 3D Printer (Client) and the Computer (Server). This implementation is based on the utilization of a NodeMCU 32S microcontroller board, which is integrated with a WiFi module. Further to that, three Rotary Encoder Modules have also been implemented. Regarding the wireless communication of the DAQ with the server, the NodeMCU 32S has been selected, since the integrated Wi-Fi Module (ESP8266-01) has an Integrated TCP/IP protocol stack, allowing real-time data transfer between the 3D-printer and the computer/server. In order to facilitate user interaction with the system, i.e., to enable the visualization of the simulation results, an Augmented Reality (AR) application has been developed, compatible with Android smart devices (see Fig. 4). More precisely, the above mentioned DAQ system, is connected to the 3D

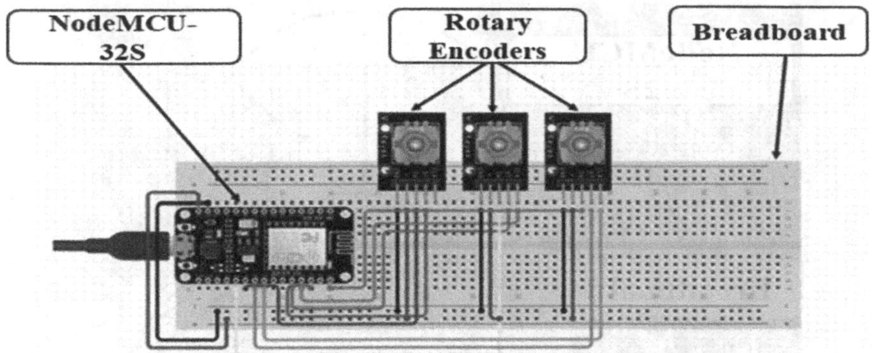

Fig. 7. DAQ (Data Acquisition) virtual prototype.

Printer via a USB cable and communicates with the printer. The three rotary encoders are connected to the system in such a way, that the movement of each stepper motor is also transferred to the encoders, providing accurate real-time position data for each axis.. Then, with the Wi-Fi Module, a webserver can be created by connecting the module to the router's network and sharing the data acquired, with the computer that is connected to the same network. By having the current position of the printer, the engineer can visualize the movement of the printer in near real-time, therefore allowing the monitoring of the process.

The distance between the two profiles of the timing belt has been measured to determine the required diameter for our pulleys, for both x and y axes, and in z axis we measured the diameter of the pulley used on the Sindoh 3D printer, which has the identical dimensions with the other two axes pulleys (i.e., x and y). The measured distance between the two sides is 12 mm, meaning that the diameter of the pulleys used should be equal to 12 mm. Therefore, to ensure a proper coupling between the pulley and the timing belt, the diameter of the 3D printed pulleys must also be the same (Fig. 9).

Having printed the pulleys for all the axes, we can start assembling the DAQ system with the pulleys and connect the system to the printer's axes. However, there were several challenges encountered while fitting the DAQ to the printer due to the enclosed space of the printer. The DAQ system, meaning the rotary encoders, needed to be installed in very tight spaces where access was difficult and collisions were possible, in order to capture the motion from the timing belts (see Fig. 10). As mentioned earlier, to acquire the position of each axis from the 3D printer, we need to connect the rotary encoders to the timing belts of each axis of the system, to enable real-time monitoring of the system. The rotary encoder modules of the DAQ system were installed to the printer with the use of a mount in the x-axis and y-axis to ensure a rigid connection to the printer's frame. Also, a double-sided tape was used to connect the mounts and the encoders to the frame of the printer. To ensure that the pulleys meshed properly with the teeth of the timing belt and to minimize the risk of skipping teeth, some pretensioning was necessary. Large jumper wires were used to connect the microprocessor with the rotary encoder modules, allowing for distant connections. However, it's important to note that when connecting

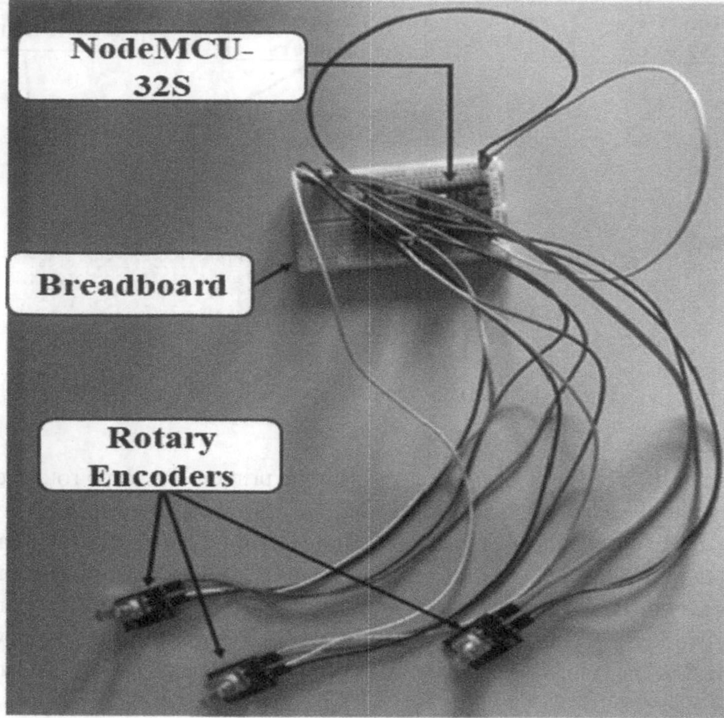

Fig. 8. Physical prototype of DAQ.

jumper cables together to extend the maximum possible distance needed to be reached, noise may be induced in the system, potentially distorting the signal.

5 Experimental Results

A laboratory machine shop produces a range of 3D printed components for quick prototyping or direct installation in assemblies. The validity of the suggested framework was evaluated using this facility; therefore, it is crucial that the component quality adheres to tolerances. Prior to implementing the Digital Twin, almost eight out of every ten parts required post-processing to meet the requisite quality. These parts were mostly complex ones with holes or other intricate geometries. However, after implementing the suggested DT framework, the engineers adapted the machine more effectively based on simulation, resulting in a significant reduction in faulty components. Moreover, with the monitoring module incorporated in the framework, engineers could quickly diagnose defective parts and halt the printing process early, saving valuable time and resources. Utilizing the DT framework, the creation of faulty parts decreased by approximately 60%, meaning that only three out of ten parts required post-processing to reach the required quality.

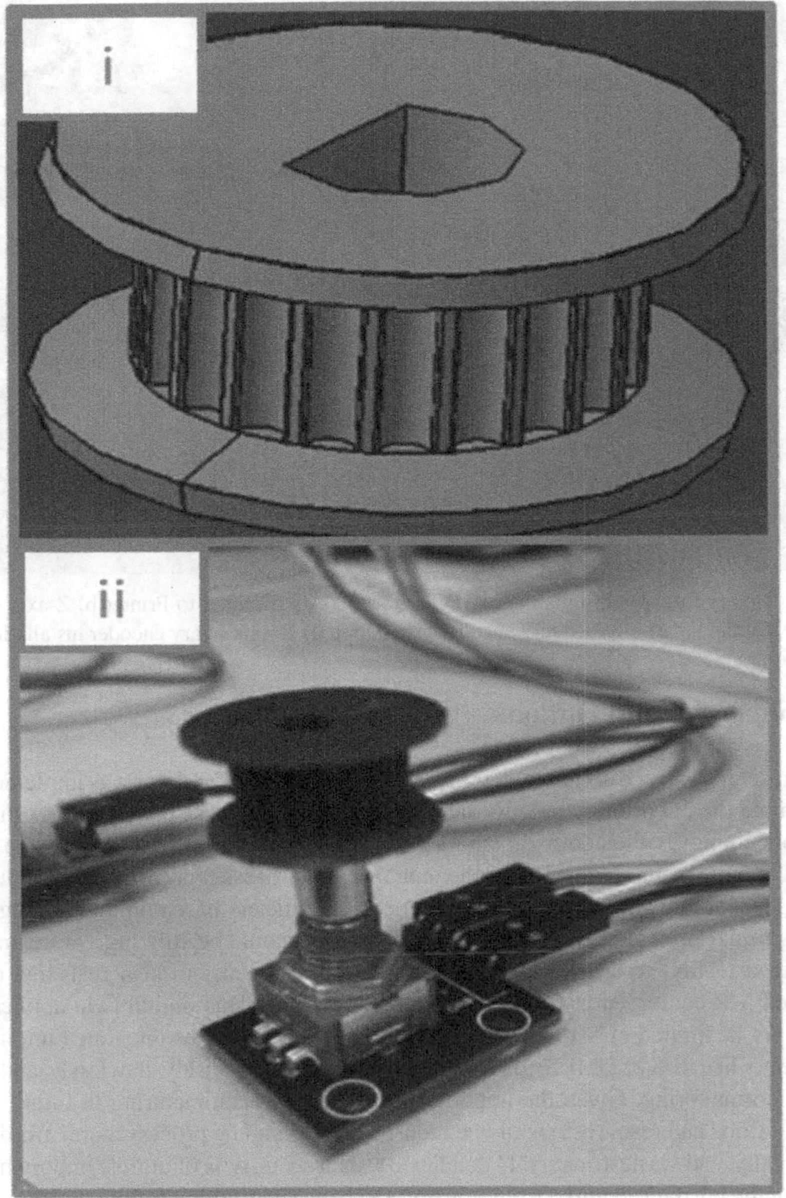

Fig. 9. a) Pulley Design CAD b) DAQ System with pulleys.

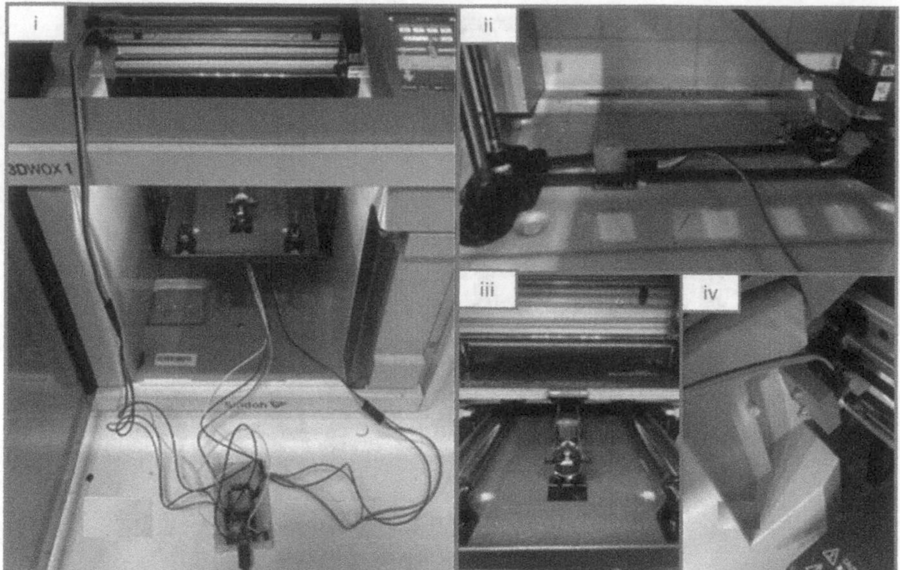

Fig. 10. Rotary Encoder Installation in 3D Printer a) DAQ installed to Printer b) Z-axis rotary encoder installation c) Y-axis rotary encoder installation d) X-axis rotary encoder installation.

6 Conclusion and Outlook

In this research work, a digital twin framework for an FDM 3D printer was implemented to facilitate the 3D printing process and the selection of process parameters. Although this work improves the additive manufacturing process for plastic materials, the integration of more technologies can further enhance the process. For instance, introducing a machine learning algorithm to suggest process parameters based on the training data could optimize print quality or speed. Another addition could be utilizing a more immersive mixed reality experience to monitor the printing process in near real-time using advanced MR equipment such as Microsoft's HoloLens. This digital twin application should not be limited only to the FDM process, but also could be integrated into metal 3D printers like SLS or DMLS, to produce structural parts precisely, flawlessly, and with real-time monitoring. Given the importance of additive manufacturing in future technology, efforts and resources should be focused on making the process more affordable, eco-friendly, and waste-friendly. In conclusion, data security is of utmost importance in handling the big data acquired from sensors, and hence encryption techniques should be used. Additionally, using UML diagrams to create class diagrams is critical in complex manufacturing systems. As technology advances, the integration of cutting-edge sensors and data analytics tools is expected to increase the precision and effectiveness of process optimization, quality control, and maintenance activities in 3D manufacturing.

References

1. Mourtzis, D., Angelopoulos, J., Panopoulos, N.: Equipment design optimization based on digital twin under the framework of zero-defect manufacturing. Procedia Comput. Sci. **1**(180), 525–533 (2021)
2. Mourtzis, D., Togias, T., Angelopoulos, J., Stavropoulos, P.: A digital twin architecture for monitoring and optimization of fused deposition modeling processes. Procedia CIRP **1**(103), 97–102 (2021)
3. Lechler, T., et al.: Introduction of a comprehensive structure model for the digital twin in manufacturing. In: 2020 25th IEEE International Conference on Emerging Technologies and Factory Automation (ETFA) 2020, vol. **1**, pp. 1773–1780 (2020)
4. Tao, F., Cheng, J., Qi, Q., Zhang, M., Zhang, H., Sui, F.: Digital twin-driven product design, manufacturing and service with big data. Int. J. Adv. Manuf. Technol. **94**, 3563–3576 (2018)
5. Zhuang, C., Liu, J., Xiong, H.: Digital twin-based smart production management and control framework for the complex product assembly shop-floor. Int. J. Adv. Manuf. Technol. **96**, 1149–1163 (2018)
6. Leng, J., Zhang, H., Yan, D., Liu, Q., Chen, X., Zhang, D.: Digital twin-driven manufacturing cyber-physical system for parallel controlling of smart workshop. J. Ambient Intell. Humanized Comput. **13**(10), 1155–1166 (2018)
7. Papacharalampopoulos, A., Giannoulis, C., Stavropoulos, P., Mourtzis, D.: A digital twin for automated root-cause search of production alarms based on KPIs aggregated from IoT. Appl. Sci. **10**, 2377 (2020)
8. Mourtzis, D., Angelopoulos, J., Panopoulos, N.: Personalized PSS design optimization based on digital twin and extended reality. Procedia CIRP **1**(109), 389–394 (2022)
9. He, B., Bai, K.J.: Digital twin-based sustainable intelligent manufacturing: a review. Adv. Manuf. **9**, 1–21 (2021)
10. Reisch, R.T., et al.: Context awareness in process monitoring of additive manufacturing using a digital twin. Int. J. Adv. Manuf. Technol. **1**, 1–8 (2022)
11. Rossi, A., Moretti, M., Senin, N.: Neural networks and NARXs to replicate extrusion simulation in digital twins for fused filament fabrication. J. Manuf. Processes **1**(84), 64–76 (2022)
12. Krückemeier, S., Anderl, R.: Concept for digital twin based virtual part inspection for additive manufacturing. Procedia CIRP **1**(107), 458–462 (2022)
13. Scheffel, R.M., Fröhlich, A.A., Silvestri, M.: Automated fault detection for additive manufacturing using vibration sensors. Int. J. Comput. Integr. Manuf. **34**(5), 500–514 (2021). https://doi.org/10.1080/0951192X.2021.1901316
14. Jaensch, F., Csiszar, A., Scheifele, C., Verl, A.: Digital twins of manufacturing systems as a base for machine learning. In: 2018 25th International conference on mechatronics and machine vision in practice (M2VIP), pp. 1–6 (2018)
15. Mourtzis, D., Angelopoulos, J., Panopoulos, N.: Development of a PSS for smart grid energy distribution optimization based on digital twin. Procedia CIRP **1**(107), 1138–1143 (2022)
16. Mourtzis, D., Angelopoulos, J., Siatras, V.: Cycle time estimation model for hybrid assembly stations based on digital twin. In: Lalic, B., Majstorovic, V., Marjanovic, U., von Cieminski, G., Romero, D. (eds.) APMS 2020. IAICT, vol. 591, pp. 169–175. Springer, Cham (2020). https://doi.org/10.1007/978-3-030-57993-7_20
17. Stavropoulos, P., Papacharalampopoulos, A., Siatras, V., Mourtzis, D.: An AR based digital twin for laser based manufacturing process monitoring. Procedia CIRP **1**(102), 258–263 (2021)

Main Event

Measuring the Phase Shift Between Hall Signals and Phase Voltages for Purpose of End Quality Control of BLDC Motor Production

Jernej Mlinarič[1,2(✉)], Boštjan Pregelj[2], and Janko Petrovčič[2]

[1] Jožef Stefan International Postgraduate School, Jamova Cesta 39, 1000 Ljubljana, Slovenia
jernej.mlinaric@ijs.si

[2] Department of Systems and Control, Jožef Stefan Institute, Jamova Cesta 39, 1000 Ljubljana, Slovenia

Abstract. BLDC motors for demanding applications require a sensor system for electronic commutation to determine the current rotor position. Often, three Hall magnetic sensors, angularly displaced by 60° or 120°, are used for this purpose. Ideally, commutation should be performed precisely at the rotor position where the back induced electromotive force (BEMF) crosses the zero value. However, in reality, the deviation (phase shift between the voltage crossing the zero value and the HALL sensor switching) is different from 0° and depends on the mechanical tolerances of motor manufacturing, sensor soldering position, and rotor magnetization repeatability. To perform comprehensive final testing of motors, a dedicated measuring method had to be developed, as professional measuring instruments (Frequency counters) are not suitable for this purpose. This is due to winding voltage not being sinusoidal but pulse-width modulated. It is also not possible to rotate the motor during testing with an additional drive. Consequently, that is why the measurement can only be performed during the coast-down period, when the rotational speed exponentially decreases. In this paper, we present a solution, developed for the EOL (end-of-line) quality assessment production of electric motors (BLDCs) at Domel company. It consists of a PCB for signal preparation, a fast USB module for simultaneous acquisition of analog signals, software for data processing, result analysis and result presentation and company database for results storage.

Keywords: Phase shift · Hall sensors · Phase voltage · End quality control · BLDC · Filtering · Run-down

1 Introduction

Owing to their affordability and good technical characteristics, BLDC (brushless DC) motors are increasingly being used and integrated into various machines and devices. While they are slightly more expensive than brushed DC motors or asynchronous AC motors, BLDC motors are primarily found in professional appliances and devices, most commonly in professional handheld battery-powered tools [1].

S. Terzi et al. (Eds.): IN4PL 2023, CCIS 1886, pp. 21–31, 2023.
https://doi.org/10.1007/978-3-031-49339-3_2

The greatest advantage of BLDC motors is their high efficiency, the ability to adjust rotational speed, and controlled torque, regulated by the motor control system [1]. Structurally and operationally, a BLDC motor is similar to a synchronous AC motor, with permanent magnets placed in the rotor, creating a rotor magnetic field that synchronously follows the stator magnetic field generated by the stator windings. It is important for optimal efficiency and effective control that the precise position of the rotor's magnetic field is known, which is determined by the rotor's position.

The rotor's position is determined by position sensors, most commonly Hall effect sensors. Typically, three Hall effect sensors are installed around the motor, positioned at 60° or 120° angles from each other [2, 3]. However, in practice, there are always slight deviations in the angular displacement during the production of electric motors. These deviations are a result of manufacturing tolerances of components, imprecise soldering of Hall effect sensors, positioning of magnetic axes in the sensor ring, and switching levels of the sensors [4]. When combined with deviations in the magnetic axes of the rotor magnets, it is evident that the measured position of the rotor, detected by Hall sensors, slightly deviates from the position of the stator field, which causes the phase shift between voltages in the stator windings and Hall signals. This phase shift between Hall signals and phase voltages later reflects in lower efficiency and larger deviations in torque regulation during motor operation.

2 Research Problem

Producers that incorporating BLDC motors into their high-tech devices aim to minimize the phase shift between Hall signals and phase voltages. Since this problem occurs due to various deviations in production process, it is sensible to measure this phase shift at the end of the production process or during the end quality control. The company Domel d. o. o. from Železniki also has this requirement.

In a laboratory environment, this phase shift (Fig. 1) can be measured using standard measuring devices while rotating the motor with an auxiliary drive. The signals from the Hall effect sensors and induced voltages in the windings are connected to the measuring device. The time difference between the zero crossings of the phase voltage and the rising or falling edges of the Hall effect signal is measured, and this difference is then correlated with the rotational speed or signal period to calculate the phase shift and can be calculated according to (1).

$$\varphi = \frac{\Delta t}{t_p} \cdot 360^\circ \quad (1)$$

where:

- φ – phase shift
- Δt – time difference between the phase voltage transition and the response of the Hall sensor signal
- t_p – period length of the signal

However, this method of measuring phase shift is not suitable for use in production as it is too time-consuming for an automated production line. It would require a special testing device to provide external rotor drive for measurement purposes. Moreover, during normal operation of a BLDC motor controlled by a BLDC controller, the voltage waveforms on the windings are not sinusoidal but pulse-width modulated. With such voltage waveforms, the phase shift cannot be accurately measured.

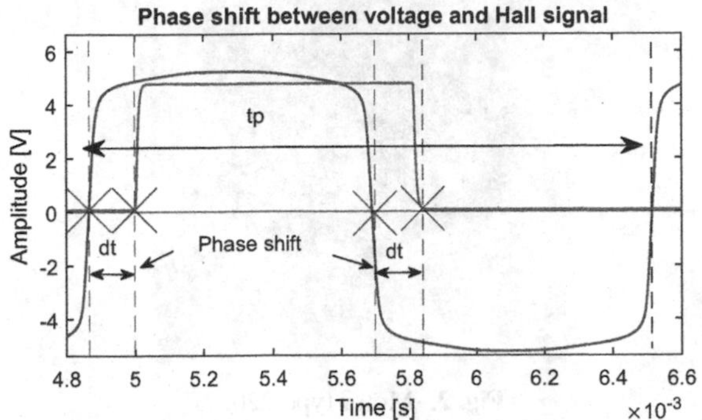

Fig. 1. Phase shift between voltage and Hall signal.

The solution to this problem is to perform the phase shift measurements immediately after turning off the motor and allowing it to coast to a stop. The motor comes to a stop within a few seconds, during which time the signal frequency changes (exponentially decreases). Due to this characteristic, measuring with standard laboratory meters is unfortunately not possible. Therefore, a new method of measuring phase shift had to be developed.

In this paper, we present the design and implementation of the procedure and algorithm for measuring phase shift. We also introduce a PCB, developed specifically for this purpose, which enables the preparation of measurement signals that are then converted into digital form by an analog-to-digital module. Finally, the results of implementing the algorithm are presented.

3 Motor Type 720

The phase shift between the Hall signals and phase voltages is measured during the final inspection of 720-type motors (Fig. 2). These BLDC motors are manufactured by Domel d. o. o. and are intended for integration into professional electric garden tools. The motor's rotor has 2 pairs of poles, and standard Hall effect sensors are used to determine the rotor position.

Fig. 2. Motor type 720.

4 The Proof of Concept

When the motor is disconnected from the power supply, it continues to rotate for a few moments until it comes to a complete stop due to the rotor's inertia. The larger the rotor's inertia and the lower the bearing friction, the longer it takes for the motor to stop. During the deceleration process, the rotating magnetic field induces a sinusoidal voltage in the stator windings. At the same time, the Hall effect sensors generate square wave signals that indicate the rotor's phase shift at specific angles. The motor typically decelerates according to a natural exponential function, resulting in a decrease in the amplitude and frequency of the induced voltage, or an increase in the signal period. This change in period is also reflected in the Hall effect sensor signals.

For the purpose of measuring phase shift, it is necessary to capture the Hall effect sensor signals and induced voltages at the correct time. These signals can then be processed subsequently. It is important to consider the time limitations for signal recording (the motor comes to a stop within 2 s, and only the initial fractions of a second are relevant for processing) as well as the sampling limitations (sampling rates of several hundred kilohertz are needed to detect phase shift at high speeds). Additionally, there are accuracy requirements set by the customer, with a desired precision of $\pm 1°$. Through experimentation and calculations, it has been determined that capturing voltage and Hall effect sensor signals for approximately 1.2 s after motor disconnection (or at a speed of 10,000 RPM) is suitable for the given case. To achieve the desired measurement accuracy, simultaneous signal sampling with a frequency of at least 500 kHz is necessary.

The phase shift is measured separately for each phase, at every transition of the phase voltage through zero for one complete rotor revolution. Since the rotor has 2 pairs of poles, during one full revolution of the rotor, there are two periods of phase voltage induced in the stator windings, resulting in a total of 4 zero crossings (2 on the rising edge and 2 on the falling edge of the voltage). These zero crossings are also reflected in the Hall effect sensor signals, with 2 transitions on the rising edge and 2 transitions on the falling edge of the signal. Considering the four signal transitions and three phases, a total of 12 measurements of phase shifts are obtained for one revolution of the motor.

5 Methodology

The previously presented concept was then implemented on the production line ML 15, located at Domel company in Železniki. This line manufactures various variants of BLDC motors of type 720. The solution presented in this paper represents an upgrade to the diagnostic system. To upgrade the system, we needed a high-speed module for synchronous sampling and A/D conversion of analog signals (with a USB connection to a computer) and a printed circuit board (PCB) for signal conditioning. Considering the requirements mentioned (high sampling frequency, simultaneous sampling of multiple input signals), we chose the NI 6343 USB module from National Instruments, which allows simultaneous sampling of 12 channels at a frequency of up to 500 kHz. We designed the electronic circuit with filters ourselves. For the development and preparation of the algorithm, we first created a program in the LabView software environment for acquiring signals from the USB module, and then we developed and prepared the delay calculation algorithm in MATLAB. Finally, we translated the developed algorithm into the C ++ programming language and integrated the solution into the software support of the diagnostic system.

5.1 USB Module for Analog Signal Acquisition

For signal acquisition, we used the USB-6343 A/D converter module with a USB output from National Instruments (Fig. 3, [5]). This is a high-performance multifunction I/O device with 16 differential analog inputs, simultaneous sampling, and 16-bit analog-to-digital conversion. It achieves a maximum signal sampling frequency of 500 kSamples/s (or 500 kHz), which we fully utilized in this case [5]. With this card, we captured 6 signals: three voltages from the stator windings and three signals from the Hall sensors.

Fig. 3. USB module NI 6343 [5].

5.2 PCB

The PCB (Fig. 4) is necessary for proper preparation of the measured signals. The induced voltage signals have a sinusoidal shape with amplitudes of 30 V or higher, while the Hall sensor signals are square waves with an amplitude of 3.3 V. Their frequency ranges from 0 Hz (DC) to 1 kHz. Due to the presence of various interfering signals from the environment and the possibility of unforeseen errors during handling of untested new products (unstable contacts, poorly welded winding connections, incorrect voltage settings, etc.), the electronic circuit ensures adequate filtering of all signals and galvanic isolation between individual channels. Special attention was given to aligning the phase shifts of the filtering circuits for the preparation of the induced voltage signals and the Hall sensor signals. These phase shifts caused by electronic filters are added to the key values of this measurement system. We have achieved a phase mismatch of less than 1° between the channels that prepare the induced voltage signals and the channels that prepare the Hall sensor signals, and this mismatch does not significantly change during operation to adversely affect the measurement results. The remaining phase mismatch is eliminated through a calibration process, where measured deviations are measured, stored, and then considered by the computer in the calculation of final results. Since the precise crossing point of the stator induced voltage through zero is crucial for measuring phase shifts, the electronic circuit nonlinearly transforms these signals during capture, intentionally amplifying this crossing point while appropriately limiting the remaining part of the signal.

Fig. 4. Developed PCB.

5.3 Development of Algorithm

Development in LabView. During the development phase, due to time constraints and the experimental suitability of the tools, we initially performed signal acquisition and drafted the algorithm using the LabVIEW environment. We chose LabVIEW because it enables easy and quick integration and operation of the A/D converter module, as the selected module and LabVIEW are products of the same company, National Instruments.

The developed program allowed for simultaneous acquisition of analog signals at a sampling frequency of 500 kHz. It captured the signals of all three phases of the stator windings and Hall sensors at the moment when we switched the motor controller to the coasting mode. These signals were then converted into digital format and stored in a binary file (BIN), which was later used for calculating the phase shifts. An excerpt of this program is shown in Fig. 5.

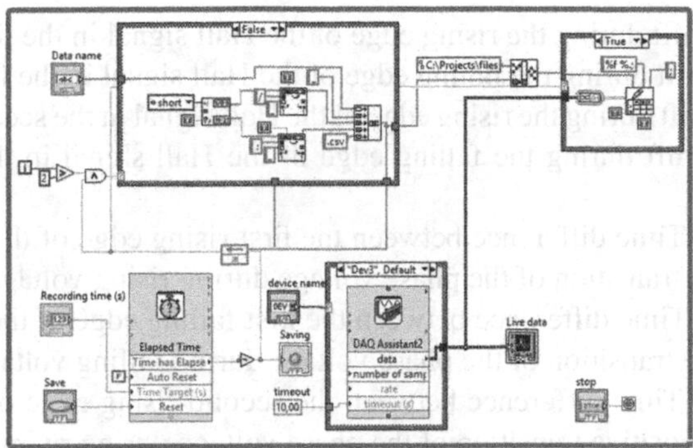

Fig. 5. Part of program in LabVIEW.

Development in Matlab. Similar to the LabVIEW tool, we also used the Matlab software for algorithm development purposes. We chose Matlab because it allows for easy and quick implementation of various algorithm variations, graphical visualization of results, statistical analysis of data, and verification of performance on different sets of measured experimental results.

In the experimental algorithm, we first open the files generated by the LabVIEW program during measurements and sort them accordingly based on their content (the signals are named PhaseU, PhaseV, PhaseW, HallU, HallV, and HallW). The algorithm then approximates the zero-crossings of the phase signals (PhaseU, PhaseV, and PhaseW), determines whether the signal is rising or falling at each crossing, and calculates the signal period. From the calculated signal period, the motor speed is then determined. Since the motor has 2 pole pairs, two consecutive periods of the signal are used to calculate the actual motor speed.

Once the measured decreasing motor speed reaches the desired speed at which we expect an appropriate measurement result (sufficient resolution and suitable accuracy) (approximately 10000 RPM), we identify the rising and falling points of the corresponding Hall signal (e.g., HallU for PhaseU signal). These points are determined as the increasing or decreasing values across a selected threshold. Figure 6 illustrates the determination of these points for one revolution, and Eqs. (2), (3), (4) and (5) depict the calculation of individual phase shift.

$$\varphi_{rise1} = \frac{\Delta t_{h1rise-f1pos}}{t_{p1}} \cdot 360^\circ \tag{2}$$

$$\varphi_{fall1} = \frac{\Delta t_{h1fall-f1neg}}{t_{p1}} \cdot 360^\circ \tag{3}$$

$$\varphi_{rise2} = \frac{\Delta t_{h2rise-f2pos}}{t_{p2}} .360^\circ \tag{4}$$

$$\varphi_{fall2} = \frac{\Delta t_{h2fall-f2neg}}{t_{p2}} \cdot 360^\circ \tag{5}$$

where:

- φ_{rise1} – Phase shift during the rising edge of the Hall signal in the first signal period
- φ_{fall1} – Phase shift during the falling edge of the Hall signal in the first signal period
- φ_{rise2} – Phase shift during the rising edge of the Hall signal in the second signal period
- φ_{fall2} – Phase shift during the falling edge of the Hall signal in the second signal period
- $\Delta t_{h1rise-f1pos}$ – Time difference between the first rising edge of the Hall signal and the first positive transition of the phase voltage during rising voltage
- $\Delta t_{h1fall-f1neg}$ – Time difference between the first falling edge of the Hall signal and the first negative transition of the phase voltage during falling voltage
- $\Delta t_{h2rise-f2pos}$ – Time difference between the second rising edge of the Hall signal and the second positive transition of the phase voltage during rising voltage
- $\Delta t_{h1fall-f1neg}$ – Time difference between the second falling edge of the Hall signal and the second negative transition of the phase voltage during falling voltage
- t_{p1} – Length of the first signal period
- t_{p2} – Length of the second signal period

To obtain more accurate and distinguishable results, we calculate the phase shifts for 10 consecutive motor revolutions, and we provide the average of the calculated phase shifts as the measurement result (the values repeat for each revolution). The final measurement results are shown in (6), (7), (8) and (9), while Fig. 7 presents a graphical representation of the measurements for one phase of a motor.

$$\varphi_{rise\_first} = \frac{\sum_{n=1}^{10} \varphi_{rise1n}}{n} \tag{6}$$

$$\varphi_{fall\_first} = \frac{\sum_{n=1}^{10} \varphi_{rfall1n}}{n} \tag{7}$$

$$\varphi_{rise\_second} = \frac{\sum_{n=1}^{10} \varphi_{rise2n}}{n} \tag{8}$$

$$\varphi_{fall\_second} = \frac{\sum_{n=1}^{10} \varphi_{rfall2n}}{n} \tag{9}$$

where:

- φ_{rise_first} – The average of ten consecutive phase shifts during the rise of the first period of the signal
- φ_{fall_first} – The average of ten consecutive phase shifts during the fall of the first period of the signal
- φ_{rise_second} – The average of ten consecutive phase shifts during the rise of the second period of the signal
- φ_{fall_second} – The average of ten consecutive phase shifts during the fall of the second period of the signal

Once we verified the algorithm's functionality, we proceeded to conduct a series of measurements on the type 720 motors. Before that, we used a function generator (Tektronix AFG 31051) to simulate the winding voltages, and its trigger output served as a simulation of the Hall sensor signal. This generator also functions as the system's calibrator in the final implementation.

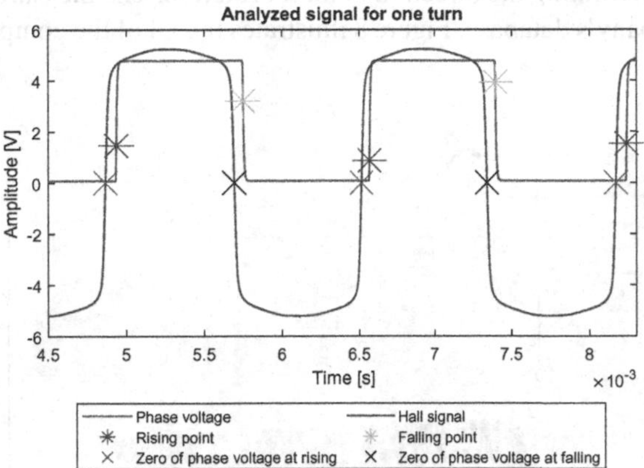

Fig. 6. Signal analysis for one turn.

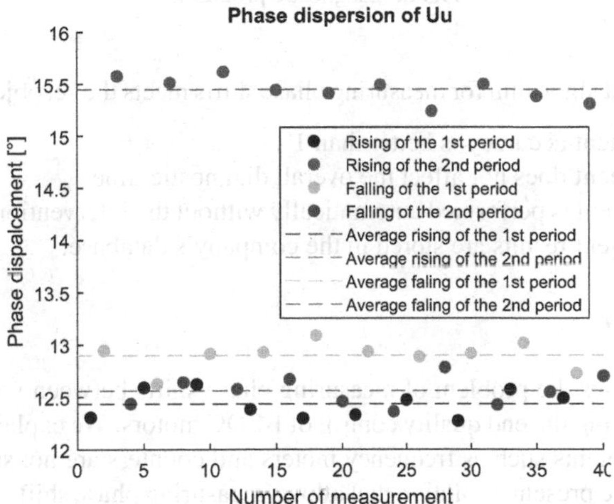

Fig. 7. Phase shift measurements, phase U.

Programming Algorithm in C++. After successful testing in the Matlab environment, the signal acquisition algorithm presented in Chapter 0 and the phase shift calculation algorithm presented in Chapter 0 were implemented as a subroutine in the C++ programming language. This subroutine was then added to the existing diagnostic program. The added subroutine functions as a specific module used only for type 720 motors with Hall angle sensors.

5.4 Results

The algorithm developed for measuring the angular position provides measurement results for all 4 voltage transitions for each phase separately, resulting in a total of 12 measurements. The measurement is performed during motor deceleration in less than 300 ms with an accuracy of 0.3° and measurement repeatability of ±0.2°. The algorithm also allows for determining the direction of motor rotation. The measurement results are stored in the company's database. Figure 8 illustrates the UI of the company's diagnostic software.

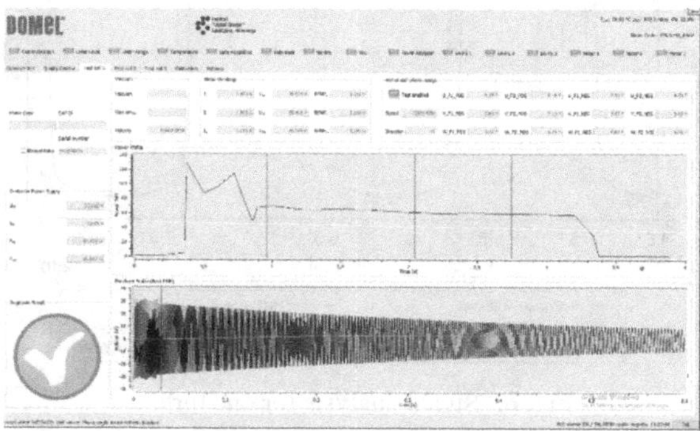

Fig. 8. Diagnostic program.

The developed algorithm for measuring phase shifts meets the set objectives, namely:

- The measurement accuracy is better than 1°.
- The measurement does not affect the overall diagnostic time.
- The measurement is performed automatically without the intervention of an operator.
- The measurement results are stored in the company's database.

6 Conclusion

The paper addresses the problem of measuring phase shifts between voltages and Hall sensor signals during the end quality control of BLDC motors. We explain why standard measuring instruments such as frequency meters and counters are not suitable for such measurements. We present a solution that allows measuring phase shifts with acceptable accuracy during the motor run-down.

The method was developed efficiently using LabView as the initial programming tool. This was followed by designing and testing the algorithm in the Matlab programming environment. In the final phase, the algorithm was converted into the C++ programming language and implemented in the diagnostic system of the ML15A assembly line at Domel.

For the implementation of the method, an A/D converter module with simultaneous acquisition of measurement channels was used, along with a specially designed PCB for signal pre-processing.

The presented measurement method is not intended as a replacement for standard measuring instruments that measure frequency, time delays, and pulse counting. Instead, it addresses the problem of measuring phase shifts in time-varying signals that occur during the coasting of electric motors.

The developed method successfully operates on the production line in a real industrial environment.

Acknowledgments. The authors acknowledge the financial support from the Slovenian Research Agency (research program No. P2-0001). The presented work is corelated to ARRS project L2-4454.

References

1. Yedamale, P.: Brushless DC (BLDC) Motor Fundamentals. Microchip Technology Inc, Chandler (2003)
2. Carolus, A., Manny, S., Mesganaw, M.: Brushless DC Motor Commutation Using Hall-Effect Sensors. Texas Instruments Inc., Dallas (2019)
3. Kolano, K.: Determining the position of the brushless DC motor rotor. Energies **13**(7), 1607 (2020)
4. Yang, L., Qu, C., Jia, B., Qu, S.: The design of an affordable fault-tolerant control system of the brushless DC motor for an active waist exoskeleton. Neural Comput. Applic. **35**(3), 2027–2037 (2023). https://doi.org/10.1007/s00521-022-07362-7
5. National Instruments USB 6343 module. https://www.ni.com/docs/en-US/bundle/usb-6343-specs/page/specs.html. Last accessed 9 Mar 2023

5G and MEC Based Data Streaming Architecture for Industrial AI

Telmo Fernández De Barrena Sarasola[1,2](✉), Juan Luis Ferrando Chacón[2], Ander García[1,2], and Michail Dalgitsis[3]

[1] Faculty of Engineering, University of Deusto, Mundaitz Kalea, 50, 20012 Donostia-San Sebastian, Spain
tfernandez@vicomtech.org

[2] Department of Data Intelligence for Energy and Industrial Processes, Fundación Vicomtech, Basque Research and Technology Alliance (BRTA), Mikeletegi 57, 20009 Donostia-San Sebastian, Spain

[3] Department of Signal Theory and Communications, Universitat Politècnica de Catalunya (UPC), Campus Nord, Carrer de Jordi Girona, 1, 3, 08034 Barcelona, Spain

Abstract. Availability of computation capabilities and real-time machine data is one key requirement of smart manufacturing systems. Latency, privacy and security issues of cloud computing for Industrial artificial intelligence (AI) led to the edge computing paradigm, where computation is performed close to the data source. As on-premise edge deployments require companies to allocate budget and human resources to acquire and maintain the required information technologies (IT) infrastructure and equipment, they are not feasible for several companies. However, 5G can merge advantages of previous alternatives. Multi-Access Edge Computing (MEC) servers deployed at the edge of the 5G network close to the final user, offer security, privacy, scalability, high throughput and low latency advantages. MECs are suitable for industrial AI, while industrial companies do not face the burden of acquiring and maintaining servers and communication infrastructures. This paper proposes a real-time high-frequency data streaming architecture to deploy Industrial AI applications at MECs. The architecture has been successfully validated with data sent through a 5G network to a Kafka broker at the MEC, where different microservices are deployed in a Kubernetes cluster. The performance of the architecture has been investigated to analyze the capabilities of 5G and MEC to cope with the requirements of Industrial AI applications.

Keywords: High frequency data streaming · Machine learning · Multi-access edge computing · 5G · IIOT · Industry 4.0

1 Introduction

The concept of the Internet of Things (IoT) is gaining importance and has had a significant impact on many areas of modern society in the last years. More and more smart environments are being created, opening new possibilities for innovative applications and developments [1], including the manufacturing field.

The development of intelligent manufacturing systems is considered to bring competitive advantages in the manufacturing industry of major countries [2]. For that reason,

S. Terzi et al. (Eds.): IN4PL 2023, CCIS 1886, pp. 32–52, 2023.
https://doi.org/10.1007/978-3-031-49339-3_3

this industry is trying to implement smart connectivity capabilities of many sensors and devices, cloud computing platforms, and software defined network control and management techniques [3]. Consequently, manufacturing enterprises are moving to develop intelligent machine tools [4], in order to maximize product quality and throughput, as well as to reduce the costs [5, 6].

Cloud computing is transforming the way data is processed. Through cloud computing models, all resources and capabilities are virtualized and provided as a service on an on-demand basis through the cloud, enabling to share computing and storage resources [7]. However, exchanging data between machines/sensors and remote cloud locations may result in delayed responses, high usage of bandwidth, and energy consumption. Another critical drawback of this approach is the security and faults of the external network [8].

To overcome those problems, fog and edge computing solutions are being developed. They are emerging computing infrastructures that bring the computation, storage and network resources closer to the places where data is generated, thus processing time-sensitive data near the source of generation at the network edge [9]. Thus, latency, real-time, network traffic and security requirements can be fulfilled while optimizing the usage of computing resources [6, 10, 11].

Multi-Access Edge Computing (MEC) is a network architecture that is gaining attention for the support of Industrial Internet of Things (IIoT) applications. It is a practical application of edge computing, proposed to be deployed at the RadioNetwork Controller (RNC), or the Base Station (BS), or gNodeB (gNB) in 5G terms [12]. MEC enables low-latency and high-bandwidth communication and provides computing resources at the edge of the network, close to the IIoT devices [4]. This allows for real-time data processing and decision making at the edge, reducing the dependence on central cloud resources and improving the overall system performance.

One of the main benefits of MEC for IIoT is the ability to perform real-time data processing at the edge of the network, this is particularly important for industrial automation and control systems, where response time and reliability are critical. To accomplish this, MEC relies on stream processing, a technique that allows for the real-time analysis of data streams as they are generated. Stream processing frameworks such as Apache Kafka, Apache Flink, and Apache Storm can be used to process data streams in real-time and make decisions based on the data. MEC also allows the use of cloud native technologies such as Kubernetes for container orchestration, to make deployment and scaling of the services more efficient.

Another important aspect of MEC for IIoT is security. Given the sensitive nature of the data being processed, and the critical nature of the IIoT systems, mechanisms such as network slicing and edge firewall can be used to guarantee secure communication and data processing. [13].

Along with cloud and edge technologies, 5G technologies are transforming the way data is processed. They are making it possible to achieve ultra-reliable low latency communications in high density heterogeneous devices and massive machine-type communications (mMTC) scenarios [14]. The combination of different technologies is expected to have impact on industrial systems, contributing to take real-time decisions and achieving efficient and responsive production systems [15].

In this paper a 5G and MEC based real-time high-frequency data streaming architecture for industrial artificial intelligence (AI) is presented. The main contributions of our paper can be summarized as follows:

- Handling real-time high-frequency data streaming in an industrial scenario.
- Presentation of an architecture for industrial use case integrated with MEC and 5G, becoming an alternative to an on-premise cabled sensors solution. This means that the user avoids acquiring and maintaining servers and communication infrastructures and just employs the needed computing resources during the time. On the other hand, thanks to the MEC, this approach enables to centralize and optimize the existing computing resources by different users depending on the requirements of each of them at different moments.

The remainder of this paper is as follows: Sect. 2 presents the related state of the art, Sect. 3 describes the considered scenario and presents the main building blocks of our solution, describing the interaction among the different entities. Sect. 4 validates the design principles of our solution through a comprehensive cloud-native testbed. Finally, Sect. 5 provides the final remarks and concludes this paper.

2 State of the Art

Due to the development of 5G, MEC is gaining attention in both industry and academics [16].

During the last years, different MEC enabled 5G use cases have been proposed in the fields of: video streaming and analytics [17], machine to machine (M2M) and massive Machine Type Communications, autonomous and connected vehicles [18], Augmented Reality (AR), Virtual Reality (VR) and Mixed Reality (MR), unnamed Aerial Vehicles (UAVs), e-Health, Smart Cities, Energy etc. [12, 19].

In the Industry 4.0 ecosystem, the scientific literature demonstrated that 5G deployment with edge computing capabilities could efficiently support production processes [20].

When working with IIoT devices under flexible and high productive scenarios, data processing limitations emerge. In this context, huge amounts of data are generated from different sources, and because of their limited computational and storage capabilities, IIoT devices cannot handle such quantity of data. For this reason, many industries, decided to use edge computing to aggregate this data and perform complex activities such as anomaly detection [21].

In [4] the concepts of digital twin and MEC are integrated, proposing a novel framework for constructing a knowledge-sharing intelligent machine tool swarm for creating smart and flexible machining processes. This enables secure knowledge sharing among different authorized machine tools in an ultra-low latency scenario. To demonstrate the feasibility of the proposed framework, a prototype system is implemented and evaluated.

In [22] a use case combining the concepts of Industry 4.0, MEC, 5G, and deep learning techniques for predicting the malfunctioning of an AGV is presented. The AGV is connected through a 5G access to its PLC, which is deployed and virtualized in a MEC infrastructure. To validate the effectiveness of the proposed solution, different experiments were made using an industrial AGV along with a real 5G network.

However, most of the MEC-related researches focus on the improvement of MEC performance from the perspectives of task offloading [23], energy optimization [24], security defense [25], etc., lacking real-world industrial scenario experiments [4]. Moreover, researchers have not found practical experiments on the predictive maintenance field and real-time data streaming in manufacturing. For that reason, in this paper a real-time high-frequency data streaming architecture to deploy Industrial AI applications at MECs is presented.

3 System Model

In this section we present the network architecture along with a cognitive maintenance use case.

3.1 Network Architecture

Our solution builds on the concept of MEC-enabled mobile networks, wherein multiple Industrial 4.0 containerized microservices are running on top of an edge-cloud infrastructure, namely the MEC site, sharing compute, storage, and network resources, and orchestrated by Kubernetes, while serving end-users in the form of IIOT devices over a 5G network, as shown in Fig. 1. Within the context of our paper, we focus on the end-user and MEC domain and consider the communication pipeline to be expressed as from producer to broker to consumer.

The MEC site is a server and service provider closer to the end user (IIoT) and implements an Industry4.0 management and orchestration (MANO) system to increase the

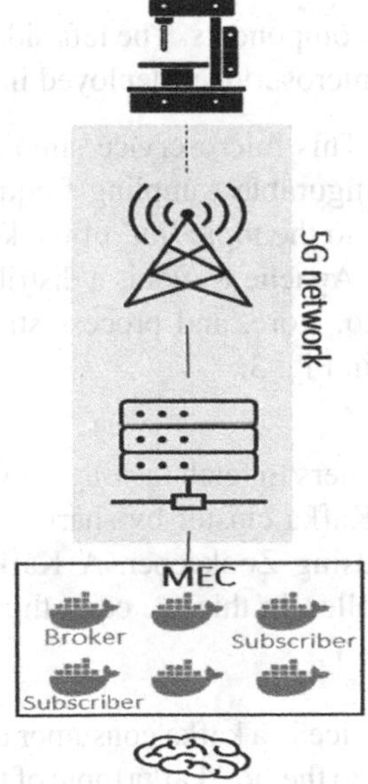

Fig. 1. Network architecture.

performance by hosting microservices (applications containerized), monitoring infrastructure, applications and communication resources, processing monitored metrics, optimizing processed metrics, and scaling resources.

3.2 Predictive Maintenance Use Case

The proposed use case is a predictive maintenance use case of a machine cutting tool, shown in Fig. 2.

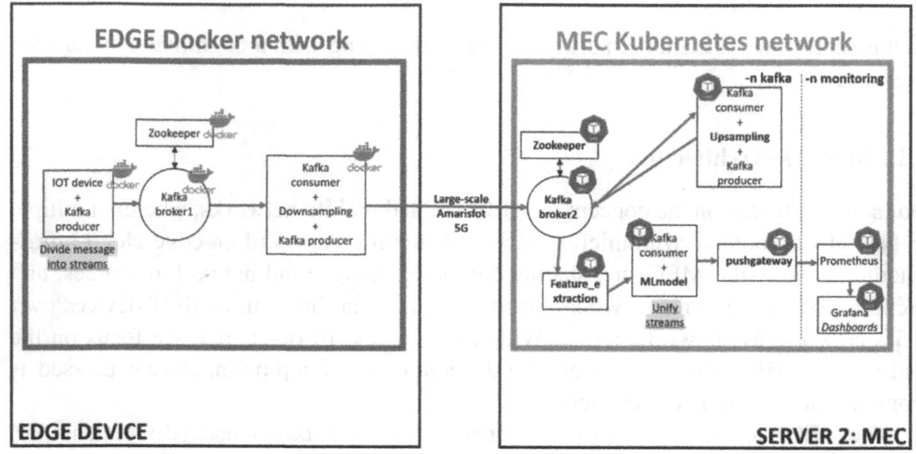

Fig. 2. Use case architecture.

We can differentiate 2 main components. The left-side black box represents an IIoT device. This is composed by 4 microservices deployed in the same Docker network:

1. Data acquisition simultator: This microservice simulates the data acquisition of 6 different sensors with a configurable sampling frequency. Each 1 s batch data is divided into streams and sent to the topic 'iot' of the kafka broker.
2. Kafka broker and zookeeper: Apache Kafka is a distributed data streaming platform that can publish, subscribe to, store, and process streams of records in real-time, which architecture is shown in Fig. 3.

   A Kafka broker allows consumers to fetch messages by topic, partition and offset. Kafka brokers can create a Kafka cluster by sharing information between each other directly or indirectly using Zookeeper. A Kafka cluster has exactly one broker that acts as the Controller. In this use case, the cluster is formed by just 1 broker and 1 topic named 'iot'.

3. Downsampler: This microservice is a kafka consumer and producer at the same time. On the one hand, it subscribes to the 'iot' kafka topic of the "kafka broker 1", receiving like this the simulated data in the data acquisition simulator. On the other hand, it

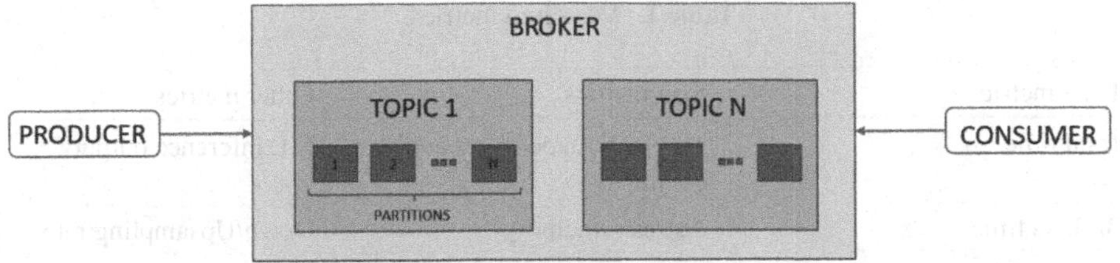

Fig. 3. Single broker Kafka architecture.

sends the data to a topic called 'upsampling' of another kafka broker ('kafka broker 2') located in the MEC through the 5G network. If needed, it downsamples the original data, to reduce the amount of data transmitted to the MEC through the 5G network.

The right-side black box represents the MEC, which is composed of different PODs, equivalent to containers, for performing the predictive maintenance task deployed in a Kubernetes cluster. This Kubernetes cluster contains 2 namespaces, 1 for performing the predictive maintenance task (kafka) and another one (-n monitoring) for monitoring different metrics, such as the architecture performance, ML model inferences etc.:

1. Kafka and zookeeper: As well as in the IOT device, in the MEC there is another kafka broker and zookeeper for connecting the different PODs with each other. There are 3 different topics: 'upsampling', 'f-extraction' and 'ml'.
2. Upsampler: This microservice subscribes to the 'upsampling' topic of the kafka broker to receive the data sent from the IoT device. If a sends the data to the 'f-extraction' topic.
3. Feature extractor: This microservice receives the data sent from the upsampler by subscribing to the 'f-extraction' topic and unifies all the streams corresponding to 1 s. After this, it extracts 5 different features from each of the sensors' data. Afterwards, it sends the features to the 'ml' topic.
4. ML model processor: After extracting the signal features, this microservice receives the features by subscribing to the 'ml' topic and it uses those features as input to make inferences with a pre-trained ML model. Throughout the whole architecture, the metrics shown in Table 1 are measured:

   These features are then sent to the pushgateway microservice.

5. Pushgateway: This is an intermediary service which allows to push the above-mentioned custom metrics to the Prometheus
6. Prometheus: Prometheus is an open-source technology designed to provide monitoring and alerting functionality for cloud-native environments, including Kubernetes. It can collect and store metrics as time-series data, recording information with a timestamp. It can also collect and record labels, which are optional key-value pairs. Apart from the custom metrics mentioned above, Prometheus can scrap other metrics of the Kafka broker, such as the Kafka broker network throughput.
7. Grafana: Grafana is an open-source interactive data-visualization platform which allows users to develop different dashboards to see their data through charts and graphs for easier interpretation and understanding.

Table 1. Measured metrics.

Time metrics	Size metrics	Other metrics
Total time	1 s batch shape (rows and columns)	ML inference output
Brokers time	1 stream memory	Down/Upsampling rate
Data read time	1 stream shape (rows and columns)	
Downsampling, upsampling, feature extraction and inference times	1 stream downsampling shape (rows and columns)	
	1 stream upsampling shape (rows and columns)	
	Number of streams created from the 1 s batch data	
	Number of unified streams to recreate the 1 s batch data	

To ensure correct time measurement in intervals in which time traces are taken on different servers, a clock synchronization has been carried out by means of a ntp server.

For sending and receiving streams, the Python "Faust-streaming" streaming message processing library has been used.

As mentioned above, each 1-s batch of data is divided into streams, as Kafka limits the stream size to 1 Mb. In the use case, streams of maximum 0.3 Mbytes are sent, as heavy messages are considered inefficient by Kafka [26].

The type of data sent from the "IOT Device" are integers. For the serialization and deserialization of messages, the Python library "ormsgpack" has been implemented, which is a library capable of serializing and deserializing messages quickly.

The simulated data acquisition rate starts at 100 kHz, and is increased every 20 s by 50 kHz, until either the network or the Kafka collapses.

4 Performance Evaluation

4.1 Experimental Setup

The hosting of the applications is performed in a Kubernetes (K8s) cluster running in a virtual machine (VM) on top of an OpenStack private cloud server. The applications are containerized as Docker containers and are deployed in the K8s cluster as Pod instances. The K8s cluster consists of only one node with both master and worker functionalities, to simplify its deployment and is divided into separated working spaces, called namespaces, to run applications in a better resource management manner. Prometheus, the monitoring tool of the whole infrastructure, is running as a Pod inside the cluster, in the namespace monitoring, and is responsible for monitoring the K8s cluster, Prometheus itself, and all the rest hosting applications.

Moreover, Prometheus retrieves metrics from a 5G network, which complements the proposed architecture and provides the communication of the Industry4.0 IoT devices. The 5G network utilized by our work is an Amarisoft proprietary solution and consists of two main components, the LTEENB and LTEMME, implemented entirely in software and running on a PC. LTEENB is an LTE/NR base station (eNodeB/gNodeB), while LTEMME is an LTE EPC (Evolved Packet Core)/NR 5GC (5G Core Network) implementation. The metrics are exposed to the Prometheus server with the help of an Amarisoft exporter running in the K8s cluster.

Finally, the K8s cluster is registered to OSM, an open-source Management and Orchestration stack aligned with ETSI NFV Information Models. The purpose of this integration is for onboarding Kubernetes Network Functions (KNFs) orchestrated by OSM, from one hand side to scale MEC's resources when it is necessary, and on the other hand side to slice the networks in order to build an infrastructure that is fully programmable, automated and designed for the Industry4.0 needs.

4.2 Evaluation Analysis

In order to evaluate the performance of the proposed architecture and the 5G, 3 different experiments have been performed. In each of them, different values of reduction and increase in signal resolution have been tested. Each of the experiments ends when either the network used, or the processing capacity (hardware) is saturated. It has been observed that the value used to reduce and increase the resolution of the data impacts on the reason of the saturation. Shows the experimental variables of the performed experiments.

- Experiment 1:

Table 2 shows the experimental variables of this experiment. The experiment starts with a sampling frequency of 100 KHz and 6 channels, without downsampling the streams, dividing the batch into 3 streams/s, being equivalent to sending 0.6 Mbytes/s.

Table 2. Experiment 1 conditions.

	Size metrics	Downsampling rate	Mbytes/sec	Streams/sec
Starting point	100kHz, 6 channels	1	0.6	3
Saturation point	150kHz, 6 channels	1	0.9	6

Fig. 4 shows the start to end spent time to send the generated data per second at a sampling frequency of 100 KHz. It can be seen how this time is between 1.18 and 1.32 s.

Figure 5 displays the times from sending 1 message among different producers and consumers. The communication between servers through the 5G network, represented by a yellow line, takes around 0.8 s, being clearly the highest time of the measured time metrics.

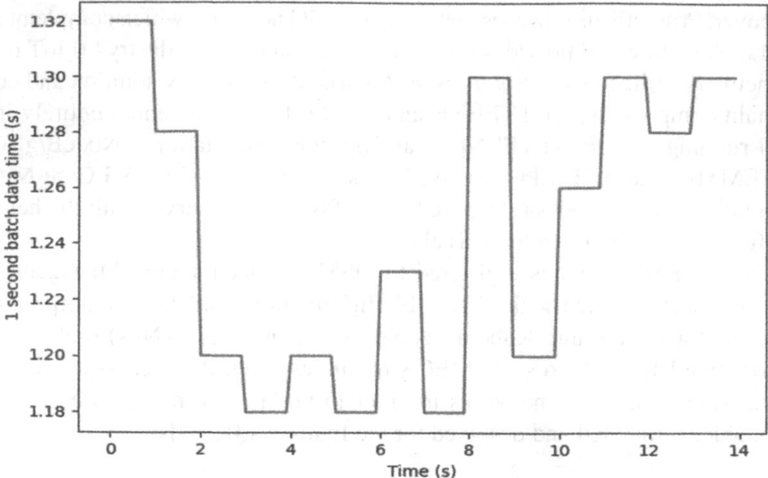

Fig. 4. Total time spent to send 1 s batch data, with 100 kHz sampling frequency, 6 channels and no downsampling rate.

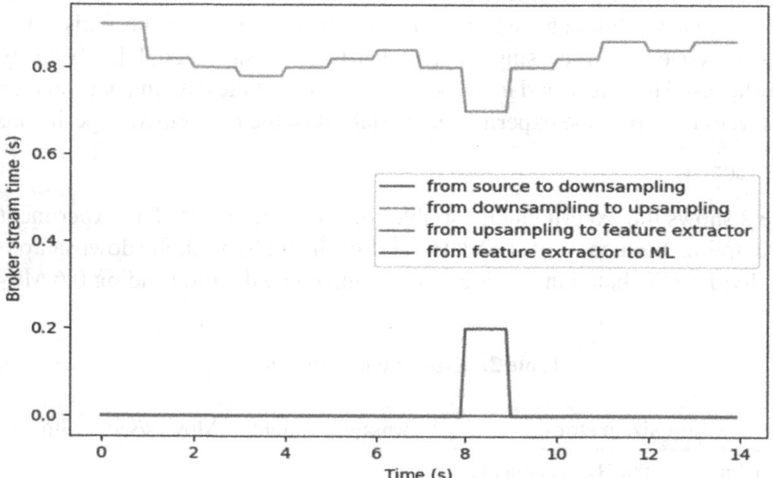

Fig. 5. Broker streams time, with 100 kHz sampling frequency, 6 channels and no downsampling rate.

Figure 6 shows the time employed to perform the downsampling and upsampling operations over a single stream, the time employed to perform the feature extraction over the 1 s batch unified data and ML inference operation. When applying those operations under 100kHz sampling frequency, the downsampling, upsampling and ML inference times are practically 0, whereas the feature extraction needs around 0.04 s.

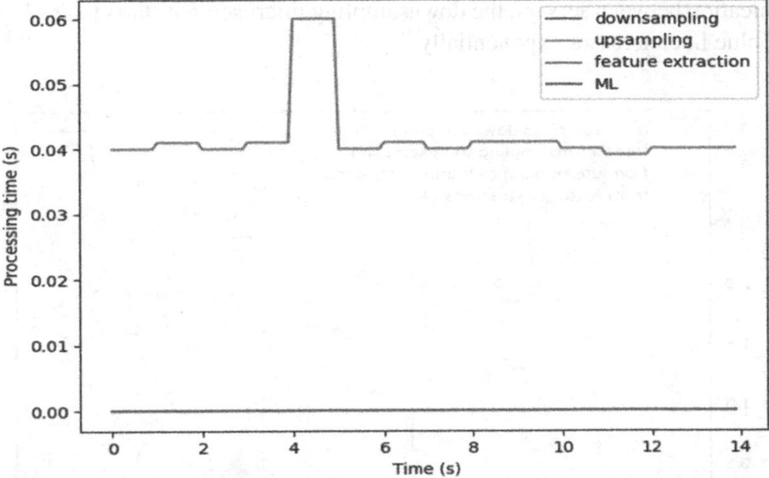

Fig. 6. Processing times, with 100kHz sampling frequency, 6 channels and no downsampling rate.

Figures 7, 8 and 9 display the same information as the one explained above but with a sampling frequency of 150 kHz. Figure 7 shows how just by increasing the sampling frequency by 50 kHz, the architecture starts to collapse.

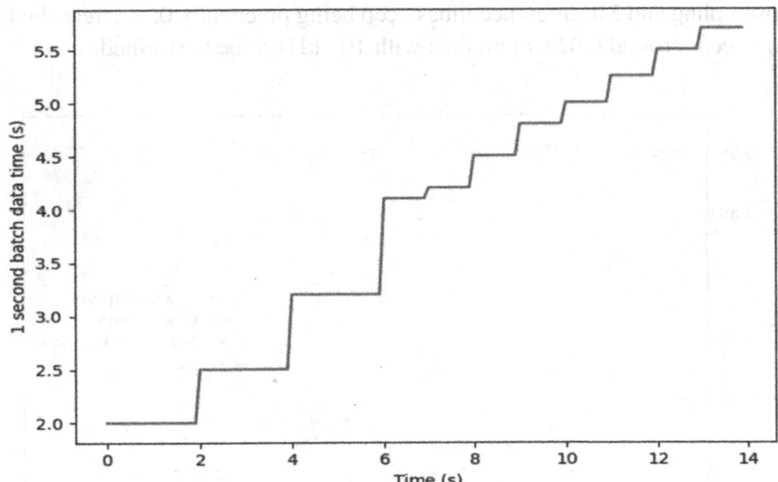

Fig. 7. Total time spent to send 1 s batch data, with 150 kHz sampling frequency, 6 channels and no downsampling rate.

Figure 8 shows how the 5G network is not able to handle the data load. It can be seen how communication between servers through the 5G network, in yellow, increases considerably to around 1.5 s. As batches of data are being generated faster than the communication between servers, the downsampling microservice starts to crash. This is why the blue line increases exponentially.

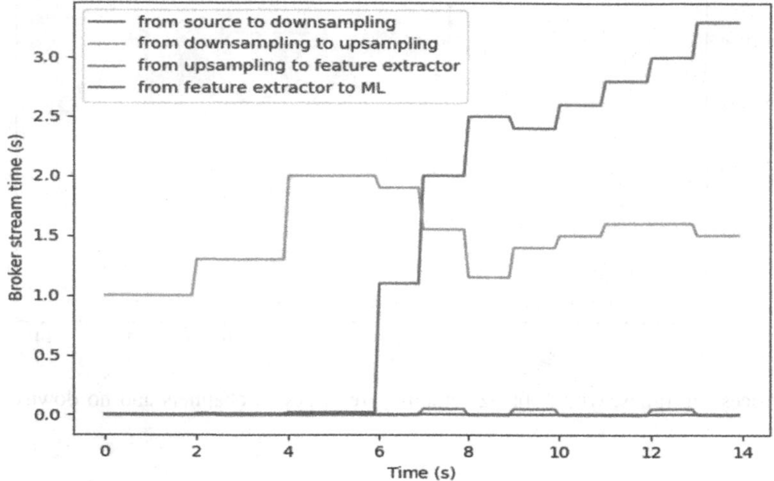

Fig. 8. Broker streams time, with 150kHz sampling frequency, 6 channels and no downsampling rate.

Figure 9 shows how by increasing the sampling frequency by 50kHz, the downsampling, upsampling and ML inference times keep being practically 0, whereas the feature extraction needs around 0.02 s more than with 100 kHz to be performed.

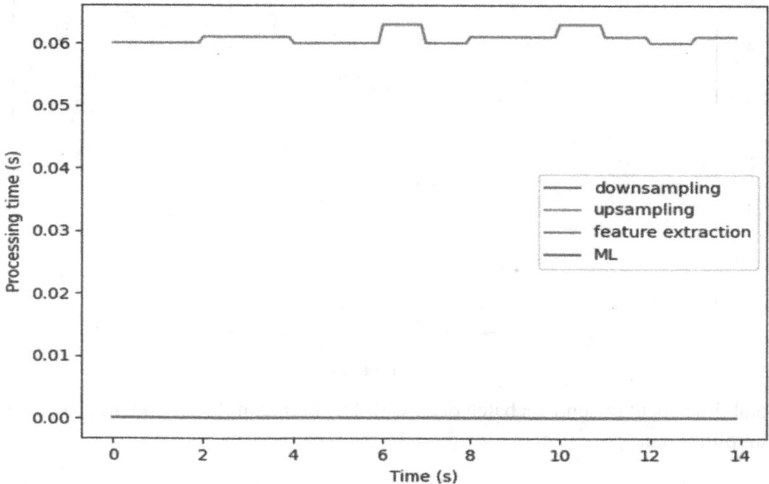

Fig. 9. Processing times, with 150 kHz sampling frequency, 6 channels and no downsampling rate.

- Experiment 2:

To solve the problem of the previous experiment and try to saturate the architecture with a higher sampling frequency, another experiment has been launched using a down-sampling rate of 2. On the one hand, this allows to reduce the load of data flow from the IIOT device to the MEC server. On the other hand, as a counterpart, the final quality of the signal is reduced, since a reconstruction is carried out and the pure original signal is not obtained.

Table 3 shows the experimental variables of this experiment. This starts with a sampling frequency of 100 KHz and 6 channels, with a downsampling rate of 2, dividing the batch into 3 streams/s, being equivalent to sending 0.6 Mbytes/s.

Table 3. Experiment 2 conditions.

	Sampling freq	Downsampling rate	Mbytes/sec	Streams/sec
Starting point	100 kHz, 6 channels	2	0.6	3
Saturation point	250 kHz, 6 channels	2	1.5	6

Figures 10, 11 and 12 show the same time metrics explained in the experiment 1, corresponding to the starting point conditions of experiment 2.

Obviously, as less data load is being transmitted from server to server due to the downsampling algorithm, the start to end spent time to send the generated data per second, displayed in Fig. 10, and the time needed to send the streams between servers is reduced. This can be seen in the yellow line of the Fig. 11, where the time is around 0.65 s, 0.15 s smaller than the one displayed in Fig. 5. Hence, as the streams must be upsampled

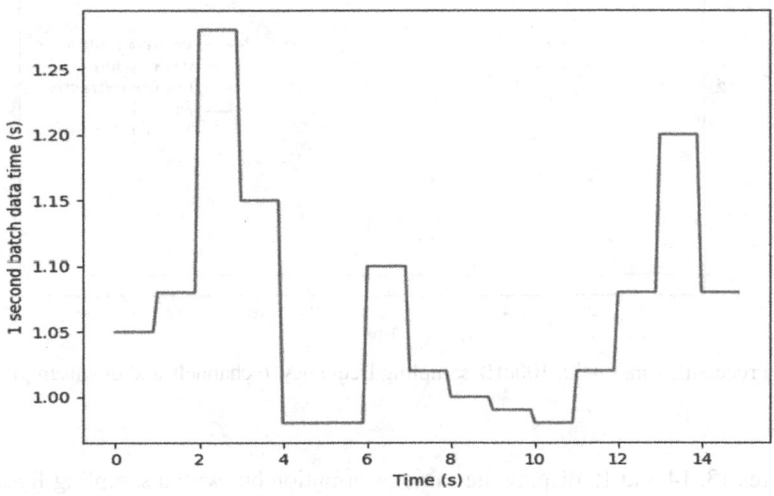

Fig. 10. Total time spent to send 1 s batch data, with 100kHz sampling frequency, 6 channels and downsampling rate of 2.

for reconstructing the original signal, Fig. 12 shows how the time needed to perform the upsampling algorithm increases to 0.01 s, while the downsampling algorithm remains practically null.

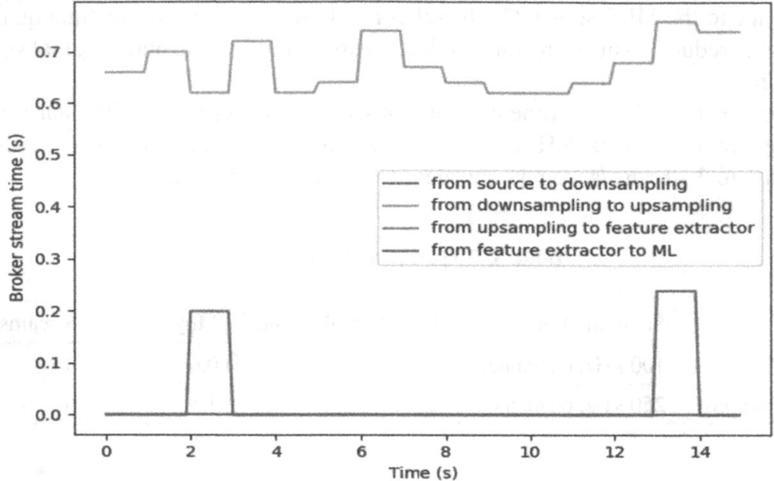

Fig. 11. Broker streams time, with 100kHz sampling frequency, 6 channels and downsampling rate of 2.

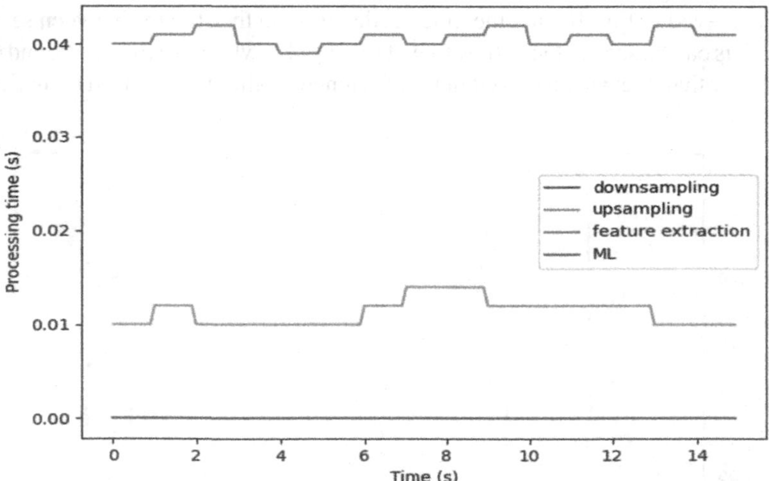

Fig. 12. Processing times, with 100kHz sampling frequency, 6 channels and downsampling rate of 2.

Figures 13, 14 and 15 display the same information but with a sampling frequency of 250 kHz. Figure 13 shows how by increasing the sampling frequency to 250 kHz, the architecture starts to collapse.

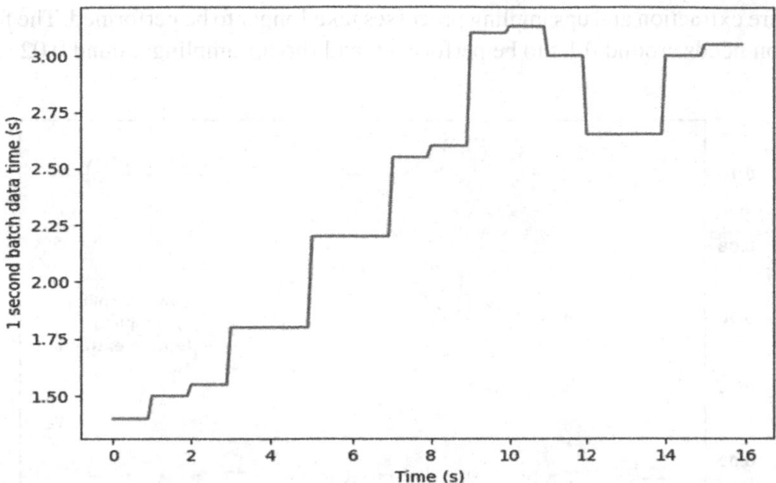

Fig. 13. Total time spent to send 1 s batch data, with 250 kHz sampling frequency, 6 channels and downsampling rate of 2.

As well as in Figs. 8 and 14 shows how the 5G network is not able to handle the data load. It can be seen again how when the communication between servers through the 5G network, in yellow, increases considerably to around 1.5 s, the downsampling microservice starts to crash. This is why again, the blue line increases exponentially.

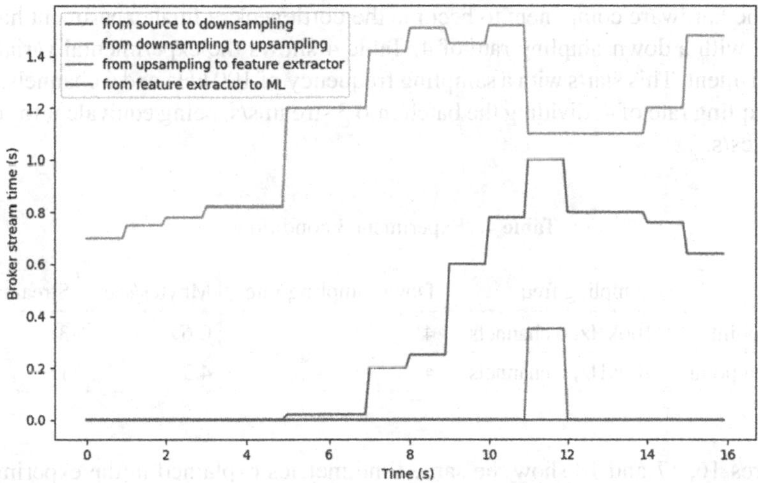

Fig. 14. Broker streams time, with 250 kHz sampling frequency, 6 channels and downsampling rate of 2.

Under these conditions, Fig. 15 shows how by increasing the sampling frequency to 250 kHz, the downsampling and ML inference times keep being practically 0. Obviously, the feature extraction and upsampling processes take longer to be performed. The feature extraction needs around 0.1 s to be performed, and the upsampling around 0.02 s.

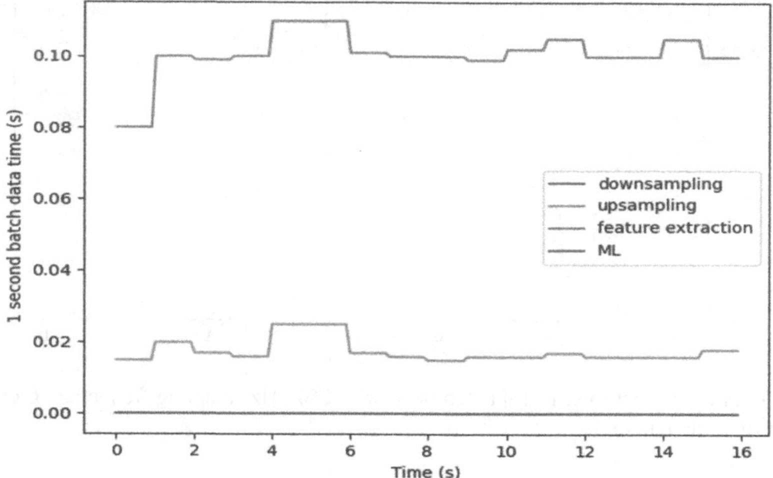

Fig. 15. Processing times, with 250 kHz sampling frequency, 6 channels and downsampling rate of 2.

- Experiment 3:

For the hardware component to become the bottleneck, a final experiment has been launched with a downsampling rate of 4. Table 4 shows the experimental variables of this experiment. This starts with a sampling frequency of 100 kHz and 6 channels, with a downsampling rate of 4, dividing the batch into 3 streams/s, being equivalent to sending 0.6 Mbytes/s.

Table 4. Experiment 3 conditions.

	Sampling freq	Downsampling rate	Mbytes/sec	Streams/sec
Starting point	100kHz, 6 channels	4	0.6	3
Saturation point	700kHz, 6 channels	4	4.2	15

Figures 16, 17 and 18 show the same time metrics explained in the experiments 1 and 2, corresponding to the starting point conditions of experiment 3.

Obviously, as less data load is being transmitted from server to server due to the downsampling algorithm, the start to end spent time to send the generated data per second, displayed in Fig. 16, and the time needed to send the streams between servers is reduced. This can be seen in the yellow line of the Fig. 17, where the time is around 0.45 s, 0.2 s smaller than the one displayed in Fig. 11. As well as in the experiment 2, as the streams must be upsampled for reconstructing the original signal, Fig. 18 shows how the time needed to perform the upsampling algorithm takes around 0.01 s, while the downsampling algorithm remains practically null.

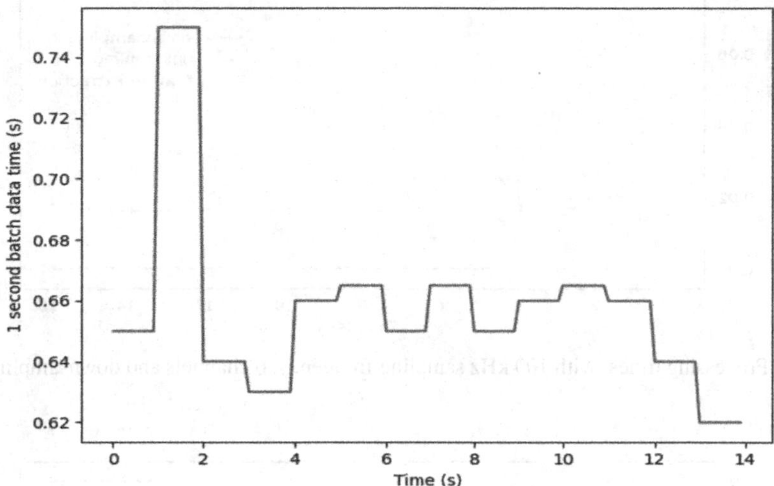

Fig. 16. Total time spent to send 1 s batch data, with 100 kHz sampling frequency, 6 channels and downsampling rate of 4.

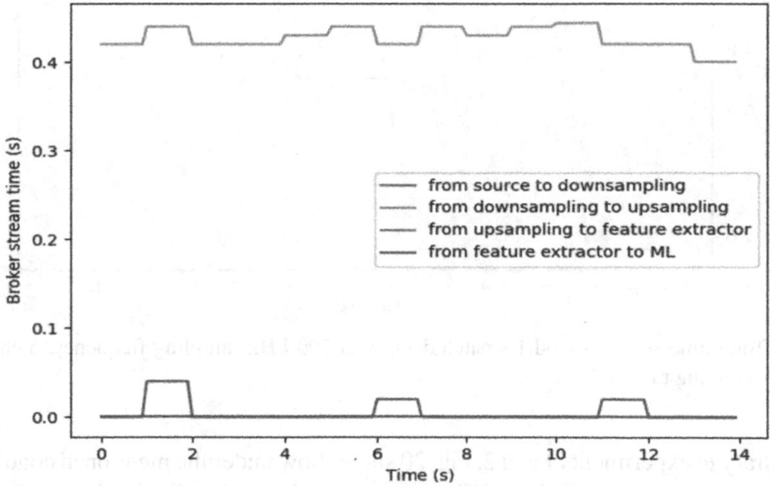

Fig. 17. Broker streams time, with 100 kHz sampling frequency, 6 channels and downsampling rate of 4.

Finally, Figs. 19, 20 and 21 display the same information but with a sampling frequency of 700 kHz. Figure 19 shows how by increasing the sampling frequency to 700 kHz, the architecture starts to collapse.

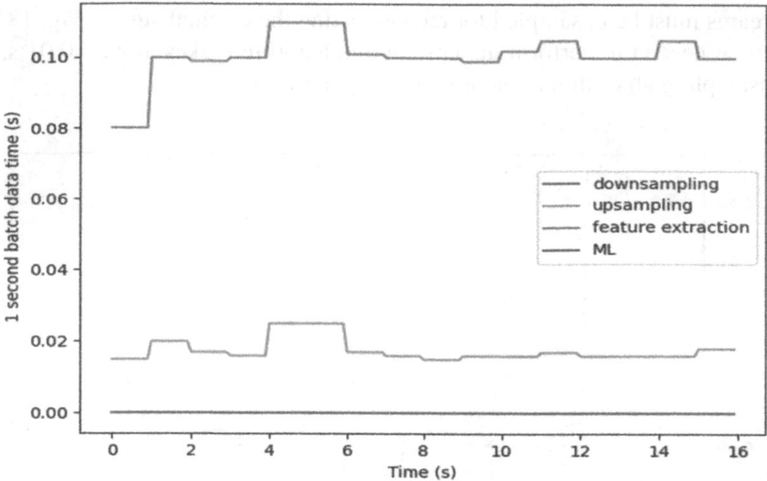

Fig. 18. Processing times, with 100 kHz sampling frequency, 6 channels and downsampling rate of 4.

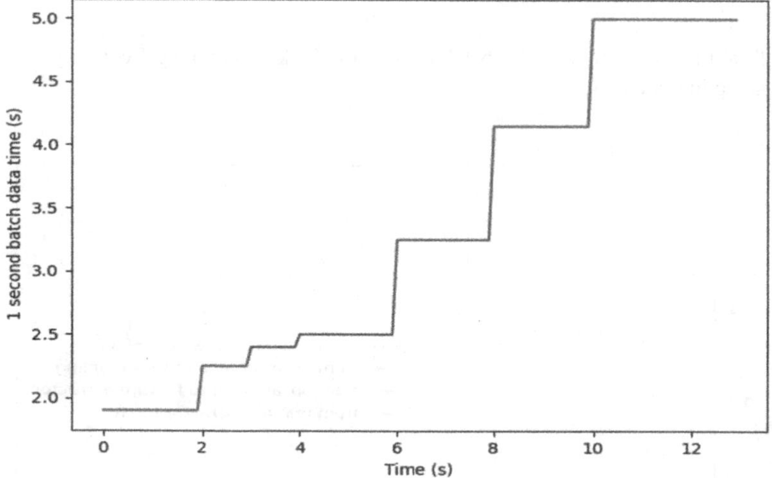

Fig. 19. Total time spent to send 1 s batch data, with 700 kHz sampling frequency, 6 channels and downsampling rate of 4.

Contrary to experiments 1 and 2, Fig. 20 shows how under the mentioned conditions, the hardware component of the MEC server is not able to handle the data load. It can be seen how in this case, first, the elapsed time from sending the streams from the upsampling to receiving them in the feature extraction consumer, plotted in green, starts to increase. This is because, as shown in Fig. 21, the feature extraction process now takes more time to be processed, blocking like this this microservice. As well, when the communication between servers through the 5G network, shown in yellow in Fig. 20, increases to around 1 s in the second 8 of the "x" axis, the downsampling micro-service starts to crash. This is why again, the blue line in that point increases exponentially.

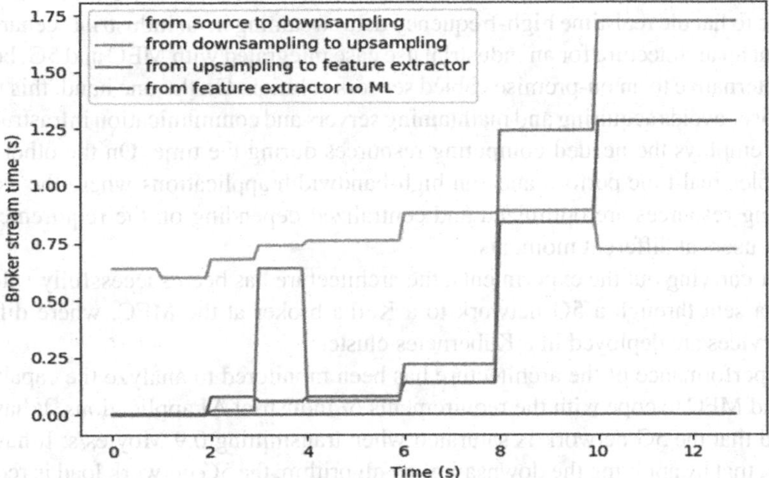

Fig. 20. Broker streams time, with 700 kHz sampling frequency, 6 channels and downsampling rate of 4.

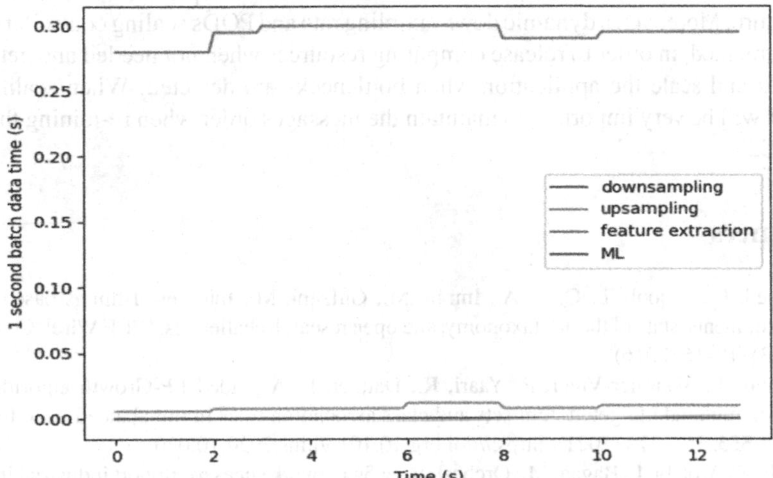

Fig. 21. Processing times, with 700 kHz sampling frequency, 6 channels and downsampling rate of 4.

5 Conclusions

In the current paper, a real-time high-frequency data streaming architecture to deploy Industrial AI applications at MECs has been presented. The main objectives of this approach are to handle real-time high-frequency data streaming in an industrial scenario and to present an architecture for an industrial use case integrated with MEC and 5G, becoming an alternative to an on-premise cabled sensors solution. On the one hand, this means that the user avoids acquiring and maintaining servers and communication infrastructures and just employs the needed computing resources during the time. On the other hand, this enables real-time performance on high-bandwidth applications where the existing computing resources are optimized and centralized depending on the requirements of different users at different moments.

After carrying out the experiments, the architecture has been successfully validated with data sent through a 5G network to a Kafka broker at the MEC, where different microservices are deployed in a Kubernetes cluster.

The performance of the architecture has been monitored to analyze the capabilities of 5G and MEC to cope with the requirements of Industrial AI applications. It has been observed that the 5G network is saturated when transmitting 0.9 Mbytes/s. It has been observed that by applying the downsampling algorithm, the 5G network load is reduced, making it possible to send higher frequency data with the counterpart of data quality loss.

Future work of this research will focus on deploying the actual architecture in a more powerful 5G network and MEC server, in order to evaluate deeper the limitations of the architecture. Moreover, a dynamic downsampling rate and PODs scaling controller could be implemented, in order to release computing resources when not needed and get more resources and scale the application when bottlenecks are detected. When scaling the PODs, it will be very important to maintain the messages order when re-joining them in the MEC.

References

1. Ahmed, E., Yaqoob, I., Gani, A., Imran, M., Gulzani, M.: Internet-of-things-based smart environments: state of the art, taxonomy, and open research challenges. IEEE Wirel. Commun. **23**(23), 10–16 (2016)
2. Shabtay, L., Fournier-Viger, P., Yaari, R., Dattner, I.: A guided FP-Growth algorithm for mining multitude-targeted item-sets and class association rules in imbalanced data. Inf. Sci. (N Y) **553**, 353–375 (2021). https://doi.org/10.1016/j.ins.2020.10.020
3. Taleb, T., Afolabi, I., Bagaa, M.: Orchestrating 5g network slices to support industrial internet and to shape next-generation smart factories. IEEE Netw. **33**(4), 146–154 (2019). https://doi.org/10.1109/MNET.2018.1800129
4. Zhang, C., Zhou, G., Li, J., Chang, F., Ding, K., Ma, D.: A multi-access edge computing enabled framework for the construction of a knowledge-sharing intelligent machine tool swarm in Industry 4.0. J. Manuf. Syst. **66**, 56–70 (2023). https://doi.org/10.1016/j.jmsy.2022.11.015
5. Liu, C., Xu, X., Peng, Q., Zhou, Z.: MTConnect-based cyber-physical machine tool: a case study. Procedia CIRP **72**, 492–497 (2018). https://doi.org/10.1016/j.procir.2018.03.059

6. Zhang, C., Zhou, G., Li, J., Qin, T., Ding, K., Chang, F.: KAiPP: an interaction recommendation approach for knowledge aided intelligent process planning with reinforcement learning. Knowl. Based Syst. **258**, 110009 (2022). https://doi.org/10.1016/j.knosys.2022.110009
7. Tao, F., Zhang, L., Liu, Y., Cheng, Y., Wang, L., Xu, X.: Manufacturing service management in cloud manufacturing: overview and future research directions. J. Manuf. Sci. Eng. **137**(4), 040912 (2015). https://doi.org/10.1115/1.4030510
8. Borsatti, D., Davoli, G., Cerroni, W., Raffaelli, C.: Enabling industrial IoT as a service with multi-access edge computing. IEEE Commun. Mag. **59**(8), 21–27 (2021). https://doi.org/10.1109/MCOM.001.2100006
9. Nikravan, M., Haghi Kashani, M.: A review on trust management in fog/edge computing: techniques, trends, and challenges. J. Netw. Comput. Appl. **204**, 103402 (2022). https://doi.org/10.1016/j.jnca.2022.103402
10. Mourtzis, D., Angelopoulos, J., Panopoulos, N.: Design and development of an edge-computing platform towards 5g technology adoption for improving equipment predictive maintenance. Procedia Comput Sci **200**, 611–619 (2022). https://doi.org/10.1016/j.procs.2022.01.259
11. Leng, J., Chen, Z., Sha, W., Ye, S., Liu, Q., Chen, X.: Cloud-edge orchestration-based bi-level autonomous process control for mass individualization of rapid printed circuit boards prototyping services. J. Manuf. Syst. **63**, 143–161 (2022). https://doi.org/10.1016/j.jmsy.2022.03.008
12. Ranaweera, P., Jurcut, A., Liyanage, M.: MEC-enabled 5G use cases: a survey on security vulnerabilities and countermeasures. ACM Comput. Surv. **54**(9), 1–37 (2021). https://doi.org/10.1145/3474552
13. Liyanage, M., Porambage, P., Ding, A.Y., Kalla, A.: Driving forces for multi-access edge computing (MEC) IoT integration in 5G. ICT Express **7**(2), 127–137 (2021). https://doi.org/10.1016/j.icte.2021.05.007
14. Cheng, J., Chen, W., Tao, F., Lin, C.L.: Industrial IoT in 5G environment towards smart manufacturing. J. Ind. Inf. Integr. **10**, 10–19 (2018). https://doi.org/10.1016/j.jii.2018.04.001
15. Cai, Y., Starly, B., Cohen, P., Lee, Y.S.: Sensor data and information fusion to construct digital-twins virtual machine tools for cyber-physical manufacturing. Procedia Manuf. **10**, 1031–1042 (2017). https://doi.org/10.1016/j.promfg.2017.07.094
16. Liang, B., Gregory, M.A., Li, S.: Multi-access Edge Computing fundamentals, services, enablers and challenges: a complete survey. J. Netw. Comput. Appl. **199**, 103308 (2022). https://doi.org/10.1016/j.jnca.2021.103308
17. Khan, M.A., et al.: A Survey on Mobile Edge Computing for Video Streaming: Opportunities and Challenges (2022). http://arxiv.org/abs/2209.05761
18. Ojanperä, T., Mäkelä, J., Majanen, M., Mämmelä, O., Martikainen, O., Väisänen, J.: Evaluation of LiDAR data processing at the mobile network edge for connected vehicles. EURASIP J. Wireless Commun. Netw. **2021**, 96 (2021). https://doi.org/10.1186/s13638-021-01975-7
19. Nowak, T.W., et al.: Verticals in 5G MEC-use cases and security challenges. IEEE Access **9**, 87251–87298 (2021). https://doi.org/10.1109/ACCESS.2021.3088374
20. Gabriel Brown: Ultra-Reliable Low-Latency 5G for Industrial Automation. Qualcomm Inc.
21. Massari, S., Mirizzi, N., Piro, G., Boggia, G.: An open-source tool modeling the ETSI-MEC architecture in the industry 4.0 context. In: 2021 29th Mediterranean Conference on Control and Automation, MED 2021, Institute of Electrical and Electronics Engineers Inc., pp. 226–231 (2021). https://doi.org/10.1109/MED51440.2021.9480205
22. Vakaruk, S., Sierra-Garcia, J.E., Mozo, A., Pastor, A.: Forecasting automated guided vehicle malfunctioning with deep learning in a 5G-based industry 4.0 scenario. IEEE Commun. Mag. **59**(11), 102–108 (2021). https://doi.org/10.1109/MCOM.221.2001079

23. Song, M., Lee, Y., Kim, K.: Reward-oriented task offloading under limited edge server power for multiaccess edge computing. IEEE Internet Things J. **8**(17), 13425–13438 (2021). https://doi.org/10.1109/JIOT.2021.3065429
24. Liu, P., An, K., Lei, J., Zheng, G., Sun, Y., Liu, W.: SCMA-based multiaccess edge computing in IoT systems: an energy-efficiency and latency tradeoff. IEEE Internet Things J. **9**(7), 4849–4862 (2022). https://doi.org/10.1109/JIOT.2021.3105658
25. Ali, B., Gregory, M.A., Li, S.: Multi-access edge computing architecture, data security and privacy: a review. IEEE Access **9**, 18706–18721 (2021). https://doi.org/10.1109/ACCESS.2021.3053233

A Classification of Data Structures for Process Analysis in Internal Logistics

Maximilian Wuennenberg(✉), Charlotte Haid, and Johannes Fottner

Technical University of Munich, Boltzmannstrasse 15, 85748 Garching Bei Muenchen, Germany
max.wuennenberg@tum.de

Abstract. Data Science plays a crucial role in driving new approaches to process optimization. With the increasing complexity of internal logistics systems, data-oriented methods have become essential in addressing the challenges that arise. However, standardized process analytics frameworks are lacking due to the heterogeneity of the underlying processes and the resulting data. This article aims to address this complexity by presenting a categorization of internal logistics data, consolidating the current state of the art. The categorization takes into account both real-world and scientifically proposed data architectures, providing a comprehensive overview. It includes a classification of comparative data fields based on their importance, the associated internal logistics processes, and potential usage scenarios. This classification is designed to cater to different use cases, such as diagnostics or prescriptive analytics. By presenting this categorization, the article enables practitioners to effectively leverage generated process data in a more goal-oriented manner. It empowers them to conduct suitable analyses tailored to their specific needs and objectives, based on the provided data architectures. In summary, this article offers valuable insights into internal logistics data categorization, providing a framework for practitioners to make informed decisions and optimize processes using data-driven approaches.

Keywords: Data analytics · Internal logistics · Process analysis

1 Introduction

1.1 Initial Situation and Motivation of the Topic

Internal logistics systems (ILS) are subject to an increasing level of digitization [1]. Processes are controlled by information technology (IT) systems such as enterprise resource planning (ERP) or warehouse management systems (WMS). The processes, on the other hand, generate data which is subsequently stored and further transferred by these systems [2]. During recent years, a wide range of process types has been adapted to this digital connection, often referred to as Industry 4.0 [3]. This development yields the potential for new types of process analysis, which are the result of recent advances in the field of data science. One example of this analysis is process mining, a method in which data is analyzed from an event-driven perspective, with the goal of obtaining insights and finding process improvement potentials [4]. To that end, the right

S. Terzi et al. (Eds.): IN4PL 2023, CCIS 1886, pp. 53–67, 2023.
https://doi.org/10.1007/978-3-031-49339-3_4

choice of application is referred to as context-aware process mining [5]. However, in order for analyses to be beneficial from a practitioner's perspective, they rely largely on the data architecture, i.e., in terms of data maturity, but also in terms of the right choice of analyzed data fields and a wise choice of data science applications [6, 7]. The main challenges faced when analyzing process data using digital methods is the heterogeneity of this data, and its high specification with regard to the respective process [8]. Depending on the IT system recording the data, and on the process type, different data structures can be generated in terms of data fields and data types. This issue becomes even more challenging given the inherent complexity and heterogeneity of ILS. Consistent documentation of the ILS process landscape, combined with involved IT systems, the generated data fields, and how they can be brought together with the objective of effective data science applications in mind [9] are all lacking. An interesting scenario from a practitioner's perspective is when a certain dataset is present regardless of any data analysis approaches yet implemented. To that end, the objective is often rather to extract as much value from the given data, instead of acquiring additional data sources.

1.2 Objective

Several recent research contributions have addressed the issue of data science in the field of ILS [2, 10–13]. However, given their focus on certain individual aspects of this ample domain, the applied data structures are highly problem-specific and thus unable to consider all facets of this field. A domain-overarching data architecture is necessary in order to ensure the broader applicability of future research [14]. A link between data creation in different IT systems and data science application with its various goals still needs to be established. To enable this link, all relevant ILS data fields must be classified according to several characteristics, including potential use cases (see Fig. 1). Therefore, this article aims to reach the following two objectives:

- Classification of ILS data which considers various IT systems and process types
- Association of relevant data structures with their potential use cases

By fulfilling these objectives, practitioners cannot just decide which data is necessary in order to execute a desired analysis type. They can also deal with the situation that a certain data structure is already given, and that as much value as possible shall be derived from it without additional data gathering effort.

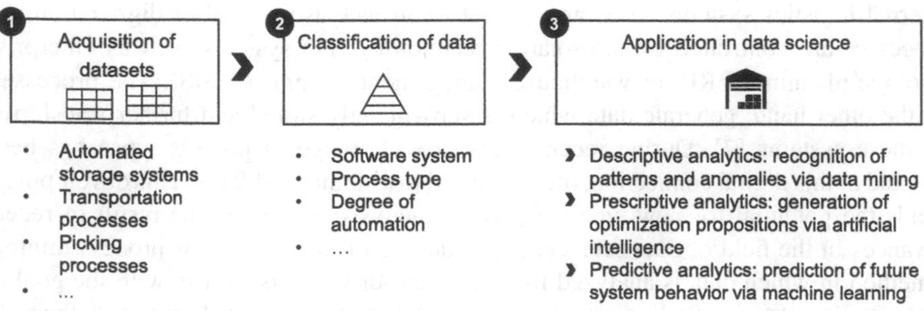

Fig. 1. Procedure for obtaining, classifying, and applying the datasets in this research.

2 State of the Art

2.1 Internal Logistics Process Landscape

ILS processes consist of several elementary activities: conveying, storing, sorting, and picking. Conveying covers all transportation processes of goods or persons within a locally limited area by technical means. Whenever goods intentionally remain in a certain position, it is considered to be a storage activity [15]. Sorting describes a diverging flow of materials so that transportation units (TU) having certain properties can be separated from others. Apart from diverging material flows, sorting also covers converging ones. All of these processes can be executed with or without the assistance of technical devices that are either human-controlled, mechanized, or self-controlled (automated) [16].

2.2 Process Control

In this article, ILS cover all enterprise activities related to conveying, storage, picking, unloading, and loading of goods, including additional processes like packaging. These activities can be executed in a manual, a partly assisted, or an autonomous manner. However, in order to enable the application of data science, each activity must leave a digital footprint. In the case of partly assisted processes, this can be achieved by, e.g., using handheld terminals or barcode scanners that allow workers to confirm executed process steps and thereby generate timestamps, locations, or order information. The generated data is then further transferred and stored, for instance in a WMS or an ERP system.

The various types of IT systems are structured based on the layer-based architecture of the automation pyramid (see Fig. 2) [17]. The pyramid contains five layers of abstraction, leading from basic sensor and actuator data up to enterprise-overarching ERP systems.

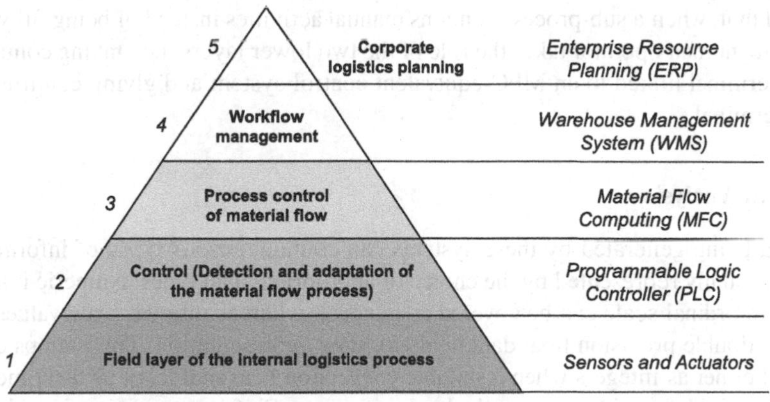

Fig. 2. Automation pyramid, adapted from [17].

The data flow in the automation pyramid is as follows: The highest layer generates a task and sends it to the lower layers, where it becomes more and more detailed. On the lowest layer, the system interacts with the physical environment. After that, the process data is in turn recorded and sent to the higher layers again. The transferred information becomes increasingly abstracted during this procedure (see Fig. 3).

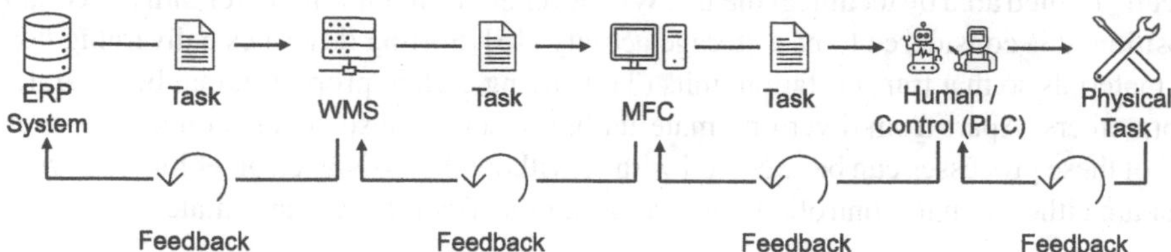

Fig. 3. Cascading data transfer between the layers of the automation pyramid.

The command chain of the automation pyramid is distributed within the following layers: on the lowest layer, the sensors and actuators of the ILS directly interact with their environment [17]. The processing of sensor inputs and generation of actuator outputs is organized on the second layer, mostly by programmable logic controllers (PLC) [17]. The latter fulfill specific material flow operations, which are generated by material flow computers (MFC) on the third layer of the pyramid. MFC decide upon the specific order in which tasks are accomplished and serve as the interface between real-time system components (PLC) and non-real-time system components (higher layers) [17]. Systems on the fourth layer (WMS and MES) are responsible for all operations in a certain sub-domain of the overall enterprise process [17]. They thereby offer the possibility for data consolidation, which is necessary for the aggregation of substantial Key Performance Indicators (KPI). Above that, the ERP system is responsible for the long-time planning of enterprise processes and the coordination of all necessary subprocesses [17]. It should be noted that, when a sub-process contains manual activities instead of being fully automated, the human operator takes the role of the two lower layers, i.e., taking commands from a terminal linked to an MFC-equivalent control system and giving confirmations to this terminal.

2.3 Data Analysis

The data being generated by these systems can contain various types of information, which is usually represented by the choice of appropriate data types. Numeric information on an ordinal scale can be covered as integers, whereas interval scale values need single or double precision float data fields for their representation. Timestamps can be recorded either as integers when a suitable conversion is available, or as datetime data. String data fields are able to cover the broadest range of information, but, since they are unstructured, their subsequent data analysis is most complicated.

Most research publications in the field of ILS processes have considered only a certain subdomain of the entire process and system landscape. For instance, machine learning is used to predict the behavior of inbound unloading processes based on historic data [13]. In a specific application of conveying operations, which are examined on the fifth layer of the automation pyramid (the ERP layer), analyses like Sankey diagrams can be deduced [2]. Another approach combines data from the fifth and fourth (MES) layer in order to set up a simulation model which can be used for process optimization [11]. Furthermore, the consolidation of process data can lead to the application of process mining. However, the underlying data structure is limited to one certain type of subprocess [12]. Also, there is one approach in which data sources from more different layers is considered: in addition to the fourth and fifth, also the second layer (PLC) is taken into account for the prediction of KPI of the ILS [10]. However, this approach only addresses the particularities of process simulation models. Finally, there is the option of deriving process optimization potentials from a combination of business process modeling and simulation models [18]. One main challenge when following this approach is the need for manual parametrization of the models, which could be automated using data science.

2.4 Summary

Condensing the findings from the state of the art leads to the following conclusion: the ILS process landscape is usually vertically structured, following the principle of the automation pyramid. Assuming a sufficient level of automation (and thus digitization) of the subprocesses involved, the generated data can be analyzed starting from a mere description of the database, up to the automated generation of recommendations for process optimization. However, existing research either only deals with isolated considerations of individual subprocesses, or is limited to a specific application scenario for the data, e.g., process simulation parametrization or process mining. As a result, the overarching consolidation of ILS process data aiming for a generalized data analysis application can be identified as a research gap being addressed by this article.

3 Sample Datasets from ILS Processes

In this article, several ILS were considered in order to obtain a fundamental database able to cover the potentially broad variety of this process landscape. These datasets were extracted both from applications within industrial companies and research projects. They have been pseudonymized and condensed for this research work. All in all, the following processes were covered (for an overview, see Table 1):

1. Automated storage system: high rack with stacker cranes (Elementary ILS process: Storage; Data transfer: between PLC and MFC layer)
2. Automated transportation process: conveying of TU in load units, several units being attributed to single tasks, executed by an automated small-parts warehouse (Elementary ILS process: Storage; Data transfer: between WMS and ERP layer)
3. Data field structure for the information interchange between MFC and WMS (Elementary ILS process: Storage; Data transfer: between MFC and WMS layer)
4. Inbound logistics: forklift trucks for the transportation from goods receipt to the storage (Elementary ILS process: Conveying; Data transfer: between WMS and ERP layer)
5. Manual picking process: picking of various articles in a shelving rack according to pick lists (Elementary ILS process: Picking; Data transfer: between MFC and WMS layer)
6. Multi-process ILS: combination of automated small-parts warehouse and stacker crane-operated high rack storage system for various articles, synchronized with transfer vehicles (Elementary ILS process: Storage, Conveying, Sorting; Data transfer: between MFC and WMS layer)
7. Standardized data transfer protocol for the operation of automated guided vehicles (AGV): communication of AGV with the overarching process control (Elementary ILS process: Conveying; Data transfer: between PLC and MFC layer) [19]
8. String-based data protocol for the information interchange between MFC and PLC (Elementary ILS process: Storage; Data transfer: between PLC and MFC layer)
9. Transportation process executed by tugger trains: data regarding the trips on different transportation routes within a production material replenishment process (Elementary ILS process: Conveying; Data transfer: between WMS and ERP layer)
10. Transportation tasks: data from conveying systems (Elementary ILS process: Conveying; Data transfer: between WMS and ERP layer)

The processes considered in this paper cover all of the elementary ILS processes. Figure 4 arranges the available datasets in the automation pyramid. Consolidation of the existing data fields within these datasets thus represents a broad overview of the ILS landscape. From this point, a framework for the classification of ILS data and an assignment to potential use cases can then be developed.

Table 1. Overview of the considered ILS sample datasets.

No. of dataset	Row No.	Column 1	Column 2										Column n
1	Header 1 2	Protocol number 123456787 123456788	Protocol time 07.07.2022 06:59 07.07.2022 07:01	Source position 01-01-017-21-3 01-01-024-23-5	Current position RE1-10 RE2-10	Target position 02-05-077-02-1 02-05-007-18-1	Loading eq. type EURO-400 EURO-700	Weight 55250 112500					
2	Header 1 2	Task number 1234565 1234566	No. of pos.in task 2 1	Material number 1120 20050 2001 41640	Source position 0000025100 5001195520	Status x y	Protocol time [1] 10.07.2022 10.07.2022	Protocol time [2] 08:42:19 14:40:46	Type/target pos. ASS ASS	Target position 1000 1000			
3	Header 1 2	Status 0 0	User B A	Protocol time 01.07.2022 05:40 01.07.2022 05:45	Current Position 1-1-5 1-2-1	Source position 0-1-1 0-1-1	Target position 5-2-5 5-2-5	Task number 120 122	No. of pos. in task 1 1	Protocol number 123454 123455	Weight 1200 1800	Loading eq. type Box Box	Quant. 3 10
4	Header 1 2	Task number 123456787 123456788	Material number 886644220 997755331	Protocol time [1] 24.06.2022 24.06.2022	Protocol time [2] 19:24:00 19:27:58	User A325KP03 A325KP02	Source position 102GKF870 161GKF378	Quantity 12 PCS 200 PCS	Target Position 082FG003 061FG374				
5	Header 1 2	Task number 123456787 123456788	Source position F01-02-C5 F01-02-C5	Target position 1OUTBOUND 1OUTBOUND	Material number A5U052125 A5U052125	Quantity 1 1	Protocol time [1] 13.07.2022 13.07.2022	Protocol time [2] 08:25:29 08:26:12	Status 050 100				

(continued)

Table 1. (*continued*)

No. of dataset	Row No.	Column 1	Column 2										Column n
6	Header 1 2	Task number [1] 123456787 123456788	Task number [2] 987654319 987654320	Protocol number 12345678 12345678	No. of pos. in task 7654320 7654321	Weight 5150 5520	Type/target pos. 2 1	Current position 2521502 2020521	Source position 0 0	Target position 2530405 0	User WMS-MFC WMS-MFC	Protocol time 03.07.2022 09:00 03.07.2022 09:00	
7	Header 1 2	Protocol number 12345676 12345677	Protocol time 15.04.2017 11:40 15.04.2017 11:40	Loading eq. type Pallet Pallet	Task number 123455 123456								
8	Header 1 2	Source position CAB01 CAB01	Type/target pos. CA1 CA1	Loading eq. type Pallet Pallet	Target position 12345 12345	Current position 01-IP01 Loop01-01	Status 0 1	Weight 1250 51000					
9	Header 1 2	Protocol number 7986281 7986282	Task number 761391 761391	Status 0 10	Source position 225 225	Type/target pos. EV-NU EV-NU	Target Position 125 125	Loading eq. type VY0105C VY0105C	User SM8-SCAN-04 SM8-SCAN-04	Protocol time 05.08.2022 14:45 05.08.2022 14:45			
10	Header 1 2	Material number 215122 *215125*	Quantity 100 150	Source position Goods receipt Goods receipt	Target position Storage 1-1 Storage 1/2L	Protocol time 24.07.2022 14:01 24.07.2022 14:15							

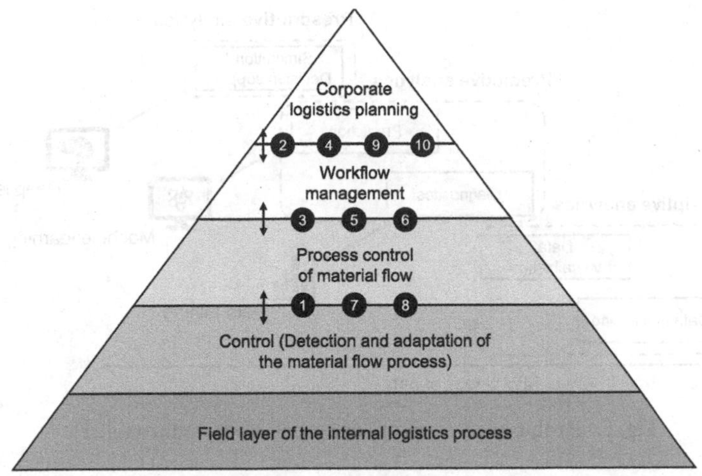

Fig. 4. Sample datasets assigned to the layer transitions of the automation pyramid.

3.1 Classification of Data Structures

As explained in the previous section, the various elementary processes of ILS are often embedded in different IT landscapes. The generated data is consolidated on several layers of the automation pyramid. In addition, the ILS processes usually differ by various characteristics. From the perspective of a practitioner, a classification of data according to a maturity model must be executed individually for each subprocess. If the data is inconsistent with its description (i.e., existing metadata), its meaningfulness is diminished [20]. The analysis of data can be grouped into three levels (see Fig. 4).

Descriptive analytics cover the consolidation and preprocessing (e.g., outlier elimination) of data fields with the objective of identifying and visualizing patterns and anomalies in the data [21]. Obtaining and consolidating the data is covered by the extract-transform-load (ETL) process [2]. More sophisticated yet, predictive analytics enable the diagnosis and monitoring of the system, thereby explaining certain phenomena in the ILS behavior [21].

As Fig. 5 shows, such objectives can still be achieved by applying data mining scenarios. Further on, a prediction model can be set up that uses algorithms to predict future behavior and the development of relevant KPI based on historic values. The key to this approach is a model using optimization metrics such that the algorithm can iteratively improve the accuracy of the prediction [22]. Therefore, machine learning approaches are necessary [23]. The mightiest and most complex level of data science, prescriptive analytics often incorporates simulation to deduce suggestions for system optimization [21]. If the model is able to identify and apply optimizations on its own, it can execute tasks similar to those of a human operations manager. The behavior of this highest level of data science can thus be classified as deep learning [22].

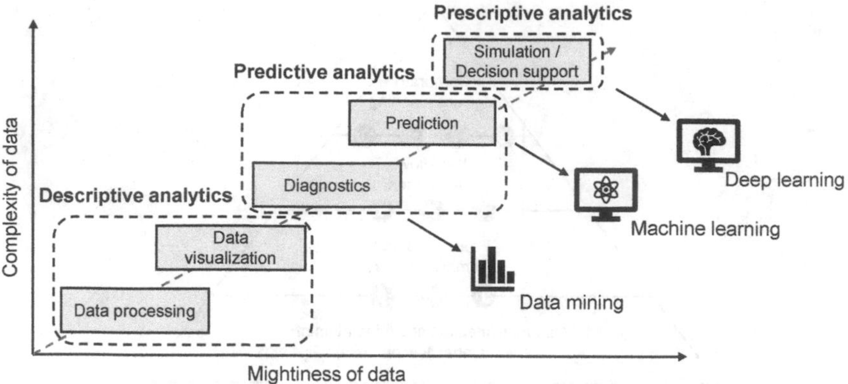

Fig. 5. Evolutionary steps of data science, adapted from [21].

3.2 Application on the Sample Data

The consolidation of all data fields from the ten ILS process datasets introduced in the previous section leads to the classification shown in Tables 2, 3, and 4.

Table 2. Data classification (Part I: core data).

No	Name of information	Exemplary data type	Process types
1	Task number	String	Storage, Picking, Conveying, Sorting
2	Protocol time	Datetime	Storage, Picking, Conveying, Sorting
3	Source position	String	Storage, Picking, Conveying, Sorting
4	Target position	String	Storage, Picking, Conveying, Sorting

The tables are sorted (column: No.) by decreasing frequency of the respective data field, No. 1 appearing in 9/10 and 26–33 in only 1. The name of information is a generalization of the (mostly different) names the respective type of process information is given in the datasets. The exemplary data type column shows how the information is represented. If different types were used among the datasets, the most general one was considered in the table (integer – float – datetime – string, with ascending generalization). The process types are created as a reference between the elementary processes covered by a certain dataset, and the datasets that cover a certain data field. Again, if several process types apply, then all are mentioned in the table.

As the separation of data fields into three different tables (the latter ones being called extended selection) indicates, not all types of process information share the same relevance for applications of data science. The information represented in Table 2 should always be present when examining the respective subprocess on any particular layer of the automation pyramid, even if the methods applied only cover elementary data mining scenarios (i.e., descriptive analytics or diagnostics). The data covered by this table

Table 3. Data classification (Part II: extended selection No. 1).

No	Name of information	Exemplary data type	Process types
5	Protocol number	String	Storage, Conveying, Sorting
6	Number of position in task	String	Storage, Conveying, Sorting
7	Current position	Integer	Storage, Conveying, Sorting
8	Type of target position	String	Storage, Conveying, Sorting
9	Loading equipment type	String	Storage, Conveying
10	Material number	String	Storage, Conveying, Sorting
11	Quantity	Integer	Storage, Conveying, Sorting
12	Weight	Integer	Storage, Conveying, Sorting
13	Status	Float	Storage, Conveying, Sorting
14	User	String	Storage, Conveying, Sorting
15	Next position	String	Storage, Conveying, Sorting

describes atomic material movements within ILS processes. Albeit being rudimentary, insights can be gathered for example by creating a histogram that depicts the time spent by TU between certain positions over a list of tasks. Data from Table 3 becomes more relevant when addressing more sophisticated process analytics approaches, i.e., it is necessary to apply approaches like machine learning models in predictive analytics scenarios to turn data into insights. Therefore, data fields in this table cover information that can be used to interpret the overall process rather than individual movements. For the creation of predictive analytics models, there is a need for data fields which describe more than just the output behavior to be predicted (e.g., the time spent within the system). Information such as material number or weight allow the prediction model to deduce an output parameter behavior that depends on those process information inputs. The information covered in this table is also typically collected by a conventional, analog value stream analysis [24]. Finally, Table 4 contains supplementary information. It is not compulsory for initial data exploration or description, and various analysis types can be used without having access to it. However, with the most complex and mighty data science applications (such as artificial intelligence as an enabler for prescriptive analytics), additional insights can be generated by considering this data. A prescriptive analytics model will usually not rely on all those fields to deduce an optimization potential, but it cannot be determined in advance which information is actually required. Just like a human process optimization expert, improvements can often only be reached when all information is made available.

Table 4. Data classification (Part III: extended selection No. 2).

No	Name of information	Exemplary data type	Process types
16	Time of task creation	Datetime	Storage, Picking, Conveying, Sorting
17	Priority	Integer	Storage, Conveying, Sorting
18	Type of source position	String	Storage
19	Quantity before task fulfillment	Integer	Storage
20	Type of task	String	Storage, Conveying
21	Previous position	String	Storage, Conveying, Sorting
22	Type of current position	String	Storage, Conveying, Sorting
23	Type of next position	String	Storage, Conveying, Sorting
24	Loading equipment ID	String	Storage, Conveying, Sorting
25	Quantity after task fulfillment	Integer	Storage
26	Length	Integer	Storage, Conveying, Sorting
27	Width	Integer	Storage, Conveying, Sorting
28	Height	Integer	Storage, Conveying, Sorting
29	Volume	String	Conveying
30	Target system of data transfer	String	Conveying
31	User person	Integer	Conveying
32	Assignment of user and person	Datetime	Conveying
33	Route	Datetime	Conveying
34	Tour	String	Conveying
35	Duration of tour	String	Conveying
36	Due date	String	Conveying
37	Starting time	String	Conveying

3.3 Results of the Application

A summarizing association of these data structures with appropriate application scenarios can be derived on the basis of the consolidation and classification of various data fields. Therefore, the user must follow several steps when implementing data science-based process analyses building on an existing database: First of all – for all existing ILS subprocesses – the existing data transfer interfaces need to be merged according to the respective layer of the automation pyramid. The data maturity must then be assessed [7]. One can then determine which subprocesses should be considered for data-based process analytics. After that, the user must check which data fields are available on the different layer transitions for each subprocess being analyzed. The potential scope of data science applications can be determined based on the importance of the data fields indicated by Tables 2, 3, and 4. Finally, a suitable set of process analytics algorithms can be selected. In this context, core data must be available for the most basic descriptive and diagnostic data mining scenarios. For more sophisticated predictive analytics use cases, the more important fields from the extended data selection must be available so that machine learning algorithms can be trained and thus generate meaningful insights. If all of the extended data fields are available, artificial intelligence is then able to determine prescriptive analytics in the form of improvement suggestions.

4 Conclusion

4.1 Interpretation

The preceding section of this article developed a classification of process data and the association of suitable data science applications for process analytics. Intended for practitioners in the domain of process analysis and optimization, this article contributes to a systematic assessment of the existing database and supports in selecting suitable algorithms able to fulfill their purpose. In an early phase of the process analysis, it can already be determined which subprocesses can be analyzed in a reasonable way, and what degree of data analysis is appropriate. Reciprocally, it can be deduced which additional data would be necessary so that a desired stage of data analysis could be executed. This means it is not necessary for practitioners to integrate specific data sources to obtain a highly specific set of analyses, but instead, the optimum of potential insights from a given data base can be drawn.

The consolidation of various sets generated by several industrial enterprises and research projects ensures the necessary generalizability of the findings. The gap in existing data science publications within the ILS domain was able to be addressed.

However, in order for data science projects to be successful, the need for process experts with a reasonable amount of implicit process knowledge still exists. That is, without this expert knowledge, an appropriate assessment of the database is not possible, and the conclusions drawn by the application of the presented findings could be misleading. This means that this research cannot fully substitute humans in ILS process analysis and optimization, but rather play an important role in supporting humans and reducing work effort, while at the same time ensuring a timely estimation of target attainment.

4.2 Limitations

The findings presented herein allow for a classification of process data enabling the reasonable selection of applications scenarios. However, target-oriented data science frameworks for all of these application scenarios are not fully present. In other words, further data science methods should be developed in addition to the research works discussed in the state of the art. Furthermore, the classification presented in this article must be tested – using various datasets and data science applications – in order to determine whether it is fully applicable in every possible scenario. Specifically, the transition between the three data tables presented is not sharp and clear. Depending on the individual circumstances, data science models to be applied might differ from the classification provided in this article. This situation leads to research tasks that need to be covered by future works.

Furthermore, the availability of data fields alone is necessary, but it is not sufficient for the application of certain data science methods. As indicated in data maturity models, the columns must be consistently filled with entries, and these entries must be meaningful with respect to the definition of the data architecture. Especially when applying methods with optimization metrics, e.g., machine learning or artificial intelligence, the generated results can only be as good as the input data.

4.3 Conclusion and Outlook

Given the data classification presented herein for optimization scenarios in the domain of internal logistics, a reasonable tool for practitioners in the operations management can be provided. Deduced from a broad set of data sources, the findings can help to successfully implement data science projects given that the knowledge of process experts is present as well. Thereby, the first research objective has been addressed. The classification allows a differentiation between descriptive analytics, predictive analytics, and prescriptive analytics approaches. Sensible analysis methods can thus be deduced following this classification. At the same time, the different types of process in the ILS domain are considered. With that in mind, also the second research objective can be considered as achieved. Industrial application projects can be set up with no need for an objective-specific integration of additional data sources in advance.

In the future, a further detailing of the entire framework by developing target-oriented process analytics applications could help to enhance the generalizability and applicability of the findings presented. Furthermore, by applying the framework to different industrial use cases, the validity of the approach could be examined with the perspective of discovering potential issues for improvement.

References

1. Vogel-Heuser, B., Konersmann, M., Aicher, T., Fischer, J., Ocker, F., Goedicke, M.: Supporting evolution of automated Material Flow Systems as part of CPPS by using coupled meta models. In: IEEE Industrial Cyber-Physical Systems (ed.) Proceedings 2018 IEEE Industrial Cyber-Physical Systems (ICPS): ITMO University, Saint Petersburg, Saint Petersburg, Russia, 15–18 May 2018, pp. 316–323. IEEE, Piscataway, NJ (2018)
2. Knoll, D., Prüglmeier, M., Reinhart, G.: Materialflussanalyse mit ERP-Transportaufträgen: Automatisierte Ableitung und Visualisierung von Materialflüssen in der Produktionslogistik. Werkstattstechnik online **107**(3), 129–133 (2017)
3. Gehlhoff, F., Fay, A.: On agent-based decentralized and integrated scheduling for small-scale manufacturing. Automatisierungstechnik **68**(1), 15–31 (2020)
4. van der Aalst, W.: Process Mining: Data Science in Action. Springer-Verlag, Berlin, Heidelberg (2016)
5. Becker, T., Intoyoad, W.: Context aware process mining in logistics. Procedia CIRP **63**, 557–562 (2017)
6. Wuennenberg, M., Muehlbauer, K., Fottner, J., Meissner, S.: Towards predictive analytics in internal logistics – an approach for the data-driven determination of key performance indicators. CIRP J. Manuf. Sci. Technol. **44**, 116–125 (2023)
7. Muehlbauer, K., Wuennenberg, M., Meissner, S., Fottner, J.: Data driven logistics-oriented value stream mapping 4.0: a guideline for practitioners. IFAC-PapersOnLine **55**(16), 364–369 (2022). https://doi.org/10.1016/j.ifacol.2022.09.051

8. Burow, K., Franke, M., Deng, Q., Hribernik, K., Thoben, K.-D.: Sustainable data management for manufacturing. In: IEEE Conference on Engineering, Technology and Innovation (ed.) 2019 IEEE International Conference on Engineering, Technology and Innovation (ICE/ITMC). IEEE (2019)
9. Wünnenberg, M., Hujo, D., Schypula, R., Fottner, J., Goedicke, M., Vogel-Heuser, B.: Modellkonsistenz in der Entwicklung von Materialflusssystemen: Eine Studie über Entwicklungswerkzeuge und Einflüsse auf den Produktentstehungsprozess. ZWF **116**(11), 820–825 (2021)
10. Vernickel, K., et al.: Machine-learning-based approach for parameterizing material flow simulation models. Procedia CIRP **93**, 407–412 (2020)
11. Milde, M., Reinhart, G.: Automated model development and parametrization of material flow simulations. In: Mustafee, N. (ed.) 2019 Winter Simulation Conference (WSC), pp. 2166–2177. IEEE, Piscataway, NJ (2019)
12. Knoll, D., Reinhart, G., Prüglmeier, M.: Enabling value stream mapping for internal logistics using multidimensional process mining. Expert Syst. Appl. **124**, 130–142 (2019)
13. Knoll, D., Prüglmeier, M., Reinhart, G.: Predicting future inbound logistics processes using machine learning. Procedia CIRP **52**, 145–150 (2016)
14. Wuennenberg, M., Vollmuth, P., Xu, J., Fottner, J., Vogel-Heuser, B.: Transformability in material flow systems: towards an improved product development process. In: Matt, D.T., Vidoni, R., Rauch, E., Dallasega, P. (eds.) Managing and Implementing the Digital Transformation: Proceedings of the 1st International Symposium on Industrial Engineering and Automation ISIEA 2022, pp. 3–14. Springer International Publishing, Cham (2022). https://doi.org/10.1007/978-3-031-14317-5_1
15. ten Hompel, M., Schmidt, T., Dregger, J.: Materialflusssysteme. Springer, Berlin Heidelberg (2018)
16. Wiendahl, H.-P., Reichardt, J., Nyhuis, P.: Handbuch Fabrikplanung: Konzept, Gestaltung und Umsetzung wandlungsfähiger Produktionsstätten. 2nd edn. Hanser, München (2014)
17. Verband Deutscher Maschinen- und Anlagenbau: Datenschnittstellen in Materialflußsteuerungen., VDMA 15276 (1994)
18. Wuennenberg, M., Wegerich, B., Fottner, J.: Optimization of Internal Logistics using a combined BPMN and simulation approach. In: Hameed, I.A., Hasan, A., Alaliyat, Abdel-Afou, S. (eds.) Proceedings of the 36th ECMS International Conference on Modelling and Simulation ECMS 2022, pp. 13–19. Pirrot, Saarbrücken (2022)
19. Verband der Automobilindustrie: Schnittstelle zur Kommunikation zwischen Fahrerlosen Transportfahrzeugen (FTF) und einer Leitsteuerung., VDMA 5050 (2022)
20. Klare, H., Kramer, M.E., Langhammer, M., Werle, D., Burger, E., Reussner, R.: Enabling consistency in view-based system development — The Vitruvius approach. J. Syst. Softw. **171**(110815), 1–35 (2021)
21. Kargul, A.: Entwicklung eines Baumaschinenmanagements zur integrativen und adaptiven Steuerung des Maschinenbestandes über den Lebenszyklus. Dissertation, Lehrstuhl für Fördertechnik Materialfluss LogistikTechnische Universität München, Garching b. München (2020)
22. Schuh, G., et al.: Data mining definitions and applications for the management of production complexity. Procedia CIRP **81**, 874–879 (2019)
23. Rebala, G., Ravi, A., Churiwala, S.: An Introduction to Machine Learning. Springer International Publishing, Cham (2019)
24. Rother, M., Shook, J.: Learning to See: Value-Stream Mapping to Create Value and Eliminate Muda, 1st edn. Lean Enterprise Inst, Boston (2018)

Harmonizing Heterogeneity: A Novel Architecture for Legacy System Integration with Digital Twins in Industry 4.0

Aaron Zielstorff[1], Dirk Schöttke[1(✉)], Antonius Hohenhövel[1], Thomas Kämpfe[1], Stephan Schäfer[1], and Frank Schnicke[2]

[1] Hochschule für Technik und Wirtschaft (HTW) Berlin, Berlin, Germany
{Aaron.Zielstorff,dirk.schoettke}@htw-berlin.de
[2] Fraunhofer IESE, Kaiserslautern, Germany
frank.schnicke@iese.fraunhofer.de

Abstract. The transition to Industry 4.0 requires the modernisation of legacy systems. This change poses challenges, in particular due to the different data formats and interfaces resulting from the heterogeneity of the components involved. To ensure seamless interoperability within Industry 4.0, a consistent data base is essential. The Asset Administration Shell (AAS), a standardised digital twin of assets, plays a key role in driving data-centric, interoperable solutions. The potential for efficient data integration means fewer errors and optimisation for the digitisation of legacy systems. This prompts an investigation into the necessary extensions and components within the AAS infrastructure to implement this process. Our paper outlines a strategy for integrating legacy systems into the AAS environment. We introduce new components that enable the modelling and embedding of information about assets throughout their lifecycle. The conceptualised architecture is designed to facilitate the assisted selection of relevant submodels, the reuse of existing resources and the automated generation of AASs. A service is proposed to verify the structure of the resulting AASs and the communication configuration. Using an articulated robot as a case study, we demonstrate the connection of data points via the OPC UA protocol. In addition, a prototype is presented that enables vertical data integration via the BaSyx DataBridge, highlighting the benefits of automated integration into AASs. The approach is versatile and is readily applicable to a variety of systems and scenarios as required.

Keywords: Digital twins · Asset administration shell · Data integration · OPC UA · Industry 4.0 · Legacy systems

1 Introduction

As digitalization advances, the efficient utilization of data has become the focus of many industrial strategies. The capability to collect, analyse, and transform data into qualified information has emerged as a pivotal factor [11]. However, despite rapid advancements in information technology, enterprises in automation face significant challenges

Funded by the German Federal Ministry of Education and Research (BMBF).

S. Terzi et al. (Eds.): IN4PL 2023, CCIS 1886, pp. 68–87, 2023.
https://doi.org/10.1007/978-3-031-49339-3_5

when integrating data from their legacy systems. This is due to the software solutions employed, which exert substantial influence on the flexibility and complexity of the system. Specifically, system interoperability and scalability present substantial challenges [16].

Based on the concept of the digital twin, the Asset Administration Shell (AAS) specification, developed by Platform Industry 4.0, creates a common understanding and guarantees interoperability through a defined metamodel [3]. The information provided by the AAS includes, among other things, documents, properties, and parameters [1].

In the industrial environment, where a variety of control components and communication protocols are utilised, the need to adapt the information provided for a unified understanding is crucial. This adaptation can be largely compensated for by using AASs and software adapters to exchange information with the assets. The use of software adapters to connect new and existing plants to the AAS is necessary because there is currently no direct integration of AASs on established industrial controls [5]. Consequently, in addition to the configuration of the controller, a configuration of the software adapters used is required. The open-source tool BaSyx DataBridge, discussed in this contribution, functions as a software adapter. The DataBridge enables connectivity to the AAS via various protocols and bus systems [13]. Depending on the use case, the extent of effort necessary in data provision and testing can vary significantly. This is largely due to manual setup requirements and the potential for overlooked mistakes. Currently, the project planning phase lacks necessary support, causing an increased complexity when configuring broad-scale solutions or adapting to altered circumstances. The research question of this paper is therefore: How can legacy devices be integrated into the AAS in a user-friendly and time-efficient manner?

To address this, an architectural concept is presented that focuses on facilitating the efficient provisioning of configuration data to the DataBridge while leveraging the existing AAS infrastructure. To illustrate this, an articulated robot use case is shown to demonstrate the transmission of data to the AAS using OPC UA.

The paper is structured as follows: Sect. 2 provides an overview of the benefits of using Digital Twins in the context of Industry 4.0 scenarios and presents existing approaches to data integration into the AAS. Section 3 discusses the current state of data integration for AASs, using the Eclipse BaSyx Middleware as an example. To illustrate the relevance of an extension concept, Sect. 4 introduces an articulated robot as an OPC UA case study. Based on the insights gained, Sect. 5 derives requirements for an architectural extension for data integration. Section 6 presents potential infrastructure components for a holistic approach to data integration. In Sect. 7, the behaviour of the components is described in detail. Building on the extension concept, Sect. 8 introduces a prototype that demonstrates the partial implementation of the presented architecture focusing on the automated configuration of data provision during the utilisation phase in the asset lifecycle. In Sect. 9, the prototype is evaluated utilizing the defined use case scenario. A forecast on future extensions for the full realization of the concept is provided.

2 State of the Art

In the realm of manufacturing automation, a fundamental distinction is made between the domains of Information Technology (IT) and Operational Technology (OT). The OT encapsulates pertinent hardware and software components that enable the monitoring of devices, processes, and events. Industrial control systems, equipped with control programs following IEC 61131-3 standards, belong to this domain and exhibit a close correlation with the operating resources of production facilities and systems [5]. This provides significant advantages in the description, commissioning, and reconfiguration of plant components.

Nevertheless, despite these connections, there are also deficits in the use of industrial controls [15]. On one hand, there is a lack of consistent self-description, maintenance information, and representation of relationships to neighbouring systems and components. On the other hand, there are discontinuities in the consistent preparation, storage, and use of information during the engineering phases. When dealing with industrial controllers (especially legacy systems), the only way to provide comprehensive information is through software adapters, connectors and gateways. For this, the communication protocol used and the data models of the partners must be known. However, if resources such as sensors only have an interface to the IT environment, which is not supported by the industrial control, the direct use of the relevant information on the part of the industrial control is not possible.

In Industry 4.0 environments, cross-sectional use of data from both IT and OT domains aspires. Peer-to-peer communication between installed devices is desirable [12]. As a solution, AASs provide an essential foundation for the provision of data across device boundaries and enable the integration of data from multiple source systems. For this, a mapping of the respective endpoints to the properties of the AAS is necessary. There are already approaches for creating and using AASs to describe assets.

In the paper [14], the authors introduced an environment for the generic preparation of AASs, which was implemented within the scope of the "OpenBasys" project. In this environment, Type 2 AASs (reactive AAS) can be realized without programming knowledge. The AAS is largely automatically generated by the operator or on request, for example, by process control, and stored in a container. The implementation is based on the reconstruction of the OPC UA data structures on the part of the assets.

By using the established AASX Package Explorer, it is also possible to prepare active AASs with their structures and embedding of relevant communication relationships. This is largely done manually, with knowledge of the data structures and formats [10].

The extension of the AAS Manager [7] provides another opportunity for the automated preparation of AASs. The authors, among other things, illustrate the process of transferring the source model (here CSV file) into an AAS-specific target model using a transformation system, consisting of a transformation interpreter and definer. The configuration by the user takes place via a user interface.

With the AAS DataBridge, it is possible to configure communication relationships between assets and existing AASs offline. It supports a variety of protocols and can be manually adjusted via configuration files. The DataBridge also provides a multitude of options for the integration of data from legacy devices.

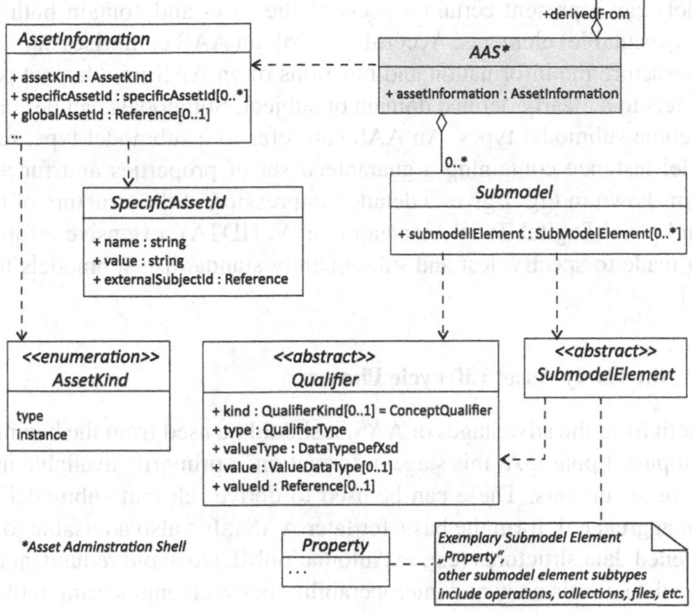

Fig. 1. Excerpt of a class diagram representing the structure of AASs [2].

3 Status Quo of AAS Data Integration

This section outlines the basic approach to asset integration into the AAS. For the realisation, it's important to distinguish between the lifecycle phases of the asset. Generally, the lifecycle can be divided into the development and production phases.

First, a brief introduction to the AAS concept is given. This is followed by a discussion of asset integration during the early lifecycle phases. Next, architectural blueprints for the vertical integration of assets with evolving data throughout the production phase are described. Finally, the BaSyx DataBridge is presented as a potential solution that serves as an adapter for integrating assets during their operational phase. Particular emphasis is placed on deployment and configuration challenges.

3.1 Asset Administration Shell

An AAS is a standardised digital representation of a physical or logical object, the so-called asset [2]. For this reason, the AAS can also be described as a digital model of the asset, which, based on metadata, serves as a machine-readable self-description of the corresponding physical or logical component. According to [4], the information model of an AAS consists of the following elements (excerpt):

- Metainformation on AASs, assets, Submodels, etc.,
- Asset-independent and asset-specific Submodels.

Submodels can represent certain aspects of the asset and contain both static and dynamic (or executable) elements. According to [6], an AAS comprises *Submodels* that are used to structure the information and functions of an AAS into distinct parts. Each submodel refers to a clearly defined domain or subject. Submodels can be standardised and thus become submodel types. An AAS can refer to a submodel type, resulting in that submodel instance containing a guaranteed set of properties and functions. The class diagram shown in Fig. 1 gives a detailed impression of the structure of the AAS.

In the Industrial Digital Twin Association e. V. (IDTA), extensive efforts are currently being made to specify, test and subsequently standardise submodels for various use cases [8].

3.2 AAS in the Early Asset Lifecycle Phases

To fully benefit from the advantages of AAS, it should be used from the beginning of an asset's development phase. At this stage, information is primarily available in the form of engineering documents. These can be used to derive relevant submodel templates which, when aggregated, form the basis for later AASs. It's also advisable to reference already modelled data structures (e.g. in AutomationML) to avoid redundant modelling and to ensure data consistency and interoperability between engineering tools.

Selecting relevant submodel templates for a specific asset and the desired use case requires expert knowledge. To successfully create AASs, both domain knowledge for implementing the use case and familiarity with the AAS metamodel and available submodel templates are essential. In addition, embedding engineering data into AASs is done manually using the AASX Package Explorer, which increases the risk of error. While embedding documents such as AutomationML files is generally possible, it requires programming effort when using a chosen AAS SDK.

3.3 Architecture Blueprints for Data Integration

In the utilisation phase of assets, the continuous updating of data in the AAS is necessary. This enables a constantly up-to-date representation of the asset and the provision of data for third-party applications. The paper [12] introduces data integration scenarios for reactive AASs. The authors distinguish between blueprints for the asset integration using different communication patterns. Figure 2 illustrates the communication relationships for the blueprints. These are:

- **Delegation:** The AAS or AAS server requests the Delegator to retrieve data from the asset. After a successful query, the data is sent to the AAS. This scheme should only be used if the frequency of queries and the amount of data is low.
- **Updater:** In this blueprint, it's not the AAS that initiates the data request. Instead, the Updater manages the data retrieval from the asset. As soon as a value is retrieved from the asset, the Updater writes it to the AAS. This method is useful when the rate of information generation is low, but data is frequently requested from possibly multiple AAS applications.

- **Event-Driven:** Here the asset is again queried by an updater. However, there's the added benefit that updating the AAS is event-based. This means that a queried value is only written to the AAS when there's a change. This blueprint should be used when both data retrieval and data production are high frequency.

3.4 BaSyx DataBridge

The BaSyx DataBridge provides the two blueprints *Updater* and *Delegator* previously described as core functionalities. Event-driven as well as static query intervals can be used. It supports various communication protocols used during the operational phase of industrial assets. Examples are OPC UA, MQTT, Kafka, and various fieldbus systems via PLC4X [13]. The DataBridge is provided as an off-the-shelf component as part of the Eclipse BaSyx middleware and can be tailored for specific use cases through configuration files without any programming effort.

Live data integration requires a data source, in this case, one or more assets, and an active (Type 2 or Type 3) AAS in a runtime environment (BaSyx middleware). It is recommended to use additional compatible components from the BaSyx ecosystem. Type 2 AASs can be created and hosted by uploading previously modeled Type 1 AAS to the AAS server. The AAS Server automatically registers the endpoints of generated AASs in the AAS Registry. AASs referenced there can be visualised via the AAS Web UI. The described architecture component structure is illustrated in Fig. 3.

Furthermore, the following prerequisites are provided for creating configuration files and commissioning the DataBridge:

- Knowledge about the communication protocols of the assets,
- Knowledge about the data structure of the assets,
- Accessibility of the assets over the network,
- Knowledge about the AAS structure,
- Accessibility of the AAS server over the network.

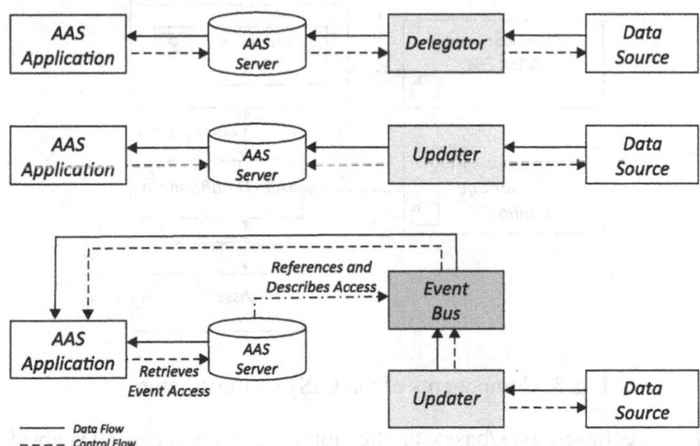

Fig. 2. Blueprints for data integration (from top to bottom: Delegator, Updater, event integration) [12].

Once all prerequisites are met, the DataBridge can be commissioned by integrating specific configuration files. In general, the following parameters must be configured:

- Access information for the data source,
- Data transformation,
- Target submodel and target property of the submodel,
- Overall structure of the integration route.

This paper focuses on the configuration of the DataBridge for OPC UA[1] during the utilisation phase of assets.

4 OPC UA Case Study

For a more detailed examination of the research question, a use case from the Industry 4.0 domain is considered. It concerns a handling system used in the automotive industry for the assembly of car parts. It consists of an articulated robot that is attached to the ceiling of the production hall via a joint. The industrial robot is equipped with a gripper that picks up vehicle parts and transports them to various assembly stations. Static information about the handling system, such as the manufacturer, product specifications and part lists are present as AutomationML files. Information about the handling system, such as the robot's joint positions, can be queried via a dedicated OPC UA server.

The data structure on the OPC UA server is based on the OPC Foundation's Robotics Nodeset. The nodeset defines a uniform structure for describing motion device systems and their components. The individual joints of the robot are defined as instances of *AxisTypes*. These contain not only static properties, such as the motion profile but

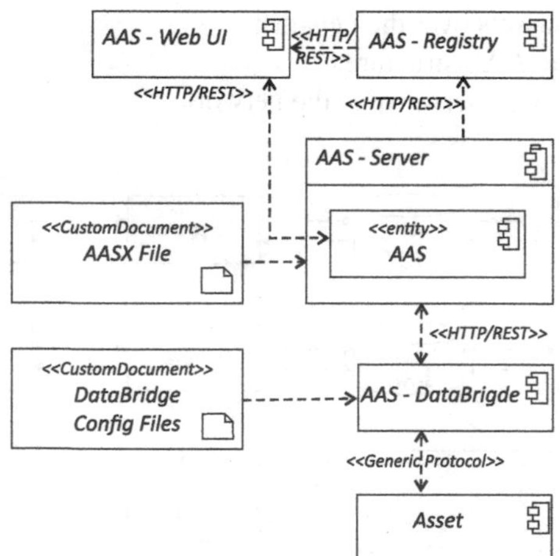

Fig. 3. Components of the BaSyx Infrastructure.

[1] https://github.com/eclipse-basyx/basyx-applications/tree/main/opc2aas/DatabridgeDemo/DatabridgeConfig.

also dynamic values. This includes joint positions and velocities obtained from the field level. An exemplary representation of the structure on the OPC UA server is shown in Fig. 4. The server consists of a total of 88 nodes and includes string, float, integer, and boolean variables as well as complex data types.

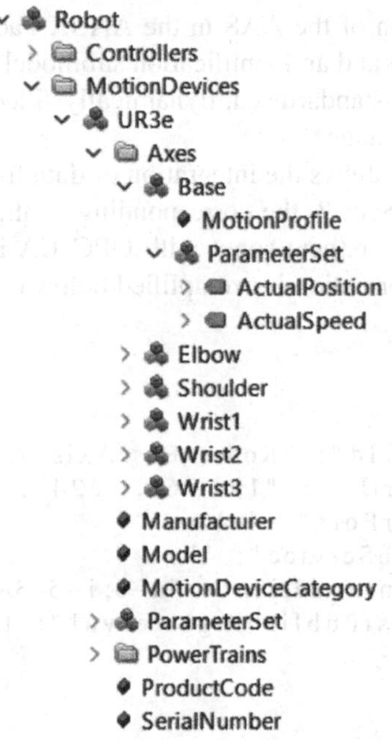

Fig. 4. Tree representation of the OPC UA Robotics Nodeset for an industrial robot.

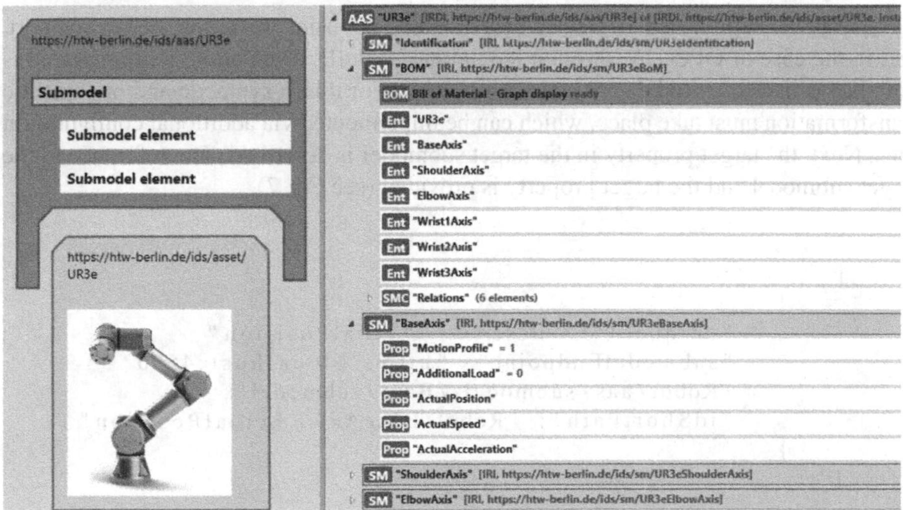

Fig. 5. AAS of an articulated robot in the AASX Package Explorer.

To create an AAS for the handling system, several submodels are used whose modeling is based on the VDMA AAS for robots. The data model is built on the OPC UA Companion Specification 40010-1 [9]. In addition to the standardised submodels for asset identification (e.g. digital nameplate) and topology overview (bill of materials), the resulting AAS also includes non-standardised submodels to describe the kinematic structure.

Figure 5 shows a section of the AAS in the AASX Package Explorer. The Bill of Materials (BOM) submodel and an Identification submodel can be seen. Dynamic joint positions are stored in non-standardised, dynamically filled submodels. These can be found at the bottom of the image.

The BaSyx DataBridge allows the integration of data from the OPC UA server into the AAS. As explained in Sect. 3, the corresponding configuration files are populated for each route from the asset (here robot with OPC UA interface) to the AAS. The configuration of access information is exemplified below (see Fig. 6).


```
[
    {
        "uniqueId": "Robot/BaseAxis/ActualPosition",
        "serverUrl": "192.168.1.224",
        "serverPort": 4840,
        "pathToService": "",
        "nodeInformation": "n=0;i=54583",
        "requestPublishingInterval": 100
    }
]
```


Fig. 6. Sample configuration of the access information in the DataBridge configuration file *opcua-consumer.json*.

The asset endpoints are described by a referable ID, using the server's URL and port, and in the case of OPC UA, through the unique NodeID. The data to be transferred is not always in the desired data format or structure. For this, a syntactic and/or semantic transformation must take place, which can be implemented via additional configuration files. Next, the target property in the target submodel is described. The reference to the target submodel and the target property is provided (see Fig. 7).


```
[
    {
        "uniqueId": "BaseAxis/ActualPosition",
        "submodelEndpoint": "http://localhost:4500
        /Robot/aas/submodels/Base/submodel",
        "idShortPath": "Robot/BaseAxis/ActualPosition"
    }
]
```


Fig. 7. Target configuration via the file *aasserver.json*.

Lastly, the integration route is configured. The previously configured components are specified in the order of their processing (see Fig. 8).

```
[
  {
    "datasource": "Robot/BaseAxis/ActualPosition",
    "transformers": [
        "dataValueToJson",
        "jsonataExtractValue"
    ],
    "datasinks": [
        "BaseAxis/ActualPosition"
    ],
    "trigger": "event"
  }
]
```

Fig. 8. Configuration of the integration route in *routes.json*.

The configuration of the integration route is done by specifying the data source, transformations, data targets, and triggers. All configuration objects are referenced by their unique ID. Writing data into the AAS in this example is event-triggered.

To put the configuration effort into perspective, this means that a total of 264 JSON objects have to be created and mapped manually to commission the DataBridge for the articulated robot. This results in a considerable amount of overhead in the configuration and testing of data provision. In particular, this is due to the lack of support for creating configuration files and identifying potential errors.

To illustrate this, an automation engineer was tasked to configure the connection of the handling system using the Robotics Nodeset via OPC UA in a non-repeated attempt. Specifically, creating the DataBridge configuration files took 3.5 h. The corresponding submodel in the AAS was set up within a further 2 h. It should be noted that the engineer had extensive prior knowledge of the AAS concept and the DataBridge implementation. Two errors occurred during the configuration, where a wrong AAS endpoint and NodeID were configured. These took another 1.5 h to locate and fix, because the DataBridge does not provide any automated configuration tests and lacks intuitive error reporting. The total time required to integrate the robot into the AAS was therefore 7 h.

The following obstacles for productive use were identified from the exemplary setup of the DataBridge:

- An AAS description must already exist,
- The manual configuration of the DataBridge is complex,
- There is no verification of the configured endpoints,
- There is also no verification of the AAS structure and content.

Thus, the DataBridge provides a purely technical solution for connecting assets to the AAS. Any adjustments on the part of the asset or the AAS require manual modification of the configuration files and increase the risk of errors.

5 Requirements for a User-Oriented Adaption

The previous sections have shown that there are challenges in integrating information across the asset lifecycle into the AAS. These challenges are particularly evident in the lack of support for selecting appropriate submodel templates, the expertise required to model AASs, and the manual configuration effort required to deploy the DataBridge for vertical asset integration in production. The main obstacle is the availability of user-oriented tools for configuring data provisioning. The following requirements for an architectural extension to the BaSyx SDK are identified as a potential solution to the challenges described:

1. **Utilization of Existing Resources:** When implementing new systems and scenarios, existing and available assets should be suggested for deployment. This approach would offers economic benefits.
2. **Automated Generation of AASs:** The creation of AASs should be automated. This particularly includes the automatic generation of AASs from the configuration of data provisioning and the selection of relevant submodels. The selection is based on information from requirements engineering, vendor information about the asset and the views of relevant stakeholders on the data in the resulting AAS.
3. **Assisted Submodel Provisioning:** The user should be supported in the selection of suitable submodels for the use case specified by them. Also relevant is the automatic assignment of asset data points to technology-related submodel data models if possible (for example when using OPC UA).
4. **Automated Configuration Tests:** Especially in manual configuration, conducting configuration tests to identify potential error sources is necessary. These tests should be performed automatically. A critical aspect is checking the accessibility of asset and AAS endpoints, as well as verifying the structure and metamodel compliance of the generated AAS.
5. **Error Reporting and Handling:** In addition to automated testing of communication routes, error reporting and their correction must also be possible. This functionality is particularly relevant for extensive data models.
6. **User-friendly Configuration Interface:** The configuration of data provisioning should be as simple and intuitive as possible for the user. This includes the graphical preparation of the configuration interface and user support through assistant functions.

The goal is to develop interoperable architectural components that can be integrated into the existing BaSyx infrastructure as APIs. These components should fulfil the requirements mentioned above and replace the manual configuration of the AAS and the DataBridge. The interfaces of the AAS server and the DataBridge remain unchanged. However, the provision of the required configuration data is automated by the new components in the architectural extension.

6 Concept for a Dynamic Asset Integration Architecture

In this section, an extension concept for the already existing BaSyx AAS infrastructure is presented. By integrating six new architectural components, this concept meets the identified requirements for the efficient commissioning of data provision from existing systems or generally from dynamic assets.

The new components are:

- Asset Catalogue,
- Submodel Template Database,
- Submodel Template Integrator,
- Data Conditioning Service,
- Configuration User Interface,
- Test Orchestrator.

A complementary component diagram, which shows both the existing infrastructure and the new components shaded in gray, is presented in Fig. 9. The new components and their functionalities are described in the following subsections.

6.1 Asset Catalogue

The Asset Catalogue aims to fulfill requirement 1 from Sect. 5. It acts as a management tool for already existing assets and associated information. These include the communication interfaces of the respective asset, associated submodels (e.g., via the *SemanticID*), and tags for asset classification to facilitate search. Classifiers are for example the asset type, the manufacturer, or provided skills represented by already existing submodels, AASs and AutomationML files (e.g. from asset vendors). Advantages of using this component arise particularly from sustainability through the reuse of assets and from the reduction of configuration effort resulting from the presence of asset-specific metadata.

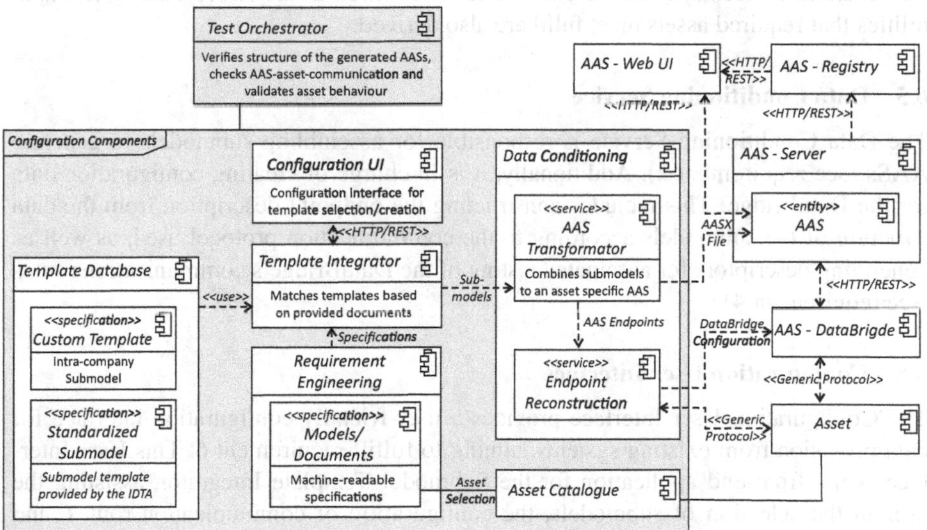

Fig. 9. Component Diagram of the Asset Integration Architecture using existing BaSyx Components.

6.2 Submodel Template Database

The Submodel Template Database is responsible for managing submodel templates, aligning with requirement 3. Here, a distinction is made between two types of submodels: Intra-Company-Submodels, which are specifically developed for assets within a company (e.g., a specific industrial robot), and standardized submodels (e.g., Digital Nameplate), provided by the IDTA.

6.3 Submodel Template Integrator

The Submodel Template Integrator enables the generation of submodels from the templates provided by the Submodel Template Database. This is achieved by matching submodel templates with asset information from the Asset Catalogue or with the specific data from the asset. An assistant service can guide the selection of submodels with the help of tags, semantic categorisations, and interface descriptions (see requirement 3). If no suitable submodel is available, there is the option to create a new one and store it in the Submodel Template Database for future uses. Furthermore, the Submodel Template Integrator acts as a backend for the Configuration User Interface. It provides information about both the existing submodel templates and the selected assets.

6.4 Requirement Engineering

Requirements engineering forms the basis for the selection of submodels. During this process, the requirements for the ASSs and the assets to be integrated are identified. Based on these requirements, a matching algorithm can suggest suitable submodel templates from the Submodel Template Database. It's also possible to integrate information from requirements engineering into the AAS. For example, engineering documents in AutomationML format could be considered. In relation to the Asset Catalogue, capabilities that required assets must fulfil are also derived.

6.5 Data Conditioning Service

The Data Conditioning Service is responsible for assembling submodels to generate AASs (see requirement 2). Additionally, it is in charge of creating configuration data for the DataBridge. This includes constructing the endpoint description from the data structure of the submodels according to the communication protocol used, as well as generating descriptors for automated testing of the DataBridge's communication routes (see requirement 4).

6.6 Configuration User Interface

The Configuration User Interface provides a user-friendly configuration interface for data provision from existing systems, aiming to fulfill requirement 6. This User Interface is the front-end application for the Submodel Template Integrator, assisting the user in the selection of submodels, the configuration of communication routes, and the assignment of asset data points to submodel properties. Moreover, it is capable of displaying errors in the configuration, for instance, after the automated testing of communication routes via the generated descriptors (see requirement 5).

6.7 Test Orchestrator

The Test Orchestrator is responsible for the automated testing of the DataBridge communication routes (see requirement 4). It is automatically triggered whenever a change in the asset or AAS data structure occurs and uses the descriptors generated by the Data Conditioning Service. The Test Orchestrator is also capable of reporting errors to the Configuration User Interface (see requirement 5).

7 Behaviour of the Extended Architecture

The behaviour of the extended architecture and the interaction of the individual components is explained below. The focus is on the processes for integrating asset-specific information into the AAS. Data generated throughout the asset lifecycle is considered. Figure 10 shows a sequence diagram illustrating the selection of submodel templates and their initialisation with asset-specific data.

Initially, the data integrator can upload machine-readable documents from requirements engineering, for example in AutomationML format, via the configuration user interface. This could be engineering models created in the SysML modelling language. Alternatively, a manual description of the use case can be submitted to suggest appropriate submodel templates. The Configuration UI then queries the Submodel Template Integrator, which acts as a backend, for appropriate submodel templates based on the information provided. It then creates search tags that are used to browse for fitting submodel templates within the template database. The submodel templates are then made available to the Data Integrator for selection and can be displayed via the configuration UI.

Another key feature is the subsequent comparison of the suggested submodel templates with the information in the Asset Catalogue. If there is also a match with the user-defined requirements, existing assets can be suggested for integration. The Template Integrator can match the submodel templates against the information in the Asset Catalogue, automatically generating submodel instances with specific asset properties.

Figure 11 shows a sequence diagram illustrating the deployment of AAS to the AAS Server and the configuration of the DataBridge. The data integrator now has the selected submodels and asset-related data as a starting point. Based on this information, static AASs are automatically generated by aggregating the submodels. For the asset usage phases, there is an option to extend the AASs with dynamic submodels through configurations via the Configuration UI. Depending on the communication protocol of the asset, the configurations for the DataBridge are created by graphically mapping submodel properties to asset-related data points, or are automatically generated from preexisting data structures, such as in OPC UA. The result of the deployment process is the provisioning of the AAS on the AAS Server and the embedding of the configurations for the DataBridge.

8 Prototype for Asset Integration

Based on the preceding architectural concept, a prototype is presented in the following section that enables the integration of data from the use case introduced in Sect. 4. The

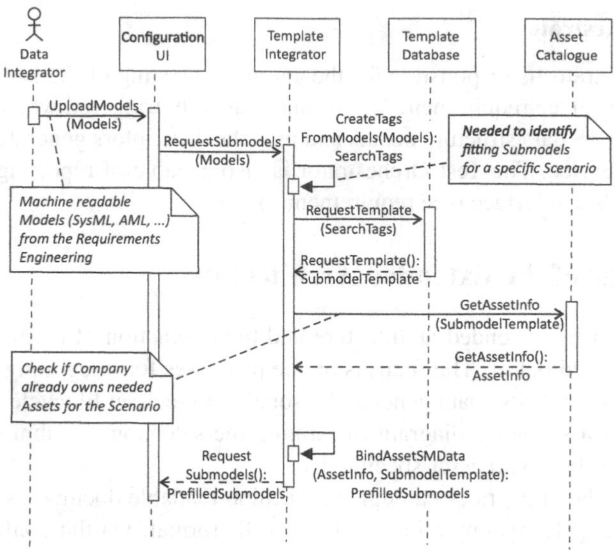

Fig. 10. Sequence Diagram visualizing the Submodel Generation from Templates based on provided Engineering Models (Excerpt).

prototype focuses on the Data Conditioning Service and its use for the OPC UA protocol. Within the context of this contribution, this component is of particular relevance as it facilitates the automatic configuration of asset connection during the production phase. Therefore, the functionalities of the other four components are not further considered.

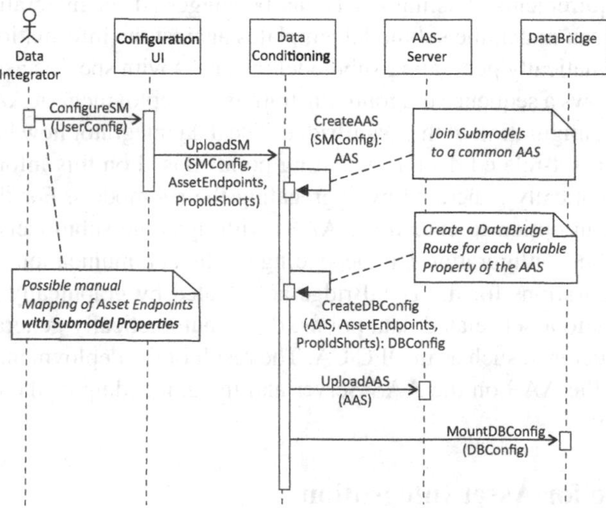

Fig. 11. Sequence Diagram of the AAS deployment based on configured Submodels (Excerpt).

Since the presented robot provides data via OPC UA, a data structure already exists on the OPC Server, which can be translated into an AAS. Thus, it is possible to implement and evaluate the Data Conditioning Service separately. Instead of using standardised and Intra-Company submodels, the OPC UA data structure is used to create AASs. Therefore, the prototype generates the AAS, which represents the same data model as present on the server.

Figure 12 depicts the prototype of the Data Conditioning Service, subsequently referred to as *OPC2AAS*[2], and its integration into the existing BaSyx infrastructure. The OPC2AAS component is itself an AAS that provides its functionality via an Operation-SubmodelElement. The AAS consists of two submodels: The first one includes the operation to start the service, whereas the second one contains automatically created DataBridge configuration files and the generated AAS as File-SubmodelElements.

The OPC2AAS Service is initiated via the operation *CreateAASFromOPC*. This operation accepts as parameters the name of the AAS to be generated and the address of the OPC UA Server. The sequence diagram in Fig. 13 illustrates the process of automatic configuration generation.

Initially, the data structure of the OPC UA Server is read. This is followed by a recursive reconstruction of the data model, starting after the root node of the server. The top level of the AAS to be generated is represented through submodels. Deeper levels use SubmodelElementCollections as a collection of subordinate elements. The deepest level of a branch is resolved through properties.

Currently, most of the basic OPC UA data types are supported, as well as complex data types such as structures and enumerations. This allows, but is not limited to, mapping OPC UA companion specifications. Custom structures and data types are also supported. At this time, OPC UA events and methods are not considered for this approach.

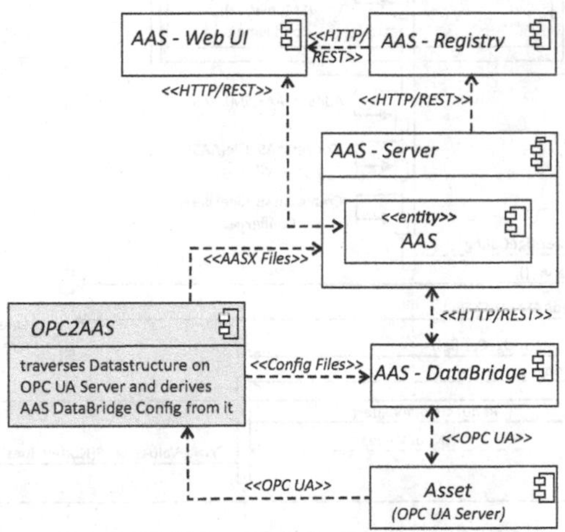

Fig. 12. Component Diagram for the OPC2AAS Prototype.

[2] https://github.com/eclipse-basyx/basyx-applications/tree/main/opc2aas.

For each property, the required JSON objects for the respective Databridge configuration files are created. After all data points of the OPC UA Server have been mapped, all previously created submodels are merged into an AAS. This is then serialized into an AASX file and provided to the data integrator as a File-SubmodelElement. The Databridge configuration files are also created via the serialization of the corresponding configuration objects and are stored as downloadable files.

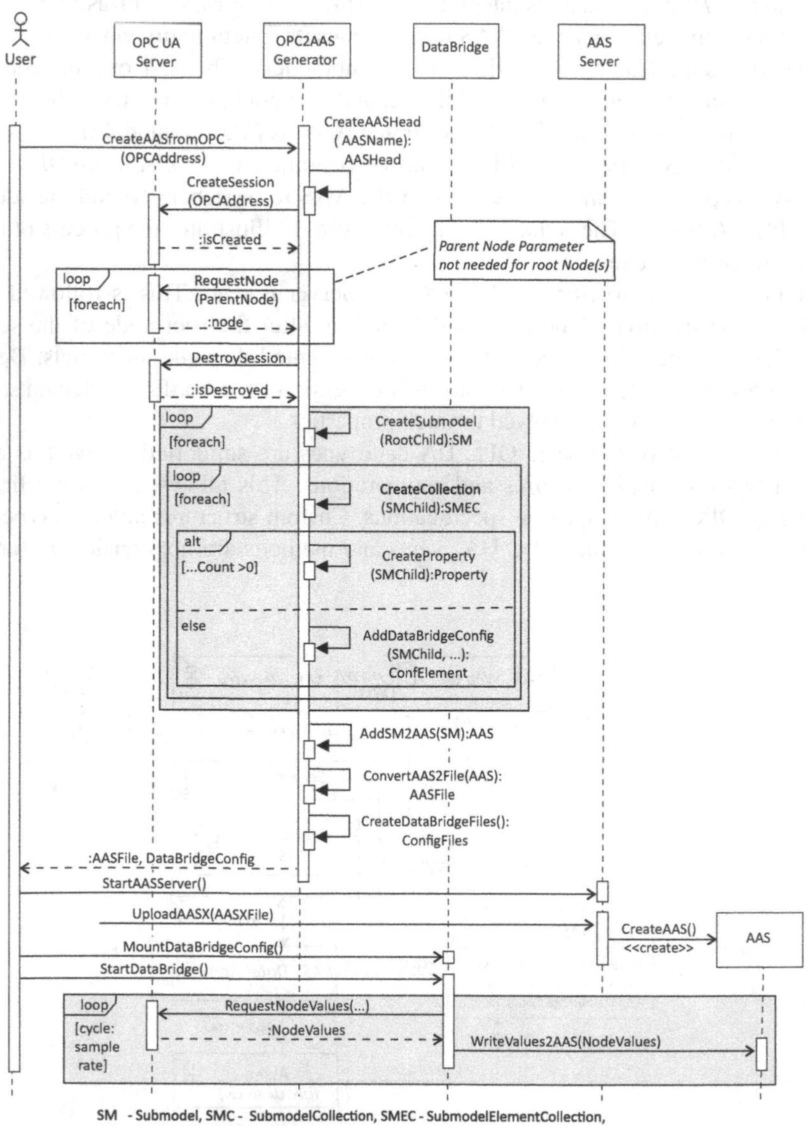

Fig. 13. Sequence Diagram for a Prototype supporting OPC UA as Asset Communication Protocol.

By uploading the generated AAS to the AAS Server, a live instance of it is initiated. Subsequently, the DataBridge can be put into operation by incorporating the created configuration files.

In the environment of the AAS Web UI[3], it is now possible to examine the AAS along with its dynamic data from the asset (in this case, the industrial robot). For instance, users can view the changing joint positions of the robot (see Fig. 14).

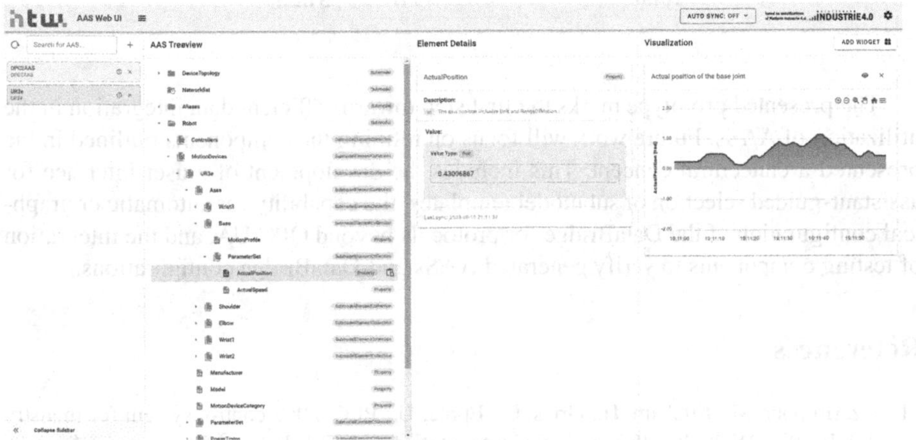

Fig. 14. AAS Web UI displaying the joint positions of the articulated robot.

9 Conclusion and Outlook

In this paper, we've underscored the significant role of Digital Twins, with a particular emphasis on Asset Administration Shells (AAS). Integrating data from legacy devices into the AAS surfaced as a notable challenge. In response, we've chosen to leverage the BaSyx DataBridge, a technical solution devised for asset connection. It lends support to an array of communication protocols, including but not limited to OPC UA. However, we've identified two major obstacles in its practical implementation: the lengthy commissioning process and the vulnerability to errors during manual configuration.

To overcome these obstacles, we've proposed an architectural concept that extends the BaSyx AAS infrastructure. Automatic configuration for asset connectivity has been identified as a vital requirement for the new architecture. Additionally, this paper introduces a prototype that implements a segment of the proposed architecture, enabling the automatic generation of AASs and DataBridge configuration files.

During the productive utilisation of the prototype in the presented OPC UA case study, it was observed that the time required for data provisioning configuration was significantly reduced. Notably, errors in the configuration were completely avoided. Table 1 illustrates the time savings achieved by the prototype.

[3] https://github.com/eclipse-basyx/basyx-applications/tree/main/aas-gui.

Table 1. Comparison of the time required for commissioning tasks between an example manual configuration and an automatic configuration.

Task	Manual	Prototype
DataBridge Configuration	3.5 h	3 min
Modelling the AAS	2 h	2 min
Error Handling	1.5 h	-
Total	**7 h**	**5 min**

The presented prototype marks the first step towards efficient data integration in the utilization of AASs. Future work will focus on refining the components outlined in the presented architectural concept. This includes the development of a user interface for assistant-guided selection of submodel templates, the capability for automatic or graphical configuration of the DataBridge for protocols beyond OPC UA, and the integration of testing components to verify generated AASs and DataBridge configurations.

References

1. Azarmipour, M., Elfaham, H., Gries, C., Epple, U.: PLC 4.0: a control system for industry 4.0. In: IECON 2019 – 45th Annual Conference of the IEEE Industrial Electronics Society, vol. 1, pp. 5513–5518 (2019). https://doi.org/10.1109/IECON.2019.8927026
2. Bader, S., Barnstedt, E., Bedenbender, H., Berres, B., Billmann, M., Boss, B.: Details of the asset administration shell: Part 1: the exchange of information between partners in the value chain of Industrie 4.0. Technical report, Plattform Industrie 4.0 (2022)
3. Bader, S.R., Maleshkova, M.: The semantic asset administration shell. In: Acosta, M., Cudré-Mauroux, P., Maleshkova, M., Pellegrini, T., Sack, H., Sure-Vetter, Y. (eds.) SEMANTiCS 2019. LNCS, vol. 11702, pp. 159–174. Springer, Cham (2019). https://doi.org/10.1007/978-3-030-33220-4_12
4. Bedenbender, H., et al.: Verwaltungsschale in der Praxis. Technical report, Plattform Industrie 4.0 (2020)
5. Cavalieri, S., Salafia, M.G.: Asset administration shell for PLC representation based on IEC 61131-3. IEEE Access **8**, 142606–142621 (2020). https://doi.org/10.1109/ACCESS.2020.3013890
6. France: Ministry of Economy and Finances, Germany: Federal Ministry for Economic Affairs and Energy (BMWi), Italy: Ministero dello Sviluppo Economico: The Structure of the Administration Shell: TRILATERAL PERSPECTIVES from France, Italy and Germany. Technical report, Plattform Industrie 4.0 (2018)
7. Garmaev, I., Miny, T., Kleinert, T., Schüller, A., Bitterlich, P.: Verwaltungsschalen aus excel?: Automatisierte erstellung von verwaltungsschalen aus bestandsdaten aus excel-tabellen. atp magazin **65**, 80–86 (2023). https://doi.org/10.17560/atp.v65i3.2636
8. Industrial Digital Twin Association e. V.: IDTA - working together to promote the Digital Twin. https://industrialdigitaltwin.org
9. OPC Foundation: OPC 40010-1 Robotics - Vertical Integration. https://opcfoundation.org
10. Ristin, M., Orzelski, A., Hoffmeister, M.: AASX Package Explorer. https://github.com/admin-shell-io/aasx-package-explorer

11. Sahal, R., Breslin, J.G., Ali, M.I.: Big data and stream processing platforms for industry 4.0 requirements mapping for a predictive maintenance use case. J. Manuf. Syst. **54**, 138–151 (2020). https://doi.org/10.1016/j.jmsy.2019.11.004. https://www.sciencedirect.com/science/article/pii/S0278612519300937
12. Schnicke, F., Haque, A., Kuhn, T., Espen, D., Antonino, P.O.: Architecture blueprints to enable scalable vertical integration of assets with digital twins. In: 2022 IEEE 27th International Conference on Emerging Technologies and Factory Automation (ETFA), pp. 1–8 (2022). https://doi.org/10.1109/ETFA52439.2022.9921728
13. Schnicke, F., Danish, M., Espen, D.: BaSyx DataBridge. https://github.com/eclipse-basyx/basyx-databridge
14. Schäfer, S., Schöttke, D., Kämpfe, T., Lachmann, O., Zielstorff, A., Tauber, B.: Migration and synchronization of plant segments with asset administration shells. In: 2022 IEEE 27th International Conference on Emerging Technologies and Factory Automation (ETFA), pp. 1–8 (2022). https://doi.org/10.1109/ETFA52439.2022.9921595
15. Wallner, B., Trautner, T., Pauker, F., Kittl, B.: Evaluation of process control architectures for agile manufacturing systems. Procedia CIRP **99**, 680–685 (2021)
16. Zeid, A., Sundaram, S., Moghaddam, M., Kamarthi, S., Marion, T.: Interoperability in smart manufacturing: research challenges. Machines **7**(2) (2019). https://doi.org/10.3390/machines7020021. https://www.mdpi.com/2075-1702/7/2/21

Approach of a Ticket-Based Test Strategy for Industry 4.0 Components with Asset Administration Shells

Dirk Schöttke[1(✉)], Aaron Zielstorff[1], Thomas Kämpfe[1], Vasil Denkov[1], Fiona Büttner[1], Stephan Schäfer[1], and Bernd Tauber[2]

[1] Hochschule für Technik und Wirtschaft (HTW) Berlin, Berlin, Germany
dirk.schoettke@htw-berlin.de
[2] EAW Relaistechnik GmbH, Königs Wusterhausen, Germany
tauber@eaw-relaistechnik.de

Abstract. Automation technology is undergoing a paradigm shift, manifested in the desire for flexible and adaptable systems. This trend is leading to an ever-increasing complexity of systems and their components. To manage this complexity, it is essential to promote interoperability between system components using Industry 4.0 components. Various software environments are available for their deployment. However, a test environment that supports essential test strategies for their verification remains to be developed. In particular, retrofitting and supporting legacy systems is a challenge. In this paper, we present a concept for a test environment based on the Asset Administration Shell (AAS), which incorporates established test methods from software engineering. This environment includes a multi-level testing process, which is able to evaluate both the structural conformance as well as the configuration and behaviour of the Industry 4.0 component. Test execution is facilitated by a ticket system that uses descriptors to enable test deployment without additional software development effort. The test environment can be seamlessly integrated into the existing AAS component landscape as an architectural component.

Keywords: Industry 4.0 component · Asset administration shell · Test scenarios

1 Introduction

The automation industry is undergoing a paradigm shift towards greater flexibility and adaptability [10]. This transition is driven by the need for greater efficiency and lower costs and is reflected in the increasing complexity of automation systems. A major challenge is the heterogeneity of components and the need for systems to communicate with each other, which makes efficient communication and integration of system components difficult [19].

The dynamic nature of current developments in automation technology is further intensified by a trend towards increased shifting of functions to control software [1,20, 22]. Centralised software enables more complex and flexible automation systems. At the same time, it also increases the complexity of the processes and the demands on the

S. Terzi et al. (Eds.): IN4PL 2023, CCIS 1886, pp. 88–106, 2023.
https://doi.org/10.1007/978-3-031-49339-3_6

software [11]. To address the increasing complexity, functionalities are progressively outsourced to "intelligent" components [18,23]. These components are able to extend and adapt their functionality autonomously and thus represent an important step towards autonomous production systems. An essential foundation for this is the interoperability of the required components, which can be ensured through the use of Industry 4.0 (I4.0) components.

I4.0 components communicate using I4.0-compliant protocols. They are organised in a service-oriented architecture (SOA) and share common semantics. Different communication protocols need to be supported to integrate assets. Information security requirements in the Asset Administration Shell (AAS) include confidentiality, integrity of data and functions, as well as availability. All I4.0 components provide their representation, including their dynamic behaviour, through information in standardised I4.0 compliant semantics.

Ensuring the quality of production environments and associated processes is a major challenge for plant operators. Modern plants, known for their desired and existing flexibility and variable designs, exhibit a high degree of complexity. This complexity results from several factors, including the heterogeneity of components, their scalability, inter-system interactions and cross-system communication [4].

The role of software solutions in shaping the flexibility and complexity of automation systems and their adaptations cannot be overlooked [5]. This is largely due to the diversity of development environments, programming languages and system platforms. In the absence of an environment for the automated preparation of Industry 4.0 (I4.0) components, they are typically prepared manually and adapted to the development environment.

Achieving general synchronisation between participants and their software solutions is a labour-intensive process under current circumstances. Nevertheless, it is crucial to ensure that I4.0 components meet their requirements and that interoperability is guaranteed [13].

Before deployment, components must undergo extensive testing scenarios to verify their required quality. Deviations from expected functionality should not only be detected during the operational phase, but ideally in advance. This requires the provision of test scenarios that coincide with the creation and updating of requirements. This includes the general description of an asset, its functionality and its ability to communicate with the AAS.

The question arises: how can the changes in functionality and evolving interfaces of I4.0 components be detected and verified? AASs, with their standardised interfaces and structure, can provide a solution to streamline and optimise testing processes. The implementation of AASs facilitates an iterative approach throughout the asset lifecycle. In addition, the standardisation of AAS submodels ensures that relevant information can be provided at all times.

The paper is structured as follows: Sect. 2 first provides an overview of the AAS concept and established test methods. The relevance of testing I4.0 components is also explained. Section 3 defines the objectives for the implementation of a test environment for I4.0 components. Based on this, the integration of existing components in I4.0 environments is presented as a use case in Sect. 4. A ticket-based testing solution is introduced in Sect. 5. In Sect. 6 the prototypical implementation of the test solution is described and evaluated. Finally, Sect. 7 concludes the paper with a summary and outlook.

2 Foundational Concepts and Context

2.1 Asset Administration Shell

An Asset Administration Shell (AAS) is a standardised digital representation of a physical or logical object, the so-called asset [2]. For this reason, the AAS can also be described as a digital model of the asset, which, based on metadata, serves as a machine-readable self-description of the corresponding physical or logical component. According to [3], the information model of an AAS consists of the following elements (excerpt):

- Metainformation on AASs, assets, Submodels, etc.,
- Asset-independent and asset-specific Submodels.

Submodels can represent certain aspects of the asset and contain both static and dynamic (or executable) elements. According to [7], an AAS comprises *Submodels* that are used to structure the information and functions of an AAS into distinct parts. Each submodel refers to a clearly defined domain or subject. Submodels can be standardised and thus become submodel types. An AAS can refer to a submodel type, resulting in that submodel instance containing a guaranteed set of properties and functions.

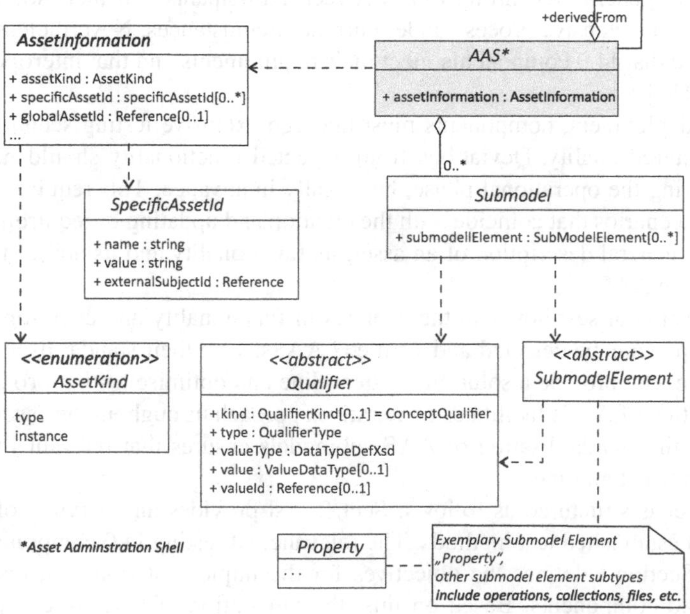

Fig. 1. Excerpt of a class diagram representing the structure of AASs.

In the Industrial Digital Twin Association e. V. (IDTA), extensive efforts are currently being made to specify, test and subsequently standardise submodels for various use cases [9]. A large number of standardised submodels already exist, which have been published by the IDTA and can be identified via their SemanticID. These include:

- Digital Nameplate: Digital nameplate that contains information about the asset,
- Handover Documentation: Documentation that contains information about the asset,
- Contact Information: Contact information that contains information about the asset manufacturer,
- Hierarchical Structures Bill of Material (BOM): Hierarchical structures that describe the relationships between assets and their components and
- Capabilities: Capabilities that the asset possesses.

The class diagram (Fig. 1) gives a detailed impression of the structure of the AAS.

There are three types of AASs (see Fig. 2). Type one AASs are represented as serialised files (XML, JSON, AASX format). Type two AASs are runtime instances installed on devices or servers. They provide an HTTP/REST interface for communication with higher-level applications and, for example, an OPC UA interface for communication with assets. Type 3 AASs are similar to Type 2 AASs and can communicate with other AASs, for example, to initiate jobs or trigger maintenance intervals. The languages for Type 3 AASs are the subject of current research [12].

2.2 Overview of Testing Methodologies

Various software development kits (SDK) are available for the implementation and use of the AAS. These enable the creation of AASs and their use. The SDKs are available in various programming languages and support the creation of AASs in types 1 and 2. The software solutions of IDTA and in particular the off-the-shelf components of BaSyx have the largest range of functions for the use of AASs.

Numerous scholars have investigated the utilization of test methods in software development. The sources referenced herein have carried out extensive discourse on software solution testing. For instance, search-based testing, suitable for robust test case coverage of the System Under Test (SUT), is discussed in [15].

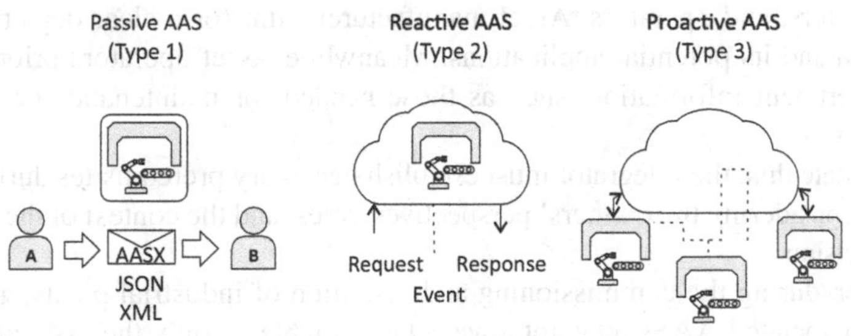

Fig. 2. Asset Administration Shell Types [3].

In [6,8,21], the method of model-based test case generation is introduced, treating the SUT as a BlackBox. By providing generated input data, it's possible to influence the internal state, with automation allowing for the evaluation of plant component quality.

Conversely, [14] discusses property-based testing where, typically, the SUT is stateless.

[17] provides an overview of different methods for testing AAS-SDKs. The authors proposed a combination of property-based and combinatorial testing as a viable approach, focusing primarily on black-box tests for Type 1 AASs de/serialization to evaluate AAS SDKs. However, it remains unclear whether an AAS-based solution has been implemented and if the future testing of I4.0 components, including the asset behavior, will be addressed.

It is essential to verify not only the AAS but also its interaction with the asset. This approach is key to a system integration process with minimum effort, which must be ensured by effective and concurrent testing. A key challenge is to manage the large number of different interfaces and their specification as described in [16], where a method for requirements-based testing of complex automation systems is presented.

Typically, isolated tests, known for their ability to reduce component complexity, have been adopted for standard software development solutions. However, these tests necessitate a robust engineering process that yields reproducible results. Therefore, future systems' test scenarios need to be deduced during the requirements determination phase. This is largely due to the increasing need for modifications during the utilisation phase of plant components and the necessity of integrating existing components into I4.0 environments.

The IDTA provides a solution for verifying the meta model conformance of submitted AASs and issues a certification. However, there's also a need to dynamically add submodels during the production phase of I4.0 components. In this context, automated testing within the existing system environment is desirable, as conditions can change even during commissioning. This applies not only to the content of the AAS, but also to their behaviour and connectivity.

2.3 Necessity of Testing Industry 4.0 Components

The AAS was conceptualized as a foundational framework for implementing digital twins, accommodating various perspectives of partners, including asset manufacturers, plant integrators, and operators. Asset manufacturers aim for a clear depiction of the specification and its potential applications. Meanwhile, asset operators prioritize easy access to pertinent information, such as those needed for maintenance or asset area modifications.

To facilitate this, the integrator must establish necessary prerequisites during implementation, considering the partners' perspectives, roles, and the context of the I4.0 component provision.

However, during the commissioning and operation of industrial plants, assets supplied with associated AASs may not always be available. If only the asset and not the AAS is provided by a supplier, the integrator is tasked with preparing the AAS. The integrator must outline a type 1 AAS based on the technical description and, if needed, set up a communication interface for a type 2 AAS. Standardized processes and a suitable toolchain are needed for this.

Upon AAS creation, it is essential to validate the syntactic correctness, completeness, and conformance of the AAS with the asset's characteristics.

The integrator is also responsible for the specification and documentation of test scenarios. If the initial conditions for asset usage change during operation, the integration process must be revisited. Here, employing AAS generators or establishing a test environment could be a viable solution.

3 Test Procedure and Goals

Each product development undergoes a two-step specification process. Firstly, the requirements specification answers the question "What is needed?", followed by the target specification, which clarifies the mode of implementation. Every attribute delineated in the target specification is assessed against the requirements specification, accompanied by integration tests wherein the product is evaluated alongside associated components such as PLCs. The objective is to preemptively uncover and avoid errors or vulnerabilities in the implementation of third-party components. The testing process should be designed with several key objectives in mind:

- Verification and validation of plant components in response to evolving requirements
- Quality assurance during operational phases
- Certification of management shells, submodels, and operations to enhance reusability
- Component evaluation based on domain-specific application scenarios
- Documentation of component behavior for validation and benchmarking purposes

4 Use Case and Requirements

4.1 Use Case

In general, the preparation of I4.0 components is not only relevant for new plants but there is also a need to integrate existing components into I4.0 environments. This is associated with considerable effort according to the existing complexity of the asset. A detailed consideration of this issue was provided by the authors in [19]. In the use case of an industrial environment, products, in this case high-quality thermal switches, were tested during production or after the manufacturing process.

To prepare, manufacture and test a product (or part of a product), processes and their associated resources are required. Therefore, the Product-Process-Resource (PPR) approach can be used. The variation of products, here using the example of thermal switches (>100 specifications in terms of design features and application), leads to a multiplicity of specifications of processes and associated resources. This means that the AAS and its submodels can be tailored to the customer's specific assets. This is essential in order to assess the use and quality of the resources used and the product manufactured.

In this environment, each product passes through predefined test scenarios. The products are placed on a special pallet carrier and made available to the respective processes. The required test frame, sequence and dwell time of the products on the test stations vary according to the product batch and are provided via a submodel.

As an example, the technological scheme (extract) of the plant environment with its processes is shown in Fig. 3. The existing plant was used with a classical and heterogeneous instrumentation (e.g. PLC, industrial robots, vision systems, etc.) and there was an overall coordination of the processes. As part of the preparation of the use case, the retrofit of plant components and their coordination was carried out using AASs.

Since data integration sometimes involves a great deal of effort, incorrect configurations should be identified at an early stage. With the preparation/provision of a test recipe, for example, the resulting I4.0 component can be evaluated.

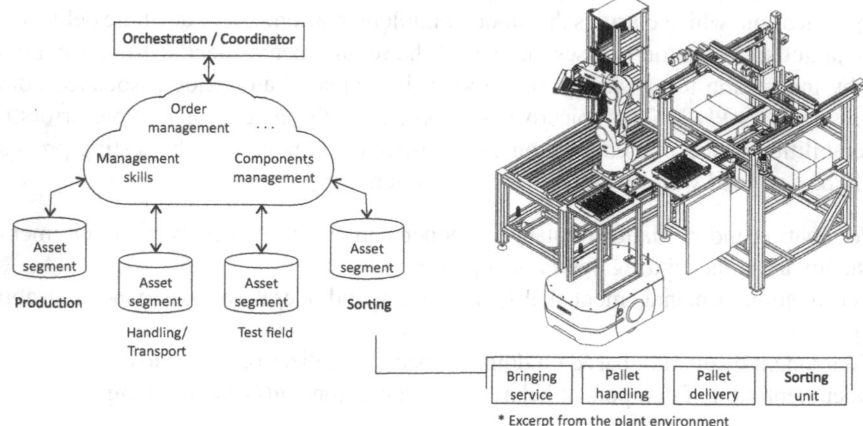

Fig. 3. Technological scheme and processes (excerpt).

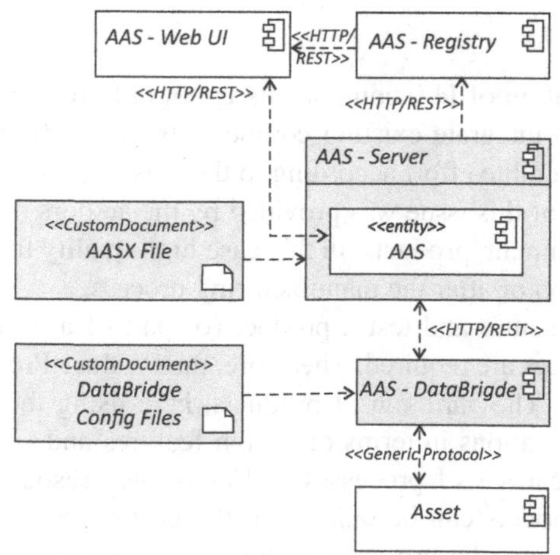

Fig. 4. Overview of the BaSyx Infrastructure (simplified representation).

4.2 Architecture Overview of in the AAS Environment

In the fundamental BaSyx architecture (see Fig. 4), the user has to configure a total of four components to use the AAS. This includes the integration into existing network structures. In general, the components are implemented as separate Application Programming Interfaces (APIs) and interact with each other via their standardised interfaces. Thus, the individual elements are interoperable and can be used as desired. Version 1 of BaSyx includes the following components:

Registry. The Registry is used to register AAS. It is used as a central repository of information to make AASs discoverable in IT networks. The Registry only contains links to existing AASs, but does not provide the content itself.

AAS Server. The AAS Server is the central component for hosting runtime instances of AASs. It allows AASs that previously existed only as static files to be uploaded and dynamically customised. The AAS Server provides the content of one or more AASs via a REST API.

DataBridge. The DataBridge can be used to integrate dynamic asset instances (e.g. PLCs or sensors) into an AAS. It supports different protocols for communicating with assets. The DataBridge populates the AAS with asset information via the REST API of the AAS server. Typically the following parameters are required:

- Asset access data (e.g. IP address, port, communication protocol, etc.),
- Data transformations (e.g., conversion of units, etc.),
- target submodel and property of the AAS as well as
- general structure of the integration route.

Web UI. The AAS Web UI can be used to visualise content from the AAS. It provides a graphical user interface that accesses the content of the AAS via the REST API of the AAS server. In particular, the UI has the ability to browse multiple AASs referenced via a registry and display their contents.

4.3 Specification of Required Functions

A comprehensive specification is essential for the implementation of the test solution. Key components are detailed below and partially summarized in Table 1 to provide an overview and classification of these elements.

The test solution should support a ticket-based test execution strategy and generate/provide evaluative test reports. This system hinges on a ticket repository utilized by the verification facility. The interaction with the ticket system can be facilitated through the services of a submodel, thus eliminating the need for the user's proficiency in specific programming languages.

Both an integrator and any component integrated within the same network can serve as the system user. Potential users of the test solution include Type 2 or Type 3 AASs,

Table 1. Requirements specification (excerpt).

Req. ID	Functionality description
Req01	The system must define the steps of the test pipeline to be performed based on a test configuration
Req02	The system must allow the user to enter the address of the registry component
Req03	The system must provide the user with the ability to initiate a ticket-oriented test process
Req04	The system must allow the user to delete and update test configurations and tickets based on the Id of the test object
Req05	The system shall provide the user with the ability to enter test configurations and tickets for each test object
Req06	The system must be able to execute a test pipeline for each test object with a valid test configuration
Req07	The system shall be capable of performing structural testing based on a structural description Derived from: Specification of a suitable format for describing the target state required
Req08	The system must generate test reports in the course of test execution
Req09	The system shall tag each successfully tested AAS
Req10	If a state machine is represented by the test object, the system shall be capable of verifying it based on a description of the behavior of the state machine by initiating transitions and evaluating states Derived from: Synchronization between the AAS and the asset must be ensured. The description of the state machine must specify the identification data of the properties that lead to the reading or setting of the current state. The current state must be able to be set and read out via the AAS
..	

software applications, and system components such as edge gateways. Essentially, any entity capable of interfacing with an AAS is considered a potential user. The BaSyx REST API [25] and BaSyx AAS Web UI [24] facilitate this interaction.

Industry 4.0 components represented by an AAS are deemed as relevant test subjects. The user or the Industry 4.0 component provides the pertinent test recipes. With the ticket-based test procedure, all three AAS versions can be tested.

During the test process, the system progresses through a test pipeline where the test solution identifies and executes the appropriate test stages based on the user's test recipe. The system must validate the AAS structure of the component under test, using the user's structure description. This process is crucial since the AAS structure can be modified at any time, for example, through the provision of an AASX file for interpretation in the BaSyx AAS Server.

The AAS's general structure, along with its submodels and the individual elements, comprise structural information. Each information unit within the AAS context, be it a submodel, property, or operation, is deemed as structural information that needs verification. Validation of an AAS or SubmodelElement, such as an operation, requires accessing or confirming the existence of a higher-level information unit. Lack of such access precludes the element's testing (Fig. 5).

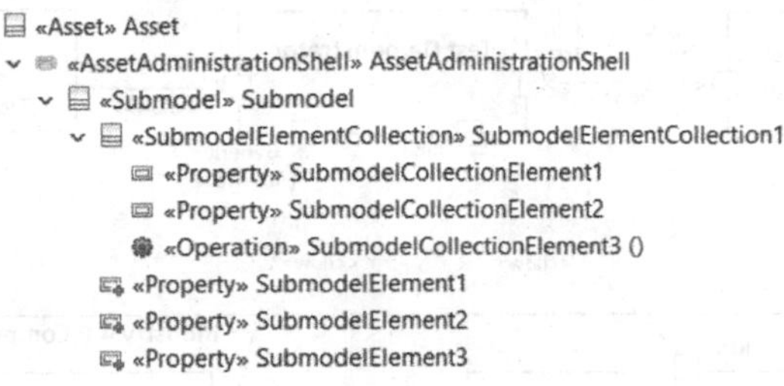

Fig. 5. Structure-oriented test execution.

In the example, a simple AAS with a submodel, three properties, and a collection of SubmodelElements is shown. The final element in the collection, intended for validation in the test pipeline, corresponds to an operation associated with a behavior. To be accessible for testing, the following must be ensured:

- the existence of the parent submodel and
- the existence of the collection of SubmodelElements.

After verifying that these are included as part of the AAS structure, the existence of the actual test object, in this case the operation, can be verified. Only after this process can the operation be considered as the object of a further stage of the test pipeline.

If a recipe describing a state machine has been provided for the test object, the correct operation of the Control Component [25] must be proven accordingly via the AAS. The following prerequisites must be met:

- Successful bidirectional communication between the asset and the AAS,
- Control of the state machine via the AAS is possible and
- The current state of the Control Component is included as a property in the AAS (and can be accessed through the REST API).

In order for the test solution to know which properties can be used to read or set the state of a Control Component, the recipe must specify the identifiers of the corresponding AAS properties. During the test, the test solution initiates transitions. After each transition, the current state of the test asset is compared with the expected state specified in the description. The behaviour provided by the asset via the AAS shall be verified by the testbed based on the corresponding description.

5 Automated Testing with AAS – Ticket Based Usage

In relation to the given use case, the following situation arises: The adaptation of the associated AAS is based on the specification of the product, in this case the thermal switch. From the AAS of the product, the relevant information (as a submodel) for configuring the resources used is extracted and assigned. The AAS configuration is made available to the AAS server in machine-readable formats such as AASX, XML or JSON.

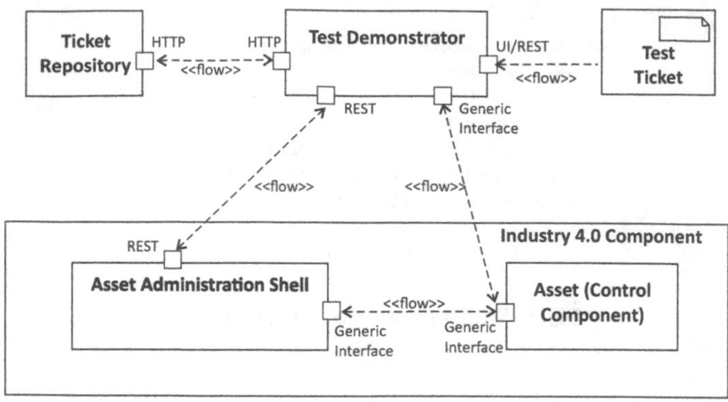

Fig. 6. Components of "ticket-based use" (excerpt).

In addition, the communication relationships to the asset must be set up via the configuration of the DataBridge, as discussed in Sect. 4. This is necessary because different resources are used during production, deployment and testing of the product. Essential configuration data is provided via a number of JSON files.

In addition, the resources must have appropriate behaviour for the specific use case. In our scenario, one of the tools used is a state machine (PackML) on the relevant PLC.

Much of the information contained in these files is manually prepared and presented in a machine-readable format. They may contain errors due to incorrect configurations, deviations from the specification or possible manipulations. Such discrepancies could consequently lead to faulty manufacturing, products and verification tests. This highlights the need to test the resulting AAS, its behaviour (i.e. process flows) and access to the assets.

The ticket-based test process (Fig. 6), applicable to all AAS types, utilizes tickets as input information, defining the test configuration and the test object's access point. Depending on the specifics, a ticket can be issued as a relational database entry or a test solution file. The first approach necessitates an interface to bypass the user's need for specific programming languages, while the second can involve direct database integration within the AAS testing software component. Passive AAS tickets may hold either the AASX file path or the file itself, while active AAS tickets must contain the test object's URL. The elements of this concept are described below:

Test Demonstrator. Users convey the test recipes to the test demonstrator through the appropriate UI or REST interface, which are then stored within the ticket repository. During testing, the test demonstrator retrieves the ticket associated with each test object and carries out the test pipeline.

Ticket Repository. The ticket repository functions as a hub for test recipes, restricting direct write access for users. User interaction with the ticket repository is managed via the test solution's AAS.

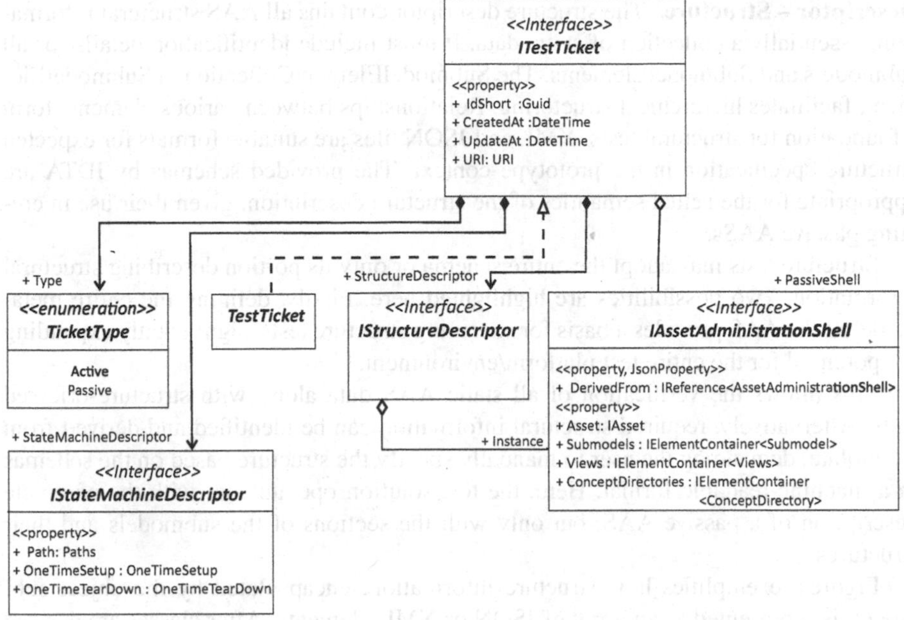

Fig. 7. Class Diagram of the ITestTicket Interface (excerpt).

Test Ticket. Throughout the test process, components with passive and active AASs can be examined. Every valid ticket, provided by the system's user, is assigned a unique identification tag by the test demonstrator.

Table 2 provides examples of possible ticket contents, including a descriptor for AAS structure evaluation and a descriptor for verifying an implemented state machine.

Figure 7 shows a class diagram for the ITestTicket interface. As detailed in the concept description, the ITestTicket interface outlines test recipe components, a placeholder for the test report, and other details. Each stage of the test pipeline requiring specific information for target-actual comparison is assigned a descriptor in the ticket.

Table 2. Data model test ticket.

Identifier	Description
Id	Global identifier
CreateAT	Time of creation
UpdateAT	Time of the last update
Type	Type of the AAS of the test object
Uri	Uri of the AAS of the test object (if active)
PassiveShell	XML content of the AAS of the test object (if passive)
StructureDespritor	Description of the target structure of the AAS of the test object
StateMachineDescriptor	Description of test scenarios of a state machine (if available)
TestReport	Test report provided by the test solution after verification

Descriptor – Structure. The structure descriptor contains all AAS structural information, essentially a collection of static data. It must include identification details for all submodels and SubmodelElements. The SubmodelElementCollection, a SubmodelElement, facilitates hierarchical structuring. Relationships between various elements form a foundation for structural tests. XML and JSON files are suitable formats for expected structure specification in the prototype context. The provided schemas by IDTA are appropriate for the actual semantics of the structure description, given their use in creating passive AASs.

Structure tests may adopt the entire schema or only its portion describing structural information. Two possibilities are highlighted here. Firstly, defining the entire metamodel of the AAS provides a basis for executing structure tests, significantly expanding the potential for the entire test platform/environment.

This allows the verification of all static AAS data along with structure-oriented tests. Alternatively, required structural information can be identified and derived from a template, demanding the user to manually specify the structure based on the schemas in a machine-readable format. Here, the test solution operates not with the complete description of a passive AAS, but only with the sections of the submodels and their structures.

Figure 8 exemplifies how structure information, encapsulated by the object submodel, is represented as an array of JSON or XML elements. After classes are derived from the schema definition, suitable libraries can deserialize the structure data. This derivation can either be done manually or by generators, such as the XML schema definition tool.

However, a more efficient alternative is the BaSyx API, which provides functionalities for serializing and deserializing AASs when dealing with external AASs.

```
{
  "assetAdministrationShells": [],
  "assets": [],
  "submodels": [],
  "conceptDescriptions": []
}
```

```
<?xml version="1.0" encoding="UTF-8"?>
<aas:aasenv ...>
  <aas:assetAdministrationShells></
       aas:assetAdministrationShells>
  <aas:assets></aas:assets>
  <aas:conceptDescriptions></aas:conceptDescriptions>
  <aas:submodels></aas:submodels>
</aas:aasenv>
```

Fig. 8. Specification JSON/XML structure of a type 1 AAS.

To extend the structure-oriented test procedure, the information can be mapped via the BaSyx interface IAssetAdministrationShell after deserializing the structure descriptor. Consequently, the test solution operates with two instances of this interface. The first instance represents the AAS of the actual test object, while the second specifies its target structure.

```
<!-- aborted => stopped -->
<path>
  <properties submodel="SM_Unit1_(SuperiorStateMachine)"
       setter="SMC_Statemachine/Prop_ControlCommand" getter="
       SMC_Statemachine/Prop_State"/>
  <state id="Aborted">
    <transition event="Clear" target="Stopped"/>
  </state>
</path>

<!-- stopped => aborted -->
<path>
  <properties submodel="SM_Unit1_(SuperiorStateMachine)"
       setter="SMC_Statemachine/Prop_ControlCommand" getter="
       SMC_Statemachine/Prop_State"/>
  <state id="Aborted">
    <transition event="Clear" target="Stopped"/>
  </state>
  <state id="Stopped">
    <transition event="Abort" target="Aborted"/>
  </state>
</path>
```

Fig. 9. Specification of state-oriented test cases (excerpt).

Descriptor – State Machine. State Chart XML specification can universally describe a state machine. Its constructs can be adopted from the specification for defining test cases, thereby enabling software-oriented verification of a state machine. This can be executed by triggering state changes and subsequently verifying if the new state aligns with the specification. The descriptor can also contain a sequence of paths, verified sequentially within the test pipeline after intermediate tests, hence considered as test scenarios.

Figure 9 illustrates a method of specifying test cases. The specification of an initial state is a prerequisite. Based on this approach, each path can be validated independently of the preceding or succeeding test case. With the unique assignment of the test path to the submodel, multiple independent state machines can also be verified.

General Procedure. Figure 10 illustrates the fundamental flow of ticket-oriented test execution, including the communication dynamics between the components. It provides the user with the flexibility to load customized test tickets into the ticket repository, inquire about them, or discard them.

During the test execution, the pertinent test ticket is provisioned. This process initiates with its instantiation and is followed by the mapping between the ticket within the repository and the ticket in the software application's context. All tickets utilized for verifying I4.0 components with active AASs contain the essential AAS's URI to establish communication. However, the reference for passive AAS tickets is made by the user. he assigned ticket is essential for preparing the TestObject class instance. If the ticket contains a URI reference, a communication link to the AAS is formed.

While passive AAS tickets encapsulate all the information necessary for test execution, the module's interface still necessitates an instance of the TestObject class to execute the test pipeline. Subsequently, the test pipeline is run. This step involves

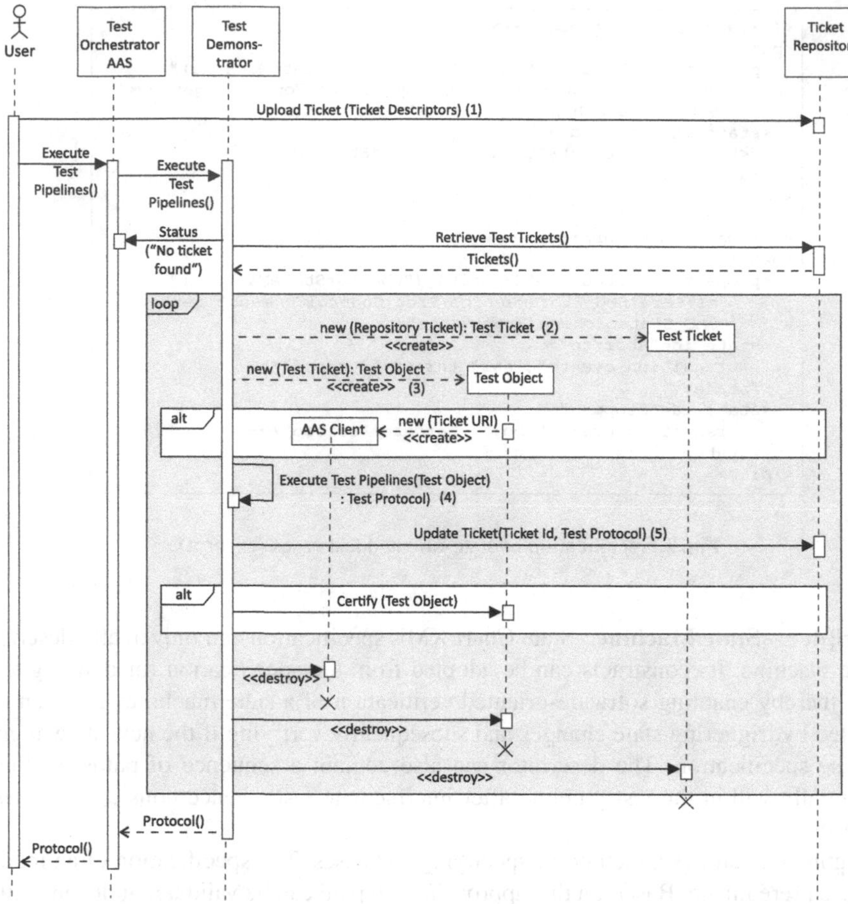

Fig. 10. Ticket-oriented test execution process (excerpt).

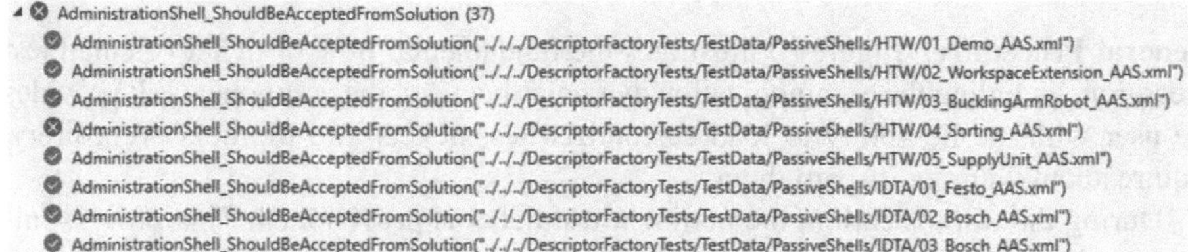

Fig. 11. Definition of valid test objects (excerpt).

associating the created test log with the test ticket and updating them in the respective directory. If no discrepancies between the test results and the ticket descriptors are identified in the pipeline, the test object is marked. After running the sequence for each test object, a comprehensive test log for all test objects is generated and provided to the user.

6 Prototype Implementation

In the prototypical implementation of the test environment, the structural verification of AAS and the state-oriented testing of Control Components (representing state machines) were realized. In this paper we focus on the structural verification of AAS. The implemented test modules are each used as stages of the test pipeline and use the .Net test framework NUnit. Figure 11 shows an excerpt of a valid test object.

6.1 Structural Tests

The first pipeline stage entails a comparative analysis between the AAS structure of the test object and the structural descriptor definition. A recursive function enables sequential traversal of the complete tree of submodels and SubmodelElements for this verification process. During each traversal step, the properties of the current SubmodelElement are compared with the information in the structural description. The sequence diagram in Fig. 12 illustrates this test case, demonstrating the comprehensive verification of an AAS's entire structure. Successful completion of the test requires an exact match between the test object's structure and the structure descriptor. Any discrepancy

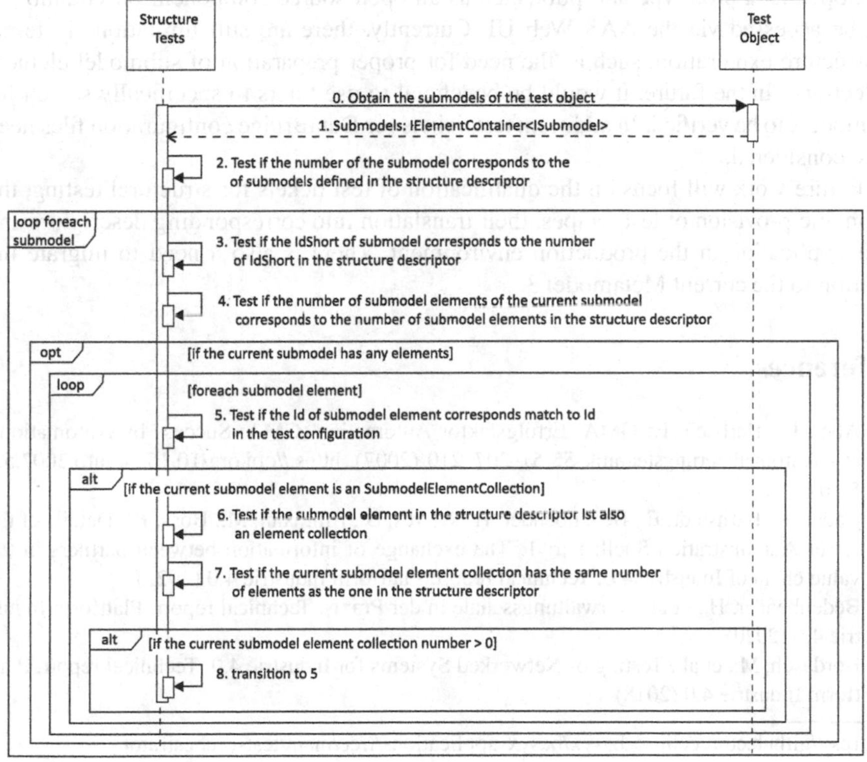

Fig. 12. Procedure AAS structure verification.

in identification data or the quantity and order of structural elements signifies a failure in the pipeline stage.

7 Conclusion and Outlook

When deploying I4.0 components in new or existing environments, it's essential to evaluate their AAS structure, behaviour and communication relationships. In particular, when alternative components are integrated into the system environment, their interoperability becomes critical. Even if the AAS content is customised, for example by assigning submodels that differ from the standardised IDTA templates, it's essential to test them, including the integration of the asset.

The ticket-based testing approach, combined with the use of a test pipeline, provides a method to efficiently test I4.0 components. The introduced test strategy provides a way to assess the AAS structure and behaviour evaluation, especially for state machines. A key feature of this solution is its accessibility to system integrators, allowing them to use it without any programming knowledge or understanding of the AAS. Test tickets facilitate the dynamic updating of target information.

The current solution only serves to demonstrate that the chosen approach of using descriptors supports the testing of I4.0 components. The architecture presented has been developed as a prototype and published as an open source component on GitHub[1]. It can be accessed via the AAS Web UI. Currently, there are still limitations in terms of structure exploration, such as the need for proper preparation of submodel element collections. In the future, it would be beneficial to use filters to specifically search for submodels to be verified. In addition, test tickets for DataBridge configuration files need to be considered.

Future work will focus on the qualification of test tickets for structural testing, the automatic provision of test recipes, their translation into corresponding descriptors and their application in the production environment. There is also a need to migrate the solution to the current Metamodel 3.

References

1. Abel, D., Harbach, F.: GMA: Erfolgsfaktor Automation (GMA: Success by Automation). at - Automatisierungstechnik **55**(5), 207–210 (2007). https://doi.org/10.1524/auto.2007.55.5.207
2. Bader, S., Barnstedt, E., Bedenbender, H., Berres, B., Billmann, M., Boss, B.: Details of the Asset Administration Shell: Part 1: The exchange of information between partners in the value chain of Industrie 4.0. Technical report, Plattform Industrie 4.0 (2022)
3. Bedenbender, H., et al.: Verwaltungsschale in der Praxis. Technical report, Plattform Industrie 4.0 (2020)
4. Bordasch, M., et al.: Testing of Networked Systems for Industrie 4.0. Technical report, Plattform Industrie 4.0 (2018)

[1] https://github.com/eclipse-basyx/basyx-applications/tree/main/test-orchestrator.

5. DIN EN 61508-3:2011-02: Functional safety of electrical/electronic/programmable electronic safety-related systems - Part 3: Software requirements. Standard, Beuth Verlag GmbH (2011)
6. El-Far, I., Whittaker, J.: Model-Based Software Testing. Wiley, New York (2002). https://doi.org/10.1002/0471028959.sof207
7. France: Ministry of Economy and Finances, Germany: Federal Ministry for Economic Affairs and Energy (BMWi), Italy: Ministero dello Sviluppo Economico: The Structure of the Administration Shell: TRILATERAL PERSPECTIVES from France, Italy and Germany. Technical report, Plattform Industrie 4.0 (2018)
8. Grochowski, M., et al.: Formale Methoden für rekonfigurierbare cyber-physische Systeme in der Produktion. at - Automatisierungstechnik **68**(1), 3–14 (2020). https://doi.org/10.1515/auto-2019-0115
9. Industrial Digital Twin Association e. V.: IDTA - working together to promote the Digital Twin. https://industrialdigitaltwin.org
10. Javaid, M., Haleem, A., Singh, R.P., Suman, R.: Enabling flexible manufacturing system (FMS) through the applications of industry 4.0 technologies. Internet Things Cyber-Phys. Syst. **2**, 49–62 (2022). https://doi.org/10.1016/j.iotcps.2022.05.005
11. Kagermann, H., Wahlster, W., Helbig, J.: Im Fokus: Das Zukunftsprojekt Industrie 4.0, Handlungsempfehlungen zur Umsetzung. Bericht der Promotorengruppe Kommunikation, Forschungsunion im Stifterverband für die Deutsche Wirtschaft e. V., Berlin (2012)
12. Kuhn, T., Schnicke, F., Oliveira Antonino, P.: Service-based architectures in production systems: challenges, solutions & experiences. In: 2020 ITU Kaleidoscope: Industry-Driven Digital Transformation (ITU K), pp. 1–7 (2020). https://doi.org/10.23919/ITUK50268.2020.9303207
13. van Lamsweerde, A.: Requirements Engineering: From System Goals to UML Models to Software Specifications. Wiley, New York (2009)
14. MacIver, D.: In praise of property-based testing. Increment - Issue 10: Testing (2019)
15. McMinn, P.: Search-based software test data generation: a survey. Softw. Test. Verif. Reliab. **14**(2), 105–156 (2004). https://doi.org/10.1002/stvr.294
16. Meinecke, K., Land, K., Jumar, U., Vogel-Heuser, B., Reider, M., Ziegltrum, S.: Anforderungsbasierter Test für die Validierung komplexer Automatisierungssysteme. at - Automatisierungstechnik **69**(6), 417–429 (2021). https://doi.org/10.1515/auto-2020-0120
17. Miny, T., et al.: Semi-automatic testing of data-focused software development kits for Industrie 4.0. In: 2022 IEEE 20th International Conference on Industrial Informatics (INDIN), pp. 269–274 (2022). https://doi.org/10.1109/INDIN51773.2022.9976069
18. Reinhart, G. (ed.): Handbuch Industrie 4.0: Geschäftsmodelle, Prozesse, Technik. Hanser, München (2017). https://doi.org/10.3139/9783446449893
19. Schäfer, S., Schöttke, D., Kämpfe, T., Lachmann, O., Zielstorff, A., Tauber, B.: Migration and synchronization of plant segments with Asset Administration Shells. In: 2022 IEEE 27th International Conference on Emerging Technologies and Factory Automation (ETFA), pp. 1–8 (2022). https://doi.org/10.1109/ETFA52439.2022.9921595
20. Thramboulidis, K.: The 3+1 SysML view-model in model integrated mechatronics. J. Softw. Eng. Appl. **3**, 109–118 (2010). https://doi.org/10.4236/jsea.2010.32014
21. Utting, M., Legeard, B.: Practical Model-Based Testing. Morgan Kaufmann, Burlington (2007). https://doi.org/10.1016/B978-0-12-372501-1.X5000-5
22. Vogel-Heuser, B., Folmer, J., Legat, C.: Anforderungen an die Softwareevolution in der Automatisierung des Maschinen- und Anlagenbaus. at - Automatisierungstechnik **62**(3), 163–174 (2014). https://doi.org/10.1515/auto-2013-1051
23. Weyrich, M., et al.: Evaluation model for assessment of cyber-physical production systems. In: Jeschke, S., Brecher, C., Song, H., Rawat, D.B. (eds.) Industrial Internet of Things. SSWT, pp. 169–199. Springer, Cham (2017). https://doi.org/10.1007/978-3-319-42559-7_7

24. Zielstorff, A., Stoehr, M., Fischer, R., Schnicke, F.: BaSyx - Fraunhofer AAS GUI - A Webapplication to select and visualize Asset Administration Shells, Submodels and Properties. https://github.com/eclipse-basyx/basyx-applications/tree/main/aas-gui
25. Ziesche, C., Espen, D., Schnicke, F.: Eclipse BaSyx Wiki - Components and their API. https://github.com/eclipse-basyx/basyx-java-components#eclipse-wiki

Balancing Risks and Monetary Savings When the Crowd is Involved in Pickups and Deliveries

Annarita De Maio[1(✉)], Roberto Musmanno[2], and Francesca Vocaturo[1]

[1] Department of Economics, Statistics and Finance "Giovanni Anania", University of Calabria, Rende, CS, Italy
{annarita.demaio,vocaturo}@unical.it

[2] Department of Mechanical, Energy and Management Engineering, University of Calabria, Rende, CS, Italy
roberto.musmanno@unical.it

Abstract. The increasing number of requests in the last-mile delivery has led to the introduction of advanced technological solutions to enhance couriers' services. In addition, innovative strategies like crowd-shipping have been introduced in order to create synergies within the territory and involve ordinary people in the transportation activity with the aim of reducing operational costs and pollution as well as of increasing the service level. We refer to a company that manages a crowd-shipping platform and provides transportation services within time windows through its own fleet of vehicles and occasional drivers. The service requests correspond to pairs of pickups and deliveries. The objective of the company is to maximize the profit by balancing risks and benefits, from an economic perspective, associated with the involvement of ordinary people in fulfilling service requests. We extend the pickup and delivery problem with occasional drivers and regular vehicles, introducing risk and compensation considerations. The computational analysis conducted through an optimization model shows how the use of occasional drivers reduces overall costs. Moreover, a series of managerial insights is provided thanks to a sensitivity analysis on the risk and compensation parameters associated with crowd-shipping service.

Keywords: Sustainable transportation · Crowd-shipping · Multi-vehicle pickup and delivery problem · Time windows · Integer linear programming

1 Introduction

In the last decades, an increase of the requests for freight transportation and parcel delivery in the urban areas has been registered, related to the fast economic development of the cities and to the massive use of e-commerce. As a consequence, the necessity of developing new strategies to improve logistics activities, while making them more sustainable and efficient, has inspired the discussion among researchers. New logistics paradigms and technologies in the last-mile segment include: vendor-managed inventory practices [1,2], city logistics solutions [3,4], parcel deliveries with lockers [5], transportation by electric and green vehicles [6] and use of drones [7]. The improvement of services provided through app-based platforms and the spread-out of the sharing economy concept [8] have allowed a fast propagation of logistics practices based

S. Terzi et al. (Eds.): IN4PL 2023, CCIS 1886, pp. 107–125, 2023.
https://doi.org/10.1007/978-3-031-49339-3_7

on components like bike-sharing [9], car-sharing or car-pooling [10], van-sharing for freight mobility [11], and ride sharing [12]. Furthermore, the diffusion of popular shipping options like the "same-day delivery" and the "one-day delivery" [13–15] has driven many companies to develop innovative frameworks and promotes crowd-shipping as one of the most hopeful transportation ways [16, 17]. Crowd-shipping refers to a logistics practice where transportation activities can be carried out by the crowd. In detail ordinary people, called *occasional drivers* (ODs), can use the free capacity of their vehicle and decide to transport parcels along their daily own trip (e.g., in the journey for going to work) and obtain a monetary reward, usually proportional to the needed deviation. In general, a digital platform is used to manage the matching between supply and demand for logistics services and to pay out the compensation related to the ODs (see [18]). This platform should be accessed in several ways, such as mobile phone or web browser, and provide the opportunity to engage a broad spectrum of people.

Crowd-shipping produces lower operating costs for companies, compared to the traditional logistics models [16]; indeed the use of ad hoc drivers is proven to provide distance savings up to 37% compared to traditional delivery systems [19]. In practice, different variants of crowd-shipping applications are used by the companies [18]. For instance Walmart, a leading company in grocery retail, introduced a system for collecting online orders and assigning them to the in-store customers [20]; Amazon introduced in 2015 an innovative service, namely Amazon Flex, now operating in 50 American cities, where ODs can receive a compensation after delivering parcels from Amazon distribution centres to final customers [21]. Crowd-shipping paradigm involves many potential benefits from the economic, social and environmental perspectives. For transportation companies, it allows to decrease the cost associated with the delivery of specific parcels, to reduce the own fleet size, to face peaks of requests in a flexible way, and to increase the service level; moreover, using ODs (already on the road) for transportation activities leads to a reduction of traffic congestion, noise and pollutant emissions within urban areas as well as of parking space for trucks [22].

The scientific literature presents several contributions on crowd-shipping in the optimization field. Archetti et al. [23] deal with the vehicle routing problem with ODs, where a set of requests known in advance is considered and each OD can satisfy only one request; the problem is solved through a heuristic algorithm and the impact of variegated compensation schemes is tested. Dalhe et al. [24] focus on the pick-up and delivery problem with ODs and time windows, with different symmetry breaking inequalities and three compensation schemes. Macrina et al. [25] discuss the opportunity for the ODs to use transshipment nodes as pick-up points, that are close to the delivery area and replenished by corporate-owned vehicles, named *regular vehicles* (RVs). In this case, the problem is solved with a variable neighbourhood search heuristic. Dehle et al. [26] deal with stochastic aspects concerning the problem; in particular, they focus on the uncertain availability of ODs. Arslan et al. [19] solve, through a rolling horizon exact approach, a dynamic pick-up and delivery problem with ad hoc drivers and dedicated vehicles in order to schedule deliveries every time a new service request arrives to the platform. The online version of the vehicle routing problem with ODs, in which new customer requests can arrive during the service time, is analysed by Archetti et al. [27]. In order to perform a real-time rescheduling of the deliveries, the authors present an insertion algorithm. The pickup and delivery problem with time windows and ODs introduced by Dalhe et al. [24] is used as a basis for their work. Generally speaking, there is a broader scientific literature that partially deals with crowd-shipping. For example, spare capacity within buses and taxis is considered for parcel deliveries within urban areas in [28] and [29], while in [30] the multi-hope multi-parcel matching problem is introduced, considering the best matching between parcels and ODs. Other studies focus on the combination of item-sharing and crowd deliveries [31] as well as on the integrated use of ODs and lockers [32,33]. For an overview about new variants, applications and recent contributions on crowd-shipping services, the reader is referred to [34,35] and [36].

Our analysis also falls into the optimization field. Specifically, the study considers a service provider, operating through a logistics platform, that manages the transportation of products belonging to different categories (personal care, home care, electronics, clothing, magazines, games and sports, etc.) and coordinates their shipping to the final customers. The service provider operates by picking and delivering products within the urban area (examples of pickup and delivery problems with only RVs in deterministic and stochastic settings are given in [37,38], respectively). In our study, transportation activities are carried out through a heterogeneous fleet of vehicles, which is composed by ODs and RVs. Obviously, the ODs are compensated for their effort. In particular, our work refers to a vehicle routing problem under time windows constraints, with the (unusual) aim of maximizing the total profit generated by the platform for serving all transportation requests from specified pairs of pickup and delivery locations. The platform has to schedule and route the RVs, considering the insertion of the ODs when it is profitable and appropriate. Generic losses lied to ODs are considered in evaluating the profit. Note that these losses can be immediately quantified in the case of package damages, delivery failures, and thefts (of components or entire products). Risks related to delay or other factors that reduce customers' trust are not easily evaluable but are equally important for the service provider in the long-term.

Various configurations of parameters are introduced and tested in this paper; a mathematical model is used as a decision support tool for the platform owner, in order to pursue the maximization of the total profit and to balance risks and monetary saving associated with the use of ODs. Indeed, in real life, it can be challenging to assess the perfect configuration for all the stakeholders. As aforementioned, the willingness to play as ODs as well as to entrust a delivery to the crowd is influenced by different environmental, social and behavioural components [18]. Buldeo Rai et al. [39] emphasize that the unknown crowd identity is an essential element of crowd-shipping and represents a substantial source of stress. In effect, although the platform registers and tracks the crowd, quality and service are more difficult to be monitored and cannot be guaranteed, as well as transparency and trust. Insecurities such as increased risk of theft, loss and damage form major barriers. Also with standard delivery, a certain amount of damage is assumed, but it is definitely less worrying and can be neglected. In order to respond to these insecurities and reassure end-users, a number of mechanisms can be introduced, e.g., a rigorous selection process or a feedback system. Here, a reliability parameter concerning ODs is considered for taking into account the aspects just described. It is worth highlighting that, in the scientific literature, an interesting analysis including profit considerations for the platform owner of a meal delivery service, based on the collaboration with riders, is introduced in [40], while Le et al. [18] underline that the ODs do not accept the assigned requests if the compensation is not considered satisfying and, as a consequence, the delivery plan would be suboptimal. The literature clearly highlights the need to simultaneously consider adequate compensation for ODs and risk associated with delivery, directly related to the reliability of the driver itself and to possible increasing costs. These considerations emphasize the importance and timeliness of our analysis focused on investigating operational variety and affect the implementation of such a service.

The remainder of this paper is organized as follows: Sect. 2 illustrates the problem and its formulation, Sect. 3 describes the experimental phase and provides managerial insights, whereas Sect. 4 summarizes some concluding remarks and future research directions.

2 Problem Description and Mathematical Formulation

We consider a directed complete graph $G = (V, A)$, in which V is the set of vertices (or nodes) and A is the set of arcs. We assume that G is an Euclidean graph, so the triangular inequality holds both in terms of cost and time matrices. We assume that the nodes in $V = \{0, 1, ..., 2n + 1\}$ (different from 0 and $2n + 1$, both describing the depot) are divided into two subsets P and D that represent the sets of pickup and delivery points, respectively. Without loss of generality, the first n nodes refer to the pickup points ($P = \{1, 2, ..., n\}$), whereas the second ones refer to the delivery points ($D = \{n + 1, ..., 2n\}$). Each service request is associated with a pickup node i and a delivery node $i + n$. A homogeneous fleet of RVs, i.e. K^r, and a fleet of ODs, i.e. K^o, are available to service the requests, with $K = K^r \cup K^o$. Each vehicle $k \in K^o$ has an origin o_k and a destination d_k, defining the set $V^o = \{o_k, d_k : k \in K^o\}$, while all RVs have origins and destinations at the depot. It is worth observing that all the ODs origins are assumed to be directly connected with the pickup nodes and all the delivery nodes are directly connected with the ODs destinations; these connections define the set A^o. Under this respect, an extended Euclidean graph $G^{'} = (V^{'}, A^{'})$ is defined, with $V^{'} = V \cup V^o$ and $A^{'} = A \cup A^o$. With each arc $(i, j) \in A^{'}$ are associated two non-negative parameters t_{ij} and c_{ij}, denoting the traversing time and the distance, respectively. Note that the distance and the traversing time for the arc $(0, 2n + 1)$ are equal to zero.

Different parameters are also associated with each node $i \in V$. In particular, we denote by f_i the service time within each node (with $f_0 = f_{2n+1} = 0$) and by e_i and l_i the earliest and the latest time to start the service, respectively. The interval $[e_i; l_i]$ represents the feasible time window for serving the corresponding node $i \in P \cup D$. There exists also a time window for $i = 0$ and for $i = 2n + 1$ in order to regularise departures and arrivals for RVs.

For each $k \in K^o$, a starting time ST_k for leaving the origin and a maximum time DT_k for reaching the destination are defined, respectively. Note that an OD is allowed to route following the scheme detailed in Fig. 1, if a request is assigned to it. In the figure, node i represents the pickup point and node $i+n$ the delivery point of a particular request. OD origins and destinations can correspond to pickup or delivery points, respectively.

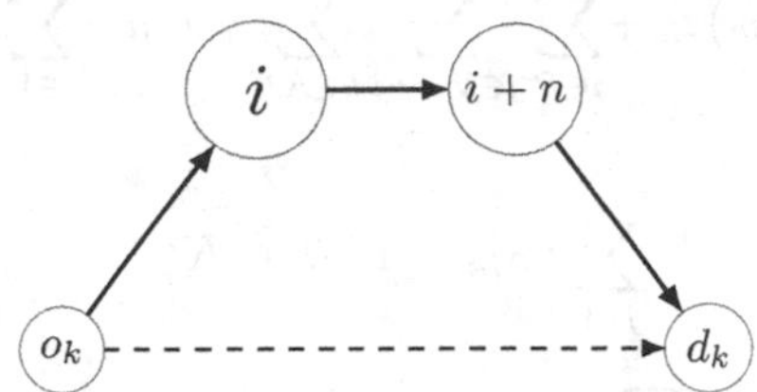

Fig. 1. OD route, if a service request is assigned to it.

Let γ_i be the price at which the service request, associated with the pickup node $i \in P$, was sold on the platform. Note that this price is defined by the platform by considering different aspects, like the distance between pickup and delivery points, as well as the type and the value of the transported good. Let θ_{ik} be the revenue related to the transportation of request $i \in P$ by OD $k \in K^o$, computed as $\theta_{ik} = \gamma_i\, \delta_k$, where δ_k is a reliability parameter (with $0 \leq \delta_k \leq 1$) associated with each $k \in K^o$. Reliability is calculated on the basis of the history of requests processed by the OD, as well as the evaluations provided on the platform by end-users. The lower the reliability of the OD, the higher the risk cost will be, associated with the non-professional driver service (e.g., damage, theft, delay) paid by the platform. Let α_k be the variable cost per unit of distance travelled by OD $k \in K^o$ and w_{ik} the distance travelled by OD $k \in K^o$ in case of transporting the request $i \in P$. Let ϕ_{ik} be a binary parameter equal to 1 if request $i \in P$ is compatible (in terms of time limits) for the OD $k \in K^o$, 0 otherwise. Let β be the unit cost per kilometre related to the RVs.

Solving our pickup and delivery problem with ODs means determining:

1. the assignment of vehicles to requests in such a way that each request is processed by an RV or, alternatively, by an OD;
2. the delivery routes for serving the requests assigned to the RVs;
3. the total profit generated by the platform implementing this service.

These decisions must be made by maximizing the total profit associated with the processed requests and by considering that the time window associated with each node needs to be satisfied and each OD can serve only one request. Finally, it is assumed that the RVs not used within the crowd-shipping service are alternatively used by the company for other professional services; therefore their non-use does not imply an additional cost. The mathematical formulation is based on the following decision variables:

- z_{ik}: binary decision variable equal to 1 if vehicle $k \in K^o$ fulfils the request associated with pickup node $i \in P$, and 0 otherwise;
- x_{ijk}: binary decision variable equal to 1 if vehicle $k \in K^r$ travels from vertex $i \in V$ to vertex $j \in V$, and 0 otherwise;

– s_{ik}: arrival time at node $i \in V$ by vehicle $k \in K^r$.

The mathematical formulation is described by (1)–(14):

$$\text{MAX} \sum_{i \in P} \sum_{k \in K^o} (\theta_{ik} - \alpha_k w_{ik}) z_{ik} + \sum_{i \in P} \sum_{j \in V: i \neq j} \sum_{k \in K^r} \gamma_i x_{ijk} - \sum_{i \in V} \sum_{j \in V: i \neq j} \sum_{k \in K^r} \beta\, c_{ij} x_{ijk} \tag{1}$$

s.t.

$$\sum_{j \in V} x_{0jk} = 1 \ \ \forall k \in K^r \tag{2}$$

$$\sum_{i \in V} x_{i,2n+1,k} = 1 \ \ \forall k \in K^r \tag{3}$$

$$\sum_{j \in V} x_{ijk} - \sum_{j \in V} x_{i+n,jk} = 0 \ \ \forall i \in P, \forall k \in K^r \tag{4}$$

$$\sum_{i \in V} x_{jik} - \sum_{i \in V} x_{ijk} = 0 \ \ \forall j \in P \cup D, \forall k \in K^r \tag{5}$$

$$s_{jk} \geq (s_{ik} + f_i + t_{ij}) x_{ijk} \ \ \forall i \in V, \forall j \in V, \forall k \in K^r \tag{6}$$

$$s_{ik} \leq s_{i+n,k} \ \ \forall i \in P, \forall k \in K^r \tag{7}$$

$$z_{ik} \leq \phi_{ik} \ \ \forall i \in P, \forall k \in K^o \tag{8}$$

$$\sum_{i \in P} z_{ik} \leq 1 \ \ \forall k \in K^o \tag{9}$$

$$\sum_{k \in K^o} z_{ik} + \sum_{k \in K^r} \sum_{j \in V: i \neq j} x_{ijk} = 1 \ \ \forall i \in P \tag{10}$$

$$e_i \leq s_{ik} \leq l_i \ \ \forall i \in V, \forall k \in K^r \tag{11}$$

$$z_{ik} \in \{0, 1\} \ \ \forall i \in P, \forall k \in K^o \tag{12}$$

$$x_{ijk} \in \{0, 1\} \ \ \forall i \in V, \forall j \in V, \forall k \in K^r \tag{13}$$

$$s_{ik} \geq 0 \ \ \forall i \in V, \forall k \in K^r \tag{14}$$

The objective function (1) maximizes the total profit for the platform, computed as the sum of the profit derived by both the OD deliveries and the RV deliveries. The constraints from (2) to (7) define the routes for the RVs. In detail, constraints (2) and (3) guarantee that each RV departs from the depot and returns to the depot at the end of the route. Constraints (4) ensure that if an RV performs the pickup operation, then it has to complete the service by visiting the delivery node. Constraints (5) and (6) concern the flow balancing and the subtour elimination, respectively. Constraints (6) also ensure consistency of time. Constraints (7) represent the precedence constraints, ensuring that a pickup is performed before its corresponding delivery. Constraints (8) ensure that a request is assigned to an OD compatible with it, whereas constraints (9) impose that each OD can serve one request at most. Constraints (10) guarantee that the service delivery is performed either by an OD or by an RV; therefore, the delivery of the same request cannot be assigned to both vehicle categories at the same time. In addition, they ensure that a service request non-fulfilled by an OD is assigned exactly to an RV. Therefore, the price γ_i in the objective function can be collected once at most. Constraints (11) impose the time window for visiting each node. Finally, constraints (12)–(14) define the nature of the decision variables. Note that constraints (6) are non-linear in this shape. In order to linearize them, an arbitrarily large parameter M_{ij} is introduced and the constraints can be expressed as follows:

$$s_{ik} + f_i + t_{ij} - s_{jk} \leq M_{ij}(1 - x_{ijk}) \qquad \forall i \in V, \forall j \in V, \forall k \in K^r. \tag{15}$$

The validity of these constraints is ensured by setting $M_{ij} \geq max\{0, l_i + f_i + t_{ij} - e_j\}$. Constraints (6) are replaced by (15). It is worth noting that the objective function of the mathematical model presented above can be decomposed in two main components. They are presented below, for better underlining the contribution of each one to the total profit and their influence in deciding whether to use ODs or RVs. The first part is related to the profit deriving from the use of ODs:

$$\sum_{i \in P} \sum_{k \in K^o} (\theta_{ik} - \alpha_k w_{ik}) z_{ik}.$$

The first contribution represents the income derived by the OD delivery activation for a request, while the second contribution is the cost of the compensation due to the driver's planned journey. It is worth observing that the deviation is obtained as the difference between the kilometres covered by the OD along the assigned route and the kilometres of its planned journey (see Fig. 1), multiplied for the unit cost. The value of w_{ik} is pre-computed for each combination of $i \in P$ and $k \in K^o$ as follows:

$$w_{ik} = c_{o_k i} + c_{i,i+n} + c_{i+n,d_k} - c_{o_k d_k}.$$

Similarly, the second profit component consists in the difference between two contributions, respectively revenue for the RV use and routing costs:

$$\sum_{i \in P} \sum_{j \in V: i \neq j} \sum_{k \in K^r} \gamma_i x_{ijk} - \sum_{i \in V} \sum_{j \in V: i \neq j} \sum_{k \in K^r} \beta\, c_{ij} x_{ijk}.$$

Since the RVs generate revenue when they perform a pickup operation, the related contribution is considered when the pick-up nodes associated with a request is visited. The objective function allows therefore to look for the combinations of ODs and RVs capable to guarantee the maximum profit.

Finally, note that the parameter ϕ_{ik} is set equal to 1 if the following conditions are satisfied, 0 otherwise:

- condition 1: $ST_k + t_{o_k i} \in [e_i, l_i]$;
- condition 2: $ST_k + t_{o_k i} + f_i + t_{i,i+n} \in [e_{i+n}, l_{i+n}]$;
- condition 3: $ST_k + t_{o_k i} + f_i + t_{i,i+n} + f_{i+n} + t_{i+n,d_k} \leq DT_k$.

It is assumed that an OD is not available to wait for fulfilling a service request. This assumption seems to be realistic. However, it is possible to consider different conditions without changing the mathematical model.

3 Computational Results and Discussion

In this section we illustrate the results provided by the computational study that was carried out on instances of various size. The model was coded in C++ and solved by using the IBM CPLEX 12.6.1. Computational experiments were carried out on a PC equipped with an Intel Core i7 dual core CPU running at 2.30 GHz, with 16 GB of RAM and the Windows 10 operating system.

3.1 Instance Generation

The instances generated for this study are divided in two sets (A and B, respectively), different for the number of available ODs that could be used in the service. The Cartesian coordinates of each node $i \in V$, as well as of each o_k and d_k, with $k \in K^o$, were randomly chosen according to a uniform distribution over a square area of 25 km^2. It is assumed that each OD has both o_k and d_k different from the others.

The set A is composed by 16 instances with an increasing number of requests to be fulfilled (from 5 to 12), with a number of available ODs equal to $|K^o| = \lceil |P|/2 \rceil$. The values of e_i and l_i, for $i \in P \cup D$, and of ST_k and DT_k, for $k \in K^o$, were randomly generated within the time horizon of one day, while the time window for the depot is fixed for all the instances: $e_0 = e_{2n+1} =$ 7:00 and $l_0 = l_{2n+1} =$ 23:00. The values of service time f_i, with $i \in P \cup D$, was randomly generated between 3 and 10 min. The company fleet is made up of $|K^r| = 4$ vehicles; it is assumed that this fleet is homogeneous and suitable for transporting different products. The travel times t_{ij} were computed considering an average speed of 30 km/h. The price γ_i at which the i-th request is sold on the platform was defined within the interval [6.00 €; 10.00 €]. In this way, it is possible to simulate the behaviour of the customers and their willingness to pay for the service provided by the platform. Note that the willingness to pay is supposed to be proportional to the perceived value of the product itself (food and beverage, personal care, home care, electronics, clothing, magazines, games, sports, etc.); see [18] for details. The reliability δ_k, $k \in K^o$, was randomly defined within the interval [0.6; 1], where the value 1 refers to a 100% reliable OD.

ODs with a reliability of less than 60% were supposed to be automatically discarded by the platform in order to maintain a certain level of service. The variable cost unit α_k, $k \in K^o$, was imposed equal to 0.5 €, while the unit cost per kilometre β related to RVs was imposed equal to 0.3 €.

The set B is an extension of the set A, composed by the same 16 instances where the number of ODs is increased (in particular, $|K^o| = |P|$). Note that each instance of the set B contains exactly the same graph G' of the corresponding instance of set A; as a consequence, the data related to depot, pickup and delivery points and to the first $\lceil |P|/2 \rceil$ ODs remain unchanged. The additional $\lfloor |P|/2 \rfloor$ ODs data are randomly generated, as described above, and added to G'. It is worth observing that the profit generated by the instances of set B may be better or equal to that of set A, due to the convenience of activating new ODs. For the computational phase, a time limit of 1,200 s was imposed for each running test.

3.2 Computational Results for Sets A and B

The results for sets A and B are detailed in Table 1. All the instances are labelled as $aXnZ$ and $bXnZ$, where X indicates the instance number and Z indicates $|P|$. Column "Instance" refers to the instance name, column "Obj.Func." reports the profit (in €) associated with the best solution found, column "Time" reports the computational time in seconds for solving the problem, columns "OD" and "RV" refer to the number of ODs and RVs routed in the solution, respectively. All the instances were solved to optimality within the time limit, so the Cplex GAP is not reported in the table.

Table 1. Results for instance sets A and B.

Instance	Obj.Func.	Time	RV	OD	Instance	Obj.Func.	Time	RV	OD
$a1n5$	15.76	7.05	1	0	$b1n5$	15.76	7.05	1	0
$a2n5$	17.00	1.09	1	1	$b2n5$	17.00	1.05	1	1
$a3n6$	21.96	9.83	1	2	$b3n6$	21.96	10.14	1	2
$a4n6$	8.66	3.32	2	0	$b4n6$	17.42	0.32	1	1
$a5n7$	30.81	12.29	1	2	$b5n7$	30.81	10.13	1	2
$a6n7$	27.84	6.71	1	0	$b6n7$	28.12	12.72	1	1
$a7n8$	32.86	184.43	1	1	$b7n8$	33.84	90.65	1	1
$a8n8$	31.01	74.93	1	1	$b8n8$	31.01	51.27	1	1
$a9n9$	30.61	572.84	1	1	$b9n9$	30.61	532.63	1	1
$a10n9$	30.79	450.91	2	0	$b10n9$	46.14	34.03	1	1
$a11n10$	48.27	1198.02	1	0	$b11n10$	48.27	1187.21	1	0
$a12n10$	47.75	952.74	1	0	$b12n10$	47.75	968.27	1	0
$a13n11$	52.75	344.97	1	0	$b13n11$	53.35	485.53	1	1
$a14n11$	53.18	838.58	1	1	$b14n11$	53.18	1120.37	1	1
$a15n12$	77.54	483.47	1	1	$b15n12$	77.97	850.25	1	2
$a16n12$	80.36	398.76	1	1	$b16n12$	80.36	361.91	1	1
Average	37.94	346.21			Average	39.59	357.71		
Tot.			18	11	Tot.			16	16

The results of set A underlines that in the 56% of the instances it is convenient to use ODs for deliveries, where a total number of 11 ODs is routed; while the percentage increases to 81% for the set B, where a total number of 16 ODs is routed. Therefore, having a greater number of ODs among the platform's users allows to reach a greater flexibility in the delivery service. Reaching a critical volume of shippers is important to increase the level of service, as well as the overall profit (see [18]). In the proposed results, the profit increases from set A to set B of about 5% on average, which is quite indicative of the potential that can be achieved on a large-scale service. Note that the real increase of profit from set A to set B is due only to 6 instances, while for the others the profit remains unchanged. This aspect is due to the scarce convenience of the ODs geographical positions, as well as to the absence of compatibility within the time windows. The largest punctual profit increase occurs in correspondence of the instance pair $a4n6 - b4n6$, equal to 101%, and of the instance pair $a10n9 - b10n9$ equal to 49.85%. It should also be noted that the presence of more ODs in set B can lead to improvements in profit, although the total number of routed vehicles does not change. This happens for example in the instance pair $a7n8 - b7n8$, where the same request is entrusted to different ODs within the two instances. It is due to the presence of a more convenient OD in the instance $b7n8$. Finally, it should be noted that the average computational time is about 350 seconds for both set A and set B, underlining that a higher number of ODs and, consequently of variables z_{ik}, does not have a significant impact on computational complexity.

In order to assess the advantage of using the crowd for deliveries instead of a fleet composed by only RVs, some tests are performed for determining comparative profit values for the objective function. In details, all the instances were run setting the compatibility parameter $\phi_{ik} = 0$, $k \in K^o$ and $i \in P$, in order to inhibit the routing of ODs and obtaining a solution with only RVs. This configuration provided a lower bound (LB) on the platform profit. On the other hand, the opposite configuration is also considered, where each OD $k \in K^o$ offers the service without receiving any compensation ($\alpha_k = 0$), with the maximum reliability level ($\delta_k = 1$). This solution allows to identify an upper bound (UB) on the platform profit, since the routing costs are minimized and the deliveries are assigned to ODs as much as possible. The LB and UB values are reported in Table 2. The table is organized as follows: column "Instance" introduces the instance name, columns "LB","Obj.Func." and "UB" report the lower bound, the profit (same value in Table 1) and the upper bound for each instance, respectively. Column "GAP" represents the percentage GAP computed as $\frac{Obj.Func.-LB}{LB} \times 100$. Column "$RV_{LB}$" indicates the number of RVs routed in the optimal solution when the use of ODs is inhibited, whereas columns "RV_{UB}" and "OD_{UB}" indicate, respectively, the number of RVs and ODs routed in the optimal solution when there is no compensation for the ODs and their reliability level is maximum. All the instances were solved to optimality within the time limit, so the Cplex GAP is not reported in the table.

The results in Table 2 show that the profit obtained by using ODs is higher than the value obtained by using only RVs in the 69% of the instances. The magnitude of this improvement (average percentage GAP) is about 19%. On the contrary, the UB value does not provide a strong indication in terms of profit, as the configuration where ODs are not remunerated and operate with maximum reliability is completely unrealistic. Nevertheless, it is worth noting how potentially high the number of compatible ODs could be (see column OD_{UB}). For example, under the ideal configuration, the results

Table 2. LBs and UBs for instance sets A and B.

Instance	LB	RV_{LB}	Obj.Func.	GAP	UB	RV_{UB}	OD_{UB}
$a1n5$	15.76	1	15.76	0.00	23.60	1	1
$a2n5$	7.47	1	17.00	127.44	17.18	1	1
$a3n6$	15.27	1	21.96	43.75	30.31	1	3
$a4n6$	8.66	2	8.66	0.00	25.71	1	1
$a5n7$	23.86	1	30.81	29.07	36.79	1	2
$a6n7$	27.84	1	27.84	0.00	33.96	1	3
$a7n8$	31.96	1	32.86	2.85	37.78	1	3
$a8n8$	29.92	1	31.01	3.64	38.36	1	3
$a9n9$	29.56	1	30.61	3.59	37.45	1	3
$a10n9$	30.79	2	30.79	0.00	47.52	1	2
$a11n10$	48.27	1	48.27	0.00	57.33	1	4
$a12n10$	47.75	1	47.75	0.00	55.62	1	4
$a13n11$	52.75	1	52.75	0.00	68.17	1	6
$a14n11$	52.57	1	53.18	1.16	67.59	1	6
$a15n12$	73.84	1	77.54	5.01	85.19	1	5
$a16n12$	78.71	1	80.36	2.10	87.30	1	5
$b1n5$	15.76	1	15.76	0.00	23.67	1	1
$b2n5$	7.47	1	17.00	127.44	17.18	1	1
$b3n6$	15.27	1	21.96	43.75	30.31	1	3
$b4n6$	8.66	2	17.42	101.27	26.87	1	2
$b5n7$	23.86	1	30.81	29.13	39.16	1	3
$b6n7$	27.84	1	28.12	1.01	35.45	1	4
$b7n8$	31.96	1	33.84	5.88	39.34	1	5
$b8n8$	29.92	1	31.01	3.64	39.40	1	4
$b9n9$	29.56	1	30.61	3.59	43.29	1	5
$b10n9$	30.79	2	46.14	49.85	48.69	1	4
$b11n10$	48.27	1	48.27	0.00	59.25	1	5
$b12n10$	47.75	1	47.75	0.00	57.35	1	5
$b13n11$	52.75	1	53.35	1.14	70.15	1	7
$b14n11$	52.57	1	53.18	1.16	69.34	1	9
$b15n12$	73.84	1	77.97	5.59	87.08	1	8
$b16n12$	78.71	1	80.36	2.10	90.75	1	8
Average				18.57			

for instance $b14n11$ show that 9 ODs are used and only the two remaining requests are processed by a RV. It can therefore be deduced that the number of used ODs is strictly dependent from the values assumed by parameters α_k and δ_k, which directly affect the final profit because of the objective function (1) structure. Since the mathematical model can be used as a decision support tool in the operational management of crowd-sourced deliveries, it is possible to select a great combination of α_k and δ_k parameters that promotes crowd-shipping activation, improving platform performances from the profit perspective. In the following, a sensitivity analysis on these parameters is presented.

3.3 Sensitivity Analysis

In order to investigate the profit trend as parameter α_k changes, a series of tests was carried out on the sets A and B, using $\delta_k = 1$, for each $k \in K^o$, and keeping the other data unchanged. In particular, the value of α_k was set equal to 50%, 100%, 150% and 200% of β (that is 0.15 €, 0.30 €, 0.45 €, 0.60 €). The results are summarised in Table 3, that is organized as follows. Column "Instance" refers to the instance name, columns "Obj.Func.", "RV" and "OD" report the objective function value, the number of RVs and ODs used within the solution, respectively, for each value of α_k. All the instances were solved to optimality within the time limit, so the Cplex GAP is not reported in the table.

The results confirm that the profit trend is always decreasing as α_k increases, because a higher remuneration for ODs erodes the profit of the platform. From the route structure perspective, the use of ODs is always convenient for values of $\alpha_k < \beta$, while above this threshold there are situations in which only RVs are routed; this happens in the 18% of the instances. The incidence becomes about 32% if $\alpha_k = 2\,\beta$. Observe also that if $\alpha_k < \beta$, the total number of ODs used is equal to 67, whereas this value is more than halved when $\alpha_k = \beta$ (number of ODs equal to 31). In contrast, the number of RVs remains almost constant. Note that, in some cases the compensation for the OD results very small or null, when α_k increases (for example, the objective function of instance $b6n7$ does not change for $\alpha_k = 0.30; 0.45; 0.60$ when only one OD is activated; indeed, in this case, the deviation is equal to zero because o_k and d_k coincide with pickup and delivery points). Generally, in order to avoid null compensations for an OD, our objective function could be lightly modified by considering a fixed cost for an OD (see the compensation schemes proposed in [24]). As an example, the evolution of the profit as α_k changes, for instance $b14n11$, is shown in Fig. 2. For representative purposes, the profit value for instance $b14n11$ was also computed with $\alpha_k = 0$, $\alpha_k = 0.05$ and $\alpha_k = 0.1$. This allows a more precise representation of the trend.

Moreover, in order to analyse the profit trend as the parameter δ_k changes, a series of tests was carried out on the sets A and B, using $\alpha_k = 0.5$, for each $k \in K^o$, and keeping the other data unchanged. In details, the value of δ_k was set equal to different reliability levels: 50%, 70%, 90% and 100% (that is 0.50, 0.70, 0.90, 1). The results are summarised in Table 4, that is organized as follows. Column "Instance" refers to the instance name, columns "Obj.Func.", "RV" and "OD" report the objective function value, the number of RVs and ODs used within the solution, respectively, for each value of δ_k. All the instances were solved to optimality within the time limit, so the Cplex GAP is not reported in the table.

In the second configuration, the results show that the profit trend is increasing as δ_k increases in the 75% of the instances, because a higher OD reliability reduces the risk cost related to damages or errors in deliveries. Nevertheless, in some cases it is not convenient to use ODs, because the unit remuneration per kilometre is not enough low.

Table 3. Sensitivity analysis on parameter α_k for instance sets A and B.

Instance	$\alpha_k = 0.15$			$\alpha_k = 0.30$			$\alpha_k = 0.45$			$\alpha_k = 0.60$		
	Obj.Func.	RV	OD	Obj.Func.	RV	OD	Obj.Func.	RV	OD	Obj.Func.	RV	OD
$a1n5$	21.54	1	1	19.49	1	1	17.44	1	1	15.76	1	0
$a2n5$	17.12	1	1	17.07	1	1	17.02	1	1	16.96	1	1
$a3n6$	26.44	1	2	24.95	1	2	23.46	1	2	21.96	1	2
$a4n6$	20.48	1	1	15.25	1	1	10.01	1	1	8.66	2	0
$a5n7$	35.29	1	2	33.80	1	2	32.31	1	2	30.81	1	2
$a6n7$	28.09	1	1	27.84	1	0	27.84	1	0	27.84	1	0
$a7n8$	33.82	1	1	33.79	1	1	33.77	1	1	33.74	1	1
$a8n8$	32.35	1	2	31.94	1	1	31.92	1	1	31.89	1	1
$a9n9$	31.63	1	2	31.54	1	1	31.52	1	1	31.49	1	1
$a10n9$	41.19	1	1	35.96	1	1	30.79	2	0	30.79	2	0
$a11n10$	49.72	1	2	48.27	1	0	48.27	1	0	48.27	1	0
$a12n10$	48.68	1	2	47.75	1	0	47.75	1	0	47.75	1	0
$a13n11$	54.02	1	2	52.75	1	0	52.75	1	0	52.75	1	0
$a14n11$	55.74	1	4	53.43	1	1	53.24	1	1	53.05	1	1
$a15n12$	79.08	1	3	77.55	1	1	77.54	1	1	77.54	1	1
$a16n12$	81.90	1	3	80.37	1	1	80.36	1	1	80.36	1	1
$b1n5$	21.54	1	1	19.49	1	1	17.44	1	1	15.76	1	0
$b2n5$	17.12	1	1	17.07	1	1	17.02	1	1	16.96	1	1
$b3n6$	26.44	1	2	24.95	1	2	23.46	1	2	21.96	1	2
$b4n6$	23.23	1	1	20.74	1	1	18.25	1	1	15.75	1	1
$b5n7$	35.29	1	2	33.80	1	2	32.31	1	2	30.81	1	2
$b6n7$	29.99	1	2	28.12	1	1	28.12	1	1	28.12	1	1
$b7n8$	33.95	1	2	33.85	1	1	33.85	1	1	33.85	1	1
$b8n8$	32.35	1	2	31.94	1	1	31.92	1	1	31.89	1	1
$b9n9$	31.63	1	2	31.54	1	1	31.52	1	1	31.49	1	1
$b10n9$	46.34	1	1	46.26	1	1	46.17	1	1	46.02	1	1
$b11n10$	49.72	1	2	48.27	1	0	48.27	1	0	48.27	1	0
$b12n10$	48.98	1	3	47.75	1	0	47.75	1	0	47.75	1	0
$b13n11$	55.93	1	4	53.60	1	1	53.41	1	1	53.22	1	1
$b14n11$	58.11	1	4	53.42	1	1	53.24	1	1	53.05	1	1
$b15n12$	79.58	1	4	78.02	1	2	77.98	1	2	77.95	1	2
$b16n12$	81.97	1	4	80.37	1	1	80.36	1	1	80.36	1	1
Tot.		32	67		32	31		33	30		34	27

The use of ODs is scarcely convenient for $\delta_k = 0.5$, where only 6 ODs are routed in total. However, after this threshold the total number of ODs increases very fast, becoming equal to 29 when the reliability is 100%. In contrast, the number of RVs remains constant. As an example, the evolution of the profit as the δ_k value changes for instance $b15n12$ is shown in the Fig. 3. For representative purposes, the profit value for instance

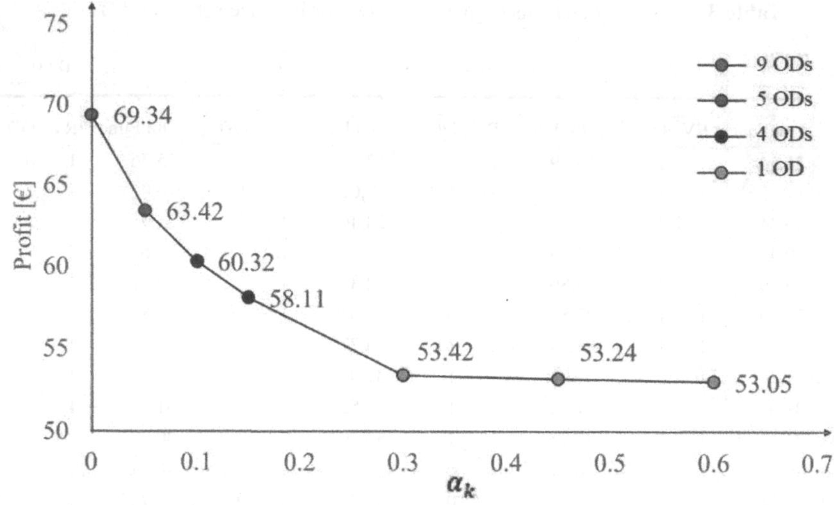

Fig. 2. The profit evolution as α_k changes for instance $b14n11$.

$b15n12$ was also computed with $\delta_k = 0.6$ and $\delta_k = 0.8$. This allows a more precise representation of the trend.

The sensitivity analysis underlines that an appropriate combination of the remuneration offered to the ODs with their reliability levels allows the platform operator to increase the total profit. Le et al. [18] clearly point out the necessity to consider insurance costs in the delivery pricing to compensate damage, as well as other factors like safety and trust. The authors emphasise that these factors are essential for the success of the platform and the achievement of the critical volume necessary to survive. Furthermore, they indicate the integration of pricing, matching, and routing into a coherent model as an open research domain. Under this respect, note that the presence of parameters γ_i, α_k and δ_k in the our model leads on this direction, while the computational experiments demonstrate the power of the analysis under the managerial perspective. Various strategies for customising the service could be implemented in this sense: rating systems for ODs to update their reliability at regular intervals, systems for calculating remuneration rates proportional to reliability, possibility to consider an increasing remuneration proportional to the OD fidelity. The model described in this paper is able to support the decision maker under these perspectives, so complex to be analysed in a more empirical way. It is worth observing that the model also considers the impact of various tariffs for different products. This perspective was not deeply investigated within the sensitivity analysis, because it is more correlated to the good nature than to the user behaviour. Nevertheless, the tariffs could be maximised, if the platform

Table 4. Sensitivity analysis on parameter δ_k for instance sets A and B.

Instance	$\delta_k = 0.50$			$\delta_k = 0.70$			$\delta_k = 0.90$			$\delta_k = 1.00$		
	Obj.Func.	RV	OD	Obj.Func.	RV	OD	Obj.Fu.nc	RV	OD	Obj.Func.	RV	OD
$a1n5$	15.76	1	0	15.76	1	0	16.06	1	1	16.76	1	1
$a2n5$	13.50	1	1	14.90	1	1	16.30	1	1	17.00	1	1
$a3n6$	15.27	1	0	17.26	1	2	21.06	1	2	22.96	1	2
$a4n6$	8.66	2	0	8.66	2	0	8.66	2	0	8.66	2	0
$a5n7$	24.07	1	1	26.11	1	2	29.91	1	2	31.81	1	2
$a6n7$	27.84	1	0	27.84	1	0	27.84	1	0	27.84	1	0
$a7n8$	31.96	1	0	31.96	1	0	32.86	1	1	33.76	1	1
$a8n8$	29.92	1	0	29.92	1	0	31.01	1	1	31.91	1	1
$a9n9$	29.56	1	0	29.56	1	0	30.61	1	1	31.51	1	1
$a10n9$	30.79	2	0	30.79	2	0	30.79	2	0	30.79	2	0
$a11n10$	48.27	1	0	48.27	1	0	48.27	1	0	48.27	1	0
$a12n10$	47.75	1	0	47.75	1	0	47.75	1	0	47.75	1	0
$a13n11$	52.75	1	0	52.75	1	0	52.75	1	0	52.75	1	0
$a14n11$	52.57	1	0	52.57	1	0	52.57	1	0	53.18	1	1
$a15n12$	75.89	1	0	75.89	1	0	76.84	1	1	77.54	1	1
$a16n12$	78.71	1	0	78.71	1	0	79.46	1	1	80.36	1	1
$b1n5$	15.76	1	0	15.76	1	0	16.06	1	1	16.76	1	1
$b2n5$	13.50	1	1	14.90	1	1	16.30	1	1	17.00	1	1
$b3n6$	15.27	1	0	17.26	1	2	21.06	1	2	22.96	1	2
$b4n6$	12.92	1	1	14.72	1	1	16.51	1	1	17.42	1	1
$b5n7$	24.07	1	1	26.11	1	2	29.91	1	2	31.81	1	2
$b6n7$	27.84	1	0	27.84	1	0	27.84	1	0	28.12	1	1
$b7n8$	31.96	1	0	31.96	1	0	32.94	1	1	33.84	1	1
$b8n8$	29.92	1	0	29.92	1	0	31.01	1	1	31.91	1	1
$b9n9$	29.56	1	0	29.55	1	0	30.61	1	1	31.51	1	1
$b10n9$	41.64	1	1	43.44	1	1	45.24	1	1	46.14	1	1
$b11n10$	48.27	1	0	48.27	1	0	48.27	1	0	48.27	1	0
$b12n10$	47.75	1	0	47.75	1	0	47.75	1	0	47.75	1	0
$b13n11$	52.75	1	0	52.75	1	0	52.75	1	0	53.35	1	1
$b14n11$	52.57	1	0	52.57	1	0	52.57	1	0	53.18	1	1
$b15n12$	75.89	1	0	75.89	1	0	76.84	1	1	77.97	1	2
$b16n12$	78.71	1	0	78.71	1	0	79.46	1	1	80.36	1	1
Tot.		34	6		34	12		34	24		34	29

operator is able to guarantee a reliable service also through ODs. As the simultaneous analysis of all these factors is complex, a decision support model becomes an effective and efficient tool for improving business performance. Finally, the selection, use and retention of reliable drivers are a guarantee for facing unexpected peaks in demand that the owned fleet cannot handle.

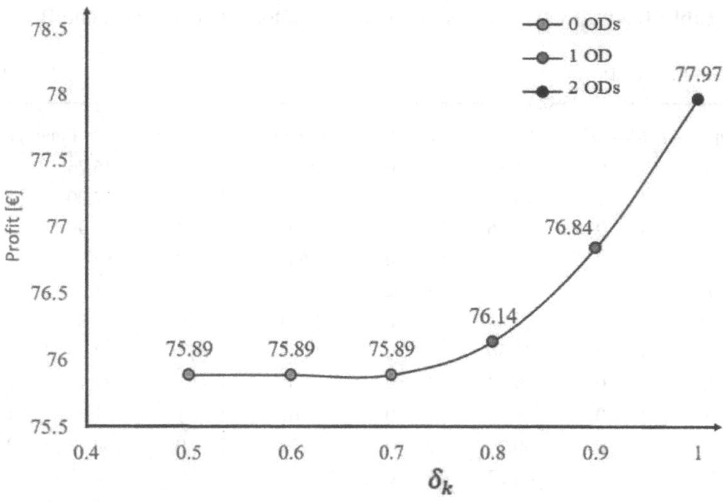

Fig. 3. The profit evolution as δ_k changes for instance $b15n12$.

4 Conclusions

A well-designed crowd logistics model can be used as decision support tool by companies to increase their profits, particularly in a urban last-mile context. A crowd-shipping framework could also improve the service level for the customers exploiting the flexibility of occasional drivers in moving within cities. From the social perspective, such initiatives have a positive impact on the reduction of freight traffic in urban areas and consequent CO_2 emissions. The integration of crowd-shipping within a broader environmental strategy can therefore improve its social benefits and facilitate its success. In this paper, we have introduced a mathematical model for a platform implementing crowd-sourced pickups and deliveries, in order to provide a decision support system for the intelligent use of regular vehicles and occasional drivers. The system has been modelled in order to consider possible configurations of revenues and costs for which the employment of occasional drivers results economically convenient for the company, balancing risks and benefits in such a service. A great level of flexibility is introduced in the mathematical formulation, allowing the customisation of tariffs for the end-users and remunerations for the occasional drivers, considering also a risk evaluation associated with the outsourcing of the delivery service to the crowd. The testing phase has evidenced that the use of occasional drivers leads to a higher profit than delivering products through only regular fleet. Furthermore, a sensitivity analysis on different parameter configurations has demonstrated the possibility to improve the total flexibility in delivery service. The ability to flexibly control remuneration for occasional drivers, proportionally considering their reliability and, as a consequence, the risk associated with delivery, enables the decision makers to increase their profits. From a tactical perspective, the platform operator could implement rating mechanisms for an evaluation of occasional drivers by end users, rewarding the most reliable drivers and ensuring higher service quality.

The model presented in this paper is only a starting point for further in-depth studies. It is empirically proven that the possibility of personalized tariffs for occasional drivers and prices of good deliveries is an important lever for profitability in conducting such a type of logistics operations, underlining the importance to expand the research from the methodological perspective. In order to overcome limitations of this work, specific algorithms could be developed for solving instances of greater size and making the system scalable on real platforms offering this kind of service. Indeed, the possibility to approach such a complex system provides optimal managerial insights for taking into account behavioural components of the users. More specifically, reaching the critical mass for such a service is deeply influenced by the willingness to play as occasional driver and the willingness to entrust freight to no professional carriers. Under this respect, managing customized tariffs can promote a higher involvement of occasional drivers and reassure final customers in delivering also fragile or valuable goods, opening new perspectives for the crowd-source business.

In future research on crowd-shipping, uncertainty could also be addressed (the reader is referred to the review of De Maio et al. [41] concerning other uncertain optimization problems in the transportation area), as well as simultaneous considerations of compensation and risk can be introduced in emerging services involving collaboration between occasional drivers, lockers, public transportation services, and drones.

Acknowledgement. The work of Annarita De Maio is partially supported by MUR (Italian Minister of University and Research) under the grant H25F21001230004. This support is gratefully acknowledged.

References

1. Laganá, D., Longo, F., Vocaturo, F.: Vendor-managed inventory practice in the supermarket supply chain. Int. J. Food Eng. **12**, 827–834 (2016). https://doi.org/10.1515/ijfe-2016-0067
2. Coelho, L., De Maio, A., Laganá, D.: A variable MIP neighborhood descent for the multi-attribute inventory routing problem. Transp. Res. Part E: Logist. Transp. Rev. **144**, 102137 (2020). https://doi.org/10.1016/j.tre.2020.102137
3. Crainic, T., Ricciardi, N., Storchi, G.: Models for evaluating and planning city logistics systems. Transp. Sci. **43**, 407–548 (2009). https://doi.org/10.1287/trsc.1090.0279
4. Montoya-Torres, J., Munoz-Villamizar, A., Vega-Mejía, C.: On the impact of collaborative strategies for goods delivery in city logistics. Prod. Plann. Control **27**, 443–455 (2016). https://doi.org/10.1080/09537287.2016.1147092
5. Schwerdfeger, S., Boysen, N.: Optimizing the changing locations of mobile parcel lockers in last-mile distribution. Eur. J. Oper. Res. **285**(3), 1077–1094 (2020). https://doi.org/10.1016/j.ejor.2020.02.033
6. de Mello Bandeira R.A., Goes G.V., Schmitz Goncalves D.N., de Almeida D'Agosto M., Machado de Oliveira C.: Electric vehicles in the last mile of urban freight transportation: a sustainability assessment of postal deliveries in Rio de Janeiro-Brazil. Transp. Res. Part D: Transp. Environ. **67**, 491–502 (2019). https://doi.org/10.1016/j.trd.2018.12.017
7. Moshref-Javadi, M., Hemmati, A., Winkenbach, M.: A truck and drones model for last-mile delivery: a mathematical model and heuristic approach. Appl. Math. Model. **80**, 290–318 (2020). https://doi.org/10.1016/j.apm.2019.11.020

8. Laporte, G., Meunier, F., Wolfer, C.R.: Shared mobility systems. 4OR **13**(4), 341–360 (2015). https://doi.org/10.1007/s10288-015-0301-z
9. Wu, C., Kim, I.: Analyzing the structural properties of bike-sharing networks: evidence from the United States, Canada, and China. Transp. Res. Part A: Policy Pract. **140**, 52–71 (2020). https://doi.org/10.1016/j.tra.2020.07.018
10. Neumann, T.: The impact of carsharing on transport in the city. Case study of tri-city in Poland. Sustainability **13**(2), 688 (2021). https://doi.org/10.3390/su13020688
11. Beraldi, P., De Maio, A., Laganá, D., Violi, A.: A pick-up and delivery problem for logistics e-marketplace services. Optim. Lett. **15**, 1565–1577 (2021). https://doi.org/10.1007/s11590-019-01472-3
12. Furuhata, M., Dessouky, M., Ordonez, F., Brunet, M., Wang, X., Koenig, S.: Ridesharing: the state-of-the-art and future directions. Transp. Res. Part B: Methodol. **57**, 28–46 (2013). https://doi.org/10.1016/j.trb.2013.08.012
13. Ulmer, M.: Dynamic pricing and routing for same-day delivery. Transp. Sci. **54**(4), 1016–1033 (2020). https://doi.org/10.1287/trsc.2019.0958
14. Laganá, D., Laporte, G., Vocaturo, F.: A dynamic multi-period general routing problem arising in postal service and parcel delivery systems. Comput. Oper. Res. **129**, 105195 (2021). https://doi.org/10.1016/j.cor.2020.105195
15. Escudero-Santana, A., Muñuzuri, J., Lorenzo-Espejo, A., Muñoz-Díaz, M.-L.: Improving e-commerce distribution through last-mile logistics with multiple possibilities of deliveries based on time and location. J. Theor. Appl. Electron. Commer. Res. **17**, 507–521 (2022). https://doi.org/10.3390/jtaer17020027
16. Punel, A., Stathopoulos, A.: Modeling the acceptability of crowdsourced goods deliveries: role of context and experience effects. Transp. Res. Part E: Logist. Transp. Rev. **105**, 18–38 (2017). https://doi.org/10.1016/j.tre.2017.06.007
17. Ulmer, M., Savelsbergh, M.: Workforce scheduling in the era of crowdsourced delivery. Transp. Sci. **54**(4), 1113–1133 (2020). https://doi.org/10.1287/trsc.2020.0977
18. Le, T., Stathopoulos, A., Van Woensel, T., Ukkusuri, S.: Supply, demand, operations, and management of crowd-shipping services: a review and empirical evidence. Transp. Res. Part C: Emerg. Technol. **103**, 83–103 (2019). https://doi.org/10.1016/j.trc.2019.03.023
19. Arslan, A.M., Agatz, N., Kroon, L., Zuidwijk, R.: Crowdsourced delivery: a dynamic pickup and delivery problem with ad-hoc drivers. Transp. Sci. **53**(1), 222–235 (2019). https://doi.org/10.1287/trsc.2017.0803
20. Savelsbergh, M., Van Woensel, T.: 50th anniversary invited article - city logistics: challenges and opportunities. Transp. Sci. **50**, 579–590 (2016). https://doi.org/10.1287/trsc.2016.0675
21. Bensinger G.: Amazon's next delivery drone: you. Wall Street J. (2015)
22. Paloheimo, H., Lettenmeier, M., Waris, H.: Transport reduction by crowdsourced deliveries - a library case in Finland. J. Clean. Prod. **132**, 240–251 (2016). https://doi.org/10.1016/j.jclepro.2015.04.103
23. Archetti, C., Savelsbergh, M., Speranza, M.: The vehicle routing problem with occasional drivers. Eur. J. Oper. Res. **254**, 472–480 (2016). https://doi.org/10.1016/j.ejor.2016.03.049
24. Dahle, L., Andersson, H., Christiansen, M., Speranza, M.: The pickup and delivery problem with time windows and occasional drivers. Comput. Oper. Res. **109**, 122–133 (2019). https://doi.org/10.1016/j.cor.2019.04.023
25. Macrina, G., Di Puglia Pugliese, L., Guerriero, F., Laporte, G.: Crowd-shipping with time windows and transshipment nodes. Comput. Oper. Res. **113**, 104806 (2020). https://doi.org/10.1016/j.cor.2019.104806
26. Dahle, L., Andersson, H., Christiansen, M.: The vehicle routing problem with dynamic occasional drivers. In: Bektaş, T., Coniglio, S., Martinez-Sykora, A., Voß, S. (eds.) ICCL 2017. LNCS, vol. 10572, pp. 49–63. Springer, Cham (2017). https://doi.org/10.1007/978-3-319-68496-3_4

27. Archetti, C., Guerriero, G., Macrina, G.: The online vehicle routing problem with occasional driver. Comput. Oper. Res. **127**, 105144 (2021). https://doi.org/10.1016/j.cor.2020.105144
28. Trentini, A., Mahléné, N.: Toward a shared urban transport system ensuring passengers and goods cohabitation. TeMA - J. Land Use Mob. Environ. **44**, 3–37 (2010). https://doi.org/10.6092/1970-9870/165
29. Serafini, S., Nigro, M., Gatta, V., Marcucci, E.: Sustainable crowdshipping using public transport: a case study evaluation in Rome. Transp. Res. Procedia **30**, 101–110 (2018). https://doi.org/10.1016/j.trpro.2018.09.012
30. Chen W., Mes M., Schutten M.: Multi-hop driver-parcel matching problem with time windows. Flexible Serv. Manuf. J. 1–37 (2017). https://doi.org/10.1007/s10696-016-9273-3
31. Behrend, M., Meisel, F.: The integration of item-sharing and crowdshipping: can collaborative consumption be pushed by delivering through the crowd? Transp. Res. Part B: Methodol. **111**, 227–243 (2018). https://doi.org/10.1016/j.trb.2018.02.017
32. dos Santos, A.G., Viana, A., Pedroso, J.P.: 2-echelon lastmile delivery with lockers and occasional couriers. Transp. Res. Part E: Logist. Transp. Rev. **162**, 102714 (2022). https://doi.org/10.1016/j.tre.2022.102714
33. Ghaderi, H., Zhang, L., Tsai, P.W., Woo, J.: Crowdsourced last-mile delivery with parcel lockers. Int. J. Prod. Econ. **251**, 108549 (2022). https://doi.org/10.1016/j.ijpe.2022.108549
34. Lyons, T., McDonald, N.C.: Last-mile strategies for urban freight delivery: a systematic review. Transp. Res. Rec. **2677**(1), 1141–1156 (2023). https://doi.org/10.1177/03611981221103596
35. Cebeci, M.S., Tapia, R.J., Kroesen, M., de Bok, M., Tavasszy, L.: The effect of trust on the choice for crowdshipping services. Transp. Res. Part A: Policy Pract. **170**, 103622 (2023). https://doi.org/10.1016/j.tra.2023.103622
36. Pourrahmani, E., Jaller, M.: Crowdshipping in last mile deliveries: operational challenges and research opportunities. Socioecon. Plann. Sci. **78**, 101063 (2021). https://doi.org/10.1016/j.seps.2021.101063
37. Ropke, S., Pisinger, D.: An adaptive large neighborhood search heuristic for the pickup and delivery problem with time windows. Transp. Sci. **40**(4), 455–472 (2006). https://doi.org/10.1287/trsc.1050.0135
38. Beraldi, P., Ghiani, G., Musmanno, R., Vocaturo, F.: Efficient neighborhood search for the probabilistic multi-vehicle pickup and delivery problem. Asia-Pac. J. Oper. Res. **27**(3), 301–314 (2010). https://doi.org/10.1142/S0217595910002715
39. Buldeo, R.H., Verlinde, S., Merckx, J., Macharis, C.: Crowd logistics: an opportunity for more sustainable urban freight transport? Eur. Transp. Res. Rev. **9**, 39 (2017). https://doi.org/10.1007/s12544-017-0256-6
40. Yildiz, B., Salvelsbergh, M.: Service and capacity planning in crowd-sourced delivery. Transp. Res. Part C: Emerg. Technol. **100**, 177–199 (2019). https://doi.org/10.1016/j.trc.2019.01.021
41. De Maio, A., Laganá, D., Musmanno, R., Vocaturo, F.: Arc routing under uncertainty: introduction and literature review. Comput. Oper. Res. **135**, 105442 (2021). https://doi.org/10.1016/j.cor.2021.105442

A Scenario Generation Method Exploring Uncertainty and Decision Spaces for Robust Strategic Supply Chain Capacity Planning

Achille Poirier(✉), Raphaël Oger, and Cléa Martinez

Centre Génie Industriel, IMT Mines Albi, Université de Toulouse, Albi, France
{achille.poirier,raphael.oger,clea.martinez}@mines-albi.fr

Abstract. Strategic Supply Chain Capacity Planning (SSCCP) is an essential activity for companies to prepare their future. However, since uncertainty became an essential factor to consider in this decision-making process, existing solutions to support this process do not fully satisfy their needs anymore. Especially in terms of uncertainty space coverage while exploring and assessing scenarios associated with uncertainty sources and decision options. Therefore, this paper introduces an approach to overcome the complexity of scenario exploration and improve the uncertainty space coverage, to better support SSCCP decision-making. This approach includes a bi-objective metaheuristic that first explores a probability-impact matrix to define a relevant subspace to consider in this uncertainty space, and then uses this subspace to explore the decision space and define a relevant subspace of this decision space to assess and display to decision-makers. Then, an implementation and experiment are described and discussed, and finally avenues for future research are suggested.

Keywords: Supply chain planning · Risk management · Robustness · Scenario generation · Metaheuristic · Decision support systems

1 Introduction

For companies, delivering products to customers is conditioned by the capacity of their associated supply chain to make the product available at the right time and place. In this regard, companies must implement decision-making processes to anticipate future capacity availabilities and requirements, and adapt either one or the other. This is called supply chain capacity planning [10]. And, when adaptation decisions require a long implementation time, for example more than a year, the associated decision-making process is usually called Strategic Supply Chain Capacity Planning (SSCCP) (or long-term supply chain capacity planning) [24]. Until a few years ago the supply chain environment was relatively stable and foreseeable [17, 19] and therefore designers of SSCCP methodologies initially based their design on this assumption [4, 19]. It is the same for the designers of software aiming at supporting these decision-making processes [22, 24]. However, this assumption has been strongly challenged during the

Supported by IMT Mines Albi.

S. Terzi et al. (Eds.): IN4PL 2023, CCIS 1886, pp. 126–148, 2023.
https://doi.org/10.1007/978-3-031-49339-3_8

past few years which have shown how supply chains are sensitive to uncertainties and difficult to predict [5,13,23]. In addition, several authors mentioned the relationship between the consideration of uncertainty in the decision-making process with the quality of the decisions made [1,11,20].

As a consequence, Oger et al. [16] proposed a Decision Support System (DSS) for undertaking SSCCP in uncertain environments. This SSCCP DSS contains an information system composed of 4 modules illustrated in Fig. 1. A major contribution of this SSCCP DSS is its ability to automatically deduce an assessment model, for any supply chain, that enables the evaluation of uncertainty and decision scenarios associated for supporting SSCCP decisions. This assessment model is compatible with all possible scenarios associated with provided uncertainty sources and decision options.

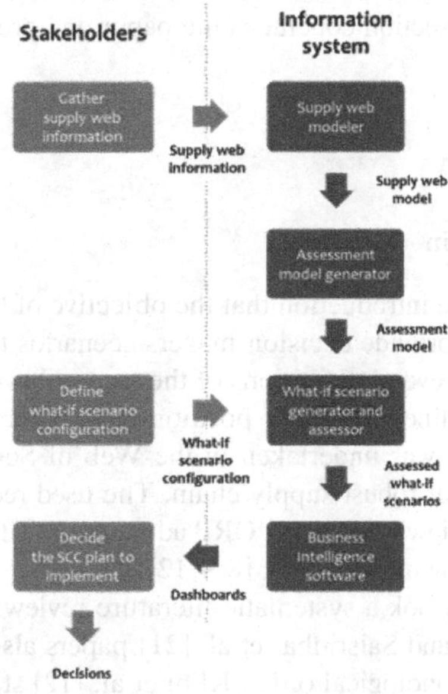

Fig. 1. SSCCP DSS proposed by Oger et al. [16].

However, a limitation of this contribution is the "what-if scenario generator and assessor" module which uses a simple cartesian product with strong filters to limit the combinatorics because the scenario space is too big to compute all scenarios for real industrial use cases. This means that the solution and uncertainty spaces are not entirely considered when defining the scenarios to assess, and that assessed scenarios are not chosen in regard to their relevance for supporting SSCCP decisions. In this paper, the "relevance for supporting SSCCP decisions" will be considered as a trade-off between the cost and the robustness of the decisions in regard to uncertainties; this will be further described in the proposition section.

Therefore, the objective of the research associated with the current paper is to propose a new approach for the "what-if scenario generator and assessor" module of the SSCCP DSS proposed by Oger et al. [16]. An approach that will enable us to better cover the solution and uncertainty spaces while assessing scenarios in regard to their relevance for supporting SSCCP decisions. The business objective is to provide decision-makers with scenarios that will help them make robust SSCCP decisions. An important hypothesis and constraint is that the assessment model that has been deduced by the SSCCP DSS must be used as a black box that takes inputs describing a scenario configuration and returns the resulting performance indicators for the corresponding scenario.

The first section of this paper introduced the context and objective of the associated research project. The second section analyzes the existing literature related to the context and objective and formulates the research question. The third section introduces the conceptual contribution to answer the research question. The fourth section describes the technical execution of the proposition and describes the metaheuristic we use. The fifth section describes the experiment, the associated results, and the corresponding discussion. Finally, the sixth section concludes the paper and provides avenues for future research.

2 Literature Review

2.1 Robust Supply Chain

It has been described in the introduction that the objective of this research is to find an approach that will enable provide decision-makers scenarios that will help them make robust SSCCP decisions. Several definitions of the term robustness can be found in the literature, so it must be defined to clearly position what is meant by robustness in this paper. Therefore, a search was undertaken in the Web of Science (WoS) database to find literature reviews about robust supply chain. The used request was the following: "robust*" (Title) and "review" OR "art" OR "advances" (Title) and "supply chain*" (Title). It returned the following 4 papers: [8,9,12,21]

Durach et al. [8] undertook a systematic literature review on supply chain robustness, and Klibi et al. [12] and Saisridhar et al. [21] papers also contain analysis of the robustness concept. In chronological order, Klibi et al. [12] states that "a supply chain network design is robust, for the planning horizon considered, if it is capable of providing sustainable value creation under all plausible future scenarios". Then, Durach et al. [8], who considered Klibi et al. [12] definition, defines robustness as "the ability of a supply chain to resist or avoid change", with the resistance being the "ability of a supply chain to withstand change" and avoidance the "ability of a supply chain not to be affected by change". Finally, Saisridhar et al. [21] defines robustness as the ability to persist without any response.

For this paper, considering previous definitions and authors' objectives, the robustness of a strategic supply chain capacity plan should be understood as its ability to maintain performance under all plausible future scenarios without the need of making any new major adaptation decision in case uncertainties occur. It implies the choice of a performance indicator which could be different from one organization to another. Therefore, it also implies the definition of a robustness indicator to compare strategic supply chain capacity plans, that should be defined in regard to the performance indicator value for all plausible future scenarios.

2.2 Robust Supply Chain Planning Models

Assessing and comparing the robustness of strategic supply chain capacity plans requires appropriate tools, and more specifically appropriate assessment models. Therefore, a search was undertaken in the WoS database to find literature reviews about robust supply chain planning models. The used request was the following: "production planning" OR "supply chain planning" (Title) AND "review" OR "art" OR "advances" (Title) AND model* (Title) AND "robust*" OR "uncertain*" (Title). It returned the following 4 papers: [6, 14, 15, 18]. Ciarallo et al. [6] is not a literature review but a model proposal, so not what we were looking for with this WoS request.

Among the 3 papers reviewing models for supply chain planning under uncertainty, Mula et al. [14] and Peidro et al. [18] consider all types of models while Mundi et al. [15] focuses on mathematical models. An interesting element to notice is that all 3 papers originate from the same research center. Each paper classifies planning models using a slightly different taxonomy, and we will mention Peidro et al. [18] who classify them in 4 categories:

- Analytical models (robust optimization, stochastic programming, game theory, linear programming, and parametric programming)
- Artificial intelligence-based models (reinforcement learning, genetic algorithm, evolutionary programming, fuzzy linear programming, fuzzy multi-objective programming, fuzzy goal programming, fuzzy numbers, multi-agent systems)
- Simulation models (discrete event simulation and system dynamics)
- Hybrid models

Most of the models studied by Mula et al. [14] and Peidro et al. [18] include only one or very few sources of uncertainties in the same model. While it has been highlighted that there are many sources of uncertainties regarding the demand, operations and supply aspects of supply chains. They recommend investigating new approaches to consider more uncertainties within the same model.

Some authors highlight that most of the methods for supply chain planning under uncertainty modeled the SC uncertainty by probability distributions, while uncertainty cannot always be modeled with probability distributions, especially for strategic planning, so other approaches such as fuzzy set and possibility theories should be investigated [15, 18].

Mula et al. [14] indicates that for complex supply chains the analytical approaches are often replaced by methodologies based on artificial intelligence and simulation. It is confirmed by Mundi et al. [15] who states that the most used approach to model uncertainty in the considered perimeter of their review is the scenario-based approach.

2.3 Research Question

Considering the context and objective described in the introduction, especially the use of an assessment model as a black box, as well as the elements found in the literature, analytical and simulation models cannot be applied to our problem. So, a solution to our problem would fall into the artificial intelligence-based models category proposed by Peidro et al. [18]. Regarding the recommendation from Mula et al. [14] to investigate new approaches for considering more uncertainties within the same model, the assessment model proposed by Oger et al. [16] is compatible with many sources of uncertainty and decisions on operations and demand, which makes it possible to consider many scenarios, but also leads to a scenario space that cannot be entirely assessed in a reasonable amount of time.

Therefore, the business objective being to provide decision-makers with scenarios that will help them make robust SSCCP decision, the research question is the following: How to search through a scenario space including decision and uncertainty variables to recommend robust decision scenarios, while relying on a black box to assess scenarios? It also leads a sub-question: what uncertainty scenarios to consider for assessing the robustness of decision scenarios considering all uncertainty scenarios cannot be explored?

The following section will described a conceptual proposition for answering these questions.

3 Conceptual Proposition

3.1 Overview

The context of this paper is to perform an SSCCP under uncertainty by using a black box to obtain the value of a key performance indicator of the supply chain for a given scenario. The value returned by this black box is the only information we can use to help the decision-maker in his process of creating a robust supply chain. To perform an SSCCP under uncertainty, we generate scenarios to see how the supply chain reacts to the decisions and the uncertainties. The utopian way would be to generate all the possible scenarios, to then analyze them in order to determine the best decisions to take considering all the possible uncertainties. This utopic method is impossible due to the fact that doing all the combinations between the decisions and the uncertainties to generate and assess all the possible scenarios would take an unreasonable amount of time.

The proposed method uses multi-objective optimization to reduce the combinatorics of the problem and to give a direction to the exploration of the scenario space. It generates scenarios by maximizing or minimizing several key performance indicators of the supply chain, thus dodging scenarios that are not relevant. The relevant scenarios are the closest to the Pareto front [2]. These scenarios give us information on the impact that the uncertainties can apply to the supply chain, weighted by their likelihood, and the protection that the decisions can apply to the supply chain, weighted by the cost of setting up these decisions. We use a multi-objective metaheuristic to approximate the best set of scenarios, i.e. the Pareto front.

The scenario generation involves two steps: instead of exploring the scenario space we first explore the uncertainty space, to then explore the decision space. The exploration of the uncertainty space identifies what are the most important uncertainty combinations the supply chain should be protected from, based on a probability-impact prioritization. Then, the exploration of the decision space identifies the decision combinations having the best trade-off between cost and their robustness in regard to the previously identified uncertainty combinations. From these two explorations we then compute scenarios to present them to the decision-maker. Figure 2 illustrates these steps.

We will first expose some definitions to clarify the elements we are working with, and the indicators that we use in this paper. Then, we will detail the exploration of both the uncertainty space and the decision space.

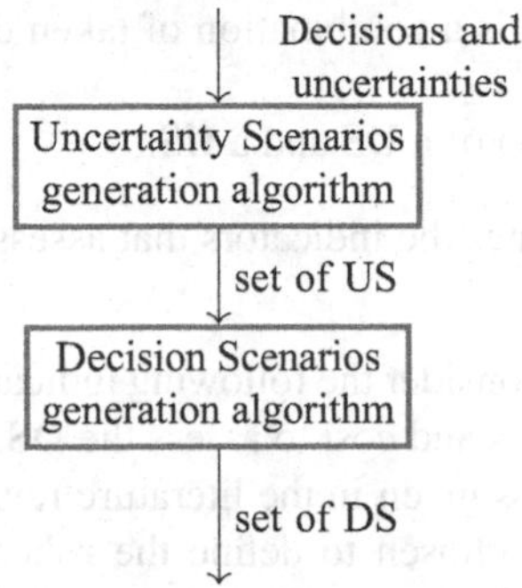

Fig. 2. Overview of our conceptual proposition.

3.2 Definitions

Elements. The SSCCP DSS creates an assessment model for the supply chain that takes a scenario configuration as input, to return the values of several key performance indicators of the supply chain for the considered scenario. The elements we work with to describe the configuration of a scenario are:

- **Decisions** that impact the supply chain, with a cost for their implementation.
- **Uncertainties** that impact the supply chain, with a given likelihood to happen.

Both the decisions and the uncertainties can impact several parameters in the supply chain: demand forecast, resources available time, bill of material, routing, supply strategies, etc. For example, a decision can be to buy equipment for a production site in order to increase the resources available time, or the launching of a marketing campaign to increase the demand forecast of a certain product. An uncertainty can be an unexpected increase in the demand forecast for a certain product, or an earthquake located near a production site leading to the decrease of its resources available time. The data behind the decisions and the uncertainties are not visible to the method. The only information we work with are whether a decision is taken or not, whether an uncertainty happens or not, and the key performance indicator of the supply chain for a given scenario. So we can generate a scenario by selecting decisions to take among the possible decisions, with happening uncertainties among the possible uncertainties. This scenario is then assessed with the assessment model generated, which returns the key performance indicators of the supply chain.

Since we work on a multi-period horizon, uncertainties can occur and decisions can be taken at different times. The proposal abstracts the temporal aspect by generating a decision and an uncertainty per period of time. It means that an uncertainty becomes several uncertainties, representing one period of time each. The same principle applies to the decisions.

From these elements, we define the following concepts to describe scenarios:

- An **Uncertainty Scenario (US)** is a combination of uncertainties that happen, among all the possible uncertainties.
- A **Decision Scenario (DS)** is a combination of taken decisions, among all the possible decisions.
- A **scenario** is a combination of a **DS** and a **US**.

The following section defines the indicators that assess the US and the DS.

Indicators. In this paper, we consider the following indicators: **impact** and **probability** to assess the US, and robustness and cost to assess the DS.

The definition of robustness given in the literature review section stated that a performance indicator should be chosen to define the robustness on. This performance indicator is called **impact** in this paper. The choice of this indicator depends on the decision-maker's goal. This proposal can take any indicator for the impact and perform the exploration accordingly, as long as it is provided as an output of the assessment model used and that it makes sense to assess the US and the DS with it. The performance indicator chosen to represent the impact is the one that the decision-maker wants to minimize or maximize. This impact is then used to define the **robustness** indicator, which represents the ability of a DS to maintain the supply chain's impact indicator to a good value under all plausible future scenarios.

In this paper, these two indicators rely on the saturation of the resources that compose the supply chain. The impact of a scenario is defined as the number of resources of the supply chain that have to be used for longer than they are available. In other words, if the utilization rate of a resource (ratio of required time over available time) is greater than 100%, then it is saturated. The required time and the available time are both obtained with the SSCCP DSS. This utilization rate indicator has been chosen for defining the impact because it is a typical indicator used for capacity planning [3]. Figure 3 displays a small example of how saturation is computed. The formula of the robustness indicator is described in the decision scenario generation section.

The **cost** indicator is the sum of the costs of all taken decisions that compose the scenario, this value is obtained with the SSCCP DSS.

The **probability** indicator assesses the likelihood of a scenario. As it is easier for the decision-maker to tell if an uncertainty is very likely, likely, or unlikely to happen, instead of giving a precise probability, each uncertainty is characterized by a probability rank, expressing its likelihood. Each probability rank has a corresponding probability value in order to compute the value of the probability indicator. These values are an approximation of each probability rank. It is important to note that this indicator does not aim at giving a precise probability for each scenario, but rather an indication of the plausibility of a scenario in order to compare the them with each other. Below is an example of 5 uncertainties with their corresponding probability rank (Table 1) and the probability value for each rank (Table 2). The number of ranks defined as well

Resources	R1	R2	R3
Required time	350h	350h	200h
Available time	400h	300h	500h
Utilization rate	87.5%	116.6%	40%
Saturated	no	yes	no

Fig. 3. Example of the computation of resource saturation.

as the associated probability value will have an impact on the results of the proposed methodology as it impacts the probability of a scenario. The choice should depend on how discriminating we want the ranks to be. For the example given in Table 2, a scenario with 3 uncertainties of rank 1 will still be more likely than one with 1 uncertainty of rank 2.

Table 1. Example for the probability ranks.

uncertainty	1	2	3	4	5
probability rank	1	1	2	2	3

Table 2. Example of probability values for the probability ranks.

probability rank	**1** (very likely)	**2** (likely)	**3** (unlikely)
probability value	80%	50%	20%

So with this example, a scenario with uncertainties 1, 2, 4 and 5 will have a probability indicator of 80% * 80% * 50% * 20% = 6.4%.

To compare the impact of two scenarios, we compare their number of saturated resources. Since it is an integer value, a lot of different scenarios can have the same impact in terms of saturation. To break the tie of two scenarios with the same number of saturated resources, we look at the sum of utilization rates of each resource. We call this new indicator the 'relaxed saturation', it is used to tell if a scenario has a higher or a lower saturation potential than another scenario with an equal saturation. An example is portrayed in Fig. 4, where we compare the utilization rates of each resource for two different scenarios. For both scenarios, only one resource (R3) is saturated. We can compute the relaxed saturation of the scenario on the right and the scenario on the left:
$S_{left} : 0.95 + 0.65 + 1.10 + 0.48 = 3.18$
$S_{right} : 0.87 + 0.65 + 1.05 + 0.55 = 3.12$

The scenario on the right has a higher relaxed saturation, so it is considered as having a higher saturation potential.

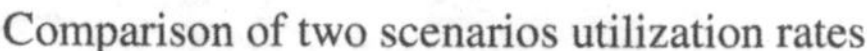

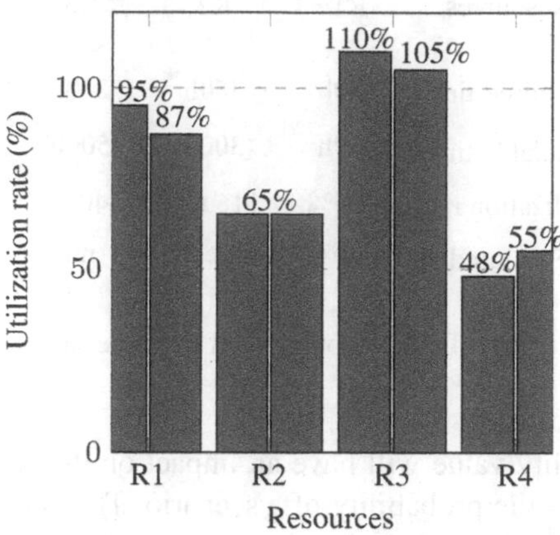

Fig. 4. Comparison of the utilization rate of each resource for two different scenarios.

3.3 Uncertainty Scenario Generation

The uncertainty space is composed of all of the US. This exploration is done to build a restricted set of US that gives a representative view of the risks the supply chain may be exposed to, i.e. a Pareto front of US with a good distribution (this is detailed below). To that extent, we want to find a US set that both covers probable and impactful US. Figure 5 represents the subspace we want to cover because it contains the US that will best assess the robustness of the supply chain.

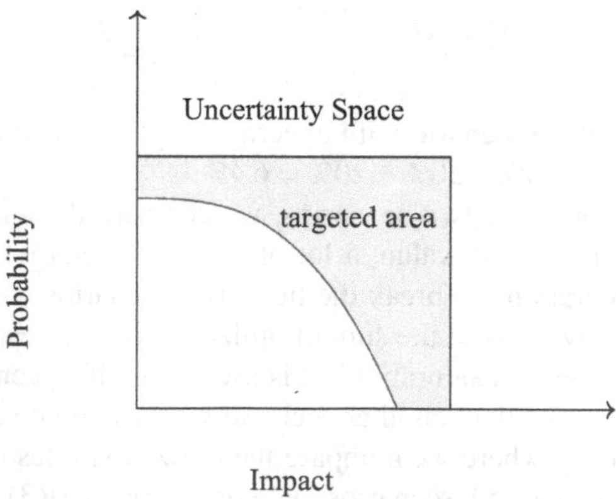

Fig. 5. Targeted area of the uncertainty space for the Uncertainty Scenarios generation.

Each US of the US set presents a trade-off between its likelihood and its impact, and to represent the uncertainty space accurately we need to have a good distribution between US that maximize the likelihood at the expense of the impact, and US that maximize the impact at the expense of the likelihood. Having too much low-impact high-probability US means that we underestimate the risks the supply chain is exposed to, and having too much high-impact low-probability US means that we overestimated the risks to which the supply chain is exposed. This is why we aim at generating a set of US whose impact gradually increases and whose probability gradually decreases. If the density of the US found is unbalanced between several zones of the targeted uncertainty subspace (i.e. the distribution is bad), it means that the zone with the lower density of US is underrepresented, leading to a DS generation that takes less account of this zone. For example, if we find a majority of US with a high impact and a low probability, and a minority of US with low impact and a high probability, the DS set generated in regard to this US set will accord a low degree of importance to the low impact US. This would lead to the generation of a DS set that are designed mostly to prevent catastrophic scenarios, whereas we want the DS to be designed in regard to the entire targeted uncertainty subspace. Neglecting the low-impact US promotes the generation of DS with more decisions to set up in order to negate the impact of the over-represented high-impact US, thus raising the cost of the DS. This distribution criterion also allows the reduction of the size of the US set. Since the DS generation is done according to the US set, the larger the US set is, the heavier the computation of the DS generation is (more detail in Sect. 3.4). To reduce the runtime, we fix a limited size for the US set. The selection of the US in the final set is done with the goal to have the best possible distribution. (more detail in Sect. 4.1: Selection and Crowding)

In the US generation, we want to maximize the likelihood and the impact of the US in order to find the most challenging set of US for the DS that will be generated at the next step. The US generation is constrained by an assessment model taking a scenario as input (i.e., a US combined with a DS). To address that, we first explore the scenario space to find scenarios with a maximal likelihood and/or maximal impact. From each scenario, we then extract their corresponding US and add it to the US set. In the end, the US set contains US that are very likely to happen and/or with a high impact, (i.e., a Pareto front of the US). We could explore a subspace of the scenario space by considering only the uncertainties with the nominal DS (i.e. working with scenarios without decisions), but it would mean that we build a set of US that assesses the robustness of the supply chain without any decisions taken. By allowing the decisions to be included in the search we consider all the forms that the supply chain can take with the given decisions. For example, if there is a high risk of a hurricane where a supplier is located but this supplier is not used in the nominal scenario, then considering only the nominal decision scenario would mean that the hurricane does not impact the supply chain, which is false. Indeed, if the decision to highly use this supplier is taken, the uncertainty of the hurricane becomes very impacting. Thus it must be taken into account before making the decision to rely heavily on this supplier.

3.4 Decision Scenario Generation

Now that we have generated a set of US with maximal impact and/or maximal likelihood, we need to generate a set of DS to be returned to the decision-makers for recommendations. This set of DS should be a subspace of the decision space composed of all the DS.

The idea is to search for DS that presents a trade-off between maximizing the robustness of the supply chain (according to the US subspace) and minimizing the costs of the decisions. Considering that, the robustness of the DS is defined in regard to the set of US defined in the previous step. Figure 6 represents the subspace we want to cover because it contains the DS that will best protect the supply chain. It is important to note that with our robustness indicator, the lower the indicator is, the more robust the supply chain is.

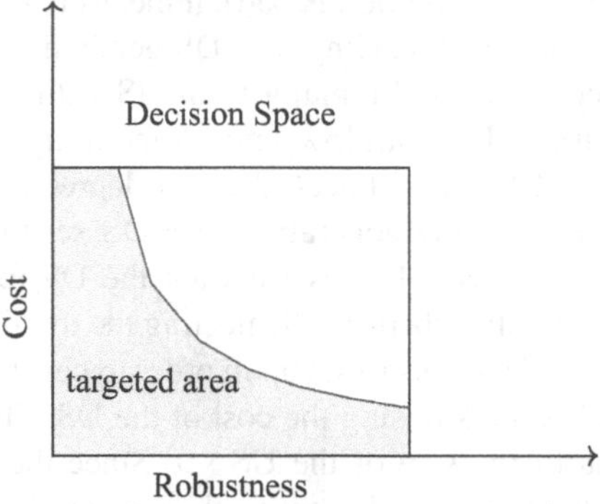

Fig. 6. Targeted area of the decision space for the Decision Scenarios generation.

In order to evaluate a specific DS, we combine it with every US of the US set (generated in the previous step), creating a set of scenarios. Once this set of scenarios is assessed, we aggregate their results to get an indicator for the studied DS to express how much it protects the supply chain against the US set. This is portrayed in Fig. 7, where the saturation of each resource is expressed by a 1 (saturated) or a 0 (non-saturated) for each scenario that represents a US of the US set. These saturations are then summed to obtain the saturation of each scenario representing a US, then the saturation of each of these scenarios is summed to obtain the saturation of the DS. We can note that there are two levels of aggregation, one at the US level, and one at the DS level.

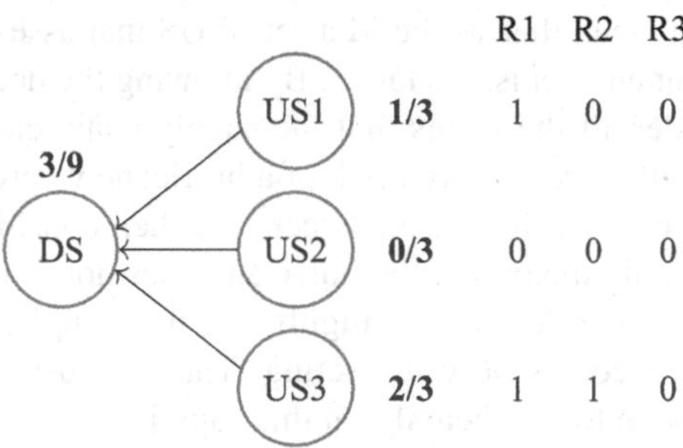

Fig. 7. Example of the aggregation of saturation for a DS, with 3 US and 3 resources.

We now have the aggregated saturation of a given DS, in relation to each US of the US set. The lower the aggregated saturation is for a DS, the better protection it offers to the supply chain from the risks approximated by the US set.

Now that we can compare two DS, we can explore the decision space to find the set of DS that will be presented to the decision-makers.

4 Technical Proposition

To explore the uncertainty space and the decision space, we use a bi-objective Genetic Algorithm (GA). It uses the dominance criterion to compare two solutions and find the Pareto front of a given space [2,7].

4.1 Exploration Method

Overview. Both the uncertainty space and the decision space are explored with a Genetic Algorithm (GA), differentiate by what a solution represents and how the objective values of a solution are computed. Figures 8 sum up how we explore these spaces with a genetic algorithm.

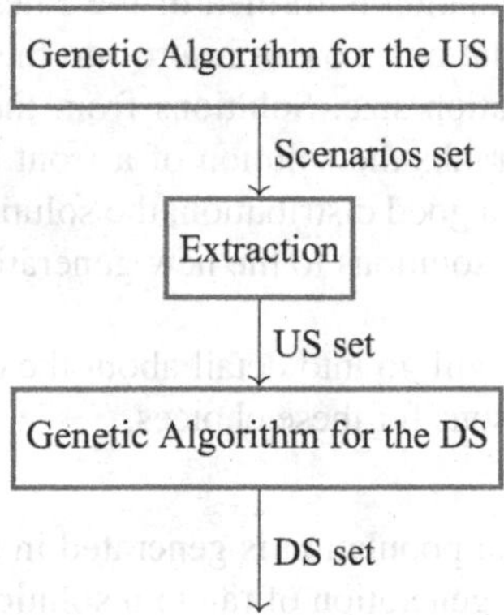

Fig. 8. How the genetic algorithm is used in the scenario generation.

For the uncertainty space, a solution is a scenario represented by a vector of binary variables, of which one part represents whether or not a decision is taken, and the part of which represents whether or not an uncertainty happens. The objective values are computed by assessing the solution scenario with the SSCCP DSS to obtain the saturation indicator and by a simple computation for the probability indicator. (full details in Sect. 3.2)

For the decision space, a solution is a DS, represented by a vector of binary variables that represent whether or not a decision is taken. The objective values are computed by generating and assessing the scenarios that result from the combination of the solution (i.e. a DS) with every US of the US set. These assessments are then aggregated to obtain the saturation indicator for the solution. The cost indicators are obtained with a simple computation. (full details in Sect. 3.2: Indicators)

Whether a solution represents a scenario or a DS, it will be treated as a binary vector for the rest of this section.

Genetic Algorithm. A GA takes as **parameters** a number of generations, a population size, and a mutation probability.

It generates an **initial population** of solutions, then improves it to create a new generation of solutions. This improvement is repeated until the number of generations specified in the parameters is reached.

To **improve** a population of solutions, an elite pool of solutions is selected to become the parent solution. This pool of parent solutions is then crossed to generate child solutions, with a chance at each crossing to have a mutation when generating a child solution.

To **select** the solutions for the next generation population, a ranking is applied to candidate solutions, composed of the parent and child solutions. It is done by computing a succession of Pareto fronts: the first Pareto front is computed to find the rank 1 solutions, these solutions are then removed from the candidates. The Pareto front is then computed for the remaining candidates to find the solutions of rank 2, and remove it from the candidates. This is repeated until all solutions are ranked.

The **next generation** population is formed of the i best rank solutions, where the ith rank is the last rank of solutions we can insert into the new generation population without exceeding the population size. Solutions from the $i + 1^{th}$ rank are selected with a crowding operator: it ranks the solution of a front by their distance from their neighbor solutions. To ensure a good distribution, the solutions with the higher distance are selected. We add crowded solutions to the new generation population until the new generation population is full.

The following subsection will go into detail about the choices made in our genetic algorithm and explain the reasons for these choices.

Initial Population. The initial population is generated in two steps: the generation of a mandatory solution, and the generation of random solution. The mandatory solutions are the unitary solution and the empty solution. The unitary solutions are all the possible solutions with only one variable to one and every other one to 0, and the empty solution is the solution with every variable to 0. These mandatory solutions are here to make sure that every decision and/or uncertainty has a chance to be considered. The random solutions are simply solutions with every bit set to 1 or 0 randomly, their role is to add diversity.

Because of the mandatory initial solutions, the size of the population must be higher than the number of variables. The gap between the number of mandatory initial solutions and the size of the population defines the number of random solutions.

Elitism. We use the ranking operator to select the elite solutions. The elite solutions are the solutions in the nth Pareto front and below. The more Pareto fronts (called **ranks** from now on) are included, the more diverse the solution can be. On the other hand, the fewer ranks included, the faster it converges. We have made the choice to select the 3 best ranks to select the elite solutions.

Crossover and Mutation. The crossover operator generates child solutions from two parent solutions. We use a random "cut" in the parent binary vectors. A cut index is chosen at random, we first generate a child whose variables take the value of parent

1 if they are before the cut index, and take the value of parent 2 if they are after the cut index. We then generate a second child with the same principle but in reverse: its variables take the value of parent 2 if they are before the cut index, and take the value of parent 1 if they are after the cut index. Here is an illustrative example:

parent 1 $[0, 0, 0, 0, 0, 0, 0, 0]$
parent 1 $[1, 1, 1, 1, 1, 1, 1, 1]$

cut at index 6

child 1 $[0, 0, 0, 0, 0, 1, 1, 1]$
child 2 $[1, 1, 1, 1, 1, 0, 0, 0]$

Every time a child solution is generated, there is a probability that a mutation occur, this probability is given in the parameters. To mutate, a variable is chosen at random among the binary vector, then its value is inverted.

The generation of a child solution can lead to an unfeasible solution because some decisions cannot be chosen simultaneously in practice (for example two different supply strategies for the same company and product). In that case, the SSCCP DSS can't assess the scenario and does not return any value for the scenario's key performance indicators. To avoid that, we generate compatible solutions from this unfeasible solution. A compatible solution is a solution where all the variables at 1 that should not be at 1 at the same time are set to 0, with the exception of at most one of those variables. Here is an illustrative example, with incompatible variables in bold:

unfeasible solution:

$[0, \mathbf{1}, \mathbf{1}, \mathbf{1}, 0, 0, 1, 1]$

compatibles solutions:

$[0, \mathbf{0}, \mathbf{0}, \mathbf{0}, 0, 0, 1, 1]$
$[0, \mathbf{1}, \mathbf{0}, \mathbf{0}, 0, 0, 1, 1]$
$[0, \mathbf{0}, \mathbf{1}, \mathbf{0}, 0, 0, 1, 1]$
$[0, \mathbf{0}, \mathbf{0}, \mathbf{1}, 0, 0, 1, 1]$

The crossover generates two child solutions unless a child solution is unfeasible, in this case, we generate as many solutions as incompatible variables (plus one for the solutions with all the incompatible variables at 0).

Selection and Crowding. The parent solutions and the child solutions are candidates for the new generation population. These candidate solutions are ranked, and the solutions of the i best ranks (Pareto fronts) are added, where the ith rank is the last rank of solutions we can insert into the new generation population without exceeding the population size. To complete the population we select solutions from the $i+1^{th}$ rank to add it to the new generation population. This selection is made with a crowding operator. This operator computes a distance value for each solution as described in [7], at the difference that the distance value is not computed with a cuboid, but by adding the difference of the values of the neighbor solutions (Manhattan distance). Here is an example with 3 solutions with their objectives values:

Solution 1: (23, 6)
Solution 2: (12, 14)
Solution 3: (5, 19)

We compute the distance value of solution 2 thanks to its neighbor solutions 1 and 3. The difference between solutions 1 and 3 on the first objective is $|23 - 5| = 18$, and $|6 - 19| = 13$ on the second objective. By adding these two differences we obtain the distance value $18 + 13 = 31$ for the solution 2.

The distance is computed for each solution, except for the two extreme solutions since they have only one neighbor solution. These extreme solutions are always kept to maintain the size of the front, so an infinite distance value is assigned to these solutions.

The candidate solutions are then added to the new generation population by ascending distance value.

This crowding is also applied to the US set for two reasons: to limit the size of the US set in order to reduce the runtime, and to ensure a good distribution between the US that maximize the likelihood at the expense of the impact, and the US that maximize the impact at the expense of the likelihood (see Sect. 3.3).

4.2 Dashboard

After the GA returns a set of US and a set of DS, we add some data to the result to ease the understanding, these data are described in the following subsection. After this adjustment, we display those results as clearly as possible to the decision-maker.

Additional Data. Before displaying the result, we choose to add every unitary US and the empty US to the US set in order to give visibility to the decision-maker on the impact of each uncertainty independently. We can do this without worrying about the distribution between US, because the DS are already computed with a set of US that has this property. This will only affect how they are displayed, and not how they are obtained.

To give the decision-maker room for manoeuvre, we define a visualization tool that we call a Pareto "band": this is a Pareto front plus a few non-optimal but close solutions. An example is displayed in Fig. 9. In our proposal, we choose to take a number of best ranks within the final solutions of the genetic algorithm to compose the Pareto band.

Displaying the Results. The resulting DS are displayed on a graph that represents their cost and their robustness indicator assessed with the US set (Fig. 9).

For each DS presented, the decision-makers can view how each US of the US set affects the supply chain with the selected DS (Fig. 10).

In addition to viewing how a DS is affected by the US of the US set, the decision-maker can view how the utilization rate of each resource of the supply for each US (Fig. 11)

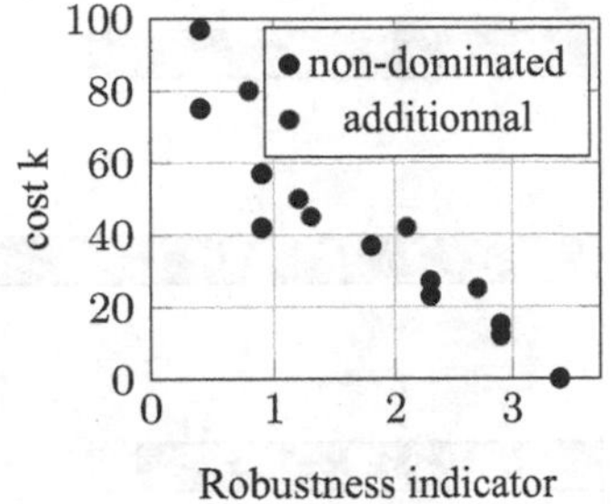

Fig. 9. Example of a Pareto "band" of Decision Scenario (DS).

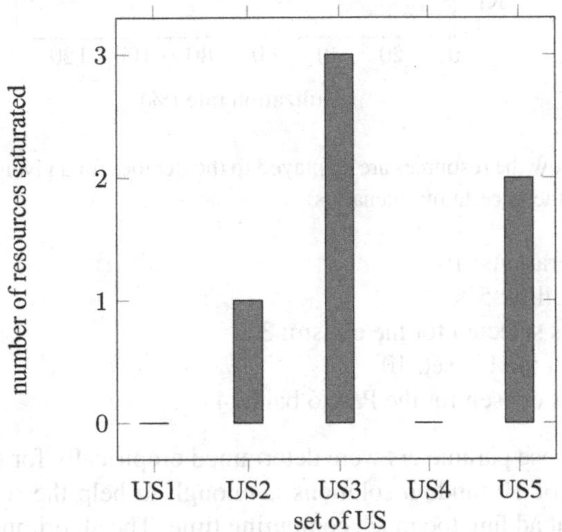

Fig. 10. Example of how the uncertainty scenario (US) are displayed to the decider for a given decision scenario (DS).

5 Results and Discussion

5.1 Use Case

The proposal is tested on an illustrative use case. The associated model, following the metamodel described in Oger et al. [16], is composed of 3 periods of time, 7 organizations, 5 product categories, 4 resource categories, 6 resources, 12 abilities, 4 demand forecast, 9 decision options (including 2 supply strategies) and 7 uncertainties. After the abstraction of the periods, we have 27 decisions and 21 uncertainties for the decision and uncertainty spaces.

The parameters for the algorithm are as follows:

- Population size: 10 random solutions + number of mandatory solutions (see 4.1: Initial Population). So 10+27+21 = 48 for the search of the US, and 10+27 = 37 for the search of the DS.

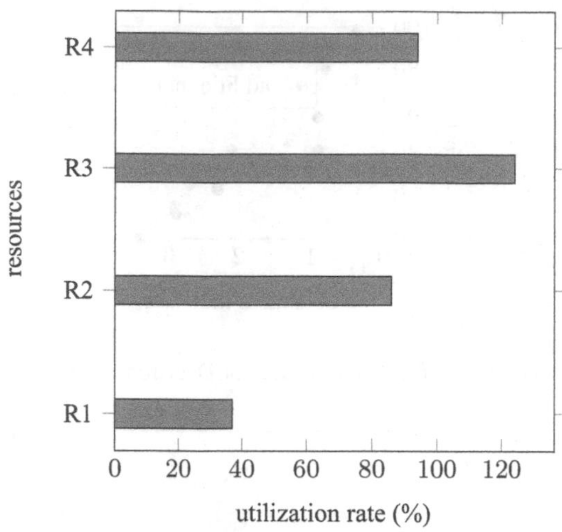

Fig. 11. Example of how the resources are displayed to the decider for a given scenario (a decision scenario with one of the uncertainty scenarios).

- Number of generations: 10
- Mutation probability: 5%
- Number of ranks selected for the elitism: 3
- Number of US in the US set: 10
- Number of ranks chosen for the Pareto band: 4

The values of these parameters were determined empirically for the considered use case. The addition of 10 random solutions is enough to help the search to reach better solutions without adding too much computing time. The algorithm converges within about 9 generations, so setting the number of generation to 10 ensure the algorithm converges and potentially find better solutions, the fewer generations the less computational time. A mutation probability of 5% is small enough to not perturb the convergence of the algorithm, but still allow him to escape local optima and find better solutions. The selection of 3 ranks for elitism enables a fast convergence and still provides good solutions. 10 US in the US set is enough to have a good distribution of probability within the selected US, the less US in the US set the less computational time. 4 ranks for the Pareto band seems a nice trade-off to have some non-optimal points beneath the Pareto front while remaining close to the front.

5.2 Uncertainty Scenarios Generation

Figures 12 compare the results of the US generation between the proposal and the initial method (filtered cartesian product). Each point is a scenario, from which the US are extracted to form the US set that will assess the DS. We have a good distribution for the high probabilities, but the density increases as the probability decreases and the impact increases. With the relaxed saturation we can see that there is a concentration of high-impacting scenarios with an almost zero probability. We expect that a portion of these scenarios will be pruned with the selection of the final US set.

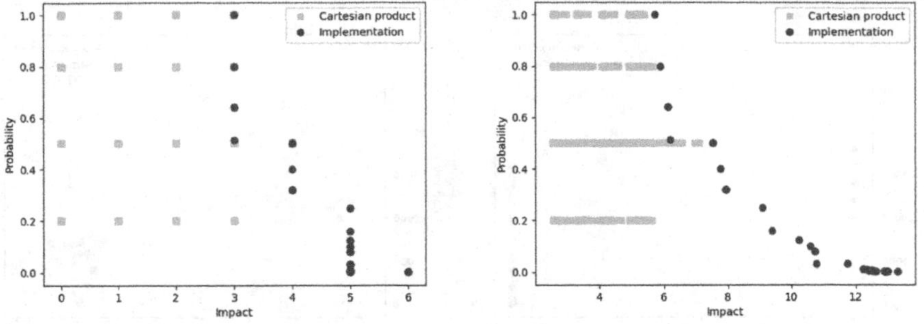

Fig. 12. Comparison of the scenarios obtained with the GA and the filtered cartesian product (left), and the same scenarios with relaxed saturation (right).

We observe that the proposed approach finds a lot more interesting scenarios than the initial method, i.e. scenarios that present a good trade-off between saturation and probability. All the scenarios from the initial method are worse or equivalent to the scenarios from the proposal. The high density of high-impacting scenarios with a low probability is due to the fact that there may be a lot of scenarios that combine several impacting uncertainties, while high-probability scenarios are obtained with the activation of a unique high probable uncertainty. A way to avoid that would be to add constraints to limit the number of activated uncertainties for the lower probability ranks.

The selection of the US to form the US set is depicted in Fig. 13. We see that the selection of scenarios corresponds to our expectation since the distribution of scenarios probability is greater than before, in addition to limiting the size of the US set. We see with the relaxed saturation that the group of impacting scenarios with an almost zero probability is well pruned, as expected.

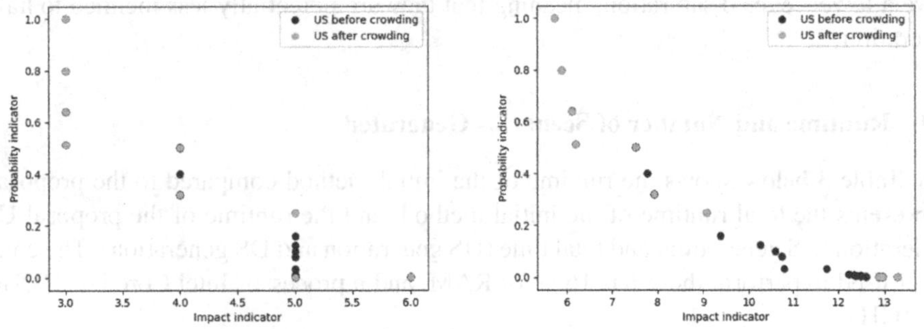

Fig. 13. Crowded Pareto front of scenarios for the Uncertainty Scenarios generation with relaxed saturation (left), and the same result with relaxed saturation (right).

5.3 Decision Scenarios Generation

Figures 14 compare the result of the DS generation between the proposal and the initial method, after the recombination. These DS are assessed with the set of US previously

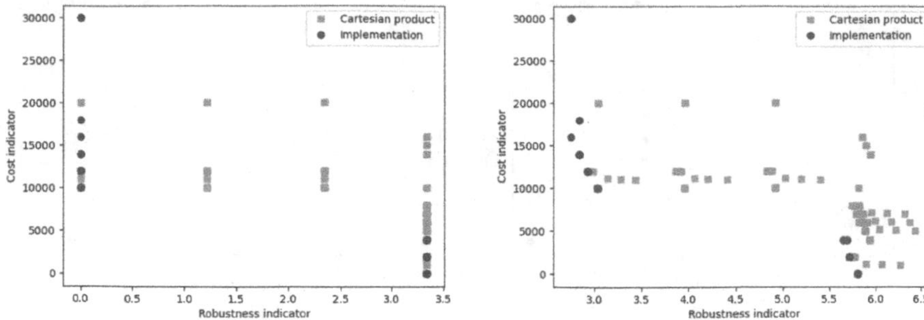

Fig. 14. Comparison of the Decision Scenarios obtained with the proposal and the initial method (left), and the same result with relaxed saturation (right).

generated and selected. We see in Fig. 14 that the scenarios are well distributed within the cost, with only 2 values for the saturation and a clear gap between them. This is due to a critical point being reached with a given combination of decisions, allowing the saturation to be nullified. This is highlighted with the relaxed saturation that barely changes within the 2 group of DS. This is because the data set is a small test case.

We observe in Fig. 14 that the DS found with the implementation are equivalent or better than the ones found with the initial method. The initial method finds a lot of DS with the same cost and various saturation, whereas the implementation finds only DS that offer a good trade-off between cost and saturation. The implementation finds only better DS for a cost under 10 000. With the relaxed saturation we see that the DS generated by the implementation are better than the one generated with the initial method, because even the DS that have the same cost and the same saturation have a lower relaxed saturation, meaning that they are potentially less inclined to have saturation.

5.4 Runtime and Number of Scenarios Generated

The Table 3 below shows the runtime of the initial method compared to the proposal. It presents the total runtime of the initial method, and the runtime of the proposal US generation, DS generation, and total time (US generation and DS generation). The computer used to perform these has 16 go of RAM, and a processor Intel Core i7-7700HQ 2.80 GHz.

Table 3. Runtime comparison (in sec).

Method	Runtime	Assessment model runtime
Initial method	24.65	27.17
US generation	9.73	9.6
DS generation	29.09	28.98
Total	38.82	38.58

The Table 4 below shows the number of scenarios generated and assessed by the initial method compared to the proposal. It presents the number of scenarios for the initial method, and for the proposal US generation, DS generation, and total (US generation and DS generation). We observe that the assessment model takes most of the runtime and that the runtime of the proposal and the initial method are close for this use case.

Table 4. Comparison of the number of scenarios generated and assessed.

Method	number of scenarios
Initial method	3388
US generation	773
DS generation	3200
Total	3973

We observe that the DS generation is the part that requires the assessment of the highest number of scenarios. The initial method and the proposal generate an equivalent amount of scenarios for this use case.

5.5 Discussion

The runtime of our proposal is equivalent to the runtime of the initial method. Further tests are needed to see how the runtime scales with the size of the data set. Besides, the quality of the results obtained with the proposal is better than the results from the initial method. First, the SD are better assessed because the US generated cover a wider space in the probability-impact space, with an even distribution. In addition to this, the generated DS offer a better protection against the saturation for a similar cost, plus some high-cost DS.

These results are slightly better than the initial method, but we need to keep in mind that this is only for a small data set. We make the hypothesis that it will perform better than the initial method in terms of quality, because the larger the data set gets, the more the combinatorics become mandatory to cover the probability-impact space and the saturation/cost space efficiently.

6 Conclusion

This paper proposes a contribution to support decision-makers in making robust Strategic Supply Chain Capacity Planning (SSCCP) decisions. The literature review section positions it in the frame of the robust supply chain planning field. It is in the continuity of the research undertaken by Oger et al. [16], which proposes a system that automatically deduces an SSCCP assessment model from supply chain data. In the initial proposal, a scenario generation and assessment module that uses a simple cartesian product with strong filters to limit the combinatorics has been implemented to illustrate the use of the assessment model. However, assessed scenarios are not chosen in regard to their relevance for assessing the robustness of the decisions. Therefore, the objective of this paper is to automate the recommendation of robust SSCCP decisions by proposing a new scenario generation approach that takes advantage of the deduced assessment model. An objective that implies the constraint of using the assessment model as a black box, and so limits possible approaches, but has the advantage of being able to automate the recommendation of robust SSCCP decisions from business data. This led to the following research question: how to search through a scenario space including decision and uncertainty variables to recommend robust decision scenarios, while relying on a black box to assess scenarios?

A conceptual proposal to answer this question has been described, it is composed of two steps: a first step to define a set of uncertainty scenarios that will be considered as the most important to be protected from, based on a probability-impact approach. A second step to define the decision scenarios to recommend, based on their performance in regard to all the uncertainty scenarios defined in the previous step. Then, this conceptual proposal has been completed with a technical proposal that uses genetic algorithms to implement the proposed approach. Finally, it has been experimented on an illustrative use case to evaluate the ability of the approach to answer the research question. During the experiment, the results have been compared with the ones obtained from the filtered cartesian product, and it has shown that the approach finds more robust decision scenarios.

This contribution should help companies gain better visibility about the robustness of their possible decisions in regard to the multitude of uncertainties. One of the difficulties of this domain is that the scenario space cannot be entirely explored because of its size, and this contribution is a step towards the improvement of the quality of the coverage (and so the visibility) to help companies make robust decisions. An important element to note is that this proposition can take into account any key performance indicators to be robust to as long as the assessment model can provide it.

However, there are still a number of limitations to be addressed to fully conclude about the proposal. First, the experiment has been performed on a small illustrative use case, testing the proposal on several real use cases would allow us to conclude on the applicability and scalability (in terms of runtime and quality of result) of the proposal. Second, a source of approximation is the choice of the probability indicator, an alternative indicator could be proposed. Finally, in the US generation step, the approach to select the US set in the crowding part is based on the Manhattan distance, a choice that could be discussed. We could study the influence of this choice by trying another approach such as Hamming distance. Third, the impact of the parameters of the algorithm could be studied in order to find a setting that can be applied to any use case, or to find a way to automate the setting of the parameters. The impact of the value for the probability ranks could also be studied to characterize the impact of these ranks and associated values on the proposed methodology.

References

1. Boonyathan, P., Power, D.: The impact of supply chain uncertainty on business performance and the role of supplier and customer relationships: comparison between product and service organizations. In: DSI Mini Conference on Services Management, Pittsburgh, USA, pp. 391–402 (2007)
2. Coello, C.A., Lamont, G.B., Van Veldhuizen: Pareto multi objective optimization. In: Evolutionary Algorithms for Solving Multi-Objective Problems (2002). https://doi.org/10.1007/978-0-387-36797-2
3. Chapman, S., Arnold, T., Gatewood, A., Clive, L.: Introduction to Materials Management, 8th edn. Pearson, Boston (2016)
4. Christopher, M., Holweg, M.: "Supply chain 2.0": managing supply chains in the era of turbulence. Int. J. Phys. Distrib. Logist. Manag. **41**(1), 63–82 (2011)
5. Christopher, M., Holweg, M.: Supply chain 2.0 revisited: a framework for managing volatility-induced risk in the supply chain. Int. J. Phys. Distrib. Logist. Manag. **47**(1), 2–17 (2017)
6. Ciarallo, F.W., Akella, R., Morton, T.E.: A periodic review, production planning model with uncertain capacity and uncertain demand—optimality of extended myopic policies. Manage. Sci. **40**(3), 320–332 (1994)
7. Deb, K., Agrawal, S., Pratap, A., Meyarivan, T.: A fast elitist non-dominated sorting genetic algorithm for multi-objective optimization: NSGA-II. In: Schoenauer, M., et al. (eds.) PPSN 2000. LNCS, vol. 1917, pp. 849–858. Springer, Heidelberg (2000). https://doi.org/10.1007/3-540-45356-3_83
8. Durach, C.F., Wieland, A., Machuca, J.A.: Antecedents and dimensions of supply chain robustness: a systematic literature review. Int. J. Phys. Distrib. Logist. Manag. **45**, 118–137 (2015)
9. Govindan, K., Cheng, T.: Advances in stochastic programming and robust optimization for supply chain planning. Comput. Oper. Res. **100**, 262–269 (2018)
10. Hopp, W.J., Spearman, M.L.: Factory Physics. Waveland Press (2011)
11. Hult, G.T.M., Craighead, C.W., Ketchen, D.J., Jr.: Risk uncertainty and supply chain decisions: a real options perspective. Decis. Sci. **41**(3), 435–458 (2010)
12. Klibi, W., Martel, A., Guitouni, A.: The design of robust value-creating supply chain networks: a critical review. Eur. J. Oper. Res. **203**(2), 283–293 (2010)
13. Kohl, M., et al.: Managing supply chains during the COVID-19 crisis: synthesis of academic and practitioner visions and recommendations for the future. Int. J. Logist. Manag. (ahead-of-print) (2022)
14. Mula, J., Poler, R., García-Sabater, J.P., Lario, F.C.: Models for production planning under uncertainty: a review. Int. J. Prod. Econ. **103**(1), 271–285 (2006)
15. Mundi, I., Alemany, M., Poler, R., Fuertes-Miquel, V.S.: Review of mathematical models for production planning under uncertainty due to lack of homogeneity: proposal of a conceptual model. Int. J. Prod. Res. **57**(15–16), 5239–5283 (2019)
16. Oger, R., Lauras, M., Montreuil, B., Benaben, F.: A decision support system for strategic supply chain capacity planning under uncertainty: conceptual framework and experiment. Enterp. Inf. Syst. **16**(5), 1793390 (2022)
17. Olhager, J.: Evolution of operations planning and control: from production to supply chains. Int. J. Prod. Res. **51**(23–24), 6836–6843 (2013)
18. Peidro, D., Mula, J., Poler, R., Lario, F.C.: Quantitative models for supply chain planning under uncertainty: a review. Int. J. Adv. Manuf. Technol. **43**, 400–420 (2009)
19. Pinon, D., Oger, R., Lauras, M.: Supply chain evolution and supply chain capability planning methodologies: a review and gap identification. In: ILS 2018–7th International Conference on Information Systems, Logistics and Supply Chain (2018)

20. Sáenz, M.J., Revilla, E.: Creating more resilient supply chains. MIT Sloan Manag. Rev. (2014)
21. Saisridhar, P., Thürer, M., Avittathur, B.: Assessing supply chain responsiveness, resilience and robustness (triple-R) by computer simulation: a systematic review of the literature. Int. J. Prod. Res. 1–31 (2023)
22. de Santa-Eulalia, L.A., D'Amours, S., Frayret, J.M., Menegusso, C.C., Azevedo, R.C.: Advanced supply chain planning systems (aps) today and tomorrow. In: Supply Chain Management Pathways for Research and Practice, pp. 171–200. InTech, Rijeka (2011)
23. Simangunsong, E., Hendry, L.C., Stevenson, M.: Supply-chain uncertainty: a review and theoretical foundation for future research. Int. J. Prod. Res. **50**(16), 4493–4523 (2012)
24. Stadtler, H., Stadtler, H., Kilger, C., Kilger, C., Meyr, H., Meyr, H.: Supply Chain Management and Advanced Planning: Concepts, Models, Software, and Case Studies. Springer, Heidelberg (2015). https://doi.org/10.1007/978-3-642-55309-7

Proposition and Evaluation of an Integrative Indicator Implementation for Logistics Management

Francielly Hedler Staudt[1](✉), Maria di Mascolo[2], Marina Cardoso Guimarães[1], Gülgün Alpan[2], Carlos Manuel Taboada Rodriguez[1], Marina Bouzon[1], and Diego Fettermann[1]

[1] Federal University of Santa Catarina, Florianopolis 88040-900, Brazil
francielly.hedler.staudt@ufsc.br

[2] University Grenoble Alpes, CNRS, Grenoble INP (Institute of Engineering University Grenoble Alpes), G-SCOP, 38000 Grenoble, France

Abstract. The growing operation complexity has led companies to adopt many indicators, making complex the evaluation of the overall performance of logistics systems. Among several studies about logistics management, this is the first one to determine an overall logistics performance indicator and evaluate its impact for logistics management. The proposed methodology encompasses four main phases: the first one defines the management scope and the indicator set, the second applies statistical tools reaching an initial model for indicators aggregation, the third one determines the global performance model, and the last phase implements the integrative indicator with its scale. The methodology is implemented in an outbound process from a Brazilian company with eight logistics KPI's. Principal Component Analysis (PCA) is used to stablish the relationships among indicators and an optimization tool is applied to define the integrative indicator scale. The global performance (GP) provided by the integrative indicator has demonstrated that even if important indicators have not reached their goal, it is possible to attain a good global performance with improvements in other areas. Thus, the framework demonstrates to be a useful solution for logistics performance management.

Keywords: Logistics performance · Integrated performance · Aggregated indicator · Indicators relationships · Decision making

1 Introduction

This digital era is turning the conventional logistics into logistics 4.0 [1]. The technological evolution, such as the application of internet of things (IoT) and digital twins have resulted in exponential growth of data [2, 3]. One new challenge that arises with logistics 4.0 is the massive amount of data that can be generated [4] and the staff has difficulties to make quick decisions with this exponential data growth [2].

S. Terzi et al. (Eds.): IN4PL 2023, CCIS 1886, pp. 149–164, 2023.
https://doi.org/10.1007/978-3-031-49339-3_9

This growing logistics complexity with the information access provided by technologies have led companies to adopt many indicators, making their management increasingly difficult. Moreover, there are indicators with different objectives (e.g., cost indicators shall be minimized, while quality indicators shall be maximized). It makes difficult the analysis of relationships among different KPIs (Key Performance Indicators) to figure out the global performance [2]. The managers can ask: "if some measures are good and some are poor, is the overall process performing well?" [5]. Therefore, problems with the comparison of performance expressions over time exist [6].

In this context, considering a set of performance indicators measured periodically, the research question is: "What is the overall performance of the system over time considering the relationship between the performance indicators?". To answer this question, the addition of an integrative indicator to the performance indicators system can be seen as a solution to facilitate manager's interpretation [7–10]. The aggregation of indicators in one metric can considerably simplify the analysis of a system, summarizing the information of a given set of sub-indicators [11]. So, the aggregated indicator provides a global overview of the performance situation interpretable by an entity not familiar with the details of the activities [9]. Works as [12, 13] affirm that the development of indicators to measure the overall logistics performance are still limited. Indeed, the literature review of [14] provides a large scope of indicators used for logistics performance management and any global integrative logistics index is cited.

Therefore, the main motivation of this work is to support manager's decisions on the logistics performance analysis, considering the indicators already used by the company and knowing that there are limits in the decision-maker's ability to process large sets of performance expressions [15]. The main gap that this paper proposes to fulfill is: how to aggregate several measures quantitatively in an integrative indicator, updated periodically, to determine the global logistics performance? The challenge is to design a structure to the metrics (i.e., grouping them together) and extracting an overall sense of performance from them.

To address this subject, the paper presents a methodology to determine a global indicator for logistics performance management. Dimension-reduction statistical tool is used to achieve the integrative indicator and optimization is used to define the indicator scale. The integrative indicator is calculated periodically allowing the company self-comparison over time. To provide the basis of the proposed methodology, a review of relevant literature regarding integrative indicators and relationships in logistics performance is presented in Sect. 2. Next, the research methodology is described (Sect. 3) and then applied in an outbound logistics process of a large Brazilian company (Sect. 4) to demonstrate its applicability for management purposes. Section 5 summarizes the conclusions and opportunities for future work.

2 Literature Review

The logistics performance literature is not new. However, [16] encouraged researches on this topic due to recent issues and problems that researchers and practitioners are facing. Initial works as [17, 18] have focused on establishing performance indicators to evaluate the logistics processes or the supply chain. As the logistics activities evolve over time, the same has happen to the measurement system. The literature on this subject has become more specific, presenting methodologies for logistics themes (reverse logistics, third-party logistics, etc.) or with focus on specific logistics processes as warehouses [19], or freight transport system [20]. In this context, the works providing frameworks to logistics performance measurement usually stops in a set of indicators definitions [21]. [22] highlights that even with several studies with frameworks, recommendations and metrics available, PMS in academic literature rarely provide guidance for implementation and use phase. [23] has focus only on the use phase of a performance measurement system, regarding the organizational changes process. In our paper, the specific phase related to implementation and use is performed to fulfill this gap.

The term performance integration is interpreted in different ways in the literature. Some researchers consider integrated performance as an indicator system framework which links the measures to strategy, and this literature is significant. Another interpretation, used in this paper, considers that the integrative indicator comes from an aggregation of several sub-indicators. In this case mathematical tools are used in order to synthesize the elementary performance expressions, representing in one indicator the global performance of the system [15]. Even if several authors have discussed the need of an aggregated measure, few works have tried to accomplish it.

Several works related to a global performance indicator usually use mathematical tools based on expert judgments as inputs to define indicators relationships (e.g., Analytic Hierarchy Process [24] or a combination of methods [25, 26]). Other papers use manager's opinion to assess indicators relations (e.g. from interviews [15, 27] or questionnaires [28, 29]). The exceptions are the works [13, 30, 31], which have defined the performance indicators relations or aggregation without human judgment. However, [30, 31] do not determine an integrative indicator, they just analyze indicators relationships. Based on the literature, this work proposes a framework to define indicators relations using a statistical tool and based on these relationships determine an integrative performance indicator for logistics management.

3 Methodology Proposition for Aggregated Logistics Performance Measurement

The proposed methodology, presented in Fig. 1, is built based on the literature review about performance management. The steps are divided in four phases as proposed by [32] for quantitative modeling research: conceptualization, modeling, model definition, implementation and update. Inside each phase, Fig. 1 shows the steps that may be carried out to achieve the aggregated performance model.

In the conceptualization phase, the step 1 *(Definition of the performance measurement scope)* is related to the activities/areas where the performance will be measured, and the step 2 (*Definition of the indicator set*) consists in choosing a group of indicators already used in company to evaluate the logistics performance. The modeling phase has three steps. In Step 1 (*Indicator time series acquisition)* data is processed and standardized. Step 2 (*Statistical tools application)* performs the dimension-reduction method, resulting in Step 3 (*Initial indicators aggregation model).* The model definition phase determines the integrated indicator equation (Step 1) and a scale for this integrative indicator (Step 2). Finally, the implementation and update phase carry out the model implementation (Step 1) and explains how and when it should be updated (Step 2).

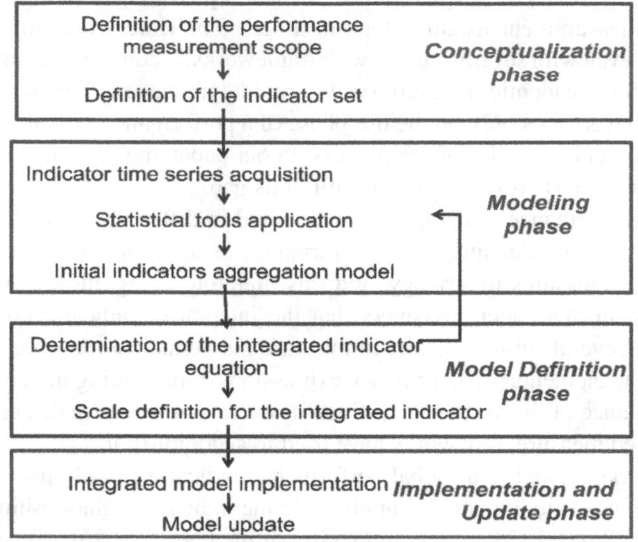

Fig. 1. Methodology steps flow.

A detailed explanation on how to perform the steps of the framework is presented on a case study in the next section.

4 Methodology Application on a Distribution Center

The enterprise which provided our case study is named DMS in this work and is a Brazilian industry founded in 1956, which is today one of the Brazilian faucet market leaders with international sales attaining every continent. The study is carried out in the company's Distribution Center (DC) located in the industrial park at Joinville city.

The industrial park produces 95% of the total company goods which are exported and distributed to all Brazilian states. The DC has 4000 m^2 and all the products produced in the industrial park are dispatch by the DC. The delivery of the products in Brazil is outsourced by freight transportation companies (one for each Brazilian region).

The case study can be considered enough general to demonstrate the methodology validation in practice, since the scope of the study covers more than one logistic activity (warehouse and transportation), and the company measures several indicators periodically for performance management.

4.1 Conceptualization Phase

Step 1: Definition of the performance measurement scope
The scope definition may be defined by the manager, who is usually the person that has a lot of indicators to analyze and will use the integrative indicator. Sometimes, there is no interest in the evaluation of some specific activities in an aggregated manner. So, the manager's participation in the definition of the measurement scope is important to increase the usability and the understanding of the integrated performance model by them.

In a meeting with the DC's manager, it was decided as scope to evaluate the outbound logistics performance (distribution center and freight transportation companies). There is a KPI group (tactical indicators) used by the DC's manager to evaluate these logistics processes, and it is difficult to verify the global performance due to indicators relationships.

Step 2: Definition of the indicator set
The proposed framework (Fig. 1) considers that indicators utilized for performance management are already derived from enterprise's strategy. There is no limit on the number of performance indicators considered for aggregation, however, a historical data (time series) of each indicator is necessary to consider the metric in the analysis.

Regarding the DC, there are many operational indicators to evaluate its processes and the freight transport companies, but it was decided to use just the KPI's since they are under manager responsibility. The indicator set is composed by 8 indicators measured in a monthly base as described in Table 1.

Table 1. The indicators used in DMS company.

Acronym	Indicator name	Indicator unit	Equation
PDS	Productivity in SKU's	SKU's packed /man.hour	$\frac{number\ SKUs\ packed}{working\ hours}$
PDR	Productivity in pieces	Pieces packed /man.hour	$\frac{number\ pieces\ packed}{working\ hours}$
FC	Freight cost from net operating revenue	%	$\frac{freight\ despenses}{net\ operating\ revenue_n}$
TP	Performance of transportation service providers	%	$\frac{orders\ delivered\ on\ time}{total\ orders\ delivered}$
SL	Service level	%	$\frac{orders\ dispatch\ on\ time}{total\ orders\ dispatched}$
OTIF	On time in full	%	$\frac{orders\ on\ time\ in\ all\ processes}{total\ orders\ delivered}$
STOCK	Finished goods stock	days of net operating revenue	$\frac{stock\ of\ finished\ goods\ (\$) x\ 360}{annual\ net\ operating\ revenue}$
ABSE	Absenteeism	%	$\frac{not\ working\ hours}{total\ hours}$

4.2 Modeling Phase

Step 1: Indicator time series acquisition
The required data to apply the proposed methodology are time series of indicators. Initially, the dataset size should be as large as possible.

Since the indicators are very heterogeneous with regard to their measurement units (e.g. $ for cost indicators, % for quality indicators), three operations should be applied on raw data [30]: filtering, homogenization and standardization. The filtering analyzes the abnormal behavior of the dataset (outliers treatment); homogenization puts all data in the same temporal frequency (it is necessary when some indicators are measured in weeks and others in months, for instance); standardization provides an auto-scaled and dimensionless data, which is defined by [33].

The time series provided by the company comprehends the monthly indicators values from January 2014 to December 2018, a total of 60 observations for each indicator. The limits are defined as mean ± 3SD (Standard Deviation). Three outliers are identified, PDS in June and November 2015; PDR in June 2015. Analyzing these data with the company members, they agreed that the indicator values are unreal. PDS in November 2015 was typed incorrectly and for the other two we agreed to change the data for the maximum time series value (without outlier).
Step 2: Statistical tools application
The statistical tools that should be used in the methodology are dimension-reduction methods. They have the potential to identify relationships between variables over time, clustering them according to the relationships and without a presumed theory [34]. The proposed dimension-reduction method to achieve indicator groups is PCA (Principal Component Analysis). PCA is a technique for reducing the dimensionality of such datasets at the same time minimizing information loss. It does so by creating new uncorrelated variables (PC's) that successively maximize variance [35].

The main outcomes provided by PCA analysis (Eq. 1) are equations in which artificial variables PC_i describe a linear combination of the observed variables X_j ($\forall j = 1, \ldots, m$ with m variables) throughout the relative weight between the original variables and the artificial ones b_{ij} [36].

$$\mathrm{PC}_i = \sum\nolimits_{j=1}^{m} b_{ij} X_j \qquad \forall\, i = 1, \ldots, n \tag{1}$$

To apply PCA, there are some conditions that the dataset should satisfy [36]: (i) the sample must be bigger than the number of variables included; (ii) the sample must have more than 30 observations; (iii) there must exist correlation among variables. Moreover, PCA is sensitive to great numerical differences among variables.

For the DMS case, PCA is performed in RStudio software using *prcomp* function (use varimax rotation to extract orthogonal components). Data entry are normalized indicator values and the PCA result is shown in Table 2.

Table 2 demonstrates the indicators versus Principal Components (PC1 to PC8), the standard deviation, the proportion variance of each PC, and the cumulative proportion of variance. The relative weight between the indicators and PCs are the cells b_{ij} in the matrix (named loadings in our work).

Table 2. PCA result.

	PC1	PC2	PC3	PC4	PC5	PC6	PC7	PC8
PDS	0.14	**−0.62**	−0.01	0.33	−0.06	0.05	0.67	0.11
PDR	0.18	**−0.55**	0.34	0.13	0.34	0.22	−0.59	−0.01
FC	−0.09	−0.14	**0.64**	−0.54	0.00	−0.45	0.19	0.07
TP	0.34	−0.29	**−0.41**	−0.04	−0.33	−0.64	−0.30	−0.05
SL	**0.56**	0.27	−0.00	−0.00	0.29	−0.05	0.05	0.71
OTIF	**0.56**	0.23	0.16	0.10	0.28	−0.10	0.20	−0.67
STOCK	0.11	−0.24	**−0.45**	−0.72	0.29	0.30	0.12	−0.10
ABSE	**−0.41**	−0.03	−0.24	0.20	0.71	−0.45	0.05	0.00
Standard Deviation	1.57	1.33	1.11	0.97	0.82	0.77	0.53	0.20
Proportion Variance (%)	30.3	22.3	15.4	11.9	8.5	7.5	3.6	0.5
Cumulative Proportion (%)	30.3	52.6	68.0	79.9	88.4	95.8	99.5	100

Step 3: Initial indicators aggregation model

One of the PCA objectives is to explain the maximum amount of variables variance in a small number of components. It is necessary to retain an appropriate number of components based on the trade-off between simplicity (retaining as few as possible) and completeness (explaining most of the data variation) [37]. Usually, the first few principal components are chosen to represent the original data [33]. If a component variance is low, it is possible to neglect this component. Kaiser's criterion rule determines that principal components with eigenvalues (standard deviation-SD) higher than 1 should be retained, since they measure the amount of variation represented by each component [38].

Furthermore, it is necessary to define the minimum loading value to consider an indicator (variable) inside a principal component (PC). According to [39], the definition of which number is considered a large or small loading is a subjective decision. For [38] items with loading score less than |0.40| were perceived as weak and should be excluded from the PC.

For the DMS case (Table 2), PC1 to PC3 are considered for the aggregation model, explaining 68% of data variance. The variables included in each PC are the indicators with loadings higher than |0.4| (in bold type).

The initial model for indicators aggregation provided by the statistical tool needs to be analyzed and refined before its implementation. To achieve it, the correlation matrix of indicators is assessed to evaluate the dimension-reduction outputs.

The objectives of the correlation matrix are: (i) help managers to understand the PCA result, since the principal components are built based on indicators correlation; (ii) identify indicators that could be discarded to improve PCA result.

For instance, if in the correlation matrix, the Person's coefficient *r* is low (e.g. value lower than 0,3), it might suggest that the indicator should be excluded from the model. After the exclusion of one indicator, the PCA needs to be performed again for the new indicator group (Step 2 in the Modeling phase, 3.2).

The correlation matrix for DMS case is performed with RStudio software and the significant correlation results (*p values* less than 0.05) are in bold in Table 3.

Table 3. Indicators correlation matrix.

	PDS	PDR	FC	TP	SL	OTIF	STOCK	ABSE
PDS	1							
PDR	**0.59**	1						
FC	−0.03	0.21	1					
TP	**0.37**	0.15	−0.15	1				
SL	−0.12	0.02	−0.18	**0.27**	1			
OTIF	−0.01	0.11	−0.07	0.21	**0.92**	1		
STOCK	0.10	0.09	−0.02	**0.28**	0.08	−0.06	1	
ABSE	−0.07	−0.13	−0.06	−0.19	**−0.42**	**−0.43**	−0.04	1

The highlighted cells of Table 3 just demonstrate the correlations with statistical significance, even if the Pearson coefficient result is low. It is possible to infer from Table 3 that FC has no significant correlation, and TP and STOCK have just low correlations. They are possible indicators to eliminate.

Three aspects are analyzed in PCA result when an indicator is removed: (i) if the number of principal components (PC) with SD > 1 is lower than the original result; (ii) if the cumulative proportion of data explained by the PC's is higher than the original result; (iii) if the indicators grouped in each component have a physical explanation in the warehouse context (considering our application).

The PCA is performed again combining the elimination of one or more indicators, however the result was not improved. Thus, PCA with eight indicators is the best result, and the final PC's equations are as follows.

$$PC1 = 0.56\ SL + 0.56\ OTIF - 0.41\ ABSE \tag{2}$$

$$PC2 = 0.62\ PDS + 0.55\ PDR \tag{3}$$

$$PC3 = -0.64\ FC + 0.41\ TP + 0.45\ STOCK \tag{4}$$

It is important to highlight that the signs of loadings in PC2 have been changed to make sense in practice. R documentation affirms that the signs are defined arbitrarily and if it is necessary to change them, it should be made for all loadings of the component.

Depending on manager objectives, it is possible to choose just one component to evaluate performance, probably the most important for company's goals. In this case, the aggregation stops here, and the manager loses a great quantity of information considered in other PCs. To consider Eq. 2 to Eq. 4 separately to analyze the outbound performance, it is necessary to develop a scale for each component, allowing the manager to evaluate each group of indicators individually. It might be an option in cases with many indicators (more than 20). However, it does not seem a practical choice if the objective is to analyze the global outbound performance. The principal component results are very subjective and difficult to compare with other components, even if there is a scale for each one to help this interpretation. Thus, we propose an aggregated expression for the component's equations.

Analyzing Eq. 2 up to 4, it could be possible to suggest by the loading values of indicators which most influence the global performance since values entries are standardized. However, for DMS case, productivity (PDS) and freight cost (FC) indicators have the highest loadings, surpassing more important indicators (pointed by DMS managers) such as service level (SL) and on time in full (OTIF). PCA defines indicators loadings based on the variables grouped in the same PC. It means that the comparison of factor loadings from different PCs to determine the most important group of indicators should be validated by company. Then, in cases that factor loadings are in tune with business reality, the global performance indicator (GP) becomes the sum of the PCs. In cases that these loadings do not match with company objectives (some indicators could be more important than others depending on the process), one possible solution is to apply different weights for each component according to its priority. Next section presents the general equation of the global performance indicator (GP).

4.3 Model Definition Phase

Step 1: Determination of the integrated indicator equation

The aggregation of the PCs in a global performance measure (GP) can be done directly as the underlying metrics are expressed in the same units of measure, which can be achieved after a normalization [7]. As the objective of the GP equation is to allow companies to adjust PC weights according to their objectives, the weighted mean is proposed in Eq. 5, where a_i are the component weights.

$$GP = \sum_{i=1}^{n} a_i PC_i \tag{5}$$

Then, if the principal components weights are defined as 1, the GP becomes the sum of the principal components, and the indicator's weights will be those defined in PCA.

In DMS study it was asked to the manager to assign weights for each PC if necessary and according to the company strategy. The weights and the final integrated indicator are demonstrated in Eq. 6.

$$GP = 0.5\ PC1 + 0.3\ PC2 + 0.2\ PC3 \tag{6}$$

To interpret the GP result (which cannot be interpreted straightforwardly) it is necessary to formulate a scale, which is developed in the next step.

Step 2: Scale definition for the integrated indicator

A scale determines the maximum and minimum values reached by a variable. The scale developed for this purpose is the interval one [40].

One possible solution to perform the scale is the use of optimization methods as described in [41]. It facilitates the inclusion of different indicator goals in the same model as well as all operation constraints. In this work the Solver tool from Excel (LP Simplex) is used to define the integrated indicator scale.

The scale for the global performance indicator GP (Eq. 6) is determined by its boundaries, i.e., the upper and lower limits that the GP indicator can attain. The GP boundaries (scale limits) are related with the maximum and minimum values that each one of the indicators can reach. Therefore, it was established that the upper and lower indicators limit are mean ± 3SD.

The optimization constraints are established by the upper and lower standardized indicators values (Table 4) before their inclusion at GP (Global Performance) equation.

Table 4. Optimization constraints and results to define GP scale.

		INDICATORS							
		PDS	PDR	FC	TP	SL	OTIF	STOCK	ABSE
Optimization constraints	Max = Mean + 3SD	51,5	546,2	2,2%	100%	100%	100%	18,94	3,0%
	Min = Mean − 3SD	34,8	297,4	1,3%	83,1%	71,5%	66,54%	6,83	−0,01
Normalized constraints	Max	3	3	3	2,22	1,85	2,14	3	3
	Min	−3	−3	−3	−3	−3	−3	−3	−3
Optimization results	Max	3	3	−3	2,22	1,85	2,14	3	−3
	Min	−3	−3	3	−3	−3	−3	−3	3

As expected, Table 4 shows that the minimization results are the lowest values for indicators like PDR and the highest value for indicators like FC (as higher FC, worst the GP result). A similar result occurred for the maximization.

The results of the model application in the DMS company are 3.65 and −4.27 as the upper and lower GP limits, respectively.

To support the scale interpretation, we transform the scale limits from −4.27 to 3.65 (optimized scale – OS) to 0 up to 100 (normal scale – NS) using traditional scale transformation rules.

Every month the GP indicator is updated, except its scale. Allowing the manager to verify your progress over time. In the next section is explained how the integrated model and scale are implemented and should be used in practice.

4.4 Implementation and Update Phase

Step 1: Integrated model implementation

The expressions that will be used by the manager for warehouse performance measurement are Eqs. 2, 3, 4, and 6. It is important to note that the factor loadings and PC weights are constants.

The integrated model should be used as any other indicator system, being updated in the same periodicity of the performance indicator measurements. It allows the managers to follow the progress of the integrated performance indicator throughout time. As the performance indicators set are also measured, it is possible to identify significant changes in indicators which alter the aggregated one. These are the main benefits of this methodology application: (i) updated periodically; (ii) the integrative indicator does not substitute other metrics. Thus, the integrated model should be refreshed as follows:

1. Calculate the indicator values in their original units of measure.
2. Standardize these indicator values according to [33].
3. Replace these standardized indicators in Eqs. 2, 3 and 4, obtaining the component values.
4. These component results are used in Eq. 6 to obtain the integrated indicator value.

These steps can be easily automatized on a spreadsheet to facilitate manager's work.

Using the dataset provided by the company (times series of 8 indicators from 2014 to 2018) the GP for each month could be calculated. Also, it was collected from the company the goals established for each indicator, and they are converted in a GP. Figure 2 demonstrates the GP results obtained for the DMS enterprise. In blue the integrative indicator value measured monthly from jan-2014 to dec-2018 and in red the company goal.

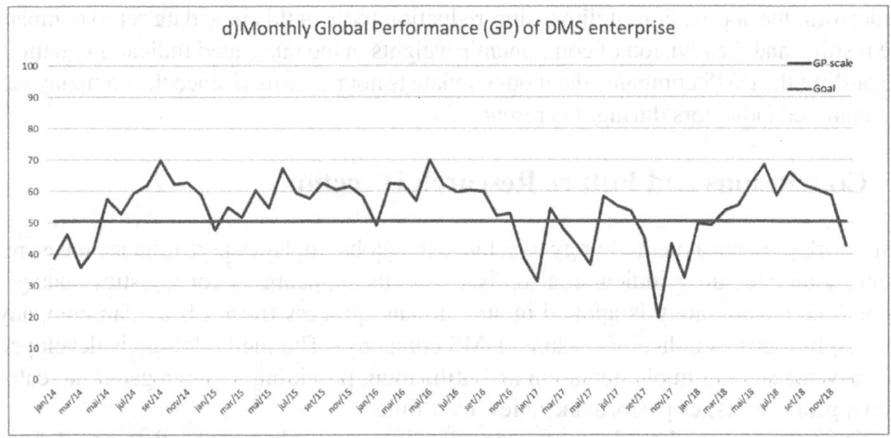

Fig. 2. GP indicator measured over time.

Analyzing Fig. 2 it is possible to see that the higher and lower GP over time are 74.73% in May 2016 and 43.76% in October 2017, respectively. The GP limits zero and

100% are not attained since the indicator limits are established higher/lower than the indicator values verified in the enterprise time series. Besides this fact, the integrative indicator presents a large variation on time, demonstrating that GP discriminates the enterprise performance in different situations and according to the established objectives.

For example, let us analyze the worst company global performance, in October 2017. At this month, the SL (72.6%), OTIF (66.7%) and ABSE (2.91%) indicators reach the worst values in the available time series, and the other indicators also have bad results. As SL, OTIF and ABSE indicators have the biggest weights in GP equation, it results in the worst GP result. For the best GP result (May 2016), the FC, TP and SL performed the best time series values, and OTIF and ABSE have good performance (92.2% and 0.64%, respectively). This result demonstrates that, even if the indicators with higher weights in GP equation are not at their best value, it is possible to attain a higher global performance with improvements in different outbound areas.

The relationship among indicators, provided by the PCA output, also helps the manager to interpret the results. For example, if PDS is improved, according to Equation PC2, PDR probably will be improved too, and a higher PC can be reached.

Thus, the decision of aggregate all indicators in a single measure (GP) provide insights about which indicators could change with a variation in one indicator, besides the overall process performance.

Step 2: Model update
The aggregated model cannot be considered as a static entity: it must be maintained and updated to remain relevant and useful for the organization [7]. The model redefinition encompasses the comparison of desired performance indicators with existing measures (to identify which current measures are kept, which existing measures are no longer relevant, and which gaps exist so that new measures are needed) [7].

Regarding this situation, our methodology proposes a periodic reevaluation of the integrated performance model. This reevaluation encompasses mainly the selection of the indicators; the application of dimension-reduction tools in this new data set to compare the results; and the revision of component's weights in the integrated indicator equation. Regarding the DMS company, the model update is not performed since the company has not changed indicators during this research.

5 Conclusions and Future Research Directions

This work presents a methodology to achieve the global logistics performance measurement by an integrative indicator, also discussing its applicability for logistics management. The methodology is applied in an outbound process from a Brazilian company with eight logistics indicators (named DMS company). The methodology is developed for easy managerial implementation and utilization, providing an aggregated indicator with a global logistics performance view over time.

The proposed methodology encompasses four main phases: the first one defines the management scope and the indicator set, the second applies multivariate statistical tools reaching an initial model for indicators aggregation, the third one determines the integrated performance model, and the last phase develops the integrative indicator's scale and implements the model.

In the DMS company application, there was eight initial indicators. To determine the indicators that should be retained in the model, an analysis of the correlation results is carried out to improve the PCA outcome. The main objective was to keep the greatest quantity of indicators as possible with a minimum number of principal components. In the DMS case all measures are maintained and compose the global performance (GP) indicator, throughout three principal components (PC's). The GP is optimized to obtain the upper and lower values of the GP scale. The optimized scale, OS, is transformed in a named "normal" scale, NS, to facilitate the interpretation of the aggregated indicator. The real case application demonstrates the usefulness of the integrative indicator and the indicators relationships for management purposes. Therefore, companies can realize the global performance of a process with the implementation of the proposed methodology and get more efficiency on the logistics management.

However, it is important to highlight some methodology's limitations as: (i) the non-linear relationships among indicators are not evaluated; (ii) the methodology considers that the enterprise already use indicators derived from enterprise's strategy; (iv) the methodology cannot be used for benchmark purposes, since each enterprise will have your aggregated indicator issued from your specific indicators.

Based on the methodology application and its limitations, it is suggested as future research directions the following developments:

- Verification of which weights should be applied to principal components if the ones defined by the company, or the ones issued from PCA.
- Analyze the impact of different scales limits in the GP interpretation.
- Test the integrative indicator methodology also including qualitative indicators, with data as good, yes, no, excellent.
- Compare GP results with the company revenue, to verify if a higher GP performance is related to a higher revenue.
- Evaluate the use of other statistical methods to achieve the integrated performance indicator.
- Analyze other methods to measure quantitatively indicator's relationships.
- Combine this methodology with systems dynamics model, where the systems dynamics can provide the relationships among variables to support model definition phase.
- Expand the methodology using big data concepts. The big data is becoming a reality in many global enterprises. The large amount of data generated by all processes based on IoE (Internet of Everything) need to be processed for performance management purposes.
- Evaluate the application of this methodology in Supply Chain Control Towers.

References

1. Zinn, W., Goldsby, T.J.: Global supply chains: globalization research in a changing world. J. Bus. Logist. **41**, 4–5 (2020). https://doi.org/10.1111/jbl.12241
2. Dev, N.K., Shankar, R., Gupta, R., Dong, J.: Multi-criteria evaluation of real-time key performance indicators of supply chain with consideration of big data architecture. Comput. Ind. Eng. **128**, 1076–1087 (2019). https://doi.org/10.1016/j.cie.2018.04.012

3. Javaid, M., Haleem, A., Suman, R.: Digital twin applications toward industry 4.0: a review. Cogn. Robot. **3**, 71–92 (2023). https://doi.org/10.1016/j.cogr.2023.04.003
4. Winkelhaus, S., Grosse, E.H.: Logistics 4.0: a systematic review towards a new logistics system. Int. J. Prod. Res. **58**, 18–43 (2020). https://doi.org/10.1080/00207543.2019.1612964
5. Johnson, A., McGinnis, L.: Performance measurement in the warehousing industry. IIE Trans. **43**, 220–230 (2010). https://doi.org/10.1080/0740817X.2010.491497
6. Clivillé, V., Berrah, L., Mauris, G.: Quantitative expression and aggregation of performance measurements based on the MACBETH multi-criteria method. Int. J. Prod. Econ. **105**, 171–189 (2007). https://doi.org/10.1016/j.ijpe.2006.03.002
7. Lohman, C., Fortuin, L., Wouters, M.: Designing a performance measurement system: a case study. Eur. J. Oper. Res. **156**, 267–286 (2004). https://doi.org/10.1016/s0377-2217(02)00918-9
8. Vascetta, M., Kauppila, P., Furman, E.: Aggregate indicators in coastal policy making: potentials of the trophic index TRIX for sustainable considerations of eutrophication. Sustain. Dev. **16**, 282–289 (2008). https://doi.org/10.1002/sd.379
9. Lauras, M., Marques, G., Gourc, D.: Towards a multi-dimensional project performance measurement system. Decis. Support. Syst. **48**, 342–353 (2010). https://doi.org/10.1016/j.dss.2009.09.002
10. Irfani, D.P., Wibisono, D., Basri, M.H.: Logistics performance measurement framework for companies with multiple roles. Meas. Bus. Excell. **23**, 93–109 (2019). https://doi.org/10.1108/MBE-11-2018-0091
11. Franceschini, F., Galetto, M., Maisano, D., Viticchi, L.: The condition of uniqueness in manufacturing process representation by performance/quality indicators. Qual. Reliab. Eng. Int. **22**, 567–580 (2006). https://doi.org/10.1002/qre.762
12. Fattahi, F., Nookabadi, A.S., Kadivar, M.: A model for measuring the performance of the meat supply chain. Br. Food J. **115**, 1090–1111 (2013). https://doi.org/10.1108/BFJ-09-2011-0217
13. Bai, C., Sarkis, J.: Supply-chain performance-measurement system management using neighbourhood rough sets. Int. J. Prod. Res. **50**, 2484–2500 (2012). https://doi.org/10.1080/00207543.2011.581010
14. Götz, L.N., Staudt, F.H., de Borba, J.L.G., Bouzon, M.: A framework for logistics performance indicators selection and targets definition: a civil construction enterprise case. Production **33**, 1–18 (2023). https://doi.org/10.1590/0103-6513.20220075
15. Berrah, L., Clivillé, V.: Towards an aggregation performance measurement system model in a supply chain context. Comput. Ind. **58**, 709–719 (2007). https://doi.org/10.1016/j.compind.2007.05.012
16. Swanson, D., Goel, L., Francisco, K., Stock, J.: An analysis of supply chain management research by topic. Supply Chain Manag. **23**, 100–116 (2018). https://doi.org/10.1108/SCM-05-2017-0166
17. Banomyong, R., Supatn, N.: Selecting logistics providers in Thailand: a shippers' perspective. Eur. J. Mark. **45**, 419–437 (2011). https://doi.org/10.1108/03090561111107258
18. Gunasekaran, A., Kobu, B.: Performance measures and metrics in logistics and supply chain management: a review of recent literature (1995–2004) for research and applications. Int. J. Prod. Res. **45**, 2819–2840 (2007). https://doi.org/10.1080/00207540600806513
19. Torabizadeh, M., Yusof, N.M., Ma'aram, A., Shaharoun, A.M.: Identifying sustainable warehouse management system indicators and proposing new weighting method. J. Clean. Prod. **248**, 119190 (2020). https://doi.org/10.1016/j.jclepro.2019.119190
20. Yazdani, M., Pamucar, D., Chatterjee, P., Chakraborty, S.: Development of a decision support framework for sustainable freight transport system evaluation using rough numbers. Int. J. Prod. Res. **58**, 4325–4351 (2020). https://doi.org/10.1080/00207543.2019.1651945

21. Ülgen, V.S., Forslund, H.: Logistics performance management in textiles supply chains: best-practice and barriers. Int. J. Product. Perform. Manag. **64**, 52–75 (2015). https://doi.org/10.1108/IJPPM-01-2013-0019
22. Ravelomanantsoa, M.S., Ducq, Y., Vallespir, B.: A state of the art and comparison of approaches for performance measurement systems definition and design. Int. J. Prod. Res. **57**, 5026–5046 (2018). https://doi.org/10.1080/00207543.2018.1506178
23. Barbosa, D.H., Musetti, M.A.: The use of performance measurement system in logistics change process: proposal of a guide. Int. J. Product. Perform. Manag. **60**, 339–359 (2011). https://doi.org/10.1108/17410401111123526
24. Dehghanian, F., Mansoor, S., Nazari, M.: A framework for integrated assessment of sustainable supply chain management. IEEE Int. Conf. Ind. Eng. Eng. Manag. 279–283 (2011). https://doi.org/10.1109/IEEM.2011.6117922
25. Kucukaltan, B., Irani, Z., Aktas, E.: A decision support model for identification and prioritization of key performance indicators in the logistics industry. Comput. Human Behav. **65**, 346–358 (2016). https://doi.org/10.1016/j.chb.2016.08.045
26. Makris, D., Hansen, Z.N.L., Khan, O.: Adapting to supply chain 4.0: an explorative study of multinational companies. Supply Chain Forum **20**, 116–131 (2019). https://doi.org/10.1080/16258312.2019.1577114
27. Orozco-Crespo, E., Sablón-Cossío, N., Taboada-Rodríguez, C.M., Staudt, F.H.: Textile sector supply chain: comprehensive indicator for performance evaluation. Rev. Venez. Gerenc. **26**, 574–591 (2021). https://doi.org/10.52080/rvgluz.26.e6.35
28. Irfani, D.P., Wibisono, D., Basri, M.H.: Design of a logistics performance management system based on the system dynamics model. Meas. Bus. Excell. **23**, 269–291 (2019). https://doi.org/10.1108/MBE-01-2019-0008
29. Gupta, A., Singh, R.K.: Developing a framework for evaluating sustainability index for logistics service providers: graph theory matrix approach. Int. J. Product. Perform. Manag. ahead-of-p (2020). https://doi.org/10.1108/IJPPM-12-2019-0593
30. Rodriguez, R.R., Saiz, J.J.A., Bas, A.O.: Quantitative relationships between key performance indicators for supporting decision-making processes. Comput. Ind. **60**, 104–113 (2009). https://doi.org/10.1016/j.compind.2008.09.002
31. Brundage, M.P., Bernstein, W.Z., Morris, K.C., Horst, J.A.: Using graph-based visualizations to explore key performance indicator relationships for manufacturing production systems. Procedia CIRP. **61**, 451–456 (2017). https://doi.org/10.1016/j.procir.2016.11.176
32. Mitroff, I.I., Betz, F., Pondy, L.R., Sagasti, F.: On managing science in the systems age: two schemas for the study of science as a whole systems phenomenon. Interfaces (Providence) **4**, 46–58 (1974). https://doi.org/10.1287/inte.4.3.46
33. Gentle, J.E.: Matrix Algebra – Theory, Computations, and Applications in Statistics. Springer, New York, NY, USA (2007)
34. Wainer, J.: Principal Components Analysis. Available at: http://www.ic.unicamp.br/~wainer/cursos/1s2013/ml/Lecture18_PCA.pdf. pp. 1–18 (2010)
35. Westfall, P.: Comparison of Principal Components, Canonical Correlation, and Partial Least Squares for the Job Salience/Job Satisfaction data analysis. http://courses.ttu.edu/isqs6348-westfall/images/6348/PCA_CCA_PLS.pdf. 1–2 (2007)
36. Manly, B.F.J.: Principal component analysis. In: Multivariate Statistical Methods: a Primer, pp. 75–90. Chapman & Hall/ CRC, Boca Raton, Florida, USA (2004)
37. Katchova, A.: Principal Component Analysis and Factor Analysis. https://sites.google.com/site/econometricsacademy/econometrics-models/principal-component-analysis. pp. 1–10 (2013)
38. Albishri, D.Y., Sundarakani, B., Gomisek, B.: An empirical study of relationships between goal alignment, centralised decision-making, commitment to networking and supply chain

effectiveness using structural equation modelling. Int. J. Logist. Res. Appl. **23**, 390–415 (2020). https://doi.org/10.1080/13675567.2019.1700219

39. PennState, E.C. of S.: Lesson 7.4 - Interpretation of the Principal Components. STAT 505 Available https://onlinecourses.science.psu.edu/stat505/node/54. (2015)
40. Jung, H.W.: Investigating measurement scales and aggregation methods in SPICE assessment method. Inf. Softw. Technol. **55**, 1450–1461 (2013). https://doi.org/10.1016/j.infsof.2013.02.004
41. Staudt, F.H., Alpan, G., di Mascolo, M., Rodriguez, C.M.T.: A scale definition for an integrated performance indicator. In: ILS 2018 - Information Systems, Logistics and Supply Chain, Proceedings, pp. 607–616. Lyon – France (2018)

Blockchain Subnets for Track & Trace Within the Logistics System Landscape

Henrik Körsgen[1(✉)] and Markus Rabe[2]

[1] TU Dortmund, IT in Production and Logistics, 44227 Dortmund, Germany
koersgen@dxk.ch

[2] TU Dortmund, Faculty of Mechanical Engineering, 44227 Dortmund, Germany
markus.rabe@tu-dortmund.de

Abstract. The advantages of track & trace solutions to enterprises that move physical goods are widespread. Yet, track & trace solutions are not a standard component of an enterprise's system landscape. While mostly being triggered by customer requests, track & trace initiatives are often siloed. Seldomly, the entire enterprise and even more rarely the enterprise's network are considered. The reasons for a siloed implementation of track & trace software are manifold. Different business priorities, adverse data sharing policies, lack of knowledge, and a lack of structured approach are a few to mention. Starting with the structured approach of the digital enterprise architecture (DEA) is a first remedy to these issues. From a technological perspective, embracing a blockchain subnet gives enterprises access to solutions for data ownership, validity, and integrity impediments. The blockchain-based subnet is compatible with a bimodal enterprise architecture. This allows enterprises to connect to their supply chain partners' logistics systems differently than to their own one. Several steps need to be considered to achieve a functional supply-chain-network-wide track & trace solution. From finding consensus among the blockchain peers to designing the track & trace block, academic input is combined to render the implementation of a blockchain-based track & trace solution possible. From a business perspective linking the requirement catalogue with the purposeful use of the latest technology follows an end-to-end approach.

Keywords: Track & trace implementation · Blockchain technology · Smart contract · Digital enterprise architecture

1 Introduction

Unexpected disruptions in the supply chain severely cast off any lead times and delivery dates promised by the sender. Enterprises are relying on receiving goods on time. Supply chains and the underlying operations often follow a clocked sequence. This sequence, for example, is crucial for supplying spare parts or semi-finished goods in just-in-time (JIT) and just-in-sequence (JIS) production lines. Any unexpected delays can result in production downtimes or financial penalties. Track & trace enables production planners and logisticians to realize supply bottlenecks early.

S. Terzi et al. (Eds.): IN4PL 2023, CCIS 1886, pp. 165–181, 2023.
https://doi.org/10.1007/978-3-031-49339-3_10

This valuable insight mitigates delays and, therefore, reduces downtime by adapting the production plan or sourcing the components somewhere else. Track & trace systems are a distinguishing factor in enhancing customer service and satisfaction [22]. They improve timeliness and correctness of transport. Regarding supply chains, the traceability, identification, and real-time tracking of goods are challenging [14]. One major issue is the collaboration of supply chain partners [14]. The more participants are part of the track & trace solution, the higher the value, but simultaneously the more difficult it is to find a common ground. Topics like data management, authorization control, and the interaction among all concerned actors need to be addressed [14]. Gnimpieda et al. proposed the design of a collaborative cloud-based platform [14]. A cloud-based platform can be connected to several layers of an IT infrastructure. Combined with suitable software, it can also handle heterogenous incoming data formats. Nowadays, data are commonly exchanged via application programming interfaces (APIs). They support and simplify back-end integration and accommodate a bimodal enterprise architecture where most of the systems of record are SAP systems. APIs are also adaptable with blockchains for executing queries and locating data [2]. Several use cases have already been identified for logistics processes. Alladi et al. showcased that several parties potentially benefit from blockchain technology (Fig. 1) [2]. Another example, the Real-Time Supply Chain architecture (RTSC) incorporates a decentralized project logistics setup [17]. The first out of the five main components is a blockchain. The reason for it being in first place is that it is the method to verify the authenticity of supply chain transactions [17].

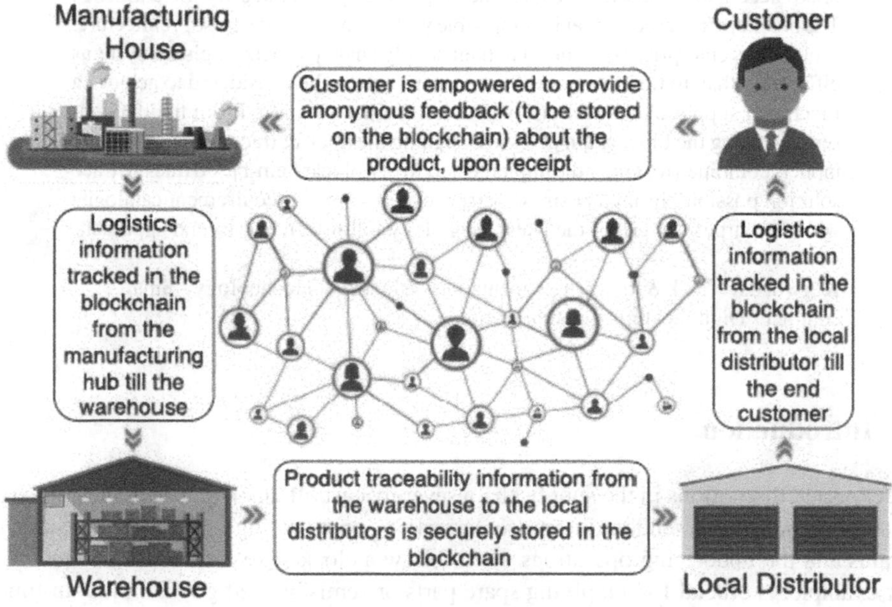

Fig. 1. Selection of blockchain applications for logistics [2].

1.1 Reasons for Blockchain Applications in the Supply Chain

The system landscape in supply chains is dominated by heterogeneous legacy systems and the synchronization of information among the members is difficult. In addition, there are latencies between the supply chain partners, as data are passed on from system to system in classic legacy systems. Due to the heterogeneity of the systems, considerable latencies can result. If a subsystem is still paper based, the communication paths between individual systems are interrupted or delayed, or the transmission of information is prevented by the failure of a central intermediary. Especially in international trade, there are delays in the flow of goods and information. A heterogeneous system landscape and heterogeneous data formats, within and across companies in the supply chain, inhibit the flow of information and create barriers [9]. Yet, many processes are still paper-based, and proofs of origin are created manually and sent physically. Copigneaux et al. found that an average of 36 original papers and 240 copies from 27 different parties are needed to trade internationally [9]. To improve planning, control, and ultimately performance, Kache and Seuring suggest exploring technical solutions such as track & trace technologies [21]. They counter the growing complexity in supply chains. Above that, track & trace solutions elevate comparability of supply chain execution costs, customer and stakeholder demand for accuracy, and timeliness of shipments, and the need to optimize the numbers of supply chain partners [5]. Further reasons are assuring regulation requirements, product tracking and diagnostics, and digital business models [8, 28].

1.2 Milestones of Blockchain Technology

The blockchain technology (BCT) roots back to 1991. The computational scientists Stuart Haber and W. Scott Stornetta researched on a computationally practical solution for time-stamping digital documents. Their intention was that these documents could not be tampered or backdated [16]. Two and a half decades later, an open source community as part of a Linux Foundation project advanced the blockchain technology by introducing Hyperledger. The project's aim is to accelerate mainstream adaptation. The open source community focused on the combination of interconnected distributed databases, modular blockchain technology, and the easy-to-use application programming interface [25]. Documented use cases are dating back to 2016 and before. Concerning track & trace in combination with BCT, one of the first examples is the SmartLog project. Its aim is to streamline the logistics value chain. Lead by the Finnish Kouvola Innovation solution provider, this project investigated the potential of self-routing containers [7]. However, before endeavouring to build a track & trace system based on blockchain technology, enterprises need to consider certain key decisions.

1.3 Digital Enterprise Architecture for Blockchain-Based Track & Trace Solutions

Since blockchain is a relatively new technology to be used for track & trace, it is recommended that enterprises invest enough time in project planning. According to the PMBOK® Guide, the first of the five project management processes is to plan scope management. Skipping the other four project management processes, scope management sheds light on how to realize a blockchain-based track & trace solution. Next to the scope statement, it entails an authorization concept and boundaries of the project [15]. The three topics scope statement, authorization concept, and project boundaries can be conceptualized in the digital enterprise architecture (DEA). It merges the technical setup with both the business it serves and the network it interacts with [23]. The three pillars business, enterprise, and network architecture give enterprises a broad but adjustable starting point for the blockchain-based track & trace solution (Fig. 2).

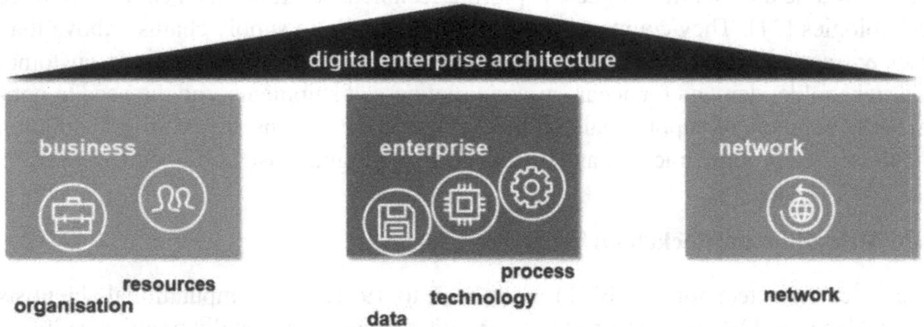

Fig. 2. Illustration of the digital enterprise architecture (DEA) concept [23].

The three pillars are subdivided into one to three building blocks. Each of these building blocks has an important stake in the key decisions for track & trace applications running on blockchain technology.

2 Preparing the Setup of a Track & Trace Blockchain

With almost one decade of blockchain evolution in the realm of supply chain management, best practices have been formed. This is also valid regarding track & trace applications on blockchains. The two major developments to mention are smart contracts and subnet blockchains. The terms subnets and subnetworks are used interchangeably. To properly make use of the latest developments, practitioners need to decide on fundamentals. These options are outlined subsequently and suggestions for the key decisions are provided.

2.1 Blockchain Design Architecture

The first key decision is about the blockchain design. It needs to be purpose-driven and, therefore, it should fit track & trace technology requirements and business goals. With these purposes in mind the participating enterprise can choose from a public, private, or consortium-based blockchain platform. Since, several partners, including suppliers, manufacturers, distributors, retailers, logistics providers, and end customers are either actively or passively involved in founding a track & trace solution (Fig. 1), the consortium-based blockchain platform is recommended. With this, the participating partners can establish a shared control and governance structure. It ensures that no single partner has centralized control over the platform, promoting fairness and collaboration. This consortium-based blockchain differs from a private blockchain. Whereas private blockchains are suitable for single enterprises, the consortium blockchain uses a permissioned network but includes multiple enterprises [12]. Above that, the consortium-based blockchain enhances data privacy by providing selective sharing and encryption mechanisms. Track & trace data contain information about product origins, manufacturing processes, and potentially employees working in the supply chain. Both a public and private blockchain are inferior to this regard. Additionally, consortium-based blockchains can offer scalability and performance benefits compared to public blockchains. By limiting the number of participating nodes, the consensus mechanisms can be more efficient, enabling faster transaction processing and higher throughput. This scalability is crucial for track and trace applications, which involve a large volume of transactions and interactions across the supply chain. Nonetheless, all participants need to agree upon the data structure, consensus mechanism, and smart contract functionality for their joint track & trace solution.

2.2 Consortium Formation

Opting for a consortium-based blockchain means that each supply chain partner is part of the network. In blockchain terms this is called a consortium of participants. The consortium should consist of trusted participants. Nonetheless, it is critical to define governance rules, roles, and responsibilities within the consortium. Dhar Dwivedi et al. recommend using a Hyperledger Fabric operating system as a platform for a consortium blockchain [12]. Such a setup serves several enterprises where a particular group of enterprises prefers to keep information private from other enterprises. Hyperledger Fabric allows a consortium to use separate channels for different subnets. A channel is a private subnet of communication between two or more peers. This channel architecture provides a certain level of privacy. For instance, peers of subnet A can be separated from peers of subnet B. This means that transaction details can be split up in different channels enabling private and confidential transactions, if required [18].

2.3 Data Integration

Once both the design of the track & trace blockchain as well as the peers of the network's consortium are defined, the data integration needs to start. It is not a prerequisite that the peers connect to the network with similar applications. However, for accelerating the implementation of the blockchain network, it is advantageous if the peers have the same connecting applications. Then, employees of the participating enterprises can share information about it and help each other to debug interfaces to existing supply chain systems. The integration to existing supply chain systems enables real-time data exchange and ensures accurate and consistent information flow across the entire supply chain. One option is to use RESTful APIs to connect with the track & trace blockchain. It is a transport standard to exchange textual data using the HTTP connectivity. RESTful APIs can connect to many types of user interfaces, devices, and enterprise systems [27]. On the one hand it allows developers to both access the supply chain applications of their peers such as an SAP system. On the other hand, RESTful APIs can extract data from the hardware devices, such as the track & trace logger, directly and communicate them back to the applications, if required [27]. Another option is professionally supported Software Development Kits (SDKs). In their experiment to create an industrial blockchain-based framework for product lifecycle management, Liu et al. have used a Hyperledger Fabric SDK. The reason is that SDKs support a variety of programming languages [24]. For the communication module of their open logistics platform, Barenji and Montreuil also chose an SDK [4]. It enables data communication between the physical module and the peers within an open logistics blockchain module. Likewise, the communication between the track & trace loggers and the track & trace blockchain network is built up (Fig. 3).

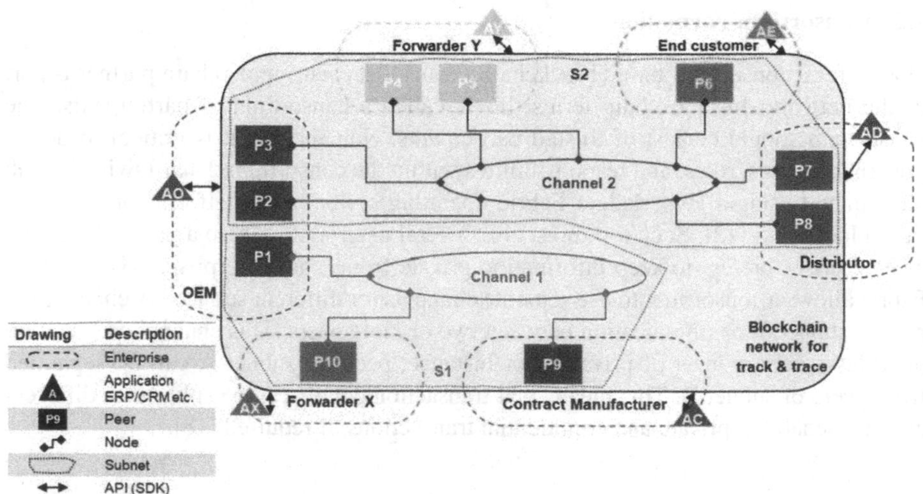

Fig. 3. Track & trace blockchain network.

2.4 Smart Contract Implementation

Smart contracts are a crucial part of the track & trace blockchain because they automate and enforce business rules within the supply chain. According to the definition by Shi-Wan et al., a smart contract is a computer program executed in a secure environment within the blockchain network. The origin of the term dates back to 1994 when Nick Szabo introduced "a computerized protocol that executes the terms of a contract" [29]. In technical terms, smart contracts link protocols with user interfaces to reinforce secure relationships over computer networks [30]. They encapsulate a business logic comprising contract terms and conditions between agreeing participants [27]. Álvarez-Díaz et al. researched on smart contracts in logistics based on the Ethereum blockchain in 2017. The purpose of their research was to develop a decentralized application. It demonstrates the flexibility and possibility to scale to an increased number of users [3]. Nowadays, distributed architectural models make decentralized applications interoperable. Consequently, inter-blockchain smart contracts are possible [32]. Furthermore, smart contracts regulate external access to the blockchain. Multiple security keys are required to trigger the smart contract. For instance, the blocks need to be validated by the peers. They validate distributed blocks independently, yet in a deterministic fashion. This ensures that ledgers remain consistent [19]. Building up on the consortium formation and the data integration, the Hyperledger Fabric offers a Fabric Contract API. Hyperledger Fabric smart contracts are also known as chain code. The fabric-contract-API provides a high-level API for application developers to implement smart contracts. The business logic of a smart contract is usually written in the programming languages Go, Node.js, or Java [20]. Such a contract interface is coded to enable one or more of the following features:

- automatic execution of contractual obligations,
- triggering payments, or
- managing inventory levels.

3 Track & Trace Blockchain Architecture

After all the four setup steps comprising the blockchain design architecture, consortium formation, data integration and smart contract implementation, are concluded, the enterprises belonging to the consortium can build the track & trace blockchain. While developing it, the participating enterprises should assure that the entire blockchain network including the interfaces to their own supply chain applications remains a transparent and auditable system. This ensures that supply chain transactions recorded on the track & trace blockchain remain valid. The peers of the network can track products' journeys, verify authenticity, and identify bottlenecks or delays in the entire supply chain. Above that, the peers can rely on an enhanced security. By leveraging the blockchain's cryptographic features, the transactions' security is enhanced. In addition, the risk of data tampering, counterfeiting, or unauthorized access is reduced. A prerequisite is a set of predefined rules that all peers of the network agree upon. They are the basis for access rights and the encryption of sensitive information.

The exit or the addition of peers have to be defined as well. Next to ex- or including the peer, the blockchain network needs to deal with the ownership and rights of the smart contracts that have been exchanged until the change in the peer group. This requires thorough contractual work before the blockchain can be put into practice. The transparency and security features might not be primary goals for developing a proof of concept. Therefore, the consortium of the blockchain should build a pilot and iteratively enhance it. The outcome of different pilot versions feeds the "plan do check act" (PDCA) cycle. With each development cycle the blockchain participants collect feedback, evaluate performance, and refine the solution based on real-world results. The blockchain network should be designed to be scalable. Hence, the larger the consortium, the more valuable is the network to all participants. The first functioning version of the blockchain network should be showcased to potential adopters. Improved efficiency, reduced costs, and increased trust are factors that lead to an expansion of the track & trace blockchain. Yet, the above three factors alone do not guarantee efficiency improvements. Proper planning, collaboration, and continuous monitoring are accompanying success factors in creating a track & trace blockchain.

3.1 Applying DEA to the Track & Trace Blockchain Network

To validate the track & trace blockchain network, it is essential to review it by means of the digital enterprise model (DEA) shown in Fig. 2. It is designed to support the implementation of track & trace systems, since it offers a holistic implementation approach [23]. So far, the business and network pillar have been focused on. The business pillar of the track & trace blockchain incorporates the automated, trusted, and integrated traceability of goods and services. The network pillar comprises the consortium of the supply chain partners profiting from efficiency improvements of the track & trace blockchain. To complete the DEA, the enterprise architecture pillar is concentrated on subsequently. So far two out of three building blocks of the enterprise architecture pillar have been dealt with. "Data" was broached in form of data integration and "technology" is an inherent part of smart contract implementation. The missing building block is the "process". To provide a complete picture of the enterprise pillar, a visualization of the track & trace blockchain is depicted in Fig. 3. This figure includes two channels. Channel 1 represents the upward supply chain from the perspective of the original equipment manufacturer (OEM). Channel 2 represents the downward supply chain from the perspective of the OEM. The track & trace blockchain network is divided into two subnets. This demonstrates the possibility to separate the peers of an enterprise's holistic blockchain network. Starting with the subnet S1, the OEM orders a component for its, e.g., precision engineering production. This component is shipped by the Forwarder X. In the case of track & trace applications, the goods movement data are completed in alignment with the physical exchange of goods. Hence, with every exchange of the goods, a smart contract is created. It entails a contractual clause in the form of a computer protocol. The exchange of goods is automatically verified while the underlying contract is executed according to the agreed terms. Furthermore, all recorded exchanges of the goods are registered as immutable objects inside the blockchain [3].

Specifically, in the example of the exchange of goods between the OEM and the Forwarder X, the goods movement event is permanently stored in the blocks of the subnet S1 (Fig. 3). Thus, Channel 1 is defining the participating peers of the subnet S1.

3.2 Advantages and Disadvantages of Blockchain Subnets

Blockchain subnets are a relatively new concept. It started with the idea of "Sharding", where a blockchain network is partitioned in smaller shards. Croman et al. were the first who discussed "sharding" as a potential approach to address blockchain scalability issues in their position paper published in 2016 [10]. The rapid growth of internet of things (IoT) applications has led to a significant role in the development of blockchain subnets. As part of their research about blockchain technology as warrant for quality of services, Viriyasitavat et al. have suggested the use of an overlay subnetwork in 2019 [30]. These two citations highlight the scalability advantages of subnets. Partitioning a blockchain network into subnets can potentially improve scalability by allowing for parallel processing of transactions. This can alleviate congestion and increase the overall transaction throughput [10]. Shortly after the enhanced scalability through subnets was thematized, the tailored consensus mechanisms were investigated. Subnets enable the adoption of different consensus mechanisms tailored to specific requirements.

This flexibility can enhance the performance, security, and energy efficiency of subnets. The main idea behind the tailored consensus mechanisms is that one consensus algorithm cannot fit every application [11]. Also, by partitioning the entire blockchain network in subnets, privacy and confidentiality is increased. Blockchain subnets can offer improved privacy and confidentiality by segregating sensitive data within specific channels. Only a certain group of peers have access to the respective channel. This helps protect the privacy of transactions and sensitive information. Finally, a significant advantage of blockchain subnets is its enhanced interoperability. Subnets can facilitate interoperability by enabling the exchange of assets, data, or information among different blockchain networks. This can foster collaboration and create a unified ecosystem across multiple chains. The latest developments on interoperability include protocols that allow cross-subnet messages to be transferred safely without any third-party involvement [13]. Such advance in the blockchain technology provides even more potential to track & trace applications based on blockchain subnets. Subnets contribute to the blockchain technology evolvement. Yet, subnets exhibit a couple of disadvantages that need to be understood. Building up the communication among enterprises not only within the subnets but also, if required, across the subnets requires additional effort. The logistics enterprise architecture becomes more complex and requires more management overhead. In particular, subnets render the blockchain more complex due to more sophisticated protocols and algorithms. Coordinating consensus mechanisms, maintaining cross-chain communication, and managing different subnets require careful design and governance. Equally, by adding another layer to the blockchain network, subnets have their own security risks. Each additional subnet introduces new attack surfaces and potential vulnerabilities.

Securing multiple channels, managing inter-chain communication, and preventing cross-channel attacks pose substantial security challenges that need to be addressed. Above that, each additional subnet needs to have a clear purpose. Without validation of its purpose, an extra subnet is a mere source for fragmentation. This can result in reduced network effects [6]. In this context the network effects diminish the more subnets exist within a blockchain system. Since less peers interact with each other, within the subnet fragmentation can hamper interoperability efforts and hinder the development of a cohesive blockchain ecosystem. Not only the creation of each blockchain network subnet requires assistance, but they also need to be supported while running. Especially coordinating consensus mechanisms across different subnets can be challenging. In case of private blockchains without a third-party certificate authority, an effective incentive mechanism must be in place to encourage participants to remain honest and cooperative within their respective subnets, too. Ensuring overall network security, fairness, and consistency while allowing for independent consensus rules requires careful coordination and potentially introduces inter-chain communication overhead.

3.3 Track & Trace Architecture Levels with BCT

For building a blockchain network based on track & trace it is essential to know about the different architecture levels. The digital enterprise architecture requirements matrix forms a helpful foundation to outline the information flow from the track & trace logger to the end user [23]. The original requirements matrix is based on the TOGAF business service layers and the ISA95 integration of corporate control systems [23]. The technical column was adopted as a link to the original table (Table 1). It highlights what the track & trace application based on BCT should resolve. In the modification for the track & trace solution based on blockchain, the two further columns blockchain level description and track & trace details are added (Table 1). Both columns provide answers to the technical challenges that need to be addressed. Part of the input for both newly added columns originates from the architecture of the proposed blockchain-based product lifecycle management figure [24]. The hardware level, L0, comprises the track & trace logger. These loggers can serve as location and event transponders. Additionally, they transmit further local information like temperature data. Liquids that need to be kept below or above a temperature threshold can be monitored. In the precision engineering industry, temperature control plays a role during transportation for optics and chemical equipment. Optical precision devices, such as lenses, mirrors, and prisms, are susceptible to changes in temperature. Temperature control during transportation helps prevent thermal expansion or contraction, which can impact their optical performance and alignment. Temperature control is even more relevant in the pharmaceutical and nutrition industries. For instance, biological and pharmaceutical products often require temperature-controlled transportation to maintain the stability of their active product ingredients. This ensures accurate analysis and prevents degradation or denaturation. In L1 the loggers are linked to smart gateways by means of smart assets such as GPS, sensors, RFID tags and readers, QR codes, etc. [24]. At this level, data is collected.

Although it is helpful to streamline the data collection devices, the smart gateway allows for gathering all the resulting data from different devices. A smart gateway is not a mandatory requirement, since a device can also directly transfer data to, e.g., a cloud. However, smart gateways are a useful middleware between the hardware and the database storage in L2. The most prevalent type of data storage is the cloud. It has replaced the former on-site or local storage. Depending on the use case, enterprises can also opt for a combination of cloud and fog data storage. Here, the installation of a smart gateway is suggested, since data security and privacy, temporary storage, data preprocessing, etc. can be conducted more efficiently with a smart gateway [1].

The blockchain level description for L2 is the blockchain information system (BIS). This component ensures that the incoming data are validated, if necessary cleaned, and encrypted. Then the final hash data, including keys, are created, and broadcasted to the blockchain network [24].

Table 1. DEA requirement matrix for track & trace blockchain.

TOGAF business service layer	ISA 95 level	Architecture level matrix		
		Technical challenge	Blockchain level description	Track & trace details
Physical	L0	IT/OT connection	Hardware	Track & trace logger
	L1	Many controllers with different data points	Smart gateway	QR code, RFID chip, Sensor, GPS, etc
Logical	L2	Real-time information access	Blockchain information service (BIS)	Database storage
	L3	Information proliferation	Blockchain network layer	Channels and subnets
Service	L4	Interoperability standards	Application layer	SCM system
	L5	User interface	Service layer	User experience

The corresponding blockchain network layer represents the core component of the entire architecture level matrix (Table 1) and the track & trace blockchain architecture (Fig. 3). Its main components are the smart contract, consensus protocol, and the underlying cryptography [24]. The consensus protocol makes sure that every new block that is added to the blockchain is a unique version of the truth that is agreed upon by all the nodes in the blockchain. The common agreement is determined by the consensus algorithm. It aims at finding a common agreement among nodes, and ultimately peers, in the blockchain network. The consensus process is a prerequisite for creating the smart contract [24]. The next level, L3, is the application layer. The track & trace blockchain network unfolds its benefits if connected to the participating enterprises' applications (Fig. 3). Behind every node there is a subnet peer and behind every peer there is an enterprise. Concerning L4, it is assumed that all the participating enterprises have at least one enterprise resource planning (ERP) system. Most likely, they also run a supply chain management (SCM) system or application. A SCM system's main purpose is to record goods movements. The technical challenge of establishing interoperability standards can often be overcome by APIs. Alternatively, SDKs can be used for connecting proprietary software, for example mobile logistics applications. Larger SCM systems are supposedly connected to the track & trace blockchain network via the BIS. The main challenge of the last level L5 is the user interface. The real-time information stemming from L2 needs to be conveyed understandably. Here, the key is designing a user interface that makes track & trace information accessible to the authorized users within the subnet, and, possibly to a restricted degree, within the entire blockchain. Processes should be monitorable across the different levels. Eventually, the user experience needs to be considered at the last level.

4 Track & Trace Data Flow and Block Structure

After finishing the preparation of the blockchain build-up and having detailed the track & trace blockchain architecture, the data flow and block structure are focused on. Both topics conclude this paper's research on how to use BCT for enhancing an enterprise's integrated traceability.

4.1 Information Flow from and to a Blockchain Network

Based on the architecture level matrix in Table 1, the information flow from and to the blockchain network is presented. Figure 4 outlines the main data flow in accordance with the levels. The six different architecture levels result in a total of eight main data flows. Four of them are executed outside and the remaining four are executed inside the blockchain network boundaries. Together they display the complete information flow from and to the blockchain (Fig. 4).

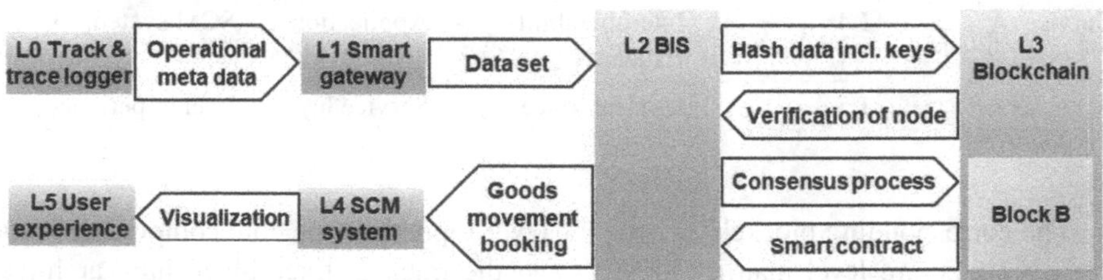

Fig. 4. Track & trace block structure.

The first data flow contains the operational meta data coming from the track & trace loggers. These meta data can be collected by various devices and technologies. The more variation in the devices and technologies, the more important becomes a smart gateway. It combines on the one hand the logger ID and on the other hand the raw data about location, events, temperature, etc. to a data set. This data set is forwarded to the blockchain information system (BIS). As a data gatekeeper for the track & trace blockchain, the BIS converts the data set into a Hyperledger Fabric data format. This is the first of the blockchain's internal operations. The second internal data flow is about the authenticity verification of the request. Either a separate requestor or a peer with a certification authority can execute this verification. The third transaction within the blockchain is considered an information since it links the block to the respective transaction. This newly created and verified block is the basis for the smart contract of the internal transaction number four. The blockchain keeps track of the relevant information and shares it with all peers within the respective subnet. In this manner, a central system for transactions is redundant and replaced by distributed blockchain models as the Hyperledger Fabric. The smart contract details are interpreted as goods movements in the adjacent systems of the involved enterprises. Referring to Fig. 4, the delivery of an optical measure equipment by the Forwarder Y to the Distributor serves as an example. After the creation of the smart contract, this information leaves the blockchain network and is issued to the adjacent SCM systems. The smart contract leads to a goods movement in both involved organisations. Ownership of the transported goods is transferred from Forwarder Y to the Distributor in this third information flow outside of the blockchain network.

The last information flow of the entire track & trace blockchain architecture concerns the visualization. The surplus or the reduction in stock of the involved SCM system is visualized in a graphical user interface. The visualization can be provided directly in the SCM system. Yet, in correspondence with the architecture level matrix, it is suggested that the resultant goods movements are displayed on a mobile application dashboard. The information flow from and to the blockchain in Fig. 4 is a simplified version. It represents the standard data flow and does not include rejections or rechecks, nor does it include data flows that skip a level.

4.2 Track & Trace Block Structure

As depicted in Fig. 4, the last two transactions inside the blockchain network also comprise the block. The block is the core of the blockchain and the smart contracts. Smart contracts refer to the blocks that are stored in ledgers owned by every peer in the blockchain network (Fig. 3). One ledger can contain several blocks. One block can comprise one or more transactions and, finally, one or more items are part of the transaction (Fig. 5). For technical reasons the block ID as well as the lock time need to be included. For giving the block a purpose, the header and at least one transaction value are added, too. With the transaction data, data fields that are specific for the track & trace layer are appended. A unique logger ID, the shipment origin, shipment destination, current location of the event, and one or more items are part of the transaction data. Last of all, the item data of the track & trace blockchain network are defined. Common value fields are the load carrier, the physical product, the product's expiry date and its owner. Another field is dedicated to the partner. This partner can be the forwarder, in case the product is being shipped, or a warehouse, in case the product is (temporarily) being stored, or a production site in case the product is being used as a component or is being modified.

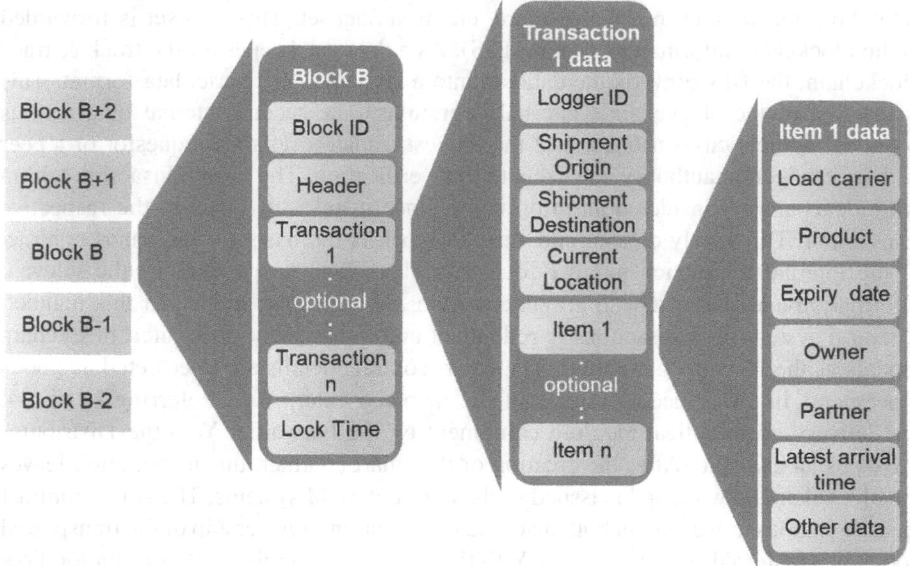

Fig. 5. Track & trace block structure.

The partner can be the same as the owner or another enterprise. It is also helpful to add a field for the latest arrival time. In comparison to the estimated arrival time, the latest arrival time needs to be updated if the shipment or production step is held up [26]. Finally, depending on the requirements within the particular subnet, other data can be added to the transaction values.

5 Conclusions and Outlook

Blockchain-based track & trace solutions are not only feasible but have future relevance. The rapid changes in technology regarding the automated traceability of goods have increased in speed with the introduction of private blockchains. Both from an academic and practitioner perspective it is difficult to follow the latest technological advancements. Second to the financial sector, the logistics sector has a wide variety of possible applications based on blockchain technology. One of them are track & trace applications. Track & trace solution implementation is a complex subject. The integration into a multi-enterprise blockchain with two or more subnets even adds complexity. Several departments within and outside of the implementing enterprise need to be involved. For this reason, the paper started with the digital enterprise architecture (DEA) model. Next to ensuring that the most important aspects are considered it also helps to understand how blockchain technology works in an intercompany setup. Although creating a consortium-based blockchain platform requires thorough planning and an agreement on several details among all participants, the advantages of using a multi-channel subnet Hyperledger Fabric for the implementation of a track & trace solution are immense. Regarding privacy, transactions are authenticated, relationships over computer networks are secured, and access is controllable. Regarding trust, all the transactions are verified and endorsed by the supply chain partners. The smart contracts, key to the track & trace application transactions, offer a database-embedded business logic that validates transactions among the peers. Furthermore, practitioners and researchers alike are hinted at the pitfalls and chances of a track & trace blockchain network. The novelty is the introduction of blockchain subnets. They offer enterprises the possibility to segregate different divisions of their business to different subnets. Hence, although being in the same blockchain network, the purchasing division can be separated from the sales division. In comparison, a blockchain with subnets can reduce transaction confirmation times. Resulting in higher processing performance of smart contracts and resource efficiency. The distributed workload across two or more subnets can reduce the storage and computational requirements for each individual node. In contrast, the limitation of this setup mainly concerns organizational challenges. The governance and the communication among the participants of the blockchain consortium require proper planning and regular agreement meetings. This applies especially at the beginning of the project when the consensus and the consensus mechanism need to be defined. With the outline of the advantages and disadvantages of subnets, enterprises obtain guidance on what topics to focus on. By splitting up the network into subnets, participants of the consortium do not need to have the same supply chain systems in the background. Also, within a single enterprise, one subnet can be connected to a system of records whereas the other subnet can be connected to a system of engagement. Depending on the track & trace use case as well as the peers connected to the blockchain channel, the subnet is compatible to an enterprise's bimodal IT. The build-up of the track & trace blockchain network including the split into two or more subnets is depicted concisely. By means of the DEA the broader architecture picture is addressed. Practitioners and academics alike are presented a path how to successfully start a track & trace integration. Combining literature with software white papers, a detailed focus on the block structure for track & trace purposes is provided. This is of importance because the block is simultaneously the core to the smart contracts. Track & trace blockchains with smart contracts offer several opportunities. From a technology perspective, the interface of a BIS with a SCM can trigger financial transaction immediately after a track & trace event. Contrarily, conventional approaches rather validate the financial transactions, succeeding an exchange of goods and services, by means of a labour-intensive check. Whole teams, often based off- or nearshored, try to verify whether the asynchronized payments, both incoming and outgoing, are correct. Concerning BCT, future research could focus on cross-operable blockchains. The latest versions of distributed architectural blockchain models offer further opportunities in collaborative manufacturing. Equally, the proposed approach, from requirement catalogue to the track & trace block, need to be tested in practice.

So far, the blockchain solution based on track & trace is a feasibility study highlighting that especially the trust barriers within a supply chain network can be overcome. Although the blockchain solution based on track & trace have already been realized in the last decade, they do not involve blockchain subnets or comprise a very few blockchain peers. The authors predict that the fast involvement of artificial intelligence (AI) will speed up track & trace solutions based on blockchain subnets. On the positive side AI might support the complex setup and on the negative side, AI might increase counterfeit and cybersecurity risks in the supply chain network.

References

1. Aazam, M., Huh, E.N.: Fog computing and smart gateway based communication for cloud of things. In: Proceedings – 2014 International Conference on Future Internet of Things and Cloud, FiCloud 2014, (August), pp. 464–470 (2014). https://doi.org/10.1109/FiCloud.2014.83
2. Alladi, T., Chamola, V., Parizi, R.M., Choo, R.: Blockchain applications for industry 4.0 and industrial IoT: a review. IEEE **7**, 176935–176951 (2019). https://doi.org/10.1109/ACCESS.2019.2956748
3. Álvarez-Díaz, N., Herrera-Joancomartì, J., Caballero-Gil, P.: 'Smart contracts based on blockchain for logistics management'. In: ACM International Conference Proceeding Series, (2020) (2017). https://doi.org/10.1145/3109761.3158384
4. Barenji, A.V., Montreuil, B.: Open logistics: blockchain-enabled trusted hyperconnected logistics platform. Sensors **22**(13), 4699 (2022). https://doi.org/10.3390/s22134699
5. Barranechea, M.J., Jenkins, T.: Digital: Disrupt or die. (2014). Available at: https://www.opentext.com/file_source/OpenText/en_US/PDF/OpenText-Article-Digital-Disrupt-or-Die-EN.pdf
6. Bharadwaj, A., El Sawy, O.A., Pavlou, P.A., Venkatraman, N.: Digital business strategy: toward a next generation of insights. In: MIS Quarterly **37**(2), 471–482 (2013). Available at: http://www.misq.org/misq/downloads/download/editorial/581/
7. Bieler, D., Bennett, M.: Disentangle hype from reality: Blockchain's potential for IoT solutions, For CIOs, (November), Forrester Research, Inc., pp. 1–19 (2016)
8. Chhikara, N., Jaglan, S., Sindhu, N., Venthodika, A.: Importance of traceability in food supply chain for brand protection and food safety systems implementation. Ann. Biol. **34**(2), 111–118 (2018)
9. Copigneaux, B., et al.: Blockchain for supply chains and international trade, Directorate-General for Parliamentary Research Services (EPRS) of the Secretariat of the European Parliament. Brussels: European Union, pp. 1–156 (2020). https://doi.org/10.2861/957600. Available at: https://publica.fraunhofer.de/handle/publica/300936
10. Croman, K., et al.: On Scaling Decentralized Blockchains: A Position Paper', Financial Cryptography And Data Security: Revised Selected Papers 20, pp. 106–125. Springer, Berlin/Heidelberg, Germany (2016)
11. de la Rocha, A., Kokoris-Kogias, L., Soares, J.M., Vukolić, M.: Hierarchical consensus: a horizontal scaling framework for blockchains. In: 2022 IEEE 42nd International Conference on Distributed Computing Systems Workshops (ICDCSW), pp. 45–52 (2022)
12. Dhar Dwivedi, A., et al.: Blockchain and artificial intelligence for 5G-enabled Internet of Things: challenges, opportunities, and solutions. Trans. Emerging Tel. Tech. (July). (2021). https://doi.org/10.1002/ett.4329
13. Gauthier, T., Dan, S., Hadji, M., Del Pozzo, A., Amoussou-Guenou, Y.: Topos: A secure, trustless, and decentralized interoperability protocol (2022). Available at: https://arxiv.org/pdf/2206.03481v1.pdf
14. Gnimpieba, D.R., Nait-Sidi-Moh, A., Durand, D., Fortin, J.: Using Internet of Things technologies for a collaborative supply chain: application to tracking of pallets and containers. In: Procedia Computer Science, pp. 550–557 (2015). https://doi.org/10.1016/j.procs.2015.07.251
15. Heagney, J.: Fundamentals of project management, 5th edn. American Management Association, New York (2016) Available at: http://lccn.loc.gov/2016004879
16. Hechler, E., Oberhofer, M., Schaeck, T.: AI and blockchain. In: Deploying AI in the Enterprise: IT Approaches for Design, DevOps, Governance, Change Management, Blockchain, and Quantum Computing, pp. 253–271. Apress, Berkeley, CA (2020). https://doi.org/10.1007/978-1-4842-6206-1_11

17. Helo, P., Shamsuzzoha, A.H.M.: Real-time supply chain: a blockchain architecture for project deliveries. Rob. Comput.-Integr. Manuf. **63**, article 101909. (2020). https://doi.org/10.1016/j.rcim.2019.101909
18. Hyperledger. 'Channels', Hyperledger-fabric docs main documentation (2022). Available at: https://hyperledger-fabric.readthedocs.io/en/release-2.2/channels.html
19. Hyperledger. The ordering service, Hyperledger-fabric docs main documentation (2022). Available at: https://hyperledger-fabric.readthedocs.io/en/release-2.2/orderer/ordering_service.html#phase-two-ordering-and-packaging-transactions-into-blocks
20. Hyperledger. Writing your first chaincode, Hyperledger-fabric docs main documentation (2022). Available at: https://hyperledger-fabric.readthedocs.io/en/release-2.2/chaincode4ade.html?highlight=API
21. Kache, F., Seuring, S.: Challenges and opportunities of digital information at the intersection of big data analytics and supply chain management. Int. J. Oper. Prod. Manag. **37**(1), 10–36 (2017)
22. Kagermann, H., Wahlster, W., Helbig, J.: Recommendations for implementing the strategic initiative INDUSTRIE 4.0. In: Final report of the Industrie 4.0 WG. National Academy of Science and Engineering, p. 82 (2013)
23. Körsgen, H., Rabe, M.: Track and trace based on the digital enterprise architecture concept. In: ICE Conference 2023. IEEE, Edinburgh, Scotland (2023)
24. Liu, X.L., Wang, W.M., Guo, H., Barenji, A.V., Li, Z., Huang, G.Q.: Industrial blockchain based framework for product lifecycle management in industry 4.0. Robotics and Computer-Integrated Manufacturing, vol. 63. Elsevier Ltd, (November 2019) (2020). https://doi.org/10.1016/j.rcim.2019.101897
25. Gupta, M.: Blockchain for dummies, IBM Limited Edition. John Wiley & Sons Inc, Hoboken, NJ (2017)
26. Schill, K., Scholz-Reiter, B.: Artificial intelligence and logistics (AILOG-2011). In: Frommberger, L. (ed.) International Joint Conference on Artificial Intelligence, pp. 1–72. Barcelona, Spain (2011)
27. Shi-Wan, L., Miller, B., Durand, J., Bleakley, G., Chigani, A.: The Industrial Internet of Things Volume G1: Reference Architecture Industrial Internet Consortium, (February), pp 1–129. Available at: https://www.iiconsortium.org/pdf/ IIC_PUB_G5_V1.01_PB_20180228.pdf (2017)
28. Stevens, A.: Supply Chain Reference Model for track and trace and serialization in the life science industry. Gartner, Stamford, USA (2015)
29. Szabo, N.: Smart contracts. Available at: https://www.fon.hum.uva.nl/rob/Courses/InformationInSpeech/CDROM/Literature/LOTwinterschool2006/szabo.best.vwh.net/smart.contracts.html (1994)
30. Szabo, N.: Formalizing and securing relationships on public networks. First Monday 2(9) (1997). https://doi.org/10.5210/fm.v2i9.548
31. Viriyasitavat, W., Da Xu, L., Bi, Z., Hoonsopon, D., Charoenruk, N.: Managing QOS of internet-of-things services using blockchain. IEEE Trans. Comput. Soc. Syst. **6**(6), 1357–1368 (2019)
32. Bellavista, P., et al.: Interoperable blockchains for highly-integrated supply chains in collaborative manufacturing. Sensors **21**(15), 1–21 (2021). https://doi.org/10.3390/s21154955

Virtual Try-On Networks Based on Images with Super Resolution Model

Franco Gallegos, Sebastian Contreras, and Willy Ugarte(✉)

Universidad Peruana de Ciencias Aplicadas, Lima, Peru
{U201610256,U20171D516}@upc.edu.pe, willy.ugarte@upc.pe

Abstract. The main job of a virtual imaging try-on is to transfer a garment to a specific area of an individual's body part. Trying to deform said garment so that it fits in a part of the desired body. Despite some research, the vast majority use a low-quality image resolution of 192×256 pixels, limiting the visual satisfaction of online users. Analyzing this visual limitation, we find that the vast majority of the algorithms use these mentioned measures to obtain better performance and optimization during their training, since while the number of pixels is smaller, in the same way, their execution time will be less in the generation. of segments or masks of garments and body parts. Despite having better performance and optimization, quality and pixel size are also of the utmost importance, since it is in the final resolution that the result for the user is appreciated. To address this challenge, we propose a super-resolution extension module, added to the ACGPN model. Such a module gets the resulting image from the ACGPN model, and then with the help of computer vision aims to increase the resolution to 768×1024 pixels with minimal loss of quality. For this, a comparison of models that perform this task of increasing the resolution is made. Finally, it is quantitatively shown that the proposal obtains better results.

Keywords: Virtual try-on · Super resolution models · Computer vision · Generative network model

1 Introduction

In 2020, e-commerce has increased exponentially thanks to digitalization and the COVID-19 pandemic.

Peruvian Chamber of Electronic Commerce (CAPECE) indicates that e-commerce in Peru increased by 50%[1], the number of new companies entering that market increased by 400% and the number of purchase shipments reached 300%. Likewise, online consumption in the fashion industry was one of the industries that increased the most, by 4,451%.

[1] Peruvian Chamber of Electronic Commerce (CAPECE) - https://www.capece.org.pe/wp-content/uploads/2021/03/Observatorio-Ecommerce-Peru-2020-2021.pdf.

S. Terzi et al. (Eds.): IN4PL 2023, CCIS 1886, pp. 182–194, 2023.
https://doi.org/10.1007/978-3-031-49339-3_11

CAPECE states that 40% of shoppers still prefer to see, touch and try on the product before buying it. Thus, in the context of online apparel shopping, shoppers are unable to try on clothes. And, consequently, they feel insecure when making the purchase and it derives in clothes returns. 15% of buyers who return clothes are because they do not fit properly at the time of delivery[2]. Similarly, Camones and Gago's study [8] shows that 15% of shoppers who return clothes are because the clothes were not what they expected.

A naive approach to this problem is to superimpose the selected clothing on the image of the person. This usually does not work because the image of the clothing must be superimposed on the image of the person taking into account several factors such as the pose of the person, body parts such as hair or arms that are placed on top of the clothing of the original image of the person. Therefore, models such as pose estimation and image segmentation must be used to obtain this information.

The studies in VITON [7], ACGPN [22], and CLOTH-VTON+ [14] propose solutions for generating clothing tests with small images, specifically 192 by 256 pixels. This is because the most used dataset for model training is VITON [7], which only has images of these dimensions. Thus, the quality of the image generated by the models are not detailed when used in a real environment.

The limitations of the model used are:

- The categories of clothing that works with the model is limited to the dataset. Specifically, the dataset used has upper clothing for men and women.
- The model only generates 2D clothing test, so it does not take into account the size of the clothing and the person.

Our main contributions are as follows:

- We developed an extension of the ACGPN [22] model, lifting the limitation of the resulting image quality, going from dimensions 192 by 256 pixels to 728 by 1024 pixels and that it can be tested with images of garments of more categories, such as: men's and women's upper clothing.

The results of our paper are divided into 2 parts. First, a Super Resolution model comparison is performed against the DressCode [16] dataset containing images of people in clothing. The comparison will have as metrics the inference time and metrics that allow measuring the quality of the image with respect to the original image. Second, from the above comparison, the super-resolution model that best fits the ACGPN model is added and a comparison is made against the ACGPN model and the Cubic Interpolation technique to enlarge the images in the VITON [7] test dataset.

The paper details the following points: First, existing solutions similar to ours will be shown in Sect. 2. Second, we will detail our contribution from the theory, dataset and methods used in Sect. 3. Also, in Sect. 4, we will comment

[2] Future of Shopping - Global Report - Snap Inc. - https://assets.ctfassets.net/inb32lme5009/qgbcw9CEHEqT6Q9iKBChz/db4138fd22e37c87fb873a3eb65486ca/Snap_-_Final_Global_Report.pdf.

on the validation performed to the proposed model and the results of the experimentation. Finally, we will discuss the main conclusions of the project and future work that can improve the line of research in Sect. 5.

2 Related Works

Now, we will explore some scientific works related to virtual clothing testing, for comparing and positioning our proposal.

Image-based virtual testing methods have recently emerged as an attractive alternative to traditional solutions. According to research [20], UVIRT is an unsupervised algorithm that leaves aside the classical algorithms that use, labeled data: segmentation mask, edges and image analysis, in order to obtain different results. Its contribution is the lower training cost and not needing to pre-process the images. Despite having quantitatively superior results in performance to C-VTON [5], being this 92.55 versus 122.83 in FID, the results show limited photorealism, that is, the resulting image presents malformations and excessive pixelation. Extending this, the algorithm used by us presents a higher quality photorealism, since images of 720×1024 pixels are used, despite being compressed to go through the virtual generation process, they tend not to pixelate excessively.

To correct this error Jun Xu et al. [21] proposed as an input a combination on attribute transformations and local representation, which focuses on having an explicit deformation (of the garment) and thus obtaining realistic results. However, its main limitation is that their proposal does not clearly deform the garment on the person if it is of very low quality or the image of the garment is not visible in its entirety. To provide a solution to these erroneous deformations, Minar et al. [14] propose CloTH-VTON+, since it uses a dataset of predefined images as pre-training along with their model that can support complex poses of the person and still have a clear deformation of the garment. Its main limitation is having results with very small images (256×192 pixels), which impairs the visibility of the result for the end user. Compared to our proposal, the results shown to the end user are in larger measurements (768×1024 pixels), since there is a module within the flow where it helps to enlarge the measurements without having much loss of sharpness for the end user. and thus obtain better visual results.

VITON-HD [3] proposes a higher quality dataset (1024×768 pixels) to alleviate the above problem, and with a normalization technique to help fit the garment details on the person. However, the normalization process causes overtraining with high cost. Compared to this proposal, we propose a training that does not lead to high cost. C-VTON [5] proposes to improve the quality of the results from various misaligned images and convincingly transfer the garment to the person. However, its limitation is to use only women's garments for training and not having easy accessibility to its proposal from a real ecommerce. Unlike our algorithm which uses images of both men and women.

In this article, we propose an extension of the ACGPN algorithm, with an enlargement of the image, greater than 192×256 pixels, with little loss of quality, using a super resolution algorithm.

3 Main Contribution

In this section, the main concepts used in our work are presented and our contribution is described in detail.

3.1 Context

Here, we present the essential concepts to understand our proposal.

Definition 1 (Computational Vision [19]): A branch of artificial intelligence that focuses on giving computers the ability to extract information from photos, videos and other visual sources. According to Szeliski's book [19], computational vision "describes the world we see in one or more images and reconstructs its properties, such as shape, lighting, and color distributions".

Definition 2 (Generative Adversarial Networks [6]): Consists of a generative system of two machine learning models, typically neural networks, that compete with each other. As mentioned in the study by Goodfellow et al. [6], the first model, called generator, is in charge of generating new data that try to simulate as much as possible real data with which the model is trained. While the second model is called discriminator, which is in charge of classifying the data it receives as real or false.

In Fig. 1 shows the classic architecture of a GAN, where it can be seen that there is a generator that produces false images and there is also a dataset from which real images are obtained. At the top is the discriminator that is responsible for discerning which of the images is true and false.

Definition 3 (VTO models [7]): Acronym for "Virtual Try-On". These are computational vision models that focus on the generation of images that allow garments to be tested virtually from images. According to the paper by Han et al. [7], the goal of VTON is, having an image of a person X and an image of a garment Y, where the image Y is transposed in a "natural" way on the image "X" preserving body parts and pose information.

In Fig. 2, the result of a Try-On model called HR-VITON is observed, which in the left column has the input images for the model, image of the person and image of the clothing, and in the right column the result of the model is observed.

Definition 4 (DressCode [16]): It is a modern dataset of paired images, between a garment and an image of a person wearing that garment. This dataset is in high resolution (1024×768 pixels), and the dress models are in full body, as well as having a wide variety of men's and women's clothing.

This dataset was proposed in order to generate a greater advance in the field of virtual testing, since the great variety, and the use of high quality images, help in the generation of tests with higher quality results.

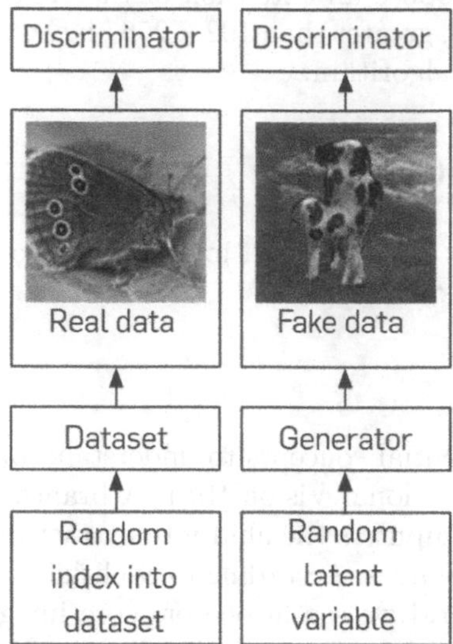

Fig. 1. Classic architecture of a GAN presented by Goodfellow et al. [6].

Fig. 2. Result of clothing test of the ACGPN model by Yang et al. [11].

Fig. 3. Example of the Dresscode dataset [16].

The Fig. 3, shows a pair of paired images, being the garment alone and the person wearing the garment.

Definition 5 (Super Resolution [23]): It is used within computational vision, since it is an algorithm based on deep learning methods, in charge of obtaining an output or result in high resolution. It should be noted that each super-resolution algorithm has a different architecture, according to its objectives and proposed optimization methods. For example, the super resolution model called SRCNN is based on a simple CNN which only uses 3 layers of convolutional networks for. training, while the FSRCNN algorithm adds more complex layers called deconvolution or transposed convolution, so it is based on nearest neighbor interpolation.

In Fig. 4, shows the common architecture of a super-resolution model, with the low-resolution image on the right side and the larger, higher-resolution image on the right.

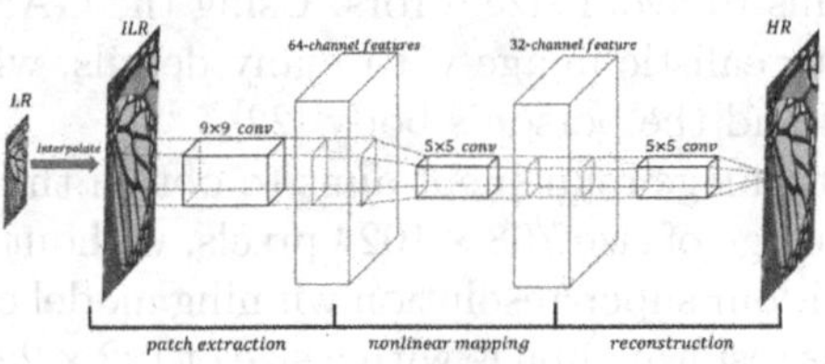

Fig. 4. Example of a super resolution architecture by Yang et al. [23].

3.2 Method

The main contribution of our proposal aims to extend the ACGPN algorithm, which generates a virtual clothing proof, with a Super Resolution model, which will help to generate larger images. Without losing much quality, since so far ACGPN only displays images with a size of 192 by 256 pixels.

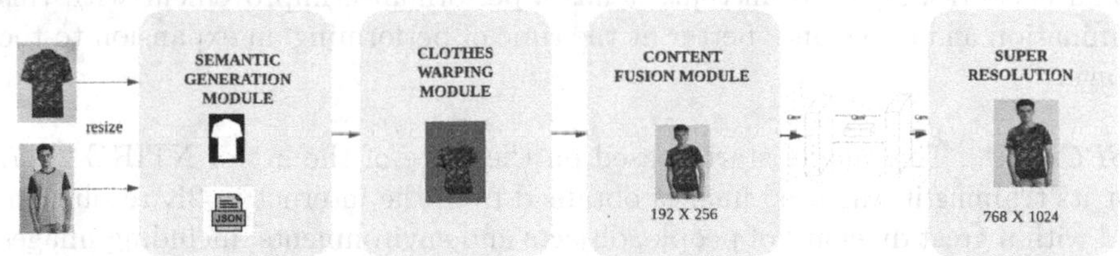

Fig. 5. Main flow of garment test generation.

In Fig. 5, we can see the main flow of our proposal, starting with the insertion of the image of the garment and the person. And in the following paragraphs the detail will be explained.

Resizing: From the algorithm, both the image of the garment and the image of the person are loaded in ".png" format, which is resized to a size of 192×256 pixels, and once it reaches these dimensions, it is saved in a folder.

Semantic Generation Module (SGM): It is a module of the ACGPN model, where through conditional generative networks (cGAN) it is responsible for obtaining the region of the garment to the smallest detail and is also responsible for obtaining the shape of the person's body, all this through the generation of masks and labels to differentiate the segmentations of the parts of the body and the region of the garment [22].

Clothes Warping Module (CWM): This module aims to adjust the incoming garment, to the region of the destination garment, using a transformation that is fed by a refinement network, this in order to generate greater detail [22].

Content Fusion Module (CFM): In this module, the region of the target garment and the region of the body parts are obtained, all in a measurement of 192×256 pixels, this to avoid size errors. Using the GAN networks, they are joined to form a photorealistic image with many details, where you can see the union of the garment and the person's body [22].

Image Refinement: Image refinement aims to obtain the resulting image and transform it into an image of size 768×1024 pixels, without losing much quality. In this module, there is our super-resolution winning model called ESPCN, where it obtains the previous resulting image with a size of 192×256 pixels and transfer through its computer networks to enlarge them to the aforementioned size and with this the final result is obtained as a better larger without much loss of sharpness.

3.3 Super Resolution Models

The 4 super resolution models to compare are presented.

EDSR [12]. It is one of the best model in Super Resolution, based on a deep neural network called DCNN, it is EDSR, its main contribution is due to the optimization in the elimination of modules that are not necessary for its conventional networks. Apart from that, it has a performance improvement with this elimination and it becomes better at the time of performing an expansion to the image.

ESPCN [18]. This model starts based on the state of the art of NTIRE 2017. For its training it was used images obtained from the internet in 2K resolution, and with a great diversity of people, objects and environments, including images with low light. After that, a series of partitions were performed, between images, compression rates per bit, CORNIA score, enlargements and reductions, all so that the algorithm can have a great capacity for any out-of-focus or out-of-square images.

FSRCNN [4]. It is a model that is based on another model called SRCNNN. The FSRCNN algorithm redesigns the base structure of the previous algorithm in order to accelerate and improve efficiency. Its structure is divided into 3 aspects. First, it introduces a convolutional layer, to map directly from the low resolution image to the high resolution. Secondly, the algorithm has a layer that transforms the image with specific dimensions to pass the process and then expand them with the result. And third, it adapts the filter sizes for each mapping.

LapSRN [10]. This model is focused on reducing the amount of parameters and the large amounts of execution times using SR algorithms. The structure of this algorithm is a deep Laplacian pyramid network, as it is based on progressively building the subband residuals of High Resolution images in the layers or levels of the pyramid. Another important feature that helps the optimization of the algorithm is that they use a preprocessing with bicubic interpolation, which extracts the features directly from the image.

4 Experiments

4.1 Experimental Protocol

This section explains the experiments and results of our project. Also, the environment is detailed so that the experiment can be replicated.

The comparison of the image size increase models and the comparison of the SR model with the OpenCV library was performed on the Google Collaborate platform with Intel Xeon CPU @2.20 GHz, NVIDIA T4 Tensor Core GPU with 12 GB RAM. The application requires Python 3.7, Pytorch 2.0.1+cu118, Pillow 8.4 and Opencv 4.7. Finally, the comparison code can be found at the following link: ""and the Rest API code at the following link: "".

Two data sets were used to perform the tests.

For the first test, 1000 images extracted from the DressCode dataset, which has images of people, were used. For this, the images were reduced to 192 by 256 pixels, pretending to be images resulting from clothing tests. Then, the models were run for each of the 1000 images measuring with the corresponding metrics and saving every 100 images a JSON file representing the metrics checkpoint. The process took more than 12 h. Finally, the last generated JSON checkpoint was loaded and the averages of each saved metric were calculated.

For the second test, we used the test version of the VITON dataset, which has preprocessed images of clothing and people. First, the clothing test generation was performed with the VITON dataset and resulted in 2032 clothing test images. Then, for each image we ran the enlargement with OpenCV's Cubic Interpolation and ESPCN model. Every 100 images, a JSON was saved containing the state of the metrics up to that point of the test. The test lasted more than 5 h. Once the process was finished, the last JSON generated was loaded and the averages of the test metrics were calculated.

Two datasets were used due to the characteristics and objectives of the tests. In the first test, the DressCode dataset was used, because the objective was to determine which of the 4 models to compare had the capacity to enlarge an image of 192 by 256 pixels to one of 768 by 1024 pixels without losing its quality and not adding more time to the inference of the ACGPN model, for which we needed a dataset containing images of size 768 by 1024 pixels approximately. The DressCode dataset has that size of images while the VITON dataset has images of 192 by 256 pixels only. For the second comparison, it was convenient to use the VITON dataset because it had the image of the person and clothing preprocessed for the ACGPN model, which reduced a significant amount of time in the testing process.

4.2 Results

Metrics : The metrics used are divided into two types, those that measure the image generated by the model against the original image (with reference) and those that measure the images generated by the model without a reference. Likewise, the first type of metrics is used for the first experiment and the second type for the second experiment.

- Metrics with reference
  1. SSIM: Measures the similarity between two images. As a research mentions [1], the similarity measurement is performed under 3 characteristics of images: Luminosity, Contrast and Structure. Also, the value range of the index is between -1 and 1, where the value 1 indicates that the images are very similar while if the value is close to -1 it means that the images are different.
  2. PSNR: This metric helps to measure the quality of the relationship between two images in terms of signal-to-noise, which is metric to measure the quality between the original image and the generated image [13]. Its metric is measured in the higher the PSNR, the better the quality of the generated image.
- Metrics without reference
  1. Sharpness: Metric that measures of measuring the sharpness or blur of an image in circumstances of blur. To calculate the sharpness, they propose, instead of measuring the width of the border by counting pixels, to calculate the difference of differences of values of the pixels with respect to the difference of pixels in a specific area [9]. To do this, a median filter is applied to the original image to remove noise and preserve edges. The edge sharpness measurement is performed for both the x-axis and y-axis. Finally, the two values are combined into one using the Euclidean norm. Its measurement range goes from 0 to the square root of 2, the closer it is to the latter, the sharper the image. It has the following equation:

$$S_I = \sqrt{R_x^2 + R_y^2} \tag{1}$$

     where,
     R_x = number of sharp pixels divided by number of edge pixels on the

x-axis.
R_y = number of sharp pixels divided by number of edge pixels on the y-axis.

2. BRISQUE: Acronym referred to as blind/reference-free image spatial quality evaluator. Metric that quantifies image losses as the presence of distortions [15]. The score is calculated by a support vector regression (SVR), which was trained with a dataset of images that have distortions known as noise and blurring. The value range of the metric goes from 0 to 100 and if the value is lower it means that it has less quality loss while if higher it means that the image possesses more distortions in the image.

Super Resolution Models Comparison. In Table 1, the results of the Super Resolution model comparison are shown. The EDSR model has the best performance in the SSIM and PSNR metrics, however, the time it takes to perform inference is more than 41 s, which makes it unsuitable for use in a real wearable test generation environment. On the other hand, the ESPCN model has the shortest inference time and its performance on the SSIM and PSNR metrics is very close to that of EDSR. This makes it the ideal model for a real environment. Therefore, this model is used for the final comparison.

Table 1. Results of the comparison of SR models using the DressCode dataset.

Models	*Time (seconds)* ↓	*Avg. SSIM* ↑	*Avg. PSNR* ↑
EDSR	41.789	**0.948**	**31.628**
ESPCN	**0.092**	0.938	30.060
FSRCNN	0.104	0.924	29.823
LapSRN	3.508	0.939	30.105

Final Comparison. In Table 2, The results of the final comparison are shown, the ACGPN model with ESPCN obtained the best score in both metrics and the time difference between the models is imperceptible in a real environment. Specifically, in the sharpness metric it obtained an improvement of 5.6% compared to the ACGPN with Cubic Interpolation, meaning that the images generated with the proposed flow have more prominent image edges than the images generated with the ACGPN flow with Cubic Interpolation. On the other hand, the BRISQUE metric tells us that the images generated with the proposed flow have fewer image distortions in the spatial domain than the ACGPN flow with Cubic Interpolation.

Table 2. Results of the final comparison.

Models	*Time (seconds)* ↓	*Avg. Sharpness* ↑	*Avg. BRISQUE* ↓
ACGPN + Cubic Interpolation	**0.002**	0.654	82.697
ACGPN + ESPCN	0.068	**0.691**	**67.348**

5 Conclusions and Perspectives

In the present work an improvement to the ACGPN virtual proof algorithm was sought, which proposed a module, with a model that allows generating proof images of clothing in sizes of 768 by 1024 pixels, this because the original model only resulted in images in resolution of 192×256 pixels, which with these low resolution measures caused a visual deficiency for the end user. For this, with the help of computer vision, a super-resolution model was used, and to demonstrate that it was one of the best, a benchmarking was performed with 4 different models, being the ESPCN model the winner.

With the experiments carried out, it was demonstrated that the ESPCN model has shown better results than the other models. Better results than the other models and also better results than the cubic interpolation model, which is frequently used in opencv. These positive results benefit the end user because they can see their clothing test images, in larger sizes and without much loss of image quality than the original, so the super resolution module helps to improve the existing ACGPN model. It is also important to mention that the project has some limitations. The first limitation of the project is that the clothing tests only work on the upper body, using only body garments such as polo shirts and blouses, and also that they only use one garment at a time. That is, the algorithm only supports one garment at a time. The second limitation is that the model cannot support the volume of the human body, so it only gives as results clothing tests in standard measurements.

Having these two limitations mentioned above, future work is proposed that can focus on them: 1) Models that can generate clothing trials with two or more garments at the same time. To do so, the model must be able to generate evidence of clothing of more types, such as lower body clothing. Since generative models are applied to more domains [17]. In this way, the user can test full body clothing sets or can make combinations with the garments. 2) Another possible approach is that the test model can generate 3D or augmented reality clothing evidence to significantly reduce confidence errors in online clothing purchases. We believe that it is necessary to recreate the image of the person with volume so that the virtual fitting generates a more realistic representation of the garment for the end user, similar to [2,24].

References

1. Borji, A.: Pros and cons of GAN evaluation measures. Comput. Vis. Image Underst. **179**, 41–65 (2019)
2. Castillo-Arredondo, G., Moreno-Carhuacusma, D., Ugarte, W.: PhotoHandler: manipulation of portrait images with StyleGANs using text. In: ICSBT, pp. 73–82. SCITEPRESS (2023)
3. Choi, S., Park, S., Lee, M., Choo, J.: VITON-HD: high-resolution virtual try-on via misalignment-aware normalization. In: CVPR, pp. 14131–14140. Computer Vision Foundation/IEEE (2021)
4. Dong, C., Loy, C.C., Tang, X.: Accelerating the super-resolution convolutional neural network. In: Leibe, B., Matas, J., Sebe, N., Welling, M. (eds.) ECCV 2016. LNCS, vol. 9906, pp. 391–407. Springer, Cham (2016). https://doi.org/10.1007/978-3-319-46475-6_25
5. Fele, B., Lampe, A., Peer, P., Struc, V.: C-VTON: context-driven image-based virtual try-on network. In: WACV, pp. 2203–2212. IEEE (2022)
6. Goodfellow, I.J., et al.: Generative adversarial networks. Commun. ACM **63**(11), 139–144 (2020)
7. Han, X., Wu, Z., Wu, Z., Yu, R., Davis, L.S.: VITON: an image-based virtual try-on network. In: CVPR, pp. 7543–7552. Computer Vision Foundation/IEEE Computer Society (2018)
8. Jara, A.C., Tello, A.M.G.: Factores que interfieren en la decisió n de compra de ropa por internet en mujeres Millennials de Lima Metropolitana. Master's thesis (2018). https://doi.org/10.19083/tesis/624072
9. Kumar, J., Chen, F., Doermann, D.S.: Sharpness estimation for document and scene images. In: IEEE ICPR, pp. 3292–3295 (2012)
10. Lai, W., Huang, J., Ahuja, N., Yang, M.: Deep laplacian pyramid networks for fast and accurate super-resolution. In: IEEE CVPR, pp. 5835–5843 (2017)
11. Lee, S., Gu, G., Park, S., Choi, S., Choo, J.: High-resolution virtual try-on with misalignment and occlusion-handled conditions. In: Avidan, S., Brostow, G., Cissé, M., Farinella, G.M., Hassner, T. (eds.) ECCV 2022. LNCS, vol. 13677, pp. 204–219. Springer, Cham (2022). https://doi.org/10.1007/978-3-031-19790-1_13
12. Lim, B., Son, S., Kim, H., Nah, S., Lee, K.M.: Enhanced deep residual networks for single image super-resolution. In: CVPR Workshops, pp. 1132–1140. IEEE Computer Society (2017)
13. MathWorks: Compute peak signal-to-noise ratio (PSNR) between images. https://www.mathworks.com/help/vision/ref/psnr.html
14. Minar, M.R., Thai, T.T., Ahn, H.: CloTH-VTON+: clothing three-dimensional reconstruction for hybrid image-based virtual try-on. IEEE Access **9**, 30960–30978 (2021)
15. Mittal, A., Moorthy, A.K., Bovik, A.C.: No-reference image quality assessment in the spatial domain. IEEE Trans. Image Process. **21**(12), 4695–4708 (2012)
16. Morelli, D., Fincato, M., Cornia, M., Landi, F., Cesari, F., Cucchiara, R.: Dress code: high-resolution multi-category virtual try-on. In: Avidan, S., Brostow, G., Cissé, M., Farinella, G.M., Hassner, T. (eds.) ECCV 2022. LNCS, vol. 13668, pp. 345–362. Springer, Cham (2022). https://doi.org/10.1007/978-3-031-20074-8_20
17. Pautrat-Lertora, A., Perez-Lozano, R., Ugarte, W.: EGAN: generatives adversarial networks for text generation with sentiments. In: KDIR, pp. 249–256. SCITEPRESS (2022)

18. Shi, W., et al.: Real-time single image and video super-resolution using an efficient sub-pixel convolutional neural network. In: CVPR, pp. 1874–1883. IEEE Computer Society (2016)
19. Szeliski, R.: Computer Vision - Algorithms and Applications. Texts in Computer Science, 2nd edn. Springer, Heidelberg (2022). https://doi.org/10.1007/978-3-030-34372-9
20. Tsunashima, H., Arase, K., Lam, A., Kataoka, H.: UVIRT - unsupervised virtual try-on using disentangled clothing and person features. Sensors **20**(19), 5647 (2020)
21. Xu, J., Pu, Y., Nie, R., Xu, D., Zhao, Z., Qian, W.: Virtual try-on network with attribute transformation and local rendering. IEEE Trans. Multim. **23**, 2222–2234 (2021)
22. Yang, H., Zhang, R., Guo, X., Liu, W., Zuo, W., Luo, P.: Towards photo-realistic virtual try-on by adaptively generating↔preserving image content. In: CVPR, pp. 7847–7856. Computer Vision Foundation/IEEE (2020)
23. Yang, W., Zhang, X., Tian, Y., Wang, W., Xue, J., Liao, Q.: Deep learning for single image super-resolution: a brief review. IEEE Trans. Multim. **21**(12), 3106–3121 (2019)
24. Ysique-Neciosup, J., Chavez, N.M., Ugarte, W.: DeepHistory: a convolutional neural network for automatic animation of museum paintings. Comput. Anim. Virtual Worlds **33**(5), e2110 (2022)

Assigning Products in a Vertical Lift Module Supermarket to Supply Production Lines

José Oliveira(✉), António Vieira, Luís Dias, and Guilherme Pereira

ALGORITMI Research Center, University of Minho, Campus Gualtar, 4710-057 Braga, Portugal
zan@dps.uminho.pt

Abstract. This paper presents the development of a mathematical model for product assignment in a Vertical Lift Module (VLM), which are increasingly employed in the industrial sector due to their advanced technology and efficient parts-to-picker process. Mathematical modelling plays a crucial role in addressing the complexity of these problems and providing intelligent and innovative solutions. Despite being a tactical problem with medium-term implications, the competitive nature of the industrial environment demands quick adjustments driven by the mass customization paradigm. This requires continuous evaluations to reconfigure the supermarket accordingly, which can be efficiently accomplished through the rapid application of artificial intelligence using advanced mathematical methods.

The proposed integer linear programming, which is based on the well-known transportation problem, features a simple objective function aimed at minimizing the number of trays in the VLM. Additionally, five constraints are included to ensure the applicability of the model to real-world scenarios. The simplicity of the AMPL implementation of the mathematical model is emphasised. Experimental computation using real data validates the proof of concept and assesses the impact of introducing new rules for product assignment. This research also explores the potential for optimising warehouse operations and suggests avenues for further investigation.

Keywords: Vertical Lift Module · Storage Location Assignment · MILP

1 Introduction

Intralogistics plays a pivotal role in modern-day supply chains, as well as to support operations management on the shop floor. As companies strive to enhance their operational efficiency, there is a growing emphasis on streamlining internal processes to reduce costs, increase productivity, and improve overall customer satisfaction. One vital aspect of intralogistics operations is the implementation of advanced storage systems that maximize space utilization while facilitating swift and accurate retrieval of goods.

This paper aims to explore the Vertical Lift Modules (VLM), a sophisticated solution that has gained significant popularity in recent years for its ability to support intralogistics operations. The VLM system represents a technologically advanced approach to inventory management, enabling companies to enhance their storage capacity, minimize handling times, and enhance overall workflow efficiency.

S. Terzi et al. (Eds.): IN4PL 2023, CCIS 1886, pp. 195–210, 2023.
https://doi.org/10.1007/978-3-031-49339-3_12

The VLM system revolves around the concept of vertical storage and retrieval, capitalizing on the available vertical space within warehouses and distribution centres. By integrating cutting-edge automation and software technologies, the system allows for seamless organization, tracking, and retrieval of items, while significantly reducing the time and effort required for manual handling.

Throughout this paper, we will delve into the core components, functionalities, and benefits of the VLM system. We will also explore how its implementation can revolutionize intralogistics operations by addressing key challenges faced by businesses, such as space constraints, order accuracy, and inventory control.

Furthermore, this paper will shed light on real-world case studies and industry best practices that demonstrate the successful integration of VLM systems in diverse sectors. By analysing these examples, we aim to highlight the system's versatility and adaptability, showcasing its ability to cater to the unique needs of different businesses.

The VLM storage system represents a ground-breaking solution for companies seeking to optimize their intralogistics operations. With its ability to maximize storage capacity, expedite order fulfilment, and enhance overall productivity, the VLM system has proven to be a game-changer in modern supply chain management. By embracing this innovative technology, organizations can position themselves at the forefront of intralogistics excellence, paving the way for sustainable growth and competitive advantage in today's dynamic business landscape.

This paper is organised as follows: The next section provides contextualization on intralogistics operations and supermarkets, along with a literature review on Vertical Lift Modules. The third section is dedicated to the modelling issues, while the fourth section presents the integer linear programming model. Section five presents and discusses the computational experiments. Conclusions and future work are highlighted in the final section.

2 Supermarkets and Intralogistics – Literature Review

In the field of manufacturing, the effective management of production lines is crucial for achieving high productivity and efficient operations. One approach that has gained significant attention in recent years is the implementation of supermarket systems. Supermarkets serve as intermediate buffers between different production stages, providing a steady supply of materials to support uninterrupted workflow. This literature review aims to explore the existing research and best practices regarding the utilization of supermarket systems in aiding production lines within various manufacturing industries.

The concept of the supermarket system originated from the principles of lean manufacturing. Lean methodologies aim to eliminate waste and optimize production processes. Supermarkets act as pull systems, where downstream processes "pull" materials as needed from the supermarket, maintaining a steady flow and reducing inventory levels. Numerous studies have highlighted the benefits of lean practices and the successful implementation of supermarket systems in improving production line efficiency, reducing lead times, and minimizing inventory costs.

The design and layout of supermarkets play a vital role in their effectiveness. Researchers have explored various factors, such as space allocation, product placement, and replenishment strategies, to optimize the performance of supermarket systems. For instance, studies have examined the impact of different supermarket designs, such as U-shaped or L-shaped layouts, on material flow, accessibility, and overall efficiency. These investigations have provided valuable insights into designing supermarkets that facilitate seamless material handling and support production lines.

Efficient inventory control is essential in managing supermarket systems. Researchers have focused on developing inventory control models, such as Kanban systems, to determine optimal inventory levels, replenishment policies, and order quantities. Moreover, studies have examined the impact of demand variability on the performance of supermarket systems and proposed strategies to mitigate its effects. Understanding the relationship between inventory management, demand fluctuations, and production line performance is crucial for achieving smooth operations in dynamic manufacturing environments.

The integration of information systems and technology has revolutionized the implementation and management of supermarket systems. Researchers have explored the use of automated identification and data capture (AIDC) technologies, such as barcodes and radio frequency identification (RFID), to track and monitor inventory levels, improve visibility, and facilitate accurate replenishment. Additionally, studies have investigated the integration of supermarket systems with enterprise resource planning (ERP) systems, enabling real-time data sharing and decision-making for efficient production line support.

Logistics management can be defined as a crucial part of supply chain management that plans, implements, and controls the efficiency of the flow and storage of goods, services, and information throughout their entire lifecycle in order to meet customer needs [1]. According to the Council of Supply Chain Management Professionals [1], logistics management activities typically include transportation management, warehousing, material handling, demand planning, inventory management, order management, and possibly third-party logistics management. Proper management aims to integrate, coordinate, and optimise all logistics activities with other elements of an organisation, including marketing, sales, production, finance, and information technology.

The storage activity does not add value to the product; however, the entire process of delivering the product to the customer relies on a set of storage and transportation activities that enable fulfilling the logistics value proposition. The presence of storage brings the product closer to the market, allowing for quicker response to the customer, significantly improving the overall service. A logistics system without storage would only be possible if there were perfect synchronisation between production and consumption, without any variability, which is simply not feasible. The need for storage infrastructure arises from the need to maintain inventory. This need arises when supply and consumption exhibit distinct behaviours over time. Therefore, the existence of inventory enables the consumption process to be independent of the supply process.

According to several authors mass customization arises from the need to offer a wide variety of products at competitive prices and short delivery times, combining product personalization with the efficiency of mass production [2–7]. However, mass customization, in addition to increasing the complexity of management operations within the factory, leads to increased costs related to production lead times, inventory, setups, and production changes [8–12].

Mass customization is a production strategy that capitalises on the efficiency of assembly lines to manufacture customised products but necessitates optimised intralogistics operations [13]. Further information about intralogistics and warehouses can be found in significant literature reviews [14–16]. In this context, supermarkets assume a vital role as decentralised storage areas, facilitating the management and replenishment of the necessary components to support the diverse customization options throughout the production process [13, 17].

Supermarkets are frequently referred to as preparation areas, emphasizing their role in temporarily storing materials and preparing unit loads such as bins or kits [18]. In certain instances, line-integrated supermarkets are employed, where each supermarket is dedicated to one or a small number of workstations [19, 20].

The Vertical Lift Module (VLM) arose in 1989 [21] and became a widely used storage solution that can be uses as a supermarket to support efficient operations in productive areas [22]. By utilising vertical space, the VLM maximises storage capacity while providing quick and organised access to items. This innovative system optimises the workflow, streamlining material handling processes and enhancing productivity in the productive area.

In the literature, VLM is referred to as a "part to picker" system, because the machine brings the items to the picker that has no need to move. The order batching problems with this type of warehouse are referred to as OFF-SP-CT-B by Pardo et al. [23] in their recent Taxonomy, that means the study is performed "OFF-offline" considering a "SP-single picker" to reduce the "CT-completion time", to form a "B-batch".

According to Pardo et al., [23] only the work of Nicolas, Yannick, Ramzi [22] is cited in their literature review related with VLM. Nicolas, Yannick, Ramzi [22] developed optimization models to minimise the total completion time for fulfilling orders using one or more VLMs. Their initial model focused on a single VLM and employed two binary decision variables within a Mixed-integer linear programming (MILP). To validate their approach, numerical experiments were conducted using real data from a hospital in France and a manufacturing company in Switzerland, utilising the commercial optimization software Cplex. While minimising total completion time is the primary objective, the authors also investigate reducing the number of visited trays as an alternative approach. This is significant because it directly impacts the operational lifespan of VLMs. The authors contend that a higher number of visited trays results in a shorter effective VLM lifetime.

The available literature also encompasses a variety of case studies and industry applications that exemplify the successful implementation of supermarket systems in diverse manufacturing sectors. These case studies provide valuable insights into the practical challenges faced, the strategies employed, and the benefits achieved. Building upon these findings, this paper presents an MILP model that assigns products to VLMs while minimizing the number of required trays. The model incorporates production data from a real-world company.

3 Modeling

This study was conducted within an automotive supplier with an exceptionally high degree of vertical integration. The company specialises in the development and manufacturing of electronic equipment, operating systems, and control devices for a diverse clientele. These products vary widely in terms of functionality and dimensions, resulting in a vast array of products that are assembled using a diverse range of components.

Within the realm of electronics manufacturing, effectively managing and organising Surface Mount Device (SMD) reels poses a significant challenge. The task of assigning thousands of SMD reels, each varying in size, to the shelves inside Vertical Lift Module (VLM) machines demands meticulous planning and strategic consideration. This complex problem encompasses several key challenges, including dealing with reel size variations, optimising space utilisation, ensuring inventory visibility, maintaining tracking accuracy, and enhancing operational flexibility.

3.1 SMD Reel Sizes

SMD reels come in various sizes, including differing widths, diameters, and heights. Managing such a diverse range of reel sizes poses a considerable challenge when it comes to allocating them to the limited tray space available within VLM machines. The goal is to maximise the utilisation of storage capacity while ensuring easy access and efficient retrieval of the required reels during the manufacturing process.

Figure 1 presents one rack that has a specific design to support the reels in their storage in the trays inside the VLM. To ensure the safe storage of reels, the rack must have appropriate dimensions that align with the reel's diameter. It is crucial to maintain the reels in a vertical position to prevent any damage to the SMD components. The dimensions of the rack should not be too short or too large in comparison to the diameter to effectively keep the reels in a vertical position. Figure 2 presents a large rack that is suitable to store a large reel properly.

3.2 Space Optimization

VLM machines are designed to optimise vertical storage space, leveraging the available height within a warehouse or distribution centre. However, determining the most efficient arrangement of SMD reels on the shelves requires careful consideration. Inefficient space allocation can lead to wasted space, decreased storage capacity, and difficulties in accessing specific reels when needed. Therefore, the problem of assigning SMD reels to VLM machine trays involves finding the optimal configuration that minimises wasted space and maximises storage efficiency.

3.3 Inventory Visibility and Accessibility

Maintaining clear visibility and easy access to the stored SMD reels is crucial for ensuring smooth and efficient operations. Assigning reels in a disorganised manner can result in difficulties locating specific components, leading to delays in production, increased

Fig. 1. A SMD Reel Storage Rack Zinc Plated with several SMD reels of different sizes.

Fig. 2. A large rack with two large reels.

handling times, and decreased overall productivity. Therefore, the challenge lies in organising the shelves in a way that provides clear visibility of the inventory, allowing operators to easily identify and retrieve the required reels without unnecessary disruptions.

3.4 Item Tracking and Retrieval Speed

With thousands of SMD reels stored within the VLM machines, accurately tracking the location of each reel is crucial for efficient retrieval. In a fast-paced manufacturing environment, delays in locating and retrieving the required reels can have a significant impact on production schedules and customer satisfaction. The problem of assigning SMD reels to the trays involves implementing efficient tracking mechanisms, such as barcode or RFID systems, that enable quick and accurate identification and retrieval of the desired components.

3.5 Scalability and Flexibility

The assignment of SMD reels to VLM machine trays must be adaptable to accommodate changes in inventory and production demands. As new reel sizes are introduced or existing ones are phased out, the system needs to be flexible enough to ad-just the trays assignments accordingly. Additionally, the ability to easily reconfigure trays assignments based on demand fluctuations or changes in production requirements is crucial for maintaining operational efficiency and responding to dynamic business needs.

Addressing the problem of assigning thousands of SMD reels of different sizes to VLM machine trays requires a comprehensive approach that balances space optimization, inventory visibility, tracking accuracy, and operational flexibility. By implementing effective strategies and leveraging advanced technologies, companies can overcome these challenges and ensure seamless storage and retrieval operations, ultimately enhancing productivity and meeting customer expectations in the electronics manufacturing industry.

4 Mathematical Model

In a simple description, we can state that our mathematical model is derived from the assignment problem's characteristics or even the transportation problem. On one hand, there is a set of (distinct) reels to be stored, and on the other hand, there is a set of (different) available places to receive the reels. Additional specific constraints are incorporated to address the particular characteristics of the real-world problem.

4.1 Notation and Assumptions

We consider the following notation:

- *N_pro*: total number of products (references).
- *N_rac*: total number of racks.
- *N_tra*: total number of trays in VLM.
- $P = \{1, \ldots, N\_pro\}$: set of indices for products.
- $R = \{1, \ldots, N\_rac\}$: set of indices for racks.
- $T = \{1, \ldots, N\_tra\}$: set of indices for trays.
- d_i:demand$\{i \text{ in } P\}$.
- c_{ij}: capacity$\{i \text{ in } P, j \text{ in } R\}$.
- p_k: place$\{k \text{ in } T\}$.

4.2 Optimisation Model

The main decision of our model is how to build the different trays from the set of products that are needed to be stored in VLM.

- $x_{ijk} \geq 0$, *integer* number plenty racks type j placed at tray k with reels of product i.
- $Y_{ij} = 1$ if product i is stored in rack j; 0 otherwise.
- $Z_k = 1$ if tray k is used to store any product; 0 otherwise.

The objective function of the assignment problem with one VLM is as follows:

$$Minimise \sum_{k \in T} Z_k \quad (1)$$

The constraints of the model are:

$$\sum_{j \in R} \sum_{k \in T} c_{ij} x_{ijk} \geq d_i, \ \forall i \in P \quad (2)$$

$$\sum_{i \in P} \sum_{j \in R} x_{ijk} \leq p_k, \ \forall k \in T \quad (3)$$

$$\sum_{k \in T} x_{ijk} \leq MY_{ij}, \ \forall i \in P, \forall j \in R \quad (4)$$

$$\sum_{i \in P} \sum_{j \in R} x_{ijk} \leq MZ_k, \ \forall k \in T \quad (5)$$

Equation (2) guarantees that are reserved enough space for the known demand and Eq. (3) establishes that the reserved space fits on the available locations within the tray. Equation (4) activates rack j when product i is stored therein. M represents a large number.

4.3 Real Problem Data

The data for this problem was obtained from a real Vertical Lift Module (VLM) used by an electronic device manufacturing company. The VLM consists of up to 62 trays arranged in two columns.

To optimise tray occupation, the company adopted six distinct rack layouts for storing the reels. Figures 3, 4, 5, 6, 7 and 8 depict these layouts in ascending order of rack width. Each layout caters to specific reel sizes, with type 1 designed for short reels and type 6 intended for very large reels.

1	2	3	4	5	6	7	8	9	10	11	12	13	14
15	16	17	18	19	20	21	22	23	24	25	26	27	28
29	30	31	32	33	34	35	36	37	38	39	40	41	42
43	44	45	46	47	48	49	50	51	52	53	54	55	56
57	58	59	60	61	62	63	64	65	66	67	68	69	70
71	72	73	74	75	76	77	78	79	80	81	82	83	84
85	86	87	88	89	90	91	92	93	94	95	96	97	98
99	100	101	102	103	104	105	106	107	108	109	110	111	112
113	114	115	116	117	118	119	120	121	122	123	124	125	126
127	128	129	130	131	132	133	134	135	136	137	138	139	140
141	142	143	144	145	146	147	148	149	150	151	152	153	154
155	156	157	158	159	160	161	162	163	164	165	166	167	168

Fig. 3. Tray type 1 layout.

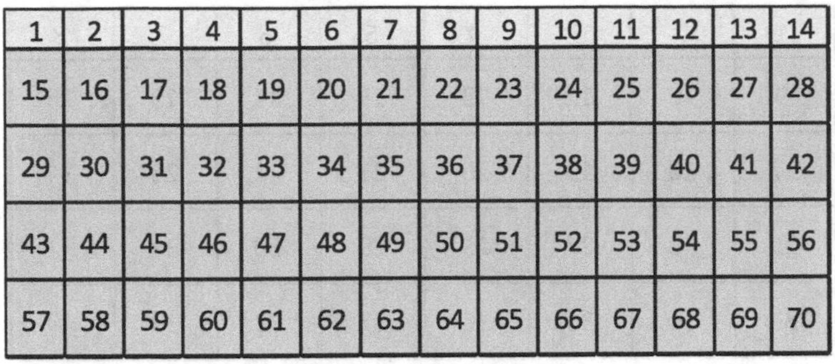

1	2	3	4	5	6	7	8	9	10	11	12	13	14
15	16	17	18	19	20	21	22	23	24	25	26	27	28
29	30	31	32	33	34	35	36	37	38	39	40	41	42
43	44	45	46	47	48	49	50	51	52	53	54	55	56
57	58	59	60	61	62	63	64	65	66	67	68	69	70

Fig. 4. Tray type 2 layout.

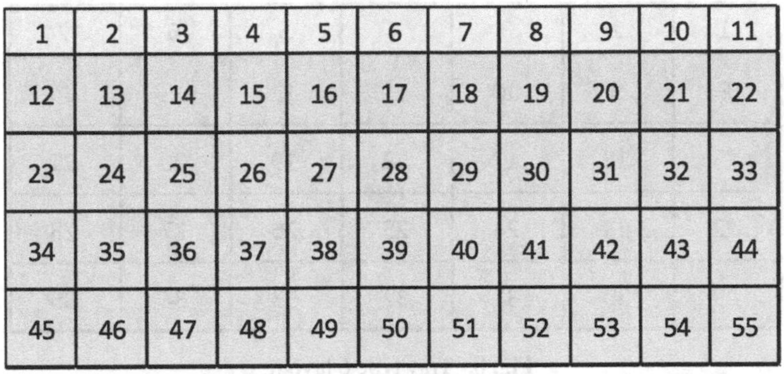

1	2	3	4	5	6	7	8	9	10	11
12	13	14	15	16	17	18	19	20	21	22
23	24	25	26	27	28	29	30	31	32	33
34	35	36	37	38	39	40	41	42	43	44
45	46	47	48	49	50	51	52	53	54	55

Fig. 5. Tray type 3 layout.

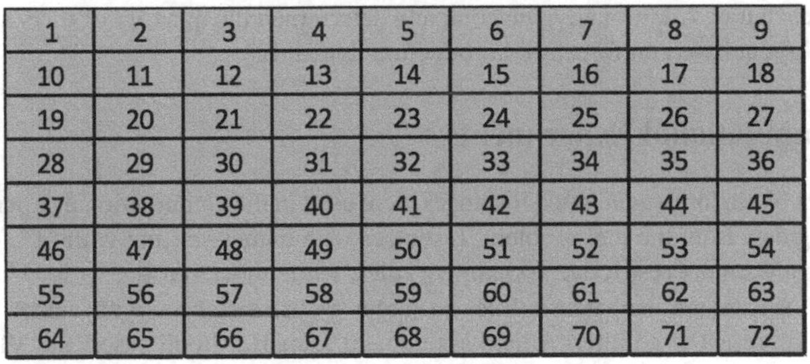

1	2	3	4	5	6	7	8	9
10	11	12	13	14	15	16	17	18
19	20	21	22	23	24	25	26	27
28	29	30	31	32	33	34	35	36
37	38	39	40	41	42	43	44	45
46	47	48	49	50	51	52	53	54
55	56	57	58	59	60	61	62	63
64	65	66	67	68	69	70	71	72

Fig. 6. Tray type 4 layout.

1	2	3	4	5	6	7	8
9	10	11	12	13	14	15	16
17	18	19	20	21	22	23	24
25	26	27	28	29	30	31	32
33	34	35	36	37	38	39	40

Fig. 7. Tray type 5 layout.

1	2	3	4	5	6	7
8	9	10	11	12	13	14
15	16	17	18	19	20	21
22	23	24	25	26	27	28
29	30	31	32	33	34	35

Fig. 8. Tray type 6 layout.

The numbered rectangles in the layouts (Figs. 3, 4, 5, 6, 7 and 8) depict the existing racks in each tray. Additionally, the company determined the quantity of trays allocated for each layout based on forecasted production demands.

5 Computational Experiments

Three sets of randomly generated instances were used in the computational experiments, collecting data from the real problem. Instances with names starting with "1" followed the company's more restrictive assignment rules, while those starting with "3" allowed for additional assignment possibilities in larger racks. Instances with names starting with "2" represented an intermediate assignment scenario. In all cases, the VLM size remains constant, consisting of a total of 62 trays of the available six layout types and 3311 racks of different sizes in line with its layout. The model was implemented in the AMPL language, and the experiments were conducted on the NEOS Server [24–26], utilising the Gurobi solver with a time limit of 28000 s.

The columns in Table 1 represent the following: Inst. - instance; P – number of different products in the instance; R – number of racks used in the solution; T – optimum or the best number of trays used in the solution; S – number of splits in the solution; CPU – time is seconds taken to obtain the solution; %TR – percentage of the total used racks in the solution; %TT – percentage of the total used trays.

Table 1. Computational results.

Inst.	P	R	T	S	CPU	%TR	%TT
1_050_1	50	269	6	0	15	8.1%	9.7%
1_050_2	50	206	4	0	2	6.2%	6.5%
2_050_1	50	188	4	1	3	5.7%	6.5%
2_050_2	50	236	4	0	9	7.1%	6.5%
3_050_1	50	282	5	1	3	8.5%	8.1%
3_050_2	50	228	5	0	13	6.9%	8.1%
1_100_1	100	472	9	2	24	14.3%	14.5%
1_100_2	100	401	6	3	7	12.1%	9.7%
2_100_1	100	600	7	2	7380	18.1%	11.3%
2_100_2	100	486	8	7	28000	14.7%	12.9%
3_100_1	100	433	9	1	840	13.1%	14.5%
3_100_2	100	607	7	1	180	18.3%	11.3%
1_200_1	200	892	15	9	180	26.9%	24.2%
2_200_1	200	803	12	6	28000	24.3%	19.4%
3_200_1	200	769	12	5	28000	23.2%	19.4%
1_300_1	300	1354	21	11	28000	40.9%	33.9%
2_300_1	300	1098	17	3	28000	33.2%	27.4%
3_300_1	300	1025	16	14	28000	31.0%	25.8%
1_400_1	400	1877	27	17	28000	56.7%	43.5%
2_400_1	400	1494	22	19	28000	45.1%	35.5%
3_400_1	400	1466	22	14	28000	44.3%	35.5%
1_500_1	500	2282	33	20	28000	68.9%	53.2%
2_500_1	500	1933	27	17	28000	58.4%	43.5%
3_500_1	500	1886	30	133	28000	57.0%	48.4%
1_600_1	600	2401	36	127	28000	72.5%	58.1%
2_600_1	600	2353	35	26	28000	71.1%	56.5%
3_600_1	600	2120	34	116	28000	64.0%	54.8%
1_760_1	760	2850	43	88	28000	86.1%	69.4%
2_760_1	760	2783	43	139	28000	84.1%	69.4%
3_760_1	760	2688	43	77	28000	81.2%	69.4%

If the CPU time is 28000, it indicates that the solution is an incumbent. One split means that the product was stored in two different trays. The objective function only minimizes the number of trays and does not consider the impact of splitting a reference into several trays. In fact, splitting the quantity of a product helps to save space in the warehouse but increases the complexity in inventory management. Although the instance set is not statistically representative, it is evident that allowing more alternatives to store reels in larger, suitable racks reduces the usage of trays and racks by around 10%. When comparing the percentages of used racks out of the total available and the percentages of used trays out of the total available, lower values can be observed in instances of type 2 and type 3, where more options for storing reels are considered.

Another concern arising from Table 1 relates to the CPU time. In fact, it was not possible to obtain the optimal value within approximately 8 h of computation for 60% of the instances. Only for instances with one hundred or fewer products was it possible to find or prove the optimal solution. While the optimal value was not attained for larger instances, the incumbent solutions that were found align with the company's objectives, accommodating the number of products in each instance as indicated by the occupation (%TR and %TT). With this in mind, new experiments were conducted using the same model and focusing on the larger instances, recording the incumbents for different CPU times (in seconds). These experiments consisted of multiple runs with varying stopping times, and it is important to note that the solver employed automatic parameters in each run, leading to a different search tree approach. Table 2 presents the incumbents' values, along with the same "key performance indicators", absolute mip gap and relative mip gap, for 12 different time stop criteria.

In less than 10 min, the best incumbents were found for all three instances. For the instance with fewer storage options (instance 1_760_1), it took less than one minute to find the best incumbent solution. While the number of racks is not included in the objective function, the search process after 30 min achieves the same values as those obtained within 8 h. The numbers for splitting fluctuate more, but they are not considered in the objective function. Both the absolute mip gap and relative mip gap show a decreasing trend with CPU time. The slight variations in some values occur because each value was obtained through independent runs, resulting in different approaches to the branch and bound search tree.

The real problem discussed in this study is a tactical one, and the decisions made should have an impact for two or three years. However, if the current demand patterns no longer align with the existing solution, a complete reset becomes necessary. In such a situation, a model aimed at minimizing changes can be applied. Companies should plan for the reset of the supermarket, which may require a significant period of non-production time.

Table 2. Results with different CPU times.

CPU_time	60	120	180	240	300	600	1800	3600	7200	10800	14400	28000
Racks												
1_760_1	2850	2850	2850	2850	2850	2850	2850	2850	2850	2850	2850	2850
2_760_1	2943	2845	2845	2880	2880	2881	2783	2783	2783	2783	2783	2783
3_760_1	2739	2739	2739	2739	2739	2688	2688	2688	2688	2688	2703	2688
Trays												
1_760_1	43	43	43	43	43	43	43	43	43	43	43	43
2_760_1	44	44	44	43	43	43	43	43	43	43	43	43
3_760_1	44	44	44	44	44	43	43	43	43	43	43	43
Splits												
1_760_1	103	88	88	88	103	88	88	88	88	88	88	88
2_760_1	51	204	204	178	178	134	139	142	139	139	139	139
3_760_1	38	38	38	37	38	100	100	80	77	80	118	77
absmipgap												
1_760_1	0.352	0.203	0.097	0.097	0.352	0.039	0.031	0.028	0.024	0.028	0.026	0.0079622
2_760_1	1.64	1.637	1.637	0.772	0.772	0.474	0.42	0.428	0.416	0.42	0.4	0.031
3_760_1	1.691	1.691	1.691	1.69	1.691	0.581	0.585	0.577	0.548	0.57	0.267	0.548
relmipgap												
1_760_1	0.00803286	0.00463365	0.00221411	0.00221411	0.00803286	0.00089020	0.00070760	0.00063912	0.00054782	0.00063912	0.00059347	0.00018174
2_760_1	0.0366374	0.0365728	0.0365728	0.0175874	0.0175874	0.0108116	0.00958182	0.00976277	0.00949057	0.00958182	0.00912554	0.00070723
3_760_1	0.0377793	0.0377793	0.0377793	0.0377569	0.0377793	0.013263	0.0133543	0.013172	0.0125103	0.0130122	0.00609575	0.0125103

6 Conclusions

The optimization of assigning different SMD reels to available positions within VLM machine can be achieved through the application of Integer Linear Programming (ILP) techniques. ILP, a mathematical optimization method, enables the allocation of discrete variables, such as assigning reels to specific positions within the VLM system. By formulating the problem as an ILP model, it becomes possible to obtain an optimal solution that takes into account various constraints and objectives.

The ILP model aims to optimise the assignment of SMD reels to available positions within the VLM system by minimising the number of used trays. The objective function takes into consideration various factors such as reel size, demand patterns, and retrieval frequency to determine the optimal allocation strategy. In the ILP model, the assignment of SMD reels to available positions (racks) is represented using decision variables. The primary variable indicates the integer value of the number of racks of type j placed at tray k to store product i. Constraints play a crucial role in ensuring that the assignment adheres to specific requirements. These constraints can include limitations on the number of reels assigned to a position, restrictions on total weight or size capacity, as well as any specific rules or guidelines governing the arrangement of reels within the VLM system. Incorporating decisions based on a mathematical approach is a pivotal means of introducing artificial intelligence to address industrial problems, offering an innovative strategy.

The ILP model is implemented in the AMPL language and solved using the Gurobi optimization solver through the NEOS Serve computation service. Thirty numeric instances were randomly generated to collect real data from a significant company in the electronics sector. The instances were divided into three sets to explore different allowed rules for the assignment. Given the complexity of the problem, proving the optimal solution within an 8-h computation time was not possible. However, both the absolute mip gap and the relative mip gap exhibit interesting values within a few minutes of computation, even for large real instances.

Further research will be conducted to expand the proposed model in order to handle multiple VLMs. Additionally, other objectives will be considered to enhance the efficiency of the picking processes. Integration of a simulation model will be undertaken to validate the effectiveness of the assignment solution. To enhance this study, we intend to extend the presented MILP model to address the proximity to production lines and to incorporate both inventory management and production planning considerations.

Acknowledgements. This work has been supported by FCT – Fundação para a Ciência e Tecnologia within the R&D Units Project Scope: UIDB/00319/2020.

References

1. Council of Supply Chain Management Professionals: Supply Chain Management Terms and Glossary Homepage. http://cscmp.org/resourcesresearch/glossary-terms. Last accessed 07 Jun 2023

2. Fatorachian, H., Kazemi, H.: A critical investigation of Industry 4.0 in manufacturing: theoretical operationalisation framework. Prod. Plan. Control **29**(8), 633–644 (2018)
3. Shukla, M., Todorov, I., Kapletia, D.: Application of additive manufacturing for mass customisation: understanding the interaction of critical barriers. Prod. Plann. Control **29**(10), 814–825 (2018)
4. Li, M., Huang, G.Q.: Production-intralogistics synchronization of industry 4.0 flexible assembly lines under graduation intelligent manufacturing system. Int. J. Prod. Econ. **241**, 108272 (2021)
5. Dörmer, J., Günther, H.O., Gujjula, R.: Master production scheduling and sequencing at mixed-model assembly lines in the automotive industry. Flex. Serv. Manuf. J. **27**, 1–29 (2015)
6. Tu, M., Lim, M.K., Yang, M.F.: IoT-based production logistics and supply chain system–part 1: modeling IoT-based manufacturing supply chain. Ind. Manag. Data Syst. **118**(1), 65–95 (2018)
7. Suzic, N., Forza, C.: Development of mass customization implementation guidelines for small and medium enterprises (SMEs). Prod. Planning Control **34**(6), 543–571 (2023)
8. Emde, S., Schneider, M.: Just-in-time vehicle routing for in-house part feeding to assembly lines. Transp. Sci. **52**(3), 657–672 (2018)
9. Zhang, Y., Guo, Z., Lv, J., Liu, Y.: A framework for smart production-logistics systems based on CPS and industrial IoT. IEEE Trans. Ind. Inform. **14**(9), 4019–4032 (2018). https://doi.org/10.1109/TII.2018.2845683
10. Ripperda, S., Krause, D.: Cost effects of modular product family structures: methods and quantification of impacts to support decision making. J. Mech. Des. **139**(2) (2017)
11. Nilsson, A., Danielsson, F., Bennulf, M., Svensson, B.: A classification of different levels of flexibility in an automated manufacturing system and needed competence. In: Towards Sustainable Customization: Bridging Smart Products and Manufacturing Systems: Proceedings of the 8th Changeable, Agile, Reconfigurable and Virtual Production Conference (CARV2021) and the 10th World Mass Customization & Personalization Conference (MCPC2021), Aalborg, Denmark, October/November 2021 8 pp. 27–34. Springer International Publishing (2022)
12. Gonnermann, C., Hashemi-Petroodi, S.E., Thevenin, S., Dolgui, A., Daub, R.: A skill-and feature-based approach to planning process monitoring in assembly planning. Int. J. Adv. Manufact. Technol. **122**(5–6), 2645–2670 (2022)
13. Napoleone, A., Moretti, E., Macchi, M., Melacini, M.: Synchronisation of material flows in mass-customised production systems: a literature-based classification framework and industrial application. Prod. Planning Control 1–19 (2023)
14. Kilic, H.S., Durmusoglu, M.B.: Advances in assembly line parts feeding policies: a literature review. Assem. Autom. **35**(1), 57–68 (2015)
15. Custodio, L., Machado, R.: Flexible automated warehouse: a literature review and an innovative framework. Int. J. Adv. Manuf. Technol. **106**, 533–558 (2020)
16. Barreto, C.G., Machado, R.L.: Dispositivos tecnológicos na coleta e separação de pedidos: revisão bibliográfica. Braz. J. Prod. Eng. **8**(6), 01–33 (2022). (in Portuguese)
17. Adenipekun, E.O., Limère, V., Schmid, N.A.: The impact of transportation optimisation on assembly line feeding. Omega **107**, 102544 (2022)
18. Ruiz Zuniga, E., Flores Garcia, E., Urenda Moris, M., Fathi, M., Syberfeldt, A.: Holistic simulation-based optimisation methodology for facility layout design with consideration to production and logistics constraints. Proc. Inst. Mech. Eng., Part B: J. Eng. Manuf. **235**(14), 2350–2361 (2021)
19. Boysen, N., Emde, S.: Scheduling the part supply of mixed-model assembly lines in line-integrated supermarkets. Eur. J. Oper. Res. **239**(3), 820–829 (2014)
20. Schmid, N.A., Limère, V.: A classification of tactical assembly line feeding problems. Int. J. Prod. Res. **57**(24), 7586–7609 (2019)

21. MHI. A history of automated vertical storage systems in the United States (White paper). Retrieved from: http://www.mhi.org. Last accessed 07 Jun 2023
22. Nicolas, L., Yannick, F., Ramzi, H.: Order batching in an automated warehouse with several vertical lift modules: optimization and experiments with real data. Eur. J. Oper. Res. **267**(3), 958–976 (2018)
23. Pardo, E.G., Gil-Borrás, S., Alonso-Ayuso, A., Duarte, A.: Order batching problems: taxonomy and literature review. Eur. J. Oper. Res. **313**, 1–24 (2023)
24. Czyzyk, J., Mesnier, M.P., Moré, J.J.: The NEOS server. IEEE J. Comput. Sci. Eng. **5**(3), 68–75 (1998)
25. Dolan, E.: The NEOS Server 4.0 Administrative Guide. Technical Memorandum ANL/MCS-TM-250, Mathematics and Computer Science Division, Argonne National Laboratory (2001). Technical report available in https://www.mcs.anl.gov/papers/TM-250.pdf. Last accessed 25 Apr 2023
26. Gropp, W., Moré, J.J.: Optimization environments and the NEOS server. In: Buhmann, M.D., Iserles, A., eds. Approximation Theory and Optimization, pp. 167–182. Cambridge University Press (1997)

Bridging the Operationalization Gap: Towards a Situational Approach for Data Analytics in Manufacturing SMEs

Stefan Rösl(✉), Thomas Auer, and Christian Schieder

Technical University of Applied Sciences Amberg-Weiden, Hetzenrichter Weg 15, 92637 Weiden, Germany

{s.roesl,t.auer,c.schieder}@oth-aw.de

Abstract. The emergence of Industry 4.0 (I4.0) technologies has significant implications for small and medium-sized enterprises (SMEs) in the manufacturing sector. Current research highlights the benefits of I4.0 technologies but often overlooks the unique challenges and needs of SMEs, particularly in the transition from implementation to routinization of data analytics (DA) in the context of I4.0 initiatives. Our paper addresses this gap by introducing a prototype of an integrated data analytics model (iDAM) specifically designed to help SMEs incorporate DA as part of I4.0. Our model was developed based on a comprehensive review of existing frameworks and methodologies. It covers three key areas (the project situation, the organization's maturity level, and the application landscape) and proposes a situational process model to bridge the implementation-routinization gap. We demonstrate and evaluate our approach using a practical, real-world use case of a multi-stage manufacturing process in an SME. The iDAM provides a structured and tailored approach to guide SMEs in operationalizing DA based on their individual maturity level and promote the use of DA methods.

Keywords: Technology adoption · Implementation · Data analytics · Manufacturing · SME · Situational method engineering

1 Introduction

Technologies such as artificial intelligence in autonomous cars or robots have played a starring role in many sci-fi movies of the past. With current technological advances, they are becoming a reality in our time. In the context of Industry 4.0 (I4.0), new opportunities are promised, many of which rely on data as the key resource and on improved data analytics (DA) as a key capability [1] for achieving economic value from data [2]. Consistent with expectations, academic literature highlights the many benefits that DA offers to manufacturing firms, including small and medium-sized enterprises (SMEs). These benefits include cost reductions, quality, efficiency, flexibility, productivity improvements, and the ability to gain competitive advantage [3].

To achieve these benefits, SMEs face many challenges [4]. SMEs' limitations regarding technology awareness and financial and personal resources can hinder the adoption

S. Terzi et al. (Eds.): IN4PL 2023, CCIS 1886, pp. 211–222, 2023.
https://doi.org/10.1007/978-3-031-49339-3_13

of DA technologies [5]. Established DA models and frameworks are developed for or by multinational enterprises and, therefore, offer little support for the specific needs of SMEs [5]. SMEs face further difficulties in adopting DA due to their focus on cost considerations and short-term benefits, lack of experience in the field, and overwhelming options and implementation technologies [3]. Additionally, SMEs exhibit substantial variations among themselves [3]. This diversity presents a challenge in developing a universally applicable model for the adoption of DA technologies and practices.

The lack of studies that focus on DA with an emphasis on supporting the operationalization of technologies from a process perspective is conspicuous. Process models ensure a standardized and systematic approach to data analytics projects. Although such methods exist in the literature, their application in practice, especially in SMEs, still needs improvement [6]. A survey of 78 professionals revealed that 82% do not follow a process methodology [7]. In contrast, 85% of the participants confirmed that following a process would be more efficient [7].

Queiroz et al. [8] distinguish different phases for the adoption of I4.0 technologies: Intention to adopt, adoption, implementation, routinization, continuance, and diffusion [8]. Their research shows that the transition from implementation to routinization is a major challenge. Consequently, our research aims to facilitate the transition from the initial use of technology to its integration into the organization. Therefore, we present a prototype model to help manufacturing SMEs operationalize DA activities and address the gaps mentioned above. The model is specifically designed to solve common issues faced by SMEs and facilitates the transition from theoretical concepts to practical use. The proposed integrated data analytics model (iDAM) for manufacturing SMEs encompasses three key areas (the project situation, the organizational maturity level, and the application landscape) and provides a situational process model to bridge the implementation-routinization gap.

The remainder of the paper is organized as follows. Section 2 presents the theoretical foundations, notable frameworks and defines key concepts. Section 3 introduces the iDAM prototype and details its components. A practice-orientated evaluation follows in Sect. 4. Finally, we provide preliminary contributions to theory and practice, limitations, and an outlook for future research.

2 Theoretical Foundation

In this section, we first define technology adoption based on the academic literature and examine its key frameworks. Second, we introduce terms and definitions related to DA and explain key methodologies.

2.1 Technology Adoption

Academic literature provides various definitions and interpretations of technology adoption. Monchak and Kim [9] offered a scientifically grounded perspective on the concept of adoption, emphasizing two fundamental aspects. (a) Adoption involves the decision-making process and acceptance of innovative technology (decision to use the innovation). (b) Adoption also encompasses the practical utilization of the innovation (putting the innovation into use). Recently, Queiroz et al. [8] refined the adoption concept of I4.0 technologies and defined two phases (adoption and post-adoption), including six distinct stages. This adoption process is presented in Fig. 1.

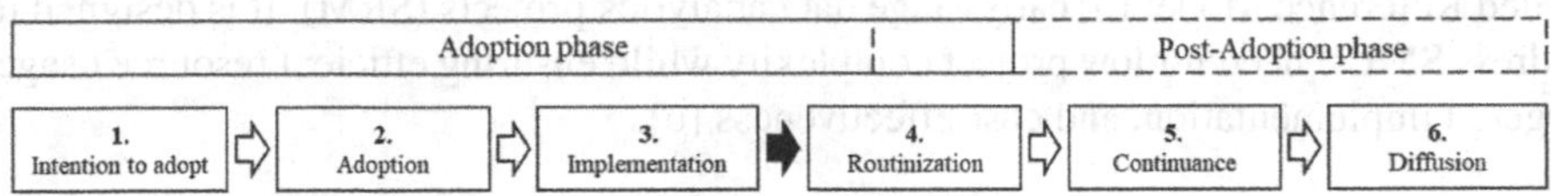

Fig. 1. Adoption stages of I4.0 technologies [8].

The first stage involves the intention to adopt (i) the technology. The next stage is focused on the acceptance of the technology (ii). The implementation stage (iii) constitutes the final stage of adoption, which includes the initial use of the technology. The adoption and post-adoption phases overlap at the routinization (iii) stage. The seamless integration of the technology into daily business processes starts here and is completed by the subsequent stages, continuance (v) and diffusion (vi) [8].

Frameworks aim to provide a systematic understanding of the acceptance and use of technologies to derive measures for technology adoption [10]. To a great extent, technology adoption literature is based on two predominant frameworks: the technology acceptance model, also referred to as TAM [11], and the technology, organization, and environment (TOE) framework [12]. Scholars believe that new frameworks keep emerging for technology adoption, including adopting I4.0 technologies in SMEs [10]. The literature analyzed showed frameworks centering on I4.0 technologies and incorporating the foundational TOE structure. Most frameworks target primarily the adoption stage intention (i) and acceptance (ii). Consequently, academic literature revealed a gap in the adoption level between the implementation (iii) and routinization (iv) stages [8].

Our research focuses on the operationalization of technology adoption, defined by the transition from implementation (iii) to routinization (iv). This operationalization is visualized as a filled arrow in Fig. 1.

2.2 Data Analytics

The central pivot of I4.0 is data and its analysis [1]. Literature lacks a consensus for using different terms to describe DA activities, but the goal remains the same: turn data into value [2]. Our research follows the definition presented by Ebrahimi et al. [13], which describes DA as a combination of tools and processes based on statistics, data mining, artificial intelligence, and diverse forms of analytics. According to their definition, DA includes the notion of data science, data visualization, and data acquisition.

In literature, the Cross-Industry Standard Process for Data Mining (CRISP-DM) is identified as the well-known de facto standard [14]. Previous reviews on data science methodologies provide more than 25 possible workflows [14, 15]. A recently published process model is presented by Schulz et al. [16]. They identified the theoretical and practical components necessary for data science process models and proposed 17 empirically grounded requirements. This group of 22 experts, nine professors, and 13 experienced practitioners revealed that well-known process models lack scientific methods and fail to meet all the identified requirements. The study's main contribution is the Data Science Process Model (DASC-PM) – "a framework that maps a data science project as a four-step process model and contextualizes it among scientific procedures, various areas of application, IT infrastructures, and impacts" [16]. Another process model is the Simplified Reference Model for early-stage data analytics projects (SRM). It is designed to address SMEs' need for low project complexity while ensuring efficient resource usage, targeted implementation, and cost-effectiveness [6].

3 Integrated Data Analytics Model (iDAM)

This section presents the iDAM, a structured framework developed to help manufacturing SMEs operationalize DA as part of technology adoption. In designing such an approach, we draw on existing frameworks and methodologies in the information systems literature. The proposed model was derived from reflections and observations made by our research team during practical DA implementations, as well as from intensive discussions with DA practitioners.

The proposed concept of the iDAM is illustrated in Fig. 2. It is composed of four pivotal elements: (A) situation, (B) maturity model (MM), (C) application landscape, and (D) situational process model. The iDAM model is portrayed with arrows to represent the workflow and the interdependencies among the various components. The information transfer is categorized as output and is systematically organized by numbers.

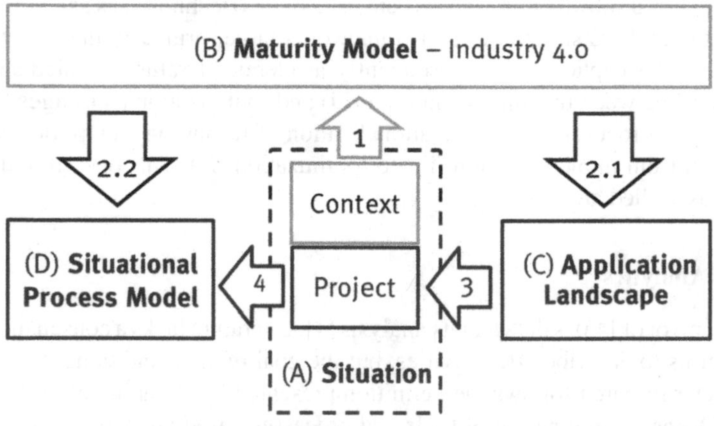

Fig. 2. General Concept of the iDAM.

The context inside situation (A) is the starting point and selects an appropriate MM (output 1). The MM assessment (B) provides information about the maturity level of an organization. It generates input to filter the application landscape (output 2.1) and influences the process model selection (output 2.2). The landscape (C) suggests a suitable application (output 3), aligning with the organization's level of maturity. Developing the use case (output 4) derived from output 3 is crucial to complete the situation (A). The maturity level (output 2.2) and the specified project (output 4) serve as input to propose a suited and situational process model (D).

iDAM provides a structured procedure for operationalizing DA and drives the integration into the business organization. By incorporating a process model into the iDAM workflow (D), we promote the practical application of data analytics methods. The iDAM prototype combines its elements into a valuable approach that facilitates the efficient realization of DA applications tailored to the organization's maturity level.

The following sections outline the components of the iDAM prototype into which selected artifacts from the knowledge base will be integrated. Selection boards are formulated in advance to ensure a streamlined workflow of the individual elements.

3.1 Maturity Model

MMs are a well-established approach in information systems that aid in creating a clear vision and outline actionable steps to guide organizations in identifying, prioritizing, and developing relevant capabilities [17]. Based on the assessed level of maturity, the process model will be selected, and the application landscape will be filtered.

A structured literature review from Hein-Pensel et al. [18] identified several I4.0 MM. We analyzed the models that are consistent with our research and used the I4.0 maturity model from Schumacher et al. [19] in our prototype. This MM is scientifically recognized and well-established. It consists of 9 dimensions, to which 62 items are assigned to assess the maturity level of I4.0. The dimensions *Products, Customers, Operations*, and *Technology* have been formulated to evaluate fundamental enablers. The dimensions *Strategy, Leadership, Governance, Culture*, and *People* are incorporated to integrate organizational aspects into the assessment. Table 1 illustrates the connection between the dimensions of the MM and their relevance to the iDAM. It also highlights the elements influenced by these dimensions for subsequent utilization.

Table 1. Connection of MM dimensions to the iDAM.

Dimension of I4.0MM [19]	Relevance to iDAM	Focused iDAM element
Customer	Low	Application Landscape (2.1)
Product		
Operation	Middle	Application Landscape (2.1) and Process Model (2.2)
Technology	High	
People		
Culture	Middle	
Leadership		Process Model (2.2)
Strategy	Low	
Governance		

3.2 Application Landscape

An application landscape consists of a set of representative applications for DA and aims to inspire project participants to identify individual use cases. It is structured into two dimensions: analytics type and project type. In the literature, the main categories of analytics are divided into three hierarchical and sometimes overlapping groups: *descriptive, predictive*, and *prescriptive* analytics [20]. Project types are clustered based on the level of clarity of question (discovery) and level of computing needs (infrastructure). Four project types are differentiated: *smaller data, well-defined, exploratory*, and *hard-to-justify* [21]. Based on these two dimensions, we provide the preliminary structure of a selection board to recommend an appropriate application in Fig. 3. Considering these two factors, we can roughly estimate the project's complexity.

		Recommended Maturity Level			
		Low	Middle		High
Dimension	Analytics Type	Descriptive	Predictive		Prescriptive
	Project Type	Smaller Data	Well-Defined	Exploratory	Hard to justify
		Low	Middle		High
		Complexity of the Project			

Fig. 3. Selection board of the application landscape.

3.3 Project Situation

A project situation is defined by the *context* and the *project* [22]. The context was set as the industrial SME environment. In a recent study, Schwarz et al. [23] focus on early-stage assessment of DA use cases by incorporating criteria that allow informed estimations of potential benefits and feasibility. Three sections are distinguished: (1) *Use case description*, (2) *use case evaluation*, and (3) *summary* (see Fig. 4). Our initial prototype draws from the framework by Schwarz et al. [23].

3.4 Situational Process Model for Data Analytics

In the context of manufacturing SMEs, their needs, and the overwhelming options of data science methodologies, our approach aims to ensure a well-suited DA workflow. Situational method engineering is a flexible methodology that enables the creation of tailored methods based on the specific situation [22]. Two mechanisms are involved in situational method engineering: configuration and composition [22]. Configuration involves adapting components of a basic method depending on specific situations [24]. Composition entails selecting and orchestrating method fragments from different base methods to generate new results [22]. Our model uses a configuration-based approach to minimize the complexity that arises from multiple options and fragments. Karlsson and

<table>
<tr><th colspan="20">1. Use Case Description</th></tr>
<tr><td colspan="5">Status</td><td colspan="5">Initiator(s)</td><td colspan="5">Problem statement</td><td colspan="5">Solution</td></tr>
<tr><td colspan="5">Addressed users(s)</td><td colspan="5">Addressed needs</td><td colspan="5">Objective KPI(s)</td><td colspan="5">Responsible(s)</td></tr>
<tr><th colspan="20">2. Use Case Evaluation</th></tr>
<tr><td colspan="20">Evaluator</td></tr>
<tr><td colspan="10">Added Value</td><td colspan="10">Strategic Fit</td></tr>
<tr><td colspan="4">Data Availability and Access</td><td colspan="4">Data Quality</td><td colspan="4">Data Security and private Constraints</td><td colspan="4">Tools and Technologies</td><td colspan="4">Expertise</td></tr>
<tr><td colspan="10">Costs</td><td colspan="10">Timeliness</td></tr>
<tr><th colspan="20">3. Summary</th></tr>
<tr><td colspan="5">Stakeholder</td><td colspan="5">Risks</td><td colspan="5">Total Score</td><td colspan="5">Conclusion</td></tr>
</table>

Fig. 4. Framework for data and analytics use case evaluation by Schwarz et al. [23].

Ågerfalk [24] propose a generic three-phase process for the situational method configuration (SMC). The three phases involve (1) defining configuration packages (CPs) for specific parts of a development situation, (2) combining CPs in configuration templates (CTs) for recurrent project characteristics, and (3) selecting an adequate CT based on the project situation [24]. We selected the following three base methodologies for our initial prototype: *CRISP-DM, DASC-PM*, and *SRM*. Based on these models, we present the selection board to support the recommendation of the base method for the SMC in Fig. 5. Once a base method is configured, the project methodology is adapted.

<table>
<tr><th></th><th></th><th colspan="6">Base Methodology for Data Analytics</th></tr>
<tr><td></td><td></td><td>SRM</td><td colspan="3">CRISP-DM</td><td colspan="2">DASC-PM</td></tr>
<tr><td rowspan="2">Dimension</td><td>Maturity Level</td><td>Low</td><td colspan="3">Middle</td><td colspan="2">High</td></tr>
<tr><td>Project complexity</td><td colspan="2">Low</td><td>Middle</td><td colspan="2">High</td><td>Very high</td></tr>
</table>

Fig. 5. Selection board of the base method.

4 Demonstration and Evaluation

The applicability of iDAM is demonstrated with a practical use case. The evaluation follows the structure proposed by vom Brocke and Mendling [25]: situation faced, action taken, results achieved, and lessons learned.

Situation Faced. We successfully demonstrated iDAM at a medium-sized machine manufacturer in a practical case study. Their key product can be categorized as a unique metal shaft with high accuracy requirements. A multi-stage manufacturing process and classical brownfield conditions represent the production environment. The organization aims at improving its operational performance, product quality, and decision-making through DA. In the ongoing digitalization project, the organization mainly acts autonomously and gets support from cross-functional teams when needed.

Action Taken. In accordance with the iDAM prototype, we started with a maturity assessment and conducted a workshop to answer the questionnaire of the chosen MM from Schumacher et al. [19]. During the assessment, we focused on the manufacturing department and collaborating teams rather than the entire enterprise. Low maturity levels were recognized, especially in the technology and people dimensions (output 2.1).

For the next phase of iDAM, it is crucial to suggest a use case from the application landscape that aligns with the maturity levels achieved. According to the selection board in Fig. 3, we chose to realize a *descriptive analysis* with the project type *smaller data* (output 3). This approach ensured clearly defined analysis goals and requires minimal effort for infrastructure setup [21].

In a workshop within the core team, we defined the use case to complete the situation. The framework in Fig. 4 provided guidance to describe and evaluate our project. To validate the practical application of the iDAM, our objective is to monitor the mileage of the x-axis (longest axis) in a grinding machine. Maintaining this critical component is essential for achieving optimal performance and meeting high-quality surface requirements. It is specified that the maintenance should be carried out annually or after the axis has reached one million meters. Data availability and quality are ensured by an existing connectivity solution on the machine controller, which stores the current position of the axis. The project aims to calculate and visualize the distance traveled along the x-axis and alert the maintenance team when one of the defined intervals is reached.

Following the selection board in Fig. 5, we defined the SRM as the base method for this practical scenario according to the estimated complexity from the project framework (output 4) and the low maturity level of supporting dimensions (output 2.2). Following the three-phase process for SMC from Karlsson and Ågerfalk [24], we defined each phase of the process model as a CP. In theory, CTs are possible for all combinations of CPs. Within our research, we identified the relevant CTs outlined in Table 2 and defined the CPs data situation, transformation, and solution container as mandatory for usage in the iDAM. To accommodate the condition monitoring use case, we opted for CT3. We deemed CP1 unnecessary due to the project description and evaluation framework (output 4) providing a clear definition. The absence of any data science aspects meant that CP4 was not a requirement, as this project solely requires descriptive data visualization. After completing the SMC approach, we can provide a tailored process model that ensures efficient use of resources and cost for our condition monitoring use case.

Results Achieved. As a practical contribution, we created an online dashboard as a maintenance support tool. It features key performance indicators, such as the average distance reached within the last 24 h, seven days, and 30 days. It also includes the mileage covered since the previous maintenance and a forecast of the estimated days before maintenance action is required. If the remaining days are exceeded, an alerting system becomes active and sends information via e-mail.

Our research demonstrated the practical applicability of the iDAM in a real-world scenario. This indicates that the prototype is effective and can be utilized in various business or academic projects. Within information systems research, prototyping already serves as a technical evaluation of artifacts [26]. In our study, the practical artifact demonstration represents the non-theoretical evaluation of our artifact's prototype at the same time.

Table 2. Configuration templates of the SRM.

	Configuration Template (CT)			
Configuration Package (CP)	CT1	CT2	CT3	CT4
CP1 = Phase 1: Definition	X	X		
CP2 = Phase 2: Data Situation	X	X	X	X
CP3 = Phase 3: Transformation	X	X	X	X
CP4 = Phase 3A: Data Analytics	X			X
CP5 = Phase 4: Solution Container	X	X	X	X

X = inclusion in the individual CT.
… = all combinations are theoretically possible

Lessons Learned. To create the theoretical evaluation, we discussed the utility of the iDAM prototype within our project team and applied a SWOT analysis. Like prototyping, feedback can be directly incorporated into subsequent construction cycles. Table 3 presents the key takeaways from the SWOT workshop.

Table 3. Key takeaways of the SWOT workshop.

Strengths	Weaknesses
• structured, transparent, and documentation • practical guidelines on where to start • optimized resource and project efficiency • tailored to the maturity • SME centric	• good knowledge of various process models needed • high methodical competency needed (SMC, applying the process models) • generic I40MM
Opportunities	**Threats**
• rapid and continuous learning • increase of the maturity levels • enhances usage of process methodologies	• overwhelming options and variations of different process models and different CTs • risk of overcomplication

5 Conclusion, Limitations, and Future Research

SMEs continue to grapple with challenges in adopting I4.0 technologies, notably DA [4]. Our paper introduces the iDAM prototype, a structured framework developed to aid manufacturing SMEs in incorporating DA activities into their routine operations. The practicality of the iDAM prototype was confirmed by a hands-on demonstration. Its design has been successfully evaluated in a SWOT workshop. Overall, the presented model facilitates smoother integration tailored to each organization's unique maturity level and individual project. Practitioners can use our prototype to realize DA applications based on their maturity and get tailored methodical support. Our research contributes to the knowledge base by introducing a practical model for the operational adoption of DA.

Our approach is limited in several aspects. The evaluation revealed the potential of the iDAM in supporting SMEs, enhancing their maturity levels, augmenting the practical application of existing DA methodologies, and providing efficient guidance in operationalizing DA. However, achieving optimal utilization of the iDAM requires extensive knowledge and methodical competence, especially when integrating the SMC approach and the generic nature of the applied MM. This requirement is misaligned with the typical needs and capabilities of SMEs, posing a risk of introducing undue complexity. The SMC approach has amplified this complexity by presenting various process models and their variations due to different CTs. The limited range of practical examples restricts the comprehensive understanding of the diverse impacts, necessitating further exploration and case studies to substantiate the findings.

Future research needs to refine the selection of process models, employing an improved MM, and further evaluation. We plan to substitute the SMC of process models by selecting an appropriate model. A study conducted by Saltz and Hotz [27] has already identified eight factors, categorized into three themes, impacting the process model selection: technical factors (exploratory data analysis, data collection, and cleaning), organizational factors (receptiveness to methodology, team size, knowledge, and experience), and environmental factors (business requirements clarity, documentation requirements, and release cadence expectations). A second area for improvement concerns the MM. The approach by Schumacher et al. [19] is often too general and does not exactly meet our specific needs. Future work could develop a specified MM to align with the specific needs in the context of the iDAM by following the approach outlined by Becker et al. [17].

References

1. Klingenberg, C.O., Borges, M.A.V., Antunes, J.A.V., Jr.: Industry 4.0 as a data-driven paradigm: a systematic literature review on technologies. J. Manuf. Technol. Manag. **32**(3), 570–592 (2021). https://doi.org/10.1108/JMTM-09-2018-0325
2. Bichler, M., Heinzl, A., van der Aalst, W.M.P.: Business analytics and data science: once again? Bus. Inf. Syst. Eng. **59**, 77–79 (2017). https://doi.org/10.1007/s12599-016-0461-1
3. Masood, T., Sonntag, P.: Industry 4.0: adoption challenges and benefits for SMEs. Comput. Ind. **121**, 103261 (2020). https://doi.org/10.1016/j.compind.2020.103261
4. Kumar, S., Raut, R.D., Aktas, E., Narkhede, B.E., Gedam, V.V.: Barriers to adoption of industry 4.0 and sustainability: a case study with SMEs. Int. J. Comput. Integr. Manuf. **36**(5), 657–677 (2023). https://doi.org/10.1080/0951192X.2022.2128217
5. Horváth, D., Szabó, R.Z.: Driving forces and barriers of Industry 4.0: do multinational and small and medium-sized companies have equal opportunities? Technol. Forecast. Soc. Change **146**, 119–132 (2019). https://doi.org/10.1016/j.techfore.2019.05.021
6. Rösl, S., Auer, T., Schieder, C.: Addressing the data challenge in manufacturing SMEs: a comparative study of data analytics applications with a simplified reference model. In: Elstermann, M., Dittmar, A., Lederer, M. (eds.) Subject-Oriented Business Process Management. Models for Designing Digital Transformations: 14th International Conference, S-BPM ONE 2023, Rostock, Germany, May 31 – June 1, 2023, Proceedings, pp. 121–130. Springer Nature Switzerland, Cham (2023). https://doi.org/10.1007/978-3-031-40213-5_9

7. Saltz, J., Hotz, N., Wild, D., Stirling, K.: Exploring Project Management Methodologies Used Within Data Science Teams (2018)
8. Queiroz, M.M., Fosso Wamba, S., Chiappetta Jabbour, C.J., de Sousa Jabbour, A.B.L., Machado, M.C.: Adoption of Industry 4.0 technologies by organizations: a maturity levels perspective. Ann. Oper. Res. (2022). https://doi.org/10.1007/s10479-022-05006-6
9. Monchak, A., Kim, D.: Examining trends of technology diffusion theories in information systems. In: ICIS 2011 Proceedings (2011)
10. Shahadat, M.M.H., Nekmahmud, M., Ebrahimi, P., Fekete-Farkas, M.: Digital technology adoption in SMEs: what technological, environmental and organizational factors influence in emerging countries? Glob. Bus. Rev. (2023). https://doi.org/10.1177/09721509221137199
11. Davis, F.D., Bagozzi, R.P., Warshaw, P.R.: User acceptance of computer technology: a comparison of two theoretical models. Manage. Sci. **35**, 982–1003 (1989). https://doi.org/10.1287/mnsc.35.8.982
12. Tornatzky, L.G., Fleischer, M., Chakrabarti, A.K.: Processes of Technological Innovation. Lexington books (1990)
13. Ebrahimi, S., Ghasemaghaei, M., Hassanein, K.: Understanding the role of data analytics in driving discriminatory managerial decisions. In: ICIS 2016 Proceedings (2016)
14. Martinez, I., Viles, E., Olaizola, I.G.: Data science methodologies: current challenges and future approaches. Big Data Res. **24**, 100183 (2021). https://doi.org/10.1016/j.bdr.2020.100183
15. Haertel, C., Pohl, M., Nahhas, A., Staegemann, D., Turowski, K.: Toward a lifecycle for data science: a literature review of data science process models. In: PACIS 2022 Proceedings (2022)
16. Schulz, M., et al.: Introducing DASC-PM: a data science process model. In: ACIS 2020 Proceedings (2020)
17. Becker, J., Knackstedt, R., Pöppelbuß, J.: Developing maturity models for IT management. Bus. Inf. Syst. Eng. **1**, 213–222 (2009). https://doi.org/10.1007/s12599-009-0044-5
18. Hein-Pensel, F., et al.: Maturity assessment for Industry 5.0: a review of existing maturity models. J. Manuf. Syst. **66**, 200–210 (2023). https://doi.org/10.1016/j.jmsy.2022.12.009
19. Schumacher, A., Erol, S., Sihn, W.: A maturity model for assessing industry 4.0 readiness and maturity of manufacturing enterprises. Procedia CIRP **52**, 161–166 (2016). https://doi.org/10.1016/j.procir.2016.07.040
20. Delen, D., Ram, S.: Research challenges and opportunities in business analytics. J. Bus. Anal. **1**, 2–12 (2018). https://doi.org/10.1080/2573234X.2018.1507324
21. Saltz, J., Shamshurin, I., Connors, C.: Predicting data science sociotechnical execution challenges by categorizing data science projects. J. Am. Soc. Inf. Sci. **68**, 2720–2728 (2017). https://doi.org/10.1002/asi.23873
22. Bucher, T., Klesse, M., Kurpjuweit, S., Winter, R.: Situational method engineering. In: Ralyté, J., Brinkkemper, S., Henderson-Sellers, B. (eds.) Situational Method Engineering: Fundamentals and Experiences, pp. 33–48. Springer US, Boston, MA (2007). https://doi.org/10.1007/978-0-387-73947-2_5
23. Schwarz, D., Mueller, R.M., List, M.: A framework for the systematic evaluation of data and analytics use cases at an early stage. In: Proceedings of the 56th Hawaii International Conference on System Sciences (2023)
24. Karlsson, F., Ågerfalk, P.J.: Method configuration: adapting to situational characteristics while creating reusable assets. Inf. Softw. Technol. **46**, 619–633 (2004). https://doi.org/10.1016/j.infsof.2003.12.004
25. vom Brocke, J., Mendling, J.: Frameworks for business process management: a taxonomy for business process management cases. In: vom Brocke, J., Mendling, J. (eds.) Business Process Management Cases, pp. 1–17. Springer International Publishing, Cham (2018). https://doi.org/10.1007/978-3-319-58307-5_1

26. Storey, M.T.: Design science in the information systems discipline: an introduction to the special issue on design science research. MIS Q. **32**(4), 725 (2008). https://doi.org/10.2307/25148869
27. Saltz, J., Hotz, N.: Factors that influence the selection of a data science process management methodology: an exploratory study. In: Proceedings of the 54th Hawaii International Conference on System Sciences, pp. 949–959 (2021)

AutoPose: Pose Estimation for Prevention of Musculoskeletal Disorders Using LSTM

Francesco Bassino-Riglos, Cesar Mosqueira-Chacon, and Willy Ugarte(✉)

Universidad Peruana de Ciencias Aplicadas, Lima, Peru
{U201816649,U201910750}@upc.edu.pe, willy.ugarte@upc.pe

Abstract. Office work has become the most prevalent occupation in contemporary society, necessitating long hours of sedentary behavior that can lead to mental and physical fatigue, including the risk of developing musculoskeletal disorders (MSDs). To address this issue, we have proposed an innovative system that utilizes the NAO robot for posture alerts and camera for image capture, YoloV7 for landmark extraction, and an LSTM recurrent network for posture prediction. Although our model has shown promise, further improvements can be made, particularly by enhancing the dataset's robustness. With a more comprehensive and diverse dataset, we anticipate a significant enhancement in the model's performance. In our evaluation, the model achieved an accuracy of 67%, precision of 44%, recall of 67%, and an F1 score of 53%. These metrics provide valuable insights into the system's effectiveness and highlight the areas where further refinements can be implemented. By refining the model and leveraging a more extensive dataset, we aim to enhance the accuracy and precision of bad posture detection, thereby empowering office workers to adopt healthier postural habits and reduce the risk of developing MSDs.

Keywords: Recurrent network · LSTM · NAO robot · Bad posture · Computer vision

1 Introduction

Office work is one of the most common jobs in our society, where we can spend up to more than 8 h sitting in front of a computer, laptop, tablet or notebook. In 2021 the average number of Europeans using a computer for work was 58% with variations between 37% and 85% depending on the country surveyed. In just 10 years the average growth per year of computer use in the workspace increased by 14%. If we estimated that this number is only going to increase (as it has been doing for a decade), it can be concluded that the number of people who end up suffering bodily pain from sitting is also going to increase [5].

Sitting for prolonged working hours can cause various fatigues both mentally and physically. In a study of 447 Iranian office workers, it was found that 48.8% of the participants did not feel comfortable at their workstation and 73.6% felt

S. Terzi et al. (Eds.): IN4PL 2023, CCIS 1886, pp. 223–238, 2023.
https://doi.org/10.1007/978-3-031-49339-3_14

exhausted during the day. Also, 53.5% suffer from neck pain, 53.2% from low back pain and 51.6% from shoulder pain [4]. Apart from muscle discomfort, it also causes increased pressure, friction and shear on the chair, and the rubbing of the chair against the skin for a prolonged time causes the skin to peel off, leading to severe pressure ulcers, leading to death [1].

To attack this problem we have to divide it in sub-problems, the difficulty encountered lays on the idea of an exponential number of ways to solve this problem based on the way that we're gonna solve each one of the sub-problems. We have to decide what tools you may or may not use. The first sub-problem we need to solve is how to estimate a pose, which can be fairly simple using tools like Open Pose [3], PoseNet [12] or Deepcut [19], which are APIs that are able to use pose estimation algorithms mainly using pre-trained models of CNN variations like Mask R-CNN [8], or straight up models like YoloV7 [22] or others pre-trained CNN architectures. The complications come in one major factor: How can we determine when a person is in a bad posture or at risk of generating muscleskeletal problems in the future? For that we need a Machine Learning model capable enough to detected what posture is and why is it harming for the worker.

Similar solutions have been reached in different papers. These vary in the way they solve the problem, for example in [5] they used weight and motion sensors in a chair. However, this does not fit our solution, since implementing a chair requires more time and money. We are looking for a solution that is quick, inexpensive and easy to use. Other solutions point to camera systems, like the one we propose, but with a different approach. In the article [13] the authors implement a camera system with a MobileNet V2 [21] neural network. However, all of the approaches proposed are not accurate classifying bad posture, being limited to basic movements and not accurately displaying the problem.

The key components of our approach are the following. We implement a LSTM model, which gives us the best accuracy and runtime from all the other models tested. We use the NAO Robot for the camera, which also gives us the ability to give the user feedback in case the worker is in a bad posture. Some complications may come when putting all the systems together and creating a application. Furthermore, the implementation and creation of a dataset that allows us to train and test our application and model.

Our main contributions are as follows:

- We have proposed a LSTM model for bad posture detection.
- We have implemented a dataset consisting of images of good and bad posture at different angles.
- We have implemented a system that allows to estimate pose and prevent muscleskeletal disorders (MSD) using the NAO robot.

This paper is divided into the following sections: In Sect. 2, we review related work on preventing MSD and pose estimation. We then discuss relevant concepts and theories related to the background of our research and describe in more detail our main contribution in Sect. 3. Furthermore, we will explain the procedures performed and the experiments conducted in this work in Sect. 4. At the end, we will show the main conclusions of the project and indicate some recommendations for future work in Sect. 5.

2 Related Works

The seating pose correction has been a concern since the office work became more and more present in the modern life. That is because this kind of sedentary work leads to back pain and other diseases that encompasses the MSD concept. The posture correction goes back to 1,850 with the invention of the corset. However, our research focuses on the pose correction to prevent aforementioned MSD's. We were able to find some other similar solution. We found some others solution to relevant problems like classifying pose, detecting wrong seating postures, and pose estimation using cameras, waves (WiFi) or sensors.

In [18], the authors propose the development of a smart chair that can classify different seating postures. The chair uses 8 sensors placed in strategic places on the chair, each one can determine the pressure applied to them and then send them via WiFi to a desktop application. They were able to classify 8 different postures, to do that they did an experiment on over 40 subjects inviting them to seat on those positions. They trained a deep learning model that is able to classify that data with a 91.68% accuracy. Our idea is different than this one in a few ways since, we are using a pose estimation system based on the input of a camera instead of sensors and instead of classifying the poses with a training data, we rely on an LSTM which will be trained based on assessments [7] that have already been studied by the corresponding scientists of the area. This means that our solution will have a more robust way to proof if the output is right or wrong than a classifier.

In [14] they explain the importance of the preventing the Work-related muscleskeletal disorders. Mostly related to the kind of labor that leaks on ergonomic assistance like tasks found in hotels, factories, construction, assembling, and big etc. They use cameras for this solution and since they try to get a real time response the model they use for predicting this is a long-short term memory neural network (LSTMNN). The LSTMNN is a model that allows inputs of sequences of data like videos. In order to determine which pose is risky or not they use Ovako Working Posture Analysis System [7] (OWAS). Which are a set of assessments that can give a score of how good or bad the posture is and that's the output they try to get. Our approach is heavily inspired by this paper since it points out the importance of preventing MSD in a work related environment and it also explains various methods that we could use to solve this problem. Our solution also uses a single camera to detect the joint positions and then a trained LSTMNN to define the risk factor on each posture and compare them with the OWAS metrics.

In [11], the authors developed a model that receives input from a system that can determine the position of a person through wireless classifier. The model would be a Support vector machine (SVM) and they intent to classify 7 daily life activities. They manage to get a 95.4% accuracy. They use 4 layers and 6 classifiers, the first classifier determines if the subject is in movement or staying. The second classifier determines if the subject is running or walking. The third classifier determines if the movement in question is a body or joint caused. The forth classifier determines if the subject is seating or standing. The other two are used to detect if the movement is caused by a feet or arm and the last one classifies the frequency or repetitions of the movement. This proposal intends to prove that the human body can reflect certain frequencies of radio waves by detecting this daily life activities. This differs from our approach solution-wise, since we intend to prevent MSD by detecting seating postures, and theirs is developing a human activity detector that is robust to environmental changes (thus the WiFi approach). They use the machine learning model SVM and we're using a deep learning approach like is the LSTM. This means that the model they trained will be able to detect human activities with high accuracy since the WiFi model they built is able to detect the pose very accurately and from there the SVM will have an easier job. On the other side our solution using a camera will probably struggle estimating the pose but the LSTM should have an easier job since it'll use a sequence of 3 or 5 frames to process the final output.

In [23], the authors developed a model monitor sleep posture in patients. That is important because it can track the progression of Parkinson's patients and epilepsy patients that often sleep in fatal postures. To achieve this they used radio frequencies. Apparently the human body can act as a reflector in low GHz frequencies. They made an experiment on 26 different homes using 26 different subjects and more than 200 nights. They achieved a precision of 83.7% with only 16 min of data. The problem they're trying to solve can relate to ours. With the difference that we're trying to prevent problems that a bad posture can lead to when we're working in a desk and they're aiming to prevent problems that bad posture can cause when sleeping. The approach they took to solve the problem differs with ours in a similar way than [18], since they'll have an easier time estimating the pose. However since in this case they're trying to detect sleeping fatal postures, we believe that in this case it would be harder to validate the output of their model even with a larger dataset although, 83.7% accuracy is really good.

In [13], the authors developed a system that is able to predict a few different types of seating postures using just the webcam that records a front view of the user. They made a variation on MobileNetV2 allowing it to use video as an input by including recurrent layers on it making the network able to use sequences of frames to determine the type of posture that is being recorded using an unsupervised machine learning approach. Ours could be considered an improvement to this solution since we're gonna use the camera in a more strategic place than the web cam. That will give a better result. However, it might be harder or more uncomfortable to use in case it becomes a product. The paper present various comparisons and between different models, the main ones he compares are a Convolutional Neural Network (CNN), a LSTM, ResNetV2 [9] a MobileNetV2 model, presenting confusion matrices and different accuracy values for different situations like the frame-rate of the camera in case they're using a recurrent neural network and different resolutions of the images in use. We will replicate this result showing process with a similar benchmark.

3 Preventing Musculoskeletal Problems with Pose Estimation

3.1 Preliminary Concepts

In this sections we will introduce in a more elaborated way the concepts we are going to use in the rest of this work. Mostly including deep learning, computer vision and ergonomics.

Definition 1: (Human Activity Recognition): HAR is a subfield of computer vision and machine learning that focuses on identifying and analyzing human activities using different methods for data collection such as cameras, sensors, radio waves, accelerometers, etc. The goal of HAR is to automatically recognize and classify human actions or behaviors in real-time, with applications ranging from surveillance and security to healthcare and sports performance analysis. This is a very broad definition and the we consider that the problem we're trying to solve is consider a sub-field related to HAR since we will use the same concept of HAR to monitor ergonomics in order to detect issues in posture.

Definition 2: (Joint angle estimation): In order to be able to detect MSD must have information about the current state of the human body. Most assessments to detect MSD require the angles between various joints in the body, such as the knee, elbow, and shoulder. With those we may be able to identify some abnormal patterns or postures that could lead to MSDs.

Definition 3: (Ergonomics): Ergonomics is the study of how to design workspaces, tools, and equipment to minimize the risk of injury or strain. By combining computer vision data with ergonomic principles, it may be possible to identify specific changes to workspaces or equipment that could reduce the risk of MSDs.

Definition 4: (Posture assessments): In ergonomics, there are some metrics used to determine the risk factor of a human posture, one of the most popular would be OWAS. Its goal is to evaluate posture and movement to assess their risk based on a set of guidelines. Its requires human input and observation but it does help as a method of validation for algorithms that try to perform similar solutions. For our case, the most useful metric would be the Rapid Upper Limb Assessment (RULA), which is used to estimate the risk of developing MSDs in the upper links, neck and trunk. It involves analyzing the worker's upper limb trunk [17].

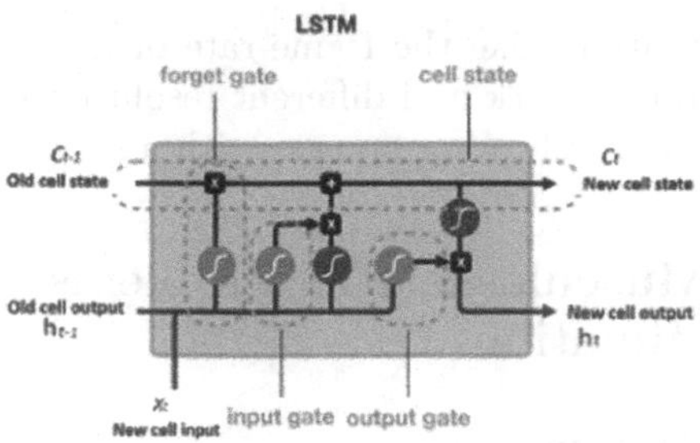

Fig. 1. Recurrent LSTM Network [10].

3.2 Method

The Model. A recurrent LSTM network will be used to realize the bad posture recognition system. This network is a type of neural network that can process data sequences and remember relevant information efficiently. The architecture is shown in Fig. 1.

Input and output size: The LSTM network will take sequences of body position landmarks as inpworked ut. The input size will depend on the number of tracking points used to represent the body position at each time instant. For example, if a tracking point-based approach is used, one could have a 2D or 3D input for each point, resulting in a multi-dimensional input. The model output could be a binary value indicating whether the pose is good or bad. Multiple LSTM layers can be used to process sequences of input data and learn more complex and higher level features. For example, an architecture with two LSTM layers could be used, where the first layer processes the input sequence and the second layer processes the output of the first layer.

LSTM layer size: The number of units in each LSTM layer is a hyperparameter to be adjusted during training. The size of the LSTM layer is related to the complexity of the model and its ability to learn more complex patterns. A layer with a larger number of units will have more capacity to learn patterns, but will also require more computational resources and may be prone to overfitting. In addition to the LSTM layers, other layers can be added to the model, such as activation layers, clustering layers, convolutional layers, etc. These layers can help extract more relevant features from the input and improve model performance.

Regularization: It is important to include regularization techniques in the model to avoid overfitting. This can be achieved by adding dropout layers, reducing the size of the layers, and increasing the amount of training data.

In summary, designing an LSTM network for bad posture estimation is a process that requires experimentation and tuning of the hyperparameters to find the architecture that best suits the data and the specific task. It is important to consider factors such as the size of the input and output, the number and size of LSTM layers, the inclusion of additional layers and regularization techniques to ensure optimal model performance.

Our Dataset. The second contribution is a dataset to train LSTM models for the detection of bad posture. In our system, it is important to have a complete dataset with the necessary frames. To achive that, we created our own dataset, based on short videos that gave us different angles to work with. First, a study had to be done on what are the most common postures of the workers, as well as the environment in which they work. Another important factor is the angle at which the camera is positioned, since the input we want to get is from the NAO robot, the angle of the images with which the model is trained with, has to be close to those that will be used with the NAO robot in the final system (which is shown on Fig. 2).

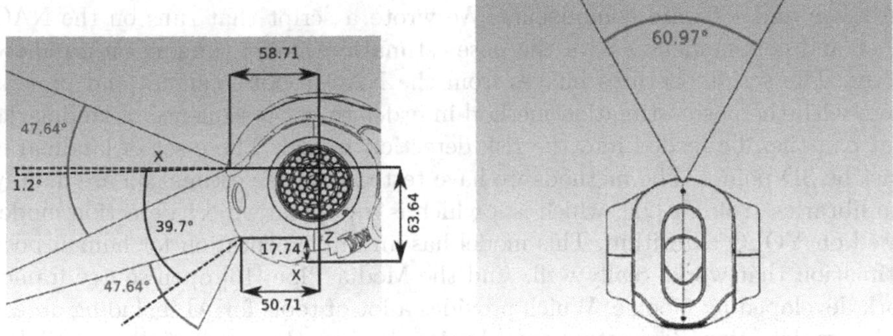

Fig. 2. Camera angles for the NAO Robot (https://www.aldebaran.com/en/nao).

Our Pose Estimation Model. The system consists of two main components: the NAO robot and the LSTM-based pose estimation model. The NAO robot is a humanoid robot designed to interact with humans in various settings, such as education, entertainment, and healthcare. In our system, we utilized the NAO robot's built-in camera to capture images of the user's posture, which is a crucial input for the pose estimation model. The images are then fed into the LSTM-based pose estimation model, which is a type of recurrent neural network that is particularly effective in modeling sequential data, such as body joint positions over time. The LSTM-based model is trained on a dataset of labeled postures, including good posture and various types of bad posture, such as slouching, leaning, and hunching. The model learns to recognize different postures and detect bad posture by analyzing the temporal patterns of body joint positions in the input images. If the model detects bad posture, the NAO robot alerts the user with a voice message, which is designed to be polite and informative, asking them to adjust their posture. The voice message is an important feedback mechanism that helps the user correct their posture and prevent MSD. This flow can be seen in Fig. 3.

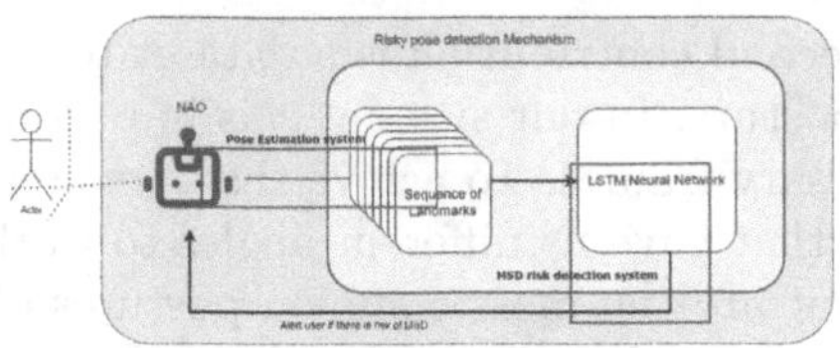

Fig. 3. System to prevent musclesqueletal problems.

To integrate the LSTM-based pose estimation model with the NAO robot, we used the Python programming language and the NAOqi SDK, which is a software development kit that provides an interface to control the NAO robot's hardware and software components. We wrote a script that runs on the NAO robot and communicates with the pose estimation model running on a remote server. The script captures images from the NAO robot's camera and process them with the pose estimation method in order to get a sequence of landmarks that can then be feeded into the risk detection model. These set of landmarks must be 3D points. The methods we have tested for pose estimation are mainly two libraries. YoloV7 [22], which is a which is a popular object detection model based on YOLO algorithm. This model has an implementation for human pose estimation that works really well. And the Media Pipe [16] open-source framework developed by Google. Which provides a lot of tools for AI including object and pose detection. The actual contribution, besides the usage of these available tools, would be the approach we're taking to improve their performance since we need them to work fast so the actual risk detection process doesn't take to long. We intend to enhance the performance of these algorithms by applying filters and preprocessing to the images as well as testing them in different aspect ratios, resolutions and fps. Also tweak the YoloV7 model a bit to make it focus on only one object in order to make it faster (Fig. 4).

Fig. 4. Pose estimation example using yolov7.

The prepossessed images are then fed into the LSTM-based pose estimation model, which outputs a binary classification result indicating whether the user is sitting in a good posture or a bad posture. If the model detects bad posture, the script triggers a voice message from the NAO robot asking the user to adjust their posture. The voice message is played through the NAO robot's built-in speaker, which is located in the head module, and is designed to be audible and clear, even in noisy environments.

4 Experiments

In this section, we will provide a concise overview of the experiments conducted in our project, focusing on the comparison of pose estimation techniques between YoloV7 and MediaPipe. We will also discuss the implementation of an LSTM model for predicting bad posture. Additionally, we will outline the necessary requirements for replicating these experiments and provide a brief discussion of the obtained results.

The first experiment in our project involved comparing the performance of two pose estimation techniques: YoloV7 and MediaPipe. Pose estimation is a computer vision task that aims to detect and track human poses in images or videos. YoloV7 and MediaPipe are popular frameworks used for pose estimation, and we chose to evaluate their effectiveness in our research.

The second experiment focused on developing an LSTM (Long Short-Term Memory) model for predicting bad posture. This experiment aimed to address the problem of identifying and predicting incorrect body postures in real-time. The LSTM model was trained on a labeled dataset that consisted of time-series data capturing different body postures and corresponding labels indicating whether the posture was correct or incorrect. The experimental setup included a diverse dataset of images and videos containing various human sitting poses.

4.1 Experimental Protocol

In this subsection, we provide details about the environment on which we conducted the experiments. This includes information about the computer hardware we used and some of the software we employed.

The following tests were executed on a laptop using an Intel i7-8750H (12) @ 2.200 GHz, 16 GB of RAM running an Arch Linux system using Xorg Display Server. The source code of the code we display here can be found at https://github.com/Cesarmosqueira/Autoposture, a requirements.txt file shows the modules we used. Some of the most worth mentioning ones are Pytorch[1], Mediapipe [16], Naoqi[2], and OpenCV[3].

4.2 Pose Estimation

In the pose estimation section you will see the proposed experiments. In this case there are two: Frames per second and 3D landmarks. The aim of these experiments is to find the library that best balances performance with accuracy when displaying results.

[1] PyTorch - https://pytorch.org/.

[2] NaoQi SDK - https://www.softbankrobotics.com/emea/en/naoqi-developer-program/.

[3] OpenCV - https://opencv.org/.

FPS. The FPS evaluates the performance in execution of the library and its capacity to be fast. The more frames per second it has, the smoother the display and the more natural the user will be able to move.

For this we tested both libraries for a period of time to get a FPS graph. All the experiments where conducted under the same machine, configuration and environment. The person used for the tests was the same and doing the same movements. We obtained the following results:

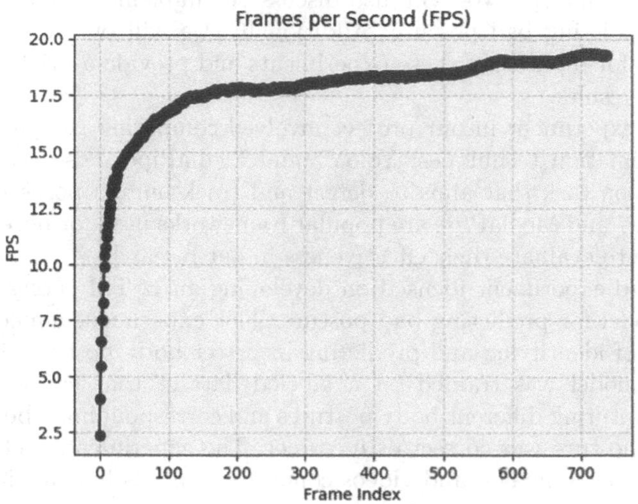

Fig. 5. Mediapipe FPS.

You can see the difference in FPS and conscientiousness between Mediapipe (see Fig. 5) and Yolo (see Fig. 6). The former shows up a little less than 20 frames per second, which is a very promising figure for these systems that require a lot of real-time processing. Meanwhile, Yolo is around 19 frames per second in the same time. This result is expected for a library like yoloV7. While is not as stable throw time as Mediapipe, is very stable for the kind of application we want. The Frames Per Second are very important but not the only metric we want, so both of them are viable options at this point.

3D Landmarks. The most important metric is the 3D landmarks of each library. These are the ones that will be sent to the lstm in order to perform the bad posture prediction. For this purpose, pose estimation was performed using the same image, to compare and contrast the results.

In Fig. 7 it can be seen how mediapipe doesn't estimate the pose properly, especially in the section of the hands and thighs. In addition, it does not have a visualization of the neck, which can be of great help for this project. In the first image of mediapipe it is possible to see clearly the torso, however in the second one it is more difficult to see and distinguish the points of the shoulder.

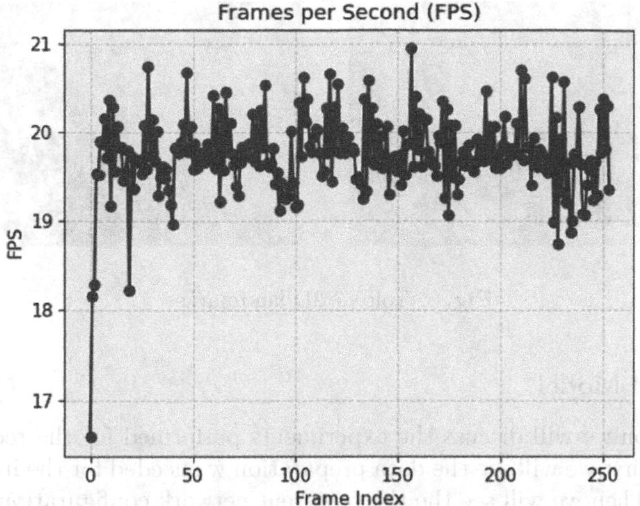

Fig. 6. YoloV7 FPS.

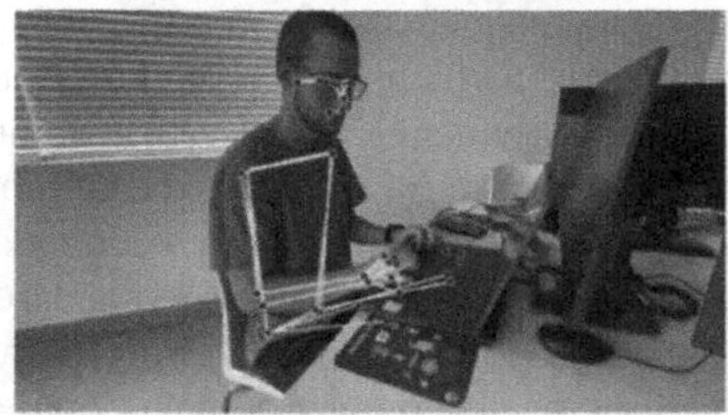

Fig. 7. Mediapipe: 3D landmarks.

On the other hand in Fig. 8 we see that yoloV7 has clearer landmarks, with color distinctions between the main body parts for understanding. It also estimates the pose more accurately, with a landmark for the neck. Also, you can see how in the second image, the torso, hands, neck and thighs are still clearly visible, giving more detail.

Results. While mediapipe has slightly better results in Frames per second, giving a better fluidity and image quality. In the 3D landmarks section it is not as accurate, not recognizing some body parts well. Meanwhile, Yolo well rounded library, giving just one frame less than mediapipe but with much better 3D landmarks. We can conclude that the better library for this applpication is YoloV7.

Fig. 8. YoloV7 3D landmarks.

4.3 LSTM Model

In this section we will discuss the experiments performed for the recurrent network lstm. First we will see the data preparation we needed for the input layer of the LSTM. Then we will see the the recurrent network configuration and finally the results obtained.

Data Preparation. In the process of recovering sequences of reference points, we establish a parameter called "sequence_length", which represents the number of frames taken into consideration to form a sequence of reference points. Additionally, we define another parameter called "gap", indicating the number of frames skipped between one set of reference points and the next in a sequence.

To capture the necessary reference points, we take samples at intervals determined by the established gap. From these captured reference points, we generate multiple matrices, with a total of "N" matrices, each having a length equal to the "sequence_length". Each matrix contains the reference points corresponding to the captured frame sequence.

Regarding the identification of the same individual in each iteration, the approach was as follow. Firstly, we identify the object with the highest number of identified reference points and store this set of reference points as "base_landmarks". Then, in subsequent iterations, we evaluate the distance between the reference points of "base_landmarks" and the reference points of other identified objects. This distance measurement allows us to determine the similarity between the reference points of different objects and establish the correspondence with the same person throughout the iterations.

To obtain a comprehensive dataset for posture classification, a script was developed where the user selects whether the posture is good or bad. The program divides each video into frames and, for each frame, the user presses a key on the keyboard to classify the posture. In the end, a CSV file is generated containing the sequence of feature points along with their corresponding posture labels.

LSTM Configuration. The LSTM model configuration consists of several components. Firstly, there is an LSTM layer, which is a type of recurrent neural network layer specifically designed to handle sequential data. It takes input sequences with a dimensionality of 57 and has a hidden size of 64. The 'batch_first=True' argument indicates that the input data has its batch dimension as the first dimension.

To prevent overfitting and improve generalization, a dropout layer is included in the model. The dropout layer randomly sets a fraction of input units to zero during training, in this case with a dropout rate of 0.2. This helps to regularize the model and reduce the likelihood of overfitting.

Following the LSTM layer and dropout layer, there are two fully connected (FC) layers. The first FC layer takes the output from the LSTM layer, which has a size of 64, and maps it to a lower-dimensional space with 32 output features. This FC layer performs a linear transformation on the input data. Finally, the second FC layer takes the output from the previous FC layer, which has 32 input features, and maps it to a single output feature. This layer is responsible for the final prediction or output of the model.

To introduce non-linearity into the model, a sigmoid activation function is applied after the final FC layer. The sigmoid function squashes the output values between 0 and 1, which can be interpreted as probabilities or binary predictions.

Overall, this LSTM model configuration is designed to process sequential data with 57-dimensional input sequences. It utilizes an LSTM layer for sequential modeling, a dropout layer for regularization, and two fully connected layers for dimensionality reduction and prediction. The sigmoid activation function is used to generate the final output of the model.

Results. To evaluate the performance of the LSTM model for the given task, an experiment was conducted using the provided code. The experiment involved preprocessing the dataset, training the LSTM model, and evaluating its performance on the test set.

First, the data was grouped by 'video' and 'group', utilizing the pandas groupby function. The sequence length was set to 10, indicating that each input sequence would consist of 10 consecutive landmarks.

The sequences and corresponding labels were then extracted from the grouped data. For each group, landmarks and labels were retrieved. Sequential subsets of landmarks were created, and the corresponding label at the last time step of each sequence was used as the label for that sequence. The sequences and labels were stored in separate lists.

The landmarks within each sequence were then normalized using the MinMaxScaler from scikit-learn. The landmarks were flattened, normalized, and reshaped back to their original shape before being stored in the normalized_sequences array.

Label encoding was performed on the labels using the LabelEncoder from scikit-learn. The normalized sequences and encoded labels were split into training and testing sets using the train_test_split function, with a test size of 20

The training set was converted into PyTorch tensors and combined into a TensorDataset. A DataLoader was created with a batch size of 16 for efficient batch processing during training.

During training, for each epoch, the gradients were zeroed, and the forward pass was performed to obtain the outputs. The loss was calculated by comparing the outputs with the labels and then propagated backward through the network. The optimizer was used to update the model's parameters based on the calculated gradients. The loss for each epoch was printed to monitor the training progress.

After training, the model was evaluated on the test set. The test set was converted into PyTorch tensors and combined into a TensorDataset. A DataLoader was created for the test set with a batch size of 16. The model's performance was evaluated using appropriate metrics, such as accuracy, precision, recall, and F1 score.

After training the LSTM, the results are the following:

Accuracy	Precision	Recall	F1 Score
67%	44%	67%	53%

The accuracy of the model indicates the proportion of correctly predicted posture labels out of the total predictions made. In this experiment, the LSTM model achieved an accuracy of 0.67, indicating that it correctly classified 67% of the posture samples in the test set.

Precision represents the proportion of correctly predicted positive labels (good posture) out of all the samples predicted as positive. The LSTM model achieved a precision of 0.44, indicating that it correctly identified 44% of the samples with good posture.

Recall measures the proportion of correctly predicted positive labels (good posture) out of all the actual positive samples. In this experiment, the LSTM model achieved a recall of 0.67, indicating that it correctly identified 67% of the actual samples with good posture.

The F1 score is the harmonic mean of precision and recall, providing a balanced measure of model performance. The LSTM model achieved an F1 score of 0.53, reflecting the trade-off between precision and recall.

These results suggest that the LSTM model shows promise in predicting good and bad posture based on the landmark sequences as input. However, there is room for improvement, as indicated by the moderate performance metrics. Further analysis and experimentation may be required to optimize the model's architecture, hyperparameters, or dataset preprocessing techniques to enhance its performance on this task.

5 Conclusions

The results obtained by the LSTM are on a good path, however, it has to be improved, increasing not only the volume of data but also its quality. By doing so we believe that the recurrent network will increase the precision, accuracy, recall and F1 Score. As it is one of the main contributions, it is important we develop a good LSTM for the correct prediction of bad posture. We also compare two main pose estimation library to see which one had better results, test them using different videos and configuration, and ended up using YoloV7, as it was the one with better results. For the dataset and data recollection we created our own dataset and preprocess it to extract the sequences of landmarks with a label to fetch the LSTM.

The next steps for developing the pose estimation for the prevention of muscleskeletal disorders, we will train the LSTM with more and better data [6], for that we will also upgrade and improve the dataset. We will also configure the NAO robot to be used as the alert and camera for the application, as similar works [2,20]. Or work with other kinds of inputs [15]. Finally all the components described must be connected and functional inside a package for easy access.

References

1. Arshad, J., Asim, H.M., Ashraf, M.A., Jaffery, M.H., Zaidi, K.S., Amentie, M.D.: An intelligent cost-efficient system to prevent the improper posture hazards in offices using machine learning algorithms. Comput. Intell. Neurosci. **2022**, 1–9 (2022)
2. Burga-Gutierrez, E., Vasquez-Chauca, B., Ugarte, W.: Comparative analysis of question answering models for HRI tasks with NAO in Spanish. In: SIMBig, vol. 1410, pp. 3–17 (2020)
3. Cao, Z., Hidalgo, G., Simon, T., Wei, S., Sheikh, Y.: OpenPose: realtime multi-person 2d pose estimation using part affinity fields. IEEE Trans. Pattern Anal. Mach. Intell. **43**(1), 172–186 (2021)
4. Daneshmandi, H., Choobineh, A., Ghaem, H., Karimi, M.: Adverse effects of prolonged sitting behavior on the general health of office workers. J. Lifestyle Med. **7**(2), 69–75 (2017)
5. Feradov, F., Markova, V., Ganchev, T.: Automated detection of improper sitting postures in computer users based on motion capture sensors. Comput. **11**(7), 116 (2022)
6. Fernandez-Ramos, O., Johnson-Yañez, D., Ugarte, W.: Reproducing arm movements based on pose estimation with robot programming by demonstration. In: IEEE ICTAI, pp. 294–298 (2021)
7. Gómez-Galán, M., Pérez-Alonso, J., Callejón-Ferre, Á.J., López-Martínez, J.: Musculoskeletal disorders: OWAS review. Ind. Health **55**(4), 314–337 (2017)
8. He, K., Gkioxari, G., Dollár, P., Girshick, R.B.: Mask R-CNN. In: IEEE ICCV, pp. 2980–2988 (2017)
9. He, K., Zhang, X., Ren, S., Sun, J.: Identity mappings in deep residual networks. In: Leibe, B., Matas, J., Sebe, N., Welling, M. (eds.) ECCV 2016. LNCS, vol. 9908, pp. 630–645. Springer, Cham (2016). https://doi.org/10.1007/978-3-319-46493-0_38
10. Hochreiter, S., Schmidhuber, J.: Long short-term memory. Neural Comput. **9**(8), 1735–1780 (1997)
11. Jiang, Y., Hu, H., Pu, Y., Jiang, H.: Wilay: building wi-fi-based human activity recognition system through activity hierarchical relationship. In: ACM MobiQuitous, pp. 210–219 (2019)

12. Kendall, A., Grimes, M., Cipolla, R.: PoseNet: a convolutional network for real-time 6-DoF camera relocalization. In: IEEE ICCV, pp. 2938–2946 (2015)
13. Kulikajevas, A., Maskeliunas, R., Damasevicius, R.: Detection of sitting posture using hierarchical image composition and deep learning. PeerJ Comput. Sci. **7**, e442 (2021)
14. Lee, Y., Lee, C.: SEE: a proactive strategy-centric and deep learning-based ergonomic risk assessment system for risky posture recognition. Adv. Eng. Inform. **53**, 101717 (2022)
15. Leon-Urbano, C., Ugarte, W.: End-to-end electroencephalogram (EEG) motor imagery classification with long short-term. In: IEEE SSCI, pp. 2814–2820 (2020)
16. Lugaresi, C., et al.: MediaPipe: a framework for building perception pipelines. CoRR abs/1906.08172 (2019)
17. McAtamney, L., Corlett, E.N.: RULA: a survey method for the investigation of work-related upper limb disorders. Appl. Ergon. **24**(2), 91–99 (1993)
18. Najafi, T.A., Abramo, A., Kyamakya, K., Affanni, A.: Development of a smart chair sensors system and classification of sitting postures with deep learning algorithms. Sensors **22**(15), 5585 (2022)
19. Rajchl, M., et al.: DeepCut: object segmentation from bounding box annotations using convolutional neural networks. IEEE Trans. Med. Imaging **36**(2), 674–683 (2017)
20. Rodriguez, R.A., Ferroa-Guzman, J., Ugarte, W.: Classification of respiratory diseases using the NAO robot. In: ICPRAM, pp. 940–947 (2023)
21. Sandler, M., Howard, A.G., Zhu, M., Zhmoginov, A., Chen, L.: MobileNetV2: inverted residuals and linear bottlenecks, pp. 4510–4520 (2018)
22. Wang, C., Bochkovskiy, A., Liao, H.M.: YOLOv7: trainable bag-of-freebies sets new state-of-the-art for real-time object detectors. CoRR abs/2207.02696 (2022)
23. Yue, S., Yang, Y., Wang, H., Rahul, H., Katabi, D.: BodyCompass: monitoring sleep posture with wireless signals. Proc. ACM Interact. Mob. Wearable Ubiquit. Technol. **4**(2), 66:1–66:25 (2020)

Towards Circular Systems: The Role of Digital Servitization in an Italian Extended Partnership

Elena Beducci(✉), Federica Acerbi, Anna de Carolis, Sergio Terzi, and Marco Taisch

Department of Management, Economics and Industrial Engineering, Politecnico di Milano, via Lambruschini 4/b, 20156 Milan, Italy
{elena.beducci,federica.acerbi,anna.decarolis,sergio.terzi, marco.taisch}@polimi.it

Abstract. "Made in Italy" products and Italian manufacturing are worldwide recognized for their quality. Nonetheless, businesses and societies are evolving, affected by structural transformations. To maintain their competitive advantage, Italian companies are asked to move towards a transformation aligned with global call for actions addressing critical issues, such as climate change. The transition of manufacturing companies, in particular Small and Medium Enterprises (SME), towards circular economy should be supported by adequate investments. To answer a national call, the Extended Partnership (EP) "Made in Italy Circolare e Sostenibile" was established. The EP aims to provide research and innovation resources to enable circular manufacturing practices in Italian companies, developing best practices to be adopted by SMEs. One of the main themes that the EP is investigating is the one of Product Service Systems (PSS), which appear as a viable path to achieve environmental sustainability. Nonetheless, resources and researches to support manufacturing companies in the path of servitization are still required. This paper aims at presenting a project, created in the context of the EP, to support companies in the development of circular PSS business models, in particular leveraging the opportunities offered by digital technologies.

Keywords: Extended partnership · Circular economy · Product service systems

1 Introduction

Italian manufacturing is globally recognized for the quality of design, materials, and technical characteristics of **"Made in Italy"** products, in particular concerning high-end and premium commodities in leading industries.

Nonetheless, the industrial context is evolving, both from a national and global perspective. The production paradigm currently in place is one of the main causes of environmental change, hence, manufacturing activities are recognised as highly impacting on the climate change issues and they will be strongly influenced by its effects in the long term [1].

In September 2015, 193 countries of the United Nations (UN) agreed about the social and environmental issues characterising the entire society and signed the **Agenda 2030**

S. Terzi et al. (Eds.): IN4PL 2023, CCIS 1886, pp. 239–249, 2023.
https://doi.org/10.1007/978-3-031-49339-3_15

for sustainable development. The Agenda 2030 is based on 17 goals to achieve sustainable development covering the three dimensions of the triple bottom line: economic, social and environmental [2]. Among these goals, the 12th "Responsible consumption and production" suggests and encourages the adoption of circular-related strategies and processes at both consumption and production sides. More precisely, the term **circular economy (CE)** represents this goal more than others. Even though the definition is blurred, and several are still present in the extant literature [3], these definitions can be summarised in the one proposed by the Ellen MacArthur foundation. According to this definition, CE is defined as an industrial economy that should be regenerative and restorative by intention and design [4]. The diffusion of this paradigm is gaining momentum especially in the manufacturing sector [5], one of the most resource greedy sectors, through the adoption of several circular manufacturing strategies like service-based business models, material recycling, product remanufacturing and reusing, industrial symbiosis networks and closed-loop supply chains establishment, and waste management practices implementation [6]. These strategies cover the three levels upon which CE can act on: the micro level (i.e. product and processes), the meso level (i.e. the factories within their supply chains or networks) and the macro level (i.e. the regions, cities etc.) [7]. The former is considered of fundamental importance to drive the entire society towards the sustainable development thanks to the help of governments. This is highlighted in the 2021 Report of World Manufacturing Forum together with the need to pursue worldwide a transformation towards sustainability and circularity-oriented practices [8]. According to the report, the countries should be guided in enhancing sustainable and circular performances to optimize resources' consumption and minimize emissions and resource waste. Therefore, within this context, to achieve longevity and maintain its competitive advantage, **Italy should pursue transformation actions** aligned with the goals of the Agenda 2030 to answer to critical issues.

To support the transformation of the Italian manufacturing context, **a substantial amount of investment is needed.** Indeed, the Italian manufacturing network is mostly composed by Small and Medium Enterprises (SMEs), which amount to the 99.9% of Italian companies [9] and often do not have the resources (both humans and financial) to keep up with the required innovation. In the last years, it emerged that the major barriers to the transformation towards circular economy for SMEs are the lack of financial and technical resources, the lack of financial support and lack of public institutional support [10].

Thus, it is necessary to support SMEs in this transition, not only to allow them to survive and eventually thrive, but also to exploit their unique characteristics which could constitute a new sustainability benchmark. Moreover, the craftsmanship characterizing Made in Italy must be protected, enhanced, and supported as a lever to both retain and attract talents, required to foster capillary innovation in the next decades.

The **Extended Partnership (EP)** positions itself in this context. In this paper the project and its main objectives are illustrated. In particular, the role of servitization and product service system (PSS) in relation to sustainability will be analyzed, presenting future researches intention in the context of the EP.

The paper is structured as follows. Section 2 is dedicated to the description of the EP, of the involved partners and of the thematic areas. Section 3 focuses on one specific and relevant theme of the EP, the digital servitization and its role in the achievement of sustainability. Section 4 discusses the creation and role of a specific project developed in the EP context focusing on the theme of servitization.

2 Extended Partnership

In Italy, in the last quarter of 2022, an Extended Partnership (EP) was established within the theme "Made in Italy Circolare e Sostenibile" answering the call of *Avviso pubblico per la presentazione di Proposte di intervento per la creazione di "Partenariati estesi alle università, ai centri di ricerca, alle aziende per il finanziamento di progetti di ricerca di base" – nell'ambito del Piano Nazionale di Ripresa e Resilienza, Missione 4 "Istruzione e ricerca" – Componente 2 "Dalla ricerca all'impresa" – Investimento 1.3, finanziato dall'Unione europea – NextGenerationEU.*

The EP focuses on three of the major industries of the Italian context which represent around the 50% of the gross domestic product (GDP) of the country [11]:

- Fashion (including fashion, apparel, leather, textile, footwear, eyewear, and accessories),
- Furniture (including furniture and interiors, contracts, exhibits, yacht design),
- Automation (including automation, mechatronics, machinery, and mechanical technologies).

The partners involved, listed in Table 1, are **both from the academic context and the industrial one**. The connection between academic and industrial realities ensure that the knowledge generated in academia can be directly exploited by industrial facilities to accomplish in concrete manners the objectives of the project. In particular, to ensure great diffusion of the actions and enhance their impacts, the main industry leaders of the selected three sectors are present within the project partners.

The EP will provide research and innovation resources, developing best practices to be adopted by SMEs. The vision of the EP is to **enable closed-loop, self-sufficient, self-regenerative, reliable, safe, and energy-aware design and manufacturing of Made in Italy products and services.**

The EP is based on eight thematic areas across which the partners are asked to collaborate based on their experiences and research fields. The topics must be addressed to answer the challenges currently impacting the design, production, consumption and End-of-Life of materials, products, related technologies, and processes. The eight thematic areas are declined in eight Spokes, illustrated in Fig. 1.

Below, the list of the topics addressed by each Spoke is reported. Above all, it is worth mentioning that the EP was designed to ensure strong collaborations among all the partners. Indeed, each Spoke is focused on a specific area, but it requires a cohesive alignment with all the other areas, thus the other Spokes. For this reason, each partner is involved in more than one Spoke based on its own experiences and can operatively work on projects which are proposed by more than one Spoke together.

Spoke 1, "**Digital advanced design: technologies, processes, and tools**", aims at mapping and developing a portfolio of digitally enhanced solutions (technologies, methodologies, and tools) for supporting, augmenting, and verifying design process

Table 1. Partners involved in the EP.

Full name of partners	Short names
Politecnico di Milano (Proposer) – Spoke Leader	POLIMI
Consiglio Nazionale delle Ricerche – Spoke Leader	CNR
Politecnico di Bari – Spoke Leader	POLIBA
Politecnico di Torino – Spoke Leader	POLITO
Sapienza Università di Roma	SAPIENZA
Università degli studi di Bergamo	UNIBG
Alma Mater Studiorum Università di Bologna – Spoke Leader	UNIBO
Università degli studi di Brescia	UNIBS
Università degli studi di Firenze – Spoke Leader	UNIFI
Università degli studi di Napoli Federico II – Spoke Leader	UNINA
Università degli studi di Palermo	UNIPA
Università degli studi di Padova – Spoke Leader	UNIPD
Aeffe Spa	AEFFE
Brembo Spa	BREMBO
Camozzi Group Spa	CAMOZZI
Cavanna Spa	CAVANNA
Italtel Spa	ITALTEL
Itema Spa	ITEMA
Leonardo Spa	LEONARDO
Natuzzi Spa	NATUZZI
Prima Additive Srl	PRIMA
Sacmi Imola S.C.	SACMI
SCM Group Spa	SCM
Stazione Sperimentale per l'Industria delle Pelli e delle Materie Concianti Srl	SSIP
Thales Alenia Space Italia Spa	THALES

and decision making, and for integrating circularity throughout the entire life cycle of products and machines.

Spoke 2, "**Eco-Design strategies: from materials to Product Service Systems – PSS**", has the objective of developing and experimenting with a portfolio of PSS eco-design strategies that support all design phases: design of PSS architecture, materials, and components; cradle-to-cradle PSS lifecycle design and impacts evaluation; service and communication design for social innovation and behavioral change.

Spoke 3, "**Green and sustainable products & materials from non-critical & secondary raw sources**" has the ambition to create products and materials for advancing

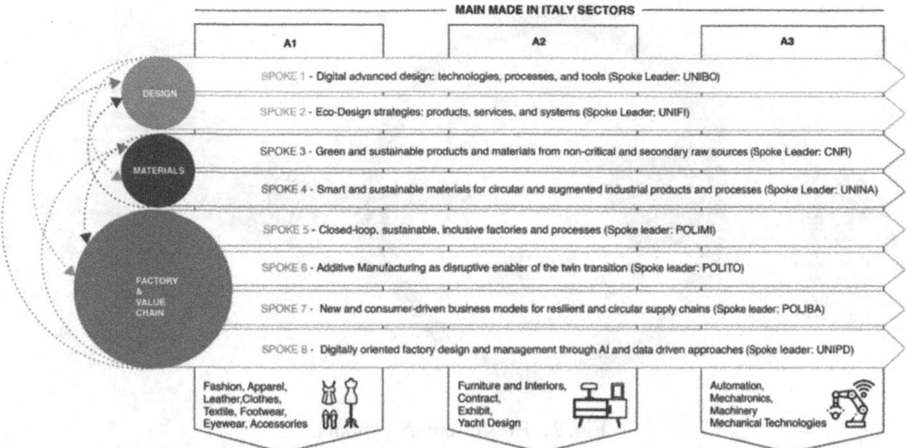

Fig. 1. Thematic Areas and Spokes.

sustainability and circularity of Made-in-Italy sectors using alternative raw sources such as waste, industrial residues, and non-critical minerals.

The Spoke 4, "**Smart and sustainable materials for circular and augmented industrial products and processes**", focuses on the conceptualizations of climate friendly products and processes and experimentation in fostering a natural oriented disruptive technology for a Green Made in Italy approach.

The Spoke 5, "**Closed-loop, sustainable, inclusive factories and processes**", aims at developing new concepts for zero-waste, pollution-free, energy-neutral, closed-loop, natural-oriented, human-centered, socially-oriented, inclusive, fully safe, self-sufficient, self-regenerative factory.

Spoke 6, "**Additive Manufacturing as disruptive enabler of the Twin Transition**", recognizes in the additive manufacturing the only viable solution to realize a new generation of green and circular products and wants to revolutionize additive manufacturing as a disrupting enabling technology of the twin transition.

Spoke 7, "**New and consumer-driven business models for resilient and circular supply chains**", has the ambition to define a new competitive paradigm, by conceptualizing, designing, and experimenting with new archetypes, methods, and solutions of restorative and regenerative business models, resilient and circular supply chains, and innovative technology-based marketing strategies.

Finally, Spoke 8, "**Digitally-oriented factory design and management through artificial intelligence (AI) and data driven approaches**", aims at developing a new concept for sustainable and resilient digital factory in which AI, digital technologies and collaborative robotics will establish a trustworthy human-machine coevolution relationship and lead to high-performance, inclusive, sustainable human-machine working systems.

The EP adopt a relevant interdisciplinary approach and cross-spoke synergies to achieve a shared vision of circularity.

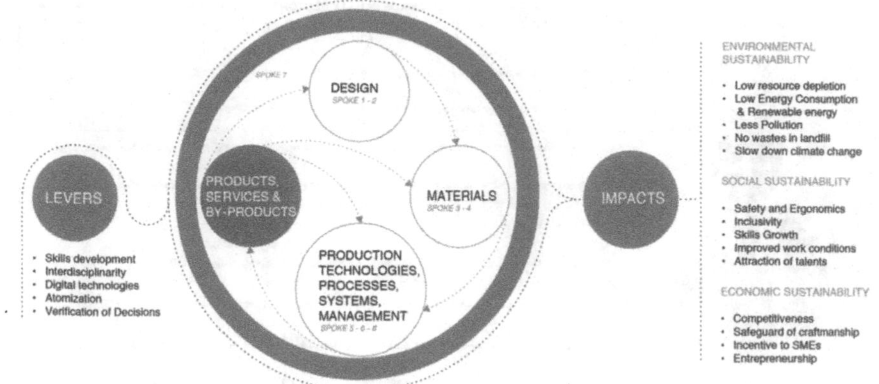

Fig. 2. EP's circularity model.

The EP structure ensures the coverage of all the key elements characterizing a circular system, Fig. 2; hence it tackles the design of both product and services including smart devises, the study of innovative materials to enhance eco-efficiency performances of products and last it covers factory and supply chain related aspects.

In the context of PE, one of the most relevant addressed themes is the one of servitization and **PSS,** which has a dedicated Spoke (Spoke 2) and can be leveraged and covered throughout the projects proposed by the various Spokes. Indeed, servitization is the basement of several circular-oriented business models applicable in both business to business (B2B) and business to customers (B2C) contexts to facilitate the achievement and improvement of circular performances. Servitization is one of the main strategies on which industrial practitioners are focusing. PSS are recognized as an opportunity to improve companies' environmental impact [12]. Moreover, digital technologies can be leveraged to support PSS, thus achieving the twin transition. Given the relevance of the topic for circular strategies and the high interest of practitioners in developing PSS offerings, the authors decided to analyze the role of digital servitization for sustainability and presenting a project developed in the context of the EP that aims at tackling this topic.

3 The Role of Digital Servitization

PSS can be defined as **systems in which products and services are optimized and integrated from a lifecycle perspective** [13]. Servitization is currently considered a common trend adopted by several manufacturing companies [14], hence around the 70% of companies in the manufacturing context have adopted servitization strategies [15].

In the industrial B2B context PSS take the name of industrial product service systems (IPS2) [12]. IPS2 has been defined by [16] as "a systematic package in which intangible services are attached to tangible products to finish various industrial activities in the whole product life-cycle". PSS offerings can be categorized in three clusters: product-oriented, in which the offering consists into a product to which services are added;

use-oriented, in which the offering is the use of product while the ownership of the good is retained by its provider; result-oriented, in which the providers and clients agree on a provided result [17].

The adoption of PSS solutions is increasingly supported by the implementation of **digital technologies** [18], which are able to improve the servitization effectiveness, facilitating the development of new pricing frameworks, business models and solutions [19].

Digitalization has been the fastest area of growth in PSS research context since 2017 [20]. Servitization and digital technologies have been researched mostly in isolation the two streams have recently been merged under the name of digital servitization [21], and still many gaps of research exist and have been identified in the extant literature. In [22], the authors identified in digital servitization an opportunity for future researches, with the need of contributions aimed at systemizing the existing knowledge since it is currently scattered across several research studies. A common definition of the phenomenon is still missing, and the existing contributions tend to focus on one or few themes only, a holistic and interconnected approach to the phenomenon is still missing [21]. [21] call for the development and proposal of descriptive models (such assessment) for practitioners to guide companies on the path towards digital servitization. [22] highlighted the need to develop new business models to facilitate servitization. [23] identify the need of researches focused on studying how IoT application can impact future business model configurations. Also, [24] call for studies related to business models archetypes for digital servitization and for the identification of strategic paths to implement digital PSS innovations.

In addition to that, also companies' resources and capabilities are fundamental to facilitate the transition, it is required to investigate how digital capabilities in servitization can generate competitive advantage, and what configurations of resources and processes are required by digital servitization [23, 24].

Digital servitization is an emerging theme that is attracting growing interest from academy and practitioners alike. It appears that there is the need for holistic descriptive models that can **guide companies in identifying a coherent and structured roadmap to overcome possible barriers and challenges faced**, exploiting all the opportunities in the **development of smart industrial product service systems**.

Although PSS configurations were initially developed to increase the price differentiation of companies, allowing to sell spare parts and additional services [25], now they represent a **viable path to achieve sustainability** [12]. PSS' providers profit from low lifecycle costs and extended assets' lifespan, thus are influenced in searching for a more efficient utilization of material [26]. PSS' environmental sustainability is impacted also by activities which are common in the PSS context, such as reuse and recycling of products, maintenance services and leasing, sharing and renting [27].

Even though digital servitization is recognized as a relevant business model to achieve environmental sustainability and to implement circular economy practices [28], only few studies address the environmental benefits of digital servitization, thus a **relevant research gap is represented by the impact of digital servitization on the circular economy paradigm.** According to [24], the extant literature still lacks an integrated framework to realize sustainable strategies through digital PSS.

The most recent researches still highlight these necessities: [29] affirms that the nature of sustainable smart PSS is under-researched from a theoretical perspective; and [30] asks for studies related to smart PSS circular business model, design processes and evaluation processes. Indeed, it is still open the gap to study how to support manufacturing companies in the design and implementation of digital PSS business models with the objective to achieve environmental sustainability.

Moreover, it is possible to observe that the interaction between digitalization, PSS and circular economy is of growing interests, and it is still a research priority [18, 31, 32] both from an academic perspective and an industrial one.

In the context of the EP, the main objectives are to develop eco-design strategies and tools to support the design and implementation of sustainable PSS businesses models, proposing methodologies for their environmental assessment and facilitate the transition. The role of digital technologies and how they can support sustainable PSS will be investigated and innovative solutions will be developed with the interaction of universities and industrial practitioners.

4 Discussions and Conclusions

The EP will focus on multiple projects involving the development of sustainable PSS business models, across distinct industrial fields and addressed in multiple spokes. The EP will offer the opportunity to connect universities and practitioners on the topic of PSS, a similar scope to the one of ASAP Service Management Forum, which is a community, involving academic research groups and companies, guiding the research on PSS at a national level [33].

The EP will have both theoretical and practical implications for the field of PSS. Thanks to the nature of the EP, which connects different universities, it will be possible to have multiple contributions focused on the theme of sustainable PSS. Independently, these contributions may support in a limited way this field of research, instead, when combined, they can achieve a higher added value to the research.

From a practical perspective, the collaboration between universities and industrial realities can facilitate the transfer of knowledge from theoretical and academic research to the industrial landscape. The involvement of industrial practitioners can facilitate the expansion of these acquired knowledge and practices to their private networks, involving both national and international realities.

One of the possible future research directions is related to one project involves Politecnico di Milano and four partner companies in the machinery sector. The project will focus on three main themes of interest: **PSS for environmental sustainability, customer needs and acceptance levels for servitization and digital technologies enabling servitization**. The project aims at developing proof of concept of business models related to PSS, with different servitization levels and different service configurations modulated according to the acceptance level of target customers. It will investigate and define target clients, their behavior model, requirements and barriers and possible involvement strategies for the facilitation of servitization. It will identify and analyses digital technologies required to enable the business models.

Acknowledgments. This study was carried out within the MICS (Made in Italy – Circular and Sustainable) Extended Partnership and received funding from the European Union Next- GenerationEU (PIANO NAZIONALE DI RIPRESA E RESILIENZA (PNRR) – MISSIONE 4 COMPONENTE 2, INVESTIMENTO 1.3 – D.D. 1551.11-10-2022, PE00000004). This manuscript reflects only the authors' views and opinions, neither the European Union nor the European Commission can be considered responsible for them.

References

1. World Manufacturing Forum: THE 2018 WORLD MANUFACTURING FORUM REPORT: Recommendations for the Future of Manufacturing (2018). www.worldmanufacturingforum.org
2. United Nations: Transforming Our World: the 2030 Agenda for Sustainable Development United Nations United Nations Transforming Our World: the 2030 Agenda for Sustainable Development. United Nations (2015)
3. Kirchherr, J., Reike, D., Hekkert, M.: Conceptualizing the circular economy: an analysis of 114 definitions. Resour Conserv Recycl **127**(September), 221–232 (2017). https://doi.org/10.1016/j.resconrec.2017.09.005
4. Ellen MacArthur Foundation: Toward the Circular Economy: Economic and business rationale for an accelerated transition, pp. 1–97 (2013)
5. Despeisse, M., Acerbi, F.: Toward eco-efficient and circular industrial systems: ten years of advances in production management systems and a thematic framework. Prod Manuf Res **10**(1), 354–382 (2022). https://doi.org/10.1080/21693277.2022.2088634
6. Acerbi, F., Taisch, M.: A literature review on circular economy adoption in the manufacturing sector. J. Clea. Prod. **273**, 123086 (2020). https://doi.org/10.1016/j.jclepro.2020.123086
7. Ghisellini, P., Cialani, C., Ulgiati, S.: A review on circular economy: the expected transition to a balanced interplay of environmental and economic systems. J. Clean. Prod. **114**, 11–32 (2016). https://doi.org/10.1016/j.jclepro.2015.09.007
8. World Manufacturing Forum: THE 2021 WORLD MANUFACTURING REPORT: DIGITALLY ENABLED CIRCULAR MANUFACTURING (2021). www.worldmanufacturing.org
9. OECD: Organisation for economic cooperation and development. financing SMEs and entrepreneurs 2022. In: Financing SMEs and Entrepreneurs 2022 (2022)
10. Dey, P.K., Malesios, C., De, D., Budhwar, P., Chowdhury, S., Cheffi, W.: Circular economy to enhance sustainability of small and medium-sized enterprises. Bus. Strat. Env. **29**(6), 2145–2169 (2020). https://doi.org/10.1002/bse.2492
11. ISTAT: Risultati economici delle imprese. http://dati.istat.it/OECDStat_Metadata/ShowMetadata.ashx?Dataset=DCSP_SBSNAZ&ShowOnWeb=true&Lang=it. Accessed 21 Jul 2023
12. Meier, H., Roy, R., Seliger, G.: Industrial product-service systems—ipS 2. CIRP Ann. **59**(2), 607–627 (2010). https://doi.org/10.1016/j.cirp.2010.05.004
13. Lindahl, M., Sundin, E., Sakao, T.: Environmental and economic benefits of Integrated Product Service Offerings quantified with real business cases. J. Clean. Production **64**, 288–296 (2014). https://doi.org/10.1016/j.jclepro.2013.07.047.
14. Landolfi, G., Barni, A., Izzo, G., Fontana, A., Bettoni, A.: A MaaS platform architecture supporting data sovereignty in sustainability assessment of manufacturing systems. Procedia Manuf. **38**, 548–555 (2019). https://doi.org/10.1016/j.promfg.2020.01.069
15. Schroeder, A., Baines, T., Sakao, T.: Increasing value capture by enhancing manufacturer commitment-managing the servitization process. IEEE Eng. Manag. Rev. **50**(3), 162–170 (2022). https://doi.org/10.1109/EMR.2022.3197075

16. Jiang, P., Fu, Y.: A new conceptual architecture to enable iPSS as a key for service-oriented manufacturing executive systems. Int. J. Internet Manuf. Serv. **2**(1), 30 (2009). https://doi.org/10.1504/IJIMS.2009.031338
17. Tukker, A.: Eight types of product–service system: eight ways to sustainability? Experiences from SusProNet. Bus. Strat. Environ. **13**(4), 246–260 (2004). https://doi.org/10.1002/bse.414
18. Raddats, C., Naik, P., Ziaee Bigdeli, A.: Creating value in servitization through digital service innovations. Ind. Market. Manag. **104**, 1–13 (2022). https://doi.org/10.1016/j.indmarman.2022.04.002
19. Le-Dain, M.A., Benhayoun, L., Matthews, J., Liard, M.: Barriers and opportunities of digital servitization for SMEs: the effect of smart Product-Service System business models. Serv. Bus. **17**(1), 359–393 (2023). https://doi.org/10.1007/s11628-023-00520-4
20. Brissaud, D., Sakao, T., Riel, A., Erkoyuncu, J.A.: Designing value-driven solutions: the evolution of industrial product-service systems. CIRP Ann. **71**(2), 553–575 (2022). https://doi.org/10.1016/j.cirp.2022.05.006
21. Paschou, T., Rapaccini, M., Adrodegari, F., Saccani, N.: Digital servitization in manufacturing: a systematic literature review and research agenda. Ind. Market. Manag. **89**, 278–292 (2020). https://doi.org/10.1016/j.indmarman.2020.02.012
22. Paschou, T., Adrodegari, F., Perona, M Saccani, N.: The digital servitization of manufacturing: a literature review and research agenda (2017)
23. Kohtamäki, M., Parida, V., Oghazi, P., Gebauer, H., Baines, T.: Digital servitization business models in ecosystems: a theory of the firm. J. Bus. Res. **104**, 380–392 (2019). https://doi.org/10.1016/j.jbusres.2019.06.027
24. Pirola, F., Boucher, X., Wiesner, S., Pezzotta, G.: Digital technologies in product-service systems: a literature review and a research agenda. Comput. Ind. **123**, 103301 (2020). https://doi.org/10.1016/j.compind.2020.103301
25. Pieroni, M.P.P., McAloone, T.C., Pigosso, D.C.A.: Configuring new business models for circular economy through product–service systems. Sustainability **11**(13), 3727 (2019). https://doi.org/10.3390/su11133727
26. Matschewsky, J.: Unintended circularity?—assessing a product-service system for its potential contribution to a circular economy. Sustainability **11**(10), 2725 (2019). https://doi.org/10.3390/su11102725
27. Annarelli, A., Battistella, C., Nonino, F.: Product service system: a conceptual framework from a systematic review. J. Clean. Product. **139**, 1011–1032 (2016). https://doi.org/10.1016/j.jclepro.2016.08.061
28. Chauhan, C., Parida, V., Dhir, A.: Linking circular economy and digitalisation technologies: A systematic literature review of past achievements and future promises. Technol, Forecast. Soc. Change **177**, 121508 (2022). https://doi.org/10.1016/j.techfore.2022.121508
29. Ries, L., Beckmann, M., Wehnert, P.: Sustainable smart product-service systems: a causal logic framework for impact design. J. Bus. Econ. **93**(4), 667–706 (2023). https://doi.org/10.1007/s11573-023-01154-8
30. Kim, M., Lim, C., Hsuan, J.: From technology enablers to circular economy: data-driven understanding of the overview of servitization and product–service systems in Industry 4.0. Comput Ind **148**, 103908 (2023). https://doi.org/10.1016/j.compind.2023.103908
31. Barravecchia, F., Franceschini, F., Mastrogiacomo, L., Zaki, M.: Research on product-service systems: topic landscape and future trends. J. Manuf. Technol. Manag. **32**(9), 208–238 (2021). https://doi.org/10.1108/JMTM-04-2020-0164

32. Bortoluzzi, G., Chiarvesio, M., Romanello, R., Tabacco, R., Veglio, V.: Servitisation and performance in the business-to-business context: the moderating role of Industry 4.0 technologies. J. Manuf. Technol. Manag. **33**(9), 108–128 (2022). https://doi.org/10.1108/JMTM-08-2021-0317
33. "ASAP SMF » Finalità e Mission. http://www.asapsmf.org/finalita-e-mission/. Accessed 27 Sep 2023

Industrial Application Use Cases of LiDAR Sensors Beyond Autonomous Driving

Olaf Poenicke(✉), Maik Groneberg, Daniel Sopauschke, Klaus Richter, and Nils Treuheit

Fraunhofer Institute IFF, Sandtorstr. 22, 39106 Magdeburg, Germany
olaf.poenicke@iff.fraunhofer.de

Abstract. This paper is giving an overview on different industrial application fields for LiDAR sensors beyond the field of autonomous driving. With insights to three specific use cases, different approaches to process the LiDAR point cloud data are described and referring results and findings of the developed applications are summarized. The application fields of the described use cases are the surveillance of industrial process environments of automated fenceless cells, the provision of visual assistance and location information for crane operators and the monitoring of the storage space occupancy in a port terminal. Based on the information from the three use cases and further general LiDAR related background an initial morphological box is drafted to enable the classification of industrial LiDAR use cases. The paper concludes with a brief overview on future work.

Keywords: LiDAR sensor · Point cloud data · Data processing · Industrial application · Transferability

1 Introduction

Throughout the last years there have been massive growth in the market for and progress in the development of LiDAR sensors, which was mainly triggered by the demands of autonomous driving. LiDAR sensors are becoming more powerful, robust, compact and affordable [1]. A result of these developments is of course, that also more and more other LiDAR-based application fields are emerging beyond autonomous driving applications. This paper aims at giving an overview on industrial application fields for LiDAR sensors beyond autonomous driving and is providing insights to three LiDAR-based Use Cases which were developed by the authors throughout the last years. Based on the Use Cases different approaches for the processing of LiDAR point cloud data are described and application specific findings are given.

The paper is first giving an overview on state-of-the-art LiDAR-based industrial applications (excluding autonomous driving applications) in Sect. 2. Then three Use Cases are described in more detail, giving the individual motivation, related work, implementation and findings (Sects. 3, 4 and 5). The paper finally concludes with generalized findings, the draft of a morphological box for the classification of industrial LiDAR applications and an outlook on future work (Sect. 6).

S. Terzi et al. (Eds.): IN4PL 2023, CCIS 1886, pp. 250–269, 2023.
https://doi.org/10.1007/978-3-031-49339-3_16

2 State-of-the-Art of LiDAR-Based Industrial Applications

This section shall give a brief overview on different industrial application fields, where LiDAR based applications are researched and developed. This overview excludes developments in the field of autonomous driving as this application field has been recently covered by other publications like Roriz et al. [1].

In general LiDAR sensors are gaining relevance in more an more application fields due to their technical features. Compared to other 3D vision technologies they offer a high range with high accuracy over long distance enabling a coverage of larger areas with few sensors. Furthermore, they are robust against ambient light and can provide additional information of 3D points like their reflectivity or in case of FMCW (Frequency Modulated Continuous Wave) LiDAR also the velocity vector.

2.1 Overview on Application Fields

Looking at industrial production environments the use of LiDAR sensors for the **perception, localization and guidance of automated guided vehicles** (AGVs) and autonomous mobile robots (AMRs) is a typical field of research and development [2, 3] as also of established industrial applications. Based on the 3D LiDAR data and trained environmental models the focus of these applications is usually on self-localization, the detection of other mobile objects and path planning. In case of AMRs with manipulators LiDAR sensors can also enhance the perception of the working environment for the planning of manipulator handlings as also collision avoidance.

A further field of use with partially well-established commercial LiDAR-based applications is the **3D scanning and mapping**, reaching from the creation of 3D models of industrial infrastructures for digital twin applications to the cartography of landscapes or of mining infrastructures. The Use Cases behind the LiDAR based generation of 3D models are of various nature. The scanning of industrial infrastructures can provide data for Building Information Models (BIM) [4] or be part of periodic inspection of infrastructure conditions [5]. LiDAR scans of landscapes or mining infrastructures can be the basis for planning activities or again for inspections. As these applications are carried out with a mobile use of LiDAR sensor(s) on various forms of vehicles, aircrafts/drones or swimming equipment, they mainly rely on the use of algorithms for the simultaneous localization and mapping (SLAM) [6]. Regarding the localization of the sensor(s) within the environment the applications can be differentiated in use cases with available GPS data and use cases in GPS-denied environments.

The use of 3D data to **derive dimensions and volumes of objects** is especially relevant in logistics related applications. In comparison to the above-mentioned application fields, logistics use cases are currently employing LiDAR sensors in defined static positions to either monitor the occupancy of storage locations [7] or to measure stored goods, like e.g., the surveying of bulk material stockpiles. Such applications make use of the known 3D data of the infrastructure to only measure the changing shapes of the handled goods. The metadata or identification of the goods need to be assigned to the 3D object data. In case of general cargo also segmentation and object classification are relevant procedures to process the LiDAR data.

For all application fields mentioned above various types of LiDAR sensors – e.g. regarding the scanning pattern and the field of view (FOV) – are employed in single or multiple sensor setups.

2.2 Introduction of Specific Use Cases

The authors of this paper have researched and developed several industrial applications based on LiDAR data in recent years. Three of these Use Cases are introduced here and are described in more detail in the following Sects. 3, 4 and 5. Especially Use Cases 1 and 2 are complementary to the application fields mentioned above. All three Use Cases are using technical installations of several LiDAR sensors and are using sensors from *Livox*. A major feature of these sensors is the use of a pseudo-random scanning pattern, which enables a higher point cloud density compared to conventional line scanning patterns [8]. However, all Use Cases have individual processing pipelines to derive application specific outputs from the LiDAR data.

Use Case 1 – LiDAR and AI Based Surveillance of Industrial Process Environments. The focus of this Use Case is to use the dynamic 3D LiDAR data to differentiate various mobile objects and humans in industrial environments. Here the typical objects of the application environment and humans have been trained to an AI model. Based on that the AI is able to detect the trained objects and humans within the scene with high reliability and low latency. The targeted application is to survey the work spaces around fenceless automated cells, which are supplied by AGVs.

Within the Use Case description in Sect. 3 the emphasis is on the AI based processing of the 3D LiDAR data, relevant challenges and approaches to further enhance the robustness of object detection.

Use Case 2 – Smart Process Observer for Crane Assistance and Automation. Within this Use Case LiDAR sensors are used to provide accurate real-time 3D data of a crane to assist the crane operator with information about the location of the crane hooks, which cannot be completely seen from the operator's cabin. Geometry fitting algorithms are used, to match the object geometries captured by the LiDAR sensors with 3D models of the relevant crane components and objects to be lifted. Thus, the operator does not need to interpret the complex 3D point cloud data.

The Use Case description in Sect. 4 focusses on the implemented geometry fitting process and the user interface as also on findings regarding the accuracy of the LiDAR measurements. Furthermore, implemented functionalities to enhance the accuracy of the localization of the crane hooks is described.

Use Case 3 – Integration of LiDAR Data into a Virtual Twin for Storage Space Monitoring. The third Use Cases describes the integration of dynamic 3D LiDAR data into the 3D model of a port. Within this so-called Virtual Twin different dynamic sensor data are integrated into a spatial 3D port model. The LiDAR data are used to monitor the occupancy of a multi-purpose storage area.

The Use Case description in Sect. 5 describes the implementation of the LiDAR measurements and the data interface to the 3D port model. Furthermore, specific challenges for the data processing and an overview on further research and development tasks are described.

3 Use Case 1 – LiDAR and AI Based Surveillance

3.1 Motivation of the Use Case

When it comes to the surveillance of industrial process environments the aim of applications is ususally to detect moving objects in restricted areas for safety reasons. Besides classical industrial safety sensors like 2D laser scanners or light curtains there are more and more 3D sensing systems available today, which enable a spatial detection of moving objects (see Sect. 3.2). However, these safety systems are only capable to detect any moving object but cannot distinguish between different object types and humans.

The aim of the LiDAR and AI based solution described in this section is to enable an object type specific detection and event generation towards the PLC of automated cells. In the Use Case scenario the system is intended to monitor the external safety zone of an autonomous and fenceless robot cell for picking of automotive components, while the internal safety zone is covered by conventional safety laser scanners. As for the logistics process the cell is supplied with load carriers by AGVs and forklift trucks. Such supply processes shall not lead to a stop of the robot, which would indeed be the case with the use of conventional safety systems. The task for the LiDAR and AI based system developed is to differentiate between uncritical known objects (AGV, forklifts), which can bring new load carriers or remove empties, and critical humans and other unknown objects. If a human or unknown object is detected within a restricted zone, the robot operation shall slow down or come to a full stop.

The Use Case with the developed application represents a technical proof of concept, which does not include a safety certification and therefor is no operational safety system. However, the technical setup of the Use Case scenario is used for the further development of the approach with emphasis on achieving a high technical availability of the system, a high robustness of the AI based object detections and low latency within the processing chain from LiDAR based scene capture to the AI based object detection and event forwarding to the PLC. An initial description of the Use Case and the system developed was described by Groneberg et al. [9]. The description in this paper includes further developments and evaluations of the system.

3.2 Related Work

Different fields of related work are relevant to the Use Case described above. Regarding the use of **safety sensor systems** for the spatial surveillance of such industrial process environments there is to mention that initial developments focussed on the use of 2D cameras. E.g., the commercial safety system of the *Pilz Safety Eye* is based on 2D imaging. For 2D imaging there has been early progress to detect and localize humans and other mobile objects, based on AI methods [10]. However, 2D imaging only allows limited spatial perception so that fusion with other technologies seemed relevant [11]. In recent years several safety certified solutions emerged based on different 3D perception principles. The solution of *VeoRobotics* employs TOF based 3D imaging [12]. So also does the integrated sensor *SafeVisionary 2* of *SICK*. The company *INXPECT* offers a spatial safety system based on radar technology, but all these systems are only capable to detect unclassified mobile objects.

Regarding the use of **AI methods for object detection** within point cloud data there have been several research publications in recent years. A comprehensive review of the developments in that field has been given by Guo et al. [13]. Furthermore, in the application field for autonomous driving the *KITTI 3D benchmark* [14] regularly evaluates AI networks processing point cloud data. The structure of *KITTI* for annotation of point cloud data was adapted by the authors. The relevant AI methods which were used and adapted in the developments described in this paper were initially described by Lang et al. (*PointPillars* [15]) and Simon et al. (*Complex YOLOv4* [16]). Specific attention needs to be given to the use of AI methods in safety critical applications, as the regulatory frameworks to enable a certification of such solutions are not in place yet (see [17]).

3.3 Implementation

The Use Case scenario and the system as it has been developed and implemented is briefly described by the Fig. 1.

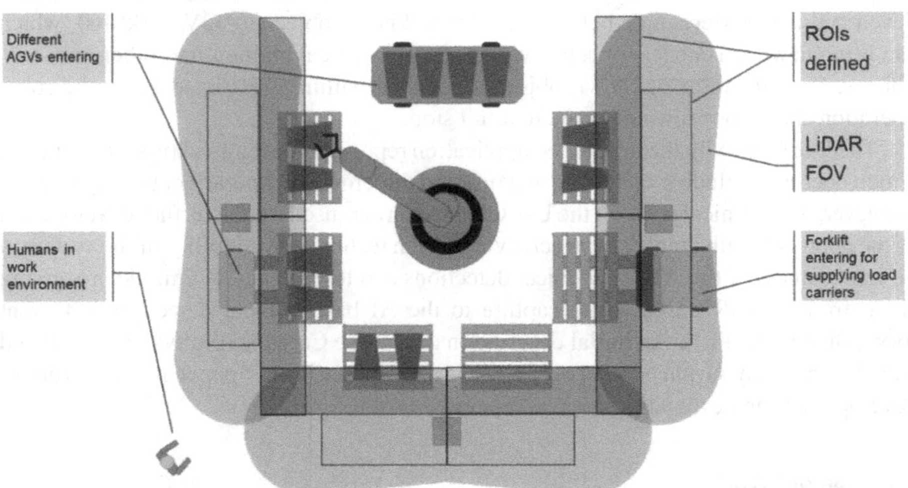

Fig. 1. Layout of the Use Case scenario with a fenceless robot cell and three LiDAR sensors installed for surveillance of the cell surrounding.

Within the scenario in total three LiDAR sensors (*Livox Horizon*) with an FOV of *81.7° x 25.1°* and a sampling rate of *10 Hz* are installed above the outer zone of a fenceless robot cell to survey the area of approx. *1.5m* in front of the cell. For the overall event space different regions of interest (ROI) are defined with different restriction level, to detect objects in these restricted areas and to trigger events depending on the type of detected object. The AI model used is executed for the data of each sensor individually. Relevant AI based detections and ROI triggered events are forwarded to the PLC of the robot cell via OPC UA.

The point clouds recorded by the LiDAR sensors are first transformed from the sensor individual coordinate systems into a uniform coordinate system. Within the uniform coordinate system, the floor is always horizontally oriented, which enables the extraction of the floor from the further data processing. Within the individual point cloud data additional filters can be applied (e.g., to reduce noise). Following the filtering the trained AI model is directly carried out on the sensor data. The AI provides the position, dimension, orientation and a confidence for the different objects detected within a frame (3D point cloud integrated over *100 ms*). Following the AI based object detection the object movements within ROIs are checked. If a human or a segment to which no class could be assigned is detected within a ROI, a referring safety event is triggered and forwarded to the PLC. Figure 2 is giving an impression of a recorded frame with several objects detected within the scene and single ROIs triggered.

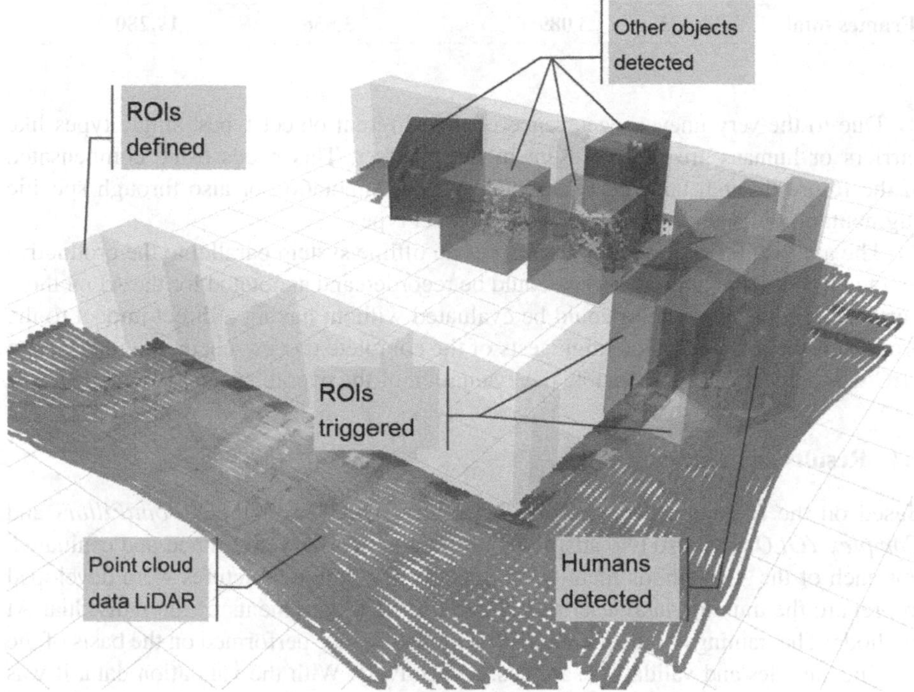

Fig. 2. Single frame from LiDAR recording with AI based detections of humans and other objects in the scene.

For the training of the selected AI networks *PointPillars* [15] and *Complex YOLOv4* [16] a significant amount of data frames was recorded, annotated and further augmented. Intermediate trials to generate synthetic training data based on 3D modelling and simulation did not show acceptable results yet. For the manual annotation a specific annotation tool was developed adopting the *KiTTI* format for annotation of object class related bounding boxes with position, orientation, dimension and flags for occlusion and truncation. Based on that a set of more than *19,000* annotated frames with more than *52,000* annotated objects was generated. The number of annotated objects as also the splitting of the data set into training, validation and testing samples is summarized in Table 1.

Table 1. Structure of the annotated LiDAR data used for AI evaluation.

Object class	Training samples	Validation samples	Test samples	Samples total
Human	12,432	3,085	3,861	19,378
AGV – Type 1	1,611	427	498	2,536
AGV – Type 2	5,656	1,394	1,759	8,809
Forklift truck	2,714	681	833	4,228
Load carriers	11,335	2,794	3,477	17,606
Frames total	**12,335**	**3,089**	**3,856**	**19,280**

Due to the very uneven occurrence of the different object types, single types like carriers or humans are more present in the data set. This needs to be compensated in the future through targeted data recording and annotation or also through specific augmentation of data of underrepresented object types.

The application developed is running as an offline system parallel to the productive robot cell. By that real process data could be recorded and annotated for the AI method. Furthermore, the application could be evaluated without having a direct impact to the process of the robot cell. For single tests of the complete process chain, the interface to PLC was activated. E.g., to enable the evaluation of the overall system latency.

3.4 Results and Findings

Based on the annotated data set, the above-mentioned AI methods *PointPillars* and *Complex YOLOv4* as also two adaptions of these networks were trained and evaluated. For each of the AI methods mentioned, specific annotation structures were developed to prepare the training data described above for the requirements of the individual AI methods. The trainings of the mentioned AI methods were performed on the basis of the training samples and validation samples, respectively. With the validation data, it was then possible to identify in each case when a single AI training is overfitted (see Fig. 3). This condition is to be avoided, because otherwise the AI is less able to generalize for incoming unknown data.

It is measured how well the respective AI method arrives at the same conclusion in different training epochs as the annotations (ground truth) in the source data. The loss rates of the AI application on the training and validation data are then compared. If the loss rate increases for the validation data (and continues to decrease for the training data), the AI is overfitting to the training data in these training epochs.

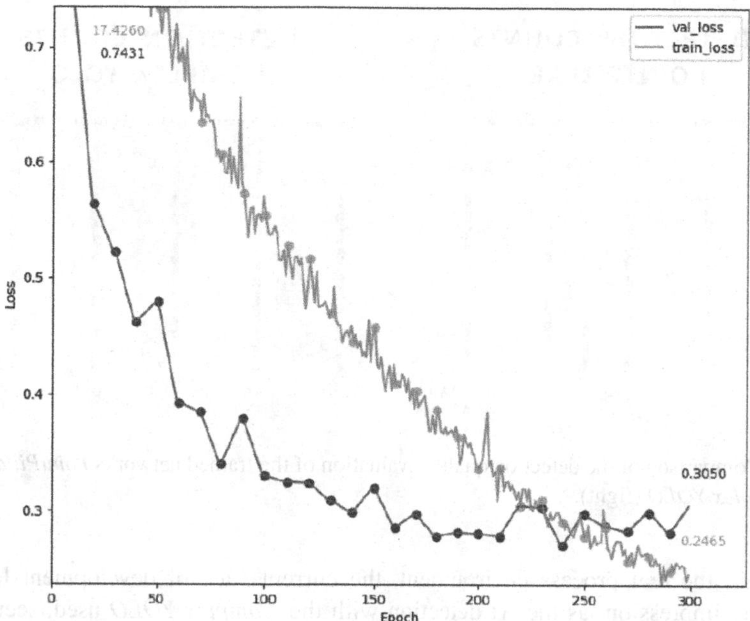

Fig. 3. Exemplary loss graph of a training (*Complex YOLOv4*), comparing the training loss and validation loss – overfitting at about epoch 230.

The four trained AI methods were evaluated with the help of the test samples. For each test sample it was checked whether the AI method arrives at the same result as the annotation of this data. On this basis, the evaluation of the AI methods could be automated and the reliability of the respective AI methods could be evaluated. As an example, the evaluation of the initial AI methods (*PointPillars* and *Complex YOLO*) is compared below in Fig. 4.

For the different object classes, the frequency with which the individual classes were detected by the AI methods is shown (normalized to *100%*). False positive and false negative detections were also included, so that detection rates above *100%* could occur (e.g., if the AI incorrectly detects a non-existent object). As a result of the evaluation, *Complex YOLO* was found to perform most reliable for the application context. In particular, the safety-critical detection of humans works much more robust and error-free with *Complex YOLO*. The developed adaption of *Complex YOLO* did not achieve significantly different results.

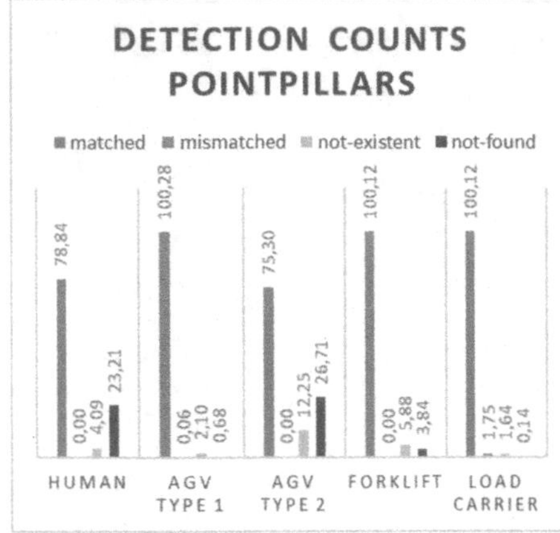

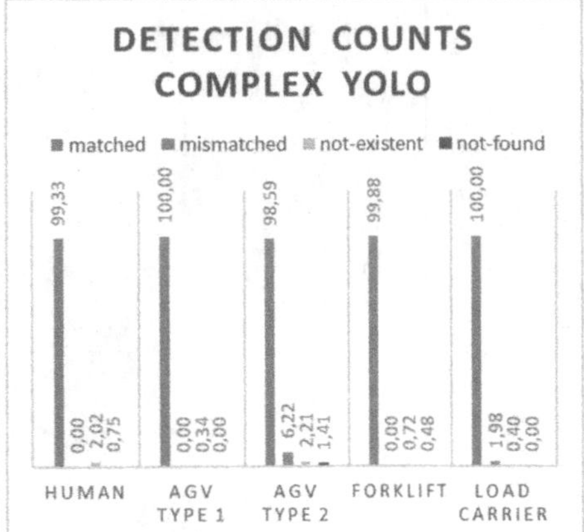

Fig. 4. Comparison of the detection quality evaluation of the trained networks *PointPillars* (left) and *Complex YOLO* (right).

Within the real process environment, the current state of development leaves a promising impression, as the AI detection with the *Complex YOLO* used, seem quite robust. Regarding the overall system latency there is room for significant improvements which can mainly be achieved by the use of more performant computation hardware and optimization of the application code. Furthermore, the use of LiDAR sensors with a higher sample rate can further reduce the latency. As the used *Livox Horizon* has a sample rate of *10 Hz* the minimum integration time for a single frame is *100 ms*.

Concerning the object detection there are single typical false-positive detections occurring, where mobile objects like the AGV are detected as human in specific locations of the working space, due to similar height and shape. Besides additional training data to make the AI detection more robust, it is currently evaluated in how far retroreflective markers enable the use of object filters complementary to the AI detection. Integrating such markers into the scene makes use of the reflectivity measure which is given by the LiDAR sensor for each individual recorded 3D point. In Use Case 2 below the use of such reflectivity information is described in more detail.

A further research and development topic is the use of different types of LiDAR sensors with the AI application, as sensors differ concerning their FOV, their resolution, their sample rate and also their scan patterns. Varying sensor characteristics can have significant effects on the usability of the available AI trainings. Thus, a change of the sensor characteristics may require additional annotation and training efforts. Therefore, the generation of synthetic training data is a highly relevant R&D topic for this application field to decrease annotation efforts significantly.

4 Use Case 2 – LiDAR Based Crane Operator Assistance

4.1 Motivation of the Use Case

Process cranes are custom-designed equipment which usually have large dimensions and are meant to operate in harsh environments and to handle large dimension objects. Thus, limited visibility of single crane components and objects to be lifted is a typical challenge for operators of process cranes. Furthermore, it is a relevant safety issue, as the limited visibility can make it difficult for the crane operator to attach loads to the crane hook securely. Non-secure lifting of loads can lead to major accidents. Because of that, technical solutions to secure the lifting process are urgently needed for large dimension process cranes.

To enhance the visibility of objects and to provide visual assistance to the crane operator the Use Case described in this section, uses LiDAR sensors to record 3D data from various crane perspectives. These 3D data are mapped to 3D models of relevant system components to provide an intuitive understandable scene to the operator. The solution developed has been initially introduced by Sopauschke et al. [18] and Lange, J. et al. [19] and has since then been developed further, including the use of retroreflective markers in the scene to enhance the accuracy and reliability for the localization of single components. The implemented system described in Sect. 4.3 is installed on a crane in a foundry, where pouring ladles with a diameter of more that *4m* need to be lifted and securely transported by the crane.

In a longer term such LiDAR installations on crane bridges will also support the perception of the working environment, which is a highly relevant aspect to further automate crane operations.

4.2 Related Work

The use of laser and **LiDAR sensors in the context of crane applications** is described in various publications and partially available as commercial solution. [20] and [21] described a system for tracking a loader crane operator and to survey the surroundings of a loader crane. A system to identify construction parts of yard cranes and to survey their surroundings in order to detect and avoid collisions between objects was described by [22]. Lange, S. et al. [23] describe the combined use of LiDAR sensors and cameras on slewing and gantry cranes for the detection of the crane grab and the localization of the goods to grab as a basis for crane automation. The detection and localization of the goods is supported by an AI based processing of the LiDAR and camera data. Florin [24] describes the established use of 2D laser scanners and the further developments to implement 3D LiDAR sensors for object detection under gantry cranes.

Within the Use Case described, main functionalities of the **data processing** are the application of geometry fitting algorithms and the use of marker detection based on reflectivity information. In parallel to the captured LiDAR point cloud data CAD models of several crane components are used in the developed solution. The process of fitting the point cloud data to the model data is called registration and is usually performed on the basis of the Iterative Closest Point (ICP) algorithm [25]. This algorithm uses a nearest neighbor search strategy to identify potential corresponding point pairs between the point cloud and the CAD model. The use of retroreflective markers for the detection and localization of objects within LiDAR point cloud data was analyzed and described by Kurz et al. [26].

4.3 Implementation

In the Use Case, a process crane was equipped with four LiDAR sensors (*Livox Horizon*) to simultaneously and continuously scan the crane's working area. The field of view (FOV) of all four sensors also covers the crane hook. As the LiDAR sensors generate a highly accurate three-dimensional image of the crane's working area with a scanning accuracy of less than *2 cm* at a distance of *20 m*, the crane hooks can be localized with high accuracy. Figure 5 shows an extract of a recording with the registration of the four sensor point clouds.

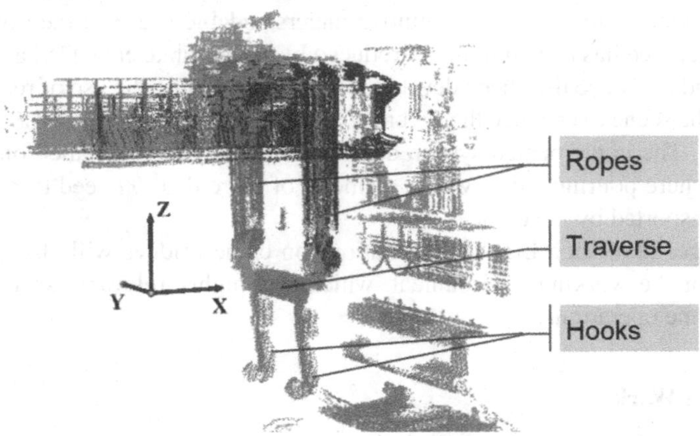

Fig. 5. Example scene with the color-coded point clouds captured by the individual sensors. A coordinate system is added for reference.

Based on the registered point clouds single crane components are detected within the overall point cloud. As the sensor perspectives create a seamless 3D image without major occlusions, the point cloud data can be matched with the CAD models of the crane components. Using this geometry fitting the ropes, the traverse, the crane hooks and the pouring ladle are detected and localized. This detection process uses prior knowledge about relationships between the components like known offsets, relative locations and maximum displacements. To reduce the number of points to be processed, a region of interest is defined within the working area of the crane. Only points within this ROI are further processed. Figure 6 shows the exemplary fitting process for the crane hooks within the point cloud.

Based on the implemented fitting algorithms the application is able to detect the crane components in most situations at a reasonable update rate. However, small movements could be noted in the fitted model positions caused by inaccurate models that do not ideally reflect the real-world situation. This of course can lead to critical situations,

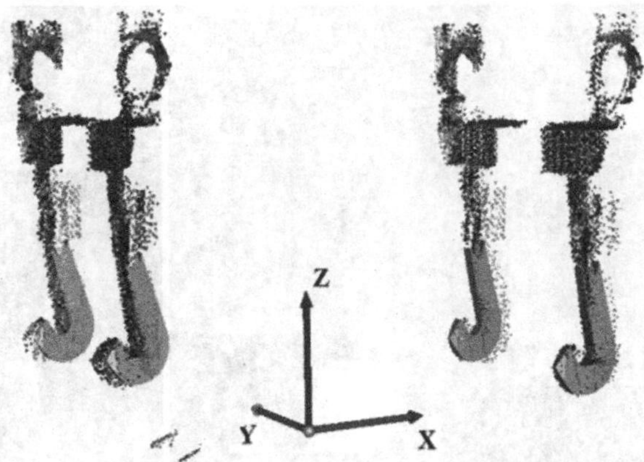

Fig. 6. Example scene with left side: initial guess of the hook's positions under the traverse, right side: hooks after registration.

when slightly incorrect position information is provided to the crane operator. Another problem of the update rate achievable with the fitting procedure occurs at faster crane trolley movements. Here a lag between the visualized point cloud data and the detected component locations can cause confusion to the crane operator.

To overcome these limitations the system was updated with functionalities to detect und to track retro-reflective markers to stabilize the detection quality and improve the detection speed. These markers were primarily mounted on the traverse (see Fig. 7) and the pouring ladle. With the LiDAR sensors capturing a reflectivity value for each point of the point cloud and with the comparably low reflectivity values within the environment of the foundry, the highly reflective markers can be clearly detected within the scene (based on a reflectivity threshold). With the known information of the marker positions, the localization of the marked object can be stabilized and detection and localization are sped up in comparison to the implementation with sole use of the geometry fitting.

In the initial implementation of the application an integration time of around *200 ms* was required to collect enough points to perform the geometry fitting based object detection and localization. Using the retro-reflective markers as the main source for object localization, the integration time can be reduced to around *100 ms*. A lower required integration time also reduces the overall latency between the LiDAR based data capture and the visualization in the user interface for the crane operator.

To visualize different levels of information to the crane operator a user interface was developed, which is displayed on a screen in the crane operator's cabin. This user interface provides different perspectives of the scene and shall support the operator in the task of securely fitting the crane hooks to the pins of the pouring ladle. Figure 8 gives an impression of the user interface.

Fig. 7. Use of retro-reflective markers – left: markers mounted on the crane traverse, right: markers visible in the 3D point cloud due to significantly higher reflectivity.

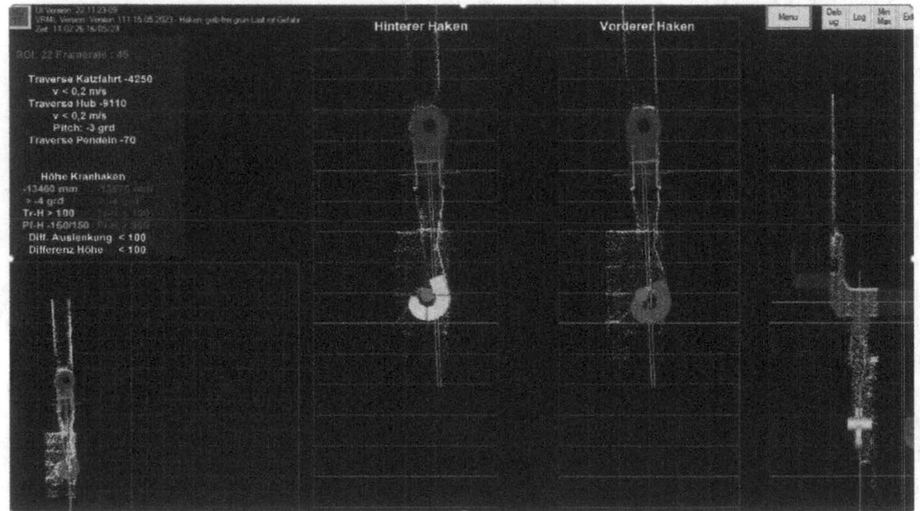

Fig. 8. Exemplary view of the user interface with different perspectives on the ROI scene of the crane hooks. The green marked hook in the middle marks, that the hook is securely fitted to the pin of the pouring ladle. (Color figure online)

Based on the localization of the relevant components the application signalizes, when the hooks are securely fitted to the pins of the pouring ladle. This is especially important, as the crane operator is not able to directly see one of the crane hooks from the operator's cabin.

4.4 Results and Findings

Besides the informational assistance the developed solution can provide to crane operators via the interface, the achievable performance of the system is relevant for potential transfer to similar applications. With the developed processing pipeline and the experience of several months of practical application of the system in a foundry the following results were achieved.

Regarding the accuracy of the object localization via the geometry fitting, the overall accuracy is within the range of ± 5 *cm*. The accuracy is actually depending on the amount of 3D points, that are captured of an individual object and also the geometric characteristics of an object. The traverse for example can be localized with a higher accuracy, as there are no occlusions of the traverse and as it has a clear geometry that supports exact matching of *x*, *y*, *z* location as also of *pitch*, *roll* and *yaw*. For other objects like the pouring ladle there are possibilities for misinterpretation due to rotation symmetry of the object. Furthermore, there are different types of pouring ladles with slight variations in size and shape which can decrease the localization accuracy. For a clear identification of the different pouring ladles, the use of different patterns of retro-reflective markers is an approach, which needs to be examined in the next steps.

The overall processing of a single frame (with LiDAR point cloud integrated over *100 ms*) takes around *250–300 ms*, which is the overall latency between the LiDAR capturing of the scene to the data processing (including the geometry fitting) to the final visualization of the localization information in the user interface. Parallel to that, the point cloud data are directly streamed to the user interface and are provided as optional visualization. However, the crane operators usually only use the localization information and the 3D model-based visualization of the relevant components (traverse, hooks, pouring ladle).

As described in Sect. 4.3 additional retro-reflective markers were integrated into the scenario to reduce the overall system latency and to further improve the localization accuracy of single components. These installations and implementations of marker tracking functionalities were carried out recently. To date the evaluation to quantify the effects of using these retro-reflective is still ongoing.

5 Use Case 3 – LiDAR Data for Storage Space Monitoring

5.1 Motivation of Use Case

The Use Case described below is situated in the process environment of a port terminal and had two different goals regarding the utilization of storage spaces. The first aim was to automatically measure and monitor the utilization of multi-purpose storage areas within the port terminal. The second aim was to further more create a real-time 3D mapping of the storage area to be integrated into a so-called Virtual Twin, which visualizes different process and infrastructure states within a spatial 3D model of the port area. This Virtual Twin for port application was described by Höpfner et al. [7].

With the installation of LiDAR sensors within the port infrastructure a dedicated storage space was permanently recorded and the captured 3D data were processed and integrated into the 3D model. The intention behind that was to enable the monitoring of the storage space utilization and to visualize currently available storage spaces, which cannot be documented in conventional ways, as the use of a multi-purpose terminal does not allow to define granular storage locations as the size of stored goods and cargo varies from small pallets, over containers up to larger machine parts or construction elements.

5.2 Related Work

The scanning of 3D contours in ports and other environments is an application area that was mainly focusing on the use of industrial line lasers [27], with commercial solutions and applications available today. E.g., the company *LASE* provides 2D laser-based solutions to automatically scan container stacks in automated or semi-automated terminals. However, such systems are creating the 3D information only in connection with the movement of cranes. For that reason, such solutions are not suitable for permanent inventory applications surveying the occupancy of storage areas.

In the past, developments focusing on continuous scanning of storage yards for bulk materials used videogrammetry and projector-contour scanning [28]. Today there are first commercial solutions available, monitoring the stock of bulk material storage locations based on static installations of LiDAR sensors (e.g., solutions of *Sachtleben Technology* or *Blickfeld*).

5.3 Implementation

For the Use Case in the port environment four LiDAR sensors (*Livox Horizon* and *Livox MID-40*) were installed on light posts of a multi-purpose terminal. With the installation spots a storage area of approx. *2,000 m²* was covered with perspective from three sides (sensor perspectives restricted due to the available installation points on light posts). Figure 9 shows the raw data recording of a single sensor in the port terminal.

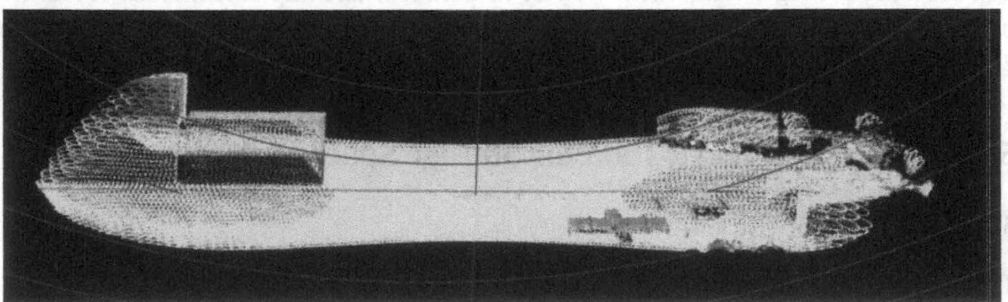

Fig. 9. Exemplary single sensor recording in the port terminal showing container stacks (left side), other stored objects and a truck delivering a container (right side).

Based on the LiDAR sensor data, a depth map was implemented to reduce the amount of point cloud data to be forwarded to the port 3D model. Such height maps were forwarded to the so-called Virtual Twin application via an MQTT interface. Due to dynamic movements in the scene (e.g., truck or crane movements in the terminal) it is not useful to permanently stream the height map to the Virtual Twin. Therefor algorithms were implemented to transmit the data event-based, when the scene is static over a defined time frame.

With the height map being forwarded to the Virtual Twin application the current status of the storage area was visualized within the Virtual Reality (VR) 3D model. Figure 10 shows the height map and its referring 3D visualization in the VR model of the port terminal. In the situation shown, mainly construction elements were stored in the terminal.

Fig. 10. Above: extracted height map of two sensor FOVs, below: visualization of the height map within the 3D port model.

5.4 Results and Findings

The development and implementation of the Use Case could not be finalized as it was initially planned within the research project, due to technical complexity in the application environment. Therefor the last step, to derive the storage space occupancy from a virtual storage location grid was not fully implemented and tested. However, it was shown, that the LiDAR sensors provide a robust data basis with good accuracy and coverage in the application environment.

The technical complexity of the Use Case is mainly due to the dynamics of different types of objects in the scene (different types of cargo, crane, trucks, reach stackers and other mobile technical equipment). This makes is complex to differentiate, which objects actually need to be registered as stored objects. Furthermore, dynamic movements cause temporary occlusions of other objects which need to be interpreted correctly. For that reason, AI based object classification and filtering of dynamic objects were identified as a major approach to drive this application forward.

Further complexity for the data processing arises from the movement of the individual sensors, although they are in static installations. With the installation on light posts of *25 m* and *35 m* height, stronger wind causes significant movements of the sensors resulting in a more or less dynamic FOV coverage of the storage area. These deviations cannot be compensated by the correction values of the sensor-internal IMU. Thus, the relative movements of the sensors make up the requirement to implement geometry fitting to map the LiDAR point clouds to actual static infrastructure elements of the port environment.

6 Transferability and Future Work

This paper gave an overview on different industrial application fields for LiDAR sensors and solutions based on dynamic 3D point cloud data provided by these sensors. Three Use Cases, the authors worked on throughout the last years, were described, giving more detail about the actual processing of the point cloud data. To enable a structural understanding of how LiDAR sensors and their sensor data can be used and thus to enable a better transferability to other application fields, this section provides the draft of a morphological box to classify LiDAR based applications. With this morphological box all the Use Cases described above can be classified.

The objective of such a morphology is, on the one hand, to map various technical parameters of sensor technology and data processing as well as the requirements in practice in a structured way. On the other hand, it enables to identify typical patterns in the classification of a wide variety of use cases, on the basis of which more efficient solution development is made possible when new use cases come up. For example, suitable LiDAR sensors as well as suitable methods of 3D data processing can be identified precisely on the basis of the specific technical requirements of a use case.

In principle this initial morphological box, that is given in Fig. 11, can be further extended, integrating also other 3D imaging sensor technologies with their advantages and disadvantages. Also, a further detailed differentiation of different sensor characteristics can be useful to enable a quick selection of suitable sensor setups out of the technical conditions and requirements of a use case.

This paper described industrial applications of LiDAR sensors beyond the field of autonomous driving. However, the further development of LiDAR sensors as also the economies of scale to make theses sensors more affordable will be mainly driven by the technical developments focusing on the automotive sector. New sensor features or development trends in this sector are of course also relevant for industrial applications. E.g., the emerging technology of FMCW LiDAR [29] will provide a velocity vector for every 3D point, which will enable new features for object detection and tracking for applications like the described Use Case 1.

	Property	Characteristics			
Sensor proper-ties	**range**	short range (<10m)	mid-range (<100m)	long range (>100m)	
	scanning pattern	regular	(pseudo) random	*other*	
	field of view	360°	view cone	dome	*other*
Installation properties	**type of installation**	mobile (free movement)	mobile (referenced movement)	quasi static	fixed static
	localisation of mobile sensor(s)	GNSS based		*other* (in GNSS-denied application environments)	
	type of setup	single sensor	multiple sensors without overlap	multiple sensors with overlap	*other*
	data processing	decentralized (edge)	sub-system	centralized (server / cloud)	
Data processing properties	**purpose**	understanding of static scene	understanding of dynamic scene	*other*	
	time criticality	none	few seconds	real-time	*other*
	major data processing methods	object segmentation	object registration	object classification	object localization
		object tracking	object measuring	mapping (e.g., SLAM)	*other*
	use of further features	none	use of reflectivity values	internal corrections (e.g., IMU)	mapped RGB image
		external calibration	background model data	*other*	

Fig. 11. Morphological box for classification of industrial LiDAR use cases.

Another relevant trend is the embedding of data processing steps and even AI based functionalities into the sensor hardware. Such developments will boost the development of novel and highly scalable LiDAR applications – e.g., in the context of safety surveillance of industrial process environments. For the training of AI based LiDAR applications furthermore the simulation of sensor data will gain further importance, as synthetic training data will be a central enabler to reduce the currently high efforts for generation of annotated training data.

Acknowledgements. Part of the developments and evaluations described in the paper were carried out in the projects *LiDAR-basierte Arbeitsraumanalyse* and *Pro-Kran* funded by the Federal State of Saxony Anhalt and the European Commission within the EFRE and REACT-EU program (funding references: FKZ 2104/00066 and 2204/00014) and carried out in the project *PortForward* funded by the EU (funding reference: 769267).

References

1. Roriz, R., Cabral, J., Gomes, T.: Automotive LiDAR technology: a survey. IEEE Trans. Intell. Transport. Syst. **23**(7), 6282–6297 (2022). https://doi.org/10.1109/TITS.2021.3086804

2. Gradu, M.: The Benefits of Advanced 3D Lidar for Autonomous Mobile Robots, SAE Technical Paper 2021-01-1015 (2021)
3. Maria, D., et al.: Environment model generation and localisation of mobile indoor autonomous robots. In: 2021 2nd International Conference on Advances in Computing, Communication, Embedded and Secure Systems (ACCESS), pp. 257–264. Ernakulam, India (2021) https://doi.org/10.1109/ACCESS51619.2021.9563306
4. Rashdi, R., Martínez-Sánchez, J., Arias, P., Qiu, Z.: Scanning technologies to building information modelling: a review. Infrastructures **7**(4), 49 (2022). https://doi.org/10.3390/infrastructures7040049
5. Kaartinen, E., Dunphy, K., Sadhu, A.: LiDAR-based structural health monitoring: applications in civil infrastructure systems. Sensors **22**(12), 4610 (2022). https://doi.org/10.3390/s22124610
6. Nam, D.V., Gon-Woo, K.: Solid-state LiDAR based-SLAM: a concise review and application. In: IEEE International Conference on Big Data and Smart Computing (BigComp), Jeju Island, Korea (South), 2021, pp. 302–305 (2021). https://doi.org/10.1109/BigComp51126.2021.00064
7. Höpfner, A., Poenicke, O., Blobner, C., Winge, A.: Use of a Virtual Twin for Dynamic Storage Space Monitoring in a Port Terminal. IN4PL 2021, Scitepress (2021)
8. Ortiz Arteaga, A., Scott, D., Boehm, J.: Initial investigation of a low-cost automotive LiDAR system. Int. Arch. Photogrammetry, Remote Sens. Spat. Inf. Sci. **XLII-2/W17**, 233–240 (2019). https://doi.org/10.5194/isprs-archives-XLII-2-W17-233-2019
9. Groneberg, M., Poenicke, O., Mandal, C., Treuheit, N.: Lidar and AI based surveillance of industrial process environments. Transp. Telecommun. J. **24**(1), 13–21 (2023). https://doi.org/10.2478/ttj-2023-0002
10. Tan, J.T.C., Arai, T.: Triple stereo vision system for safety monitoring of human-robot collaboration in cellular manufacturing. In: 2011 IEEE International Symposium on Assembly and Manufacturing (ISAM), pp. 1–6. IEEE (2011)
11. Frese, C., Fetzner, A., Frey, C.: Multi-sensor obstacle tracking for safe human-robot interaction. In: ISR/Robotik 2014; 41st International Symposium on Robotics, pp. 1–8. VDE (2014)
12. Moel, A.: How collaborative is your manufacturing application? In: Quality Magazine, vol. 61, 2nd edn. BNP Media (2022)
13. Guo, Y., Wang, H., Hu, Q., Liu, H., Liu, L., Bennamoun, M.: Deep learning for 3D point clouds: a survey. IEEE Trans. Pattern Anal. Mach. Intell. **43**(12), 4338–4364 (2020)
14. Geiger, A., Lenz, P., Stiller, C., Urtasun, R.: 3D Object Detection Evaluation 2017. Karslruhe Institute of Technology, last checked 04.08.2022, available online at http://www.cvlibs.net/datasets/kitti/eval_object.php?obj_benchmark=3d
15. Lang, A.H., Vora, S., Caesar, H., Zhou, L., Yang, J., Beijbom, O.: Pointpillars: fast encoders for object detection from point clouds. In: Proceedings of the IEEE/CVF Conference on Computer Vision and Pattern Recognition, pp. 12697–12705 (2019)
16. Simon, M., Milz, S., Amende, K., Gross, H.M.: Complex-YOLO: Real-time 3D Object Detection on Point Clouds. arXiv preprint arXiv:1803.06199 (2018)
17. Becker, N., Junginger, P., Martinez, L., Krupka, D.: KI in der Arbeitswelt – Übersicht einschlägiger Normen und Standards. Gesellschaft für Informatik e.V. (GI) (2021)
18. Sopauschke, D., Trostmann, E., Richter, K.: Smart process observer for crane automation. In: Kabashkin, I., Yatskiv, I., Prentkovskis, O.: Reliability and Statistics in Transportation and Communication, Bd. 640, pp. 177–190. Cham: Springer International Publishing (Lecture Notes in Networks and Systems) (2023)
19. Lange, J., Richter, K., Sopauschke, D.: Intelligenter Prozessbeobachter für die Kranautomatisierung. In: Scholten, J.: 31. Internationale Kranfachtagung – Digitalisierung, Innovation, Produktsicherheit. Selbstverlag der Ruhr-Universität Bochum (2023)

20. Miądlicki, K., Saków, M.: LiDAR based system for tracking loader crane operator. In: Trojanowska, J., Ciszak, O., Machado, J. M., Pavlenko, I. (eds.) Advances in Manufacturing II: Volume 1 - Solutions for Industry 4.0, pp. 406–421. Springer International Publishing, Cham (2019). https://doi.org/10.1007/978-3-030-18715-6_34
21. Miadlicki, K., Pajor, M., Sakow, M.: Loader crane working area monitoring system based on LIDAR scanner. In: Hamrol, A., Ciszak, O., Legutko, S., Jurczyk, M. (eds.) Advances in Manufacturing, pp. 465–474. Springer International Publishing, Cham (2018). https://doi.org/10.1007/978-3-319-68619-6_45
22. Jeong, H., Hong, H., Park, G., Won, M., Kim, M., Yu, H.: Point cloud segmentation of crane parts using dynamic graph CNN for crane collision avoidance. JCSE **13**, 99–106 (2019). https://doi.org/10.5626/JCSE.2019.13.3.99
23. Lange, S., Berroa, J., Bockelmann, P., Busemann, B., Diederichsen, R., Eickmeier, L.: Steuerung von Kranen mit Künstlicher Intelligenz: Kran-AI KAI. In: Scholten, J.: 31. Internationale Kranfachtagung – Digitalisierung, Innovation, Produktsicherheit. Selbstverlag der Ruhr-Universität Bochum (2023)
24. Florin, J.: Einsatz von Mehrlagenscannern (LiDAR) zur Automatisierung von Krananlagen in der Industrie. In: Scholten, J.: 31. Internationale Kranfachtagung – Digitalisierung, Innovation, Produktsicherheit. Selbstverlag der Ruhr-Universität Bochum (2023)
25. Besl, P.J., McKay, N.D.: Method for registration of 3-D shapes, pp. 586–606. SPIE (1992). https://doi.org/10.1117/12.57955
26. Kurz, G., Scherer, S.A., Biber, P., Fleer, D.: When Geometry is not Enough: Using Reflector Markers in Lidar SLAM. Online available at http://arxiv.org/pdf/2211.03484v1 (2022)
27. Chun, T.-W., Kim, K.-M., Lee, H.-G., Nho, E.-C.: Fast scanning method for container stacking profile with one laser sensor. Industrial Electronics Society, 2003. In: IECON '03. The 29th Annual Conference of the IEEE (2003)
28. Ou, J., Zhou, J., Zhu, X., Yuan, Y., Shang, Y., Zhang, X.: Large stack-yard three-dimensional measurement based on videogrammetry and projected-contour scanning. Opt. Eng. **51**(6) (2012) Springer
29. Richter, M.: FMCW-LiDAR: Game-Changer für autonomes Fahren. Elektronik Praxis. Online: https://www.elektronikpraxis.de/fmcw-lidar-game-changer-fuer-autonomes-fahren-a-18e9a5141fb4e0f9180dea63f5aba17a/ (last checked: 24.07.2023) (2020)

When the Learning Lab Embraces Digitalisation: The Development of a Digital Learning Lab for the SMILE Project

Marco Dautaj[1,2](✉), Franco Chiriacò[1], Sergio Terzi[1], Margherita Pero[1], Nizar Abdelkafi[1], and Maira Callupe[1]

[1] Dipartimento di Ingegneria Gestionale, Politecnico di Milano, via R. Lambruschini 4, 20156 Milan, Italy
{marco.dautaj,franco.chiriaco,sergio.terzi,margherita.pero, nizar.abdelkafi,maira.callupe}@polimi.it

[2] University School for Advanced Studies IUSS Pavia, Palazzo del Broletto, Piazza Vittoria 15, 27100 Pavia, Italy

Abstract. The impact COVID-19 generated on people routine linked with the rapid digitalization has led the educational approach to the need of a fundamental shift. In response to these evolving circumstances, SMILE (Smart Manufacturing Innovation, Learning-Labs, and Entrepreneurship) has undertaken a comprehensive initiative in order to move from the traditional learning labs towards digital ones. This digital transformation aims to enhance students' learning experiences and problem-solving capabilities by leveraging technologies and innovative approaches. Digital Learning Nuggets are central to this paradigm shift, which are small units of interactive and engaging educational content. These nuggets have proven instrumental in augmenting students' comprehension and retention of subject matter while fostering a more personalized learning journey. Moreover, the integration of MIRO, a collaborative software platform, further drives students' learning by facilitating interactive discussions and fostering teamwork in a virtual environment. SMILE's digital learning lab (SMILE DLL) serves as the foundation for the upcoming Hackathon, an event characterized by the collaboration between academia and industry. In collaboration with various companies, this experiential learning initiative offers students the opportunity to tackle problems posed by these organizations. Participants gain invaluable insights into real-world applications of their knowledge and are better equipped to address complex issues in a professional context. The Hackathon represents the link between academia and industry, fostering a dynamic environment where students can apply theoretical concepts in order to solve real problems. This immersive learning experience not only fosters their critical thinking and analytical skills but also nurtures creativity, adaptability, and teamwork, paramount attributes for today's competitive job market.

Keywords: Digital learning lab · Smart manufacturing · Education

S. Terzi et al. (Eds.): IN4PL 2023, CCIS 1886, pp. 270–284, 2023.
https://doi.org/10.1007/978-3-031-49339-3_17

1 Introduction

In the last decades, there has been an emergence of innovative learning models that take place in a variety of spaces beyond the physical one. This was demonstrated by the introduction of Massive Online Open Courses (Nykvist et al., 2021) and Learning Management Systems from the 2000s (Turnbull et al., 2021), and it was further accelerated by COVID-19 (Belton et al., 2021). Nowadays, the classroom is no longer perceived as the only conducive Learning Space (LS), and the learning experience is perceived as made up of Learning Activities (LAs) situated in various spaces. Therefore, providing LSs other than classrooms, and adapting the LAs to the setting, is very important for Higher Education Institutions (HEIs).

Several publications have attempted to construct models of LSs to support academics working in the field to recognize commonalities and differences in what often are implicit conceptualizations of relations between LSs and LAs. Generalized representations of the LS support the understanding of the concept and embrace contributions from relevant domains (Ellis and Goodyear, 2016). Historically, the study of LSs in HEIs has not attracted particular attention from researchers. For long time, learning in HEIs was considered independent of the spaces in which it was located, in contrast to schools where the design of LSs and its contribution to learning have been under continuous exploration (Clark, 2002).

Looking at the German and more widely European experience, we can identify that in the last years, several educational institutions have invested in the creation of new types of learning environments and spaces, in which trainees could physically work with and within manufacturing facilities and new technologies for experimenting and learning how to use them. Strictly speaking, the concept of a teaching laboratory is not new; it was the main approach since the second industrial revolution used by industrial schools for training apprentices on manufacturing jobs (Ghergo, 2020). What is new, however, is the level of complexity of the solutions that are created within such laboratories. In effect, during the last decades, work-integrated/work-based/active learning (Cunningham and Dawes, 2016) became a major pedagogical paradigm to rethink the didactic and LAs inside and outside institutional context (mainly schools), capable of engaging learners more actively and innovatively. The pedagogical principle of work-based learning provides a holistic learning experience, that combines reflection on theory and practical activities, by relying on a circular training approach, which enables learning-teaching dynamics between teacher and student and also between students. In the tertiary and technical educational context, work-based learning is recognized as a valuable pedagogical approach for developing graduate employability, increasing employment prospects, and contributing to deepening educational experiences while promoting other learning outcomes (Rowe et al., 2021).

For the purpose of our research project, we investigate how LAs and LSs, in which technical education takes place, should be designed to assure that trainees acquire a proper level of competencies. Indeed, in the state-of-the-art section, we show that this topic has to be discussed more intensively by the academic community. This investigation found its practical application in the development of a deliverable of the SMILE[1] project we are working on with other European partners. This deliverable represents the concept and prototype of SMILE Digital Learning Lab which will support innovation activities at HEIs and provide tools for collaboration between students involved in innovation development, academics and entrepreneurs. DLLs of HEIs will be linked to allow international cooperation and easy access to innovation ecosystems of distant regions. Moreover, the DLL proposed will serve as the foundation for the upcoming Hackathon, an event characterized by the collaboration between academia and industry in the development of solution provided by students, researchers and professionals to real companies' challenges.

Based on these premises, this study aims at contributing to the SMILE addressing one of the main goals of the project, which is to pioneer the development of an immersive and cutting-edge virtual environment, widely referred to as the Digital Learning Lab. This digital environment has been meticulously crafted to provide an educational experience that enables students to shift from traditional learning to an innovative approach for knowledge acquisition.

2 State of the Art

In recent decades, society witnessed an increase in the pace of development of technologies that affect many societal areas, as well as a huge shift in the economic model. Manufacturing is undergoing many transformations that have the potential to increase efficiency and reshape the way of doing things (Albukhitan, 2020). Green and sustainable transformation and technological evolution bring challenges for organizations due to resulting increased complexity in manufacturing, and then more demanding requirements from engineering graduates and technical students (Manyika et al., 2017). The discussion about the skills that engineering and technical students need to develop to face real challenges has been ongoing for decades (Latha and Prabu, 2020). However, the innovations brought forward by these transformations are drastically impacting the workforce due to the automation of tasks, the increase in high-skill activities, and a higher degree of complexity (Bonekamp and Sure, 2015). Practitioners emphasize the importance of acquiring knowledge and skills in areas such as energy, automation, data analysis, and software development, as well as skills such as interdisciplinarity, collaborative work, problem-solving, and innovation (Jerman et al., 2020). Despite this, Jerman et al. provide evidence that a knowledge gap is widespread, pointing to employability mismatches between the market requirements and the educational credentials of graduates, which should increase their competencies and skills towards smart manufacturing topics.

[1] SMILE (Smart Manufacturing Innovation, Learning Labs, and Entrepreneurship) is an EIT project for the acceleration of institutional change about increasing innovation and entrepreneurial capacities and integration into regional innovation ecosystems, using the EIT Knowledge Triangle Model extended by civil society (quadruple model) as the main driver for systemic institutional change.

HEIs are expected to prepare graduates with the required skills to support companies in remaining competitive. Often, the advances in technology raise doubts about whether this can be achieved with standard educational models (Doherty and Stephens, 2021). The acquisition of knowledge and the development of skills are downstream in the educational path that the students navigate throughout their careers. Addressing the challenge presented above requires an understanding of three key factors that shape students' learning experience: (i) the contents that students should learn, (ii) how these contents are assimilated and should be taught (Learning Activities – LA), and (iii) how the spaces where learning takes place should be designed (Learning Spaces – LS) (Barker et al., 2006).

Research regarding the integration of technology in education has gained relevance due to COVID-19, which has transformed the learning processes and caused modification in LSs and LAs (López-Belmonte et al., 2021). Building upon established research about online learning, several works are dedicated to discussing the development of LS using technologies to provide holistic and self-sufficient experiences for learning (Kanetaki et al., 2022). While there is often a tendency to consider digital practices as disembodied, these cannot be separated from the physical learning context nor the emotional aspects it entails (Pischetola, 2022). Literature shows the rise in the adoption of spaces such as Teaching Factories (Abele et al., 2018; Kreß et al., 2023), Makerspaces, and Fab Labs (Stickel et al., 2019). The implementation of these LSs is highly driven by technology with few works discussing their pedagogical and spatial foundations. Thus, an approach driving the design of LS and LA to maximise the efficiency and effectiveness of the learning experience is required.

The last two decades have clearly shown the relevance of manufacturing in our Society, at the global and national levels. Industrial "manu-facere" is a fundamental factor of collective well-being and global economic value. According to the World Manufacturing Foundation (WMF, 2022), over 70% of world trade is directly linked to industrial activities, and over 60% of job positions are linked to manufacturing while manufacturing – with its related services – contributes to the growth of the global GDP by roughly 40%. Italy – with its manufacturing specializations (Aerospace, Automation, Automotive, Cosmetics, Defence, Fashion, Furniture, Machinery, Packaging, Textile, etc.) – is globally among the top ten Countries, just after Germany, being strictly rooted in its inventing and production capabilities accumulated during hundreds of years (with its craftsmen, its Small and Medium Manufacturing Enterprises, its public engineering-oriented companies).

At the same time, it should be clearly stated how manufacturing could also have negative impacts on our Society: global warming (according to the UN, up to 61% of CO_2 emissions are still coming from manufacturing, (UNCTAD, 2020)), air and water pollution, resources depletion, land degradation, solid wastes, etc. Because of this, another manufacturing model should be developed to support sustainable and circular manufacturing.

This issue has been clear in Europe for several years (e.g., the European Industrial Emissions Directive 2010/75, as well as the Sustainable Consumption and Production Action Plan 2008/397). The creation of a more Sustainable Economy and Society should pass from the consolidation of more sustainable and circular manufacturing (Kopp,

2006). As the European experience has already demonstrated, more Sustainable Development could be established by making proper use of the new emerging technologies. Among these, digital technologies are mature enough to play a relevant role. Not by chance, the paradigm of Industry 4.0 – coined in Germany and diffused in Europe in the last 10 years (e.g., (Davies, 2015)) – is deeply rooted in this vision, of a more sustainable, resilient, and circular manufacturing.

To recapitulate, (i) manufacturing is relevant for Society, (ii) manufacturing should evolve for becoming more Sustainable, (iii) while embracing new technologies, (iv) whereas the most emerging and promising technologies are the digital ones.

In this transformation, human resources play an important role, as they should make this evolution possible, by changing mindsets and habits, creating new solutions, adopting inventions, and using new knowledge, skills, and competencies. One problem should be recognized. In an advanced society such as the European one, there is a dramatic shortage of skills and competencies needed to run such a transition (Cornerstone People Research Lab, 2022). There is a need for highly skilled people that are trained on these technologies (McKinsey, 2021).

In Italy, the "skill gap" in the manufacturing domain is terrific: the job market (Excelsior Unioncamere, 2022) is currently missing hundreds of thousands of persons (technicians, operators, engineers, etc.) with enough competencies for supporting different actors in the market such as companies and public institutions. This is the result of many factors, for example, families that have often not pushed their children to manufacturing-related jobs, considered a "dark and unpleasant job" and policymakers who have not understood the drivers of the real economy, as well as educational players (schools, institutes, universities, etc.) that have not paid proper attention to manufacturing and have not invested sufficiently in proper educational approaches.

If we look at other European countries, which are anyhow suffering from the general lack of competencies, it can be seen some relevant differences. One of the authors' interests is in the educational system and the educational practices put in place to create and support the needed skills. By looking at Germany, it can be observed how technical education has been deeply supported during the last decades in order to generate enough professionals with the required skills (OECD, 2010).

3 Learning Lab Methodology

Before providing a definition for a learning lab, it is fundamental to introduce and define the concept of laboratory learning. As highlighted by (Sanchez et al., 2022), current literature poorly addresses the definition of such a concept, despite the plethora of definitions of laboratory learning and learning lab in HEI. On the top of our knowledge, among the few contributions present in the literature, laboratory learning is defined as "learning that takes place in a space where students can observe, practice, and experiment with objects, materials, phenomena, and ideas either individually or in groups." (Ka Yuk Chan, 2012).

As highlighted in the first part of this definition, the focus is on students, which can be hands-on while being actively engaged in the learning process, contrary to frontal lectures, which constitute a unidirectional approach for conveying knowledge. Moreover, this learning approach provides students with the capabilities to build true understanding (Ka Yuk Chan, 2012) and develop soft skills and digital skills, support reflexivity and foster the evolution of attitudes towards teaching and learning (Sanchez et al., 2022). Consequently, the learning laboratory, or simpler "learning lab", is the space where people work applying laboratory learning. Some examples of learning lab in a HEI are those depicted in Figs. 1 and 2. Indeed, a laboratory is intended to be a place dedicated to work, and specifically in our case to manufacture, as well as a place dedicated to scientific experimentation (Sanchez et al., 2022).

Fig. 1. Learning Lab (MEL LAB) at Politecnico di Milano

Fig. 2. Learning Lab (Educafè) at Politecnico di Milano

According to the advent of the most recent technologies, which have transformed the learning processes and caused the modification of LSs and LAs (López-Belmonte et al., 2021), the recent COVID-19 pandemic forced people to stay at home, drastically limiting or even eliminating the possibility for people to meet in presence, such space is not restricted just to the physical one. Not by chance (Ka Yuk Chan, 2012) highlights in her work the multiplicity of forms of space in which learning laboratory can take place, where among others can be found physical laboratory space, as well as the e-learning management system, and computer-simulated virtual laboratories. Furthermore, following the study by (Sanchez et al., 2022), a learning lab is defined as "a physical, digital and human space for observation, experimentation, and evaluation, to rethink and enrich learning and teaching attitudes and practices at the university". Again, the multiplicity of forms of spaces is considered. Indeed, the digitalization of LA and LS has led to the definition of Digital learning labs (DLL).

"Digital learning labs" is an innovative tool that complements innovation development and educational resources of HEI, where educators, external experts from outside of the HEI system (e.g., start-up entrepreneurs), and students can analyse different real market opportunities using digital lab environments by experimenting with a range of emerging technologies and generate solutions in the context of SM. This definition of DLL is the result of an open discussion among the partner of the SMILE project.

Often such a type of learning lab is associated with the actual physical laboratory and the actual components in a confined space that a user can remotely access through a computer (Ka Yuk Chan, 2012). However, the selection of the form of LS strongly depends on various factors such as university strategic policy, resource availability, teacher's initiative, and laboratory design, as well as students' cohesiveness (Hofstein and Lunetta, 2004).

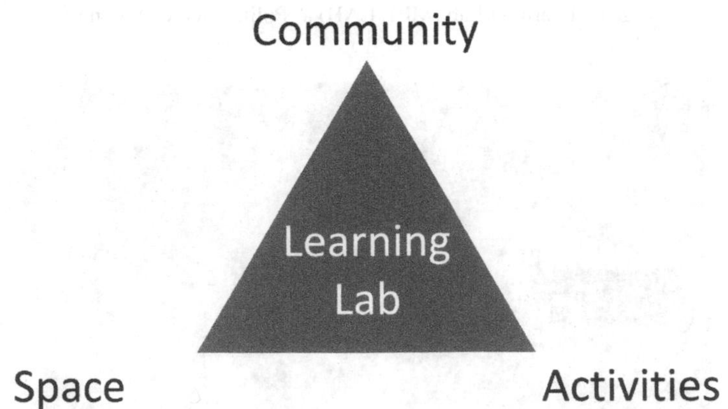

Fig. 3. The learning lab as a 3-dimensions model (Sanchez et al., 2022)

On the top of our knowledge, the structure of a learning lab is built upon three key dimensions, which are space, activities and communities (Fig. 3).

In particular:

- The learning space is defined as the physical-digital space where laboratory learning takes place, respectively encompassing different physical rooms properly designed for the purpose of the lab, and digital communication platform(s) for storing and disseminating resources among peers and within the team, if any (Sanchez et al., 2022).

- Learning activities are "concrete learning scenarios designed, organized or facilitated by the learning lab" (Sanchez et al., 2022). In other words, they represent the tasks carried out by people embedded in the laboratory learning within the learning space.
- Finally, the last dimension of the learning lab is the community, defined by (Preece et al., 2003) as a "flexible organization oriented towards shared goals, a collective experience and a "shared microculture" based on values, practices, conversational rules, and behaviours". In other words, it embeds people that carry out laboratory learning and perform learning activities within the learning space.

All these three dimensions, generally intended to be physical, can be digitalised to develop what has been defined as "digital learning lab". As already mentioned, the shift towards a DLL implies the application of digital tools that allow people to create a digital community able to carry out activities in a digital space. Having a space where the different members of the laboratory can meet represents a crucial part in the creation of the learning lab. When dealing with a DLL, such space consists in the reshaping of the physical one into the digital one resorting to software able to recreate physical rooms in which students can join as it was a physical learning lab. This software is of different type according to the type of activities they can support. In this study we focus on collaboration and environment tools. Digital collaboration tools are defined by Salopek (2000) as "the use of technology to enhance and extend the abilities of individuals and organizations to collaborate, independent of their vertical area." Such technologies are clustered into videoconferencing tools (e.g., Microsoft Teams, Skype, Webex), communication and messaging tools (e.g., Microsoft Outlook, Microsoft Teams, WhatsApp, Google mail), file sharing systems (e.g., Internal Intranet System, SharePoint, Google-Drive, Microsoft OneDrive), and finally, project management tools (e.g., Trello, Jira, Microsoft Project) (Andersson and Mutlu, 2020). In addition to these technologies, there are also further collaboration platform where participants of the DLL can carry out activities and organize the work. Example of such software are Miro, Mural, and Microsoft White Board.

4 Result

As introduced in the previous section, DLL complements innovation development and educational resources of HEI where educators, external experts from outside of the HEI system (e.g., start-up entrepreneurs), and students can analyse different market opportunities by using digital lab environments and experimenting with a range of emerging technologies to generate solutions in the context of SM.

For the creation of the SMILE digital learning lab, we resort to the model in Fig. 3. Such a model consists of three dimensions: community, learning space, and learning activities.

Regarding the community dimension, the learning lab is intended to be exploited by HEIs that belong to the EIT community and those that do not, with the objective of developing skills and capabilities in smart manufacturing. The community consists of all people involved in the teaching–learning interaction. Students, professors, laboratory experts, and tutors interact in the learning space to share knowledge, skills, and capabilities to fulfil hands-on activities. Because it is a learning lab, students are the major target when defining the community.

Once participants have been defined, the second step is to create a space, in our case digital, where participants can interact with each other and perform individual or group activities.

In the SMILE project, the main activity defined is a Hackathon. The hackathon will offer a holistic and immersive learning experience for students with the opportunity to apply their skills, collaborate with peers, and achieve targeted resources. This approach fosters critical thinking, problem-solving, teamwork, and creativity, and enables students to improve and achieve their learning goals. Companies will present different challenges for the hackathon. These challenges are designed to give students the possibility of working on real-world problems and enabling them to apply their knowledge and skills in practical situations to elaborate solutions. Companies participating in the hackathon will bring specific challenges they are currently facing or new ideas they want to explore. These challenges will focus mostly on smart manufacturing and will consist of a clear problem statement, goals, and preferences. Students that participate in the hackathon can choose a challenge that matches their interests, skills, and expertise. They will then work as a team to find a solution to the chosen challenge while using their collective knowledge and skills. Teams will have access to a digital classroom, digital learning nuggets, Miro, and other tools to collaborate for problem resolution. Each challenge will present unique opportunities and challenges that require innovative thinking and interdisciplinary approaches. Thus, students will need to analyse the problem, conduct research, brainstorm ideas, model solutions, and refine their ideas.

Throughout the hackathon, group members will receive guidance and support from mentors, industry experts, and academics. The challenges aim to foster critical thinking, creativity, collaboration, and problem-solving skills among the participating students. At the end of the Hackathon, teams will present their solutions to a panel of judges, which may include representatives from the participating companies. Students can showcase their innovative ideas, demonstrate their problem-solving abilities, and receive feedback from industry experts. The challenges provided by companies in the Hackathon offer a platform for students to apply their knowledge and facilitate networking and potential career opportunities. Companies may also recognize the talent and skills demonstrated by the students and consider recruiting them for internships, projects, or future employment.

For the purpose of supporting these activities, we resort to multiple digital learning spaces:

- *Pre-created digital learning nuggets* (Fig. 4) and specific multidisciplinary teaching materials on Smart Manufacturing Innovation and Entrepreneurship will be provided. The SMILE project intends to provide participants of the hackathon with 20 knowledge nuggets uploaded on YouTube for free in order to be consulted whenever participants want. Such materials standalone mini learning activities, usually with a length of less than 5 min, that would vary in the concept learners undertake in a particular context in order to attain specific learning outcomes (Polsani, 2003). Within the SMILE project, knowledge nuggets are videoclip on different and specific topics having in common the key pillars of the project itself, namely smart manufacturing, innovation, and entrepreneurship. For the creation of each videoclip, with a length of maximum 10 min, the project partners designed the contents – PowerPoint presentation and text – following the text has been turned into videos thanks to Synthesia. This software allows people to make video content without cameras, microphones or studios just leveraging artificial intelligence (AI). The outcome consists in a high-quality video with an AI avatar speaker that can replicate the natural voice sounding of more than 120 languages. Examples of the topic covered are the application of the business model Canvas for the smart manufacturing, the evolution of manufacturing and main global trends, the entrepreneurial strategies for smart manufacturing.

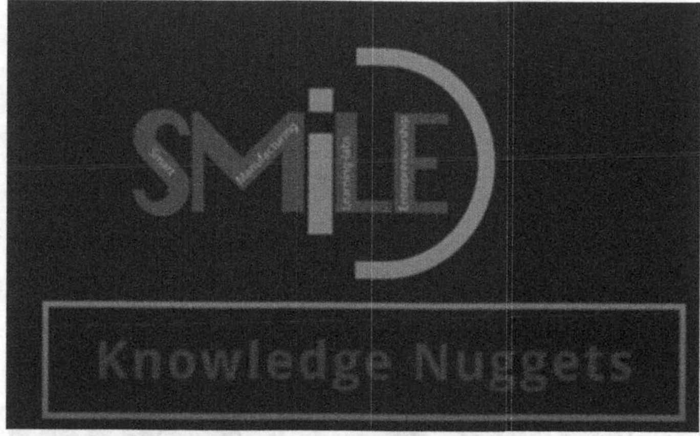

Fig. 4. SMILE Digital Learning Nugget

- *Collaborative visual platform (e.g., Miro* (Fig. 5): This platform allows students to communicate, collaborate and interact in a virtual space. Through the collaborative visual platform, students can share ideas, brainstorm solutions, create visuals, and collaborate in real-time on projects. This platform facilitates effective teamwork, creativity, and communication amongst participants, and enables collaboration to solve the challenges posed during the hackathon. This platform allows students to communicate, collaborate and interact in a virtual space. Through the collaborative visual platform, students can share ideas, brainstorm solutions, create visuals, and collaborate in real-time on projects. This platform facilitates effective teamwork, creativity, and communication amongst participants, and enables collaboration to solve the challenges.
- *Online communication platforms, such as Zoom or MSTeams* (Fig. 6): This digital space will be used for synchronous interaction among students and with the companies and for the presentation to companies. Indeed, such tools, also known as video-conferencing tools (Salopek, 2000; Andersson and Mutlu, 2020), present different features for the user; such as for example phone-calls, audio conferencing, chatbox, as well as desktop sharing (Gierszewska, 2013). In their designated function,

such communication tools effectively encompass verbal communication, coordination, and make a valuable contribution to remote decision-making while remaining cost-effective.

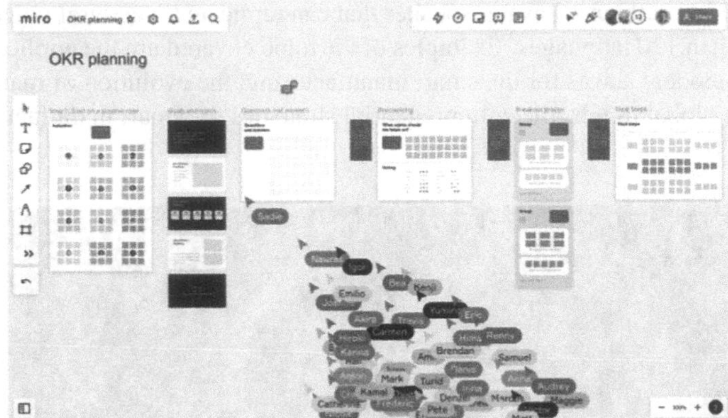

Fig. 5. Example of the use of the Miro collaborative environment

Fig. 6. Example of the use of the Microsoft Teams (Tuttotech.net)

5 Discussion

In the discussion, we reflect on digital learning. As the activity is still ongoing, we reflect, in particular, upon the pre-created digital learning nuggets. They were used by HEIs to ameliorate and improve students' strengths and abilities. First, they increase accessibility and convenience, allowing students to access educational content anytime, anywhere, through digital devices. This flexibility supports education, allowing individuals to learn at their own pace and time. Second, digital learning nuggets provide very small learning experiences, delivering information in small, manageable amounts. This strategy helps students stay focused and motivated by avoiding information overload. Students can participate in specific topics of interest or areas, in which they need to improve, facilitating targeted learning experiences. By combining digital learning nuggets with digital learning labs, students can access specific information that gives them the knowledge and guidance they need to solve real problems.

The use of digital learning nuggets in combination with digital learning labs offers many benefits. First, it helps students to be prepared for lab assignments by providing relevant background information, concepts, and ideas. These pre-assessment materials ensure that students have a foundational understanding before participating in the digital learning lab, thus greatly improving their practical learning experience. Furthermore, digital learning nuggets can serve as examples and materials for use in the lab. Students can consult them for guidance, techniques, problem-solving advice, or explanations of underlying principles. This allows students to navigate lab assignments independently, thereby developing critical thinking and problem-solving skills.

Moreover, for the future, we believe that digital learning nuggets should be equipped with interactivity and feedback that enhances the learning experience. They can be developed using interactive simulations, virtual experiments, or data analysis tools that allow students to manipulate variables, observe results, and draw conclusions. These interactive elements allow students to explore different scenarios, test hypotheses and gain a deeper understanding of the topic.

Within this Digital Learning Lab, students are empowered to actively engage and collaborate with their peers, amplifying their abilities to tackle real-world challenges with ingenuity and creativity. By leveraging the latest advancements in technology, SMILE fosters an atmosphere of interactivity, enabling students to seamlessly interact with the virtual environment, each other, and a vast array of educational resources. In this dynamic and collaborative educational approach, students have the opportunity to develop skills such as critical thinking, problem-solving, communication, and teamwork.

6 Conclusion

The changes occurred in the technology landscape have strongly affected manufacturing, thus requiring workers to acquire knowledge and skills in areas such as energy, automation, data analysis, and software development, as well as skills such as interdisciplinarity, collaborative work, problem-solving, and innovation (Jerman et al., 2020). At the same time, also due to the recent COVID-19 pandemic, the way of learning and teaching has radically changed. Following this trend, this paper proposes the important dimensions to be considered when designing a Digital Learning Lab aimed at teaching interdisciplinarity, collaborative work, problem-solving, and innovation skills. Specifically, the digital learning lab encompasses digital learning nuggets and a challenge-based activity proposed by companies.

Digital learning labs exhibit some limitations. First, a problem related to data privacy and security can emerge. Since the environment is entirely managed online, the protection of sensitive information (e.g., students-side, company-side) should be ensured. Second, technical problems (e.g., hardware malfunctions, software glitches, etc.) may hinder the progress of the hackathon. Third, hands-on experience may suffer, especially if team members are not present in the same physical space.

For future research, studies should delve into understanding the impact of digital learning labs on student learning outcomes. Furthermore, they can investigate ways to improve personalisation within DLL to meet individual student needs. Research should also be conducted on inclusive design, ensuring that all students, including those with disabilities, can access this educational approach. Lastly, it is of paramount importance to address the digital divide, by exploring strategies that ensure that all students have equal access to digital learning lab.

Lastly, the expected number of participants for the Hackathon (that will be run at the end of November 2023) will be characterized by at least 30+ students from SMILE's consortium. In order to guarantee the best experience for students participating in the Hackathon, a set of 20 pre-created digital learning nuggets will be put at their disposal to enrich their knowledge. Furthermore, students will have the possibility to use MIRO (collaborative platform) directly within Zoom (communication platform).

Acknowledgements. This project has received funding from EIT RawMaterials under grant agreement ID 10044 (correspondent to the project shortly entitled "SMILE", "Smart Manufacturing Innovation, Learning-Labs, and Entrepreneurship").

This study was carried out within the MICS (Made in Italy – Circular and Sustainable) Extended Partnership and received funding from the European Union Next-Generation EU (PIANO NAZIONALE DI RIPRESA E RESILIENZA (PNRR) – MISSIONE 4 COMPONENTE 2, INVESTIMENTO 1.3 – D.D. 1551.11-10-2022, PE00000004). This manuscript reflects only the authors' views and opinions, neither the European Union nor the European Commission can be considered responsible for them.

References

Abele, E., Metternich, J., Tisch, M., Reitberger, T.: Learning Factories: Concepts, Guidelines, Best-Practice Examples (2018).https://doi.org/10.1007/978-3-319-92261-4

Albukhitan, S.: Developing digital transformation strategy for manufacturing. In: Procedia Computer Science, The 11th International Conference on Ambient Systems, Networks and Technologies (ANT)/The 3rd International Conference on Emerging Data and Industry 4.0 (EDI40)/Affiliated Workshops, vol. 170, pp. 664–671 (2020). https://doi.org/10.1016/j.procs.2020.03.173

Andersson, H., Mutlu, A.: Digital Collaboration Tools. What Types of Frustrations do Managers Experience? Lund University (2020)

Barker, L., et al.: The research agenda for the new discipline of engineering education. J. Eng. Educ. **95**, 257–258 (2006)

Belton, B., et al.: COVID-19 impacts and adaptations in Asia and Africa's aquatic food value chains. Mar. Policy **129**, 104523 (2021). https://doi.org/10.1016/j.marpol.2021.104523

Bonekamp, L., Sure, M.: Consequences of industry 4.0 on human labour and work organisation. J. Bus. Media Psychol. **6**, 33–40 (2015)

Clark, H.: Building Education: The Role of the Physical Environment in Enhancing Teaching and Research. Issues in Practice. Institute of Education, 20 Bedford Way, London, WC1H 0AL, England (2002)

Cornerstone People Research Lab: Thriving In The Global Skills Shortage: Your Path Through The Wilderness [WWW Document]. eLearning Industry. https://elearningindustry.com/free-ebooks/thriving-in-the-global-skills-shortage-your-path-through-the-wilderness (2022). Accessed 25 Jul 2023

Cunningham, I., Dawes, G.: The Handbook of Work Based Learning. Routledge, London (2016). https://doi.org/10.4324/9781315557342

Davies, R.: Industry 4.0: Digitalisation for productivity and growth [WWW Document]. European Parliament. https://www.europarl.europa.eu/thinktank/en/document/EPRS_BRI(2015)568337. Accessed 25 Jul 2023

Doherty, O., Stephens, S.: The skill needs of the manufacturing industry: can higher education keep up? Educ. Training **63**, 632–646 (2021). https://doi.org/10.1108/ET-05-2020-0134

Ellis, R.A., Goodyear, P.: Models of learning space: integrating research on space, place and learning in higher education. Rev. Educ. **4**, 149–191 (2016). https://doi.org/10.1002/rev3.3056

Excelsior Unioncamere, 2022 [WWW Document]. https://excelsior.unioncamere.net/pubblicazioni/2022. Accessed 25 Jul 2023

Ghergo, F.: Storia della Formazione Professionale in Italia. Gli anni 1860–1879. CNOS-FAP, Roma (2020)

Gierszewska, M.: Exploratory study on how virtual teams create, share and manage knowledge. Dissertation Thesis, Business Innovation, Birkbeck College. https://aisel.aisnet.org/ (2013)

Hofstein, A., Lunetta, V.: The laboratory in science education: foundations for the twenty-first century. Sci. Educ. **88**, 28–54 (2004). https://doi.org/10.1002/sce.10106

Jerman, A., Pejic Bach, M., Aleksic, A.: Transformation towards smart factory system: examining new job profiles and competencies. Syst. Res. Behav. Sci. **37**, 388–402 (2020). https://doi.org/10.1002/sres.2657

Ka Yuk Chan, C.: Laboratory learning. In: Seel, N.M. (ed.) Encyclopedia of the Sciences of Learning, pp. 1705–1708. Springer US, Boston, MA (2012). https://doi.org/10.1007/978-1-4419-1428-6_966

Kanetaki, Z., et al.: Grade prediction modeling in hybrid learning environments for sustainable engineering education. Sustainability **14**, 5205 (2022). https://doi.org/10.3390/su14095205

Kopp, U.: The EU SDS process [WWW Document]. European Sustainable Development Network. https://www.esdn.eu/fileadmin/ESDN_Reports/2006-May-The_EU_SDS_process.pdf (2006). Accessed 25 Jul 2023

Kreß, A., et al.: Revision of the learning factory morphology (May 24, 2023). In: Proceedings of the 13th Conference on Learning Factories (CLF 2023). https://ssrn.com/abstract=4458050 or https://doi.org/10.2139/ssrn.4458050

Latha, S., Prabu, C.B.: Vuca in engineering education: enhancement of faculty competency for capacity building. Procedia Comput. Sci. **172**, 741–747 (2020). https://doi.org/10.1016/j.procs.2020.05.106

López-Belmonte, J., Costa, R., Moreno Guerrero, A., Marín-Marín, J.-A.: Co-word analysis and academic performance of the term TPACK in web of science. Sustainability **13**, 1–20 (2021). https://doi.org/10.3390/su13031481

Manyika, J., et al.: Jobs Lost, Jobs Gained: Workforce Transitions In a Time of Automation. McKinsey & Company (2017)

McKinsey: Mind the [skills] gap [WWW Document]. McKinsey. https://www.mckinsey.com/featured-insights/sustainable-inclusive-growth/chart-of-the-day/mind-the-skills-gap (2021). Accessed 25 Jul 2023

Nykvist, S., Langseth, I., Haugsbakken, H.: The role of a learning support team in transforming online learning. In: EDULEARN21 Proceedings, pp. 11567–11567 (2021). https://doi.org/10.21125/edulearn.2021.2421

OECD report: Vocational Education and Training in Germany: Strengths, Challenges and Recommendations (2010)

Pischetola, M.: Teaching novice teachers to enhance learning in the hybrid university. Postdigit. Sci. Educ. **4**, 70–92 (2022). https://doi.org/10.1007/s42438-021-00257-1

Polsani, P.: Use and abuse of reusable learning objects. J. Digital Inf. **3**(4) (2003). https://jodi-ojs-tdl.tdl.org/jodi/article/view/jodi-105

Preece, J., Maloney-Krichmar, D., Abras, C.: History of emergence of online communities. Encycl. Community (2003)

Rowe, A., Jackson, D., Fleming, J.: Exploring university student engagement and sense of belonging during work-integrated learning. J. Vocat. Educ. Training (2021). https://doi.org/10.1080/13636820.2021.1914134

Sanchez, E., Paukovics, E., Cheniti-Belcadhi, L., El Khayat, G., Said, B., Korbaa, O.: What do you mean by learning lab? Educ. Inf. Technol. **27**, 4501–4520 (2022). https://doi.org/10.1007/s10639-021-10783-x

Salopek, J.J.: Digital Collaboration, Training & Development, vol. 54, no. 6, pp. 39–43 (2000). http://www.lusem.lu.se/library. Accessed 28 Sep 2023

Stickel, O., Stilz, M., Brocker, A., Borchers, J., Pipek, V.: Fab:UNIverse – Makerspaces. Fab Labs Lab Managers Acad. (2019). https://doi.org/10.1145/3335055.3335074

Turnbull, D., Chugh, R., Luck, J.: Issues in learning management systems implementation: a comparison of research perspectives between Australia and China. Educ. Inf. Technol. **26**, 3789–3810 (2021). https://doi.org/10.1007/s10639-021-10431-4

UNCTAD: The Sustainable Manufacturing and Environmental Pollution Programme [WWW Document]. United Nations Conference on Trade and Development. https://unctad.org/news/sustainable-manufacturing-and-environmental-pollution-programme (2020). Accessed 25 Jul 2023

WMF: World Manufacturing Foundation [WWW Document]. World Manufacturing Foundation. https://worldmanufacturing.org/ (2022). Accessed 25 Jul 2023

Case Fill Rate Prediction

Kamran Iqbal Siddiqui(✉), Madeleine Mei Yee Lee, Thomas Koch, and Elenna Dugundji

Massachusetts Institute of Technology, Cambridge, MA 02142, USA
kamranis@alum.mit.edu, {madeleinelee,thakoch,elenna_d}@mit.edu

Abstract. Stockouts present significant challenges for Fast-Moving Consumer Goods (FMCG) companies, adversely affecting profitability and customer satisfaction. This research investigates key drivers causing Case Fill Rate (CFR) to fall below target levels and identifies the best model for predicting future CFR for the sponsor company. By utilizing feature importance techniques including Shapley additive explanations (SHAP) value plots, we conclude demand forecast error is the most critical driver influencing CFR. Machine learning classification and regression techniques were deployed to predict shipment cut quantity. To improve longer-term forecasts, a combination of models should be incorporated, along with extended historical data, promotions data, and consideration of exogenous variables. In conclusion, companies should prioritize forecasting accuracy and optimize inventory policy to improve CFR in the long run.

1 Introduction

Fast-Moving-Consumer-Goods (FMCG), products intended for everyday consumption, are valued at over $10 trillion USD, and projected to reach $15 trillion USD in 2025 (Bhandalkar, 2025). The FCMG industry is often faced with challenges driven by the high complexity of supply chains and wild fluctuations of demand due to frequent promotional campaigns and changes in consumer behavior. Recent events like COVID-19, the Suez Canal blockage, US port congestion and geopolitical issues in Europe have led to massive supply chain disruptions. These disruptions include raw material and labor shortages, reduced transportation and production capacities and major hikes in freight and utility tariffs, which have further enhanced the vulnerability of the FMCG industry, causing a ripple effect of customer demand being unfulfilled. These disruptions have become increasingly frequent in the last decade, driving the urgency of companies to build a resilient and robust supply chain network to proactively mitigate the negative impact of such scenarios. The sponsoring company, an FMCG company with multiple product lines, is also vulnerable to these disruptions. The research focused on one product line due to the business maturity with well-established customer demand patterns.

The company used Case Fill Rate (CFR) as a performance metric to evaluate their performance against customer orders and set a predetermined CFR target level that they wanted to attain. CFR was computed by dividing total shipments by total customer orders. Multiple factors, including demand forecast, inventory levels, and production

S. Terzi et al. (Eds.): IN4PL 2023, CCIS 1886, pp. 285–303, 2023.
https://doi.org/10.1007/978-3-031-49339-3_18

planning, influenced CFR performance. The sponsor company employed the term "cut" to describe ordered volumes that were unable to be fulfilled.

A low CFR translates to lost sales, which in turn contributes to losses in net profit margin. Furthermore, lost sales negatively impact customers' loyalty and brand confidence, as switching costs for FMCG products are relatively low. A recent study (NielsenIQ, 2022) reports that 70% of consumers will purchase an alternate brand if their regular choice is out of stock. With the further pressure of rising inflation, consumers are more price sensitive and therefore actively seeking alternate brands that are priced lower. Moreover, it is exceedingly difficult to regain customers if their trust in the brand is diminished. Consequently, the company will need to increase spending on advertising and marketing campaigns to regain market share and customer loyalty. Occasionally, there are contractual penalties that are required to be paid by the sponsoring company when customer orders are unfulfilled due to CFR being below the target level.

The objective of the research project was to gain a better understanding of the major risk factors that had contributed to the consistently low CFR over the past three years. Additionally, the project aimed to develop a predictive model that could estimate future CFR based on the key risk drivers identified through the analysis of data from the previous three years.

A data-driven approach was hypothesized to be the most appropriate approach for this research, which was divided into two stages. First, the major risk drivers that was driving the low CFR in the past three years were identified, which also set the feature of future case fill rate projection. Second, the major risk drivers identified in the first stage were used as variables to be incorporated into a model that could predict CFR for the upcoming weeks so that the company could take appropriate actions to mitigate this loss.

To build a CFR prediction model for the sponsor company, our project plan included reviewing literature related to inventory management, demand forecasting challenges, supply chain metrics, and stock out impacts, as well as machine learning algorithms used in similar projects. We collected and examined quantitative data from the sponsoring company and conducted weekly meetings with key stakeholders to collect qualitative data such as operations and logistic network and identify key business variables related to the project. Descriptive analytics were performed on the data for preliminary data validation. Multiple machine learning techniques were used for pattern recognition, identifying key variables, and predictive models. Based on the machine learning technique that provided the best output, model validation was performed using a test dataset. Lastly, we formulated managerial insights and recommendations for the company as well as areas for future research.

2 Literature Review

To dive deeper into the core problem of the research – identifying the major risk driver(s) causing a low CFR and how can we predict CFR – we reviewed literature on: (1) inventory management in FMCG and demand forecasting challenges, (2) supply chain metrics & impact of stock outs, and (3) big data and machine learning algorithms, as these are most relevant to this research project.

2.1 Inventory Management in the FMCG Industry

Fast-moving consumer goods (FMCGs), as the name suggests, refer to everyday products that sell quickly at a relatively low cost to a broad consumer base. To cater to this dynamic demand and to mitigate this quick turnover challenge, companies must maintain optimum inventories both on the shelves as well as in different echelons in their supply chains (ITC Infotech, 2022). FMCGs generally operate on a built-to-stock model, as they have shorter lead times to fulfill customer orders so they must invest in finished goods inventory to cover forecasted demand while minimizing their financial exposure (Gundogdu and Maloney, 2019).

One major challenge in supply chain management is determining the optimal inventory level for each level of the supply chain (Inderfurth, 1991). Insufficient inventory can result in stockouts and a decrease in the customer base, while excess inventory can lead to high costs such as storage and financial expenses. Inventory, or safety stock, is typically kept in a supply chain to cover inefficiencies such as demand forecast accuracy, supply plan compliance, delays in production and upstream supply chains, transportation disruptions, logistics disruptions, and so on. Inderfurth (1991) emphasized that safety stock is a critical component of inventory management, and it acts as a buffer to compensate for demand forecast inaccuracy and demand fluctuations, which will be discussed in the next section.

Demand Forecasting. Maintaining high forecast accuracy for a consumer goods company is a major challenge, as sales operations are heavily dependent on the accuracy of the demand forecast. However, research by EKN Research (2022) has shown that the average forecast accuracy for the consumer goods industry is approximately 60% irrespective of the forecast method used.

Operating with high accuracy in demand forecast allows a company to maintain low inventories in terms of safety stock and reap the financial benefits that come with this. Conversely, a high forecast error requires greater investment in safety stock inventory to cover demand variation. Gruen (2002) suggests that approximately 47% of stock out events are due to poor demand forecast accuracy, which leads to either understocking or overstocking of inventory. Overstocking inventory has a negative financial impact on the organization, whereas understocking inventory leads to stock outs, loss of sales, and damage to brand confidence, which jeopardizes customer relationships (Raman and Kim, 2002).

Moreover, poor demand forecast accuracy also leads to multiple supply chain inefficiencies, such as increased logistics costs to expedite the shipments, and reallocation of inventory from sub optimal regions within the network to fulfill backorder. Low forecast accuracy over time also causes a bullwhip effect from upstream to manufacturing, resulting in frequent production plan changes. Suppliers in the upper echelons tend to build more inventories within the network to cater to sudden demand variations (Chen et al, 2000).

Demand Uncertainty Caused by Discounts and Promotions. In the FMCG industry, sales promotions and discounts are key marketing strategies to boost sales. Products can be selected for promotion for multiple reasons like slow moving or dead inventory, high sales targets, and remaining shelf life. However, the main goal of all promotions is to boost sales. Sales promotions are mainly of two types: trade and consumer sales promotions. Trade promotions are used to boost primary sales and are targeted to the trade (retailers, wholesalers, distributors) in the form of discounts, commissions, and incentives so that they stock more products, give better visibility to the product, and thus generate more sales from the end consumers. Consumer promotions are sales promotion activities, they are targeted directly toward the end consumer and are advertised in public media to attract the attention of the masses (Nigam, 2016). Promotional activities vary from region to region and are highly influenced by local consumer buying patterns.

Promotions drive an increase in sales revenue of approximately 45% as compared to non-promotional sales. Promotions entice consumers through a financial incentive.

Selected products are put on promotion by manufacturers and sometimes retailers, to increase the customer base, increase the retailer's margin for the product (Zoellner and Schaefers, 2015), promote brand switching, and market new products (Blattberg and Neslin, 1993).

2.2 Supply Chain Metrics and Impact of Stock Outs

In supply chain, the main goal is "to get the right product in the right quantity in the right place and at the right time, at minimum total cost" (Carvalho et al., 2022). The KPIs or metrics are selected based on their relevance and impact on the supply chain process efficiency for the organization. To build an efficient supply chain, companies tend to follow numerous supply chain metrics or key performance indicators (KPIs) to gauge and improve their processes (Lohmann et al., 2004). These metrics vary at each echelon and function of the supply chain. All these KPIs and performance drivers contribute to the efficiency of the organization's supply chain to achieve customer satisfaction by fulfilling demand. For example, in the upper echelon of the supply chain, demand forecast accuracy is used to gauge the deviation of actual demand from forecasted demand within the demand planning function, whereas total cycle time measures the time required to convert raw materials into finished products within the production function (Drew Editorial Team, 2022). Conversely, OTIF (On-Time-In-Full) and Case Fill Rate (CFR) are commonly used metrics in the lower echelons to measure the performance of customers' orders fulfillment and the ability to deliver as per the promised date (Calhoun, 2022). In this research, the sponsoring company uses CFR as a key metric and a benchmark to measure the performance of customer delivery.

Product stock outs remain a key challenge for consumer goods industries and the entire world saw the severe effects of stock outs during COVID pandemic (EKN Research, 2022). In a detailed study, EKN Research (2022) published the below statistics on the impact of out-of-stock events in fast moving consumer goods industry.

- In North America, out-of-stock events cause an annual loss of approximately $129.5 billion while in Europe, 7–10% of annual sales are lost due to stock-outs. Accumulated losses from overstocking and stock-outs are worth $1.1 trillion every year.
- The average stock-out rate is around 8% for all categories while the out-of-stock rate exceeds 10% for promotional products.

- It is more likely that consumers switch brands rather than switch stores/retailers however, repeated out-of-stock products lead to 70% of consumers switching stores/retailers rather than searching for an alternative brand.
- Inaccurate demand forecasts have the highest contribution (47%) to out-of-stock events.

As the objective of this research is to predict the CFR impact caused by stock out events using the data driven approach, we will discuss the topics of big data and machine learning algorithms in the next section.

2.3 Big Data and Machine Learning Algorithms

Big data is defined as distributed computing architectures that consist of three Vs: big volumes, more velocity, and a great variety (Henry, 2019). Big data is incredibly valuable for businesses of all industries to increase productivity and competitiveness. Manyika et al. (2022) projected that if the private sector efficiently leveraged big data to promote operational efficiency and quality, profit margins could grow by up to 60%. The data avalanche generated by a vast amount of transactional data in the FMCG business had proficiently enhanced advanced analytical to drive revenue growth. For example, the history of sales data and promotion activity provided vital insight into consumers' behavior in relation to price changes, empowering companies to develop marketing strategies to influence customers' purchases (Infosys, 2022).

Big data has empowered machine learning and predictive analytics with advanced algorithms to improve forecast accuracy within the supply chain, compared to traditional forecast models. Machine learning is mainly classified into supervised and unsupervised learning. Supervised learning requires pre-defined labels and is designed to train the algorithm in classifying data and high accuracy of predictive outcome, while the latter does not require pre-defined labels (Dickson, 2022). Chase (2016) discussed that traditional forecasting models based on times series are restricted to only a few variable factors like demand history. In contrast, forecast models based on machine learning can incorporate unlimited variable factors that are relevant to the forecasting model to improve robustness and accuracy. A study by Carbonneau et al. (2008) showed that forecast error in machine learning techniques is lower compared to traditional techniques such as naïve and moving average.

Supervised Machine Learning. Classification and regressions are main algorithms in supervised learning. Regression algorithms such as linear regression and logistic regression examine the correlation between independent and dependent variables and predict target output, such as stock out rate (linear regression) and stock out events (logistic regression). Algorithms like Support Vector Machine (SVM), Decision Tree, and Random Forest, group test data into specific categories to predict target output. These algorithms can also be applied to identify root causes in prediction models.

In our study, we will use multiple supervised learning algorithms including decision tree, naïve bayes to identify the key variables that have the most impact on a low CFR, and we further develop a predictive model to forecast CFR using both regressions and classification algorithms to test the correlation between multiple variables.

Unsupervised Machine Learning. In contrast to supervised learning, unsupervised learning not require target labels (Alzubaidi, 2020). Clustering and dimensionality reduction are algorithms within unsupervised learning commonly used to explore segmentations based on similar data points to understand the most influential dependent variables, detect anomalies using pattern recognition, and gain hidden insights. Examples of unsupervised learning include K-means, Nearest Neighbor, Principal Component Analysis. We do not apply unsupervised learning in this study.

3 Data

The research analyzes the performance of one product line of the sponsor company. The study is focused on that one product line as the first step, analyzing the orders received, forecasting accuracy, ability to fulfill this demand i.e. Case Fill Rate and inventory management for that product line. The research provided cut quantity prediction, insights, and recommendations to the sponsor company to address the following questions:

- What are major risk drivers causing CFR below target level for the last 3 years?
- Which risk drivers are relevant to predict future CFR?
- What is the best model to project future case fill rate driven by identified risk driver?

3.1 Business Understanding

The dataset provided by the sponsor company contained three years of sales transactional data, including details on customer purchase history, inbound and outbound shipment of distribution centers, daily inventory levels, demand forecast, manufacturing plans, SKU master data, and labor capacity as shown in Table 1.

Table 1. List of key features from the dataset

Table	Feature	Description
Daily Forecast	Forecast Date	Date for which forecast was created
Daily Forecast	Forecast Quantity	Forecast value in SU, this is forecast for one day (Forecast Date)
Daily Forecast	Forecast Generated Date	Date when forecast was generated
Daily Forecast	Location	Distribution Center code – ship from location
Daily Forecast	Product ID	Distribution center identifier, ship from location
Inventory	Calendar Date	Date, all values are reported in the end of the day of calendar day

(*continued*)

Table 1. *(continued)*

Table	Feature	Description
Inventory	Available Stock on Hand	Stock available for shipment
Inventory	Days forward Coverage	Coverage (in days) of available stock, taking into consideration current forecast
Inventory	Plant ID	Distribution Center code – ship from location
Inventory	SKU ID	SKU Product Identifier
Order Deliveries	Product ID	SKU Product Identifier
Order Deliveries	Material Available Date	Date on which product must be ready to be shipped based on customer requested delivery time
Order Deliveries	Plant ID	Distribution center identifier, ship from location
Planned Production	Calendar Date	Planned production date generated
Planned Production	Ship From	Shipped from Location
Planned Production	Actual SOH	Actual Stock on hand available
Planned Production	Material	Finish product code

Daily Forecast. This table contains the forecasted demand for each SKU for the next 60 days. The system uses statistical forecasting by analyzing historical sales data, demand patterns, and incorporates relevant factors like promotion data to generate the forecast 60 days prior to the actual date. The demand planner reviews and validates the forecast plan on a weekly basis and adjusts before finalizing the plan for production.

Planned Production Plan. This table contains information on the planned quantity for production, actual quantity produced, and projected inventory consisting of stock on hand, inventory inflow, and outflow.

Inventory. This table contains information on the stock on hand level, safety stock levels, and demand for the current week plus the expected demand for the next 1 to 25 weeks. If the stock on hand is higher than the shipment cut quantity, the data will be dropped from the dataset for modelling.

Order Delivery. This table contains information on the orders placed by customers, including the timestamp of the order, the required delivery date, and the actual shipment creation date. If the total ordered quantity is not shipped in full, the remaining quantity is considered as a shipment cut.

Master Data. This table contains the specifications and characteristics of each product, including packaging, sizes, and minimum quantity per stocking unit.

3.2 Data Preprocessing

Data Cleaning. During the data cleaning phase, the dataset containing over 5 million rows was reviewed to ensure the integrity of the data for the model. Null, outlier, and inconsistent data were identified and handled. Null data were either dropped or replaced using mean imputation or the previous value. Outliers were identified using quartiles and removed from the dataset. Inconsistent data such as negative purchase order quantity was also removed prior to modeling. Besides, inconsistent data like negative purchase order quantity is also removed from the dataset prior to modelling.

Data Integration. Data integration was a significant effort, as the dataset consisted of multiple tables with different datatypes and data structures. Detailed data manipulation was necessary to ensure the correctness of the output data. For example, the date format varied in most tables, including yyyymmdd, mm-dd-yy, and ddmmyyy, requiring extra care in formatting prior to merging and joining the dataset. Additionally, data in different tables consisted of multiple types, requiring changing data types of features, scaling numerical values, and encoding numerical values to categorical values as a prerequisite to fitting them into the model. The tables in the database are linked together based on key attributes such as SKU, plant, and date, which act as the essential conditions for joining the tables.

Feature Selection and Reduction. Feature selection is done to help reduce the complexity of the data, improve accuracy, and increase efficiency for computation time for modelling. In feature reduction, the number of features in the dataset is reduced by selecting a subset of the most informative and relevant features for a particular modeling task. Besides, some features with common attributes are grouped together. For instance, features related to customer behavior, such as monthly order frequency and order volume may be grouped together to create a composite feature that captures the overall behavior of the customers as one feature. Similarly, features related to product attributes, such as SKU type (liquid or powdered) or packaging size, may be grouped together to simplify the analysis or modeling task.

Date Aggregation. This is a key step in data preprocessing before we can proceed with modelling. This was a process of combining multiple data points into a single data point to create a more manageable and informative dataset. This step helped reduce the noise in the data, improve the accuracy and reliability, simplify modelling and address data quality issues. The dataset provided by the sponsor company contained the daily transactional data for sales however orders from customers are not on a daily cycle basis due to which there is high random variation in the data, there were some dates with zero orders and some with very large orders, this variation was reduced by aggregating the data on a weekly basis.

4 Exploratory Data Analysis

Data visualization is an essential tool that provides insights into trends and patterns, making data more interpretable and understandable. Data visualization also allows users to detect anomalies in historical data easily. The research includes diverse data visualizations for readers and the sponsoring company which provide insights for informed decision making. To identify the major driver of a low case fill rate, statistical methods such as SHAP (Shapley Addictive Explanation) values are utilized to identify the factors strongly associated with low case fill rates and cut quantity. SHAP values provide a measure of feature importance, indicating the extent to which each factor contributed to the overall performance of the system. By incorporating both decision tree analysis and SHAP values, this study aims to comprehensively identify and understand the drivers of low case fill rates.

4.1 Feature Importance

SHAP Value Bar Plot. To further investigate the primary causes of low case fill rate, we applied the SHAP (SHapley Additive exPlanations) value technique. This approach quantifies the contribution of each feature in driving low case fill rate, using cut quantity as the target variable. In this analysis, cut quantity represents unfulfilled portion of an order (total order minus delivered quantity).

Based on the result from SHAP Value bar plot in Fig. 1, features with the highest SHAP value were "Forecast" and "Forecast Error", which indicates that discrepancies between the forecasted quantity and the actual quantity ordered by customers had a significant impact on the final prediction of "Cut Quantity". A high SHAP value suggests that both forecast and forecast error are the major driver of high cut quantity that contribute to the low case fill rate. The feature "Available Stock "also had a high SHAP Value, indicating that the available stock is a major determining factor contributing to cut quantity.

In contrast, although the feature "Available Stock" had a high feature value, it had a relatively low SHAP value for the target variable of "Cut Quantity". This suggests that while the availability of stock is important in the model, it may not have as much of an impact on the final cut quantity compared to the forecasted quantity and forecast errors. However, the results still suggest that available stock is a major driver of low case fill rate, indicating that it is critical to plan for adequate stock to meet customer demands and prevent stockouts.

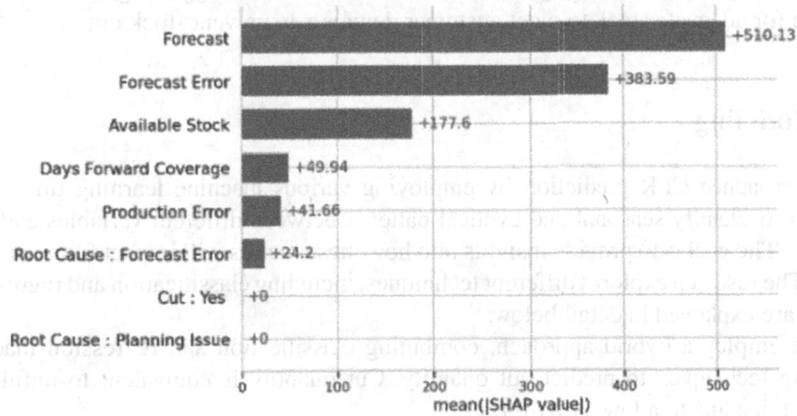

Fig. 1. SHAP Value Bar Plot

SHAP Value Beeswarm Plot. We employ a beeswarm plot in Fig. 2 to visualize the distribution of SHAP values for each feature in the model to make prediction using cut quantity as a target predictor. In this analysis, the results show that forecast, forecast error and available stocks represents the highest feature predicting the target variable, indicating that these features have a high significance to the target variable's prediction.

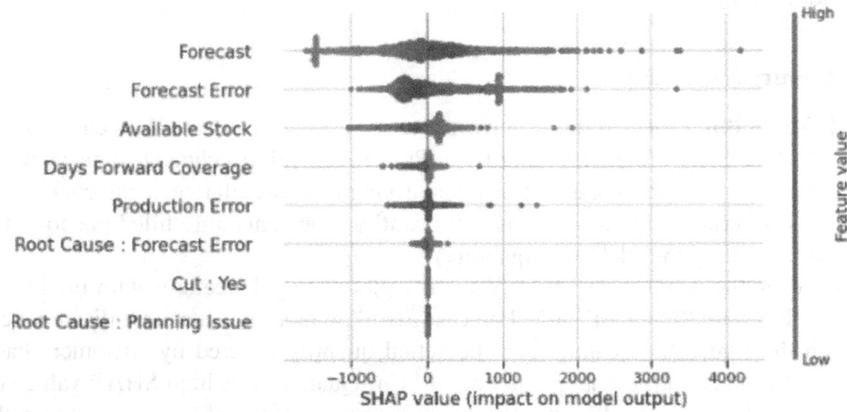

Fig. 2. SHAP Values Beeswarm Plot

Forecast and forecast error show that there are high feature values with high SHAP values, indicating that the higher the forecast and the forecast error, the higher the cut quantity leading to a low case fill rate. The result suggests that the discrepancies between forecast quantity and actual quantity ordered by customers are the major drivers driving a low case fill rate.

In contrast, the features of available stock have a high feature value but a relatively low SHAP values for target variable, which is cut quantity. This indicates that the lower the available stock quantity, the higher the cut quantity will be. The result suggests that the available stock is also a major driver of low case fill rate, suggesting that it is critical to plan for adequate stock to meet customer demands to prevent stock out.

5 Modeling

We approached CFR prediction by employing various machine learning time series models to identify seasonal and cyclical patterns between different variables and case fill rate. The goal is to provide insights into how these factors will impact future case fill rates. The research explores different techniques, including classification and regression, which are explained in detail below.

We employ a hybrid approach, combining classification and regression machine learning techniques to predict cut quantity. Cut quantity is equivalent to unfulfilled demand, leading to a low case fill rate.

An alternative approach involves a dual forecasting method, predicting inventory availability and order quantity on future dates. The target variables are inventory availability and forecasted order quantity received. We report on this second approach elsewhere.

5.1 Hybrid Classification and Regression Model for Cut Quantity Prediction

We used a hybrid model in predicting cut quantity. In our two-step approach, we first utilize classification methods to predict whether there will be a cut on a given day (binary outcome). Then, we apply regression methods to predict the magnitude of the cut quantity for the days identified as having cuts. This allows us to effectively estimate both the occurrence and the magnitude of cut quantities in our case fill rate predictions.

Data Preparation and Train-Test Split. Before applying the models, we split the dataset into training and testing sets, with the training set comprising data before January 1, 2022, and the testing set containing data from January 1, 2022, onwards. This separation ensures that the models can be evaluated on unseen data, providing a more accurate assessment of their performance.

Classification Models. We begin by employing various classification models to predict the occurrence of cuts, including Random Forest, Logistic Regression, Naïve Bayes, Decision Tree, and K-Nearest Neighbors. Our predictor variables for the classification models are forecast error, production error, projected inventory for 30 days, and forecast order for 30 days. The performance of each classification model is evaluated based on accuracy, precision, recall, specificity, and confusion matrix.

Regression Models. Once we have identified the days with cuts using the classification models, we then proceed to predict the magnitude of the cut quantity for these days. For this purpose, we tested several regression models, such as Linear Regression, Ridge Regression, Lasso Regression, Elastic Net, Random Forest Regression, Gradient Boost Regression, and Support Vector Regression. The performance of each regression model is assessed using root mean square error (RMSE).

Model Evaluation and Selection. Our goal is to identify the most suitable combination of classification and regression models for predicting the occurrence and magnitude of cut quantities, which ultimately determine the case fill rate. We compare the performance of our baseline model (based on forecast error, production error, projected inventory for 30 days, and forecast order for 30 days) with other advanced classification and regression models, selecting the best-performing models based on accuracy, RMSE, and confusion matrix.

5.2 Performance Measure Metrics

To evaluate the performance of our models in predicting case fill rate, we employ a range of metrics suitable for classification and regression models. Here, we explain each metric and how it applies to predicting case fill rate.

Confusion Matrix. The confusion matrix is a table that compares the predicted and actual values for each category. It is particularly useful for classification problems, as it helps to identify where the model is making accurate predictions and where it may be misclassifying data. By analyzing the confusion matrix, we can better understand the model's performance in predicting whether there will be a cut on a given day.

Recall. Known as sensitivity or true positive rate, recall measures the proportion of true positive predictions out of all actual positive cases. It assesses the model's ability to identify days with no cuts on a given day. High recall values indicate a lower rate of false negative predictions.

Specificity. Known as true negative rate, specificity measures the proportion of true negative predictions out of all actual negative cases. It evaluates the model's ability to correctly identify days with cuts. High specificity values indicate a lower rate of false positive predictions.

Root Mean Squared Error. RMSE measures the difference between the predicted and actual values. It is a common metric used for regression and forecasting problems, as it indicates how well the model is predicting cut quantity versus the actual value.

By employing these metrics, we comprehensively evaluate the performance of our models.

5.3 Modelling Results and Validation

Building on the insights from exploratory data analysis in Sect. 4, we explore various machine learning methods to predict case fill rate. We discuss the outcomes derived from our Hybrid Classification and Regression Model using different features. We then present the performance metrics of our baseline model and the other classification and regression models. We discuss the accuracy and confusion matrix of each classification method comparing them to identify the best model of predicting cut category. We review the RMSE of each regression method to identify the best model of predicting cut quantity.

Baseline Hybrid Classification and Regression Model Performance. The baseline model, which combines Logistic Regression for classification and Random Forest Regression for regression, uses the following features:

- Forecast error moving average of past 7 days.
- Forecast error moving average of past 14 days.
- Projected inventory quantity for next 7 to 30 days
- Forecasted order quantity for the next 7 to 30 days.

The binary target variable in the classification model is cut category. If cut category is equals to 1, it represents that there is a cut for the given day, in contrast, 0 represents no cut for the day with ordered quantity fulfilled. The continuous target variable in the regression model is magnitude of the cut quantity for the days identified as having cuts.

The performance of the baseline model is shown in Table 2, using Logistic Regression for binary classification of days having a cut or not, and Random Forest Regression for prediction of cut quantity for a day having a cut.

Table 2. Baseline Hybrid Model Performance Metrics

			Predicted	
			TRUE	FALSE
Logistic Regression	Actual	TRUE	199	1
		FALSE	12	5
	Accuracy		0.94	
	Precision		0.94	
	Recall		1.00	
	Specificity		0.29	
Random Forest	RMSE		557	

Feature Importance Analysis. To ensure robustness of our model, we conducted a feature importance analysis to identify the most important predictors. Our results showed that forecast error of the last 7 days and forecast error of the last 14 days are the most significant predictors for the model. Consequently, we excluded the less important features and reran the models using only significant predictors. The performance of the more parsimonious baseline model is shown in Table 3.

Table 3. Baseline Hybrid Model Performance Metrics using only significant predictors

			Predicted	
			TRUE	FALSE
Logistic Regression	Actual	TRUE	200	0
		FALSE	14	3
	Accuracy		0.94	
	Precision		0.93	
	Recall		1.00	
	Specificity		0.18	
Random Forest	RMSE		557	

The Logistic Regression model achieved an accuracy of 0.94 and a precision of 0.93. This model showed no false positives but had a higher number of false negatives (14) compared to the model with more features.

Performance of Alternative Classification Models. After removing less important feature and keeping only Forecast error 14 days and Forecast error 7 days, we reran the model with different classification methods with results shown in Tables 4, 5, 6 and 7.

Naïve Bayes Classifier. The Naïve Bayes model showed an accuracy of 0.92. The model had a higher number of false positives (5) but lower false negatives (12) compared to the baseline Logistic Regression model using only significant predictors.

Decision Tree Classifier. The Decision Tree model resulted in an accuracy of 0.92. This model had a higher number of false negatives (15) and false positives (3) compared to the baseline model, indicating a lower performance in correctly classifying both positive and negative instances.

Support Vector Machine Classifier. The SVM model achieved the highest accuracy among all classifiers (0.94) and the highest precision (0.94). This model showed no false positives and, together with Naïve Bayes, had the lowest number of false negatives (12) compared to other models.

Gradient Boost Classifier. The Gradient Boost Classifier model showed an accuracy of 0.92. This model had a higher number of false negatives (15) and false positives (2) compared to the baseline model, indicating a lower performance in correctly classifying both positive and negative instances.

Table 4. Performance of Naïve Bayes Classifier (days having a cut or not)

			Predicted	
			TRUE	FALSE
Naïve Bayes Classifier	Actual	TRUE	195	5
		FALSE	12	5
	Accuracy		0.92	
	Precision		0.94	
	Recall		0.98	
	Specificity		0.29	

Table 5. Performance of Decision Tree Classifier (days having a cut or not)

			Predicted	
			TRUE	FALSE
Decision Tree Classifier	Actual	TRUE	197	3
		FALSE	15	2
	Accuracy		0.92	
	Precision		0.93	
	Recall		0.99	
	Specificity		0.12	

Table 6. Performance of Support Vector Machine Classifier (days having a cut or not)

			Predicted	
			TRUE	FALSE
Support Vector Machine (SVM) Classifier	Actual	TRUE	200	0
		FALSE	12	5
	Accuracy		0.94	
	Precision		0.94	
	Recall		1.00	
	Specificity		0.29	

Table 7. Performance of Gradient Boost Classifier (days having a cut or not)

			Predicted	
			TRUE	FALSE
Gradient Boost Classifier	Actual	TRUE	198	2
		FALSE	15	2
	Accuracy		0.92	
	Precision		0.93	
	Recall		0.99	
	Specificity		0.12	

Our comparative analysis of different classifiers models revealed that the Support Vector Machine (SVM) model outperformed the other models in terms of accuracy and precision. This indicates that the SVM model is most effective in classifying and predicting cut quantities for case fill rate. However, as case fill rate emphasizes cut quantity (actual negative values), the SVM and Naïve Bayes models perform best in predicting actual negatives (specificity) while SVM and Logistic Regression models have higher recall, indicating that they perform better in identifying actual positives.

Considering both recall and specificity, after SVM, the Logistic Regression model appears to be a good choice for predicting actual negatives, as it has a perfect recall and the relatively high specificity among the top-performing models in terms of recall.

Performance of Alternative Regression Models. After classifying days that have a cut, we evaluated cut quantity using different regression models to predict the magnitude of cut quantity in each day that cut category is equals to 1 from predicted from the classification model. The models evaluated include Support Vector Regression (SVR), Gradient Boost Regression, Multi-layer Perceptron (MLP) Regression, Ridge Regression, Elastic Net Regression and Lasso Regression.

Results evaluated using Root Mean Squared Error (RMSE) are shown in Table 8.

Table 8. Performance of Alternative Regression Models for prediction of cut quantity

Random Forest (Baseline)	RMSE	557
SVR	RMSE	1023
Gradient Boost Regresssor	RMSE	854
MLP Regressor	RMSE	1195
Ridge	RMSE	786
Elastic Net	RMSE	786
Lasso	RMSE	786

The Random Forest model serves as a baseline for comparison, achieving an RMSE of 557. Comparatively, the Lasso, Ridge, and Elastic Net models show similar performance, with RMSE values around 786. These results indicate that these models are less effective than the Random Forest model for predicting cut quantity in this imbalanced dataset.

The SVR, Gradient Boost Regressor, and MLP Regressor models have varying performance. The SVR and MLP Regressor models have higher RMSE values (1023 and 1195, respectively), indicating they are less accurate compared to other models. The Gradient Boost Regressor, with an RMSE of 854, is more accurate than the SVR and MLP Regressor models but still less accurate than the Random Forest model.

Although the RMSE results perform well, these values may not provide an accurate representation of the model's performance given the imbalanced nature of the dataset. Most of the data consists of days with no-cut quantity, while cut quantities greater than 1 constitute only a minor portion of the values. As a result, the imbalanced dataset may result in deceptive RMSE values, as they may not adequately reflect the model's ability to predict the less frequent cut quantities.

6 Discussion

This research presents a few limitations. First, the dataset used in this study covers a three-year period, which may impact the model's ability to effectively learn patterns and generalize to new data points, particularly in the context of machine learning. Furthermore, the absence of certain data points such as promotional data and market indices may hinder the model's ability to learn from the available training data and create accurate predictions. A larger and more comprehensive dataset could lead to improved model performance and more accurate predictions. Besides, the dataset used is also imbalanced in nature, which may have led to biased model performance and less accurate prediction for underrepresented classes. Future research could explore techniques specifically designed for handling imbalanced data, such as oversampling the minority class, under sampling the majority class, like cut category.

Second, certain products in the market have short life cycles, which means that they are available for a limited period. As a result, there may be insufficient training data for these specific products, which could have hindered the model's ability to accurately predict their demand and associated cut quantities. Future research could explore strategies for handling short life cycle products, such as developing specialized models or leveraging transfer learning techniques.

7 Conclusion and Recommendations

7.1 Managerial Insights

This research project identified the key drivers that influence the Case Fill Rate (CFR) for a sponsor company. We found several factors that impact CFR and inventory prediction, and we provided recommendations for companies to help improve their forecasting accuracy and inventory availability, which would lead to a better case fill rate.

Forecast error and demand variability are critical factors that impact the Case Fill Rate (CFR) for companies, especially in industries with high demand variability such as Consumer Packaged Goods (CPG) companies. Therefore, improving forecast accuracy should be a priority to optimize inventory policy and increase CFR. It is crucial to incorporate the impact of promotions and exogenous factors, such as trade and retail promotions, market index and economic indices during forecasting, as these factors can significantly impact sales volumes and inventory levels. By addressing these factors and incorporating forecasting error and demand variation into their inventory policy, companies can optimize inventory levels and meet customer demand effectively.

The second part of our research aimed to develop a model that can predict inventory for a period of 13 weeks in advance. However, our analysis revealed that this can be a challenging task due to various factors, as discussed previously. These include the high variability in inventory availability and order demand caused by factors such as promotions and the irregular order patterns typical in B2B businesses. Nonetheless, we suggest that utilizing advanced forecasting techniques, such as machine learning models that incorporate time series and exogenous variables, could help improve prediction accuracy. It is essential to consider the strengths and limitations of such models to ensure they are suitable for specific business needs.

Aggregating data from SKU level to the brand level can potentially improve forecast accuracy as a whole and be helpful in certain situations, such as ordering raw materials and production resource planning. However, this may not meet the specific business requirement of the company sponsoring the study since forecasting order demand by brand may not account for the unique demand patterns of individual SKUs. This is particularly crucial as the delivery of a specific SKU may not be substituted by another SKU, making it necessary to forecast by SKU level to ensure optimal inventory levels and meet customer demand.

7.2 Future Research

We recommend that future research explore the use of more advanced machine learning techniques, such as Reinforcement Learning or Deep Reinforcement Learning, to better understand the intricate relationships between features and impact of case fill rate.

Additionally, future research could consider incorporating more external data points, including a larger training dataset, promotional activities, market indices, and competitor pricing, to enhance the predictability of cut quantity and its impact on case fill rates.

Market indices offer valuable insights into overall economic conditions and consumer trends, which may directly affect product demand. Including this information in the models can help account for wider market influences when forecasting cut quantities and case fill rates. Similarly, promotional activities can have a significant impact on demand patterns. Incorporating these factors into the models can better capture the effects of sales promotions, discounts, and other marketing efforts on inventory levels. Competitor pricing data can also be a beneficial input, providing a deeper understanding of the competitive landscape and its influence on customer preferences and purchasing behaviors. By incorporating additional data points, the model can more effectively capture the comprehensive market dynamics that influence order quantity and projected inventory, leading to improved case fill rate projections.

By employing advanced machine learning techniques and integrating more external data points in future research, we believe there is potential to develop more accurate and reliable models for predicting cut quantities and case fill rates. This would enable the creation of more robust and adaptive models that can effectively forecast cut quantities and case fill rates while considering additional data points.

References

Alzubaidi, Z.Y.: A comparative study on statistical and machine learning forecasting methods for an FMCG company. Rochester Institute of Technology, Scholar Works **96** (2020)

Bhandalkar, S.: FMCG Market Expected to Reach $15,361.8 Billion by 2025, Allied Market Research. https://www.alliedmarketresearch.com/press-release/fmcg-market.html. Last accessed 1 Dec 2022

Blattberg, R.C., Neslin, S.A.: Chapter 12 sales promotion models. In: Eliashberg, J., Lilien, G.L. (eds.) Marketing, Handbooks in Operations Research and Management Science, vol. 5, pp. 553–609. Elsevier (1993)

Calhoun, S.: On-Time, In-Full (OTIF): A Key Supply Chain Metric. https://www.veryableops.com/blog/on-time-in-full-otif. Last accessed 1 Dec 2022

Carvalho, H., Naghshineh, B., Govindan, K., Cruz-Machado, V.: The resilience of on-time delivery to capacity and material shortages: an empirical investigation in the automotive supply chain. Comput. Ind. Eng. **171**, 108375 (2022)

Carbonneau, R., Laframboise, K., Vahidov, R.: Application of machine learning techniques for supply chain demand forecasting. Eur. J. Operat. Res. **184**(3), 1140–1154 (2008)

Chase, C.W.: Machine learning is changing demand forecasting. The J. Bus. Forecast. **35**(4), 43–45 (2016)

Chen, F., Drezner, Z., Ryan, J.K., Simchi-Levi, D.: Quantifying the bullwhip effect in a simple supply chain: the impact of forecasting, lead times, and information. Manag. Sci. **46**(3), 436–443 (2000)

Dickson, B.: Machine learning: What's the difference between supervised and unsupervised? TheNextWeb.Com [blog]. Advanced Technologies & Aerospace Collection. https://www.proquest.com/blogs-podcasts-websites/machine-learning-what-s-difference-between/docview/2407960774/se-2?accountid=12492. Last accessed 1 Dec 2022

Drew Editorial Team. 10 Key Performance Indicators for production management. http://blog.wearedrew.co/en/10-key-performance-indicators-for-production-management. Last accessed 1 Dec 2022
EKN Research: Plugging Out-of-Stock Gaps in Consumer Goods, RIS News, https://risnews.com/ekn-research-plugging-out-stock-gaps-consumer-goods. Last accessed 1 Dec 2022
Gruen, T.W.: A Comprehensive Guide to Retail Out-of-Stock Reduction in the Fast-Moving Consumer Goods Industry. https://www.nacds.org/pdfs/membership/out_of_stock.pdf. Last accessed 1 Dec 2022
Gundogdu, B., Maloney, J.: Comparison and financial assessment of demand forecasting methodologies for seasonal CPGs. In: Supply Chain Management Capstone Projects, Massachusetts Institute of Technology (2019)
Henry, J.: Data Analytics and Machine Learning Fundamentals Live Lessons Video Training, 1st edn. Addison-Wesley Professional (2019)
Inderfurth, K.: Safety stock optimization in multi-stage inventory systems. Int. J. Product. Econ. **24**(1), 103–113 (1991)
Infosys BPM, Big Data Analytics in CPG: Insights Into Its Benefits. https://www.infosysbpm.com/blogs/retail-cpg-logistics/why-big-data-and-analytics-is-a-must-for-profitable-growth-in-cpg.html. Last accessed 1 Dec 2022
ITC Infotech, Inventory Management and Optimization for an FMCG Manufacturing Company. https://www.anylogic.com/resources/case-studies/inventory-management-and-optimization-for-an-fmcg-manufacturing-company/. Last accessed 1 Dec 2022
Lohman, C., Fortuin, L., Wouters, M.: Designing a performance measurement system: a case study. Eur. J. Operat. Res. **156**(2), 267–286 (2004)
Manyika, J., Chui, M., Brown, B.: Big data: The next frontier for innovation, competition, and productivity | McKinsey. https://www.mckinsey.com/capabilities/mckinsey-digital/our-insights/big-data-the-next-frontier-for-innovation. Last accessed 1 Dec 2022
Nielsen IQ, Can the FMCG industry afford to lose billions from empty shelves? https://nielseniq.com/global/en/insights/education/2022/can-the-fmcg-industry-afford-to-lose-billions-from-empty-shelves/. Last accessed 1 Dec 2022
Nigam, A.: Product promotion effectiveness: root causes of stock-outs by. In: Supply Chain Management Capstone Projects. Massachusetts Institute of Technology (2016)
Raman, A., Kim, B.: Quantifying the impact of inventory holding cost and reactive capacity on an apparel manufacturer's profitability. Product. Operat. Manag. **11**(3), 358–373 (2002)
Zoellner, F., Schaefers, T.: Do price promotions help or hurt premium-product brands? the impact of different price-promotion types on sales and brand perception. J. Advert. Res. **55**(3), 270–283 (2015)

A Continuous Review Policy for Warehouse Inventory Management

Andrew Mohn, Charles Snow, Yusuke Tanaka, Thomas Koch, and Elenna Dugundji(✉)

Massachusetts Institute of Technology, Building E40, Cambridge, MA 02142, USA
{admohn,charlessnow,yusuket}@alum.mit.edu, {thakoch,elenna_d}@mit.edu

Abstract. A continuous review policy (CRP) was used to simulate the inventory of finished product, raw material and packaging material at a warehouse. The ordering points were simulated based on the minimum order quantity and the production forecast. The safety stock levels did not impact the ordering points in this scenario because the demand was known and did not deviate. The simulation results showed that the average weekly number of pallets received at the warehouse was 341, with a standard deviation of 115 pallets. The aggregated ordering volume was fairly volatile, but the warehouse inventory levels were fairly uniform over time. The overall bin occupancy remained below 1,700, less than 20% of the total warehouse capacity. This suggests that the CRP is a good inventory management policy for products with known and stable demand. However, the volatile ordering volume could be a problem if there are constraints on processing incoming deliveries to the warehouse.

Keywords: Continuous review policy · Warehouse inventory management · Finished product · Raw material · Packaging · Production schedule · Purchasing strategy · Safety stock

1 Introduction

1.1 Infrastructure

The sponsor company owns a warehouse operated through an automated storage and retrieval system (AS/RS) with capacity of more than 9000 storage bins [1]. The bins have four different sizes and can each accommodate goods of different size and weight. In addition to this warehouse, the sponsor company currently rents 2200 slots of storage space from a third party warehouse provider. The expenditure of this warehouse rental is greater than the operating cost of the owned warehouse and hence renting is to be minimized or ideally to be avoided altogether.

S. Terzi et al. (Eds.): IN4PL 2023, CCIS 1886, pp. 304–316, 2023.
https://doi.org/10.1007/978-3-031-49339-3_19

1.2 Product Categories, Testing and Storage Policy

This warehouse space (both rental and owned) is used to store

- Raw Material
- Packaging Material
- Finished Product

Once raw material leave the warehouse towards the production site, work in progress ("Half Finished Products") are stored at the production site during formulation and packaging and only returned to the warehouse as finished product (see Fig. 1). All three above-mentioned categories undergo batch-based testing procedures before they can be released for production (raw material, packaging) or final distribution (finished product). The duration of this testing process depends on the type of product and ranges between one and several weeks.

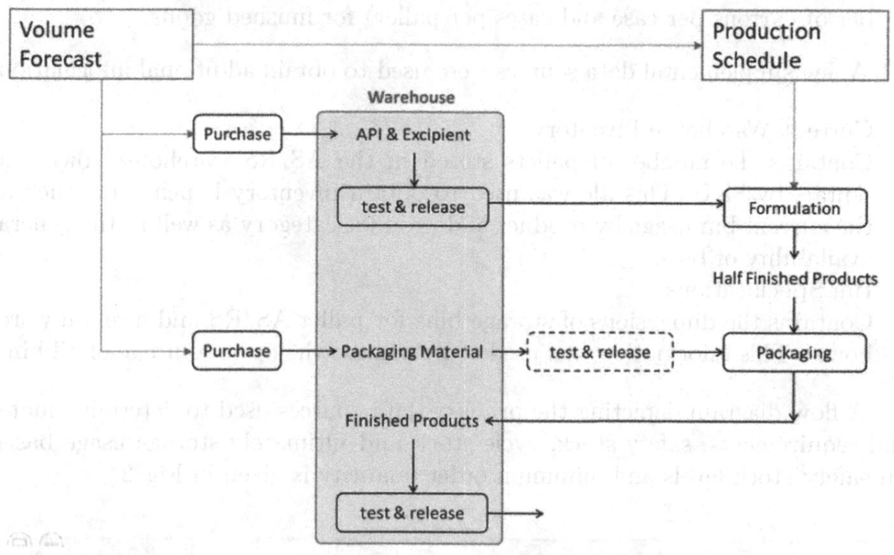

Fig. 1. Purchasing, Warehousing and Production Process Overview.

1.3 Product Portfolio, SKUs, and Warehouse Usage

The examined warehouse hosts a total of about 38 different finished products which account for roughly 40% of the warehouse space used. The packaging material used comprises about 197 different stock keeping units (SKU) and equally accounts for roughly 40% of the inventory in terms of the number of bins used. The remaining 20% of warehouse space is used for storing the raw materials comprising 64 different products.

2 Data

All data were provided in separate documents. The primary data sources are:

1. Actual Production Schedule & Production Forecast
   Contains the actual production schedule for 2022 and first half of 2023 as well as a monthly forecast up until 2025.
2. Bill of Materials (BOM)
   Contains the bill of materials for each product, the order lead time as well as machining and packaging times.
3. Raw Material Pallet Quantity
   Contains information on which measurement unit (kilograms, pieces, bags...) is used for each raw material and packaging and how many of them constitute one pallet.
4. Finished Product Information
   Contains product information such as dimensions and packing details (number of cartons per case and cases per pallet) for finished goods.

A few supplemental data sources were used to obtain additional information:

- Current Warehouse Inventory
  Contains the number of pallets stored in the AS/RS warehouse (own and rental) by SKU. This file was used to obtain inventory benchmarks such as the current bin usage by product and product category as well as the general availability of bins.
- Bin Specifications
  Contains the dimensions of storage bins for pallet AS/RS and a rental warehouse. This information was used to determine the optimal usage of all bins.

A flow diagram depicting the primary data sources used to determine material requirements, safety stock, cycle stock and ultimately storage usage based on safety stock levels and minimum order quantity is given in Fig. 2.

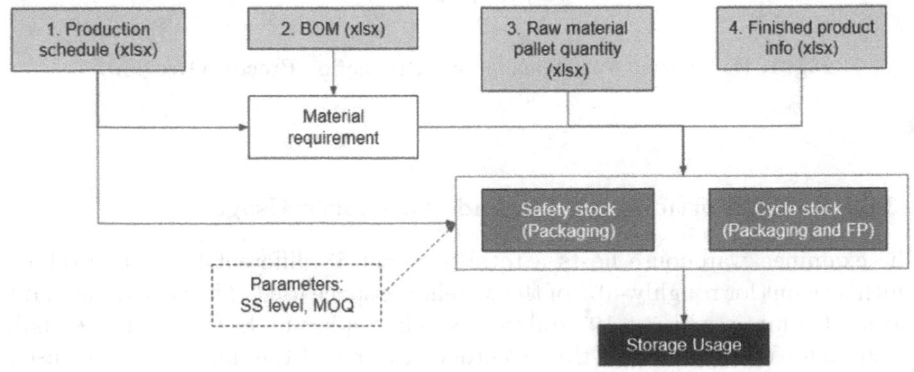

Fig. 2. Primary Data Sources to Determine Storage Usage.

3 Exploratory Analysis

3.1 Total Monthly Production Volume

The actual production volume in 2022 is heavily marked by two COVID-19 related lockdowns which resulted in a drastic decrease of production output in January and July 2022. However, the other months logged an erratic production volume (see Fig. 3).

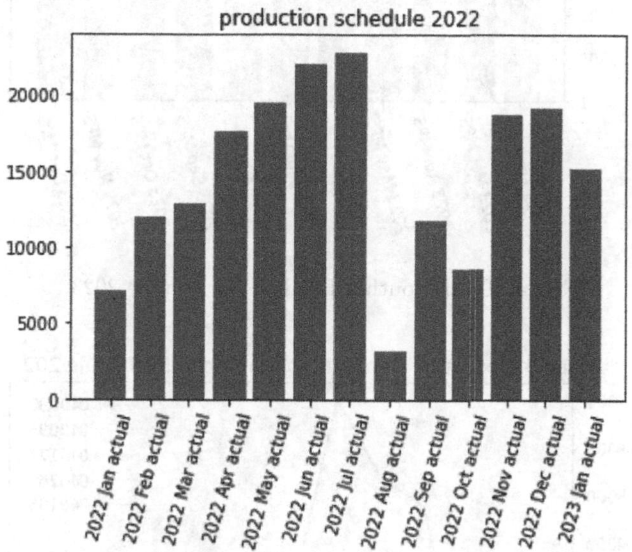

Fig. 3. Total Monthly Production Volume 2022.

Compared with the production forecast for 2023 (see Fig. 4), it appears the values in 2022 may have little predictive value since there are no apparent patterns of seasonality or annual repetition in the limited time series.

3.2 High Volume Products

The factory lockdowns are mirrored in the production quantity of the top five finished products by volume but it is also visible that they do not seem to follow any trend or order amongst each other. The order of those top ranking products changes significantly in most months in both the actual monthly production schedule throughout 2022 (see Fig. 5) as well as the monthly forecast for 2023 (see Fig. 6).

The vast differences in production volumes between different products can be seen in the current inventory snapshot with a typical exponential distribution. The top 15 products account for 87% of all finished product storage volume (see Fig. 7).

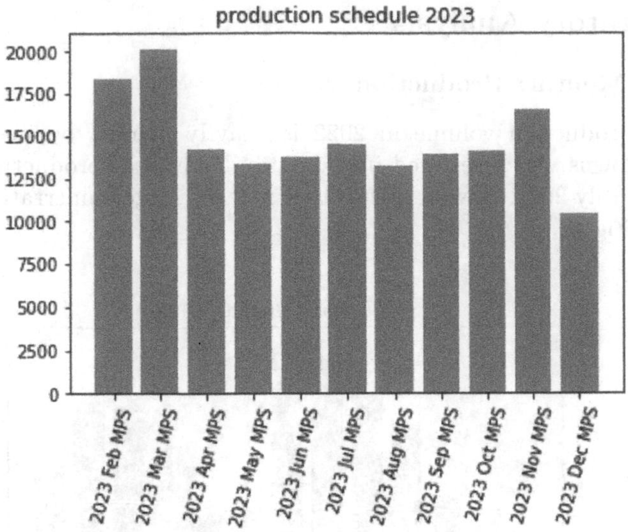

Fig. 4. Total Monthly Production Volume 2023.

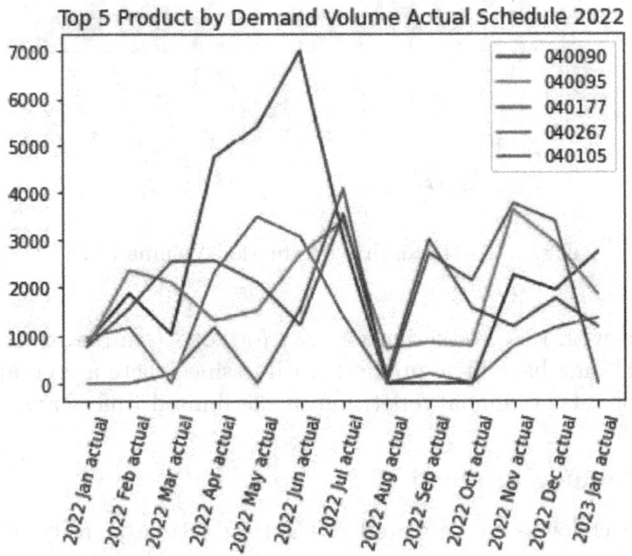

Fig. 5. Actual Monthly Production for Top 5 High Volume Products 2022.

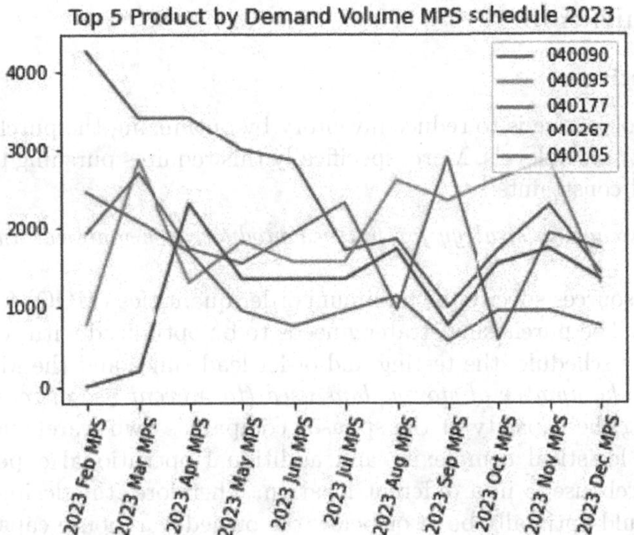

Fig. 6. Monthly Production Forecast for Top 5 High Volume Products 2023.

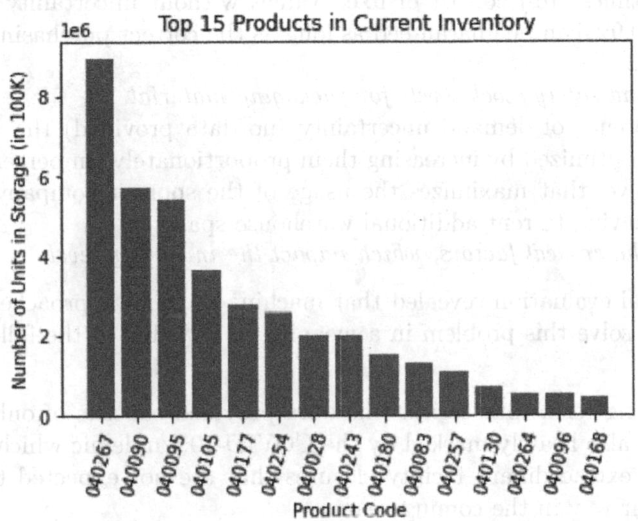

Fig. 7. Storage Volume for Top 15 Products in Current Inventory.

4 Optimization

4.1 Objective

The general objective is to reduce inventory by optimizing the purchasing strategy and safety stock levels. More, specifically this requires pursuing the following subgoals and constraints:

1. *Define purchasing strategy for finished product, raw material and packaging material*
   The data sources specify the minimum order quantities (MOQ) for purchased materials. The purchasing strategy needs to be optimized with respect to the production schedule, the testing and order lead times and the MOQ.
2. *Minimize the number of storage bins used (to prevent use of rental space)*
   Surpassing the capacity of the sponsor company's own warehouse results in increased logistical complexity and additional operational expenses as the rental warehouse is in a different location. Therefore, the desired maximum usage should optimally be at or below the owned warehouse capacity of 9000 bins.
3. *Maintain service level of* $\geq$ *99.9%*
   As all data provided by the sponsor company (production schedule, purchasing lead times etc.) consist of fixed values without uncertainty, the service level of 99.9% can be guaranteed as long as the correct purchasing points are identified.
4. *Recommend safety stock levels for packaging material*
   In the absence of demand uncertainty (no data provided) the safety stock levels are optimized by increasing them proportionately (in percent) up to an optimal level that maximizes the usage of the sponsor company warehouse without having to rent additional warehouse space.
5. *Identify the critical factors, which impact the inventory level*

The initial evaluation revealed that machine learning approaches cannot be employed to solve this problem in a meaningful way due to the following characteristics:

- Lack of long term time series. The data provided consists of only two years which are also heavily marked by the COVID-19 pandemic which resulted in repeated, extraordinary facility closures that are not expected to repeat in any similar way in the coming years.
- There is no discernible pattern in the current data. Thus, it became clear that the creation of a neural network approach as was explored in the beginning will not yield any useful results.
- The provided production schedule is the actual manufacturing plan and has no element of uncertainty. Therefore, there is no unknown variable that needs to be predicted.

Therefore, the best and easiest approach to solve the optimization proved to be the use of a continuous review policy that is based on arithmetic operations only.

4.2 Selected Approach

A continuous review policy (CRP), also known as the continuous review inventory system, is a type of inventory management strategy that uses regularly monitoring the inventory levels of products and ordering additional supplies when necessary to avoid stockouts as well as overstocking [2,3]. Under the CRP, a predetermined inventory level, known as the reorder point, is established. When the inventory level reaches this point, an order is placed to replenish the inventory. The reorder point is calculated by considering:

1. Lead time for replenishment
2. Demand rate for the product
3. Desired level of safety stock

The CRP helps to ensure that the right amount of inventory is available at the right time to meet the demand. It also helps to minimize inventory holding costs and reduce the risk of stockouts, or in the current scenario with fixed demand prevents them altogether. In the sponsor company scenario

1. The *lead time* does not only include the purchasing but also the testing lead time and provided as fixed numbers in weeks.
2. The *demand rate* for each product is fixed by the production schedule. There is also a testing time for finished product post-production. Thus, the testing duration needs to be taken into account to calculate warehouse occupancy. It is however already considered in the production schedule, i.e. the production readiness date is prior to and excluding this testing period.
3. The sponsor company is using a set of minimum *safety stock* levels by product but also requested to optimize those. Hence, safety stock is considered as a variable subject to the optimization within the constraint of the existing warehouse space.

4.3 Assumptions

In order to carry out the calculations and optimization described in the following sections a number of assumptions needed to be made.

- Packaging material is being stored in the warehouse while waiting for release. For the duration of the testing procedure whose length depends on each packaging material individually, the packaging material is stored inside the warehouse but can not be released for production yet.
- Packaging material can either be stored in the large bin types in their original pallet or the pallet can be split in half and then stored in the small bins types.
- Since the individual measurements for packaging material was not provided, the simulation assumes that all packaging material uses the same full pallet measurements regardless of the exact material.
- The minimum order quantities (MOQ) are fixed by the suppliers and cannot be changed.

- To simplify the production forecast each month is considered to comprise four full weeks, thus one year consists of 48 calculator weeks. Moreover, the simulation does not consider any holidays and assumes that the production volume is consistent throughout all four-week periods.
- The production volume per month is equally distributed over four weeks. The demand is linear and uniform for the intra-month period.

4.4 Pipeline and Data Processing

The main challenge for processing the provided data and building the pipeline is the diversity of formats and units. For example, safety stock levels are provided as "weeks" and units of the finished products are listed as packs in some files and units or thousand units in others and eventually stored as pallets in the bins. Therefore, the pipeline includes a series of conversions in order to connect all data sources as well as a number of assumptions detailed above.

5 Result

5.1 Ordering Points

Simulation of the inventory using the continuous review policy (CRP) outlined above allows the calculation of ideal ordering points [4]. For each product, the ordering point is different and depends on the minimum order quantity (MOQ) as well as the production forecast (see for example, Fig. 8).

Under the CRP, the safety stock levels do not impact the ordering points in this particular scenario since the demand is known and does not deviate and as a result the safety stocks are actually never used. This is expected to be different in reality with uncertain demand.

In total, 341 pallets of packaging material are received at the warehouse on weekly average, with the standard deviation of 115 pallets. In aggregation, the ordering points result in a fairly volatile overall ordering volume which is an interesting and potentially problematic aspect to consider in case there are any constraints on processing incoming deliveries to the warehouse (see Fig. 9). No such constraints are known to the authors and hence have not been taken into consideration for this evaluation.

5.2 Inventory Levels

The warehouse inventory levels are the mirror image of the ordering points. In line with the periodic but irregular ordering points, the inventory levels for each product spikes with an incoming order followed by a stock level decrease of varying pace until the safety stock level is reached (see for example, Figs. 10 and 11).

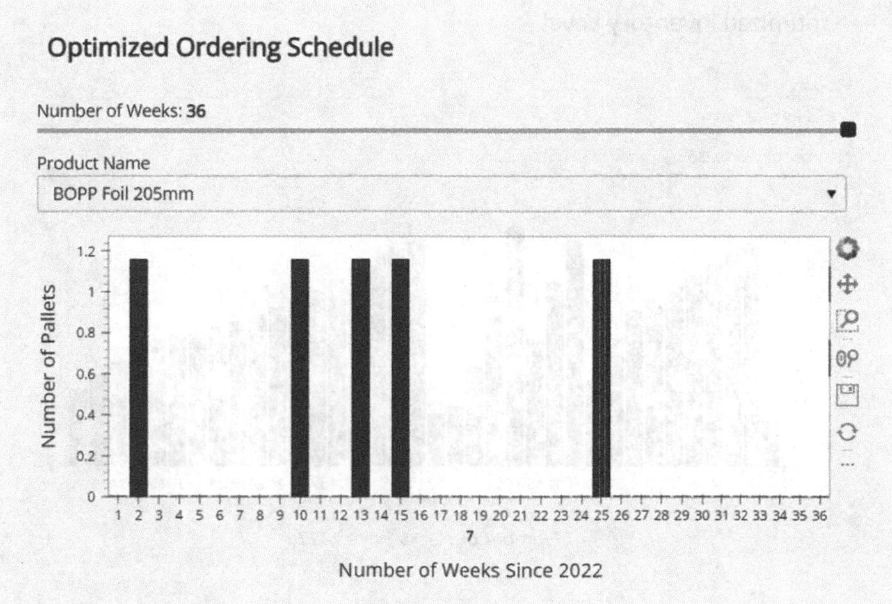

Fig. 8. Optimized Ordering Schedule for Example Product.

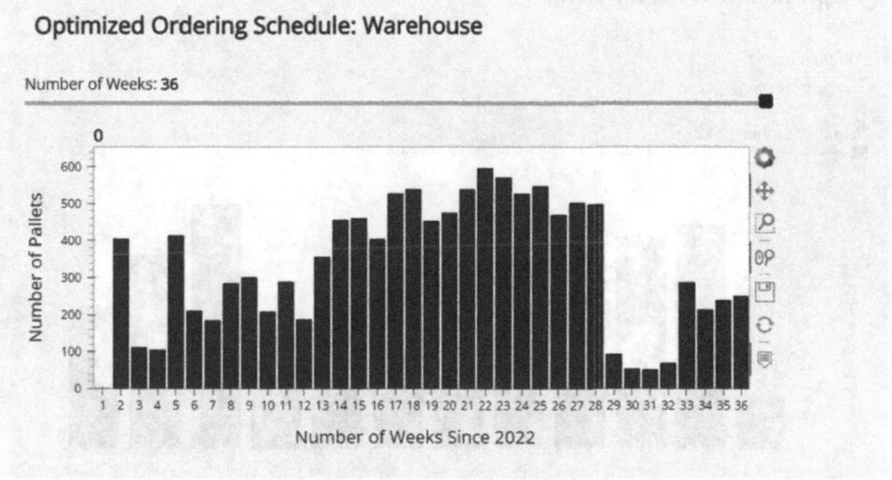

Fig. 9. Optimized Ordering Schedule for Warehouse.

In total, 1,336 pallets of packaging material are stored at the warehouse, with the standard deviation of 89 pallets. Unlike the ordering volume, the aggregate stock levels are fairly uniform over time and do not show the same degree of erratic fluctuation as order volume (see Fig. 12).

Fig. 10. Optimized Inventory Level for Example Product, 36 Weeks.

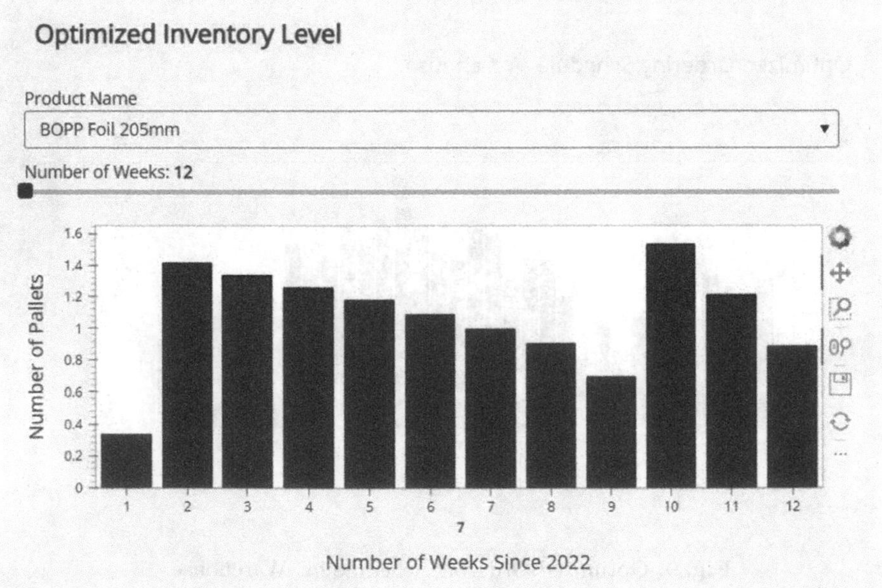

Fig. 11. Optimizes Inventory Level for Example Product, 12 Weeks.

In this simulation it is also visible that the overall bin occupancy remains below 1700. This corresponds to less than 20% of the total warehouse capacity of over 9000 and is thus well below the targeted value of 40% of the total capacity.

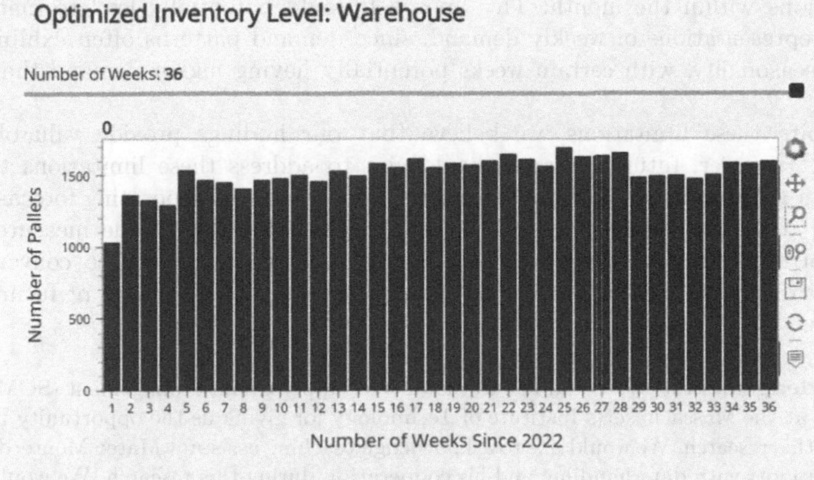

Fig. 12. Optimized Inventory Level for Warehouse, 36 Weeks.

5.3 Limitations

This study is subject to several limitations that may have affected the accuracy of our results and the applicability of our conclusions. We outline these limitations below to provide a comprehensive understanding of the context within which our findings should be interpreted.

Firstly, the absence of variance data for the forecast made it challenging to accurately determine the safety stock. Safety stock calculations rely heavily on the variability of demand and supply. As such, without variance data, our analysis might not accurately reflect the real-world scenario of the safety stock required to mitigate the risks associated with unpredictable fluctuations in supply and demand.

Secondly, the packaging material measurements presented another limitation. The simulation was conducted under the assumption that all packaging material uses the same full pallet measurements, regardless of the specific material in question. This assumption oversimplifies the complexity associated with different materials, each likely having unique measurements. Consequently, the simulation results may not accurately reflect situations where packaging materials differ in their dimensions.

Thirdly, there was a lack of inventory value and holding cost data. Without this information the cost of holding inventory was not taken into consideration. It would be assumed that finished product would have a higher value than packaging material, so would in turn be more costly to hold in inventory.

Lastly, the method used for the conversion of monthly production forecast data into weekly data posed a limitation. By dividing the monthly forecast uniformly over the weeks in each month, we failed to account for possible weekly fluctuations within the month. This approach could potentially lead to inaccurate representations of weekly demand, since demand patterns often exhibit weekly seasonality, with certain weeks potentially having higher demand than others.

Despite these limitations, we believe that our findings provide valuable insights. However, future research should aim to address these limitations to provide a more accurate and robust analysis. Specifically, incorporating forecast variance data into safety stock calculations, considering the unique measurements of different packaging materials, and refining the approach to convert monthly data into weekly data could greatly enhance the accuracy of future analyses.

Acknowledgements. We would like to thank the Supply Chain Management (SCM) program at the Massachusetts Institute of Technology for giving us the opportunity to conduct this research. We would like to acknowledge teaching assistant Mateo Monterde for his support with data handling and his cooperation during this research. We would also most gratefully like to acknowledge project team members Tobi Lorch and Hongkai Wang for their contribution to the work.

References

1. Bartholdi, J., Hackman, S.: Warehouse and Distribution Science (0.98.1) (2019). https://www.warehouse-science.com/book/editions/wh-sci-0.98.1.pdf. Accessed 1 Sept 2023
2. Bookbinder, J.H., Tan, J.Y.: Strategies for the probabilistic lot-sizing problem with service-level constraints. Manage. Sci. **34**(9), 1096–1108 (1988)
3. Caplice, C.: MITx Supply Chain Management MicroMasters Credential: Supply Chain Analytics (2023). https://www.edx.org/learn/supply-chain-design/massachusetts-institute-of-technology-supply-chain-analytics. Accessed 1 Sept 2023
4. Jalali, H., Nieuwenhuyse, I.V.: Simulation optimization in inventory replenishment: a classification. IIE Trans. **47**(11), 1217–1235 (2015)

17th IFAC/IFIP International Workshop on Enterprise Integration, Interoperability and Networking

Industrial Communication with Semantic Integration Patterns

Georg Güntner(✉), Dietmar Glachs, Stefan Linecker, and Felix Strohmeier

Salzburg Research Forschungsgesellschaft mbH, 5020 Salzburg, Austria
{georg.guentner,dietmar.glachs,stefan.linecker,
felix.strohmeier}@salzburgresearch.at

Abstract. Digital twins have emerged as a key technological concept in the manufacturing industry. They form an information hub for industrial equipment and interact with dedicated applications in the operational manufacturing network. Digital twins consume and deliver information from machines to basically all connected applications. This results in complex integration requirements. The paper builds on previously designed semantic interoperability concepts for data-driven digital twins. It gives an overview of semantic data integration standards and provides insights into the current implementation of semantic integration patterns. Based on the challenges of the underlying research project "i-Twin", semantic integration patterns provide standardized communication channels for operational management systems and connected assets. They build on the services of the semantic data integration middleware and use semantic connectors to bridge the proprietary data objects with an I4.0 compliant information model based on the asset administration shell (AAS). Semantic integration patterns will reduce the integration effort for equipment manufacturers and software providers, thereby accelerating automation and digitalization processes.

Keywords: Asset administration shell · Asset management · Digital twin · Middleware · Patterns · Semantic interoperability

1 Introduction

1.1 Data Integration as a Challenge in Industrial Digitalization

In recent years, industrial digitalization has become a significant driver for improving productivity, plant availability, sustainability, and resource efficiency. Large initiatives have been formed to support the digital transformation by supporting standardization projects, collecting success stories, organizing expert congresses to exchange methodology and technology. Examples of these basically similar industrial digitalization initiatives are the German "Plattform Industrie 4.0" [1], and the American "Industry IoT Consortium" [2].

Digitalization led to a tremendous increase of the complexity of the communication between machinery and manufacturing IT systems: Industry 4.0 transformed almost

S. Terzi et al. (Eds.): IN4PL 2023, CCIS 1886, pp. 319–335, 2023.
https://doi.org/10.1007/978-3-031-49339-3_20

every new machine and component into an intelligent networked asset. And this trend is even more reinforced by digital retrofitting approaches of existing formerly not connected equipment.

When data is exchanged between each machine and each application, as well as between each of these applications, the situation of a production network shown in Fig. 1 arises: the classic automation pyramid [3] is dissolved, because machines and control devices (edge layer) continuously supply data to all those IT systems (application layer) that need this data for monitoring, surveillance, analysis, and control processes. The heterogeneity and multitude of common protocols and standards place complex demands on data integration, digital communication, and interoperability.

The manual or automatic procedures used to address data integration issues vary fundamentally:

- in the openness of and access to the messages or control units,
- in the communication protocols used, and
- in the adaptability to different applications.

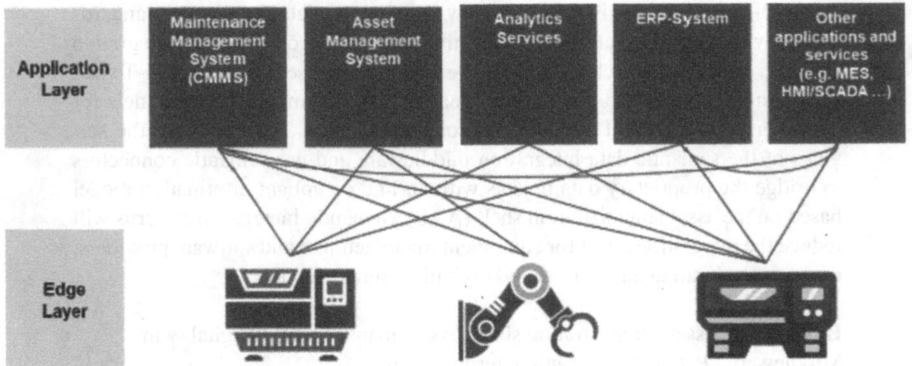

Fig. 1. Direct communication between machines and applications.

It is not uncommon that selected solutions result in a "vendor lock-in effect", associated with high integration efforts and costs, because the sender of a message must know the recipient and its programming interface exactly and map the information to the recipient's information model. An example of such a situation are alert messages generated by different machines that are to be forwarded to a maintenance management system or to an AI software via an HMI/SCADA system.

1.2 Digital Twins as Information Hubs

In modern manufacturing networks, digital twins are an increasingly adopted concept for the digital representation of industrial assets, including their components, control devices, software, as well as spare parts [4]. Digital twins provide a key technological concept for the digital transformation of automation and production processes.

Digital twins exchange information with all connected applications in the operational manufacturing systems and thus establish an information hub for industrial data integration. Therefore, digital twins and associated information models are naturally at the centre of interoperability considerations: Solutions to provide open, standards-based, self-describing (semantic) interfaces between participants in a manufacturing ecosystem can significantly reduce integration efforts.

The importance of the digital twin concept is underlined by a lot of ongoing standardization initiatives, e.g., the "Digital Twin Framework for Manufacturing" [5], the "Digital Factory Framework" [6], and the "Reference Architecture Model Industrie 4.0 (RAMI4.0)" along with the Asset Administration Shell (AAS) [7]. Furthermore, industrial and research associations have been founded to support standardisation, provide training, and contribute to open-source development in the area of digital twins. A prominent example is the Industrial Digital Twin Association [8].

The role of digital twins as information hubs in manufacturing networks gave birth to the research ideas addressed in a project entitled i-Twin ("Semantic Integration Patterns for Data-driven Digital Twins in the Manufacturing Industry"). In this project a research consortium made up of software providers, manufacturers and researchers designs integration patterns aiming at a reduction of integration efforts: By means of semantically described standardized integration patterns the implementation of digital twins is simplified, the interoperability is increased, and vendor lock-in effects are reduced.

1.3 Structure of the Paper

As the basic concepts of Semantic Integration Patterns were described in [9], we only summarize these concepts here with respect to readability and refer to details in the references. The focus of the paper is to describe the implementation of the components forming the Semantic Integration Patterns, i.e., the use of the Asset Administration Shell as core information model.

The remainder of the paper provides an update and focused view of the state of the art in industrial information integration (Sect. 2), a conceptual overview of the Semantic Integration Patterns (Sect. 3), and insights into the current state of the implementation of the Semantic Connectors (Sect. 4). Finally, Sect. 5 summarizes the main findings and gives an outlook of the future research.

2 Basic Concepts of Industrial Information Integration

In general, industrial information integration refers to the process of connecting and harmonizing various data sources, systems, and technologies in an industrial setting. The goals of such an endeavour can include the streamlining of operations, the optimization of processes, enhanced efficiency, supply chain optimisation, enabling predictive maintenance, cost reductions and many more. Furthermore, industrial information integration can be seen as an enabler for Industry 4.0 [10].

In this section we give an overview of industrial information models with a focus on the support of semantic interoperability. We then outline the concepts of data integration architectures and messaging infrastructures.

2.1 Industrial Information Models

Information models are formal descriptions of (parts of) the world, usually consisting of entities, attributes, and relationships. They exist in a whole range of levels, with interdisciplinary (or global) information models being the most general-purpose and use-case-related information models being among the most specific. In the manufacturing domain, industrial information models (IIMs) provide domain-level information models for the management of the asset life cycle as well as for production and maintenance processes.

When building an IIM, entities model real world objects, e.g., machines, parts, processes, or persons. A machine is described by static or dynamic attributes, e.g., the manufacturer, the year of construction, and actual (dynamic) and maximum (static) power consumption. Finally, relationships form another modelling concept of IIMs connecting entities.

A major goal of IIMs is interoperability, which is the ability of systems, devices, and applications to connect and communicate with each other regardless of manufacturer. IIMs are available in different technologies and specification languages.

Well-established standards in specific manufacturing domains, such as ISA-95 [11], Weihenstephan Standards [12] and EUROMAP [13], are currently mapped into modern, more expressive languages, including the Asset Administration Shell, OPC UA and AutomationML (see below). Correlations and connections between these three IIMs are provided in a discussion paper [14] from leading industry organisations (Microsoft, KUKA, Siemens, a.o.) and associations (AutomationML e.V., IDTA, OPC Foundation, VDMA).

In the remainder of this section, we initially give an overview of data dictionaries and semantic vocabularies for IIMs. With AAS, OPC UA and AutomationML, we then present three promising IIMs.

Data Dictionaries and Semantic Vocabularies. With respect to the support of data dictionaries and semantic vocabularies in IIMs, the digital exchange format IEC 61360 [15] for commonly shared concepts represents the industrial counterpart of the semantic web technology for vocabularies and is an integral part of newer IIIMs. IEC 61360 allows for the definition of hierarchical concept classes, their properties and unit of measures. It also supports the assignment of predefined value lists to properties in a general manner or when used in combination with distinct concept classes.

ECLASS [16] is a well-known common data dictionary based on the mentioned IEC 61360 format and provides a cross-sector standard for classification of products and services. Using such standardized reference data is a core concept for the data exchange with other companies, or with other business domains. The thirty-nine subject areas covered by ECLASS include electrical engineering, construction, logistics, food, medicine optics, automotive and others.

A recent European study underlined the impact of semantic technologies and semantic enrichment on improved data quality [17]. In the manufacturing domain, the representation of self-contained knowledge about assets is supported by the RDF data model for the Asset Administration Shell.

The Industrial Ontologies Foundry [18] provides reference ontologies to support manufacturing and industry needs. The work is conducted in different working groups, addressing topics such as maintenance, supply chain, production planning.

Likewise, the Smart Applications REFerence [19] ontology provides a shared model of consensus that facilitates the matching of existing assets in the smart applications domain.

RAMI4.0 and AAS. To address interoperability in horizontal and vertical integration scenarios, the "Reference Architecture Model Industrie 4.0 (RAMI4.0)" [7] includes a meta-model standard called "Asset Administration Shell (AAS)" [20]. An Asset Administration Shell represents an information model for the digital description of physical assets (with properties and capabilities) and thus provides the implementation of the digital twin for Industry 4.0.

In the AAS, properties and capabilities are organized in submodels, containing standardized elements describing characteristics, configuration parameters, states, and executable services of the asset. Each asset consists of a multitude of submodels covering distinct aspects of the asset, such as technical data, operational data, documentation or simply a digital nameplate identifying the asset. Standardization of submodels is an ongoing process: currently about 80 submodels for a variety of use cases are under development or fully specified [21]. For a technology independent data exchange, several serialization mappings, such as JSON, XML, RDF or OPC UA [22], AutomationML [23] as well as a package file format for AAS [24] are provided. The AAS is always coined with its functional counterpart, the interactive I4.0 component [25]. This ensures, the asset is (1) uniquely identifiable and (2) the asset can communicate with other I4.0 components [26].

Semantic Interoperability is a fundamental aspect of the AAS meta-model. The AAS supports data interoperability by providing references to standardized and corporate data dictionaries (e.g., ECLASS) and ontologies as a fundamental part of the AAS data model [27, 28]. However, it has to be stated clearly, that the current version of the specification emphasizes the use of data dictionaries and, while clearly offering conceptual integration, leaves some open space with the respect to the use of upper-level ontologies, e.g., the Industrial Ontologies Foundry [18] providing reference ontologies to support manufacturing and industry needs, or the Interoperable Knowledge Language (IKL) enabling interoperability among advanced reasoning systems as an extension to Common Logic [29].

OPC UA. With OPC UA, the OPC Foundation developed an open standard for the exchange of machine information via internet protocols (TCP/IP, HTTP). In addition to the transport of measured and controlled variables from and to the machines, OPC UA supports sector-specific extensions ("Profiles") of the information models based on companion specifications (CS). Notable among others are OPC UA for Machinery, Robotics and Machine Vision [30] also supported by the "universal machine technology interface" [31].

OPC UA also provides standards and technologies for interoperability on several aspects of the RAMI4.0 architecture model, using both, PubSub and Client/Server communication including but not limited to:

- Field level data exchange, e.g., for "horizontal" real-time device-to-device communication between production process steps along the shopfloor (UAFX),
- OT information exchange with PLCs (OPC UA TCP), e.g., for requesting specific information PLCs,
- IT network communications (OPC UA over MQTT), e.g., for event-based reporting of alert messages,
- Edge-to-cloud communication (OPC UA REST), e.g., for reports to cloud dashboards or remote service interfaces.

Furthermore, security features such as secure transport, authentication mechanisms or access control are also defined.

While OPC UA is focusing on the operational phase of the asset lifecycle, AAS provides features to cover the whole lifecycle, including Beginning-of-Life and End-of-Life.

AutomationML. AutomationML, developed by AutomationML e.V., is an XML-based data modelling language, which is applied mainly in the engineering design phase in shopfloors up to whole production lines [32]. It uses CAEX to represent hierarchical structures and allows to reference or include external documents (such as images and icons, function blocks or kinematic and geometry models). AutomationML supports semantic references to external models like ECLASS.

2.2 Data Integration Architecture and Communication Networks

Data Integration Architecture. A look at the current situation in the manufacturing industry reveals that data integration solutions, if existent at all, mostly rely on proprietary interfaces: This is a result of a lack in standardization of information models and messaging infrastructures at the time when the systems were developed. Such proprietary solutions create vendor lock-in effects and result in high integration efforts. With the broad acceptance of standardized industrial information models as described in Sect. 2.1 the situation changed, and new data integration architectures were enabled.

In this context, the recent revival of a concept for data sharing is worth considering: Dataspaces were introduced in computer science more than 15 years ago as a shift from a central database to storing data at one source and referencing it [33]. The recently published International Data Spaces Reference Architecture Model (IDS RAM) [34] describes the components and their requirements in detail. Gaia-X [35] was formed as a European initiative to establish a federated and secure framework for sovereign data exchange. Gaia-X is taking the dataspace concept one step further and considers generic data-related services (e.g., storage, web servers) to enable interoperability between different cloud providers and IT infrastructures. Promising software components, such as the "Eclipse Dataspace Connector" [36] are already available.

Messaging Layer. The job of the messaging layer is to enable the exchange of data between different software modules (or applications). It implements the necessary communication mechanisms and provides a convenient interface for interaction. The different modules then do not need to care about the technical details but utilize the messaging layer.

Existing technologies in the Industry 4.0 space follow different approaches concerning messaging. While data formats like AutomationML have no necessity to specify how data is transmitted, standards like OPC UA are very flexible and support multiple communication protocols (e.g., binary, web service). On the device-level, MQTT is often used as a lightweight and reliable communication mechanism but apart from MQTT there are numerous technologies available, both proprietary and open.

Messaging layers usually don't reinvent the wheel but use existing technologies. Modern, broker-based message-oriented middleware (MOM) systems provide the perfect starting point for such an endeavor. In such systems, a central component called a "broker" acts as an intermediary.

The broker receives messages from the message source and delivers them to the message sink(s). Next to other benefits, the use of a message broker (such as MQTT or Kafka) enables the loosely coupled exchange of data. The source (or producer, sender, or publisher) doesn't need to know who the destination (or consumer, receiver, or subscriber) is/are and vice versa. Furthermore, so called topics are used to organize different forms of data. The source publishes to some topic, while the destination subscribes to some topic (hence the term "publisher subscriber", that is often used in this context or short "PubSub"). All of this makes MOMs very flexible and scalable and a great fit for I4.0. While MQTT and Kafka were originally designed for rather distinctive use cases (MQTT was designed for resource-constrained devices behind fragile networks while Kafka was designed for high-throughput data streams within data centers), both somewhat evolved and can be used interchangeably here.

3 Semantic Integration Patterns

The challenges with respect to data integration in networked manufacturing environments and the interoperability requirements of digital twins acting as information hubs between machines and applications led to the research design of the i-Twin project: in this project, a concept called Semantic Integration Pattern forms the core of the design of a semantic integration middleware interacting with the edge and the application layer by means of Semantic Connectors.

Semantic Integration Patterns aim at supporting an automated exchange of data in production networks. They include both, the communication between assets and applications, and the communication between the different applications. Such communication requires shared information models and data exchange formats. The respective communication tasks remain domain specific. Typical examples for such communication patterns are:

- Request of the recent maintenance history by an edge controller to inform maintenance staff about recent problems and activities.
- Request of the reasons for downtimes by a dashboard application to calculate the overall equipment efficiency (OEE).

3.1 Definition and Purpose

Semantic Integration Patterns address domain-specific communication requirements in manufacturing networks. They define the respective endpoints of a communication as well as the data to be exchanged in the process.

Assets and applications benefit from a networked environment by simply providing their functionality or by using functionality available in the network.

The pattern specification is abstract and may be individually extended. Patterns may also evolve over time and newer versions can be provided.

For simple use, the patterns are self-contained and complete: all required elements are contained within the SIP.

Semantic Integration Patterns use the Asset Administration Shell (AAS) as shared information model, in particular the AAS submodel and its contained elements. While the communication paths are covered with the respective submodel elements Operation (Request/Response) and Event (Publish/Subscribe), the payload data is modelled with submodel elements. According to our design, each of the elements in a SIP must have a semantic identifier pointing to the full data specification from external semantic catalogues. The semantic identifier is a mandatory requirement for later retrieval of the pattern itself or its constituting elements.

At runtime, each I4.0 component can load a pattern from a central repository using its semantic identifier. The communication elements (Operation, Event) contained with the pattern are also found using their semantic identifiers. However, it is essential that at least one I4.0 component exists in the network which realizes an operation or subscribes to events with the communication element's semantic identifier.

The semantic interoperability middleware takes care of the available patterns and whether they are active at runtime.

3.2 Semantic Interoperability Middleware

The architectural design presented in [9], is based on a three-tier architecture with the application layer, the edge layer, and the central data integration layer. Participating applications and assets are active I4.0 components. They are equipped with their own individual AAS and expose their data and functionality to the network. In our design, assets and applications adhere to the AAS information model [20] and communication rules [25].

The architectural design in Fig. 2 shows the data integration layer as a central contact point for I4.0 components and contains the following building blocks:

- The *Asset Repository* serves as the central contact point for submodel templates.
- The *Asset Directory* maintains a mapping of asset identifiers and their associated I4.0 service endpoint. This implies, that active I4.0 components register with the Asset Directory during startup, indicating the I4.0 compatible endpoint as well as the semantic identifiers they are responsible for. During shut down, the I4.0 component de-registers from the directory. Hence, the *Asset Directory* enables the search and retrieval of active I4.0 components implementing a requested functionality based on the functionality's semantic identifier.

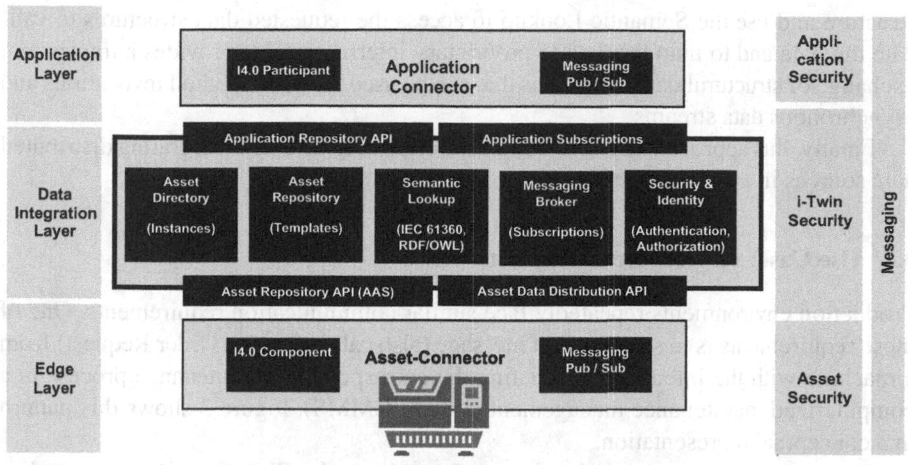

Fig. 2. Data Integration Layer: building blocks.

- The *Semantic Lookup* provides the domain specific vocabulary to all I4.0 components. It allows the definition of abstract concept classes including their properties. Built on technology standards such as IEC 62832 (Digital Factory framework), RDF/OWL, IEC 61360 (Semantic markup) it allows storing well-known vocabularies such as ECLASS, but also loading RDFS/OWL based ontologies for semantic definition of data structures.
- The *Messaging Broker* provides the asynchronous transport mechanism. Each of the Connectors uses a Broker for publishing to or subscribing event channels.
- The *Security & Identity* component finally manages the Authentication and Authorization of any communication request in the network. This component builds on the OAuth 2.0 standard.

3.3 Semantic Connectors

In the conceptual design as described in [9], Semantic Connectors provide a standardized interface to the manufacturing applications based on the AAS meta-model. Conceptually we distinguish two types of connectors:

Asset connectors interact directly with the asset's control device or facilitate OPC UA or similar methods to obtain the asset's details, for example to obtain or update the value of a property or to invoke a control command.

Application Connectors expose a standard compliant interface in the exact same way as asset connectors. Effectively, they transform both the applications methods and the exchanged data into the standardized I4.0 world (see Sect. 4 for details of the implementation).

In conjunction with the Data Integration Layer, the Semantic Connectors represent the core of the Semantic Integration Patterns (SIPs). They use the structural settings available in the Asset Repository and instantiate the respective AAS models. Application Connectors use the semantic identifiers retrieved from the instantiated AAS model structure and use the Semantic Lookup to access the requested data structures to validate the data and to map the data to proprietary interfaces. This provides a transparent exchange of structural data definitions that can be used for both, method invocations and asynchronous data streams.

Finally, this approach allows to build data-driven digital twins integrating distributed data sources in a standardized way.

3.4 Use Case: Service Order Request

Production environments repeatedly face similar communication requirements. One of these requirements is to send an alert message (also called Service Order Request) from a machine with the intention of initiating the corresponding maintenance process in a computerized maintenance management system (CMMS). Figure 3 shows this pattern in a conceptual representation.

The form of the service order request depends on the CMMS used. To generalize this request, IDTA has set up a process to standardize a corresponding AAS submodel. The resulting submodel is currently in final review.

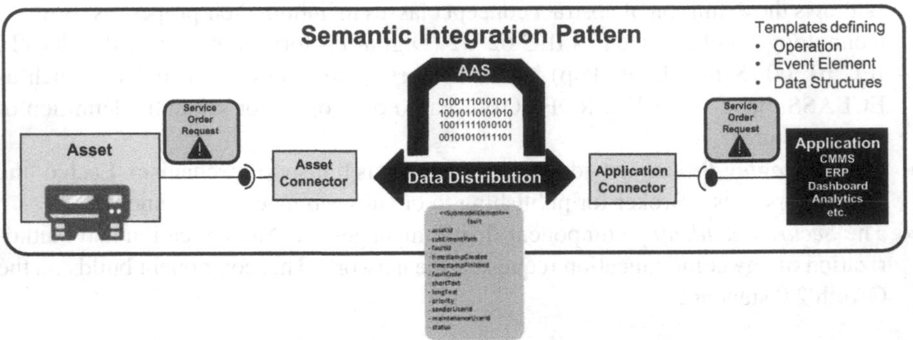

Fig. 3. Semantic Integration Patterns in use: service order request.

However, to send the service order request a machine does not need to know which CMMS is in use, nor does it need to know where and how this CMMS can be reached. It only needs to know the process of the service order request and be able to fill out the corresponding information model. Thus, a machine only needs fill the data structure of the service order request and the possibility to send this request.

This is where the Semantic Integration Patterns come into play: They allow the abstract definition of the structure of a service order request with the elements of the AAS. Simple attributes are mapped with property elements, defining the data type and, if applicable, also permitted value ranges or value lists. Property elements are combined into complex structures or concept classes and modelled as Collection elements. Each of these elements are additionally equipped with a semantic identifier, thus explicitly referencing external dictionary entries, or pointing to Concept Descriptions in the scope of the AAS.

The structure defined in this way is abstract and represents a template. Only an instantiation of the template makes this structure available at runtime.

4 Implementation

4.1 Implementing Semantic Connectors

A Semantic Integration Pattern represents common communication patterns. Given the AAS specification, communication capabilities belong either to the AAS itself (REST API of the I4.0 component), or they are explicitly added by means of the model elements for *Operation* and *Event* element. Each of the elements reference the respective payload data.

While *Operation* elements specify AAS elements as input and output variables, the *Event Element* must have a reference to the observed AAS element. Consequently, when requesting an operation execution or when triggering an event, the transferred user data conforms to the referenced AAS elements. Transferring full AAS metadata is discouraged, instead, the *value-only* representation of the referenced elements is preferred.

Using the *value-only* representation has several advantages: (i) the transmitted data is reduced to the minimum. (ii) the transmitted structure can easily be applied to full AAS structure, e.g., for validation, and (iii) it can finally be mapped to an application specific object.

The semantic connector itself provides the connection points to the proprietary IT application to enrich its data with semantics.

4.2 Semantic Integration Patterns in Use

In our design approach of the Semantic Integration Patterns (SIP), each application should reside in its own world and does not need to adopt the information model of the semantic middleware, e.g., the AAS meta-model. It is the task of the semantic connector to map and validate all application specific to the SIP's payload objects, e.g., the observed element of an *Event Element*, or the input or output variables of an *Operation*. For this purpose, the *value-only* representation of the payload's model element is used.

Consequently, the I4.0 component needs to load a SIP to have the communication elements available at runtime. For this, the semantic connector uses the Asset Repository to obtain the patterns definition. Once the SIP is loaded, an *Operation* or *Event Element* is located on behalf of their respective semantic identifier and finally activated by providing the requested data object:

Firstly, it is obvious, that the proprietary object is mappable to the payload object's *value-only* representation as defined in the SIPs data specification. Secondly, issuing a communication is only meaningful, when the operation is effectively executed, or the triggered event is handled. For this, the connector uses the Asset Directory and verifies, that at least one I4.0 component in the network, implements the activated Operation element or subscribes to the triggered Event Element.

Activation of Patterns. Semantic Integration Patterns are modelled as generic templates and specify both, the communication elements, and the communication payload data.

Template elements however are not active. Therefore, it is required to create instances of the SIP elements at runtime while retaining the semantic reference to the template element. This is especially important when realizing the recipient of a communication pattern, e.g., providing the functionality for accepting method execution requests. For I4.0 components, the use of a SIP only requires (i) retrieval of the pattern using its semantic identifier and (ii) issuing a method execution or publishing an event using the I4.0 components proprietary data objects.

Figure 4 provides an overview of the necessary steps to activate a Semantic Integration Pattern. These 6 steps are subsequently described in more detail:

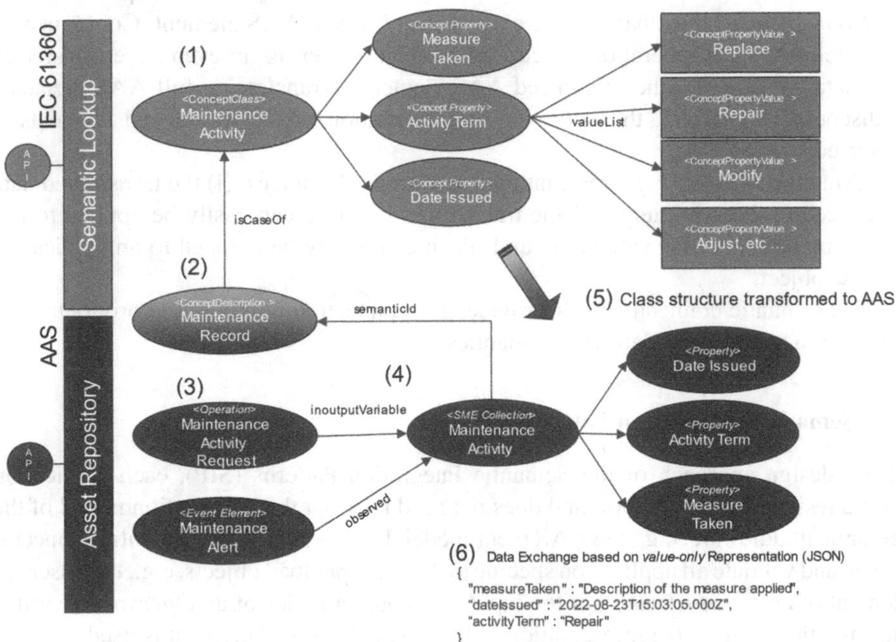

Fig. 4. Semantic Integration Patterns: activation in 6 steps.

1. Payload Semantics: The architecture of the integration middleware proposes the use of a sematic lookup component providing semantic definitions of data elements used in the Digital Factory. For SIPs, the overall structure of the communication objects including their detailed properties (data type, units, value lists) are to be managed. It is essential, that the semantic information model supports at least concept inheritance and the assignment of properties to classes. The industrial standard IEC 61360 as well as RDFS/OWL based ontologies support this concept inheritance.
2. Semantic Catalogue: Within the AAS meta-model, the Concept Description integrates external semantic definitions into the AAS world. Following the *isCaseOf*

relationship, any I4.0 component or the central Asset Repository can resolve and verify the semantics if necessary. As for the released AAS meta-model [20], the concept description may contain data specification data from the external catalogue, e.g., a Submodel Element Collection references the Concept Classification (IEC 61360) or the corresponding RDFS Class, a Submodel Data Element however references the Concept Property or the RDFS Data Property defining the data type, value range and the like. This external data can be placed with the concept description, thus easily distributed to I4.0 components using the standardised API's.

3. Defining Semantics for AAS Elements: Most AAS meta-model elements inherit from *HasSemantics*: they maintain a semantic identifier, pointing to an AAS template element of the same type.
4. Mastering the template-instance relationship: At runtime, instance elements maintain (i) the reference to its constituting template element and (ii) the reference to the concept description (e.g., the template's semantic identifier). That way, structure (template) and meaning (concept description) are set.
5. Applying structure: Proprietary data objects from I4.0 components are mapped to newly created AAS instance elements by adhering to the template-based data structure for objects and the semantic definition of data elements (data types, value lists).
6. Recreating domain objects: When using the *value-only* serialization modifier [25], the resulting output corresponds to the structure from the semantic lookup system and may be converted to proprietary domain objects as expected from the I4.0 component.

Validation. The semantic connector provides generic access methods allowing the surrounding application to use its own data objects when communication with the outer world. To ensure validity of the provided data objects, the connector validates the incoming objects.

To achieve this, the semantic connector uses the *Value Only* serialisation available in the AAS specification to map arbitrary objects to the template elements representing the SIP's payload data structure. Effectively, passing an arbitrary object as an operation's input parameter results in the following steps:

- The provided object is transformed into the supported serialisation format, e.g., JSON.
- The serialized object is applied to the operation variable, e.g., the data of the JSON tree is type-safely mapped to the values of the input variable.
- The input parameter's AAS value element is enriched based on the semantic definitions. E.g., an instance element is dynamically instantiated at runtime based on the semantic specifications from the templates.

As a result, the connector maintains the full AAS meta-data structure corresponding to the semantic definitions. When issuing an execution request, the connector facilitates the Asset Directory and retrieves the I4.0 component, responsible for answering the method invocation [25]. The returned results are processed the exact same way as the input variables. Thus, the following principles for SIP-based communication are valid:

- Only the semantic identifier is required when initiating a pattern-based communication.

- The responsible I4.0 component is identified and contacted automatically by the semantic middleware.
- Input or output variables are accepted/provided as proprietary objects but validated against structure and data type.

During this validation process, only existing AAS elements are mapped. The determination of mandatory or optional elements in complex data structures is currently not specified in the AAS metamodel. In addition, the *OperationVariable* element denoting an input or output parameter lacks a mandatory/optional indicator. For improved validation, the use of *Qualifier* or *Extension* elements would be a valuable option.

5 Conclusions

5.1 Summary

In our paper we presented the challenges of industrial digitalization with respect to data integration and interoperability issues. We described digital twins as information hubs for industrial communication networks, including machines (edge layer) and various IT systems (application layer). As a potential solution for interoperability requirements, we provided an overview of promising recently developed industrial information models with inherent semantic extensions (i.e., AAS, OPC UA, AutomationML).

The core of the paper is dedicated to the description of the design and implementation of a semantic data integration middleware with a three-tier approach (application, data integration, and edge layer) which was developed in the research project i-Twin. The project defines Semantic Integration Patterns as a concept providing standardized communication channels for manufacturing systems and connected assets (e.g., service order request, maintenance history request, provision of OEE calculation, exchange of equipment component structure). We outlined the implementation of the Semantic Connectors bridging the proprietary data objects of operational systems with an I4.0 compliant information model based on the Asset Administration Shell. Thus, we showed the intermediate results of the development of Semantic Integration Patterns as an interoperability concept for digital twins.

5.2 Outlook

Among the beneficiaries of the semantic integration middleware layer and the Semantic Integration Patterns, we identified factories, equipment manufacturers, service providers, application developers, system integrators, and edge developers. The proposed approach aims at:

- reducing integration efforts (access to type-based equipment and application profiles),
- speeding up the commissioning and the integration design phase for assets as well as for applications,
- integrating asset descriptions from equipment manufacturers in a standardized format with semantically described data points, thereby speeding up data point engineering and mater data engineering,

- providing secure access and distribution of data between manufacturing applications including validation.

The research activities in i-Twin will be continued with the publication of the final system architecture and the final version of the description of the Semantic Integration Patterns. The implementation of the semantic integration middleware and the Semantic Connectors is continued in a hackathon in late 2023 and continuously published on the project's GitHub repository [37]. The software is validated in a laboratory setup at Salzburg Research and in an industrial application scenario at Innio Jenbacher, in which an industrial communication platform based on the semantic integration concepts is set up which allows for a map-based visualization of the plant's machine status by merging MES and CMMS data.

In the project consortium, there are ongoing exploitation activities to develop a pattern-based integration of edge controllers, OT software, and a computerized maintenance management system.

Thematic extensions of the addressed research challenges will be sought by entering a closer alliance with the Gaia-X community (i.e., Manufacturing-X and the national Gaia-X Hubs in the manufacturing domain). The contributions to further standardization of AAS (see below) and to the development of AAS submodels will be continued in cooperation with IDTA and the InterOpera project [38].

With the latest release of the AAS specification, a mature information model fostering interoperability is available. The Semantic Integration Patterns propagated in this work use the AAS specifications to simplify communication with predefined AAS template elements as well as the transmitted user data. Semantic information models such as IEC 61360 and RDFS/OWL support the complete description of the exchanged data. With stronger support of upper-level ontologies (e.g., IOF [18], IKL [29]) in the standardization of the AAS information model, such concepts will be applicable in the future design of Semantic Integration Patterns The runtime aspect of Semantic Integration Patterns however is subject to the implementation of the Semantic Connector which needs to deal with the patterns definition obtained from an AAS repository and by adhering to the provided semantic definitions.

While instantiating AAS elements from templates and maintaining the semantic relationship is already a well-known step, validation of the data exchanged is currently limited to checking the structure of the data and for the data type safety. Although there are eligible workarounds, a thorough validation, whether all required operation parameters are provided or whether all mandatory structure elements are filled is currently not foreseen with AAS meta-model elements.

Acknowledgements. The research presented in this paper has been conducted in the i-Twin project (title: "Semantic Integration Patterns for Data-driven Digital Twins in the Manufacturing Industry"), which is funded by the Austrian Federal Ministry for Climate Action, Environment, Energy, Mobility, Innovation and Technology (BMK) and the Austrian Research Promotion Agency (FFG) within the research programme "ICT of the Future". The project has a duration of 27 months and will end in March 2024.

References

1. PI40. Plattform Industrie 4.0. https://www.plattform-i40.de/ (2023)
2. IIC. Industry IoT Consortium. https://www.iiconsortium.org/ (2023)
3. Åkerman, M.: Implementing Shop Floor IT for Industry 4.0. Gothenburg, Doctoral thesis, Chalmers University of Technology (2018)
4. Kritzinger, W., Karner, M., Traar, G., Henjes, J., Sihn, W.: Digital twin in manufacturing: a categorical literature review and classification. IFAC-PapersOnLine **51**(11), 1016–1022 (2018). https://doi.org/10.1016/j.ifacol.2018.08.474
5. ISO/DIS 23247-1: Automation Systems and integration – Digital Twin framework for manufacturing, Part 1: Overview and general principles. https://www.iso.org/standard/75066.html (2021)
6. IEC 62832-1: Industrial-process measurement, control and automation – Digital factory framework – Part 1: General principles. https://standards.iteh.ai/catalog/standards/iec/cfef54c6-c080-4e1d-980a-a7d53a784409/iec-62832-1-2020 (2020)
7. DIN SPEC 91345: Reference Architecture Model Industrie 4.0 (RAMI 4.0). https://www.beuth.de/technische-regel/din-spec-91345/250940128 (2016)
8. IDTA: Industrial Digital Twin Association. https://industrialdigitaltwin.org/ (2023)
9. Strohmeier, F., Güntner, G., Glachs, D., Mayr, R.: Semantic integration patterns for industry 4.0. In: Proceedings of the 3rd International Conference on Innovative Intelligent Industrial Production and Logistics (S. 197-205). Valetta, Malta: Institute for Systems and Technologies of Information, Control and Communication (2022). https://doi.org/10.5220/0011550100003329
10. Li, D.X., Xu, E.L., Li, L.: Industry 4.0 state of the art and future trends. Int. J. Product. Res. **56**, 2941–2962 (2018). https://doi.org/10.1080/00207543.2018.1444806
11. ANSI/ISA-95: https://en.wikipedia.org/wiki/ANSI/ISA-95 (2023)
12. WS: Weihenstephan Standards – The communication interface for your machines. https://www.weihenstephan-standards.com/en/ (2022)
13. EUROMAP: EUROMAP-OPC-UA interfaces for plastics and rubber machinery. https://www.euromap.org/opcua%5Fplatform/ (2021)
14. Drath, R., et al.: Diskussionspapier – Interoperabilität mit der Verwaltungsschale, OPC UA und AutomationML (2023)
15. CDD: IEC61360 Common Data Dictionary (CDD). https://en.wikipedia.org/wiki/IEC%5F61360 (2017)
16. ECLASS: ECLASS e.V. https://eclass.eu/ (2023)
17. EC DIGIT: European Commission: Data Quality Management. https://joinup.ec.europa.eu/sites/default/files/document/2019-09/SEMIC%20Study%20on%20data%20quality%20management.pdf (2019)
18. IOF: Industrial Ontologies Foundry. http://industrialontologies.org/ (2021)
19. ETSI STF 578: Smart Applications Reference Ontology, and Extensions. Official ETSI portal for SAREF. https://saref.etsi.org/ (2021)
20. AAS Part 1: AAS Part 1: Metamodel. From IDTA – Der Standard für den Digitalen Zwilling: https://industrialdigitaltwin.org/wp-content/uploads/2023/06/IDTA-01001-3-0%5FSpecificationAssetAdministrationShell%5FPart1%5FMetamodel.pdf (2023)
21. IDTA Submodels: IDTA Submodels. Industrial Digital Twin Association. https://industrialdigitaltwin.org/en/content-hub/submodels (2023)
22. IEC 62541: OPC Unified Architecture, Parts 1–14. https://opcfoundation.org/developer-tools/specifications-unified-architecture (2020)
23. IEC 62714: Automation ML (Automation Markup Language). http://automationml.org/ (2022)

24. AAS Part 5: AAS Part 5: Package File Format (AASX). https://industrialdigitaltwin.org/en/wp-content/uploads/sites/2/2023/04/IDTA-01005-3-0%5FSpecificationAssetAdministrationShell%5FPart5%5FAASXPackageFileFormat.pdf (2023)
25. AAS Part 2: AAS Part 2: Application Programming Interfaces. IDTA – Der Standard für den Digitalen Zwilling. https://industrialdigitaltwin.org/wp-content/uploads/2023/06/IDTA-01002-3-0%5FSpecificationAssetAdministrationShell%5FPart2%5FAPI.pdf (2023)
26. Ye, X., Hong, S.H.: Toward industry 4.0 components: insights into and implementation of asset administration shells. IEEE Ind. Electron. Mag. **13**(1), 13–25 (2019). https://doi.org/10.1109/MIE.2019.2893397
27. AAS Part 3a: AAS Part 3a: Data Specification – IEC 61360. Retrieved from IDTA – Der Standard für den Digitalen Zwilling. https://industrialdigitaltwin.org/en/wp-content/uploads/sites/2/2023/04/IDTA-01003-a-3-0%5FSpecificationAssetAdministrationShell%5FPart3a%5FDataSpecification%5FIEC61360.pdf (2023)
28. Belayev, A., et al.: Plattform Industrie 4.0. Modelling the Semantics of Data of an Asset Administration Shell with Elements of ECLASS: https://www.plattform-i40.de/IP/Redaktion/DE/Downloads/Publikation/Whitepaper%5FPlattform-Eclass.pdf (2021)
29. Hayes, P., Menzel, C.: IKL Specification Document. https://www.ihmc.us/users/phayes/IKL/SPEC/SPEC.html (2006)
30. OPC UA: OPC UA Specification Documents. https://opcfoundation.org/developer-tools/documents/?type=Specification (2023)
31. UMATI. https://umati.org/ (2023)
32. Drath, R., Luder, A., Peschke, J., Hundt, L.: AutomationML – the glue for seamless Automation Engineering (Bd. ETFA.https://doi.org/10.1109/ETFA.2008.4638461). IEEE International Conference on Emerging Technologies and Factory Automation, ETFA (2008)
33. Halevy, A.Y., Franklin, M.J., Maier, D.: Dataspaces: a new abstraction for information management. In: Lee, M., Tan, K.-L., Wuwongse, V. (eds.) DASFAA 2006. LNCS, vol. 3882, pp. 1–2. Springer, Heidelberg (2006). https://doi.org/10.1007/11733836_1
34. IDSA: IDS Reference Architecture Model. International Data Spaces. https://internationaldataspaces.org/publications/ids-ram/ (2023)
35. Gaia-X Consortium: Gaia-X Federation Services. http://gxfs.eu (2023)
36. Eclipse Foundation: Eclipse Dataspace Components. https://projects.eclipse.org/projects/technology.edc (2023)
37. i-Twin-Repo: i-Twin GitHub Repository. https://github.com/i-Asset/asset-repository (2023)
38. InterOpera: Digitale Interoperabilität in kollaborativen Wertschöpfungsnetzwerken der Industrie 4.0. https://interopera.de/ (2023)

Strategic Roadmap for Digital Transformation Based on Measuring Industry 4.0 Maturity and Readiness

Sandro Breval Santiago[1] and Jose Reinaldo Silva[2(✉)]

[1] Federal University of Amazonas, Manaus, AM, Brazil
sbreval@ufam.edu.br

[2] University of São Paulo, Polytechnic School, São Paulo, Brazil
reinaldo@usp.br

Abstract. Digital transformation emerged as a strategic imperative for organizations in the era of Industry 4.0. As disruptive technologies reshape industries and business models, organizations must navigate this evolving landscape to remain competitive and relevant. Maturity models directed to Industry 4.0 offer a valuable framework to assess an organization's current state, identify gaps, and develop a strategic roadmap for successful digital transformation. Digital transformation is a complex and multifaceted journey that requires a well-defined roadmap to guide organizations through leveraging digital technologies and capabilities. Therefore, a practical and sound approach to developing a roadmap is the basis for achieving a successful digital transformation strategy. A structured approach, based on building blocks, can lead to a systematic plan to implement digital initiatives. In this article, we will explore creating a roadmap to digital transformation using building blocks.

Keywords: Maturity model · Industry 4.0 · Digital transformation · Service science · System engineering

1 Introduction

The primary challenge for manufacturing organizations is shifting from a cost-based approach to a highly value-added competitive advantage. Currently, such effort led to the implementation of Industrie 4.0, expected to offer the necessary added value by aiding businesses and making essential adjustments for excellence and flexibility, thereby leveraging the increasing demand for personalized and higher-quality products. Manufacturing processes must become more flexible, digitalized, interconnected, and responsive to demand. Instead of undertaking a time-consuming and costly integration process, Industrie 4.0 transforms traditional industrial equipment and processes into distributed cyber-physical systems orchestrated through IoT platforms. According to some authors [19], the Fourth

Supported by University of São Paulo and Federal University of Amazonas.

S. Terzi et al. (Eds.): IN4PL 2023, CCIS 1886, pp. 336–347, 2023.
https://doi.org/10.1007/978-3-031-49339-3_21

Industrial Revolution, also known as Industry 4.0, is the most influential driver of innovation in the upcoming decades, ushering in the next wave of advancements. As a result, crucial elements of Industry 4.0, including real-time capability, interoperability, and the integration of horizontal and vertical production systems through ICT systems, are perceived as the solution to businesses' challenges in maintaining competitiveness. These challenges encompass globalization and intensified competition, the unpredictability of market demands, shortened innovation and product life cycles, and the increasing complexity surrounding product development. Hence, recognizing the significance of this new landscape concerning corporate competitiveness, this study aims to develop a model for assessing industries' readiness to implement Industry 4.0 (I4.0) paradigms. In line with this approach, the model establishes an optimal level of preparedness for I4.0 based on existing enabling technologies and their respective prerequisites - ensuring a model system approach. Through a comparison of the current state of the company with the "ideal standard" provided by the model, it becomes possible to identify the managerial actions to be planned for enhancing the company's competitiveness in alignment with I4.0 paradigms. In practice, Industrie 4.0 concepts and systems design are being used by manufacturing organizations across a range of industrial sectors. The automobile, transportation, aerospace, and heavy machinery industries are examples of such sectors. Each industrial sector has distinctive qualities, leading to various paths toward digital transformation, which is also heavily influenced by the manufacturing company's strategic position along the supply/value chain. The proposal is, therefore, to establish a sound academic framework over which it is possible to adapt the roadmap for digital transformation to the specificity of each sector.

2 Current Roadmap Initiatives Toward Industrie 4.0

Different industrial organizations predominantly implement Industrie 4.0 concepts through pilot projects resembling feasibility studies rather than undergoing a comprehensive digital transformation. However, these pilot initiatives often fail to showcase the complete potential of digital transformation due to their limited scope, as they used to overlook vital organizational components such as structure and culture [28].

The main challenge faced in implementing the Industrie 4.0 paradigm in these businesses stems from a lack of comprehension regarding the connection between the business and technological aspects at the organization's strategic and tactical levels. Additionally, there is a failure to meet production demands, further complicating the adoption of Industrie 4.0 [2,12,34].

In reality, numerous businesses treat digital transformation IT projects like standard projects. However, the fundamental challenge lies in genuinely understanding the driving force behind this transformation process [11,21] and finding a proper project management approach. The proposed framework presented in this article is a reference model that suits this demand.

2.1 The Referencial Approach and Methodology

We conducted an actual validation case study and a comprehensive literature review to create the roadmap model. Through the literature review, we synthesized a generic "Digital Transformation Process" that centers around capability maturity and the alignment of business and IT aspects. This process serves as the foundation for our roadmap model.

The Industrie 4.0 roadmap is designed based on the organization's current state of digital transformation through a readiness assessment. This assessment helps to determine the organization's current maturity level. The primary objective of the roadmap is to elevate the organization's maturity level from its existing state, allowing it to progress and advance in the context of Industrie 4.0 implementation.

We propose a set of variables as the primary reference to match the current maturity and readiness with the intended transformation. At this point, a proper adaptation would emerge depending on the strategy of the company and the sector involved. However, even if not fully shown in this article, proper project management is highlighted, integrating MBSE (Model-Based System Engineering) and Goal-oriented development, which is more suitable for strategic development.

3 The Reference Model Background

The reference model background is based on three sound approaches:

1. Maturity and readiness evaluation, using PIMM4.0, developed by one of the authors [4];
2. Requirements and strategic analysis based on goal-oriented approach;
3. Using Model-based System Engineering to analyze the relationship between the organization and the environment, composed of concurrents, supporters, and supporting ecosystem.

In the following, we shortly describe each of these issues.

3.1 Maturity and Readiness Analysis

The model for measuring the maturity and readiness of Industry 4.0, PIMM 4.0, was developed in Brazil with a dimensional view of the value chain, encompassing the following dimensions:

1. Product: the level of customization and digital values of the product portfolio;
2. Manufacturing: which identifies characteristics of the production process;
3. Strategy: capturing the organization's positioning regarding Industry 4.0;
4. Business model: which examines the business ecosystem and organization's agility;
5. Interoperability: verifying the level of vertical and horizontal integration;

6. Logistics: which highlights responsiveness and supply chain visibility;
7. People and Culture: which indicates people's readiness and cultural scope;

The dimensions and their respective variables were chosen based on the following steps: a) a systematic review of the literature; b) interviews with experts and c) tests with industrial companies. Therefore, with the creation of dimensions, modeling was developed using structural equations.

The model uses a multivariate analysis and structural equations to provide a clear view of the relationships between measurable variables. Data sources originate from multi-view and multi-level data collection, ensuring accuracy and consistency in measuring maturity and readiness.

Experts were consulted regarding the weights of the variables in each dimension. They assigned weights from 1 to 2, which made up the calculation of the degree of maturity and readiness. To compose the roadmap variables, variables with weight 2 assigned by the experts were chosen.

The model also presents four measurement levels:

1. Digital: focused on the initial phase of system and logistics integration, with low organizational scope and evidence of connectivity. Checks the level of interoperability and integration of systems, logistics, and their functional links, considering the factory data collection automation and its usability.
2. Technological: looks for important system initiatives with reduced interoperability, beginning with automation in operational areas and evidence of low logistics integration. This level demonstrates the existence of integrated systems by measuring interoperability, M2M, and evidence of logistical visibility.
3. Transition: evaluate the high integration between sub-systems allowing high visibility, along with significant automation initiatives with capacity gains, transparency levels, and predictive capabilities. Focus on systems and interoperability combined with data collection, manufacturing data usage, M2M, and control and automation with other functionality in the organization, including adherence to the business model and strategy.
4. Advanced: Advanced system and logistics interoperability permeating all organizational levels, evidence of self-optimization in processes. The relationships between the integrated systems demonstrate the interoperability with aspects of the autonomous and independent supply of the production lines (for specific segments) and the customization capacity and digital values in the portfolio aligned with the value chain.

The collected data and evaluation of measurement levels is the start of a strategic analysis where the company business goals should match and limit the roadmap toward I4.0.

3.2 Strategic Analysis Using Goal-Oriented Approach

Creating a thorough roadmap for Industry 4.0 adoption requires strategically using building pieces like portfolio, digitalization, business model, technology preparedness, visibility, and vertical and horizontal integration. Each building component reflects a crucial element that helps a business successfully transform. In order to fulfill changing client demands, the portfolio development block comprises reviewing the current product/service offers and finding potential for customization and digital upgrades.

However, it is crucial to establish that the roadmap relies on an institution's digital transformation instead of just technological improvements. Improving operations and decision-making includes digitalization and requires integrating cutting-edge technology like IoT, AI, and data analytics. However, those enhancements must fit a general strategy and revision of goals. The business model building block focuses on value propositions and revenue streams through new partnerships and ecosystem interactions.

Therefore, the organization's capacity to adopt and adapt to Industry 4.0 technologies depends on its technological readiness. The priority for real-time data access and analytics depends on the visibility to support data-driven insights and quick decision-making. Vertical integration guarantees smooth communication between all company divisions, from the shop floor to the top management. Achieving end-to-end optimization and horizontal integration requires an internal collaboration structure and a continuous understanding between clients and stakeholders. Organizations may create a roadmap that encourages innovation, efficiency, and competitiveness in the Industry 4.0 landscape by carefully aligning these building elements, positioning them for long-term growth and success in the digital age (see Fig. 1).

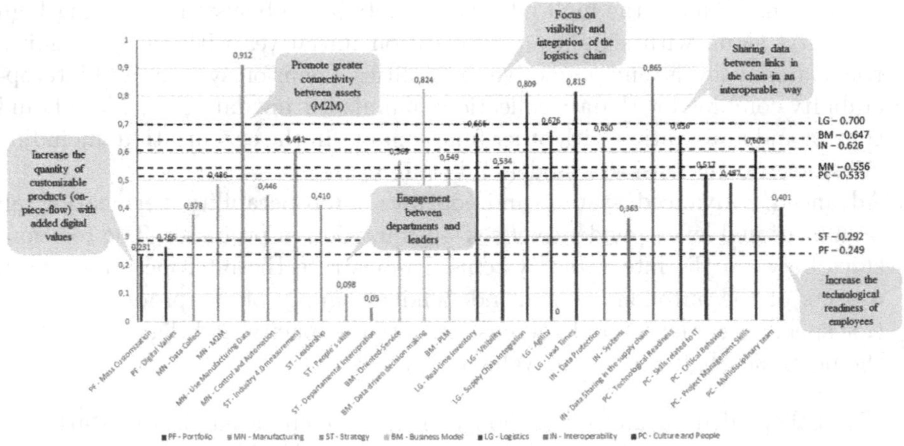

Fig. 1. Building blocks for the industry 4.0 roadmap.

The roadmap is a strategic process that demands design methods and criteria for analyzing and evaluating returns. Therefore, a systematic approach should rely on adapted System Design Methods.

3.3 The MBSE Integration Analysis

A strategic process for digital transformation supposes that the new automated approach fits the main objectives of the transformation as well as its business process, which means that a better positioning of the organization is the target. Therefore, a goal-oriented design method should be a reference for this strategic planning, integrated vertically with the shop floor and the production.

Although experience determines such a design's success, it is impossible to trust in a heuristic and intuitive approach, given the risks involved. Thus, the question is to find a hybrid, integrated, and sound design method to support the development of the strategic roadmap, which puts together the application environment, the ecosystem, the other systems, and possible conflicts for one side, and the technology available and further tendencies, together with the readiness and maturity of the organization.

The proposal is for them to fit System Design with goal-oriented methods - suitable to strategic planning. The academic challenge is that system design methods are eminently functional and not goal-oriented. However, goal-oriented methods are typically defined for software engineering or extended to products or processes but not necessarily for systems design.

We propose to enhance the goal-oriented approach [3,23] and others dealing with Systems Design, following the approach of the "Seven Samurais of System Design" proposed by James Martin [25] and supported by the International Council on Systems Engineering [8].

Briefly, the system already in development creates a new environment for goal-oriented processes [29] directed to the transformation strategy from I3.0 or earlier approach to I4.0 [26]. The direction reinforces automation and cloud manufacturing [30]. Model-based Systems Engineering references the method. However, it must take as input some parameters and vectors extracted from maturity and readiness analysis (a system called PIMM4.0 that was already developed). In the next section, we highlight this feature extraction.

4 Case-Study Analysis

We present a home appliance and television manufacturing company as a case study. The company has automatic insertion lines (SMD) and final assembly lines. It has two manufacturing plants: one dedicated to the assembly of air conditioners and another to the production of televisions and mobile phones. In this study, we focused on the plant for televisions and cell phones, analyzing the maturity and readiness of management, logistics, manufacturing, maintenance, and quality.

The analysis was performed using a platform developed by one of the authors, PIMM4.0, collecting data concerning the dimensions: products, manufacturing, strategy, business model, logistics, interoperability, and people-culture. Data from 86 employees were collected in the platform, composing a substantial view of people-culture.

Data were analyzed, verifying the existence of biases in the areas, revealing 12 employee responses identified as being in line with the rest of the sector. Interviews and direct observations focused on these cases. Reports consolidate the analysis indexes for each dimension.

The proposed model uses the multivariate approach for the relational analysis, composing the degrees of maturity and readiness for each dimension. Structural equation modeling is a multivariate technique combining multiple regression (dependency relationships) with factor analysis (representing unmeasured concepts and factors with multiple variables) to estimate interrelated dependency simultaneously.

In PIMM4.0, the structural equation model captures statistical causal relationships between variables. Understanding the causal sequence between variables can explain how a specific stimulus determines a given effect and potentially test a hypothesis numerically [16]. In addition, it is possible to test and estimate causal relationships based on statistical data and qualitative causal assumptions. Such an approach can enable the simultaneous testing of numerous dependency relationships.

The theoretical model comprises a Structural Module formed by seven constructs (Latent Variables) representing the studied elements and a Measurement module formed by 48 indicators for measuring the constructs (Observable Variables). The relationships between the models and their respective representations are shown in Table 1.

All variables in this study have an Average Variance Extracted (AVE) greater than 0.5, indicating that the variables have a convergent validity. Property measurement scales are presented in Table 1.

The reliability for each construct indicates the level of internal consistency and all scales have a Cronbach's alpha above 0.6, indicating that the scales are reliable. Indicator reliability describes the extent to which a variable or set of variables is consistent regarding what it intends to measure. The reliability of one construct is independent of and calculated separately from that of other constructs. The researcher can monitor reflective indicators' loadings to assess indicator reliability.

Considering the possibility of customization and introducing digital values, the portfolio is the basis for the strategic roadmap. By embracing customer-centricity, flexible manufacturing, data-driven decision-making, and advanced technologies, manufacturers are poised to meet the growing demand for personalized products/services while achieving greater efficiency and sustainability [35].

M2M communication [5,22] composes the backbone of Industry 4.0 by enabling real-time data transfer and decision-making, enhancing efficiency, and reducing downtime [6]. At its core is the ability of machines and devices to communicate with each other, collect vast amounts of data, and seamlessly interact to optimize production processes [28].

The synergy between strategy and product lifecycle management (PLM) has assumed paramount importance for manufacturing enterprises [13,21]. Tech-

Table 1. Dimensions and variables of the PIMM4.0 model.

Dimension	Variables	Factors Loadings	AVE	Cronbach
Products	Mass Customization	0.231	0.590	0.595
	Digital Values	0.266		
Manufacturing	Data Collect	0.378	0.670	0.769
	M2M	0.486		
	Use of manufacturing data	0.912		
	Control and automation	0.446		
Strategy	Industry 4.0 measurement	0.611	0.624	0.661
	Leadership	0.410		
	People's skills	0.098		
	Departmental interoperation	0.05		
Business Model	Oriented Service	0.569	0.672	0.603
	data-driven decision making	0.824		
	PLM	0.549		
Logistics	Real-time inventory	0.666	0.501	0.742
	Visibility	0.534		
	Supply Chain Integration	0.809		
	Agility	0.676		
	Lead times	0.815		
Interoperability	Data Protection	0.650	0.741	0.648
	Systems	0.363		
	Data sharing	0.865		
Culture and People	Technological readiness	0.656	0.595	0.694
	IT Skills	0.517		
	Critical behavior	0.487		
	Project management	0.605		
	Multidisciplinary team	0.401		

nology advancements and market dynamics become increasingly unpredictable, demanding a well-defined strategy that aligns with PLM practices and becomes the linchpin of sustainable competitiveness. Effective PLM, encompassing product design, development, production, and end-of-life considerations, allows for rapid adaptation to changing customer demands and market trends. Simultaneously, a robust strategy ensures that PLM efforts remain focused, relevant, and aligned with overarching business objectives [27]. Together, these elements create a dynamic framework that enables manufacturers to navigate the complexities of Industry 4.0 [19], optimizing product development cycles, reducing time-to-market, and enhancing overall operational efficiency [24].

Supply chain visibility has emerged as a pivotal factor in modern manufacturing. The technologies drive visibility and transformative effects on manufacturing operations, leading to efficiency and overall competitiveness [17,32]. The contemporary manufacturing landscape must gain real-time, end-to-end visibility, turning the supply chain into a strategic imperative. Heightened visibility is possible by the integration of technologies such as the Internet of Things (IoT), big data analytics, and blockchain [7], which facilitate the tracking and monitoring of goods, materials, and information as they traverse the supply network [1,10,33]. However, those technologies should not be the start of the strategy.

The transition towards Industry 4.0, characterized by automation, artificial intelligence, and the Internet of Things (IoT), has redefined the skills required for the modern manufacturing workforce [9]. The readiness of individuals to adapt to these technological changes is a pivotal factor in the industry's success [14].

Vertical and horizontal integrations in manufacturing are also critical dimensions. Vertical integration, involving the seamless connection of different levels of the production process, from suppliers to customers, ensures a cohesive and efficient flow of information and materials [10]. Manufacturers use it to optimize processes, reduce lead times [15], and enhance supply chain visibility, ultimately improving overall operational efficiency and customer satisfaction. Horizontal integration involves the integration of various functions and processes within the manufacturing facility, promoting cross-functional collaboration, data sharing, and real-time decision-making. It enables the convergence of technologies like IoT, AI, and automation to create interconnected systems that react dynamically to changing conditions [20,31]. Vertical and horizontal integration in Industry 4.0 fosters agility, responsiveness, and innovation, enabling manufacturers to thrive in an increasingly competitive and dynamic global marketplace [18].

The dimensions collected from this company to compose the goal-oriented analysis are shown in Table 2.

Table 2. Dimensions and variables of the PIMM4.0 model.

Building Blocks	Results	PIMM4.0	Actions
Portfolio	0.248	0.994	Introduce digital values into products
Manufacturing	0.556	2.222	Increase automated data collection
Strategy and business	0.523	2.093	Align Industry 4.0's KPI
Supply Chain Visibility	0.675	2.700	Increase visibility into logistics chain
Readiness Technological	0.503	2.010	Team with technological readiness
Vertical Integration	0.363	1.452	+ interoperability between internal links
Horizontal Integration	0.865	3.460	+ interoperability between external links

5 Conclusion and Further Work

The fundamental elements of a strategy plan for implementing Industry 4.0 concepts in contemporary production can be taken as building blocks to start the design of a roadmap for I4.0. We identified these building blocks conceptually and applied them to a case study, shown in Table 2. The identification was performed using a system developed by one of the authors, PIMM 4.0. These building blocks highlight the significance of comprehending the dimensional variables and factor loadings inside the PIMM4.0 model, emphasizing the value of customization and the infusion of digital values. Additionally, M2M communication is the foundation for Industry 4.0, enabling real-time data exchange and optimization of production processes.

Additionally, the interplay between strategy and product lifecycle management (PLM) emerges as a crucial driver of sustainable competitiveness in the continually changing manufacturing scene. Rapid innovation is made possible by solid strategy and efficient PLM methods.

We mentioned that the building blocks should feed a modeling process to formalize the strategy, providing resources to test and anticipate risk analysis. Such a method relies on goal-oriented requirements and, therefore, is suitable to receive the building blocks as goals. The next step will be to develop a framework to perform the process modeling.

The general discussion underlines the complexity of implementing Industry 4.0 in contemporary manufacturing, emphasizing the fundamental elements required for success. It becomes clear that a comprehensive grasp of dimensional variables - factor loadings within the PIMM4.0 model - the possibilities for customization and digital integration are the foundation for building a strategic roadmap.

Acknowledgements. Special thanks to University of São Paulo and Federal University of Amazonas.

References

1. Alcácer, V., Rodrigues, J., Carvalho, H., Cruz-Machado, V.: Industry 4.0 maturity follow-up inside an internal value chain: a case study. Int. J. Adv. Manuf. Technol. **119**, 5035–5046 (2022). https://doi.org/10.1007/s00170-021-08476-3
2. Almada-Lobo, F.: The industry 4.0 revolution and the future of manufacturing execution systems (MES). J. Innovation Manag. **3**, 16–21 (2016). https://doi.org/10.24840/2183-0606_003.004_0003
3. Alrajeh, D., Cailliau, A., Lamsweerde, A.: Adapting requirements models to varying environments. In: Proceedings of ACM Conference. ACM (2020)
4. Azevedo, A., Santiago, S.B.: Design of an assessment industry 4.0 maturity model: an application to manufacturing company. In: Proceedings of the International Conference on Industrial Engineering and Operations Management, Toronto, ON, Canada, pp. 23–25 (2019)
5. Bi, Z., Xu, L.D., Wang, C.: Internet of things for enterprise systems of modern manufacturing. IEEE Trans. Ind. Inform. **10**, 1537–1546 (2014). https://doi.org/10.1109/TII.2014.2300338
6. Burns, T., Cosgrove, J., Doyle, F.: A review of interoperability standards for industry 4.0. In: Procedia Manufacturing, vol. 38, pp. 646–653. Elsevier B.V. (2019). https://doi.org/10.1016/j.promfg.2020.01.083

7. Caiado, R.G.G., et al.: A fuzzy rule-based industry 4.0 maturity model for operations and supply chain management. Int. J. Prod. Econ. **231**, 107883 (2021). https://doi.org/10.1016/j.ijpe.2020.107883
8. Cloutier, R., Hutchison, N. (eds.): Guide to theSystems Engineering Body of Knowledge. INCOSE (2023)
9. Com, W.A., Oberer, B., Erkollar, A.: International journal of organizational leadership leadership 4.0: digital leaders in the age of industry 4.0. Int. J. Organ. Leadersh. **7**, 404–412 (2018)
10. Demir, S., Gunduz, M.A., Kayikci, Y., Paksoy, T.: Readiness and maturity of smart and sustainable supply chains: a model proposal. EMJ - Eng. Manag. J. (2022). https://doi.org/10.1080/10429247.2022.2050129
11. Facchini, F., Digiesi, S., Pinto, L.F.R.: Implementation of i4.0 technologies in production systems: opportunities and limits in the digital transformation. In: M., P.A.L.F.A. (ed.) Procedia Computer Science. vol. 200, pp. 1705–1714. Elsevier B.V. (2022). https://doi.org/10.1016/j.procs.2022.01.371
12. Ghobakhloo, M., Iranmanesh, M.: Digital transformation success under industry 4.0: a strategic guideline for manufacturing SMEs. J. Manuf. Technol. Manag. **32**, 1533–1556 (2021). https://doi.org/10.1108/JMTM-11-2020-0455
13. Ghobakhloo, M., Fathi, M.: Corporate survival in industry 4.0 era: the enabling role of lean-digitized manufacturing. J. Manuf. Technol. Manag. **31**, 1–30 (2020). https://doi.org/10.1108/JMTM-11-2018-0417
14. Gorecky, D., Schmitt, M., Loskyll, M., Zühlke, D.: Human-machine-interaction in the industry 4.0 era. In: Proceedings - 2014 12th IEEE International Conference on Industrial Informatics, INDIN 2014, pp. 289–294. Institute of Electrical and Electronics Engineers Inc. (2014). https://doi.org/10.1109/INDIN.2014.6945523
15. Govindasamy, A., Arularasan, A.: Readiness and maturity assessment model to measure the industry 4.0 ecosystem. In: Kannan, R.J., Geetha, S., Sashikumar, S., Diver, C. (eds.) International Virtual Conference on Industry 4.0. LNEE, vol. 355, pp. 57–67. Springer, Singapore (2021). https://doi.org/10.1007/978-981-16-1244-2_5
16. Hair, J.F., Ringle, C.M., Sarstedt, M.: PLS-SEM: indeed a silver bullet. J. Market. Theory Pract. **19**, 139–152 (2011). https://doi.org/10.2753/MTP1069-6679190202
17. Ivanov, D., Dolgui, A., Sokolov, B.: The impact of digital technology and industry 4.0 on the ripple effect and supply chain risk analytics. Int. J. Prod. Res. **57**, 829–846 (2019). https://doi.org/10.1080/00207543.2018.1488086
18. Jepsen, S.C., Mork, T.I., Hviid, J., Worm, T.: A pilot study of industry 4.0 asset interoperability challenges in an industry 4.0 laboratory. In: IEEE International Conference on Industrial Engineering and Engineering Management, vol. 2020, pp. 571–575. IEEE Computer Society (2020). https://doi.org/10.1109/IEEM45057.2020.9309952
19. Kagermann, H.: Change through digitization—value creation in the age of industry 4.0. In: Albach, H., Meffert, H., Pinkwart, A., Reichwald, R. (eds.) Management of Permanent Change, pp. 23–45. Springer, Wiesbaden (2015). https://doi.org/10.1007/978-3-658-05014-6_2
20. Kim, J.H.: A review of cyber-physical system research relevant to the emerging it trends: industry 4.0, IoT, big data, and cloud computing. J. Ind. Integr. Manag. **02**, 1750011 (2017). https://doi.org/10.1142/S2424862217500117
21. Kohnová, L., Papula, J., Salajová, N.: Internal factors supporting business and technological transformation in the context of industry 4.0. Bus. Theory Pract. **20**, 137–145 (2019). https://doi.org/10.3846/btp.2019.13

22. Kusiak, A.: Smart manufacturing. Int. J. Prod. Res. **56**, 508–517 (2018). https://doi.org/10.1080/00207543.2017.1351644
23. Liaskos, S., Khan, S.M., Myloupolos, J.: Modeling and reasoning about uncertainty in goal models: a decision-theoretic approach. Softw. Syst. Model. **21**, 1–24 (2022). https://doi.org/10.1007/s10270-021-00968-w
24. Mansour, H., Aminudin, E., Mansour, T.: Implementing industry 4.0 in the construction industry- strategic readiness perspective. Int. J. Constr. Manag. **23**, 1457–1470 (2021). https://doi.org/10.1080/15623599.2021.1975351
25. Martin, J.: The seven samurai of systems engineering: dealing with the complexity of 7 interrelated systems. In: Proceedings of INCOSE Symposium. INCOSE (2004)
26. Nakayama, R.S., Spinnola, M.M., Silva, J.R.: A multilayer proposal to a smart home applied to healthcare. Polytechnica 144 (2021). https://doi.org/10.1016/j.cie.2020.106453
27. Narula, S., Prakash, S., Dwivedy, M., Talwar, V., Tiwari, S.P.: Industry 4.0 adoption key factors: an empirical study on manufacturing industry. J. Adv. Manag. Res. **17**, 697–725 (2020). https://doi.org/10.1108/JAMR-03-2020-0039
28. Schuh, G., Scheuer, T., Nick, G., Szaller, A., Vargedo, T.: A two-step digitalization level assessment approach for manufacturing companies. In: Procedia Manufacturing, vol. 54, pp. 25–30. Elsevier B.V. (2020). https://doi.org/10.1016/j.promfg.2021.07.005
29. Silva, J.R., Macedo, E.C.T., Correa, Y.G., Medeiros, R.F.: A multilayer proposal to a smart home applied to healthcare. Polytechnica **4**, 1–14 (2021). https://doi.org/10.1007/s41050-021-00029-7
30. Silva, J.R., Vital, E.L.: Toward a formal design to service-oriented cloud manufacturing. In: Anals of the Automatica Brazilian Congress, vol. 2. Automatica Brazilian Society (2020). https://doi.org/10.48011/asbav2i1.1241
31. Tao, F., Cheng, J., Qi, Q., Zhang, M., Zhang, H., Sui, F.: Digital twin-driven product design, manufacturing and service with big data. Int. J. Adv. Manuf. Technol. **94**, 3563–3576 (2018). https://doi.org/10.1007/s00170-017-0233-1
32. Tjahjono, B., Esplugues, C., Ares, E., Pelaez, G.: What does industry 4.0 mean to supply chain? Procedia Manuf. **13**, 1175–1182 (2017). https://doi.org/10.1016/j.promfg.2017.09.191
33. Wagire, A.A., Joshi, R., Rathore, A.P.S., Jain, R.: Development of maturity model for assessing the implementation of industry 4.0: learning from theory and practice. Prod. Plan. Control **32**, 603–622 (2021). https://doi.org/10.1080/09537287.2020.1744763
34. Wang, S., Wan, J., Zhang, D., Li, D., Zhang, C.: Towards smart factory for industry 4.0: a self-organized multi-agent system with big data based feedback and coordination. Comput. Netw. **101**, 158–168 (2016). https://doi.org/10.1016/j.comnet.2015.12.017
35. Wang, Y., Ma, H.S., Yang, J.H., Wang, K.S.: Industry 4.0: a way from mass customization to mass personalization production. Adv. Manuf. **5**, 311–320 (2017). https://doi.org/10.1007/s40436-017-0204-7

MBSE- Based Construction Method of Unified Information Model for Production Equipment

Jun Li[1,2], Keqin Dou[1,3(✉)], Yong Zhou[1], Jinsong Liu[1], Qing Li[2], and Yiqiang Tang[1]

[1] China Industrial Control Systems Cyber Emergency Response Team, Beijing 100040, China
dkq1989@163.com

[2] Department of Automation, Tsinghua University, Beijing 100084, China

[3] University of Chinese Academy of Sciences, Beijing 100049, China

Abstract. Under the background of the integration and development of next-generation information technology and the manufacturing industry, production equipment has evolved into Cyber-Physical System (CPS), which seamlessly combine embedded computing, network communication, and high-performance control. In this context, the information model of production equipment has gradually become a pivotal aspect supporting the visualization of the physical operation status of production equipment, optimizing decision-making in the digital realm, and enabling communication and interaction mapping in the cyber-physical space. Based on the model-based systems engineering (MBSE) principle, a unified information model for the whole manufacturing process of production equipment is proposed to solve the problems of diverse information types, diverse expression forms and complex model heterogeneity in the field of production equipment information modeling. From the perspectives of communication, knowledge, and geometry, the management activities of production equipment are analyzed, function modules are assigned, and information elements are defined. Consequently, a holistic information model for production equipment is formulated to support the integration of multidimensional models and realize the optimization and control of heterogeneous production equipment, which providing valuable reference for developers and practitioners of the production equipment information model.

Keywords: Production Equipment · Information Model · Cyber-Physical · System · Model-based System Engineering

1 Introduction

The manufacturing industry is the material foundation and industrial mainstay of the national economy, and is an important symbol to measure the level of science and technology and comprehensive strength of a country. As the basic carrier of manufacturing activities, production equipment is the core asset of manufacturing enterprises, and its management level directly affects the production, operation, supply and other value-creating activities. With the integration of new information technology and manufacturing industry, the level of digitalization, networking, and intelligence of production

S. Terzi et al. (Eds.): IN4PL 2023, CCIS 1886, pp. 348–367, 2023.
https://doi.org/10.1007/978-3-031-49339-3_22

equipment continues to improve, and the interaction between the environment and supporting equipment becomes more and more close. Production equipment is no longer just a mechanical product composed of physical structure, but to accelerate the transformation to the virtual and real mapping, interactive drive and real-time interaction of the digital twin of production equipment. Its operation mode, management mode and management objectives have undergone fundamental changes, which put forward higher requirements for the interconnection, innovation and optimization of production equipment, transformation and upgrading [1].

The production equipment information model integrates and consolidates a large amount of industrial technology principles, industry knowledge, perception information, geometric features, and other different types of data, and encapsulates them into modular model components [2]. These components become the key to support the realization of ubiquitous connectivity, dynamic perception, efficient control and intelligent optimization of production equipment, and also an important guarantee for giving full play to the value of production equipment assets and the effectiveness of digital management. Domestic and foreign academia and industry have carried out a lot of research, exploration and application of production equipment information model, and relevant international standardization organizations and industrial enterprises have developed various industrial communication protocol specifications with independent intellectual property rights from their own advantages. Based on various communication protocols, the relevant production equipment communication integration standards are published, and the interconnection requirements of production equipment information are proposed from multiple levels and multiple dimensions, laying the foundation for production equipment bidirectional mapping, information interaction and sharing, and seamless service integration.

The internal information associations and intricate interaction logic of the production equipment management activities throughout the manufacturing process are complex, requiring an urgent need for a unified information model to provide a standardized and comprehensive definition of the information pertaining to these activities. Therefore, this study mainly focuses on the intelligent optimization and control requirements of multi-heterogeneous production equipment in the intensive manufacturing workshop. It deeply analyzes the concept, research status, and existing problems of the unified information model for production equipment. Based on the theory of information physics systems, a method for constructing a unified information model for production equipment throughout the entire manufacturing process is proposed. From the three dimensions of communication, knowledge and geometry, the operation and control activities of production equipment are analyzed, the function modules are assigned, and the information elements are defined. The unified information model of production equipment for the whole manufacturing process is constructed to facilitate the observation of multi-dimensional information related to equipment management activities, enable knowledge search, reasoning, and closed-loop control feedback. On this basis, a multi-dimensional model fusion application scheme for production equipment based on the unified information model of production equipment is proposed to support the realization of virtual-real mapping, dynamic interaction and collaborative optimization.

2 Related Works

2.1 Information Model Concept Differentiation

Information model is a simplified description of objects in the real world for a certain purpose, aiming to realize the abstract cognition and expression of real-world objects in the information world, and its concept and definition gradually evolve with the development of science and technology and the change of industrial needs. Early information models can be regarded as human thinking models, which mainly describe and explain the characteristics and activities of objects in the real world based on human thinking patterns and linguistic organization. In the 1960s and 1970s, with the popularization of computer applications, the regular and structured representation and storage of information in computers were promoted, and the concept of information model came into being [3]. In the 1990s, in order to meet the needs of multi-class information system architecture design and integrated interconnection, the information model added elements such as object attributes and association relations on the basis of the original regular description. In recent years, with the continuous breakthrough and development of the new generation of information technology, the concept of information model covers more and more contents and broader boundaries. Yu Runcang, academician of the Chinese Academy of Engineering, pointed out that the information model integrates multi-dimensional, multi-scale and multi-domain holographic information, which can realize the digital expression of the dynamic change process of data, processes and resources at different stages [4]. At the same time, information model has also been widely used in many fields such as architecture, city, industry, etc., such as Building Information Modeling (BIM) [5], City Information Modeling (BIM) [6], Common Information Model (CIM) [7], Industrial Internet Information Model (3IM) [8], etc.

From the perspective of the development of information model, information model has gone through the evolution process from the abstraction of objective objects, the abstraction of data features in computers and information systems, and then to the abstract of multidimensional information resources. Its positioning has also continued to extend from the initial cognitive expression to regularization description, relationship definition and digital expression of holographic information. Combined with the object and scope of this study, the information model in this study mainly refers to a regular expression model used to describe the object, the attribute of the object and object relationship.

2.2 Unified Information Model of Production Equipment

As an entity that frequently interacts with operators, supporting equipment, digital system, physical environment, etc., production equipment needs to describe and express the information involved in a unified, complete and accurate manner through information models. Since production equipment itself is a complex system involving multidisciplinary fields, multi-production processes and multi-component elements, domestic and foreign research institutions, industrial enterprises and standardization organizations all study production equipment information models from their own industry fields and application needs, and pay different attention to the specific content of information model standardization and unification.

In terms of the regularization expression of the attributes of production equipment itself, in order to unify the definition rules and description methods of various attribute elements of production equipment in computer systems, various research institutions and international standardization organizations have carried out research on production equipment data dictionary for the unified semantic description of key attribute elements of various production equipment. International Electrotechnical Commission (IEC) has formulated IEC61360-4 international standard for general data dictionary [9], and the ECl@ss of Germany has formulated a unified data and semantic system in the industrial field [10]. Based on data dictionary, relevant production equipment manufacturers have established production equipment information models for general fields or specific objects, so as to realize the unified query, statistics, exchange and processing of production equipment information in the computer system, and support the unified semantic expression and information exchange of production equipment information inside and outside the enterprise.

In terms of transmission and interaction of production equipment information, in order to solve the problems of different communication methods, complicated protocols and difficult data transmission of multi-type heterogeneous equipment, relevant international standardization organizations, industrial enterprises and research institutions have developed various industrial communication protocol standards with independent intellectual property rights from their own interests. The International Electrotechnical Commission has developed the FDI Field Equipment Integration Standard IEC 62769 [11], which is used to describe the field communication integration of production equipment. The OPC Foundation proposed the unified OPC UA architecture IEC 62541 [12], which provides a cross-platform general framework for the establishment of the information model of production equipment and supports the interconnection and interoperability of equipment, system and environment based on OPC UA.

In terms of bidirectional mapping between physical entity and digital virtual body of production equipment, in order to solve the problem of unified integration and accurate expression of multi-level, multi-dimensional and full-life cycle information of production equipment, research institutions and standardization organizations in various countries have carried out research and exploration on production equipment information models. In 2015, the Industry 4.0 platform released the Industry 4.0 Reference architecture model (RAMI 4.0) [13], which innovatively proposed the concept of asset management shell to describe industrial asset information and functional applications of production equipment. In recent years, digital twins [14] and information physical systems [15] have established multi-dimensional, multi-disciplinary and multi-physical digital models of production equipment in a digital way to simulate and describe the geometric form, attribute elements and behavior rules of production equipment.

2.3 Research Gaps

Based on the above in-depth analysis of the development status of the production equipment information model, it is found that the current research on the unified information model of production equipment still has shortcomings in terms of general framework, coverage and expression depth, etc., which is difficult to meet the operation management requirements of multi-type heterogeneous production equipment under the background of the rapid development of industrial Internet, digital twin and other technologies. The details are as follows:

The lack of unified and comprehensive description of multi-type heterogeneous production equipment information makes it difficult to support the in-depth analysis and accurate regulation of production equipment operation control activities. At present, the information generated by the operation of production equipment has exploded, and the fields and dimensions involved have continued to extend and expand. However, the current production equipment information models often start from a single domain or a single dimension of application requirements, and there is no interaction between the different types of production equipment information models. Therefore, it is necessary to establish a unified information model of production equipment with different content, standardized semantics and consistent format to support the application of data integration sharing and information fusion of production equipment in operation management activities.

The lack of unified associated description of operation activity information of production equipment for different application scenarios, and it is difficult to support integrated control of production equipment operation activities throughout the whole manufacturing process. At present, most of the production equipment information models focus on a single activity such as operation management and maintenance of production equipment, and lack the description rules of the internal logic and correlation of the operation information of production equipment in different scenarios, which cannot support the unified semantic expression of all kinds of information of production equipment throughout the whole manufacturing process. For example, the information exchange between equipment maintenance and equipment operation management activities is not smooth. This results in difficulties in timely updating equipment running status assessment information based on equipment maintenance and repair information, thereby leading to low efficiency in equipment operation management and inability to reflect equipment operation status accurately. Therefore, it is necessary to build a unified information model of production equipment covering the whole manufacturing process to support the information interconnection, and virtual and real bidirectional mapping of production equipment in the whole manufacturing process.

The lack of unified definition of correlation and constraint rules of production equipment attribute information, state parameters, control logic, etc., which is difficult to support high-level applications such as equipment predictive maintenance, fault diagnosis, and remote operation and maintenance. In the practical application process, production equipment is often interrelated with supporting equipment and digital system to form a complex production system with hierarchical structure and correlation relationship, which puts forward higher requirements for the granularity and correlation of information expressed by the production equipment information model. Therefore, it is necessary to build a unified information model of production equipment that can uniformly express the operation logic and correlation of production equipment, so as to meet the needs of intelligent management and control of production equipment for the whole manufacturing process.

3 Analysis of Construction Requirements of Unified Information Model of Production Equipment Based on Cyber-Physical System

Currently, production equipment has evolved into a cyber-physical system (CPS) integrating embedded computing, network communication, high-performance control and physical environment [16]. Based on the closed loop channel of data interaction between physical space and cyber space, production equipment CPS can converge, integrate and transmit the physical status data of itself in physical space through communication perception, thus completing the information transmission between physical space and cyber space. In the cyber space, it can form standardized and modular knowledge units and functional components of production equipment based on data extraction, and assemble them to form digital virtual body of production equipment. Besides, through knowledge acquisition, combined user requirements and application scenarios, production equipment operation decision knowledge is obtained. Then, it can complete feedback control from the cyber space of production equipment to the physical space, and visually display the operating status, production schedule, decision basis of production equipment in the physical space based on digital virtual objects, and further form a production and manufacturing system based on automatic information flow, which enabling intelligent perception, dynamic analysis, scientific decision making and precise execution.

At present, the operation management and control system of production equipment generally manages, controls and maintains the equipment as a cyber-physical system (CPS). The production equipment CPS puts forward higher requirements for the collection, transmission, processing and application of production equipment information, and needs a clearly expressed, semantically complete and structurally consistent production equipment information model as the foundational support, as shown in. Figure 1 ext, we analyze the unified attribute content of production equipment CPS in the whole manufacturing process of physical space, cyber space and virtual-real mapping process. In the physical space, we pay more attention to the visual display of the operating conditions of production equipment, and mainly focusing on the consistent description of the geometric feature information such as the appearance shape, size, internal structure, spatial pose and assembly relationship of various production equipment. In the cyber space, we pay more attention to the construction, updating and reasoning logic of production equipment digital virtual body assisted decision-making knowledge, which mainly focusing on the consistent expression of production equipment expert knowledge, empirical parameters, operating criteria, correlation and other domain knowledge. In the process of virtual-real interaction, we pay more attention to whether the production equipment data can be stably collected and whether the control instructions can be effectively fed back. We mainly focus on the consistency definition of communication transmission parameters such as data format, instruction coding, control logic, interaction mode, transmission configuration, etc. in the data exchange process between equipment entity and digital virtual entity. Therefore, this study constructs a unified information model of production equipment from dimensions of communication, knowledge and geometry, in order to solve the problems of irregular information expression, incomplete content and unsmooth interaction between physical space, cyber space of production equipment.

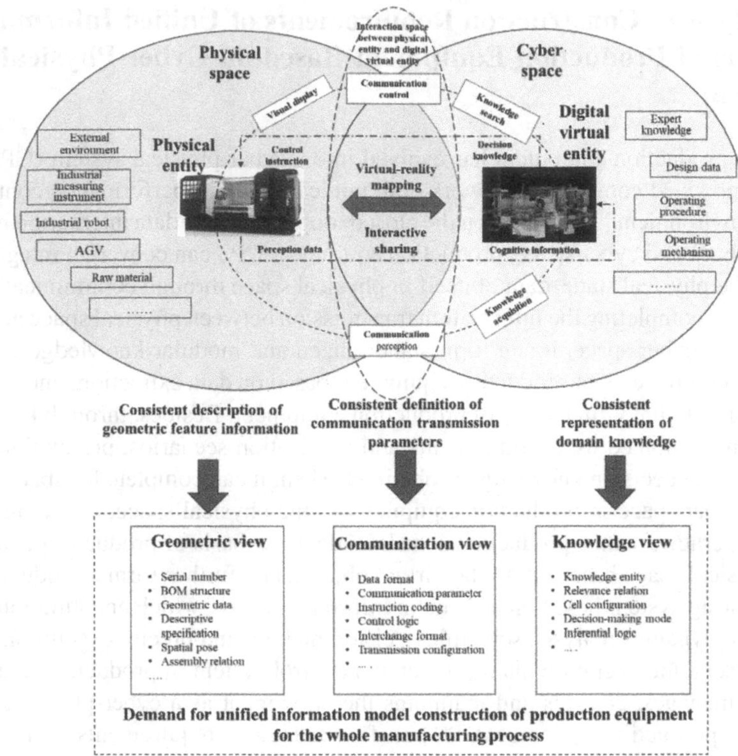

Fig. 1. Unified information requirement analysis framework of production equipment based on CPS

4 Construction Method of Unified Information Model for Production Equipment in the Whole Manufacturing Process

4.1 Technical Route for Construction of Unified Information Model for Production Equipment Based on MBSE

As a complex engineering system integrating virtual and real world, production equipment CPS needs to rely on MBSE to carry out the construction and application of unified information model for production equipment. MagicGrid is an MBSE methodology mainly applied to the forward development of complex products. Based on the issues that need to be addressed during different stages of product development, MagicGrid divides the design process into problem domain, solution domain, and implementation domain. Within each domain, it is further divided into four parts: Requirement, Behavior, Structure, and Parameter, comprehensively expressing the product attributes throughout various stages of development. Starting from the knowledge, communication and geometry dimensions of production equipment, this study refers to the MagicGrid methodology to vertically build the research process of requirement analysis-activity behavior-function module-information model (RAFI, Requirement-Activity-Function-Information), and horizontally build the progressive research method of problem domain, solution domain and implementation domain, forming a matrix technical route for the construction of unified information model for production equipment, as shown in Fig. 2.

From a vertical perspective, through the demand analysis of production equipment operation control information oriented to the whole manufacturing process, MBSE method is applied to complete user demand analysis, management activity definition, function module analysis and information model construction. According to the demand input, the problem domain conducts equipment activity content decomposition, function module division and entity object recognition from the whole; based on the specific activities, functions and entities input from the problem domain, the solution domain conducts the behavior definition of management activities, the construction of attribute set of function modules and the analysis of entity attribute relationship; Based on the behavior, functional requirements and relationship constraints input by the solution domain, the implementation domain applies SysML (System Modeling Language) to design equipment activity elements, attribute parameters and information elements of specific application scenarios, and finally completes the realization of the unified information model of production equipment from the global system to the local details and even the specific scenarios.

Horizontally, in the management activity analysis stage, the content of production equipment management activities is analyzed layer by layer in the problem domain, the behaviors and actions of production equipment management activities are analyzed in detail in the solution domain, and the activity elements are designed and activity diagrams are drawn in the implementation domain based on the specific requirements of equipment operation control by expanded SysML. In the stage of function module assignment, the function modules of production equipment are decomposed in the problem domain, the attribute set of function modules of production equipment is constructed in the solution domain, and the attribute parameters of function modules are defined and module diagrams are drawn in the implementation domain based on the expanded SysML through the specific requirements of function modules of equipment. In the stage of information model construction, relevant information entities are identified in the problem domain according to the management activities and functional applications of production equipment, entity relationship diagrams are adopted in the solution domain to describe and analyze the entity attribute relationship network of production equipment information, and unified information elements of production equipment are constructed in the realization domain based on the specific application scenarios of management activities of production equipment. Thus, the unified information model of production equipment for the whole manufacturing process is constructed.

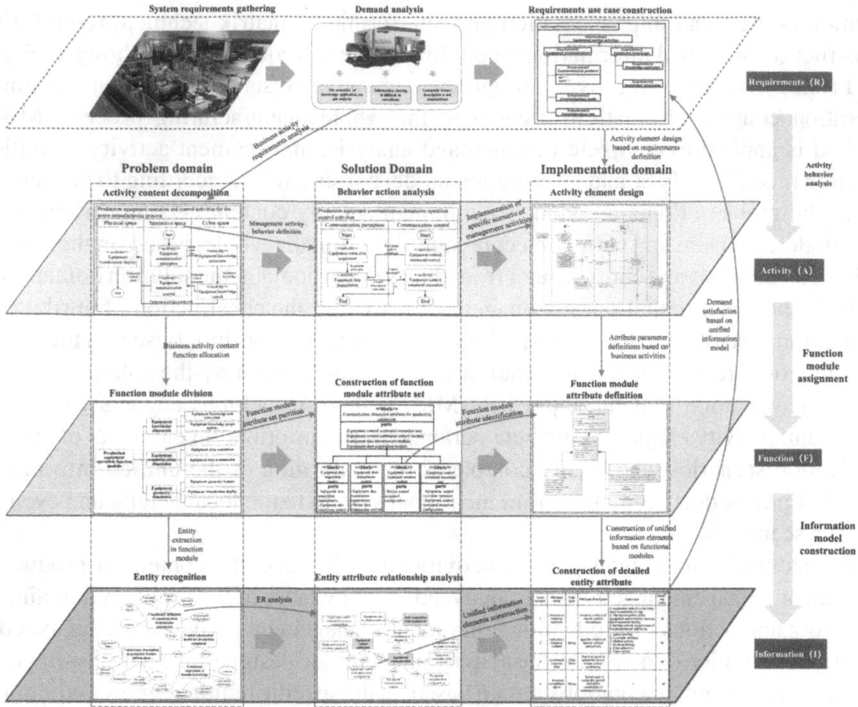

Fig. 2. Technical route for construction of unified information model for production equipment in the whole manufacturing process.

4.2 Research on Management Activities of Production Equipment

Problem Domain: Activity Content Decomposition. Based on the operation control requirements of production equipment, this study conducts a content analysis of management activities, clarifies the operational logic of management activities, and decomposes and obtains specific details of activities. According to the operation and control requirements of production equipment, the operation process of equipment is divided into five primary activities: communication perception, operation control, knowledge extraction, knowledge search and visual display. Based on this, from the perspectives of communication, knowledge, and geometry, the operational logic of management activities in the context of operation management of production equipment is further clarified. From the perspective of communication, operation management of production equipment mainly focuses on information interaction between cyber space and physical space, including data collection and transmission, as well as the issuance and execution of control instructions. The knowledge dimension mainly focuses on extracting and abstracting relevant knowledge within the cyber space of production equipment, forming a knowledge graph for knowledge search and reasoning, and assisting in control decision-making. The geometry dimension mainly focuses on real-time linkage and updating of geometric feature models of physical entities of production equipment, and visualizing the current operational status of production equipment (see Fig. 3).

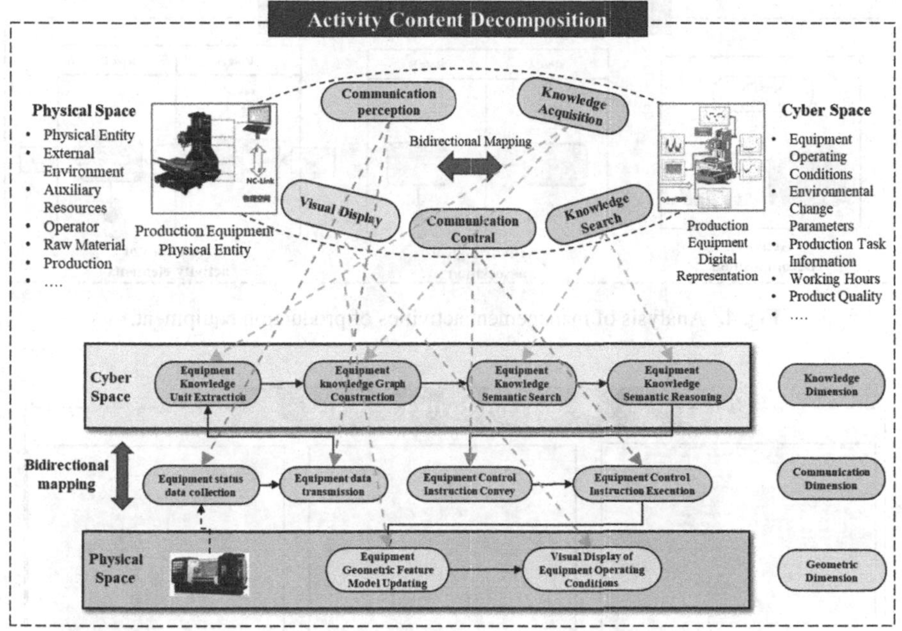

Fig. 3. Decomposition of management activities of production equipment.

Solution Domain: Behavior and Action Analysis. Based on the requirements, operational logic, and relationships of specific activities related to each dimension of production equipment, the activities are broken down into several sub-actions. By analyzing the relationships and input-output parameters between sub-actions of specific activities in management of production equipment, the logical relationships between each sub-action are established, thus clarifying the behavioral rules and operational logic of the management activities. Based on the decomposition of activities into sub-actions and their relationships, relevant elements such as input-output, associated roles, and process sequences are added to assemble the activity elements and form a generic description scheme for management activities of production equipment. By analyzing the operational logic of subdivided activities in cyber space, physical space, and the bidirectional mapping between them in operational and control of production equipment, it provides logical reference for the design of management activity elements in the subsequent sections (see Fig. 4).

Implementation Domain: Activity Element Design. Based on the specific requirements and operational logic of management activities, the expanded SysML is used to perform functional decomposition, activity analysis, and action specification for application activity elements in specific scenarios. The sub-actions, activity nodes, and activity partitions are assembled to generate a complete activity diagram, providing dynamic descriptive information of system functionality. This process lays the foundation for the construction of a unified information model for production equipment. (see Fig. 5).

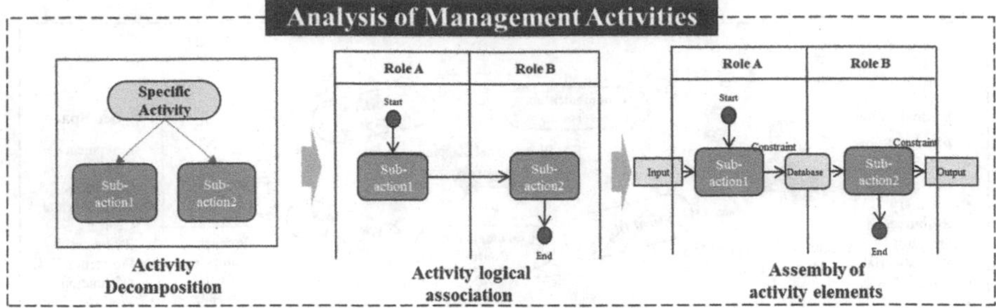

Fig. 4. Analysis of management activities of production equipment.

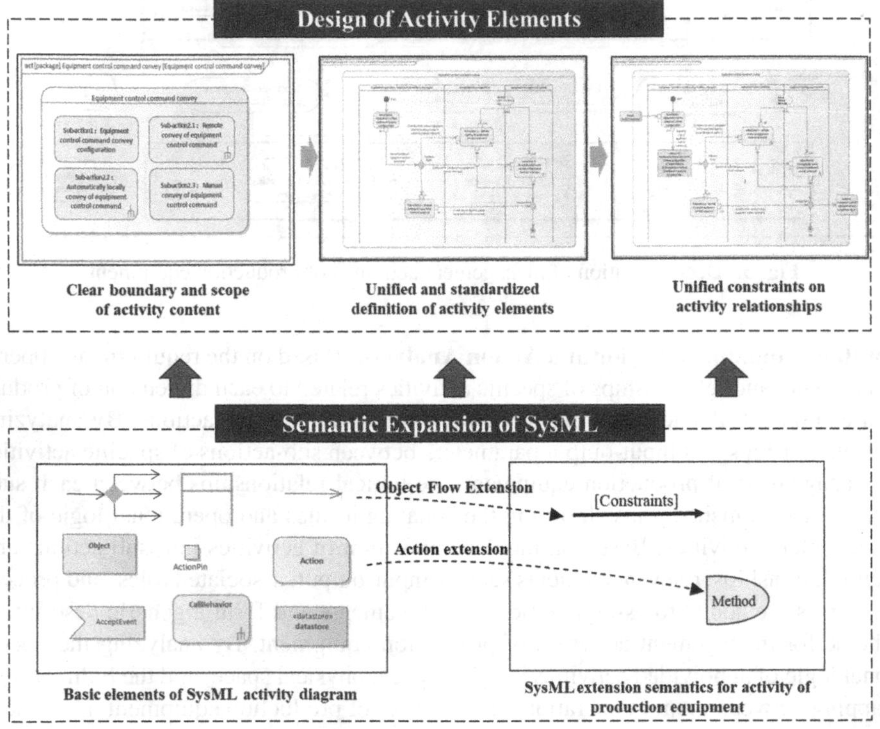

Fig. 5. A method for describing management activities of production equipment based on SysML extension.

4.3 Allocation of Production Equipment Operation Management Function Modules.

Problem Domain: Function Module Division. Building on the decomposition of management activities of production equipment, the management function modules of production equipment are defined. In this regard, three dimensions are considered: communication, knowledge, and geometry. The boundary scope and expressive content of each function module of production equipment are analyzed in depth to clarify the fundamental functional applications. In the communication dimension, the focus is on the perception and acquisition of the operating status of production equipment, as well as the feedback control. This dimension is divided into four primary function modules: equipment data acquisition, equipment data transmission, equipment control instruction issuance, and equipment control instruction execution. In the knowledge dimension, the emphasis is on acquiring and applying knowledge of production equipment operation and management. This dimension is divided into three primary function modules: equipment knowledge unit extraction, equipment knowledge graph updating, and equipment knowledge semantic search/reasoning. In the geometry dimension, the focus is on the visualization requirements of the operating and controlling processes of production equipment. This dimension is divided into two primary function modules: equipment geometric characteristics and visual display of equipment running status. Based on the decomposition of the primary function modules, the content expressed in the cyber-physical space is discussed. According to the three dimensions of knowledge, communication and geometry, it is further decomposed into secondary and even tertiary function modules. (see Fig. 6).

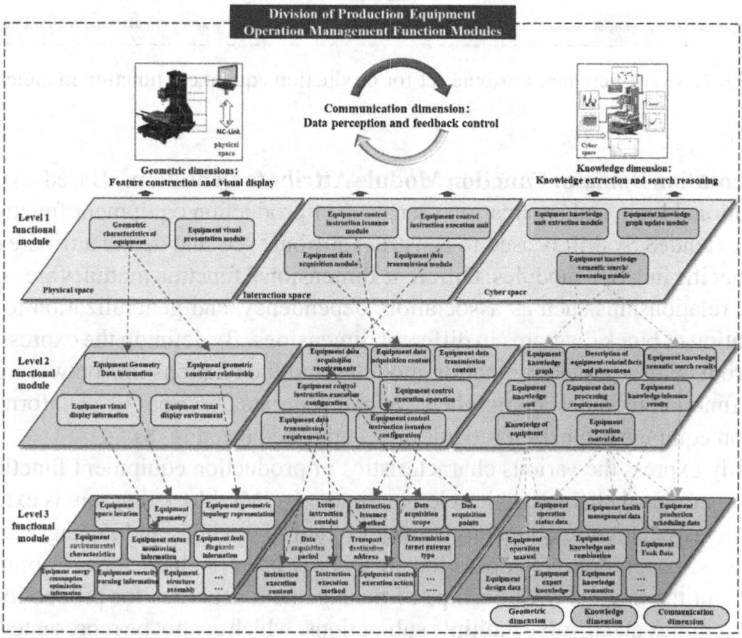

Fig. 6. Division of production equipment operation management function modes.

Solution Domain: Construction of Function Module Attribute Set. Based on the decomposition mentioned above, the construction of attribute sets for various function modules of production equipment is carried out to clarify the functional attribute elements included in specific activities. In the activities of production equipment operation management, there is a mutual influence between action behavior, function modules, and attribute elements. Changes in activity behavior lead to changes in function modules, which further result in changes in attribute elements. Therefore, this study extracts relevant attributes for specific management activities of production equipment and obtains the corresponding attribute elements related to these activities. According to the hierarchical relationship of function modules, the activity-related attribute elements and function modules are mapped and designed to match, and the attribute elements of corresponding function modules are obtained. Subsequently, specific functional attribute elements are combined and assembled, which form a complete set of function modules for production equipment in specific scenarios (see Fig. 7).

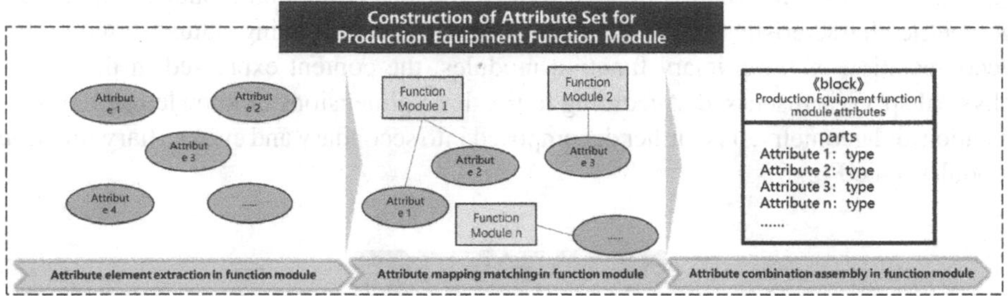

Fig. 7. Construction of attribute set for production equipment function modules.

Implementation Domain: Function Module Attribute Definition. Based on the internal operational logic and application scenarios of production equipment function modules, the extended SysML is used to construct attribute sets and define attribute parameters for specific function modules. Different-dimensional function modules are combined based on relationships such as association, dependency, and generalization to support the formation of block diagrams in different dimensions. By defining the expressive content of production equipment function modules and the relationships between different types of function modules, comprehensive and accurate descriptions of information of production equipment function modules are supported (see Fig. 8).

To fully express the various characteristics of production equipment function modules, the operational characteristics element in the SysML block diagram is extended to express the association relationship between function modules and management activities. The <<operation >> operation in SysML usually characterizes some simple behavior, but the internal relationships of management activities for production equipment are complex and involve multiple sub-actions, which cannot be represented only by <<operation>>. Therefore, this study extends the <<activity>> 'activity behavior' element in the SysML block diagram block based on stereotype to support the complete expression of behavior characteristics related to production equipment function modules (see Table 1). Using the extended SysML, attribute sets are constructed and attribute parameters are defined for specific function modules. Different-dimensional function modules are combined based on relationships such as association, dependency, and generalization to support the formation of block diagrams in different dimensions.

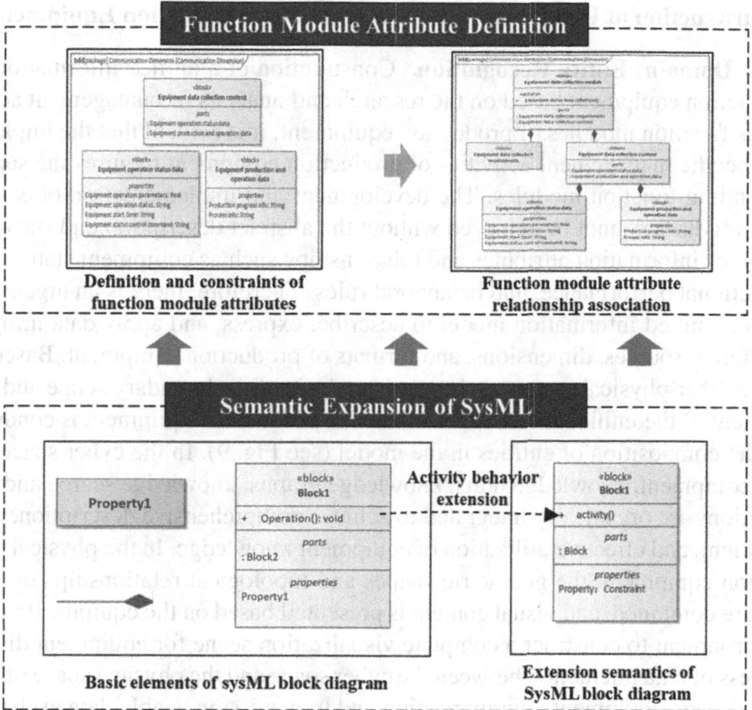

Fig. 8. SysML-based method for defining attribute parameters of production equipment function module.

By defining the expressive content of production equipment function modules and the relationships between different types of function modules, comprehensive and accurate descriptions of relevant information regarding production equipment function modules are supported.

Table 1. Semantic extension of SysML for the functional field of production equipment.

Name	Symbol	Extension	Description	Rule
Activity behavior	«block» Block1 + activity() parts : Block properties Property: Constraint	Expand the operational semantics in behavioral characteristics and add active behavioral elements within the module	Activity behavior is used to associate equipment operation control activities	1. In the process of production equipment operation and management, support the execution of related equipment operation and management activities through the<<activities>>in the production equipment function module; 2. The<<activity>in the production equipment function module can call one or more<<actions>>.

4.4 Construction of Unified Information Model for Production Equipment

Problem Domain: Entity Recognition. Construction of a unified information model for production equipment based on the research and analysis of management activities, as well as function modules of production equipment, it is evident that the implementation of specific management activities of production equipment requires the support of corresponding function modules. The development and implementation of equipment function modules cannot be achieved without the abstract description and standardized definition of information attributes and relationships such as equipment status parameters, functional performance, and behavioral rules. Therefore, there is an urgent need to establish a unified information model to describe, express, and apply data information from different sources, dimensions, and formats of production equipment. Based on the theory of cyber-physical system, a thorough analysis of the boundary scope and expressive content of the unified information model for production equipment is conducted to clarify the composition of entities in the model (see Fig. 9). In the cyber space of production equipment, knowledge units, knowledge graphs, knowledge search and reasoning functions are organically integrated to achieve comprehensive description, efficient management, and effective utilization of equipment knowledge. In the physical space of production equipment, the geometric shapes and topological relationships of physical entities are combined, and visual content is presented based on the equipment visualization environment to construct a complete visualization scene for equipment display. In the process of data interaction between the cyber space and the physical space of production equipment, equipment communication and transmission enable data exchange and instruction control among equipment and management systems, thus supporting equipment data collection and equipment control instruction delivery and execution, realizing collaboration and linkage between equipment and interconnection between equipment and systems.

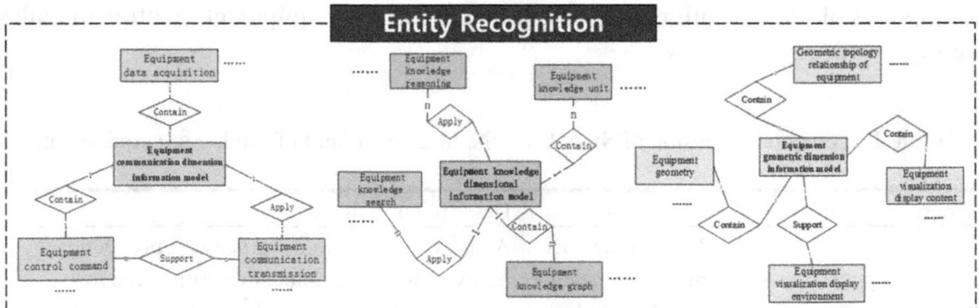

Fig. 9. Entity recognition of unified information model for production equipment.

Solution Domain: Analysis of Entity Attribute Relationship. Based on the analysis results of management activities and function modules of production equipment, and with reference to the semantic norms of entity relationship diagrams (ER diagrams), an analysis of entity properties and relationships for production equipment is conducted. Using the basic elements of entities, attributes, and relationships, an ER diagram is created to analyze the structure and relationships of the unified information model for production equipment, and achieve a visual representation of the internal logic of the information model (see Fig. 10). By constructing a unified information model for production equipment, the consistency description of production equipment in the cyber-physical space is supported, and the unified description, recognition, and application of various types of information for production equipment are realized. This analysis provides a foundation for the development of the unified information model for production equipment and supports the visualization of its logical structure and relationships. The resulting model enables the integration and standardization of equipment information, facilitating its use across different systems and contexts.

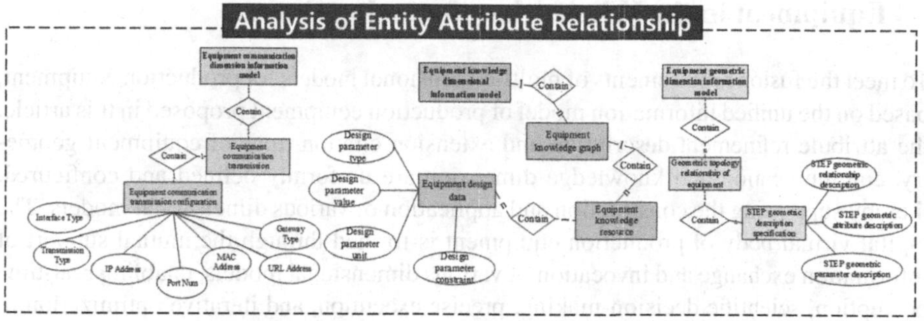

Fig. 10. Schematic diagram of production equipment entity attribute relationship analysis.

Implementation Domain: Construction of Detailed Entity Attribute. Based on the analysis results of entity properties and relationships, a unified information model for production equipment is constructed to facilitate the unified construction and description of information from different dimensions. The aim is to provide a standardized and unambiguous set of descriptive rules for the fundamental properties, status, and knowledge of production equipment. The syntax and structural rules are presented in Table 2. In accordance with the GB/T 33863.3 and GB/T 33863.5 standards, the attribute data types should be defined. The modeling rules are denoted by "M" for mandatory and "O" for optional. Based on the construction rules of the unified information model for production equipment, models are developed for knowledge, communication, and geometry dimensions. Each dimension provides a unified description for the attributes of the production equipment information model. This ensures consistency across different dimensions and facilitates the integration and standardization of production equipment information. The unified information model for production equipment serves as a foundation for capturing and representing various aspects of production equipment information, enabling comprehensive and standardized descriptions.

Table 2. Rules for constructing a unified information model for production equipment.

Number	Attribute name	Data type	Attribute description	Attribute value	Modeling rule
X	The name of attribute	Data type for attribute	Explanation of attribute meaning	The value of attribute	M/O
...	...	...	...	...	...

5 Application of Unified Information Model of Production Equipment in the Whole Manufacturing Process

To meet the fusion requirements of multi-dimensional models for production equipment, based on the unified information model of production equipment proposed in this article, the attribute refinement description and extension citation rules of equipment geometry, communication and knowledge dimension are uniformly defined and configured, thereby supporting the construction and application of various dimensional models. The digital virtual body of production equipment is formed through the mutual support of information exchange and invocation of various dimensional models, enabling real-time perception, scientific decision-making, precise execution, and iterative optimization of production equipment in the information physical space (see Fig. 11).

Based on attribute definitions such as equipment communication transmission configuration, equipment control command execution configuration, and equipment operational state data acquisition, the communication model constructs external communication links for production equipment by parsing equipment communication protocols, the transmission of information such as equipment start stop time, usage status, and operation status is pushed to the geometric model for visual display. Furthermore, equipment control commands are generated using control decision strategies derived from the knowledge model, enabling intelligent optimization of the operational state of production equipment. Additionally, the human-machine interaction information from the geometric model is transformed into equipment communication control commands, facilitating real-time interactive feedback control of the equipment.

Based on attributes such as equipment monitoring knowledge information, equipment knowledge search, and equipment knowledge reasoning, the knowledge model converts equipment operational data transmitted by the communication model into status monitoring knowledge, which is then used to detect potential fault signs, optimize production scheduling indicators, and optimize equipment performance optimization strategies during equipment operation through equipment knowledge search and reasoning engines, and transmitted to the geometric model to support the visualization of equipment operation control. Furthermore, the equipment operation control knowledge is updated and stored promptly based on the results of equipment operation control.

Based on attribute specifications such as human-machine interaction information and equipment geometry structure, the geometric model provides information on geometric topology relationships and spatial coordinates for the digital representation of equipment. By collecting data from communication model, the current operating status of equipment is dynamically displayed in the informational space. Leveraging the knowledge search and reasoning results from the knowledge model, visual simulation of equipment fault mechanisms, production scheduling, and performance optimization are conducted, presenting equipment operation control scenarios in a concise and intuitive manner.

To meet the operational and control requirements of production equipment, the interaction and real-time computation of data among various dimensional models are conducted by invoking the communication, knowledge, and geometric models. The digital representation of equipment orderly integrates information, including equipment communication data, operational control knowledge logic, and geometric spatial positions, and updates relevant information in real-time to the corresponding model, achieving the fusion application of multi-dimensional models of equipment to support intelligent decision-making and optimized execution of management activities, such as equipment fault diagnosis, production scheduling, and performance management.

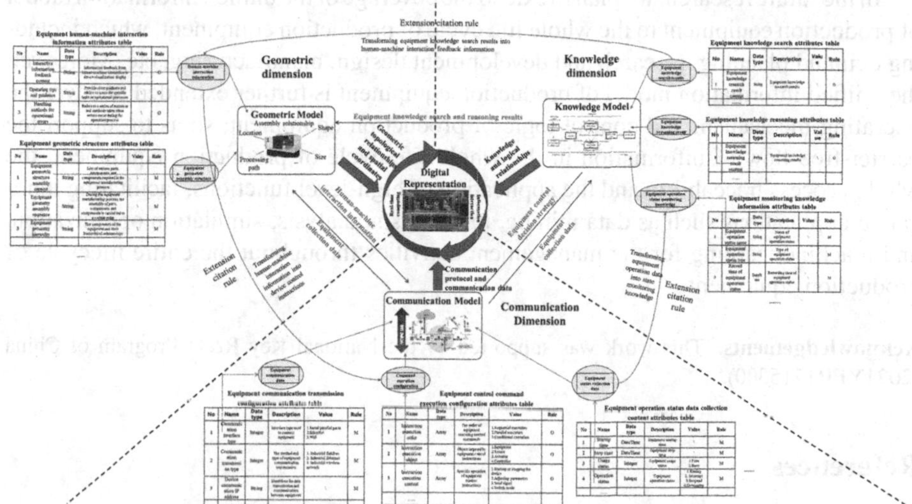

Fig. 11. Application of unified information model of production equipment in the whole manufacturing process.

6 Summary and Prospect

This study provides an in-depth analysis of the concept, research status, and existing problems of the unified information model for production equipment. Besides, based on the theory of information physics systems, a demand analysis for the construction of a unified information model for production equipment is carried out, and the construction method of the unified information model of production equipment throughout the whole manufacturing process is proposed. In addition, from the three dimensions of communication, knowledge, and geometry, we conducted the analysis of production equipment management activities, the allocation of function modules and the definition of information elements, and extend the SysML system modeling language combined with the requirements of production equipment operation and management. Finally, according to the specific concepts and constraints in production equipment management activities and function modules, we constructed a unified information model of production equipment for the entire manufacturing process, which can realize unified description, expression, and application of multi-dimensional information for production equipment. On this basis, a fusion application scheme for multidimensional models of production equipment is presented based on unified information model. Through the interactive sharing among the communication, knowledge, and geometric models of production equipment, it supports bidirectional mapping, scientific decision-making, and iterative optimization between physical entities and digital representations of production equipment, and offers valuable insights and references for developers and practitioners of production equipment information model.

In the future research, we plan to extend the coverage of the unified information model of production equipment to the whole life cycle of production equipment, which including demand planning, research and development design, manufacturing, etc. Moreover, the unified information model of production equipment is further extended to cover the operating mechanism and control logic of production equipment, so as to support the barrier-free flow of information in the whole life cycle of production equipment, the whole process traceability and the application of high-level functions, facilitating innovative applications such as data mining, mechanism analysis, simulation optimization, and machine learning for the management activities throughout the entire lifecycle of production equipment.

Acknowledgements. This work was supported by the National Key R&D Program of China (2021YFB1715300).

References

1. Jun, L., Yong, Z., Xin, L., et al.: Model architecture and multi-dimensional model fusion method for production equipment. J. New Industrialization **13**(Z1), 32–44 (2023)
2. Jiashun, L., Jianhua, L., Zhibin, W., et al.: Integrated information model for complex cables in virtual environment. Comput. Integrated Manuf. Syst. **19**(05), 964–971 (2013)
3. Codd, E.F.: A relational model of data for large shared data banks. Commun. ACM **13**(6), 377–387 (1970)
4. Runcang, Y., Cheng, L., Ruijun, Z., et al.: Mining information model: the development direction of mining informatization. China Mine Eng.. **47**(05), 1–3+13 (2018)
5. Taylor, J.E., Bernstein, P.G.: Paradigm trajectories of building information modeling practice in project networks. J. Manag. Eng. **25**(2), 69–76 (2009)
6. Xu, Z., Qi, M., Wu, Y., Hao, X., Yang, Y.: City information modeling: state of the art. Appl. Sci. **11**(19), 9333 (2021). https://doi.org/10.3390/app11199333
7. Gomez, F.J., Vanfretti, L., Olsen, S.H.: CIM-Compliant power system dynamic model-to-model transformation and modelica simulation. IEEE Trans. Industr. Inf. **14**(9), 3989–3996 (2017)

8. Yu, S., Huang, Y., Du, T., Teng, Y.: The proposal of a modeling methodology for an industrial internet information model. PeerJ. Comput. Sci. **8**, e1150 (2022). https://doi.org/10.7717/peerj-cs.1150
9. IEC 61360-4:2005: Standard data element types with associated classification scheme for electric components – Part 4: IEC reference collection of standard data element types and component classes. International Electrotechnical Commission (IEC) (2005)
10. Klein, M., Leitzgen, M., Weyrich, M.: Description of an intelligent resource unit for a smart production. In: Proceedings of the 2016 IEEE 21st International Conference on Emerging Technologies and Factory Automation (ETFA). IEEE, Berlin, Germany (2016)
11. GB/T 41771.1-2022/IEC 62769-1:2021. Field Equipment integration-part 1: Overview. State Administration of Market Regulation (2022)
12. GB/T 33863.1-2017/IEC/TR 62541-1:2010, OPC Unified Architecture Part 1: Overview and Concepts. State Administration of Market Regulation (2017)
13. Baicun, W., Fei, T., Xudong, F., et al.: Smart manufacturing and intelligent manufacturing: a comparative review. Engineering **7**(6), 738–757 (2021)
14. Fei, T., Weiran, L., Meng, Z., et al.: Digital twin five-dimensional model and its applications in ten fields. Comput. Integrated Manuf. Syst. **25**(01), 1–18 (2019)
15. GB/T 40021-2021, Cyber-physical systems--Terminology. State Administration of Market Regulation (2021)
16. Zhongjie, W., Lulu, X.: A review of research on information physics fusion systems. Acta Automatica Sinica **37**(10), 1157–1166 (2011)

Decentralized, Autonomous Setup and Access to Data of Independent Partners in a Hyper Connected Ecosystem

Frank-Walter Jaekel[1(✉)], Eckart Eyser[2], Robert Schwengber-Walter[3], Robert Harms[4], and Kai Grunert[5]

[1] Fraunhofer Institute for Production Systems and Design Technology (IPK), Pascalstr. 8-9, 10587 Berlin, Germany
frank-walter.jaekel@ipk.fraunhofer.de
[2] TresCom Technology GmbH, Wilhelm-von-Siemens-Straße 23, 12277 Berlin, Germany
[3] Innomotics GmbH, Nonnendammallee 72, 13629 Berlin, Germany
[4] 5thIndustry GmbH, Karl-Marx-Allee 92, 10243 Berlin, Germany
[5] T-Labs, Chair of Service-centric Networking (SNET), Technische Universität Berlin, Ernst-Reuter-Platz 7, 10587 Berlin, Germany

Abstract. The paper express results about a project on hyper-connected ecosystem of industrial networks and especially the services infrastructure developed during the project. A specific aspect is the concept and related feasibility study to establish an autonomous and distributed data management using the web presents of potential network partners. The question of the approach was "How to allow the accessibility of required information on demand everywhere and independent from a specific platform or cloud infrastructure for every partner or company within a business network". It starts with the accessibility of information as a major asset for decision making. During the project, industry partners insist on reducing the preparation effort for participation in the partnership and therefore data provision had to be supported with services. The paper provides insides of the work done, the findings and results. The briefly described demonstrator illustrates the usage of the service prototypes and early application cases.

Keywords: Value chain · Distributed information access · Hyper-connected ecosystem

1 Introduction and Background

The successful implementation of future-oriented technologies, especially with an increasingly pronounced digitization of production and company processes, requires the availability of information about the current information needs of persons, IT systems or companies at any time and from any location. In fact, business process management (BPM) approaches address similar topics already with the cross-organizational business processes (CBP) [1] in terms of distinguish between private and public company information as well as access rights for detailed information. In this way enterprises provides

S. Terzi et al. (Eds.): IN4PL 2023, CCIS 1886, pp. 368–379, 2023.
https://doi.org/10.1007/978-3-031-49339-3_23

so called public information for other companies and organizations within enterprise networks to form CBPs. The hyper-connected ecosystem of industrial networks provides a set of services to realize such concept like CBPs using the web presents of enterprises. It goes beyond the individual productions and focuses on the networking of companies that are in the digital transformation.

In this context, digital twins, as a consistent collection of data on a specific product, plays a major role in the networking of information. All required information should be immediately available at any location independent if they are statically or dynamical. In fact, state changes of objects should be immediate available in the related web representation applying edge computing and IoT (Internet of Things) technologies.

In the hyper-connected ecosystem of industrial networks project the need for information networking and corresponding digital components of corporate networks to achieve the availability of necessary data and its demand-based preparation has been determined through workshops and exchanges with industry and reported in a reference model for operating in the hyperconnected ecosystem. This also included work on identifying standards, terminologies and ontologies as well as company, product and service profiles identified in this context, such as those used by the big and small partner companies. The discussion of flexibility versus fixed terminology led to a configurable definition of terms when defining company profiles, which can include different terminologies depending on use. The profiles can be used to configure bots (e.g. scraper) that find and provide data about the companies in the profile. In addition, potential new partners can also be found. The feasibility of this approach was demonstrated using prototypes, but also its extensibility by external partners such as suppliers from partner companies.

This approach allows data to be made available in a decentralized manner without having to be entered into a dedicated platform. The data therefore remains the responsibility of the company providing the data. The different services were tested separately and used in particular for feasibility analysis. Finally, the prototypes of services were transferred to a common demonstrator in order to be able to show their interaction. The communication between the partners and services was tested along typical application processes in a practical value-added network.

The result of the approach related to "Hyperconnected Ecosystem for Industrial Networks" are services and interface catalogues as well as prototypes for the demand-oriented choreography of partner networks for flexible, semi-automatic and agile adaptation to the market as well as its prototypical implementation supported by reference models.

This goal was achieved through the new results for managing information via the partners' web presence using flexible company descriptions (profiles) and a service infrastructure for using the data. Initial states of the results were already communicated in a number of scientific publications such as the definition of the "Hyperconnected Ecosystem for Industrial Networks" [2, 3], the situation related to standards and ontologies [4] and the potential usage of digital twins [5].

The current paper will express the project approach as well as details about the feasibility tests and demonstrator for further development of the "Hyperconnected Ecosystem for Industrial Networks" as well as initial industrial feedbacks. The next chapter gives a brief overview of the state of the art. It was analyzed at the beginning of the project, but also further developed during the project period due to new emerging technologies such as chatGPT and industrial network design approaches. This is followed by a motivation chapter that expresses the demand for data accessibility, which is addressed in the next chapter of the project approach. The current status of the implementation approach is given by an demonstrator or show case illustrating the use of the project results. Finally, an initial evaluation of the results is provided.

2 State of the Art

Both in research and in industry, there are approaches that pursue similar goals. In terms of industry, one of the most similar services is ScoutBee's search and partner selection approach [6]. They provide a valuable service for very large organizations but they also work on a higher degree of automatization of the search and selection strategies. It is still an open question how far these strategies can be atomized and therefore be available for a wider range of organizations including also small and medium size companies.

In terms of research current activities in projects such as GAIAX [7], BASYS [8], CATENA-X [9] has been considered especially in terms of data and interface related options like Eclipse Dataspace Connector (EDC) [10], OPC-UA [11]. The core of CATENA-X is very close to the objectives of the "Hyperconnected Ecosystem for Industrial Networks" such as easy, interoperable, independent of platforms and ecosystems, decentralized. It has with EDC a technology to interconnect data sources.

A selection of different technologies for the realization of the communication were investigated and partly tested by the creation of prototypes. Feasibility studies were performed using BASYx [12] and the use of OPC-UA as well as concepts for the asset administration shell (AAS) [13]. BASIYx is an Eclipse based development environment developed within the BASYS project and representing a potential implementation of an AAS. Also, OPC-UA has been tested building prototypes of the partner matching. It was followed by a comparison made with CATENA-X, particularly with regard to the EDC.

The results were used to develop services, in particular the Matcher service described later, and to provide the interface of the IoT Edge connection. The data management keeps still a challenge within and across industrial partners. Platforms and clouds. We checked terminologies as well as ontology approaches like terminology e.g. ECLASS [14], product model e.g. STEP [15], master data quality e.g. ISO8000 [16] and ontology frameworks to provide a consolidated ontology set [17]. Main parts of this analysis have been already published in the paper and presentation "Towards Standardization of Ontologies in Research and Industry" [4].

A further upcoming related innovation is the use of AI like chatbots for partner findings and selection. Initial tests with chatGPT provide first results but very depending on the questions and without partner evaluations. However, this might be added in later work via an applications build on chatbots. In the feasibility checks and demonstrator, we use SpaCy [18] for text analysis together with a scraper for analysis of different web content.

3 Motivation and Approach

Whether we are talking about Industry 4.0, 5.0, devices paying attention to human emotions, smart factories or IoT, it simply won't work without an information baseline. Master data, transaction data and various data sources are needed to feed the related IT applications.

Data usually needs to be transferred to different systems and platforms. This requires interfaces between different data sources or manual operations. Within an organization, concepts such as interface management, enterprise service buses, data lakes or an enterprise-centric information model partially considered to create single entry points or clear rules for data management. From experiences in industry this is still implemented in the digital transformation process which requests a higher degree on the organization of data and data sources. Therefore, also the opportunity to make data available within their web presents increases.

In a network of business partners, it requires data concepts across platform and cloud infrastructures. An idea developed within the hyper connected ecosystem for industry is the change from pushing data to different platforms considering different formats and understandings to pulling data form the web presents of an organization. In an initial attempt just the existing and available company data are used via fetching the data from the web. After initial successful tests also specific and critical data are demanded. This required an enrichment of the company web presents with secure sections. Here also data about machinery or order states were provided. The security of the data against unauthorized access is defined via so-called trust circles and realized in the prototype as access rights to data [3]. The access rights are defined by the partner who provides the data.

Each partner within a circle of trust shares access rights with other partners in the circle. Of course, the level of openness can be aligned individual. This allows the automatic fetching of specific detailed data from each of the partners in this trust cycle. In the demonstrator this is just given by access rights to the specific areas of the web presents of the partner.

A major challenge is the provision and availability of information without losing track of the different platforms. This is true for individuals as well as for companies in particular. We approach the topic from the other side - in contrast to the provision of data in different infrastructures, the data is provided by individual companies or persons for collection by services that collect this data and forward it for further processing. The protocol can be designed in such a way that each transaction is registered. In addition, only released data can be accessed by a partner via access rights. However, a specific platform is not required. The principle is similar to the semantic web approach of the w3c community. The CATENA-X project addresses a similar decentralized data management by the following statement: "participation in a data room are each on the side of the partners" (https://catena-x.net/en/offers/edc-the-central-component).

In terms of the "Hyperconnected Ecosystem for Industrial Networks" information provision is less formal because of the use of related text analysis services and web bot capabilities. Effectively we defined a concept of services to form an ecosystem for decentral data provision, search and collection of data on demand, generic matching on the data and provision to the production process. This includes static data as well as dynamic data like the status of equipment or an order status within production. The ontology can be flexible configured related to the demand of a request. This was required because within the project concerning hyper connected ecosystem we intended to keep the scope open and do not focus on one application area. Other existing platforms in this direction keeps usually a specific focus and therefore also based on a specific ontology.

4 Project Approach

At the beginning about 3 years ago, the question was "How to allow the accessibility of required information on demand everywhere and independent from a specific platform or cloud infrastructure for every partner or company within a business network". This has been addressed by an initial reference model after consultations and workshops with industrial companies (small and big). At this stage, reflections were made on social network infrastructures, because although these networks are quite similar, more attention needs to be paid to security and handling requests from industry in relation to business services such as supporting the creation and execution of value networks and the bundling of service offerings.

The small enterprises involved belong to industrial networks in Berlin. The requirements developed in workshops with the partners of these networks were transformed into a set of services divided into basic and business services.

The project work was guarded by an analysis of existing approaches from state of the art in companion with feasibility studies. Related to the different approaches and the requirements from small and medium size companies a major demand for acceptability was the effort to participate in the future ecosystem.

This added to the project approach the identification and automatic fetching of the required information instead of entering the partner information in the next platform. This also contributes to the flexibility in terms of scoping because the possible differences in products and service definition are now managed by configuration of data delivery services. The description of a shaft for electrical machines, for example, differs considerably from the properties of an electrical circuit board. We had both in the project to create a broader area of application. Therefore, it was difficult to develop a common ontology. Instead, the ontology should simply be imported as a kind of configuration for the different services and information stores. Related to this demand, we have defined a profile service that can be adapted to a specific ontology.

To check the feasibility of the approach and later to create show cases. The following components were developed for a first version of the "Hyperconnected Ecosystem for industrial networks" in the form of services:

- A profile service based on a modelling engine for the flexible mapping of company, product and service profile content. It provides a flexible definition of partner profiles in terms of product, services and its capability descriptions.
- A scraper for filling the company profile structure with data by fetching it from the web. A simple synonym mechanism is used in the profiles to also consider alternative designations of characteristics. In addition, current status data can be transferred to the profile via this scraper by considering the partner URL and if available the access rights.

- A matcher to search for partners via the profiles has been developed and implemented as a service. The service has a Rest API and can be accessed via the web. The target is to correlate the demands of customer processes with the suppliers.
- Since the demonstrator requires an MQTT connection for the flexible exchange via Pub/Sub, another service was created that translates the data from the MQTT protocol into a Rest protocol.
- The entire process is created, managed and executed in a open-source process management system.
- A network service has been developed to create and manage supply chains in the Hyperconnected Ecosystem and the necessary assets for data exchange.
- An IoT connector between equipment and the company web presents has been build by an industry partner to express the connection between the internal data and the web.

The services can be extended or replaced by other services as needed. The system is thus a network of different services that can be used flexibly, including the profiles that are implemented in the demonstrator. The feasibility was demonstrated by test examples with industrial partners and also proven with the structure of the demonstrator. For example, climate data or availability data can be collected by the scraper via a calendar function and made available in the profile data.

The demonstration and proof of feasibility of the cloud and service architectures defined in the project is shown in a demonstrator environment consisting of decentralized distributed applications. The communication between the partners is tested along typical application workflows. As shown in Fig. 1, these are the distributed applications of the different apps described before. In the architecture MQTT as well as REST protocols are used in combination with JSON descriptions of the content.

The scraper can either update data directly via specified URLs and corresponding access rights in the profiles (mode 2) or also identify other possible partners on the Internet in a first mode.

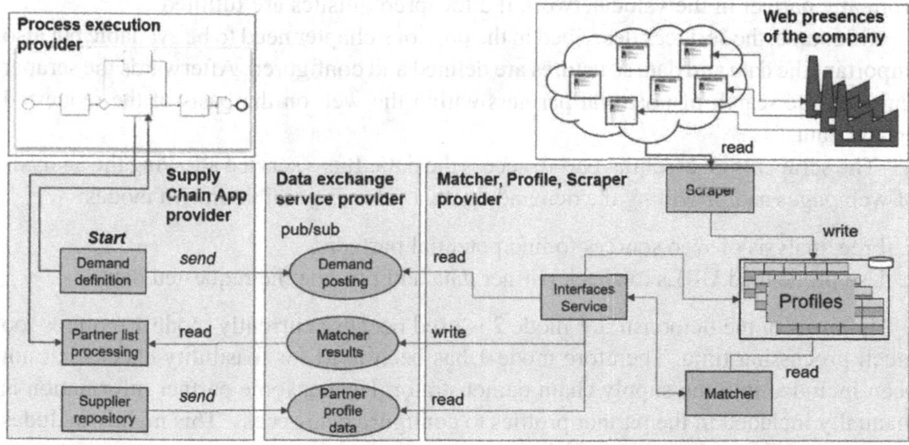

Fig. 1. Communication between different providers across platforms using pub/sub.

The services offered here are not tied to a specific platform or cloud. However, it has been shown that the connection of services that communicate directly with each other requires an exchange standard. This should be as generic as possible and independent of the exchanged data. In the future, this format can replace the proprietary JSON format, which is optionally used via MQTT and Rest. OPC-UA and AAS (Asset Administration Shell) were investigated as part of the project. However, due to time constraints, they could not be fully implemented in the demonstrator. There is potential here for future work and the development of further services.

Another need for development is the expansion of profile data, which is also offered as a service in the Demonstrator. Services can be created here that cover specific areas such as electrical systems, electronic components, etc. In the demonstrator, according to the project partners, we have concentrated on shafts for electrical machines and circuit boards.

Legal issues (e.g. contract law, supply chain regulations) and possible cyber-attacks were excluded from the research project. These must be ensured in an industrial implementation along with points of robustness of the networked services and their protection against cyber-attacks and data loss.

The different services are used for feasibility analyses and first tests with end users. Afterwards they are combined into a demonstration of the potential capabilities of an initial core of the hyperconnected ecosystem. In the following chapters, we will present briefly the demonstrator to give an insight into the services in order to demonstrate the feasibility of the interaction of the services.

5 Show Case and Demonstrator

The show case relates to a realization of a supply chain within the "Hyperconnected Ecosystem for industrial networks". In the project it has been selected as a typical example of a group of companies working together. The structure of the demonstrator illustrates that cross-company access to data across different data sources is possible from any partner in the value network if a few prerequisites are fulfilled.

Of course, the services described in the previous chapter need to be available but also important the data and data structures are defined and configured. Afterwards the scraper can start the search of potential partners within the web on the basis of the requested profile data.

The scraper is an essential part to access the data. It is a service allowing the analysis of web pages and providing the demanding data. This is possible in two modes:

1. Free analysis of web sources to find potential partners,
2. Use predefined URLs to check partner data and provide the requested data.

In terms of the demonstrator mode 2 is used because currently mode 1 requires too much processing time. Therefore mode 1 has been used for feasibility checks but not been included into the supply chain demonstrator. Hence, some partner information is manually included in the partner profiles to configure data access. This mainly includes the partner URL and the name of the partner.

Subsequently, further information can be pulled from the partner websites. For the future, it is planned to also enable mode 1, as searching for partners even in a manual way is quite time-consuming.

After this step, freely available data has been transferred to the profiles. To obtain more detailed data, the access rights must be observed. A partner belongs at least to a corresponding circle of trust and thus has the necessary access rights. In the case of the demonstrator, it is the access rights to the climate cabinet data that are used by the scraper and encrypted in the profile data.

This enables the desired exchange of partner data, their products and services as well as other offers, e.g. free resource capacities such as a climate cabinet in our example. The data is both static information and dynamic status information such as the current temperature or the occupancy of resources. It can also be data about the progress of work or the quality of orders and products.

The approach covers a very wide range of topics, each with its own terminology and ontology. Therefore, the terminology needed in each case be defined via profiles of the potential partners for the respective products or services. These profiles are preferably filled by the respective web presences of the potential providers. Provider data are for example descriptions of products, services and delivery conditions, etc. Detailed information of a digital twin of the partner or the corresponding products can also be used (see, Fig. 2).

The initial terminology used in the demonstrator has been derived mainly from two product scopes as well as from partner information and service definitions. On a generic level we take the term "capability" to describe product and service specifics which is enriched with synonyms to allow also a free search within the internet.

The scraper works best on structures like tables and formatted text. It can also run on free text but the results are more accurate if the data is given in table form.

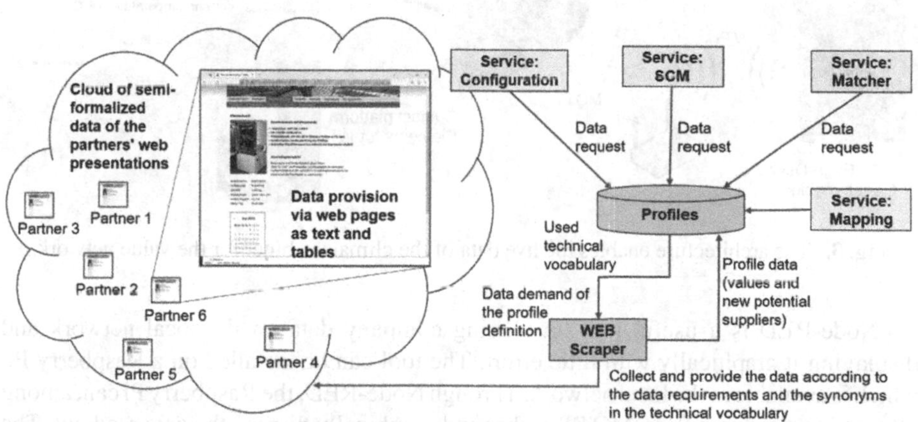

Fig. 2. Use of partner data from the web.

For the demonstrator a project partner (a small supplier company) has provided a climate cabinet with state data on the Internet. The climate cabinet can be booked as a service. To transfer the data of the climate cabinet to the web the following edge device has been provided by the industry partner.

The company data can in fact be transmitted to various online portals. One possibility is to transmit the data from the edge device directly to the company website by means of an http request. This request is evaluated on the website and the data is displayed on a page that is only accessible to logged-in users.

We have used this method to display the current data of our climate cabinet (status and temperature) on companies' webpage. The data is transferred in a simple comma-separated values (CSV) format. In our case it looks like this: Status; Temperature; (for example: ON; 25.45;).

Another possibility is to transfer the company data from the edge device to an MQTT broker via the MQTT publish command. The MQTT broker could, for example, be hosted by a third-party provider or set up directly on the server of the company website. With the help of a script on the server of the corporate website (for example in Node.js or PHP), the data can be read from the MQTT broker and displayed on the website. In this case, we transfer the data in JSON format. Each sensor is a separate object and contains all the data to be transmitted. An example is the temperature for a thermocouple on the demonstrator (see Fig. 3).

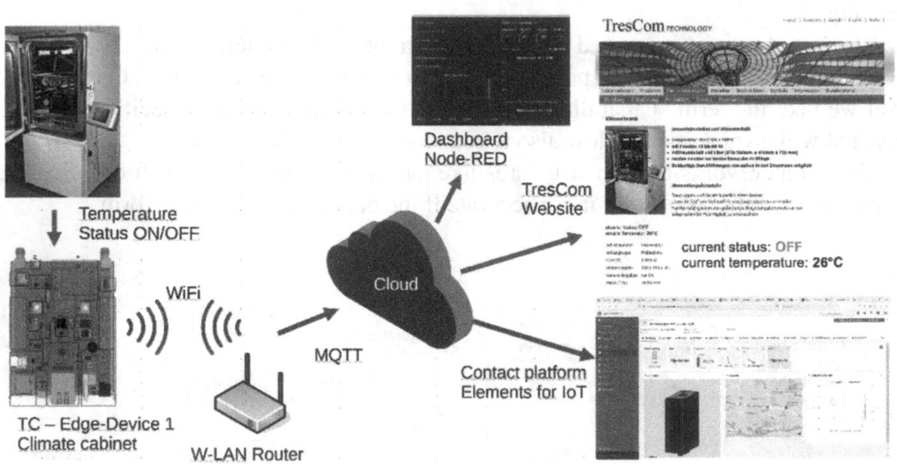

Fig. 3. The architecture enables the live data of the climate cabinet for the value network.

Node-RED is a useful tool for sharing company data on the local network and displaying it graphically with little effort. The tool can be installed on a Raspberry Pi, which is available in the local network. Through Node-RED, the Raspberry Pi can, among other things, connect to an MQTT broker and graphically display the data read out. The tool can also evaluate the data from an http request. Among other things, Node-RED also supports the TCP, UDP, WebSocket and BLE protocols.

Corporate data can be configured for different tasks. One possibility is to display the data on a website or in various other applications. Here, the data is displayed in a readable way for a user and can be used for resource planning, for example. A case is the availability of a climate cabinet and possible logs for the run times that a user has booked.

Another option for displaying data is the digital twin, where the current live data of the process being monitored is displayed. A third way to use the data is machine to machine (M2M) communication. Here, the edge device not only takes over pure monitoring tasks, but can also intervene in processes under certain circumstances. This can happen when defined limit values for a sub-process are reached and the edge device interrupts the process to avoid dangerous situations. Or another machine / process evaluates the incoming data and causes the edge device to switch off certain processes. Here, partners in the network such as the client of the service can intervene and stop the process if it could be dangerous for the test.

Furthermore, the edge device offers the possibility to integrate additional sensors that do not have their own connection to the internet into an existing system. Additional sensors can, for example, communicate with the edge device via bluetooth and send their own data away.

Various protocols such as HTTP, MQTT, OPC-UA, CoAP or others can be made available for the transport of data. This simplifies the integration into already existing systems. The data format of the user data can be adapted to the corresponding protocol. It is possible to transmit data in JSON or CSV format.

Now we have the data structures, the access to the company data and the fetching of the data via the scraper service. In the next step it is used to establish the supply chain via supply chain management component and workflow system. For this purpose, requirements must be defined for each process step that describe the goal of the process step. In the demonstrator, this is stored as follows: The entire process is created, managed and executed in the open source process management system.

Using MQTT, the process steps are sent to the supply chain app, where each step is supplemented with further requirements. Now a "matching" can take place for each process step, which compares the stored requirements with the profile data. For this purpose, the process step enriched with technical and non-technical requirements is published via MQTT and received and further processed by the matcher service. As a result, a list of suppliers that can perform this step is returned for each process step. A request for the process step is then sent to the relevant suppliers as a possible order. They can decide whether they want to process the order. After that, the project manager still has to agree to an offer before a supplier for a step is determined.

This process repeats itself for all process steps in the supply chain and can also be repeated at runtime if a supplier suddenly drops out due to delivery problems, for example. In this way, an automated and efficient formation of a partner network that takes over the handling of a supply chain is possible.

6 Evaluation, Conclusion and Next Steps

The analysis of the networking in the Hyperconnected Ecosystem has uncovered some potentials that become visible through an increase in efficiency and/or a faster processing / response time. Savings of resources, utilization of capacities and further synergies between the companies improve the competitiveness at the production.

The network, which is set up as a model and examined with various actors, has shown valuable insights into partnership cooperation and feasibility. The networking of companies and employees could be implemented quite quickly through a trusting relationship with each other. The technical possibilities of data exchange are available in principle and could be sufficiently demonstrated and tested in an exemplary manner.

Another promising approach is the use of technologies such as the Internet of Things (IoT), blockchain and artificial intelligence (AI). The IoT can help collect real-time data from sensors on manufacturing machines and products to monitor the quality and condition of goods like presented with the edge device. In the future, this will depend on how the challenges of security and desired data transparency on the network are further addressed.

Blockchain technology can ensure transparency and security in supply chain transactions. However, there are currently still some challenges to overcome for practical and secure use especially in terms of complexity and costs.

AI can help to predict trends and demand in the future and thus minimize the risk of over- or underproduction. This technology has not yet been considered in the course of the project. However, AI is already helping to analyze the web pages and find information about the partners. Industrial-Strength Natural Language Processing" SpaCy is used for this purpose.

In production, the continuous use of product and process data in the network to increase efficiency and the sustainable availability of the product will be essential in the future. The networking of manufacturing partners and the provision of information and data in the digital twin over the entire product life cycle form the basis for new, targeted services and the maintenance of competitiveness.

With IoT solutions (edge device), live data can be made available. The status and temperature of the climatic chamber as well as the current temperature and vibration data of the electric drives in the testbed of the feed the digital product twin as well as the availability of the resource in the Hyperconnected Ecosystem. However, the real-time capability is somewhat limited and should not be used for safety-relevant evaluation. These evaluations may have to take place in the upstream edge device. IoT solutions help to accelerate and optimize downstream services for the entire manufacturing network as assistance systems and data loggers.

A need for development is the expansion of profile data, which is also offered as a service in the demonstrator. Here, services can be created that cover specific areas such as electrical systems, electronic components, etc. In the demonstrator, we have concentrated on shafts and circuit boards in accordance with the project goals. Legal issues (e.g. contract law, supply chain regulations) and possible cyber-attacks were excluded from the research project. These must be ensured in an industrial implementation just as much as points of robustness of the networked services and their protection against cyber-attacks and data loss.

We will continue to work on these topics and investigate the possibilities of uses in terms of business models especially related to existing enterprise networks.

Acknowledgement. Foundations of the described work has been developed in the scope of a project of the Werner von Siemens Centre (https://wvsc.berlin/) WvSC.EA "Electric motors 2.0" supported by the European Regional Development Fund (EFRE).

References

1. Born, M., et al.: ATHENA framework for cross-organizational business processes. In: Nitto, A.S., Traverso, P., Zwegers, A. (eds.) At Your Service: Service-Oriented Computing From an EU Perspective. Page MIT Press Series on Information Systems, MIT, Press (2009)
2. Jaekel, F.-W., Zelm, M., Chen, D.: Service modelling language applied for hyper connected ecosystem. In: Proceedings of the 2nd International Conference on Innovative Intelligent Industrial Production and Logistics (IN4PL 2021), pp. 209–215. SCITEPRESS – Science and Technology Publications, Lda (2021)
3. Jäkel, F.-W., Gering, P., Knothe, T.: Hyperconnected Ecosystems für industrielle Netzwerke. Zeitschrift für wirtschaftlichen Fabrikbetrieb **116**(12), 872–876 (2021). https://doi.org/10.1515/zwf-2021-0212
4. Jäkel, F.-W., Young, B., Zelm, M.: Towards standardization of ontologies in research and industry. In: AFIN 2022: The Fourteenth International Conference on Advances in Future Internet. IARIA (2022). ISBN: 978-1-68558-008-79
5. Jäkel, F.-W., Gering, P., Knothe, T.: The use of digital twins to overcome semantic barriers in hyperconnected ecosystems for industry. In: I-ESA Workshops 2022. Martin Zelm, Andrés Boza, Ramona Diana León, Raúl Rodríguez-Rodríguez: Proceedings of Interoperability for Enterprise Systems and Applications Workshops co-located with 11th International Conference on Interoperability for Enterprise Systems and Applications (I-ESA 2022), Valencia, Spain, 23–25 Mar 2022. CEUR Workshop Proceedings 3214, CEUR-WS.org (2022)
6. Scoutbee: https://scoutbee.com/
7. GAIAX: https://www.gaia-x.eu/what-is-gaia-x/data-spaces
8. BASYS4.0: https://www.basys40.de/. Last access 1 Feb 2022
9. CATENA-X: https://catena-x.net/en/. Last access 1 Sep 2023
10. CATENA-X and EDC: https://catena-x.net/de/angebote-standards/edc-die-zentrale-komponente-fuer-die-navigation. Last access 1 Sep 2023
11. OPC-UAL: https://opcfoundation.org/. Viewed on 30 Aug 2021. letzter Zugriff 01 Aug 2021
12. BASYSx: https://www.eclipse.org/basyx/?target. Last access 1 Feb 2022
13. BMWI, Details of the Asset Administration Shell. https://www.plattform-i40.de/IP/Redaktion/EN/Downloads/Publikation/Details_of_the_Asset_Administration_Shell_Part1_V3.html. Last access 1 Feb 2022
14. eCl@ass: https://www.eclass.eu/en/index.html. Last access 1 Feb 2022
15. STEP: https://www.iso.org/standard/59780.html. Last access 1 Sep 2023
16. ISO8000: https://www.iso.org/standard/70095.html. Last access 1 Sep 2023
17. Industrial Ontologies Foundry (IOF): https://www.industrialontologies.org/
18. SpaCy: https://spacy.io/. Last access 1 Feb 2022

Human-Centric Digital Twins: Advancing Safety and Ergonomics in Human-Robot Collaboration

Ben Gaffinet[1,2(✉)], Jana Al Haj Ali[2], Hervé Panetto[2], and Yannick Naudet[1]

[1] Luxembourg Institute of Science and Technology, Belval, Luxembourg
{ben.gaffinet,yannick.naudet}@list.lu
[2] Université of Lorraine, CNRS, CRAN, Nancy, France
{jana.al-haj-ali,herve.panetto}@univ-lorraine.fr

Abstract. Human-Robot Collaboration combines the reliability of robots with human adaptability. It is a prime candidate to respond to the trend of Mass Customization which requires frequent reconfiguration with variable lot sizes. But the close contact between humans and robots creates new safety risks, and ergonomic factors like robot-induced stress need to be considered. Therefore we propose a human-centric Digital Twin framework, where information about the human is stored and processed in a dedicated Digital Twin and can be transmitted to the robot's Digital Twin for human-aware adaptations. We envision and briefly discuss three possible applications. Our framework has the potential to advance collaborative robotics but inherits technical challenges that come with Digital Twin based approaches and human modelling.

Keywords: Human-Robot collaboration · Human digital twin · Cognitive digital twin · Human-Centric system

1 Introduction

Human-centric systems are designed following the human centered design paradigm which focuses on people's needs first [12]. Important pillars of the design philosophy are, among others, usability, accessibility, ethical considerations and user empowerment. The paradigm has been applied successfully to develop, for example, healthcare information systems, interfaces for user electronics or Smart Homes, especially for elderly care. Human-centric systems are not only implemented to support consumers or patients, but also workers in an industrial context. In manufacturing, the collaboration between humans and robots can benefit from human-centric design approaches.

Where appropriate, industry has adopted automation to enabled efficient and cost-effective production of large lot sizes, keeping unit cost down. But the high upfront cost of fully automated systems are prohibitive for small production

S. Terzi et al. (Eds.): IN4PL 2023, CCIS 1886, pp. 380–397, 2023.
https://doi.org/10.1007/978-3-031-49339-3_24

runs. Additionally it is costly to change the configuration of a fully automated production line, leading to limited flexibility when it comes to customizing a product for a customer segment or an individual's specific demands. As a polar opposite manual labor is highly flexible and, provided the right training and instructions, can customize products quickly to respond to demand, but at a high unit cost. Therefore a compromise between cost-effectiveness and flexibility is desirable for products that should be highly customizable with variable lot sizes [41]. A prime candidate to achieve this is Human-Robot-Collaboration (HRC) (see Fig. 1) which combines the repeatability, accuracy and strength of robots with the flexibility and versatility of humans.

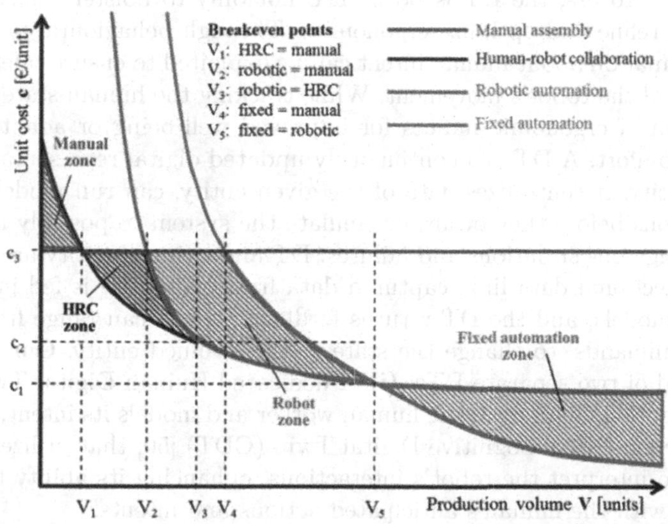

Fig. 1. Economic viability of HRC as presented in [45]. The blue zone represents the production volumes for which HRC provides the best unit cost and thus is economically viable. (Color figure online)

Interactions between humans and robots have evolved over time, starting with mere coexistence in the same physical space with completely independent operations. Eventually the interactions between humans and machines deepened, Wang et al. [64] distinguished between Coexistence, Interaction, Cooperation and Collaboration between Humans and Robots. For the remainder of this paper we exclusively focus on Human-Robot-Collaboration, which means that both actors are sharing the same workspace, resources and tasks while direct physical contact is allowed.

With the close contact between robots and humans comes a non-negligible risk of injury which motivates extensive research into robot safety methods and collision avoidance in particular. Real-time situational awareness is a common challenge and required to estimate distances or distinguish voluntary from accidental contact. Robots need to be more flexible and adaptable in their programming to work with the uncertainty that human behaviour introduces into the system. Nonetheless successful HRC implementations can improve ergonomics [39] by minimizing mental and physical fatigue by assigning repetitive and heavy lifting tasks to the robot. But poorly implemented systems can induce stress in the human worker and erode trust in the machine thus there is a need to track the human state and ergonomic metrics for good collaboration.

In the field of system control, safety has always been a major concern for industrial setups. Recognizing this, the Digital Twin (DT) has been identified as a practical and efficient solution. Given its potential, we are inclined to propose a framework that integrates DT. By emphasizing human interaction and involvement in the process, the DT is positioned not only to bolster safety measures but also to refine and optimize ergonomics. Through behavioural models additional information about human intent can be exploited to ensure safety through adaptation of the robot's movement. While tracking the human state allows the computation of ergonomic indices for improved well-being or adapt operation speed for comfort. A DT is a continuously updated digital representation of the twinned entity. It centralizes data of the given entity, can run models to simulate situations before they occur, or emulate the system to possibly mitigate or prevent dangerous situations and failures. DT and twinned entity are connected via a bi-directional data link; captured data from the entity is fed into the DT to update models; and the DT returns feedback, which can range from suggestions to commands, to change the state of the twinned entity. Our framework is composed of two separate DTs; **(i)** A dedicated Human Digital Twin (HDT) [49] which gathers data from the human worker and models its intent, behaviour and well being; **(ii)** A Cognitive Digital Twin (CDT) [50] that utilizes cognitive functions to interpret the robot's interactions, enhancing its ability to align its operations with the human's anticipated actions and intents.

The remainder of the paper is structured as follows; Sect. 2 presents the state of the art for assembly tasks in HRC work cells with a special focus on the limitations and challenges in safety and ergonomics; in Sect. 3 we present a DT based approach to address perceived gaps in the state of the art; Finally in Sect. 4 we conclude and provide research directions.

2 State of the Art

Multiple core challenges of HRC are succinctly expressed by Wang et al. [64]: *"An essential aspect of HRC is how to cope with human ergonomics, process time, emotions and reaction during collaboration, and safety aspects."*

While a wide array of challenges exist in HRC we choose to focus on, and explore, two dimensions: **safety & ergonomics**. Both lead back to problems with real-time situational awareness and integrating information about the human state and behaviour. Therefore human-centered approaches are particularly applicable to address these challenges. It was in this context that the notion of DT was introduced. DTs offer a precise digital replica of a real system or process, enabling detailed simulations and analysis. These tools are proving essential in tackling and solving the challenges of HRC. In what follows, we explore in depth the applications and implications of DTs in this context.

2.1 Safety

The merits of HRC are discussed in [33] where Kruger et al. make the case for how robot reliability and human adaptability can enable a new generation of assembly processes. Safety becomes a prime concern as soon as the physical separation between human workers and industrial robots is no longer guaranteed. HRC, by definition, allows physical contact between human workers and robots making physical separation inherently impossible.

In the industrial sector, many robots operate as Cyber-Physical Systems (CPS), optimized for performance and the completion of specific tasks. Faced with the rapid evolution of HRC, Yilma et al. [67] introduced an innovative approach to Industry 4.0, based on the Cyber-Physical-Social Systems (CPSS) paradigm. While human aspects and subtleties are frequently omitted from traditional CPS-centric models, the CPSS methodology aims to resolve this omission. It aims to strengthen collaboration while guaranteeing security. Thanks to artificial intelligence, CPSS can assimilate and interpret human behaviors, making robots, especially those based on CPS, more effective collaborative allies.

In [63,64] the causes for HRC accidents are organized in three categories; Engineering failures, human errors, and poor environmental conditions. For robotics and machinery in general, engineering failures are addressed in the design phase and guidance is provided in ISO 13855 [28]. The unavoidable physical contact between robots and humans in HRC setups required an adaptation of standards, which lead to ISO/PDTS 15066 [29]. It provides valuable guidance on risk assessment, safety features, workspace design as well as task and process design. Overall safety in robotics is a well researched subject, nonetheless the challenging context of HRC requires further investigation on how to enable setups that can operate at relatively high efficiency and speed without compromising safety.

Research in HRC safety can be categorized into three categories; **(i)** understanding injury mechanisms and related standards; **(ii)** limiting the severity of an impact; **(iii)** active collision avoidance. In the first category, Haddadin et al. [22–24] made major contributions with their work on injury mechanisms of collisions that might occur during HRC task execution. Further research from Haddadin et al. [21] establishes that safety is guaranteed for robot velocities below 2.7 m/s and in [25] the link between mass, velocity, impact geometry and resulting injury is described in detail. Instead of limiting operational velocity, Laffranchi et al. [36] proposed to regulate the energy of the system instead. Earlier research in [66] analyses pain tolerance of humans and establishes an early method to reduce robot velocity upon impact, which allows the human operator to reflexively withdraw and avoid serious injuries and pain. More recent research introduces additional constraints to the control algorithms based on newly introduced safety indicators [46]. Depending on the distance between robot and human operator the kinetic and potential energy in the system is reduced to limit the energy that could be dissipated in the event of a collision.

Detecting collisions and reacting appropriately represents a second major category of research in HRC safety. Unmitigated movement of a robot after an unwanted collision can lead to severe pain and injury. As contact between robot and human is expected in HRC it is not appropriate to stop operations as soon as any physical contact occurs, instead more subtle methods are required. On the hardware level the addition of joint torque sensors enabled a new set of safety features. Tonietti et al. [61] adjusts the stiffness of actuation to inherently guarantee safety. Park et al. [55] developed a passive safety mechanism through non-linear stiffness. During normal operations high stiffness is maintained, but upon impact, that exceeds a set threshold force, the stiffness drops quickly. In contrast Geravand et al. [20] base their control architecture on the motor currents and joint velocity without the need of additional torque sensors. Kokkalis et al. [30] compare provided motor currents with the expected current needed for the planned trajectory to limit forces during contact. In a similar approach [48] uses reference torque and actual torque to the same end, while [40] use Neural Networks to detect torque disturbances. A last set of approaches uses additional external sensors, such as optical cameras [15,19,34] or depth sensors [10,17] to detect collisions.

Avoiding collisions altogether is approached from different angles by researchers. A large swath of research uses on or the combination of detection systems such as, time of flight cameras (or other depth sensors) [1,3,18] or optical [60] cameras. Creating 3D models of the robot, environment and/or human worker is sometimes used in addition to the chosen sensing systems [47,65] to enable better distance estimations. Some approaches put the human worker at the center of their investigation by tracking their movement, either with wearables or external cameras to ultimately include human behaviour [69] as a parameter for robot adaptation [37]. Augustsson et al. establish safety zones [6] based on which the robot can adapt when a human enters the zone. In this case the data about the human is communicated to the robot for adaptations. Efficient real-time communication is generally a challenge and includes communicating the human position to the robot as well as changes in assembly order or settings to the human [7].

Decades of Robotics safety research have lead to hardware adaptions, and methods that substantially reduce the risk of severe injuries. Force and speed limits, alongside collision detection and appropriate reactions upon impact mitigate both pain and injury severity. But, we believe that further research is desirable in the field of collision avoidance. Increased situational awareness, including the internal state of the human operator (e.g. stress, behavioural patterns), could enable less restrictive and more dynamic speed adaptations and enable increased efficiency of HRC work cells. In Sect. 3 we introduce a DT based approach to address the perceived limitations of traditional setups.

2.2 Ergonomics

In HRC setups robots should support the human worker to fulfill the defined task as a human-robot team and adapt their own behaviour to make the human comfortable, improve ergonomics performance and keep task completion time low [64]. Ergonomics encompasses not only physical stress, which can be induced by e.g. lifting heavy loads, but also mental stress. Both mental underload, from monotonous tasks, and overload, typically from overstraining or high pace, need to be addressed in HRC research.

A necessary component of HRC is that the human team member accepts to work with the robot. Poorly adapted robot movement can induce stress, erode trust and ultimately lead the the loss of propensity to work with the robot. Trust is a major parameter for successful HRC setups and has been studied extensively by Hancock et al. [26]. The dominant factor that can erode trust is the performance of the human-robot team, while environmental and human factors have a more limited impact. The distance between human and robot alongside the robot's movement speed has a direct impact on induced stress [4]. The more general impact of robot movement on the human affective state has been investigated in [35]. Adapting the robot's movement by designing human-aware systems is a promising approach that has found success in the field.

Research addressed the problems through better motion planning based on human-aware systems. The movement needs to be predictable, and perceived as safe. Multiple paper seek to improve motion planning and task allocation by including information about the human worker; such as the human's goals [56], mental model [52], perception of robot movement [13,54], next subtask [27] or intended motion [62].

Many promising approaches to improve fluency of HRC systems and ergonomics rely on understanding the human worker's behaviour and state better. In Sect. 3 we propose the use of HDT to gather human worker data and relevant models for better adaptive systems.

2.3 Digital Twins

Safety, a long-underestimated major concern in robotics research, has become a central preoccupation as intelligent collaborative robots, commonly known as cobots, are increasingly integrated into various industries. These cobots are equipped with sensors that enable them to detect and react to their environment, guaranteeing safe physical interactions with humans. These sensors not only detect the presence of humans and potential obstacles, but also gather complex data on cobot movements and forces, such as joint position and compliance monitoring. Faced with this safety challenge, it is imperative to develop advanced simulation models known as digital twins (DT). These are defined as, "*A set of adaptive models that emulate the behaviour of a physical system in a virtual system getting real time data to update itself along its life cycle. The digital twin replicates the physical system to predict failures and opportunities for changing, to prescribe real time actions for optimizing and/or mitigating unexpected events observing and evaluating the operating profile system*" [58]. These DT enable scenarios to be recreated [57] and tested virtually [32]. This data-driven approach ensures that cobots can interact safely with humans, marking a significant advance in automation within the manufacturing sector. Safety in HRC setups is further delved into with a study [11], where a mixed-reality approach is proposed to enhance safety. This method employs sensors to measure the real-time safety distance between humans and cobots. Further enhancing the capabilities of DT, Droder [14] introduces a machine learning method for industrial cobots to avoid obstacles and people, using the nearest neighbor approach for trajectory planning and neural networks for detection.

With the aim of allowing DTs in virtual reality to guide the safe implementation of human-robot collaboration strategies in future factories, Oyekan [53] established a DT workshop to study human responses to both predictable and unpredictable cobot motions. The findings indicated that real-world human reactions to robotic behaviors were consistent with those observed in the DT virtual environment. It is essential to create an accurate and consistent DT model that captures the physical components and their interactions. With this in mind, a quadruple DT model has been suggested [42], encompassing separate models for the cobot, the individual, the collaborative framework, and their interrelationships.

In the field of ergonomics, the introduction of Digital Human (DH) technology to the DT-controlled HRC represents a significant step forward, emphasizing human centricity in a production context. This system [44] captures and simulates operator movements and physical constraints in real time, providing a precise ergonomic assessment platform. It is structured around three integrated modules: the first is a virtualized robotics module offering direct, real-time control of the PLC; the second is a DH module specifically dedicated to the analysis and simulation of operator actions; and finally, a production management module which guarantees adapted planning taking ergonomic criteria into account.

The DT has been employed in the design and reconfiguration of assembly systems. Kousi et al. [31] has modeled production parameters at different levels and updates them dynamically using data from 2D-3D sensors, combining geometry and semantics to obtain an overview of the production process.

DT functions, like monitoring, prediction and optimization, offer effective strategies for HRC assembly. Malik's [43] study introduces a DT framework aimed at optimizing the design, construction, and control of human-machine assembly collaborations. Through computer simulations, a constantly updated digital model of the collaborative environment is maintained, ensuring timely improvements and mirroring the physical setup. Similarly, Bilberg's [8] research focuses on an object-oriented simulation of a flexible assembly cell, integrated with a cobot to work alongside humans. Beyond traditional virtual models, this DT emphasizes real-time control, dynamic task allocation between the cobot and human, and adaptive cobot programming based on the task sequencing.

DT, while useful in a variety of fields, have certain limitations when applied to HRC. One major limitation is their limited ability to anticipate and adapt to unpredictable human behavior in dynamic work environments. In addition, DT may struggle to model safety accurately enough to ensure safe interactions between cobots and human workers. This highlights the need for a better understanding of the human processes at the core of these interactions. The notion of cognition focuses primarily on knowledge and understanding [50]. It encompasses the processes by which sensory inputs are transformed, stored, and used [51], including aspects such as attention, reasoning, learning, memory, perception, problem solving, and knowledge representation, among others [2].

In an HRC context, where safety and ergonomics are major concerns, it becomes clear that advanced cognitive capabilities are required. This is where the Cognitive Digital Twin (CDT) comes in, which is "*a digital representation of a physical system that is augmented with certain cognitive capabilities and support to execute autonomous activities; comprises a set of semantically interlinked digital models related to different lifecycle phases of the physical system including its subsystems and components; and evolves continuously with the physical system across the entire lifecycle*" [70]. The CDT possesses knowledge manipulation and problem-solving abilities. These cognitive capabilities include detection, reasoning, and self-learning, enabling continuous and proactive adaptation.

Research such as that conducted by Shi et al. [59] on a CDT framework for manufacturing systems with HRC based on 5G communication networks illustrates the increasing importance of CDT in the manufacturing field. The concept of CDT in [68], thus provides the ability to dynamically handle more complex and unpredictable situations through enhanced computational capabilities. As an emerging concept, CDT has not yet been widely implemented and verified in the industry. Most published studies explore the theoretical perspectives of CDT or focus on its vision. Nonetheless, there are ongoing studies and projects targeting its practical feasibility in diverse industry scenarios. Notably, the active EU project COGNITWIN [70] aims to enhance the cognitive capabilities of existing process control systems to enable self-organization and address unpredicted behaviors.

3 Proposed Research

In this section we propose a DT based approach to respond to challenges in HRC safety and ergonomics. We propose an adapted architecture for DTs of agents and discuss their application in the context of HRC. Two functionalities of DTs are of interest, namely emulation and simulation.

3.1 Single Agent Digital Twin

For each physical entity, or more precisely agent, we propose to instantiate a dedicated DT that gathers all the data coming from the twinned entity, and holds all the models describing and acting upon the twinned entity. Additionally the ability to receive data from the environment or other physical entities is required to provide the relevant context for some of the models. Figure 2 depicts the essential elements and their interactions required to build a DT of an agent. *Data* from the *Twinned Agent* is fed to the *Agent Digital Twin* and stored in the *Data Storage* alongside data from the *Environment* that is needed to give required context. *Data* is used by the *Models* to track and predict parameters of the *Twinned Agent*. The result of running a model can be fed back into the *Data Storage* to update relevant parameters or trigger a feedback to the *Twinned Agent*. For cobots the feedback could be a change in operational mode while a human agent can not be directly controlled but only influenced via suggestions. The last element is the *Agent Digital Twin*'s interaction with other agents in the system. Through and *Access Interface* data can be shared between agents and fed to the relevant models to adapt behaviour accordingly. The *Co-Simulation Interface* provides the ability to run simulations of what-if scenarios involving multiple agents. In this case simulated data needs to be provided as both the physical *Environment* and *Twinned Agent* are decoupled for simulation runs.

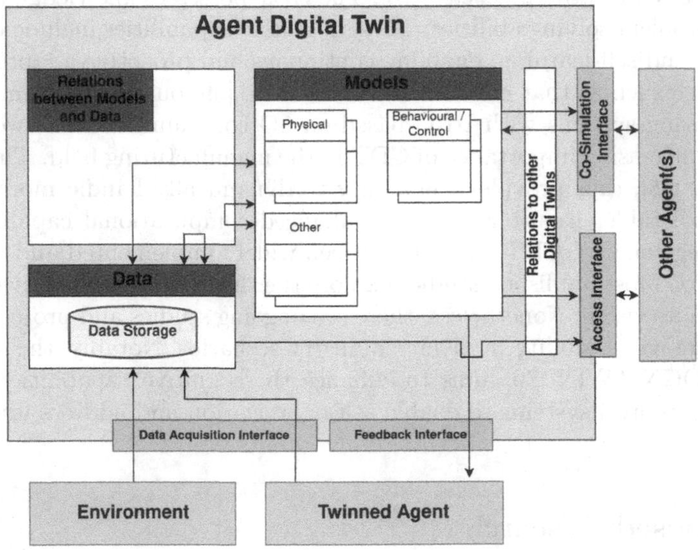

Fig. 2. Digital Twin Architecture for an Agent. Adapted from the Human Digital Twin reference architecture proposed by Löcklin et al. [38]. In the context of HRC the agent is either a human or a robot.

3.2 Digital Twins for Human-Cobot Collaboration Systems

Considering the specific case of an HRC scenario, there will be two DTs; a *Human Digital Twin* and a *Cognitive Digital Twin*, see Fig. 3 for the proposed

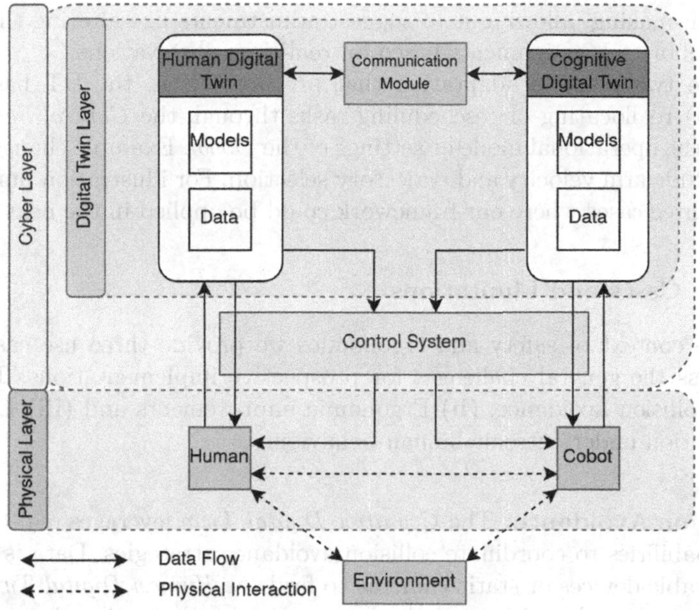

Fig. 3. Digital Twin based approach for HRC systems with one human worker and one Cobot. Dashed lines represent physical interactions while full lines represent data flows.

architecture. The physical layer is composed of a *Human* alongside a *Cobot*. Both agents have physical interactions with each other and the *Environment* itself. Data is gather from both agents to feed into their respective DTs, which follow the previously described architecture from Fig. 2. A *Communication Module* enables the exchange of data between both DTs. Each DT can run models to track the state of the system and send feedback to its twinned entity. Feedback to the *Physical Layer* is managed by a *Control System*, which can reallocate and reschedule tasks dynamically, or change the operational mode of the *Cobot*.

The *Human Digital Twin* gathers data from the human worker, which can include static data (e.g. age, skills, personality) and live data (e.g. biometrics, video, sound). Through models meaningful information, such as ergonomic indices, can be computed, stored and shared with the *Cognitive Digital Twin* and *Control System*. Receiving live information about the state of the human worker is the backbone of human-aware cobot adaptation.

The *Cognitive Digital Twin*, on the other hand, utilizes data received from the *Human Digital Twin*, along with its own data and knowledge models, to perform more advanced analyses. The *Cognitive Digital Twin* harnesses its cognitive functions to perform various tasks. Through perception, it interprets sensory data like facial expressions and voice tone. It employs reasoning to detect patterns and anomalies, drawing from its memory of past experiences. This informs its decision-making, allowing it to suggest adjustments like altering the cobot's parameters or task assignments based on real-time observations.

We see two possible adaptation that are possible in the DT based HRC system; **(i)** reallocating or rescheduling tasks through the *Control System*, **(ii)** changing the operational mode or settings of the *Cobot*. Example changes for the *Cobot* include arm velocity and trajectory selection. For illustration purposes we describe three cases where our framework could be applied in the next Sect. 3.3.

3.3 Use Cases and Limitations

Given the context of safety and ergonomics we provide three use cases below and discuss the general challenges for prospective implementations. The cases are; **(i)** Collision avoidance, **(ii)** Ergonomic improvements and **(iii)** Emulating cobot reaction under extreme human behaviour.

I - Collision Avoidance: The *Cognitive Digital Twin* leverages real-time emulation capabilities to coordinate collision avoidance strategies. Data is gathered from wearable devices or static cameras to feed *the Human Digital Twin*, which calculates estimated positions of the human operator's head and arms. Simultaneously, data concerning the cobot's joint and end effector positions is continuously monitored and shared with the *Cognitive Digital Twin*. The *Communication Module* facilitates data exchange between human and cobot positions, which is then analyzed by a collision avoidance model stored within the *Cognitive Digital Twin*. The advantage is the possibility to connect models from the *Human Digital Twin*, for example a intention model, with the collision avoidance model of the *Cognitive Digital Twin*. The adaptive behaviour can incrementally be enhanced by considering increasingly complex aspects of human behaviour.

II - Ergonomic Improvements: In an analogous fashion information from the human worker can be fed to a dedicated model of the *Cognitive Digital Twin* to adapt the cobot's movement in order to decrease induced stress. To improve the human's comfort not only the movement of the cobot can be adapted but also the allocation of tasks. The *Control System* is kept up to date about the task progress of both agents but can also receive information about the state of the human worker. A threshold based approach could be used to trigger dynamic reallocation of tasks when stress or fatigue increases too much.

III - Emulating Cobot Reactions Under Extreme Human Behaviour: The DT framework can be used to run emulations by decoupling the physical entities from the system and feeding in emulated data. In the context of HRC this opens up the possibility to test the cobot's adaptive response under extreme human behaviours without putting any human at risk of injury. The ability to emulate edge cases becomes especially important if the adaptive behaviour relies on Machine Learning, knowledge-based systems (symbolic AI) or hybrid approaches. Such integrated approaches can show unintended behaviour when encountering edge cases, making emulation vital.

Related Works: Attempts to better account for the human factor in industrial contexts exist. The novelty of the present proposal are the dedicated DTs for each entity with a particular focus on HRC. Ascone et al. [5] consider Human-Machine Systems and propose a holistic framework for DTs of such systems. They argue that humans are an inseparable part and propose capturing human data and building human models. But they consider one single DT for the whole system without having a dedicated DT for each agent. Bousdekis et al. [9] consider a Manufacturing System which includes operators alongside machines and processes. DTs for both the machines and humans are proposed to detect abnormal situations and support the operator's activities. The solution is not focused on HRC but rather on joint decision making between the operator and an AI system. Endo et al. [16] implement a Human Digital Twin to minimize the physical load of a worker that is working alongside a robot. In the use case both the robot and human pick items from boxes and store them in a cart without entering in direct contact. Two DTs a instantiated with a physical load model for the human and progress tracking of the overall process. The solution enables the dynamic reallocation of tasks and successfully decreases the work performed by the human and maximizes the usage of the robot.

Proposed Experimental Validation: In the context of Industry 4.0, where cyber-physical systems play a key role, we propose to apply the framework to a case of human-robot collaboration (HRC). More specifically an assembly task performed jointly by a human and a cobot. We envision a shared workstation where the cobot and human share resources to assemble a specific product, without the need to move away from the workstation. An expected challenge is to reduce the complexity of the human model to a minimal amount of parameters (e.g.: stress or fatigue) while maintaining the ability to meaningfully adapt the cobot's speed and trajectory selection. A second challenge, which is common in DT based approaches, is the requirement for real time operations, thus implementations that rely on computationally expensive methods are not viable. Through a questionnaire it is possible to assess the amount of stress experienced by participants for an adaptive and non-adaptive system. We would judge an implementation as successful if stress is reduced without significantly increasing the overall cycle time.

4 Conclusion and Discussion

We discussed how a human-centric, DT based, approach can be applied to respond to challenges in Human-Robot Collaboration (HRC). We explored, in detail, the state of the art two particular problems; safety & ergonomics. Extensive safety research has established limits to velocity and energy for human safety. Furthermore methods to limit the severity of an unwanted collision are well established. The most challenging approach to safety is avoiding unwanted collisions altogether, which requires excellent situational awareness. Ergonomics research established a link between robot movement and the human's feeling of safety, trust and stress. The human experience and well-being can be improved through adaptive motion planning and dynamic task allocation but requires a good understanding and tracking of the human state.

From the challenges in safety and ergonomics we identified situational awareness to be particularly important for successful HRC implementations. To achieve excellent situational awareness it is necessary to track the human state and account for the behaviour and intent of humans. As an additional benefit ergonomic adjustments could be made using the tracked data about the human worker.

In our discussions on HRC, we have highlighted the growing importance of safety, particularly with the emergence of collaborative robots. These cobots, equipped with advanced sensors, guarantee safe interactions with humans. Having explored the state of the art in the application of DT in HRC, it is clear that DTs play an essential role in simulating and predicting interactions to enhance safety. Digital Human (DH) technology reinforces this vision by faithfully reproducing human movements to provide a complete ergonomic assessment. However, despite the considerable advantages of DHs, they face the challenge of anticipating unpredictable human behavior. This is where the CDT comes in, adding advanced cognitive capabilities to traditional DT. Although CDTs represent a promising advance, their practical implementation remains largely theoretical.

We proposed a DT based framework where each agent has its own dedicated Agent Digital Twin (see Fig. 2). Applied to a HRC system it translates to a human and a cobot, each with their DT (see Fig. 3). Through a communication module, data can pass between the DTs to run models that require awareness of each other's state. The Human Digital Twin is designed with the explicit role of gathering the data about the human, and running models, required for human-aware approaches to safety and ergonomics. Likewise, the Cognitive Digital Twin is designed to analyze this data in greater depth, thus enabling anticipatory adaptations during human-robot interactions. We briefly presented three use cases for our framework; **(i)** Collision avoidance models can be supported with human intent models; **(ii)** Stress can be reduced by adapting the cobot's movement or dynamically reassigning tasks, **(iii)** Cobot reactions under extreme human behaviour can be emulated without putting humans at risk.

Human-robot collaboration, particularly through the use of a DT, presents multiple challenges. The intrinsic complexity of human behavior poses modeling difficulties, often resulting in discrepancies between the DT's predictions and real-world outcomes. Additionally, these models might lack the adaptability to cope with rapid behavioral changes, necessitating substantial data for training. The real-time demands of tools like Computer Vision can introduce performance bottlenecks, making the system's speed a paramount concern. Task design for such collaborations is crucial; poorly planned interactions can lead to inefficiencies or even failures. Navigating the regulatory landscape while employing these technologies is another consideration. Moreover, when tapping into personal data, such as biometrics, there's an added emphasis on securing that data, ensuring its safety and confidentiality.

With a view to future research directions in human-robot collaboration, the distinction between HDT and CDT models is crucial. For HDT, a thorough exploration of human models is necessary to ensure a faithful, nuanced digital representation of the individual. At the same time, for CDT, it's crucial to identify and integrate the cognitive functions representative of robots. Once these elements have been established and differentiated, they can be applied to specific use cases, laying the foundations for more harmonious and productive human-robot collaboration.

Acknowledgement. This work has been partially supported by the ANR French National Research agency and the FNR Luxemburgish National Research funds project AI4C2PS (INTER/ANR/22/17164924/AI4C2PS), 2023–2025.

References

1. Ahmad, R., Plapper, P.: Safe and automated assembly process using vision assisted robot manipulator. Procedia CIRP **41**, 771–776 (2016)
2. Al Faruque, M.A., Muthirayan, D., Yu, S.Y., Khargonekar, P.P.: Cognitive digital twin for manufacturing systems. In: 2021 Design, Automation and Test in Europe Conference & Exhibition (DATE), pp. 440–445 (2021). https://doi.org/10.23919/DATE51398.2021.9474166. ISSN 1558-1101
3. Anton, F.D., Anton, S., Borangiu, T.: Human-robot natural interaction and collision avoidance in flexible manufacturing cells. IFAC Proc. Vol. **45**(6), 835–840 (2012)
4. Arai, T., Kato, R., Fujita, M.: Assessment of operator stress induced by robot collaboration in assembly. CIRP Ann. **59**(1), 5–8 (2010)
5. Ascone, C., Vanderhaegen, F.: Towards a holistic framework for digital twins of human-machine systems. IFAC-PapersOnLine **55**(29), 67–72 (2022)
6. Augustsson, S., Christiernin, L.G., Bolmsjö, G.: Human and robot interaction based on safety zones in a shared work environment. In: Proceedings of the 2014 ACM/IEEE International Conference on Human-Robot Interaction, pp. 118–119 (2014)
7. Augustsson, S., Olsson, J., Christiernin, L.G., Bolmsjö, G.: How to transfer information between collaborating human operators and industrial robots in an assembly. In: Proceedings of the 8th Nordic Conference on Human-Computer Interaction: Fun, Fast, Foundational, pp. 286–294 (2014)
8. Bilberg, A., Malik, A.A.: Digital twin driven human-robot collaborative assembly. CIRP Ann. **68**(1), 499–502 (2019). https://doi.org/10.1016/j.cirp.2019.04.011. https://www.sciencedirect.com/science/article/pii/S000785061930037X
9. Bousdekis, A., Apostolou, D., Mentzas, G.: A human cyber physical system framework for operator 4.0 – artificial intelligence symbiosis. Manuf. Lett. **25**, 10–15 (2020)

10. Casalino, A., Guzman, S., Zanchettin, A.M., Rocco, P.: Human pose estimation in presence of occlusion using depth camera sensors, in human-robot coexistence scenarios. In: 2018 IEEE/RSJ International Conference on Intelligent Robots and Systems (IROS), pp. 1–7. IEEE (2018)
11. Choi, S.H., et al.: An integrated mixed reality system for safety-aware human-robot collaboration using deep learning and digital twin generation. Robot. Comput.-Integr. Manuf. **73**, 102258 (2022). https://doi.org/10.1016/j.rcim.2021.102258. https://www.sciencedirect.com/science/article/pii/S0736584521001381
12. Cooley, M.: On human-machine symbiosis. In: Gill, K.S. (ed.) Human Machine Symbiosis. Human-Centred Systems, pp. 69–100. Springer, London (1996). https://doi.org/10.1007/978-1-4471-3247-9_2
13. Dragan, A., Srinivasa, S.: Integrating human observer inferences into robot motion planning. Auton. Robot. **37**, 351–368 (2014)
14. Dröder, K., Bobka, P., Germann, T., Gabriel, F., Dietrich, F.: A machine learning-enhanced digital twin approach for human-robot-collaboration. Procedia CIRP **76**, 187–192 (2018). https://doi.org/10.1016/j.procir.2018.02.010. https://www.sciencedirect.com/science/article/pii/S2212827118300295
15. Ebert, D.M., Henrich, D.D.: Safe human-robot-cooperation: image-based collision detection for industrial robots. In: IEEE/RSJ International Conference on Intelligent Robots and Systems, vol. 2, pp. 1826–1831. IEEE (2002)
16. Endo, Y., Maruyama, T., Tada, M.: DhaibaWorks: a software platform for human-centered cyber-physical systems. Int. J. Autom. Technol. **17**(3), 292–304 (2023)
17. Fischer, M., Henrich, D.: 3D collision detection for industrial robots and unknown obstacles using multiple depth images. In: Kröger, T., Wahl, F.M. (eds.) Advances in Robotics Research, pp. 111–122. Springer, Heidelberg (2009). https://doi.org/10.1007/978-3-642-01213-6_11
18. Flacco, F., Kroeger, T., De Luca, A., Khatib, O.: A depth space approach for evaluating distance to objects: with application to human-robot collision avoidance. J. Intell. Robot. Syst. **80**, 7–22 (2015)
19. Gecks, T., Henrich, D.: Human-robot cooperation: safe pick-and-place operations. In: IEEE International Workshop on Robot and Human Interactive Communication, ROMAN 2005, pp. 549–554. IEEE (2005)
20. Geravand, M., Flacco, F., De Luca, A.: Human-robot physical interaction and collaboration using an industrial robot with a closed control architecture. In: 2013 IEEE International Conference on Robotics and Automation, pp. 4000–4007. IEEE (2013)
21. Haddadin, S., Albu-Schaffer, A., De Luca, A., Hirzinger, G.: Collision detection and reaction: a contribution to safe physical human-robot interaction. In: 2008 IEEE/RSJ International Conference on Intelligent Robots and Systems, pp. 3356–3363. IEEE (2008)
22. Haddadin, S., Albu-Schäffer, A., De Luca, A., Hirzinger, G.: Evaluation of collision detection and reaction for a human-friendly robot on biological tissues. In: Proceedings IARP 2008 (2008)
23. Haddadin, S., Albu-Schäffer, A., Hirzinger, G.: Safety evaluation of physical human-robot interaction via crash-testing. In: Robotics: Science and Systems, vol. 3, pp. 217–224. Citeseer (2007)
24. Haddadin, S., Albu-Schäffer, A., Hirzinger, G.: Requirements for safe robots: measurements, analysis and new insights. Int. J. Robot. Res. **28**(11–12), 1507–1527 (2009)
25. Haddadin, S., et al.: On making robots understand safety: embedding injury knowledge into control. Int. J. Robot. Res. **31**(13), 1578–1602 (2012)

26. Hancock, P.A., Billings, D.R., Schaefer, K.E., Chen, J.Y., De Visser, E.J., Parasuraman, R.: A meta-analysis of factors affecting trust in human-robot interaction. Hum. Factors **53**(5), 517–527 (2011)
27. Hawkins, K.P., Vo, N., Bansal, S., Bobick, A.F.: Probabilistic human action prediction and wait-sensitive planning for responsive human-robot collaboration. In: 2013 13th IEEE-RAS International Conference on Humanoid Robots (Humanoids), pp. 499–506. IEEE (2013)
28. ISO: ISO 13855 safety of machinery - positioning of safeguards with respect to the approach speeds of parts of the human body (2010)
29. ISO: ISO/TS 15066 robots and robotic devices - collaborative robots (2016)
30. Kokkalis, K., Michalos, G., Aivaliotis, P., Makris, S.: An approach for implementing power and force limiting in sensorless industrial robots. Procedia CIRP **76**, 138–143 (2018)
31. Kousi, N., et al.: Digital twin for designing and reconfiguring human-robot collaborative assembly lines. Appl. Sci. **11**, 4620 (2021). https://doi.org/10.3390/app11104620
32. Kritzinger, W., Karner, M., Traar, G., Henjes, J., Sihn, W.: Digital twin in manufacturing: a categorical literature review and classification. IFAC-PapersOnLine **51**(11), 1016–1022 (2018). https://doi.org/10.1016/j.ifacol.2018.08.474. https://www.sciencedirect.com/science/article/pii/S2405896318316021
33. Krüger, J., Lien, T.K., Verl, A.: Cooperation of human and machines in assembly lines. CIRP Ann. **58**(2), 628–646 (2009)
34. Krüger, J., Nickolay, B., Heyer, P., Seliger, G.: Image based 3D surveillance for flexible man-robot-cooperation. CIRP Ann. **54**(1), 19–22 (2005)
35. Kulic, D., Croft, E.A.: Affective state estimation for human-robot interaction. IEEE Trans. Robot. **23**(5), 991–1000 (2007)
36. Laffranchi, M., Tsagarakis, N.G., Caldwell, D.G.: Safe human robot interaction via energy regulation control. In: 2009 IEEE/RSJ International Conference on Intelligent Robots and Systems, pp. 35–41. IEEE (2009)
37. Liu, H., Wang, Y., Ji, W., Wang, L.: A context-aware safety system for human-robot collaboration. Procedia Manuf. **17**, 238–245 (2018)
38. Löcklin, A., Jung, T., Jazdi, N., Ruppert, T., Weyrich, M.: Architecture of a human-digital twin as common interface for operator 4.0 applications. Procedia CIRP **104**, 458–463 (2021)
39. Lorenzini, M., Lagomarsino, M., Fortini, L., Gholami, S., Ajoudani, A.: Ergonomic human-robot collaboration in industry: a review. Front. Robot. AI **9**, 262 (2023)
40. Lu, S., Chung, J.H., Velinsky, S.A.: Human-robot collision detection and identification based on wrist and base force/torque sensors. In: Proceedings of the 2005 IEEE International Conference on Robotics and Automation, pp. 3796–3801. IEEE (2005)
41. Lu, Y., Adrados, J.S., Chand, S.S., Wang, L.: Humans are not machines-anthropocentric human-machine symbiosis for ultra-flexible smart manufacturing. Engineering **7**(6), 734–737 (2021)
42. Ma, X., Qi, Q., Cheng, J., Tao, F.: A consistency method for digital twin model of human-robot collaboration. J. Manuf. Syst. **65**, 550–563 (2022). https://doi.org/10.1016/j.jmsy.2022.10.012. https://www.sciencedirect.com/science/article/pii/S0278612522001832
43. Malik, A.A., Bilberg, A.: Digital twins of human robot collaboration in a production setting. Procedia Manuf. **17**, 278–285 (2018). https://doi.org/10.1016/j.promfg.2018.10.047. https://www.sciencedirect.com/science/article/pii/S2351978918311636

44. Maruyama, T., et al.: Digital twin-driven human robot collaboration using a digital human. Sens. (Basel Switz.) **21**(24), 8266 (2021). https://doi.org/10.3390/s21248266
45. Matthias, B.: Industrial safety requirements for collaborative robots and applications. In: ERF 2014 Workshop: Workspace Safety in Industrial Robotics: Trends, Integration, and Standards (2014)
46. Meguenani, A., Padois, V., Da Silva, J., Hoarau, A., Bidaud, P.: Energy based control for safe human-robot physical interaction. In: Kulić, D., Nakamura, Y., Khatib, O., Venture, G. (eds.) ISER 2016. SPAR, vol. 1, pp. 809–818. Springer, Cham (2017). https://doi.org/10.1007/978-3-319-50115-4_70
47. Mohammed, A., Schmidt, B., Wang, L.: Active collision avoidance for human-robot collaboration driven by vision sensors. Int. J. Comput. Integr. Manuf. **30**(9), 970–980 (2017)
48. Morinaga, S., Kosuge, K.: Collision detection system for manipulator based on adaptive impedance control law. In: 2003 IEEE International Conference on Robotics and Automation (Cat. No. 03CH37422), vol. 1, pp. 1080–1085. IEEE (2003)
49. Naudet, Y., Baudet, A., Risse, M.: Human digital twin in industry 4.0: concept and preliminary model. In: IN4PL, pp. 137–144 (2021)
50. Naudet, Y., Panetto, H., Yilma, B.A.: Towards cognitive interoperability in cyber-physical enterprises. In: 22nd IFAC World Congress, IFAC 2023. Preprints of the 22nd IFAC World Congress Yokohama, Japan, 9–14 July 2023, 2023 the authors. Accepted by IFA (2023). https://hal.science/hal-04189335. Issue: 755-766
51. Neisser, U.: Cognitive psychology. New York, Appleton-Century-Crofts (1967). http://archive.org/details/cognitivepsychol00neis
52. Nikolaidis, S., Shah, J.: Human-robot interactive planning using cross-training: a human team training approach. In: Infotech@ Aerospace 2012, p. 2536. AIAA (2012)
53. Oyekan, J.O., et al.: The effectiveness of virtual environments in developing collaborative strategies between industrial robots and humans. Robot. Comput.-Integr. Manuf. **55**, 41–54 (2019). https://doi.org/10.1016/j.rcim.2018.07.006. https://www.sciencedirect.com/science/article/pii/S0736584517303150
54. Pandey, A.K., Alami, R.: Mightability maps: a perceptual level decisional framework for co-operative and competitive human-robot interaction. In: 2010 IEEE/RSJ International Conference on Intelligent Robots and Systems, pp. 5842–5848. IEEE (2010)
55. Park, J.J., Lee, Y.J., Song, J.B., Kim, H.S.: Safe joint mechanism based on nonlinear stiffness for safe human-robot collision. In: 2008 IEEE International Conference on Robotics and Automation, pp. 2177–2182. IEEE (2008)
56. Pellegrinelli, S., Admoni, H., Javdani, S., Srinivasa, S.: Human-robot shared workspace collaboration via hindsight optimization. In: 2016 IEEE/RSJ International Conference on Intelligent Robots and Systems (IROS), pp. 831–838. IEEE (2016)
57. Ramasubramanian, A.K., Mathew, R., Kelly, M., Hargaden, V., Papakostas, N.: Digital twin for human-robot collaboration in manufacturing: review and outlook. Appl. Sci. **12**, 4811 (2022). https://doi.org/10.3390/app12104811
58. Semeraro, C., Lezoche, M., Panetto, H., Dassisti, M.: Digital twin paradigm: a systematic literature review. Comput. Ind. **130**, 103469 (2021). https://doi.org/10.1016/j.compind.2021.103469. https://www.sciencedirect.com/science/article/pii/S0166361521000762

59. Shi, Y., Shen, W., Wang, L., Longo, F., Nicoletti, L., Padovano, A.: A cognitive digital twins framework for human-robot collaboration. Procedia Comput. Sci. **200**, 1867–1874 (2022). https://doi.org/10.1016/j.procs.2022.01.387. https://www.sciencedirect.com/science/article/pii/S1877050922003969
60. Tan, J.T.C., Arai, T.: Triple stereo vision system for safety monitoring of human-robot collaboration in cellular manufacturing. In: 2011 IEEE International Symposium on Assembly and Manufacturing (ISAM), pp. 1–6. IEEE (2011)
61. Tonietti, G., Schiavi, R., Bicchi, A.: Design and control of a variable stiffness actuator for safe and fast physical human/robot interaction. In: Proceedings of the 2005 IEEE International Conference on Robotics and Automation, pp. 526–531. IEEE (2005)
62. Unhelkar, V.V., et al.: Human-aware robotic assistant for collaborative assembly: integrating human motion prediction with planning in time. IEEE Robot. Autom. Lett. **3**(3), 2394–2401 (2018)
63. Vasic, M., Billard, A.: Safety issues in human-robot interactions. In: 2013 IEEE International Conference on Robotics and Automation, pp. 197–204. IEEE (2013)
64. Wang, L., et al.: Symbiotic human-robot collaborative assembly. CIRP Ann. **68**(2), 701–726 (2019)
65. Wang, L., Schmidt, B., Nee, A.Y.: Vision-guided active collision avoidance for human-robot collaborations. Manuf. Lett. **1**(1), 5–8 (2013)
66. Yamada, Y., Hirasawa, Y., Huang, S., Umetani, Y.: Fail-safe human/robot contact in the safety space. In: Proceedings 5th IEEE International Workshop on Robot and Human Communication, RO-MAN 1996 TSUKUBA, pp. 59–64. IEEE (1996)
67. Yilma, B.A., Panetto, H., Naudet, Y.: A meta-model of cyber-physical-social system: the CPSS paradigm to support human-machine collaboration in industry 4.0. In: Camarinha-Matos, L.M., Afsarmanesh, H., Antonelli, D. (eds.) PRO-VE 2019. IAICT, vol. 568, pp. 11–20. Springer, Cham (2019). https://doi.org/10.1007/978-3-030-28464-0_2
68. Yin, Y., Zheng, P., Li, C., Wang, L.: A state-of-the-art survey on augmented reality-assisted digital twin for futuristic human-centric industry transformation. Robot. Comput. Integr. Manuf. **81**, 102515 (2023). https://doi.org/10.1016/j.rcim.2022.102515. https://www.sciencedirect.com/science/article/pii/S0736584522001971
69. Zhao, X., Pan, J.: Considering human behavior in motion planning for smooth human-robot collaboration in close proximity. In: 2018 27th IEEE International Symposium on Robot and Human Interactive Communication (RO-MAN), pp. 985–990. IEEE (2018)
70. Zheng, X., Lu, J., Kiritsis, D.: The emergence of cognitive digital twin: vision, challenges and opportunities. Int. J. Prod. Res. **60**(24), 7610–7632 (2022). https://doi.org/10.1080/00207543.2021.2014591. https://www.tandfonline.com/doi/full/10.1080/00207543.2021.2014591

Cost-Benefit Evaluation of Digital Twin Implementation for Pharmaceutical Lyophilization Plant

Ramona Rubini[1,2](✉), Rocco Cassandro[3], Concetta Semeraro[4], Zhaojun Steven Li[3], and Michele Dassisti[2]

[1] Department of Agricultural and Environmental Sciences, University of Bari, Bari, Italy
ramona.rubini@uniba.it

[2] Department of Mechanical, Mathematics, and Management (DMMM), Polytechnic University of Bari, Bari, Italy
michele.dassisti@poliba.it

[3] Department of Industrial Engineering and Engineering Management, Western New England University, Springfield, MA 01119, USA
{rocco.cassandro,zhaojun.li}@wne.edu

[4] Department of Industrial and Management Engineering, University of Sharjah, 27272 Sharjah, UAE
csemeraro@sharjah.ac.ae

Abstract. The pharmaceutical industry continually seeks advancements to improve manufacturing processes, ensuring product quality, regulatory compliance, and operational efficiency. Lyophilization, a critical process for preserving pharmaceuticals and biological materials, necessitates innovative solutions for optimization and risk mitigation. This research investigates the cost-benefit analysis of implementing a Digital Twin for a pharmaceutical lyophilization plant, focusing on system resilience. The research addresses disruption scenarios affecting the manufacturing process and evaluates the potential benefits and costs associated with Digital Twin integration. The methodology encompasses data collection, system resilience assessment, and cost-benefit analysis. The outcomes indicate the transformative potential of Digital Twin technology in enhancing operational resilience and reducing disruption rates.

Keywords: Digital Twin · Lyophilization · Resilience · Cost-Benefit Analysis · System Disruption

1 Introduction

The pharmaceutical industry, characterized by its strict quality standards, regulatory demands, and the critical importance of product integrity, continually seeks innovative ways to enhance the efficiency and reliability of its manufacturing processes.

Within the spectrum of pharmaceutical manufacturing procedures, the freeze-drying process, commonly referred to as lyophilization, plays a crucial role in ensuring the stability and efficacy of pharmaceutical products. This process holds particular significance

S. Terzi et al. (Eds.): IN4PL 2023, CCIS 1886, pp. 398–407, 2023.
https://doi.org/10.1007/978-3-031-49339-3_25

as it allows for preserving delicate pharmaceuticals and biological materials [1]. In this context, the integration of Digital Twin technology has emerged as a promising solution for process optimization and risk mitigation [2].

The main research question of this study is to assess the cost-benefit implications of implementing a Digital Twin for a pharmaceutical lyophilization plant. A preliminary system resilience analysis serves as the foundation for this evaluation since Digital Twins improve the reliability and resilience of systems through prognostic monitoring.

Lyophilization is susceptible to various perturbations, encompassing technical, managerial, organizational, and personnel-related factors [3]. These perturbations can lead to production delays, product quality deviations, and regulatory non-compliance [4].

Therefore, the fundamental challenge is whether investing in Digital Twin technology can improve resilience to disruptive perturbation while also considering the financial implications.

A multi-faceted approach is adopted to address this research problem. It involves assessing the resilience of the lyophilization plant to various types of perturbation, quantifying the costs associated with Digital Twin implementation, and analyzing the potential benefits, both in terms of enhanced operational resilience and economic gains.

The purpose of the research is to offer a methodology for performing a cost-benefit analysis of implementing a Digital Twin to improve a lyophilization plant based on a resilience analysis. Two different situations are considered for this comparison, considering disruptions that could potentially affect the pharmaceutical manufacturing process:

- Evaluate the existing state of the lyophilization plant, assessing its vulnerability, operational efficiency, and overall resilience without any additional technological interventions. Analyze how technical, managerial, organizational, and personnel-related disruptions can impact the system.
- Analyze the cost-effectiveness and potential advantages of integrating a Digital Twin into the existing operational setup. The Digital Twin not only replicate the physical system but is capable of identifying improvement opportunities through resilience efficiency. Evaluate the Digital Twin's ability to anticipate, simulate, and mitigate disruptions across the technical, managerial, organizational, and personnel domains.

The research focuses on the second scenario, wherein the Digital Twin emerges as a transformative technology capable of proactively recognizing system vulnerabilities and recommending changes or improvements based on a resilience analysis.

2 State of the Art

As industries attempt to reduce disruptions, streamline operations, and guarantee product quality, the drive to make manufacturing processes more resilient has recently gained much traction.

In the dynamic landscape of pharmaceutical manufacturing, maintaining a leading position in technological advancements is crucial to guarantee product quality, adhere to regulatory requirements, and optimize operational efficiency. Industry 4.0 advent triggered the adoption of cutting-edge technologies and the requirement for connected, intelligent manufacturing systems. Central to Industry 4.0 is the concept of the "Smart Factory", which entails the integration of physical production systems such as Cyber-Physical Systems (CPS), Internet of Things (IoT), Prognostics and Health Management (PHM), and Big Data Analytics (BDA), among the others. This consolidation enables the comprehensive collection, analysis, and exploitation of vast amounts of data generated throughout the production chain, thereby facilitating real-time decision-making, process optimization, improved quality control, and enhanced flexibility to meet ever-changing market demands [5, 6].

In particular, Digital Twins are virtual representations of physical systems, processes, or objects, providing a mirror image of their real-world counterparts. DT provides continuous monitoring, analysis, and optimization by empowering real-time monitoring and synchronization of data [7].

Within the pharmaceutical manufacturing sector, resilience has emerged as a critical imperative in Industry 4.0 [8]. In this context, resilience refers to maintaining critical functions and recovering swiftly in the face of disruptions. Such disruptions can range from technical issues such as equipment failures and power outages to managerial challenges such as scheduling errors and decision-making delays. Furthermore, organizational and personnel-related factors, such as supply chain disruptions or workforce inefficiency, can also impact resilience [3].

The integration of Digital Twin with resilience analysis has emerged as a promising approach to address these challenges [9]. Digital Twins use sensors to monitor the system continuously. These sensors capture data, which is then analysed by AI algorithms, enabling real-time detection of faults and anomalies [10].

Furthermore, Prognostic Health Management (PHM) leverages the power of data analytics and machine learning to predict machinery's future health and performance [11]. Hence, patterns [12], trends [13], and anomalous behaviour [14] can be identified to address potential system failure.

When coupled with resilience analysis, these approaches enable organizations to identify potential points of failure, develop proactive strategies for mitigation, and enhance overall system resilience. While the potential benefits of digital twins and resilience-focused strategies in pharmaceutical manufacturing are evident, the associated costs represent a significant consideration. The investment required for acquiring, implementing, and maintaining Digital Twin technology is substantial. Therefore, it is imperative to carefully consider the cost-benefit trade-offs to ensure that the advantages of enhanced resilience outweigh the financial commitments.

Despite the growing interest in Digital Twin [2], and resilience analysis [15–19], few studies systematically address the comprehensive assessment of the cost-effectiveness of Digital Twin adoption within pharmaceutical manufacturing, particularly concerning lyophilization processes.

3 Methodology

A methodology to perform a cost-benefit evaluation of Digital Twin implementation for pharmaceutical lyophilization plants is proposed. The methodology aims to enhance the system's resilience while considering four categories of disruption.

As shown in Fig. 1, the methodology is composed of three main steps. The first step involves a data collection process. Thus, historical data, failure reports, and expert interviews constitute valuable sources for gaining insights into the freeze-dryer system, its historical performance, and the impact of previous disruptions. A foundational understanding of the system's behaviour and vulnerabilities is developed.

The second step involves a system resilience assessment to understand how the lyophilizer responds to potential disruptions. Failure Modes, Effects, and Criticality Analysis (FMECA) is employed as a structured and systematic method to conduct this assessment. FMECA is a systematic and structured methodology used to identify potential failure modes of equipment, systems or products, assess their consequences, and prioritize maintenance actions based on their criticality [20]. Potential failure modes or disruptions that could occur in the systems are identified. For each identified failure mode, the effects or consequences on the freeze-dryer are analyzed. A severity rating (S), e.g. 1 to 10, is assigned to each failure mode based on the potential impact. A higher severity rating indicates a more severe impact on the system and the process. A probability rating (O), e.g. 1 to 10, is assigned to each failure mode based on its probability of occurrence. A higher probability rating indicates a higher likelihood of the failure mode occurring. Then, the system's ability to detect or anticipate each failure mode before it affects the system is evaluated by assigning a detection rating (D), e.g. 1 to 10, for each failure mode. A higher rating indicates a better ability to detect the failure mode. The Risk Priority Number (RPN) is determined by the product of these three indicators, severity, occurrence, and detectability (1).

$$\mathrm{RPN} = \mathrm{S} \times \mathrm{O} \times \mathrm{D} \tag{1}$$

This yields a numerical value representing the risk associated with each failure mode.

Additionally, disruption impact indices are introduced to characterize the potential impact of each disruption type on the failure mode. These indices are determined based on expert analysis considering the particular system and its vulnerability. The relative influence of organizational, management, technical, and personnel-related disruptions on the failure mode's impact is described by disruption impact weights (w_O, w_M, w_P, w_T). The combination of disruption impact weights and the disruption impact indices contribute to defining the Overall Disruption Impact (ODI) for each failure mode (2).

$$\mathrm{ODI} = w_O d_O + w_M d_M + w_T d_T + w_P d_P \tag{2}$$

Therefore, the RPN and the ODI define each failure mode in terms of disruption's influence on failure, severity, occurrence, and detectability. This analysis forms the basis for the Failure Mode, Effect, Criticality, and Disruption Analysis (FMECDA), ultimately pinpointing the critical component that requires improvement.

The third step involves a cost-benefit evaluation of integrating a Digital Twin in the lyophilization plant, considering the disruption impact rates and the implementation costs. The potential benefits of incorporating a Digital Twin into the current system are determined, including enhanced operational efficiency, reduced downtime, proactive maintenance, improved production quality, and informed decision-making. Then, the costs associated with Digital Twin integration are quantified in the Cost of Investment (CI):

$$CI = C_a + C_{int} + C_{p\_train} + C_{setup} + C_m \tag{3}$$

C_a represents the cost of technology acquisition. It is related to the cost of acquiring necessary technology components such as software licenses, hardware, sensors, communication devices, and other technological infrastructure essential for the Digital Twin system.

C_{int} represents the cost of Digital Twin integration in the exisitng system. This includes costs related to modifying the existing infrastructure and ensuring clear communication between the Digital Twin and the physical system.

C_{p_train} represents the cost of training the plant personnel to effectively use and manage the Digital Twin system. This includes training sessions, workshops, and procedures.

C_{setup} represents the cost of setting up the infrastructure to support the Digital Twin system. This includes costs related to networking, server setup, cyber-security protocols and additional equipment needed to support the system.

C_m represents the expenses required to maintain and update the Digital Twin system. This includes costs for regular software updates, hardware maintenance, addressing technical issues, and ensuring the system is up-to-date with the latest technologies and security measures.

An evaluation of the Return on Investment (ROI) (4) offers insights into the cost-effectiveness of this implementation. The calculation of ROI involves comparing the benefits gained from the Digital Twin integration against the costs incurred (3).

$$ROI = \frac{Net\,Gain\,from\,Investment}{CI} \times 100 \tag{4}$$

The Net Gain from Investment is the positive difference between the benefit gained and the total costs associated with the Digital Twin integration, these costs include technology, infrastructure, implementation, personnel training, and maintenance expenses. A positive ROI indicates that the benefits outweigh the costs, providing a strong rationale for the implementation.

4 Case Study

4.1 Scenario 1

The freeze-dryer system at the actual state is analyzed. The central component of the system is the freeze-dryer, consisting of a chamber with multiple shelves where the pharmaceutical products are placed. It includes the refrigeration system, vacuum pumps, condenser, and heating elements. The lyophilizer conducts a cyclical process of freezing the product, reducing pressure to sublimate the frozen solvent, and collecting the vapour in the condenser. Thus, the plant comprises various mechanical parts such as valves, pumps, compressors, condenser coils, and shelves. Moreover, the Supervisory Control

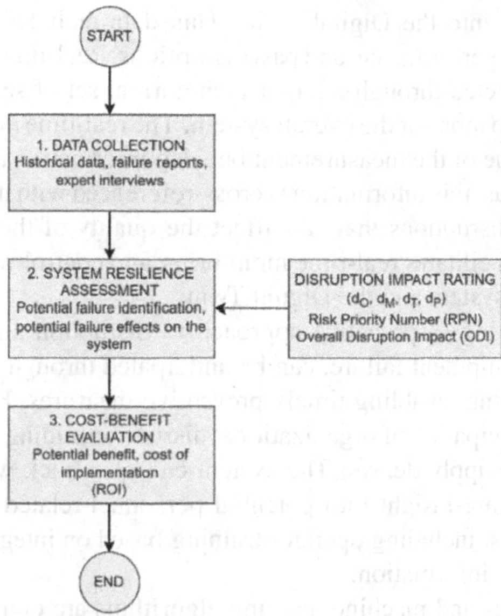

Fig. 1. Three steps methodology for evaluating the integration of a DT in a pharmaceutical lyophilization plant.

And Data Acquisition (SCADA) system and Programmable Logic Controller (PLC) monitor and control in real-time the process. This oversight is complemented by sensors and actuators, providing continuous monitoring of critical parameters. Any deviations trigger alerts, and a visual interface keeps operators and supervisors informed. Qualified operators are responsible for the freeze-dryer setup, automatic product loading and unloading phase monitoring, and process parameter monitoring. Supervisors oversee the operations, ensuring adherence to protocols, and making critical decisions for process optimization and decision-making.

A detailed comprehension of the lyophilizer system is achieved through analyzing historical data of the last years, plant visiting, and interviewing plant staff. Consequently, its previous performance, maintenance history, and past disruption have been determined.

The FMECDA analysis is performed and potential failure modes, their severity, occurrence, and detectability ratings are identified. Thus, the disruption impact rates are obtained. Technical disruptions have affected the system by 50% (equipment failures, failure in the loading system), organizational disruption by 33% (supply chain delay for raw materials, packaging, and spare parts), and personnel-related disruptions by 17% (workforce shortage). Management disruptions have a relatively minimal impact.

4.2 Scenario 2

The integration of a Digital Twin enriched with prognostic capabilities emerges as a promising solution to reduce disruption rates within the system. This Digital Twin, which is connected to the physical system, replicates its behaviour in real-time and forecasts potential future states. Historical and real-time data from the freeze-dryer system are integrated into the Digital Twin. This data includes information on past operations, equipment performance, and past disruptions. Real-time data from the freeze-dryer system are collected through a larger than current set of sensors and Internet of Things (IoT) devices to monitor the overall system. The real-time monitored data include not only the point value of the measurement but also information about the parameter's acceptable ranges. Thus, this information is cross-referenced with historical process data to identify potential disruptions that can affect the quality of the processed products. The SCADA system facilitates real-time monitoring and control while serving as a link between the physical system and the Digital Twin.

The integration brings a proactive approach to disruption anticipation. Technical disruption, such as equipment failure, can be anticipated through real-time monitoring and predictive modelling, enabling timely preventive measures. Hence, historical data integration allows anticipation of organizational disruption, aiding in the proactive management of potential supply delays. The system can also track workforce availability and efficiency, providing insight into potential personnel-related disruptions and taking proactive measures, including operator training based on integrated procedures and regulatory compliance information.

Advanced analytics and machine learning algorithms are employed to analyze the integrated data, enabling the Digital Twin to identify patterns, deviations, and emerging trends. Moreover, predictive models are implemented within the Digital Twin to forecast potential disruptions and failure modes. These predictive models use prognostic analysis based on historical and real-time data, aiding in anticipating potential failure modes before they manifest in the physical system. Hence, the Digital Twin provides insights into disruptions' likelihood and potential impact. This proactive prediction paves the way for preemptive actions and strategic measures, aiming to significantly reduce disruption rates and fortify the system's resilience against disruptions. Moreover, it forms the basis for preventative actions and strategic initiatives, driving a significant reduction in disruption rates and strengthening the system's resilience against various potential disruptions.

This scenario introduces robust cybersecurity solutions and communication protocols, ensuring the security and efficiency of data exchange between the physical system, sensors, actuators, and the Digital Twin. This integration significantly enhances operational resilience and overall efficiency within the lyophilization plant.

5 Conclusion

The present stage of the research has laid the foundation for assessing and enhancing the resilience of lyophilization plants through the integration of innovative technologies, such as Digital Twin.

Two scenarios are analyzed to evaluate the potential impact of implementing a Digital Twin in a pharmaceutical lyophilization plant. As depicted in Table 1, Scenario 1 represents the current state of the lyophilization system, without additional technological integration. This scenario emphasizes cost-efficiency while acknowledging its vulnerability to disruptions. On the contrary, Scenario 2 introduces the integration of a Digital Twin enriched with prognostic capabilities, focusing on proactive disruption prevention, enhanced operational efficiency, and improved production quality.

The comparative analysis highlights that Scenario 2 presents a promising avenue for future implementation, effecting a transformation from a reactive to a proactive, resilient, and efficient system. It amplifies the overall resilience of the freeze-dryer through disruption rate reduction.

However, it is essential to acknowledge that implementing a Digital Twin is not without challenges. It requires a significant investment in technology acquisition, integration, personnel training, and maintenance expenses.

Table 1. Disruption rates and associated benefits for Scenario 1 and Scenario 2 in the lyophilization plant.

Scenario	Disruption rate				Benefits
	d_O	d_M	d_T	d_P	
Scenario 1	33%	0%	50%	17%	Low costs, Operational continuity,
Scenario 2	−10%	0%	−15%	−5%	Proactive disruption prevention, Enhanced operational efficiency, Improved production quality

To propel the study towards a comprehensive and actionable outcome, several key future developments are recommended.

Firstly, the development of a comprehensive mathematical method is necessary. This method should facilitate a meticulous investigation into the cost-benefit analysis of various innovative implementations, starting from the disruption level, the perturbed information, and the FMECDA analysis. Such a mathematical approach would provide a structured and quantitative framework for evaluating the financial implications and potential advantages associated with each implementation, aiding informed decision-making.

Moreover, long-term monitoring with sensors and data analysis using analytical techniques on different lyophilization plants can yield a profound understanding of disruptions and system behaviour. This will enable the derivation of more precise and insightful conclusions, laying the groundwork for effective resilience enhancement strategies.

Additionally, the creation of simulation models replicating the lyophilization process and disruptions would be instrumental. These models could be used to simulate the impact of various disruptions and technology integrations, offering a virtual platform for cost-benefit analysis. Such simulations would provide a safe and controlled environment to analyze the potential outcomes of different strategies before actual implementation.

Furthermore, the implementation of this simulation algorithm in the proactive-based Digital Twin would enhance the overall system's resilience.

These future developments will pave the way for practical and impactful recommendations, contributing to the resilience and efficiency of lyophilization processes within the pharmaceutical industry.

Acknowledgements. This work was supported by the Italian Ministry of University and Research under the Programme "Department of Excellence" Legge 232/2016 (Grant No. CUP - D93C23000100001)". The authors thank Sanofi s.r.l. for partially funding this research.

References

1. Bhambere, D., Gaidhani, K., Harwalkar, M., Nirgude, P.: Lyophilization/freeze drying – a review. World J. Pharm. Res. **4**, 516–543 (2015)
2. Chen, Y., Yang, O., Sampat, C., Bhalode, P., Ramachandran, R., Ierapetritou, M.: Digital twins in pharmaceutical and biopharmaceutical manufacturing: a literature review. Processes **8**(9), 1088 (2020). https://doi.org/10.3390/pr8091088
3. Rubini, R., Cassandro, R., Caggiano, M., Semeraro, C., Li, Z.S., Dassisti, M.: The human factor and the resilience of manufacturing processes: a case study of pharmaceutical process toward industry 5.0. In: Borgianni, Y., Matt, D.T., Molinaro, M., Orzes, G. (eds.) Towards a Smart, Resilient and Sustainable Industry, pp. 96–107. Springer Nature Switzerland, Cham (2023). https://doi.org/10.1007/978-3-031-38274-1_9
4. Aytug, H., Lawley, M.A., McKay, K., Mohan, S., Uzsoy, R.: Executing production schedules in the face of uncertainties: a review and some future directions. Eur. J. Operat. Res. **161**(1), 86–110 (2005). https://doi.org/10.1016/j.ejor.2003.08.027
5. Baheti, R., Gill, H.: Cyber-physical systems. Impact Control Technol **12**, 1–6 (2011)
6. Lee, J., Bagheri, B., Kao, H.-A.: A Cyber-Physical Systems architecture for Industry 4.0-based manufacturing systems. Manuf. Lett. **3**, 18–23 (2015). https://doi.org/10.1016/j.mfglet.2014.12.001
7. Semeraro, C., Lezoche, M., Panetto, H., Dassisti, M.: Digital twin paradigm: a systematic literature review. Comput. Ind. **130**, 103469 (2021). https://doi.org/10.1016/j.compind.2021.103469
8. Debnath, B., et al.: Assessing the critical success factors for implementing industry 4.0 in the pharmaceutical industry: implications for supply chain sustainability in emerging economies. PLOS ONE **18**(6), e0287149 (2023). https://doi.org/10.1371/journal.pone.0287149
9. Zhou, C., et al.: Analytics with digital-twinning: a decision support system for maintaining a resilient port. Decis. Support. Syst. **143**, 113496 (2021). https://doi.org/10.1016/j.dss.2021.113496
10. Gao, Z., Cecati, C., Ding, S.X.: A survey of fault diagnosis and fault-tolerant techniques-part I: fault diagnosis with model-based and signal-based approaches. IEEE Trans. Industr. Electron. **62**(6), 3757–3767 (2015). https://doi.org/10.1109/TIE.2015.2417501
11. Guo, J., Li, Z., Li, M.: A review on prognostics methods for engineering systems. IEEE Trans. Reliab. **69**(3), 1110–1129 (2020). https://doi.org/10.1109/TR.2019.2957965
12. Semeraro, C., Lezoche, M., Panetto, H., Dassisti, M.: Data-driven invariant modelling patterns for digital twin design. J. Ind. Inform. Integr. **31**, 100424 (2023). https://doi.org/10.1016/j.jii.2022.100424
13. Cattaneo, L., MacChi, M.: A digital twin proof of concept to support machine prognostics with low availability of run-to-failure data. IFAC-PapersOnLine **52**(10), 37–42 (2019). https://doi.org/10.1016/J.IFACOL.2019.10.016
14. Kaul, T., Bender, A., Sextro, W.: Digital twin for reliability analysis during design and operation of mechatronic systems. In: Proceedings of the 29th European Safety and Reliability Conference, ESREL 2019, pp. 2340–2347 (2020). https://doi.org/10.3850/978-981-11-2724-30876-CD

15. Su, Q., Moreno, M., Ganesh, S., Reklaitis, G.V., Nagy, Z.K.: Resilience and risk analysis of fault-tolerant process control design in continuous pharmaceutical manufacturing. J. Loss Prev. Process Ind. **55**, 411–422 (2018). https://doi.org/10.1016/j.jlp.2018.07.015
16. Khoirani, A.B., Masruroh, N.A., Yu, V.F.: Development of a supply chain disruption optimization model. In: 2022 IEEE International Conference on Industrial Engineering and Engineering Management (IEEM), pp. 919–923 (2022). https://doi.org/10.1109/IEEM55944.2022.9989585
17. Alexopoulos, K., Anagiannis, I., Nikolakis, N., Chryssolouris, G.: A quantitative approach to resilience in manufacturing systems. Int. J. Prod. Res. **60**(24), 7178–7193 (2022). https://doi.org/10.1080/00207543.2021.2018519
18. Dormady, N.C., Rose, A., Roa-Henriquez, A., Morin, C.B.: The cost-effectiveness of economic resilience. Int. J. Prod. Econ. **244**, 108371 (2022). https://doi.org/10.1016/j.ijpe.2021.108371
19. Ghorbani, E., Hajiabadi, M.E., Samadi, M., Lotfi, H.: Providing a preventive maintenance strategy for enhancing distribution network resilience based on cost–benefit analysis. Electr. Eng. **105**(2), 979–991 (2023). https://doi.org/10.1007/s00202-022-01710-5
20. Automotive Quality and Process Improvement Committee: Potential Failure Mode and Effects Analysis (FMEA) Including Design FMEA, Supplemental FMEA-MSR, and Process FMEA (2021). https://doi.org/10.4271/J1739_202101

Author Index

S. Terzi et al. (Eds.): IN4PL 2023, CCIS 1886, pp. 409–410, 2023.
https://doi.org/10.1007/978-3-031-49339-3